PRINCE VON BÜLOW

MEMOIRS

MEMOIRS OF
PRINCE VON BÜLOW

I

From Appointment as Secretary of State for
Foreign Affairs to Morocco Crisis, 1897-1903.

II

From Morocco Crisis to Resignation of the
Chancellorship, 1903-1909.

III

The World War and the Collapse of Germany,
1909-1919.

IV

Early Years and Diplomatic Service, 1849-1897.

*THE volumes are arranged in the order in
which they were written.*

BÜLOW AND HIS SUCCESSOR BETHMANN-HOLLWEG

At the Lehrter station in Berlin, before Bülow's departure, 17th July 1909

PRINCE VON BÜLOW

MEMOIRS

1903-1909

LONDON & NEW YORK

PUTNAM

FÜRST VON BÜLOW DENKWÜRDIGKEITEN, ZWEITE BAND
First published in Germany November 20th, 1930

PRINCE VON BÜLOW *MEMOIRS* 1903-1909
First published in England November, 1931

Translated from the German by

F. A. VOIGT

PRINTED IN GREAT BRITAIN.
CHISWICK PRESS: CHARLES WHITTINGHAM AND GRIGGS (PRINTERS), LTD
BRUNSWICK PARK ROAD LONDON N.11.

CONTENTS

CHAPTER I

CHAPTER IV

CHAPTER V

CHAPTER VI

CHAPTER VII

CHAPTER VIII

CHAPTER IX

CHAPTER X

CHAPTER XI

CHAPTER XII

CHAPTER XIII

CHAPTER XIV

CHAPTER XV

CHAPTER XVI

CHAPTER XVII

CHAPTER XVIII

CHAPTER XIX

CHAPTER XX

CHAPTER XXI

CHAPTER XXII

CHAPTER XXIII

CHAPTER XXIV

CHAPTER XXV

CHAPTER XXVI

CHAPTER XXVII

CHAPTER XXVIII

CHAPTER XXIX

CHAPTER XXX

CHAPTER XXXI

CHAPTER XXXII

LIST OF ILLUSTRATIONS

CHANCELLORSHIP 1903-1909

THE MEMOIRS OF
PRINCE VON BÜLOW

CHAPTER I

The Morocco Affair—Queen Marie Christine of Spain—Metternich's despatch concerning Morocco—Prince of Reuss on St. Petersburg—Admiral Tirpitz in St. Petersburg—The 1903 Elections to the Reichstag—Socialist gains increased—A parliamentary duel with Bebel—The Jesuit Law ; abrogation of paragraph 2—William II's feeling on the Jesuits—The attitude at Court—Letters from Cardinal Kopp and Franz Arenberg—The Kaiser's Mediterranean trip in March 1904—Professor Theodor Schiemann—The Kaiser's eagerness for a meeting with President Loubet—Return via Karlsruhe— Eckardstein in Karlsruhe—Motor racing in Homburg.

FOR some time past I had been keeping my eye on Morocco, fully aware of a possible, ever closer *rapprochement* between France and England, through the exchange of Morocco for Egypt.

In Vienna, during the Kaiser's visit there, I had had a chance of renewing my information on the subject. I had been received by Queen Marie Christine of Spain, a woman of great insight and decision, to whose dignity and intelligence the Spanish dynasty owed its survival of the disastrous Spanish peace with America.

She had told me in confidence that France, for some time past, had been trying to persuade the Spanish Government to an offensive-defensive alliance, but that, so far, Spain had not accepted, in spite of urgent French importunities.

France, together with this alliance, had suggested a partition of Morocco, on the basis of which the French would receive the North and Spain the South. The Queen expressed the opinion that France had used King Edward's mediation to get England's consent to this plan. For herself all Spain really asked was not to be left with empty hands since, in view of traditional Spanish claims to Morocco, and of that country's geographical position, this might mean a collapse of the Spanish dynasty.

II.   B

Back in Berlin I asked our ambassador in London to draft me his opinion on this matter. Count Metternich based his reply on an article in a great English newspaper which had suggested that, throughout the Boer War, the attitude of the German Government, in particular that of the Chancellor and of the Secretary of State for Foreign Affairs—of the Kaiser even, had all undoubtedly been pro-English, but that the German people had displayed, throughout the whole of that period, more animosity, envy and hatred of England than the people of any other country. Since Germany, through the surprising development of her industry, the growth of her overseas interests—a commerce that, nowadays, had begun to extend all over the world—and the construction of a large new fleet, was from day to day becoming her most serious rival, England was forced to regulate her policy accordingly.

French competition had long ceased to be dangerous to England, Russia was only dangerous in Asia. Germany was the one real menace. Metternich, however, added that he did not believe in any durable friendship between Great Britain, Russia, and France. A temporary Anglo-Russian *rapprochement*, the co-operation, *ad hoc*, against Germany, of England, France, and Russia, was quite feasible. Should this ever actually materialize, even though it might last some time, it would still be premature to speak of any German isolation. On the one hand Austria was dependent on her German alliance, while, on the other Russia, if our policy were calm and skilful, would be equally disinclined to win back Alsace for the French, or to destroy German trade to oblige England.

Metternich's unofficial, but none the less reliable information suggested conflicting streams of Russian opinion: a distrust in Russian Government circles of Republican and atheist France as against the old Slav hatred of the German. All would depend on our own political skill. He closed his letter as follows:

I repeat and emphasize my opinion that the British Government does not desire a rupture, and will not lightly undertake any step against us. But anti-German feeling in England is so decided that, on any major international issue, no British Government, even with the best will in the world, would be free to take our side. The best we can hope for the moment is the maintenance of what diplomatic language calls " correct and friendly " Anglo-German relationships.

Ever since you have guided our policy our position in Russia has slowly but steadily improved. I think it would be a great mistake to force this amelioration.

On the 4th October 1903 Metternich reported on Morocco:

Should England, France and Spain agree to a partition of Morocco we could only inform these powers from the outset that, unless we ourselves were included in it, we could never recognize such a scheme. We should be bound to protest at any disregard of our considerable commercial interests on the Atlantic coast. It may be objected that an empty protest not re-enforced by threats and active diplomatic pressure, is usually more dangerous than letting matters slide. It is always possible, of course, to apply such pressure, but might be dangerous. Should England make any important Moroccan concession to France she will endeavour, in return, to free Egypt from all international fetters. The French have long since made up their minds to this, and would gladly, in return for Morocco, relinquish to England the little remaining Egyptian influence they possess. Obviously we could only embark on any active anti-British policy in Egypt if England were to oppose us in Morocco. Mere suspicion of that would not suffice, unless we wished to force the British Government to an attitude inimical to us on principle.

If [Metternich concluded] England agrees with France in spite of everything, for a complete partition of Morocco— though, since the relinquishment of the few remaining French rights in Egypt would not outweigh any British surrender in Morocco, I still consider this unlikely—she can only be impelled by the desire to consolidate her new French entente, *à tout prix*. Should the partition be arranged behind our backs any pressure we could bring to bear on France would be far more effective than a protest to England. We could suggest to the French Government—*le cas échéant*—that we are convinced that France is far too prudent to jeopardize the excellent Franco-German relations so carefully fostered for over thirty years. There would be no necessity to mobilize an army corps for that . . . and neither would the French! Nevertheless Morocco is quite a serious " little game of bluff ".

Finally Metternich warned me against any premature German participation in the Morocco question, and especially against an inopportune press campaign.

If necessary, and at the right moment, we shall be able to get all we want by the use of heavy diplomatic artillery. But if we bring up our batteries too early that will only give our opponents time to take cover and prepare their defences. When is this psychological moment due? Only further developments, and a fairly complete knowledge of Anglo-French agreements can show us that.

Not long after the meeting of our Kaiser with the Russian Imperial couple at Wolfsgarten, I had received a not uninteresting letter from Prince Henry VII of Reuss, my former chief, the patron and friend of many years. He wrote of events in Russia and conditions at the Russian Court. He had just received a visit from his niece, the Grand Duchess Vladimir, at his estate, Trebschen, in the Neumark. He remarked as follows, à propos of that charming lady's confidences:

All I have managed to gather has left a very disturbing impression. The good will and clearer intelligence of Tsar Nicholas fail in their effect because of a complete lack of energy or interest in State Affairs. Moreover certain influences which can only be described as pernicious, are beginning to make themselves felt. These influences, feminine in origin, with a very dubious admixture of mysticism, emanate from the Montenegrin princesses, who wield so decisive a power over the reigning Tsarina that even the Dowager Empress cannot combat it. One instance is the disfavour which overtook Witte when he refused to grant the ruler of the Tcherna Gora as much money as the daughters would have liked. The Grand Duchess Vladimir is convinced that the mystic preoccupations of this clique form a grave danger to the dynasty. The Russian people scents corruption, and the Little Father's prestige suffers accordingly. All this is being carefully used by the Nihilists to undermine Imperial prestige still further. Revolution, to-day, has changed its tactics. The *mot d'ordre* is no longer to assassinate a sovereign, but to discredit dynastic infallibility with the people. At the top there is utter ignorance of this danger, and the belief that "all is for the best," etc. No one has a chance of being listened to unless he can paint it all in glowing colours. Everybody else is ignored. No one who tells the truth can get a hearing, but is jealously watched and pushed aside.

To these views of his niece, the Grand Duchess, the Prince added:

It is fortunate that the Tsar is so well disposed towards our Emperor. Though the sea itself is a fickle and unstable element the rendezvous arranged on it may be to the good—especially since the eternal feminine is excluded from them. But the

greatest care is advisable that no exaggerated advances be made.
Their effect would be exactly the opposite of what was intended.
The passion for the Ally on the Seine appears to be artificially
stimulated. With regard to Lambsdorff the Grand Duchess
thought he lacked much of what goes to the making of a statesman, but that he was reliable.

A week before the visit of the Grand Duchess Vladimir to
Trebschen, Tirpitz had been in St. Petersburg. The Kaiser had
ordered him to deliver to the Tsar some sketches of our battleships
in course of construction, and to explain that our naval power
remained concentrated in the North Sea. Tirpitz was to satisfy the
Tsar that the rumour spread by the French press that we intended to
turn Danzig into a naval base was unfounded. The Admiral had,
of course, no opportunity of observing the intimate life at the Tsar's
Court, but he was received there with great distinction. He lunched
at Tsarskoe-Selo with their Majesties, in the innermost circle. The
Grand Dukes Alexei Alexandrovitch and Alexander Mikhailovitch,
hitherto reported anti-German, were very friendly. Vice-Admiral
Avellan, who had led the Russian squadron to Toulon thirteen years
previously, showed himself especially well-disposed.

The 1903 elections in Germany had brought the Social Democrats great gains. William II was too intelligent not to feel that,
by his speeches and "gestures," he himself had done much to
increase them. But, as was unluckily too often his habit, he shut
his eyes to his own responsibility and, *proprio motu*, sent me a telegram, not in cipher, announcing that it was all the same to him
whether red, black, or yellow monkeys gambolled in the Reichstag
cage. This schoolboy joke was never allowed to reach the public—
a fine proof of the loyalty and discretion of our telegraph officials.
To me it was less the Socialist gains which seemed significant, than
the belief, now gaining ground all over Germany, and becoming in
many cases almost an article of faith— that the Socialist movement
could never be brought to a standstill, but must roll ahead like some
elemental force—like the sea or an avalanche. I therefore sought
an opportunity for a reckoning with the Socialists. I was convinced
that, at the psychological moment, it would be necessary to dissolve
the Reichstag, so as to bring about one better constituted. Fully
determined to uphold law and order, I was as opposed as ever to any
measure of unprovoked violence, much more so to a *coup d'état* or
infringement of the sworn constitution. I believed and still believe
that, in the long run, no great social tendency or undercurrent can
be successfully fought with other than intellectual weapons—reason,

that is to say, and common sense. These need not exclude strong measures in case of necessity. The spoken word is undervalued in Germany. Without pretentions to the temperament or gifts of a Faust many of our German Philistines crassly repeat Faust's dictum:

" *Ich kann das Wort so hoch unmöglich schätzen.*" [1]

In actual fact the value of words is incalculable. I doubt whether, in 1906, we should have won such brilliant victories over Socialism if my Reichstag speeches of the previous months had not been circulated in millions of copies, and paved the way for our victory.

If I fought the Socialists it was not because I failed to understand their essentially justified aspirations. Still less did I oppose them from the standpoint of any narrow class consciousness, or from reasons of personal egotism. But I was convinced that in Germany above all any Socialist rule would mean the end of the greatness, power, and prosperity of the Empire. The virtues as much as the weakness of the German national temperament make Socialism a danger to Germany.

The German is more doctrinaire than other races. Far less than the English, French, or Italians can he distinguish between the theory of a case and its practise. His doctrinaire obstinacy makes him run his head against a brick wall. When, during my term of office, an international conference met in Berne to attempt to regulate the hours of women's and children's labour, Alexandre Millerand, then one of the leaders of the French Social Democrats, later president of the French Republic, said to my brother Alfred, who was then German representative in Berne: " Do try to control your bureaucrats who have been sent from Berlin for this Congress. They are more doctrinaire and unpractical than even our most stupid Socialist dreamers. *Que diable, avant tout il faut que l'industrie marche!* "

The type of Millerand, Briand, Albert Thomas, Lloyd George, Crispi, Fortis—the type, that is to say of demagogue who worries his way through to sensible statesmanship, is to be found, again and again in England, Italy, and France, to the lasting benefit of these countries. In Germany he is rare. We Germans have not yet produced a Clemenceau, who, once he became a minister, ordered the troops to fire on strikers and coldly replied when his previous speeches were contrasted with this cruel episode: " *A présent je suis de l'autre côté de la barricade.*"

[1] " I cannot rate the spoken word so high."

CHANCELLOR PRINCE VON BÜLOW

National feeling is, in reality, much stronger among our neighbours than among ourselves. The French Socialist wishes a socially
organized France to dominate Europe, because France—the France
of 1789, is " *la mère de la révolution.*" In the same way the French
clerical demands that France—" *le fils aîné de l'église* "—shall pre-
dominate in the Catholic world. The French Socialist wants to rise
above the fog and poverty that surround him, the German to drag
down others into the depths. Even the German's greatest talent,
his gift for organization—has largely aided the growth of Socialism,
though it has led at the same time to its petrifaction. Sidney
Sonnino said to me during the winter 1914-1915: " I certainly
admire the German gift for organization. But when, as with you,
it is allowed unlimited scope it leads to arterio-sclerosis—to mental
calcification." During the Great War Balfour made much the same
remark; *i.e.* that German organization was a danger to the whole
world, but that, perhaps this was the very talent which made us
such bad psychologists.

In the course of my oratorical duel with Bebel (December 10th,
14th, and 15th, 1903)[1] I hauled over the coals the whole programme
and attitude to life of German Social-Democracy. Perhaps I was
successful chiefly because I spoke extempore, save for a few concrete
references from notes, on the scandals in the Forbach garrison, and
the exaction of tolls on the canals.

My fierce attacks on the intolerance displayed by Bebel at the
Dresden Social-Democratic Congress were appreciated even by a
considerable section of the Left. The revisionistic Socialists
smirked in silence. Though I gave Social-Democrats full marks
for discipline and capacity for sacrifice I placed them bottom for
clarity of programme or positive achievement. I was, unfortunately,
foretelling the future only too well.

I have often been asked the origin of a rhyme I flung at Bebel's
head:

> " *Und willst du nicht mein Bruder sein
> So schlag' ich dir den Schädel ein.*"[2]

I did not know it then, nor do I to-day. This bit of doggerel came
into my head while I was speaking, and must, I suppose have been
with me since my childhood at Frankfurt, Sachsenhausen or
Bonames where many memories of 1848 were still fresh.

The highly intelligent Frau von Kotze, Prince Bismarck's niece

[1] Prince Bülow's *Speeches*. Complete edition, vol. ii, p. 1 *et seq.* Compressed
edition, vol. iii, p. 10 *et seq.*
[2] " Be my brother or I'll crack your skull."

and the daughter of his beloved Malle (*née* von Arnim-Kröchlendorff) wrote to me as follows, à propos of the Reichstag debate:

All the passionate love of country which lies dormant in my veins as a Bismarck was fired as I read your speech. Never, since Bismarck's death, has such a speech been heard in the Reichstag. It makes one's heart leap up to hear the leader of the nation use such bold, plain, challenging words—words which are not mere words but acts! You redouble our confidence in you; encourage the belief that, perhaps, many things to-day might be otherwise if your wishes had not met such insurmountable obstacles. Every patriot must cherish the fervent wish to see you remain many years the head of the government. I hope that, from anyone so steeped up to the neck in the old traditions as myself, this wish will show you how deeply and sincerely I rejoiced.

The poet, Ernst von Wildenbruch, wrote me:

Again, as so often before, you have been inspired to give its final expression to a deep, and very wide-spread feeling. If now I endorse with all my heart, and pronounce a fervid "Amen," to each powerful and significant word you uttered, the general feeling of peace and ultimate serenity which your speech as a whole has left on my mind, is due to the knowledge that we Germans have placed at the helm a man of such breadth of vision, and at the same time such iron determination as yourself.

Another poet, Adolf Wilbrandt, wrote:

MY DEAR—AND VERY HONOURED—FRIEND,
Splendid! Before I start my daily round as a dramatist I feel I simply must let you know how enchanted I am with your last Reichstag speech. I only wish I could have listened to it. You rode the grey horse Bebel magnificently!

From Hamburg the shrewd and matter of fact Ballin wired as follows:

Must ask Your Excellency's permission to say how enthusiastic I feel at your latest speech against Bebel. A real word in season. The whole country has been waiting for such a speech. It will win Your Excellency friends and admirers far beyond the frontiers of the Fatherland.

On looking back, years later, at these debates I find my old conviction re-enforced that our present politician's habit of referring to long, carefully prepared, manuscript speeches—of lecturing, in a word, rather than speaking—is largely responsible for the admitted lifelessness of our arid sessions in the Reichstag. Such monologues, at the mercy of every heckler, without direct answer for one's opponent, can never hope to attain the spontaneity, the immediate vital appeal of French debate, which really *is* a discussion of current events and far surpasses ours in vivacity and interest.

At each Reichstag session the clerical Centre would move the abrogation or, failing that, the amendment of the so-called " Jesuit Law " (of July 4th 1872), concerning the Society of Jesus. It was not simply a question of the basic intention of this law as set down in paragraph 1 which forbade all activity of the Order within the Reich. What the Centre demanded was the suppression of paragraph 2, which provided that members of the Order, or of any affiliated body, might, if of foreign birth, be expelled without further cause from German territory. If they were German subjects, domicile in specified districts and localities might either be forbidden or imposed on them. I was no friend of discriminatory laws, except in the case of our Eastern Provinces where Polish agitation was so vehement as to place us in a state of self-defence. In German Poland the continued existence of the Prussian State, and German culture were at stake, but it struck me as unfair that members of the Jesuit Order should be the only German subjects whose legal right to a home was denied, or, in any case, curtailed. For many years the Conservatives, as well as the great majority of Liberals, had voted regularly for the motion that paragraph 2 of the Jesuit Law should be repealed.

Already on 3rd February 1903, I had answered the member Spahn, in the Reichstag, to the effect that, in my opinion, questions of religious belief within the Reich, no longer needed for their solution the application, merely because they belonged to the Jesuit Order, of any special restriction to German subjects.

On 8th March 1904, at a session of the Federal Diet, I procured the abrogation of paragraph 2 and, on the same day, the Kaiser's signature to the joint recommendation of Diet and Reichstag.

This signature was not easily obtained. Like most Protestants and even a certain number of Roman Catholics, William II had a strong prejudice against Jesuits. Whenever he examined a document which contained even a passing mention of the sons of St. Ignatius Loyola he never failed to write " devil's brood " or " sons of hell " in the margin.

Opposition in the Diet had chiefly come from Saxony, and from the Thuringian States. The wise and far-seeing King Albert had never lost sight of the fact that Saxony was the cradle of the Reformation, and that Saxons, by an overwhelming majority, held fast to their

Protestant faith. His brother and successor, King George, and his sons and grandsons, were all ultra-clerical in outlook, and took every occasion to demonstrate the fact. It was therefore not a very edifying spectacle when, by express command of his sovereign, the Minister for Ecclesiastical Affairs in Saxony stated, in the Saxon Lower House that, by unanimous decision in the Cabinet, the Saxon vote in the Diet had been against the abrogation of paragraph 2.

To the lively applause of the, then, very loyal Saxon Chamber the Minister added that this action on the part of the Cabinet had met with special approval from His Majesty—that it deserved the sincerest, deepest gratitude of all Saxons. For me this meant, of course, a stab in the back, an attack neither sincere nor very courageous, engineered from purely particularist, dynastic motives. There is a certain irony in the fact that the Crown Prince George of Saxony should have joined the Catholic priesthood after the revolution and become, as Father George of Saxony, a member of the Jesuit Order. The debates which, in the Prussian Diet, led to the abrogation of paragraph 2, afforded me ample opportunity to convince myself of the unreliability, and utter insincerity of our politicians, of no matter which shade of opinion.

After the retirement of the far more capable Count Stirum the deputy Heydebrand had imposed himself on the Conservative Party as its leader. He denounced me with the most effective dramatic pathos of which his little figure was capable: " Thus far, Mr. Chancellor;—but no further! "

Those in high places, he added, did not consider Protestant interests enough: the Executive displayed no firmness towards ultramontanism, etc. In the course of the debate I was able to observe Herr von Heydebrand inciting the deputy Sattler, an avowed hater of Catholicism, to even fiercer onslaughts on the Government.

Sattler was a man of some merit who, soon afterwards, died of a painful disease. Herr von Heydebrand, a few years later, was to break from the National-Liberals and, with crude ill manners and a deplorable lack of political intelligence, throw himself into the arms of the Centre Party!

The highest note was struck by the National-Liberal leader, Professor Friedberg. I can see him still adjuring me in a high-pitched voice and pointing an accusing finger:

" When some future Treitschke is inspired to relate the internal policy of Prussia in this year of grace 1904, you Chancellor Bülow, who re-opened our doors to the Jesuits, will receive scant praise."

It was my privilege, in 1917, to see the same Dr. Friedberg, then Vice-President of the Prussian Council of Ministers, emerge from the Council Room, arm in arm with Premier Hertling—" two minds and but a single thought "—with Hertling who, all his life, had been a staunch supporter of the Jesuits!

> All the world's a stage
> And all the men and women merely players

as Shakespeare's melancholy Jacques remarks to his exiled Duke.

I had certainly the laugh on my side when I asked a deputy who, the year before, had voted the abrogation of paragraph 2, and was now attacking me for agreeing with him, whether his previous vote had been registered with a mental reservation, in the hope that the Government would not agree. I added that this seemed to me Jesuitical!

In face of these attacks, mostly inept, my deepest instincts came to the surface, and I declared how much I could sympathize with John Huss as he watched the " silly old woman " bring her faggots to add them to his stake—" *Sancta simplicitas* "!

This abrogation brought me into much disfavour, particularly among the Kaiserin's ladies-in-waiting. At the time of the Boer War I had received many abusive letters, some of them signed and some anonymous, calling me " England's lackey," " traitor to the Fatherland," etc. Now it was my dear wife's turn, who had always kept well apart from politics. For weeks she was deluged with letters, with post-cards even—from zealous, mostly anonymous Protestants, who sharply reproved her for being a Catholic and so betraying her husband and her country to the Jesuits. In some instances these were accompanied with threats. They all went into the waste-paper basket.

A friendly aide-de-camp in their Majesties' suite described in a letter the following scene:

> During dinner last night one of Her Majesty's ladies said with a sigh: " The Chancellor has a Catholic wife and a Catholic adjutant, the hereditary Prince von Salm; even his private secretary Geheimrat Schefer is also said to be a Catholic. In any case his best friend Prince Franz Arenberg is a zealous Catholic, and escorts Madame von Bülow to mass every Sunday, at St. Hedwigs'. How will it all end?" The Kaiserin did not reply, and the Kaiser also remained silent, but seemed perturbed.

I did not let such a mixture of malice and stupidity annoy me. I can quite well understand the widespread Protestant mistrust of the Society of Jesus. Many Catholics even regard this Order with suspicion. No writer has criticized the Jesuits more sharply than Pascal in his immortal letters, *Les Provinciales*, and yet Pascal was one of the greatest Catholics of all time. It was a Catholic who said: "*O vos, qui cum Jesu itis, non ite cum Jesuitis.*" A Tyrolese Catholic, Hermann Gilm, in his *Jesuit Songs*, pilloried this Order as no one else has ever done. But, on the whole I do not believe that in countries with a strong Protestant majority—in England or the United States—the Jesuits can do much harm. On the other hand the histories of Austria, France, and Poland, show all the harm they can do in Catholic countries, by their violent fanaticism, narrow-mindedness, and love of power. In a nation like the German, where the two faiths are almost numerically equal, the Order has not always contributed to a good understanding between the Protestant and the Catholic. So much the more necessary therefore for the Protestant half of our people to maintain the rights and dignity of the Protestant Church, in broad-minded tolerance, though with a firm upholding of its faith. Here I must assert emphatically that there are not only clever and capable but good and noble men among the Jesuits, men imbued with a spirit of the finest idealism. During the Franco-Prussian War of 1870 I served in the same squadron as a Westphalian Baron, von Böselager. He attracted me. He was a young man of exceptional gifts and cultivation, and at the same time a very efficient soldier. No King's Hussar could surpass his keenness on duty, his untiring zeal on patrol, his bravery during an attack. We held long religious conversations in the spirit of the great dictum "*In necessariis unitas.*" After the campaign Böselager handed over his considerable fortune to charitable institutions, and entered the Jesuit Order. When, years later, I asked one of his relatives for news of him, I learned that Carl Böselager had succumbed to a plague epidemic in the marshy lowlands of the Ganges, having tended the sick, and comforted the living to the end. *Ave pia anima*!

When I had achieved the abrogation of paragraph 2, Cardinal Kopp wrote to me as follows:

I beg Your Excellency to accept an unobtrusive word of thanks for Your settling of the Jesuit question. This storm, which seems to me largely artificial will, I hope, soon subside. I trust that, on the other hand we Catholics will long remember the sacrifices made by Your Excellency to further this peaceful achievement.

In unchanging loyalty and homage,
G. CARDINAL KOPP.

My dear old friend Prince Franz Arenberg wrote:

> Julius Bachem the editor of the *Kölnische Volkszeitung* has just told me that the second edition of the Catholic State Lexicon is completed, and that it has been decided to present you with a copy de luxe. They all know how grateful they ought to be to you for all the attacks you have brought on yourself in their interests, and they hope this gift will give you some proof of their grateful devotion. It gives me much pleasure to be able to transmit this demonstration of their gratitude.

Arenberg added later in conversation: "As a Centre Party man I thank you. As a friend I say 'Now stop!' Whenever any German Party has got all it can reasonably expect it always ends by becoming arrogant, and then the Government gets sick of it." Within two years this prophecy had been realized.

In March 1904 the Kaiser took his first Mediterranean trip. The Hamburg-America Line had placed one of its finest liners at his disposal. This enabled His Majesty to invite a great many of his friends. On the Kaiser's return the Chief of the Military Cabinet, Count Dietrich Hülsen, a man of considerable common sense said to me:

"Why did you send us that awful Schiemann? He is a parasite, a toady, and a climber. The three together are too much of a good thing." When to-day I look back on my life I am forced to admit that, since, as a general rule, to err is human, I often, in my own particular case, had the misfortune to err in personalibus. When I became State Secretary for Foreign Affairs Waldersee and Holstein called my attention to a Baltic Professor of History, Herr Theodor Schiemann, who was then in very straitened circumstances. I asked him to dinner; he seemed very well up in Russian history. Since history has always specially interested me, and I had, during my stay in Russia, made a point of studying its past, I was delighted with my new acquaintance though I found his obsequious manner rather objectionable. He really did seem very badly off, and I helped him from time to time out of the small funds at my disposal for such purposes. I also granted his urgent request to be presented to H.M. the Kaiser and, after a dinner at which His Majesty was present, I gave him a chance to go through his paces. He related for the Imperial edification such events as the execution of the unhappy Tsarevitch Alexei by his father, Peter the Great; the murder of Tsar Peter III by his wife, the Empress Catherine; the suffocation of Tsar Paul with the secret knowledge, if not connivance, of his wife and his eldest son, Tsar Alexander I. Finally I placed him on the list of suggested invitations for the Kaiser's Mediterranean trip. Schiemann looked not merely half-starved, which touched my wife's soft heart from the beginning, but also down at heel. I bought him a complete new outfit for the journey. He received two new lounge suits—a smart navy blue, and a light grey—in which he could appear without embarrassment as a member of the Imperial suite.

But, as with so many other professors, the atmosphere of the court went to his head. His toadying obsequiousness increased; he was for ever scandal-mongering, and, worse still, became, as time went on, the cause of many political *contretemps*. In those days he was writing a weekly review of foreign affairs for the *Kreuzzeitung*, and nearly every article contained a panegyric in my honour. Later these essays appeared in book form. I have them still, bound in red morocco, in a neat little row in my library. Since their binding is red they could not blush when Schiemann, after my resignation, changed from a fulsome eulogist to a spiteful enemy.

While the Emperor sailed the Mediterranean, Loubet, the French President, visited Rome. William II would have liked only too much to meet him, and was very pre-occupied with the ceremonial proper to such an event. It seemed to him out of the question to let the band on any German boat play the "Marseillaise" on such an occasion. "That would be contrary to my legitimist principles," wrote the Kaiser. But he was willing to concede the military march "*Sambre et Meuse*" to the President, although that too had been baptized in blood at the Revolution. I pointed out to His Majesty that really he had no need to worry, since it was highly unlikely that the President would summon up the courage for such a meeting, and so incur the wrath of the French Chauvinists—Déroulède and the "*Ligue des Patriotes*." He would be particularly unwilling to do so at that moment, since he was engaged in affronting the Pope in an effort to win over the Italians. Nevertheless the Kaiser held fast to his plan with an obstinacy peculiar to himself whenever a personal inspiration was involved.

His Majesty's original intention had been to put in at Corfu before he finished his trip. There he was to have met his sister, Princess Sophie of Greece, and at the same time to have visited the Achilleon, the beautiful château of the Empress Elizabeth of Austria, of which he had heard much, which he wished to own, and did in the end actually purchase. Suddenly now, and without his having informed me in Berlin, the course of the Imperial vessel was changed. It made for Genoa instead of for Venice and Corfu, since the Kaiser hoped to catch President Loubet on his return journey

from Naples to France. To put it quite bluntly he wished to pounce
on the President somewhere between Naples and Genoa. Our
Ambassador to Rome, Count Monts, informed me on 31st March
1904 that His Majesty insisted on disembarking at Genoa. He
wrote:

Since the 29th, the date provisionally arranged for this,
clashes with President Loubet's departure from Naples, it has
been confidentially suggested by the Italians, that a change in His
Majesty's itinerary might be advisable. His Majesty, however,
has refused a parallel programme in which Major von Chelius
worked out a landing in Trieste. Since a visit to the Adriatic,
and especially to the Island of Corfu was already planned for the
end of the trip, this return to the Mediterranean, for the special
purpose of disembarking at Genoa, may be interpreted by the
Italians as intentional. This, above all, would have a bad effect
on King Emanuel, and might do serious injury to the excellent
results of the Naples interview. The Italian Court would be
obliged to arrange an official reception at Genoa. A German
Emperor, on a ship escorted by a squadron, cannot land in the
guise of a private gentleman. The best that could be provided
to meet our Kaiser could only be an Italian prince—most probably the Duke of Genoa—since the King, at the same moment
will be personally supervising the embarkation of President
Loubet at Naples. Comparisons, neither pleasing for His Majesty
nor good for the public, might be drawn. Apart from this, if our
Kaiser crosses, so to speak, in the wake of the French squadron,
the rumour that His Majesty is eager for a personal talk with the
French President, will begin to come to life again. I have had
several discussions of this matter with Herr von Tschirschky, the
Foreign Office representative on board the Imperial ship. The
latter is of opinion that only Your Excellency in person is likely
to persuade His Majesty, in the light of the above, against returning via the Mediterranean. Even so it will not be easy to induce
His Majesty to alter his programme, since he himself has said to
several adjutants, though never directly to Herr von Tschirschky,
or myself, that he is anxious to meet the French squadron on its way
from Naples as though by accident. Since even a Nelson did not
succeed in meeting the fleet on its way to Egypt it would surely
be a difficult task for Commodore Usedom to catch up with the
ironclads of the Republic on the high seas. Finally I would
respectfully venture a personal observation: during my stay at
Naples certain of His Majesty's remarks seemed to point to a

repetition of this Easter trip next year. This, despite all rumours to the contrary, seems to tally with a very noticeable friendliness displayed by His Majesty towards the King, and with his readiness to bestow decorations and orders on everybody who happened to be suggested to him, and even, at times, in excess of these suggestions.

On 2nd April Monts added this postscript:

At the moment of going to post I received a telegram from Tschirschky. He urgently requests Your Excellency to preserve completest secrecy as to His Majesty's wish to meet the French fleet in the Mediterranean. Our naval and diplomatic sources of information would be painfully compromised, debarred from future service abroad, and so made useless.

The Kaiser, in the end, was forced to console himself by admiring the beauties of Sicily. They aroused his naturally impressionable and beauty-loving spirit to enthusiasm. The cathedral of Palermo, with its tombs of Frederick II, the inspired and unhappy Emperor, and of his father, the mighty Henry IV, evoked many Hohenstaufen memories in him. In Sicily the family is forgotten and these memories are almost effaced. Considerable surprise was therefore felt when the Kaiser, on his return, replied to an address of the mayor of Karlsruhe with the remark that he had just come from a country where the memory of the old German emperors was more faithfully cherished and kept alive than anywhere. This speech (delivered on 28th April 1904) I toned down as far as possible before publication. In spite of this there was a general shaking of heads. His capacity for being intensely moved by the most various and conflicting impressions was both William II's charm and his misfortune.

When I reached Karlsruhe, a few hours before the Kaiser, to receive him, I found a cipher telegram from the Foreign Office informing me that von Eckardstein, the ex-Secretary of Embassy, had also just left for Karlsruhe. [*The publishers wish to dissociate themselves from the following statements, which are included in order to preserve for English readers the full text already available in the German edition. This passage has historical value, not as a comment on the person concerned, but as an indication of the Imperial Chancellor's point of view.*] Richthofen, the Secretary of State, who had sent this message, informed me further that he had heard, from a trustworthy and very important Berlin banker, that Eckardstein was heavily involved in bear speculations. It would therefore be as well to keep my eye on him in all his relations with the Kaiser.

Eckardstein had retired some while previously, at a moment when, notwithstanding certain things I disliked about him, I was considering him for a minor Embassy. He had given, as the reason for his retirement, the fact that his wife could not manage to live anywhere but in England, and that considerable financial interests bound him to his wife's country. A few years later it was discovered that Eckardstein was already too involved in risky, large scale, Stock Exchange speculations, to make it safe for him to live far from the City.

I soon learned what had brought him to Karlsruhe. The Kaiser, with his accustomed frankness, informed me that Eckardstein had given him a " first-rate " piece of advice. He was to take the earliest chance that offered—*e.g.* the imminent unveiling of a war memorial at Metz or Saarbrücken—to " turn a cold douche on Paris." This would raise Imperial prestige and take the French down a peg. The advice was doubly dangerous since His Majesty resented the French President's Mediterranean escape from the meeting so ardently desired. I succeeded in preventing this false step in the direction advised by Eckardstein, and a little later was rewarded by H.M.'s complete *volte-face* into the arms of " La belle France."

His Majesty was at Homburg attending some automobile races, and a French car won. As the Kaiser handed the victor a trophy awarded by the Kaiserin, several Frenchmen present began to shout " *Vive l'Empereur!* " The Kaiser was so pleased with this demonstration that he wired off at once to President Loubet:

> Hasten congratulate you on victory just obtained by French industry, and which I had great pleasure in witnessing. Reception given the victor by crowd goes to prove how much a triumph gained by hard work and intelligence can do to engender sentiments free from rivalry.

His Majesty, in the first white heat of enthusiasm, had gone even further than the above. My friend, Cabinet Councillor von dem Knesebeck, who in my absence was entrusted with the drafting of the telegram, succeeded in putting through this reasonable version. Loubet's reply was dignified and restrained.

I had received the following telegram from His Majesty:

> Gordon Bennett race went splendidly; huge crowd, with many French; a Frenchman won. President Paris Automobile

Club and members of Committee presented to me. All, *proprio motu*, cheered me in the name of France. Cheer taken up with enthusiasm by the many hundreds of French men and ladies present. Shouts on all sides "*Vive l'Empereur!*" and "*Vive l'Impératrice!*" The French attitude irreproachable. Tribunes, in the style of Jacobi's Roman Circus splendidly arranged. General satisfaction and enthusiasm and really remarkable organization —the whole thing went off brilliantly. Am convinced the two countries have taken a definite step towards reconciliation.

This little incident shows once more how inclined William II always was to set quite an exaggerated value on events of no political significance. In the present instance the shouts of "*Vive l'Empereur!*" had electrified him. Yet, as Bismarck had already bitterly observed, on the occasion of the new Emperor's demand that his mother should visit Paris—a visit which, as everyone knows, was a fiasco: "The Prussian 'Hurrah' is no longer good enough for our Sovereign. He hankers for a French '*Vive l'Empereur!*'"

The Kaiser's naïve subjectivism—his egocentric attitude to life, to give the thing its fashionable cliché—were also displayed in the matter of the motor-car itself. When the first cars appeared in Unter den Linden, His Majesty had not yet begun to use them. He was for ever raging against these vehicles because they frightened his horses. He demanded that they should be controlled and placed under police supervision, and once remarked in my hearing:

"I only wish I could put a bullet in the . . . of every chauffeur I meet."

But when he himself began to drive one, and his chauffeurs were "Honk-honking" merrily everywhere, he became a fanatical motorist, apt to consider any criticism as almost a personal affront.

CHAPTER II

*The Hereros rising—Wars must be made with more than military
weapons—The Russo-Japanese War—Kuropatkin—Edward VII
visits Kiel—My interview with the Emperor and Tirpitz—Arrival
of Edward VII at Kiel—The King of England gives me an interview
—The Press of both countries—Speeches at Kiel—Visit of King
Edward to Hamburg—My interview with Lord Selborne—The Kiel
Regatta.*

IN the year 1904 two questions especially engaged my attention:
firstly the rising in our South-West African colonies; secondly,
and to a far greater extent, the war between Russia and Japan.
In Germany it was everywhere asserted that the Herero rising had
been engineered by the English. I did not believe it then nor do
I to-day. There have always been such risings in African colonies,
especially in newly-conquered colonies, and in every part of the
Dark Continent. The rising was serious, but thanks to the sustained
endurance and valour of our men, it was quelled, though with a
grievous loss of men and property. The splendid behaviour of the
troops was a fine proof that, despite a long peace, our people still
retained their military virtues. I could, with justice, write in my
Deutsche Politik,[1] that those famous men who fought and died on
desert soil deserved a lasting place in their country's memory. On
the book's appearance in 1916 I added: " May this blood not
have been shed in vain. May South-West Africa, the oldest of our
colonies—the great territory where, inspired by Bismarck, Germans
first trod African soil be ours again with its diamond fields when
this war is ended—and for ever."

Providence has denied us this wish. In the Great War, at the
end of an heroic resistance, South-West Africa was wrested from
Germany. In 1904 the South-West African rising marked a crisis in
our Colonial policy, but, at the same time, a turn for the better. All
our colonies were developing well. German appreciation of their
value and significance had begun to penetrate into every class of the
people. The disastrous peace, the collapse of the glorious German
Empire, destroyed, with many others, these fine hopes.

I am reminded, in spite of myself, on looking back at the South-

---

[1] Prince Bülow, *Deutsche Politik* (popular ed., p. 107).

West African rising, of an incident which came vividly into my mind more than once in the course of the Great War. In the spring of 1904 General von Trotha, a smart Foot Guardsman, had been entrusted with the conduct of operations in South-West Africa. To dispose of the Hereros more quickly he suggested that they should be driven—women, children and all—into a waterless desert, where a certain and lingering death would confront them. I informed His Majesty that I would never give my consent to this suggestion. The Kaiser, at first, seemed surprised, then he began to grow agitated. To my contention that such action would be unchristian he replied that Christian precepts were not applicable to heathens and savages. I said to him: " I will dispense with the Sermon on the Mount, and set aside all theological arguments. All I need quote is a very profane thinker—Talleyrand, who said when the Duke of Enghien had been shot: ' *C'est pire qu'un crime, c'est une faute.*' Your Majesty's ' No quarter ' speech has already done much harm, although it was only an intimation. If, now, you proceed from theory to practice, you will do harm that no results can justify. Wars are not fought by military weapons alone; politics must also carry weight."

The Kaiser became very angry, and we did not part on good terms. But a few hours later I got a letter from him, to say that he yielded to my objection. With that mixture of kindliness and wit which so often characterized him he signed himself:

WILLIAM I. R.
qui laudibiliter se subjecit.

I am convinced that if, throughout the Great War, the Kaiser had had at his side a Chancellor worth the name, instead of four non-entities, we should have used no military methods whose practical value was not worth the moral and political harm they did us. Wars are, in the long run, won or lost on a political not a military basis. I should like here to emphasize the fact that our severest military measure during the war never touched those extremes of cruelty practised in Hamburg by Davoust, by Mélac in the Palatinate, by Kitchener in South Africa, or that blockade which, in the Great War, the English engineered against us, and which caused the deaths by slow starvation, of thousands of innocent German women and children. This was far more abominable than either the shooting of Nurse Cavell, or the sinking of the " Lusitania." But, just as when war was declared, we put ourselves in the wrong by clumsy diplomacy, so, as the war continued, was our policy of " frightfulness " the result of the same stupidity and awkwardness. There, too, we were " sheep in wolves' clothing."

Count Osten-Sacken, an old and experienced diplomat had already, in conversation, in the autumn of 1903, justifiably compared the friction between Russia and Japan, which preceded the outbreak of war, with the origins of the Mexican adventure. The Russo-Japanese and Franco-Mexican wars alike arose out of shady Stock Exchange speculations. They were similar also in the circumstance that the military enterprises inspired by jobbers were camouflaged with patriotic phrases as far-seeing political action. Rouher, in France, had called the Mexican expedition: " *La plus grande pensée du règne.*" In Russia the *camarilla* surrounding the Tsar—Grand Dukes, who wanted to make money on the Jalu River, persuaded him that their " policy of expansion " would revive the glories of Imperial policy under Peter, and Catherine the Great. All the more comprehensible therefore, the uneasiness of the Pan-Slavs, who wished to see Russia husband her resources for Europe, in particular for the Balkans. Kuropatkin was appointed to the supreme command of the Russian Army in Manchuria. Till then he had been the idol of Russian patriots. He was considered not merely a brilliant swashbuckler à la Skobelev, but even a very great strategist, of almost Napoleonic dimensions. I met him more than once in society, and at intimate dinners in St. Petersburg. He impressed by sitting and saying nothing, which was generally considered very profound. Instead of talking he would drink off one glass of vodka after another, and this delighted everyone as a proof of the genuine Russian temperament. The poor man was to encounter the same fate as Gyulai, Benedek, Trochu—as Bazaine, Lebœuf, and many another general, who first were overrated, then despised.

Tsar Nicholas had stumbled into war. Conflict with Japan had seemed to him always a possible, at times a likely contingency. But he had not believed that war would be so sudden. On the night before the Japanese torpedo boats attacked the Russian fleet outside Port Arthur the Tsar, at a court ball in St. Petersburg, honoured the Japanese ambassador with a long and gracious conversation. Later, as the ball progressed, the Japanese, with Asiatic inscrutability, remarked to the Japanese Ambassadress, Countess Alvensleben: " The poor Tsar doesn't know that all the time he is talking to me here his navy in Port Arthur is being sunk by ours."

Even after the naval battle at Chemulpo, which actually gave the Japanese possession of Korea, the Tsar replied to Chamberlain Benckendorff's question whether, in view of the war with Japan, the forthcoming Court balls should not be cancelled: " It will never come to anything serious. *Les Japonais n'oseront pas.*"

Later a Russian lady said to me: " *Les impériaux dans tous les pays ne veulent jamais croire et admettre ce qui ne leur convient pas.*" She might have quoted the Latin phrase: " *Quos deus perdere vult prius dementat.*"

In May, with new life and budding trees, a longing for action would stir the impulsive heart of the Kaiser, not always for his good. In the spring of 1904 he astonished me by announcing that his uncle King Edward had intimated his intention of coming to Kiel. I felt an instant doubt whether the initiative had ever really come from King Edward.

Later I learnt that the Kaiser, through his brother Prince Henry, had sent a special message to the King that he particularly wished to receive his visit at Kiel. The idea of leading the English Monarch straight into the workshop of our navy, and demonstrating its rapid development, *ad oculos*, made me uneasy. I would very much rather have suggested a visit to Berlin, to Wilhelmshöhe with its charming surroundings, to Homburg with motor tours in the Taunus, and trips on the Rhine. One day, as I pondered all this, Tirpitz called. He had just been informed, by a telephone call from the Kaiser, of the alleged English request to visit Kiel. The thought of a meeting in Kiel was equally unwelcome to us both. He felt sure the Kaiser's childish vanity would not rest until he had bragged to the Englishman of the recent progress of our navy. Bragging, said von Tirpitz, was a vice the Kaiser could never be rid of. The only thing, therefore, to be done was to see that no really important excuse for bragging presented itself. Whatever happened we should have to prevent the Kaiser from massing the fleet in Kiel: the fewer ships he displayed to the English there the better. We decided to go together at once and lay our views on the subject before His Majesty, and so left Berlin for the Neues Palais.

When I suggested to the Kaiser that I should have preferred a meeting at Homburg, Wilhelmshöhe, or Berlin, rather than at our greatest naval port, he replied somewhat irritably that his uncle had so far refused a visit to Berlin, and that he did not want to have to " beg " for one. I had foreseen this excuse, and showed him a telegram from the archives (I had brought it with me in my pocket) proving that, some time previously, King Edward had expressed a wish to visit Berlin. It was the Kaiser himself who had found this visit inconvenient and postponed it. Then there was nothing left for His Majesty but to announce the fact that he had already wired to his uncle to say how delighted he was at the prospect of his visit to Kiel. The thing was done and could not be undone. The Secretary of State for the Navy next suggested, in a detached and measured tone, that it would be better not to parade the whole of our naval forces at Kiel.

The Kaiser, who for some time had not liked Tirpitz, abruptly declared that it was childish to imagine the English not fully informed of our naval strength, from the smallest pinnace to the biggest warship. Tirpitz replied that he had no doubt of it, but that there was a difference between King Edward, and the admirals and naval officers of his suite, being informed by despatches from the English naval attaché in Berlin, and occasional reports from spies and agents, and their seeing with their own eyes the entire strength of our fleet manœuvre in front of them. The English especially were open to direct impressions.

I emphatically supported these very judicious representations, till at last the Kaiser agreed to let Tirpitz send as few or many ships to Kiel as he chose. It transpired, however, the next day, that His Majesty in the course of the night, had directly instructed the Naval Cabinet to send everything, down to the smallest boat, to Kiel. Even now to " show them what he could do " was the thing the Kaiser wanted most.

On June 25th the King of England was due to arrive in Kiel. The Kaiser was eager to receive his uncle, whose course lay through the Kaiser Wilhelm Canal, in Brunsbüttel. I had trouble in dissuading him from this by pointing out how inconvenient it would be for King Edward, no longer in his prime, to be roused between four and five in the morning. The Kaiser insisted that, at least he should go aboard the King's ship and be the first to welcome his uncle. When King Edward received this message he insisted with his usual tact that he, as guest, felt obliged to pay the first visit to his host.

The Kaiser did all in his power to make the reception as brilliant as possible. As the French put it, he " had put the little pots inside the big ones " (" *il avait mis les petits pots dans les grands* "). Every Cabinet Minister had been ordered to Kiel for the reception of His Britannic Majesty, and unless I am mistaken, the Secretaries of State as well. A whole troop of Excellencies, magnificent in Orders and gold braid, were arranged in a dignified row along the shore. All the Royal Princes had been ordered to swell the Guard of Honour drawn up on the landing stage. His Majesty was so flurried that, no sooner had his uncle set foot on land, than, with friendly little pokes in the ribs, he stimulated to ever greater empressement, the generals and admirals requisitioned to compose his personal suite.

His uncle looked as calm as he looked agitated. He had brought
the First Lord of the Admiralty, the Earl of Selborne, Admiral
Prince Louis of Battenberg, and Count Gleichen, the English
military attaché in Berlin, with him. The two last were German by
birth: Battenberg, the son of Prince Alexander of Hesse and the
Polish Countess Hauke; Gleichen, a son of Prince Victor of
Hohenlohe-Langenburg, and an Englishwoman, Miss Seymour. As
is usual with German renegades, both did their best to hide their
origins under exaggerated British jingoism. Battenberg was a
brother-in-law of Prince Henry of Prussia, Gleichen a cousin of the
Empress Augusta Victoria: they, therefore, both heard more than
was good for us.

The day the English arrived, a banquet took place on board the
"Hohenzollern." The Kaiser had drafted the speech he intended
for this occasion with my help. It did no particular harm that he
should have insisted on retaining a phrase in which King Edward
had "most kindly" consented to take part in the German regatta-
week. In return for this, he allowed my sentences to stand to the
effect that the German Navy, built to guarantee our soil and commerce, was destined for the maintenance of that peace which the
German Empire, in concert with the other great powers, had upheld
for thirty years and would maintain.

"Everyone is aware that your Majesty's thoughts and actions
are equally directed towards this goal—the maintenance of peace!
Since I too have devoted all my energies to this end may God grant
success to our common effort."

At the close there came a passage, suggested by William II,
recalling an unforgettable hour together, when King and Kaiser,
son and grandson, had stood side by side at the death-bed of the great
Queen Empress, the ruler of those Dominions now governed by
King Edward in her stead.

King Edward answered in German, in an extempore and very
cordial speech. It touched him to know that his efforts to keep the
peace had found such recognition: he was happy in the certainty
that the German Emperor had the same objective as himself:

"May our two flags wave side by side for all time, in defence of
the peace and well-being not only of our own countries but of every
other nation."

With a reference to Queen Victoria's memory, sacred alike to
son and grandson, King Edward raised his glass in honour of their
German Majesties.

Next day, after a luncheon party on board the "Meteor" the
King conversed for nearly an hour with me alone. The rumour is

entirely groundless, though later it was fairly widespread, that on that occasion, I suggested an Anglo-German alliance to King Edward. Nobody could seriously imagine me tactless enough to have put such a proposal, *ex abrupto*, to the King of England after luncheon; more especially since a proposed alliance between the English and ourselves had, some years previously, been frustrated by the unwisdom of German public opinion, and the opposition of the then British Prime Minister. In that talk together on board the " Meteor," the King first talked of the Far East. " The Russians," he said, " have only themselves to blame for their misfortunes. Their diplomacy is as bad as their strategy on land and sea. The Japanese have done brilliantly everywhere. Besides they are morally in the right. Russia had neither right nor reason for going to Port Arthur. She has no business whatever in Korea, and has snatched Manchuria from the Chinese in the most brutal fashion."

The King then said that, if Russia had listened to him, war could have been avoided. " At the end of November," he said, " when the Tsar was staying in Spala, I transmitted to him the very moderate conditions on which Japan would have been ready to come to an understanding. The Tsar delayed his reply to these conditions too long, partly no doubt because of the death of little Princess Elizabeth, which made a very deep impression on him. The Japanese kept on repeating that, if Russia did not send her answer soon, they would not be able to control their popular feeling for war. It was too late when the Tsar at last decided to accept Japanese conditions. The leading men in Japan had decided on war in the meantime."

King Edward made no secret of the fact that he hoped for a speedy peace in the Far East, and desired very soon to offer his services as mediator. The Japanese would not be difficult.

When I objected that, after such defeats Russia could scarcely make peace without severely affecting her prestige, the King remarked that he did not see how Russia's position could be improved.

" No Russian success seems likely either on sea or land, and the wisest thing her government could do would be to conclude the speediest possible peace on the best terms they can get."

This led King Edward to the " yellow peril " proclaimed so urgently by the Kaiser. He said that, in contrast to his nephew, and as he hoped in agreement with myself, he could not see that it existed.

" The Japanese are a brave, chivalrous and intelligent people— every bit as civilized as Europeans from whom nothing except the colour of their skins distinguishes them. It would be regrettable if fear of the Yellow Peril, which in my opinion does not even exist, were to influence German policy in any anti-Japanese direction."

I answered His Majesty quite decidedly that our attitude in the Russo-Japanese War would continue as neutral and stable as hitherto. We did not dream of any interference.

I then expressed my thanks to the King for his toast of the previous day. That exalted gentleman answered that a smooth and friendly relationship with Germany had always been a heartfelt wish of his. "For this reason," he added, "I am personally grateful to you for the firm and courageous stand you took in the Boer War. It wasn't so easy for you in those days. It is really unfortunate that the German and English peoples cannot understand each other better. It is all the more difficult to fathom because the individual German who comes to England soon feels at home there and can recognize the great qualities of the English, while on the other hand all the English living in Germany have nothing but praise for the energy and efficiency of the Germans, in every branch of Science and Art, and latterly in commerce and industry also."

I allowed myself a smiling interruption. "With the exception of Mr. Saunders." [1]

Saunders was in those days German correspondent to the *Times*. He had, as I explained to Mr. Balfour, during my English visit in 1899, done nothing but stir up anti-German feeling in the most perfidiously spiteful manner. His Majesty heartily agreed.

"The Press," he said with emphasis, "is mainly responsible for all the misunderstandings which have arisen between Germany and England. I won't go into the question which has been most to blame, the English press or the German. I can only say that between England and Germany there is unfortunately much ill-feeling, though certainly no unbridgable division of interest. Any conflict between these countries would be the greatest misfortune that could befall the world, and especially Europe. But it won't ever come to that. It would not only be a great misfortune but a great piece of folly into the bargain. People in Germany and England should really try not to be too suspicious and too sensitive. There is a widespread conviction in England that the Germans are only building their navy with the intention of falling on England, as soon as they have made it strong enough, of ruining her for ever, either by breaking her commerce or even by an invasion. I do not share this belief. I even do my best to oppose it. But you must understand that since England's safety depends on the safety of her fleet the British Admiralty builds two new English ships to every one

[1] English in original.

German. In Germany people are inclined to look upon friendly relations between England and either France, Russia, Italy or Spain, as a direct threat to themselves. But such alliances are only inspired by the same spirit of defence as the Triple Alliance and the German Navy. If Berlin and London keep clear-headed and don't do anything too stupid, the tension between Germany and England is bound to relax as time goes on; just as, gradually, even far greater menaces between France and England, England and Russia, have been dissipated."

Towards the end of our talk King Edward, on his own initiative, touched on the " agreement " (of April 8th), concluded by Balfour's Cabinet with France, on arbitration in Colonial disputes. It had been signed on the day when the Kaiser visited Malta on a Mediterranean cruise. It consisted of three declarations: (1) England had promised to take no steps towards changing the *status quo* in Egypt; France to demand no term of evacuation. (2) France had given her word not to change the political status of Morocco; England recognized that France, as a neighbouring state to Morocco, had the right to maintain peace there, and in case of necessity assist the Sultan in his administrative reforms with military or financial re-enforcements. (3) Frontier and tariff differences of long standing between both countries, in Senegambia, on the Niger, in Siam and Madagascar, as well as such time-honoured disputes as the contentions on New-foundland fisheries, and the legal status of New-Hebrides natives, were to be settled by arbitration in a spirit of mutual concession.

On this very important agreement to whose conclusion he himself had greatly contributed, King Edward remarked:

" No such particular agreements would be necessary between England and Germany, since there are no concrete, conflicting political interests. With France things are different. Understanding, in her case, with regard to old and difficult points of contention, had become an absolute necessity. But this understanding of France with England is not directed against Germany. There is no thought of isolating Germany. On the contrary my one desire is to reduce all points of friction between the Great Powers, and to secure as long as possible for Europe that universal peace which is as much to England's interest as to Germany's. I shall also do my uttermost to reduce the points of conflict of England and Russia. Peace is an universal necessity, since all countries groan alike under the burden of their armaments taxation."

The King also said *en passant* that he would regret it if conflicts arose in the Near East.

" I am for peace everywhere. It is true that there is not much to be done with regard to the Sultan and the Turks. The former is unteachable, and the latter are a decadent people. The future in the Balkan Peninsular lies with the Rumanians, Greeks, and Bulgars."

He went on to speak of his niece, the Crown Princess Marie of Rumania, with great affection. He could not understand why the Kaiser always spoke of her so slightingly. A little coquetterie and a flirtation every now and then, were surely permissible in a young and pretty woman. Moreover rumours were always exaggerated. Unkind remarks of the Kaiser's had come to her ears and prejudiced her against the German Emperor.

"And also of course her husband," King Edward added with a laugh. "It is not wise to play the schoolmaster everywhere."

King Edward regarded internal conditions in Russia very pessimistically. He compared General Bobrikov to the High Bailiff Gessler. Of Tsar Nicholas he spoke with all the affection of a kinsman. Our talk ended with these words which the King pronounced in balanced serious tones:

"Patience and mutual tact will little by little bring back our peoples into the paths of better mutual understanding. I shall continue to have great confidence in you, in your ability and sincere love of peace."

The length of our interview had seemed to preoccupy the Kaiser: he did not, however, interrupt us, but remained on the quarter-deck out of earshot, busy lecturing the naval officers present, on naval construction.

I have reproduced this talk almost textually. On account of its historic importance I had it noted down almost at once. I reproduce it here from my notes. On looking back on it I am convinced that King Edward's whole policy was directed towards preventing our alliance with Russia. He wanted to keep us apart.

With an eye to all future possibilities he certainly was trying to cultivate the French, as well as the Russians, the Japanese, America, Italy and Spain. I have already mentioned, in connection with the Great Paris Exhibition of 1878, how King Edward, although of pure German origin—a Coburg on his father's side, and on his mother's a Guelph—much preferred the French to ourselves; how, during our war against Denmark, and the war of Prussia against Austria, he publicly showed his hostility to the Bismarckian, the great, the mighty Germany, especially during the Franco-Prussian War. King Edward, on suitable occasions, was fond of giving his nephew a sly rap over the knuckles. But he never wanted a war with us.

[*The publishers wish to dissociate themselves from the following statements which are included in order to preserve for English readers the full text already available in the German edition. This passage has historical value, not as a comment on the distinguished Englishmen concerned, but as an indication of the Imperial Chancellor's point of view.*] Between uncle and nephew many corners might slowly have been rounded if the latter had not constantly annoyed his uncle, by an exhibition of what was perhaps his worst fault—tactlessness. I have already said that the King's *bête noire* was Lord Lonsdale, that disreputable person who was not only in debt, but head over ears in debt. Why should just this *mauvais sujet* have been chosen as the Kaiser's bosom friend. Nobody in Germany or England could understand it. The German invitation asking Lord Lonsdale to come to Kiel put the King of England out of humour from the outset. It had been impossible to prevent this noble lord's receiving an invitation. The office of Imperial Chancellor, rightly understood and discharged, is enough to fill up the whole of one good workman's time. But to handle the Kaiser properly and keep in constant touch with him in the interests of the country, the necessity of repairing his little slips, or rather of preventing them from happening, required a double supply of time and strength.

King Edward was very annoyed at finding Lonsdale, whom he heartily detested, at Kiel. He demanded that at least the Kaiser should show himself particularly gracious to his own particular friend, Sir Thomas Lipton, the tea magnate, whom he had brought to Kiel. But this was not to be achieved.

The Kaiser asserted that his uncle had borrowed millions from the immensely wealthy Sir Thomas, who provided the whole of England with Ceylon tea, and was rolling in money. He could not, he said, encourage this undignified connection. By all the laws of common sense it should have been a matter of indifference to the Kaiser on what basis his uncle's friendship for Lipton, who was neither stupid nor uninteresting, reposed. Had the Kaiser possessed a grain of worldly wisdom he could have given his uncle great pleasure by paying just such little attentions to this nabob as would have predisposed in his favour the Sovereign of that universal empire, whom he fêted so impetuously: " *Pour être aimé il faut être aimable,*" as Marco Minghetti used to say.

The speeches exchanged on June 25th had been reasonable: but two days later at the Imperial Yacht Club, William II made a speech which, although highly characteristic of his nature, was rather naïve than statesmanlike. He began by eulogizing the King, as Admiral of the Royal Yacht Squadron, to which England owed the development and flourishing condition of this magnificent sport. He went on to say that in England he had served his seaman's apprenticeship, and added: " When, as a little boy, I was allowed to visit Plymouth and Portsmouth, hand in hand with kind aunts and friendly admirals, I admired the proud English ships in those two superb harbours. Then there awoke in me the wish to build ships of my own like these some day, and when I was grown up to possess as fine a navy as the English."

This childhood memory almost moved His Majesty to tears. He called for three cheers, in real honest jack-tar fashion, for King Edward. When the requisite " Hip-hip-hip hurrahing " had died down the King of England replied.

His speech was in German, and I again admired his ironic gift of rising to every situation. His reply was a mixture of good-natured sarcasm and friendly thanks for his reception:

" My dear Willy, you have always been so very nice and friendly with me that I find it difficult to express my gratitude for all your kindness in a way that would really do you justice. I am proud to have become a member of this club. I thank you a thousand times for all your good wishes, and drink your health as Admiral of the Imperial Yacht Club."

While the Kaiser was making his speech, I had forbidden the representative of Wolff's Agency to wire to Berlin before I had corrected it. As soon as I had the shorthand notes in my hands I composed, as often before on such occasions, another, equally friendly, but more sober Imperial address, which I gave back to Wolff's for transmission. Afterwards when the Kaiser read it in the *Kieler Zeitung*, he said to me, without any anger, but in a somewhat mournful voice: " You've made me another new speech—and you've left out just the best bits."

I replied calmly but seriously: " Believe me Your Majesty— this is far better for Yourself and everyone concerned. If you describe our fleet, constructed with such heavy cost, sometimes with danger, so sentimentally, as the outcome of your own personal inclinations and juvenile memories, it will not be easy to obtain further millions for naval construction from the Reichstag."

The Kaiser grunted: " Ach, that damned Reichstag." But there the matter rested for the moment.

Next day King Edward went to Hamburg. His visit to our greatest trading centre went off extremely well. It was the brightest spot in the whole visit. The King had always liked Hamburg. He was in the best of humours at the banquet the city gave him, freer and more jovially at ease than among all the uniforms at Kiel.

He said, in a short address that, when he returned to his own country, he would be sure to seize every opportunity of telling his English subjects how well and pleasantly Hamburg had received him. He was perfectly aware that this reception was not meant only for himself but for the great Empire whose ruler it had pleased God to make him.

An incident helped to increase the King's good humour. On the table stood some magnificent goblets, masterpieces of goldsmith's craft. When the King admired them the mayor begged him to accept them as souvenirs of the City of Hamburg.

The King who, like many other sovereigns, really enjoyed being given little presents, accepted them with evident pleasure, saying that he would always consider them a token of the good relations which, for centuries, had subsisted between this great city and England.

On his return from Hamburg the King told me that he had telegraphed to England, to his Secretary of State for Foreign Affairs, Lord Lansdowne, to say he could not have had a better reception in any English city.

On June 29th I had a long talk with the Earl of Selborne. He told me much about Lord Salisbury who had passed away a few months previously at Hatfield. He had been intimate with that great English statesman and was, I believe, his son-in-law. He told me among many other things that Salisbury had always been in favour of a good understanding with Germany. But he had not wanted an alliance because he was opposed on principle to English commitments in Europe. He once told our Ambassador that he considered the sea and her chalk cliffs were England's best allies. Although he valued Chamberlain's talents, he did not much care for him personally, and considered him too reckless and impulsive in his handling of foreign policy. Even during his last illness, Lord Salisbury urged upon his sons and his intimate friends the necessity for England to remain on terms of amity with Germany, in spite of occasional friction. A war between the two nations would be a European catastrophe, with no good results for either.

How lovely Kiel Bay looked, sparkling in the June sunshine! Everything there, Kiel Week, all the gay doings in Kiel, were William II's creation. Nowhere did he feel more at his ease. For him it was a kind of equivalent to the growling of cannon, the gallop of neighing steeds for Napoleon, the parade ground of Krasnoie-Selo for Nicholas I, of chamois hunting for the Emperor Maximilian I, of museums and picture galleries for the Medici. At the beginning of my Chancellorship he was all impatience to see me at

Kiel; each year I had to accompany him there, though often I found it hard to leave Berlin. I am still very grateful to the Emperor for all the kindliness and attention which he would lavish upon me at Kiel, and yet I can never remember those days without a certain feeling of uneasiness. Usually we would embark before 6 a.m. in the " Meteor." It was not the getting up early that I minded, it was the desolate boredom that ensued. Yachting did not interest me, and on the " Meteor " it was the sole topic of conversation. After several days, I would attempt to take refuge in one of the two little cabins reserved for guests. Nothing to read on board but English novels, which I would devour from beginning to end. I can still remember *Peter Simple* with gratitude, a naval romance which describes in the most innocuous fashion the charming adventures of a midshipman: there was *Japhet in Search of his Father*, and *David Copperfield* and many more.

From time to time, I would put in an appearance on the bridge to see how much longer our pleasure trip would be likely to last. My best hour was mid-day lunch, well-prepared by an English cook, with an assortment of good iced drinks. As a rule our programme was the following: at the moment when we embarked on the " Meteor " the two English skippers were in charge—skipper is the name which the English give the captains of their yachts—His Majesty would be eaten up with the urge to take the helm himself, but he knew that the skippers would not approve. Their professional reputation was at stake, they wanted to win the races and were convinced that the thing would be impossible if once they let the Emperor take the helm. The latter would then do his best to cajole them and win them over with friendly words. He became hail-fellow-well-met with them, slapped them on the shoulder, offered them cigarettes. Usually he managed to win them over. Sooner or later the moment would arrive when everything would depend on his bringing the yacht round her goal, so that she neither struck the buoy that lay there, nor swept round too far from it, which would have meant a loss of time. If the Kaiser steered himself we regularly hit the buoy. His sorrow was always the same; the skippers grunted and swore in English. Prince Henry, a yachting expert, would wear a disapproving air—some impertinent aide-de-camp would remark with a melancholy smile, " Every time he steers her it's the same."

CHAPTER III

Visit of the German Fleet to Plymouth in July 1904—*Count Metternich's report—Explanation of this letter—Preparation of the Russo-German Commercial Treaty—Negotiations—Count Witte, his methods of negotiation—The murder of Plehve, the Russian Minister of the Interior—Commercial Treaty with Rumania and negotiations for a Treaty with Austria-Hungary—Marriage of the Crown Prince— The Prospective Princesses—Betrothal to Princess Cecilie of Mecklenburg.*

ON the last day of the Kiel visit, King Edward proposed to the Kaiser that the German fleet be sent to Plymouth to pay a visit to this big English naval harbour. That, at least, is what the Kaiser declared. I thought at the time, however, that the proposal might have come from William II himself. It is probable that he had hoped to make a powerful impression in England with his bright, stately ships—to make even a moral conquest at any rate to "show what he could do." But the visit of our navy to Plymouth was a failure. We had a cold reception by the English Navy, and the general public was unfriendly. English newspapers published articles in which we were accused of trying to spy out English ports. One important English newspaper even made the foolish suggestion that the German naval authorities wanted to discover and test a suitable place for an invading army to land in England.

Our Ambassador in London, Count Metternich, wrote to me that our visit to Plymouth had not had a very good reception in the English press. The newspapers affected to feel suspicious of this " investigation " of English ports. Referring to the repeated, and somewhat tactless efforts of our Kaiser to make friends in England, the Ambassador added: " It is not dignified to demand more love from people than they are inclined to give. Everything in its own time." Some days later, I received a letter from Metternich which was more disquieting. He wrote to me on July 9th 1904:

In another letter written to-day, I have informed you of the excellent impression made in England by the King's visit to Kiel. The Prince of Wales, the Duke of Connaught, the Princesses, all have expressed themselves as delighted with this successful trip. This feeling is not confined to the Court—it seems to be general. You know that I do not set much store by gossip and scandal and am not inclined to form hasty conclusions. My conviction, therefore, that we have to deal with a secret conspiracy against Anglo-German understanding, is all the more disturbing. The publicists, particularly in the reviews, give information which I can only attribute to diplomatic whispers from a foreign source. The Englishman, even the educated Englishman, is apt to think that his monthly reviews exert no political influence because they are only read by the few. I am not of that opinion. The impulse which influences the masses proceeds from the few, and even abstract scientific thoughts, if they are deep and stirring and contain a new truth, will form the minds of a new generation. I have often deduced, from his pseudonym, the real name of a contributor to reviews, but the veil has remained drawn over the source of his information. Before Kiel, a general attempt was made to cast suspicions upon us and to warn people against us, not only in the political reviews, but at Court as well. I know for certain that strong influences were brought to bear upon King Edward to keep him from going to Kiel. Among the diplomats, there are only three who have the King's ear: the Portuguese Soveral, the Austrian Mensdorff and the Russian Benckendorff. Soveral is not an intriguer, nor is he anti-German. He could even be very useful to us if he were not afraid of causing displeasure and of being snubbed in the most exalted places in our country. I deplore this, and would like to think that His Majesty is not always rightly informed about Soveral. Like all Southerners and, indeed, many a Northerner, he is vain, and if I were sure that he would be well-treated in passing through (that is to say, by His Majesty), I would have Henry Pless invite him to Fürstenstein. But unless he were going to be received by His Majesty, I do not think, as far as I know him, that he would go to Berlin. The days when he was " the blue monkey " are passed. He is now a rather important and generally popular personality, and if his vanity were tickled and he were singled out for special distinction by His Majesty, he might be of great use to us in opposing these libels and suspicions which he now leaves unopposed. Soveral said to me recently, in a long talk I had with him, that King Edward had come back from Kiel extraordinarily satisfied. Soveral, who is a clever man and probably knows him extremely well, says that the King has always striven for good relations with Germany. His traditions and his own feelings point that way, and any unpleasant-

ness with Germany always reacts upon him. Soveral did not
conceal from me that we have a secret enemy, whose hand could
often be discerned, but who always vanished before the moment of
discovery. He could not or would not say who the enemy was.
I do not think that Soveral is diabolical enough to tell me this, if
he were the secret enemy himself. It is to Austria's interest that
German and English policy should follow the same lines. For
this reason, I do not think that Mensdorff intrigues against us.
I have never heard so, and have no reason to think it. He
might join in the gossip and sympathize if a Royal personage
thinks he has a " grievance " against us, but I am convinced that
he is politically on our side. I even know that it was very disagreeable to him when Anglo-German relations grew worse. There
remains Benckendorff. Friction between England and Germany
would accord with his political interests. I have had several long
conversations with him in which he poses as very pro-German.
But he may cherish the idea that good relations between Russia
and Germany are just as useful as bad ones between Germany and
England. He is very suave and clever, and until I learn that I
am making a mistake, I shall apply the principle to him: *à larron,
larron et demi*. He may safely repeat everything I say to him
both here and in St. Petersburg. Although I do not like to make
accusations that are not supported by concrete facts, I feel bound
to let you know that I have heard on many sides that Benckendorff
tried to prevent King Edward's visit to Kiel. Of all rumours,
perhaps Court rumours are the least trustworthy. But the con-
census of opinion is, after all, striking. If one has a hidden
adversary whom one cannot catch, nothing, of course, could be
more clumsy than to brand him openly in public or in the press.
This would only make him more spiteful and cautious. The only
possible plan of action is to appear to notice nothing, but to be
watchful for some concrete fact to emerge. In this game of
intrigue against the German Empire, the Embassy must also
take some knocks. It amuses me to hear myself described as a
dangerous man, who is always overreaching poor Lansdowne
and the Foreign Office, and, as a man virulently anti-English,
only desirous of England's ruin. But, unhappily, the Embassy
has attackers in its own ranks. As far as I am concerned, it is a
matter of indifference what people say about me personally. I
can always defend myself if it is worth the trouble. But it is
utterly unjustifiable for a former member of the Embassy, out of
spite and disappointed hopes, to try to undermine the position of
younger members of the Embassy by virtue of his own social

standing. I consider this an unpatriotic act, which even wounded vanity and an exaggerated opinion of one's own importance, cannot justify. It is spread abroad that Victor Eulenburg, who has won himself an excellent position in a surprisingly short time, is very unpopular with the English, and that he was only sent here as a kind of spy of His Majesty's, to report on the tea-table tittle-tattle of London. As this story is going the rounds, I went in pursuit of it and was able to trace at least one half of it to its originator. The following little scene is from an absolutely trustworthy source: King Edward, in the rear of his box at the Opera, was smoking a cigarette in the company of the gentleman who told me the story. With much rubbing of hands and bowing, Alfred Rothschild entered uninvited to enquire after the exalted gentleman's health and the Kiel trip. He also asked what H.M. the Kaiser thinks of the war in the Far East, and to this the King gave short and evasive replies. Rothschild then mentioned that a new Secretary, Count Eulenburg, is at the German Embassy, and, as he heard, very unpopular. The King said he knew nothing about it. On the contrary in Kiel, young Eulenburg had made himself quite useful—he had, at my request, discussed some small details about orders and decorations with the gentlemen in the King's suite. Rothschild, when asked, declared that Eckardstein told him that Eulenburg is very unpopular here. The King's companion joined in the conversation, saying that this was not true, that Eulenburg, on the contrary, is very much liked, that he is a very pleasant person, and that Eckardstein only says such things against the German Embassy out of pique, because he is no longer attached to it, and because he wanted to be an Ambassador himself. Whereupon the King: " Good Heavens, no! That would never do! "[1] Alfred Rothschild, quiet and puzzled, saw too late that he had done his friend and favourite, Eckardstein, a bad turn. Whether Eckardstein also spread abroad the tale of Eulenburg's secret reports to His Majesty, I do not know, but as both stories are always told together, it is probable that they are from the same source. You will not, I am sure, permit my story of the private talk in the opera box to go back to Eckardstein or A. Rothschild. Personally, I have always cultivated the best relationship with Rothschild, and he has, on more than one occasion, proved himself helpful and friendly.

I must add a short commentary of my own to this letter of our London Ambassador. The Marquis of Soveral, as first Secretary

---

[1] English in the original.

GATHERING OF THE BÜLOW FAMILY

Photo taken in the year 1903.   In the centre Count Bernhard von Bülow

of the Portuguese Embassy in Berlin in the 'eighties, had played a certain part under the old régime in Berlin society. He was universally popular, a frequent guest at the " love-feasts " of the Lancer and Cuirassier Guards, and a great ladies' man. The old Kaiser who, in common with his generation, delighted in a man of elegant manners, especially if he were a graceful flirt, conferred many distinctions on Soveral. Berlin has always had the habit of nick-naming people. Prince Charles' Chamberlain, Count Gerhard Dönhoff, who was a famous gourmand, was called the " Truffle Grave." I have already related that my grand-uncle, Colonel Count Wilhelm Redern, was called the " Cloud Pusher," because of his stiff walk and his way of raising his nose in the air, while his brother, Count Heinrich Redern, who was not very talented but had an enormous mouth, rejoiced in the sobriquet, " Bread Monkey." Soveral, because of his Southern blue-black hair, was called the " Blue Monkey." Under the new régime, which began in 1888, Court manners became, unfortunately, less tactful than of old. It delighted William II to refer to Soveral in conversation as the " Blue Monkey " and, intending it only as a jovial witticism, he even called him so to his face. This was not only in very bad taste, it was unwise. Transferred to London as Ambassador, the Marquis of Soveral soon became a favourite and friend of both King Edward and Queen Alexandra, was highly popular in London society, and had great social and political influence. The story is told of the famous English seaman, Sir Walter Raleigh, that once when Queen Elizabeth was getting out of her carriage on a wet day, he laid his costly cloak down before her so that she should not soil her white satin slippers. Soveral is said to have performed this courtly action for a lovely lady of the Embassy, and because of such anecdotes, London's upper ten thousand found him interesting. I had always been on very good terms with Soveral, but my efforts to persuade the Kaiser to win him back were as unavailing as my long years of endeavour to make His Majesty regard the Japanese more tolerantly.

Count Benckendorff, who was at that time Russian Ambassador in London, was of German origin. The career of his family was characteristic of conditions in old Russia. When Tsar Paul I heard the English Ambassador call a certain Prince Dolgoruki a *grand seigneur*, he said to him angrily, and not unjustly: " *Sachez, Monsieur, que dans mon pays on n'est grand seigneur que quand je parle à quelqu'un et pendant que je parle à quelqu'un.*" The wife of this same Tsar Paul, Tsarina Maria Feodorovna, a Württemberg Princess, was looking for a trustworthy governess for her children. This was an important matter to her because of her husband's changing and unreliable moods.   A former Russian Governor of the Baltic Provinces called her attention to the well-educated daughter of an artillery Major from Riga, called Benkendorf.   Father and daughter did not belong to the old Baltic nobility and were not related to the Beneckendorff-Hindenburg family of the Marches, of which the famous Field-Marshal is a member.   Fräulein Benkendorf from Riga proved an excellent governess for the Imperial children, who retained an affectionate memory of her.   She herself married Herr von Lieven, a man of the Baltic nobility who, thanks to his wife, became later an Ambassador in London, and a Prince.   She was also able to assist the careers of her brothers.   Mephistopheles says that the relations of the flea that the king loved would soon be great folks at Court.   A Benckendorff (the feudal-looking " c " was placed before the " k " in the family name later, and the " f " at the end was doubled) became chief of the Third Department, that is, of the political Secret Police, under Tsar Nicholas.   In those days, this was the most important position in Russia.   Another married the daughter of Alopeus, the Russian Ambassador in Berlin.   He, too, was a soldier of fortune.   His real name was Fuchs and he had started life as a theological candidate at Bonn.

Many a German made a great career for himself in the Russia of the seventeenth, and even of the eighteenth and the nineteenth centuries—Cancrin, born at Hanau, and the son of Professor Krebs, advanced, under Nicholas I, from a humble post in the salt works at Staraya Russa, to the position of Finance Minister which he held for many years, and eventually was made Count Cancrin—Brunnov, originally a tutor, became Ambassador in London—and the sons and grandsons of the comedy writer Kotzebue, he who was murdered by a student named Sand, became generals, admirals, ambassadors and governors-general.   The documents subsequently published by the Bolsheviks, show fairly conclusively that the Ambassador Benckendorff, of whom Metternich wrote, was endeavouring, by means of anti-German intrigues, to make St. Petersburg forget his German origins.   But Metternich's news of Eckardstein disturbed me most of all.   [*The publishers wish to dissociate themselves from the following statement which is included in order to preserve for English readers the full text already available in the German edition.   This passage has historical value, not as a comment on the person concerned, but as an indication of the Imperial Chancellor's point of view.*]   A few years later, the scandalous divorce proceedings instituted by Eckardstein against his wife, brought about his final social and moral downfall.

Count Victor Eulenburg, a son of the then Lord Chamberlain, and later Minister of the Household, was an uncommonly efficient, gifted, and decent young man, who had been my adjutant for several years. As Chancellor of the Realm, I had three adjutants, all of whom died young. I bear all three in grateful memory. My first was the Hereditary Prince Emanuel of Salm-Salm, who later married an Austrian Arch-Duchess. He met with a hero's death during the Great War as Cavalry Captain in the Gardes-du-Corps. At the beginning of the war, he was surprised by the English in India, whither he had gone tiger-shooting. Interned by the English, he managed, with the help of his wife's aunt, Queen Christine of Spain, to get permission to return to Germany. In Gibraltar he was taken a second time, but his constant pleading, with the Queen as intermediary, gained him his freedom once more. He went immediately to the Eastern Front, and there joined his regiment, which had just finished a successful engagement against the Russians. As his comrades greeted him joyfully, one last Cossack bullet struck Emanuel Salm on the temple. He sank down without a word, without a cry of pain. Solon the wise would have ranked him, together with Tellos of Athens, as one of the few truly blessed mortals. The beautiful verses which Ernst Moritz Arndt wrote on Friedrich Friesen, who fell in the Ardennes in 1814, might have been written for Emanuel Salm:

War je ein Ritter edel
Du warst es tausendmal
Vom Fusse bis zum Schädel
Ein lichter Schönheitsstrahl.[1]

His successor, Count Victor Eulenburg, succumbed at a comparatively early age to tuberculosis, contracted during an expedition to Abyssinia. A great future had lain before him, so unusual were his gifts. My last adjutant was Erich von Schwartzkoppen, son of the distinguished commander in the war of 1870-1. He was a typical example of those Prussian officers produced by the Cadet Corps, who are efficient, devoted to duty, and possess such military and human qualities as no one could copy, to quote Bismarck. He, too, died young.

I had convinced myself by a careful study of the international, political, and commercial situation, that we must, above all else, come to an understanding with Russia. If this were accomplished, Rumania, Austria-Hungary, Switzerland and the other countries

[1] " If ever there was a noble Knight, you were he, a thousand times over, one bright sunbeam from top to toe."

would follow. I was also of the opinion that we should deal most easily with the former Minister of Finance, now the Russian Premier, Sergei Iulievitch Witte. But how was I to approach him? I remembered that Witte had told me at our last meeting in St. Petersburg, that there were two big financiers in Europe in whom he had unbounded confidence—Rothschild in Paris and Ernst Mendelssohn in Berlin. I got into touch with the latter who combined cleverness and business acumen with absolute reliability and warm patriotism. He was able to approach Witte by secret and safe methods. In this way I enquired if Witte were inclined to treat with me direct in the matter of a new Commercial Treaty and, should this be so, how best to open negotiations. Witte, up to this moment, had been in the habit of using certain Russian newspapers as mediums for violent polemics against German desires and demands for commercial treaties. This, however, did not disturb me. "*La langue*," said Talleyrand, "*a été donnée à l'homme pour déguiser ses pensées.*" Not long afterwards, Herr von Mendelssohn told me that Witte would be glad to deal with me directly. To bring this about, the best thing would be for the German Kaiser to broach the subject in as natural and discreet a manner as possible in his correspondence with Tsar Nicholas. Kaiser William, who acquiesced in my plans, permitted me to draft one or two letters to the Tsar. We wrote approximately as follows: To keep relations between Russia and Germany unclouded it was advisable to cease the wearisome tariff squabbles and to come to an understanding on an economic basis. But if German bureaucrats and Russian *tchinovniks* were entrusted with this task, there would be no end to it. It would be more practical to shut up two real statesmen together, the greatest economic and financial authority in Russia, Herr Witte, and the German Chancellor, so that they might as quickly as possible reach an understanding satisfactory to both parties. They need not exactly meet in prison. Witte could come to Norderney, where the German Chancellor always spent the hot summer months and where the bracing sea air would give new resilience to Sergei Iulievitch. The Tsar wrote a letter of cordial agreement.

In the course of July Witte arrived in Norderney. He brought a large staff of officials with him, among them the former Russian Financial Attaché in Berlin and later Minister of Commerce, Timiriaseff, who was a good musician and a wily negotiator. I, too, had summoned a large number of leading officials to the island, among them Posadowsky, Podbielski, Wermuth, Körner, and a number of excellent auxiliaries, including Kapp and Göbel. Wolf-

gang Kapp was born in New York, the son of a Westphalian who, in
September 1848, when twenty-four years old, had been one of the
revolutionary hotheads who had attempted to break up the National
Assembly at Frankfurt by force of arms. Forced to fly to America he
had, nevertheless, remained a good German, and returned to Germany
in 1870. He wrote an excellent book, which I have mentioned
elsewhere, dealing with the disgraceful traffic in soldiers practised
by petty German Princes. Kapp's son entered the Prussian Ministry of Finance as a young auxiliary and became Landrat of the
district of Guben. There he showed himself to be an extreme
Conservative, living in constant feud with the member for the
Constituency, the Liberal Prince Henry Carolath, although the
Prince had a gentle amiable nature, which had won him the nickname of " Butter Henry." In 1900 Wolfgang Kapp became
Councillor in the Prussian Ministry of Agriculture, Domains and
Forests, and acted as Commissioner for this Ministry at the Commercial Treaty negotiations at Norderney in 1904. He was a
thorough and industrious official of a highly honourable character,
a patriot and an idealist, but he neither realized his own limitations,
nor was he capable of an understanding of the wider aspects of the
general position. As self-appointed Chancellor of the Reich during
the spring " putsch " in 1920, he was a tragi-comic figure, reminiscent partly of the Captain of Köpenick, and partly of General
Claude François de Mallet who, in October 1812, immediately
after Napoleon had evacuated the burning city of Moscow, proclaimed himself Governor of Paris and wielded power for twenty-
four hours. These exciting future events could not be foreseen by
the modest Commissioner, who followed his chief in Norderney,
the jovial Podbielski, at a respectful distance. Kapp was to lose his
position and his livelihood as the result of petty and spiteful attacks
launched against him by Bethmann-Hollweg, from the height of
his Chancellor's seat in public sessions in the Reichstag during the
Great War.

In Norderney I established such close relations with Witte
that he dined at our house every night. After dinner there were
two or three hours of pleasant conversation. Witte was outspoken
about everything, and this is the first requisite if people, who meet
often, are not to bore one another. He was not in his monarch's
good graces and had a decided grudge against him. Nor did he
love the Tsarina Alexandra Feodorovna, whom he accused of
inciting her husband against him. For that end she had used the
approved means of telling the Tsar that St. Petersburg society
regarded him as a puppet in Witte's hands. She had even drawn

a small caricature of Witte with his massive figure and rough-hewn features, holding in his hand a little marionette which possessed the finely drawn face of the alleged autocrat. Witte humorously described how, with the help of a French spiritualist, a Monsieur Philippe, the Montenegrin Grand Duchesses managed to draw the Tsar and Tsarina into their net. The medium called up the spirit of Tsar Alexander III. When asked what advice he had for his son, the spirit urged loyal adherence to the paternal heritage, particularly with regard to the Alliance with France. At the end, he called to his terrified son, in sepulchral tones: " *Et surtout, n'oublie pas de donner beaucoup d'argent au Prince de Montenegro, mon meilleur ami.*" I, for my part, determined that such machinations should never gain a foothold at our Berlin Court and in our clear Berlin atmosphere. Witte described his dismissal to me as follows: " When I had finished my usual report, the Daklod, as we say in Russia, on the day appointed for it, the Tsar, who was seated at his writing table, stared straight in front of him in an embarrassed manner. Then he said gently, and without looking at me, that he had the impression of late that my health was poor, and he did not wish me to overwork. Therefore he would relieve me of my post of Finance Minister, and nominate me chief of the Council of Ministers." Witte continued, as the colour mounted to his face in wrathful remembrance of the situation: " Then I lost patience. So much falsity and hypocrisy enraged me. I said to the Tsar: I don't understand why you play such a game with me. The post of President of the Council of Ministers is a pure sinecure in Russia. You might just as well have sent me to Siberia or the Caucasus." After a short pause, Witte continued, not without a certain emotion in his voice: " Now you will see that the Tsar has good qualities too. The same evening he sent me a thick envelope containing 400,000 roubles." Witte was apparently proud of this consolation prize.

Witte was a convinced partisan of friendship between Russia and Germany. It was not that he cherished a special affection for the Germans. He preferred Paris to Berlin, and he liked the French, personally, more than the Germans. The English and Americans impressed him to a high degree. But he was convinced that the fate of the Russian dynasty depended upon the maintenance of peace and good relations between Russia and Germany. He was a firm monarchist, in spite of his feelings towards the present Tsar, and in spite of his occasional leanings towards Liberalism. As far back as 1904 he was of the opinion that the fall of the monarchy in Russia would be the signal for anarchy, misery, and the downfall and

ruin of the great Empire. Like many other Russian statesmen,
Witte disapproved and despised the pro-Slav enthusiasm for the
Balkan nations. The sacrifice of Russian blood and money was
rewarded with rank ingratitude by these nations without exception
—the Serbs, the Bulgarians later, and the Greeks and Rumanians
on every possible opportunity. Russia had no need to expand: rather,
she was already too vast. Not only in Siberia and Turkestan,
but in the Caucasus and even in European Russia, there were
enormous tracts of country waiting to be ploughed and cultivated,
illimitable riches were waiting to be mined. The possession of
Constantinople would be a doubtful blessing to Russia. Tsar
Nicholas I once wrote in a firm hand, on the margin of a dispatch
which contained the statement that the orthodox cross must again be
placed on the Church of St. Sophia: " In theory this is all very
well, but in practice, Constantinople would be a possession of doubtful value to Russia, a source of weakness rather than of strength.
Are we to have three capitals? St. Petersburg, the creation of the
greatest Russian Emperor, we can never give up—still less can we
give up Holy Mother Moscow—are we to have Byzantium also? "
Witte himself was decidedly against any extension of the Russian
Empire in Europe. Eastern Prussia? Russia had enough Germans
already. Posen? Russia had enough Poles. Galicia? Russia had
enough Jews. The chief reason why Witte was an upholder of
peace and unity with the German neighbour, however, lay in the
conviction which, I hear, he held to his dying day, that war between
Russia and Germany might possibly lead to the fall of the Hohenzollerns, and would certainly mean the end of the Romanovs. He,
too, thought that such a war would only promote revolution.

The negotiations for the Commercial Treaty generally took
place in the morning, but sometimes we met in the afternoon also.
Witte and I were unanimous in our desire to regard the whole
problem broadly, and not to stumble over petty details. It could
not be denied that he was more broad-minded than my respected
German colleagues. After my people had argued with Witte's
staff for a while, he used to send me a slip of paper on which was
written: " *Mettons fin à ces commérages inutiles! Je vous propose la
solution suivante. . . .* " His suggestions were always practical and
usually acceptable. When one of the German delegates protested
that, unless Witte gave way on a certain point, it might be possible
for us to get a Bill hurried through the Reichstag demanding that
the Government should not give way to Russia on this particular
point, Witte replied with a smile: " And with one short telegram
I can bring about an Imperial ukase raising all our demands by

400 per cent. *Laissons ces enfantillages!* " Of course, I would not permit myself to be bluffed by him, knowing that this was a form of art particularly dear to Russians. One afternoon, after an unusually violent discussion which led nowhere, Witte sent one of his secretaries to me to enquire at what time next day the Berlin express left the Norddeich terminus of the railway opposite the island of Norderney. After an hour, I sent him a message that I had arranged for a saloon car for his journey from Norddeich to Berlin, in consideration of the long hours of travelling he had before him from Berlin to St. Petersburg. He did not broach the subject of his departure again.

A scene that occurred during one of the last sessions is unforgettable. Witte, who had spent the previous evening in my villa talking animatedly until far into the night, took a slip of paper from his pocket, and made a little speech in which he said that in recognition of the goodwill displayed by the German delegation, and to express his own personal regard for the German Chancellor, he wished to make us some not inconsiderable concessions of his own free will. He had barely read these out, when the Under-Secretary of State, Wermuth, who sat next to me, said in bad French, although I did my best to prevent him: " When the Russians are in the mood for giving, the Germans ought to put forward four or five other claims which would give the Russian concessions their full value." Witte replied coolly: " *J'ai voulu vous faire plaisir mais comme vous semblez mal comprendre mes mobiles et mes intentions, je retire ce que j'ai dit.*" Wermuth was a hard-working, well-informed, but not very sensitive official. He was the son of King George of Hanover's former Chief of Police, an official, who through his reactionary attitude in the last few years before the catastrophe of 1866, had made himself much hated, and was, perhaps, respected by the blind King for that reason. At the time, the street urchins of Hanover sang:

> *Du hast den groben Tschirnitz,*
> *Hast Liebig, den süssen Friseur,*
> *Du hast den bitteren Wermuth,*
> *Mein Georgie, was willst Du noch mehr?* [1]

Tschirnitz was a General Adjutant, much feared on account of his harsh manners, and Liebig was the particular favourite of the

---

[1] You have the rude Tschirnitz,
You have Liebig the sweet young hairdresser,
You have Wermuth the bitter,
My Georgie, what more can you want?

last Hanoverian king. When the son of Wermuth supported me during these commercial treaty negotiations, he was distinctly agrarian, and was much afraid of annoying the Conservatives. In those days it would have been difficult to believe that later on, when he was Mayor of Berlin, he would get on extremely well with the Majority Socialists, and even with the Independents and Communists in the " Red [1] House in the Königstrasse."

Körner, the director of the Commercial-Political Department in the Foreign Office, was a strong supporter of mine. In the old days, in the Saxon Ministry of Finance, his father had worked on customs questions. It was said of the son, that he grew up amongst statistics and tariff ordinances as other children grow among rocking-horses and boxes of bricks. Witte was impressed by his ability and knowledge and also liked his manners. During the discussion of a tariff which was important for Chemnitz industry, Witte said: " *Je vous cède cette position pour faire plaisir à M. Körner qui est Saxon.*" Twenty-one years later, when the German Republic wished to negotiate customs duties with Soviet Russia, this distinguished official of the old régime was appealed to and asked to conduct the negotiations with the New Russia.

When I announced to Kaiser William that Witte and I had come to an agreement, the Kaiser sent me the following telegram:

> Your announcement filled me with great satisfaction and much pleasure. After years of painful endeavour, the great work has succeeded, thanks to your never-ceasing industry and self-sacrificing devotion. May our people and our Fatherland come to realize what you have achieved for them by signing this Commercial Treaty, and may they give you just as warm and sincere thanks as I do now. Enjoy your holidays in deserved peace.

When I returned for a few days on pressing business to Berlin, I met my friend Witte on a morning ride in the Tiergarten. From a good distance away, he called out to me excitedly: " Good news! Plehve's just been murdered! " The Russian Minister of the Interior, an enemy of Witte, had been killed on 28th July by an anarchist's bomb, while on his way to the station in Warsaw. Plehve was one of those Russian Germans who, though less cruel than the real Russians, make themselves more hated because of their systematic harshness and rigour. He was a type often seen in Russia since the time of Peter the Great. The son of an impoverished

---

[1] The Town Hall, called " Red " not only because of its red bricks but because of its Socialist-Communist majority.

East-Prussian landlord, he was taken as a child to Russian Poland where his father had bought a small farm. Young Plehve grew up a Pole. Later on, his father moved into central Russia where the son changed from Pole to Russian as quickly as he had changed from German to Pole. " Wilhelm " Plehve had turned into a Polish " Wáclaw," and this " Wáclaw " developed later on into a Russian " Viatcheslav " with the same speed and simplicity. Plehve possessed uncommon capacity for work, a hard fist, unbreakable will-power and great personal courage. Constantly threatened by bombs and bullets, he always drove in an armoured carriage and only told the driver his destination at the last moment. Everybody was convinced that he was a marked man, and that, sooner or later, he would be blown up. He had inspired a great passion in the wife of a French military attaché. She declared hysterically that her greatest pleasure was to share the danger of sudden death with the man she loved. She was not with him in the carriage on the day Plehve was hit by the bomb.

A fortnight after Plehve's murder, the long hoped-for son was born to Tsar Nicholas II. He was given the typically Russian name of Alexei Nikholaievitch, and on the day of his birth was nominated chief of a Finnish Life Guard Regiment, an East Siberian Cavalry Regiment, chief of all Cossack Regiments, and placed at the same time, *à la suite* of two Guards and four line Regiments. All these distinctions, which appear so puerile to-day, could not prevent the poor child from meeting an early and terrible end, a fate which appears all the worse because the boy was sickly from birth. Alexei Nikholaievitch was haemophilitic. His godfathers were Kaiser William and King Edward. The former was represented at the christening at St. Petersburg by his brother Henry who, on his return, could not express in sufficiently warm terms the Imperial couple's joy at the birth of an heir. Tsarina Alexandra Feodorovna was appointed chief of a Dragoon Regiment as a reward.

Germany was assured against economic isolation by the conclusion of a Commercial Treaty with Russia. The fact that confidential and friendly relations existed between the most distinguished Russian statesman and myself was no small matter for us. I wished also to achieve a Commercial Treaty with Rumania, and to this end, invited my old friend, the Rumanian statesman, Demeter Sturdza, to Homburg, where I spent a few weeks in the autumn. We came to an understanding in a short time. Count Posadowsky had been very helpful in bringing about the tariff duties, and as I wished to give him the pleasure of personally concluding an important treaty, that with Austria-Hungary, I sent him to Vienna for this purpose. I soon saw that an exceptional capacity for work and an unique knowledge of economics are not all that are required of a negotiator, in short, that diplomacy, to use Bismarck's words, is not as Germans sometimes think, a science, but an art. Posadowsky soon stuck fast in Vienna. Instead of taking conditions as they were and making the best of them, he started to lecture Austria-Hungary on the drawbacks of dualism. The obvious disadvantages of such a constitution were undeniable, but the Austrian negotiators were not in a position to alter matters, and in any case had no desire to be taught how to do so by a stranger. " *Je sais bien que je suis laid*," said the Frenchman in the story, " *mais je n'aime pas qu'on me le dise.*" As the relations between Posadowsky and the delegates of the Dual Monarchy became less friendly, our Secretary of State of the Interior saw that he could get no further. Whereupon, instead of quietly admitting it—*non omnia possumus omnes*, he accused our Ambassador, Count, afterwards Prince, Karl Wedel, of not giving him sufficient support. Wedel, an old Guards Lancer, took the matter as a personal insult, and was on the point of challenging Posadowsky to a duel. I had to call Posadowsky back to Berlin, and carry on the negotiations there with the Austrian delegates sent from Vienna. Half a century before, Jacob Grimm had written that in formal questions, where relatively unimportant points are in debate, the Germans are more quarrelsome and opinionated than any other nation. In big questions, the Germans usually manœuvre more clumsily than other people.

Among the Austrian delegates, with whom we soon came to a complete understanding in Berlin, I especially noticed Baron Max Beck, who impressed me by his adroitness. He had been the juridical adviser of the Archduke Francis Ferdinand in the prepara-tions for the marriage of His Royal Highness to Sophie Chotek. In his breast pocket he carried a portrait of the Archduke, arm-in-arm with the lady of his choice, which bore the inscription: " From the happy pair to its sincere friend." When soon afterwards, as Austrian Premier, Beck introduced a Bill based on universal suffrage, which was desired by both Clericals and aristocrats, he fell into deep disgrace with the changeable Archduke. Even clever people too frequently forget the wise counsel of the Psalmist: " Put not your trust in Princes" (Psalm 146, 3). The conclusion of the remaining Commercial Treaties I left to my trusted colleagues, in particular, to His Excellency von Körner.

The marriage of the Crown Prince had been occupying the mind of his mother, Kaiserin Auguste Victoria, for some time. In her simple piety and rigid morality, she wished her sons to marry early, and so enter the holy married state as pure and unsullied as possible. A daughter of the Duke of Cumberland was first considered for the eldest son. The Kaiserin, herself the daughter of an unsuccessful pretender, felt an understandable sympathy for the house of Guelph, which, like that of Holstein, had fallen a victim to the larger policy of Bismarck. Philip Eulenburg, with great personal skill had established good relations with the Cumberland family, and was eagerly endeavouring to smooth the way for the union Her Majesty wished. But his efforts shattered on the *vis inertiae* of the Duke Ernst August of Cumberland, who so enraged Kaiser William by his passive resistance that he once wrote on the margin of a letter from Eulenburg: " Before I let the impertinent Guelph climb to Brunswick's throne, I'll see him rot! " This did not prevent William II from giving his charming and only daughter to the son of this impertinent Guelph with Brunswick's throne as dowry. The Kaiserin next considered one of the two daughters of Prince Albert of Saxe-Altenburg, and a Prussian Princess. At Her Majesty's desire, I asked the two young ladies to dine. They looked very pale; at table, one of them felt indisposed. I had the impression that they were both too delicate for the exhausting position of a German and Prussian Crown Princess. Both married later on, the one a Prince Reuss, the other a Count Pückler.

Prince Henry XVIII of Reuss was one of my oldest and most trusted friends. It is well known that all Reuss Princes bear the name of Henry, in honour of one of the greatest German Emperors, the Hohenstaufen Emperor, Henry VI. They are distinguished only by their numbers—the elder branch counting to one hundred, the younger beginning with number one again every century. As they do not want to be called by their numbers in the family circle, they all have nicknames: the distinguished Ambassador in St. Petersburg, Constantinople and Vienna, Prince Henry VII of Reuss, was called " Septi "—another Reuss, Prince Henry IX, bore the jesting title " Pio Nono," another was " Enrico," and so on. The principality of Reuss was the smallest German Federal State. When Frederick the Great, on a journey through his country, was greeted by a Prince Reuss at the frontier, he addressed him with the words: " *Voilà deux souverains qui se rencontrent.*" Prince Henry XVIII of Reuss, who was married to a Princess of Mecklenburg, called my attention to a cousin of his wife, Princess Cecily of Mecklenburg-Schwerin. The idea of this union pleased the Kaiserin from the first. She did not even object to the eccentric mother of Princess Cecily, the Grand Duchess Anastasia, a daughter of Grand Duke Michael Alexandrovitch of Russia.

When the betrothal was accomplished, the Grand Duchess Louise of Baden said to me: "You will all be satisfied with her and so will the country. Young Princess Cecily has a wider vision and more *savoir faire* than most German Princesses, and for goodness of heart and strength of character, she is second to none." At all times, Princess Cecily fully justified this opinion of her. The grace and charm of her manner and appearance won all hearts. Everyone who came in contact with her respected her intelligence, her desire to improve her mind, the seriousness of her views and her sense of duty. She deserves the praise Heinrich von Kleist awards Queen Louise in one of his poems. Crown Princess Cecily bore misfortune nobly when it fell on her young shoulders. On September 4th 1904, the Kaiser told me at the autumn manœuvres of the 9th Army Corps in Altona, that the betrothal of the Crown Prince and Princess Cecily had taken place at Castle Gelbesande near Doberan. Beaming with pleasure, the Kaiser proclaimed the news that evening during the course of the gala banquet at Altona. The Kaiserin drank to me with tears of emotion in her eyes.

CHAPTER IV

*Death of Prince Herbert Bismarck(September 18th 1904)—His character
—Outbreak of Russo-Japanese War—Count Metternich's letter on
the Dogger Bank incident—Giolitti visits Homburg—The Kaiser
urges alliance with Russia—The Imperial hunt in Silesia; unfavourable influences—A report from Herr von Schön—Anti-English feeling
in William II—The question of Danish neutrality—Anxious letters
from Philip Eulenburg—A New Year's Eve talk with William II;
1904—My efforts to raise his Majesty's spirits.*

FOR some time past alarming rumours had been circulating on
the state of Prince Bismarck's health. It seemed hard to
believe that this imposing figure, the very picture of health
and energy was already marked down by death. All the greater
therefore was the shock of the sudden news which surprised me on
September 18th 1904. I have had five really close friends:
Herbert Bismarck, Philip Eulenburg, Franz Arenberg, Bodo
Knesebeck, Frederick Vitzthum. I think Herbert was the closest—
perhaps because of the great admiration that continued throughout
my life, which I had felt, in my earliest childhood for his father.
My earliest memory of Herbert is of playing with him in the pretty
garden of our house in the Mainzerstrasse in Frankfurt and with
his brother, Bill, and our little friend Christa Eisendecher, who was
later to become Countess Eickstedt-Peterswaldt. There was a streak
of Germanic brutality in both brothers. Herbert and Bill both
wanted to make little Christa kiss a fat toad. My brother Adolf
and I defended her, and this led on to a pitched battle. Years later
life had drawn us together again. During my term of office in
St. Petersburg I had approached Herbert closely in a political
sense, and there had resulted between us a protracted political
correspondence.

After his father's fall, in the August of 1890, Herbert had
visited me in Wildbad, where I was spending some weeks with my
wife. All that he told me of the break between the great Prince
and the Kaiser could only enhance my loyalty to the former. Herbert had watched my political career, from my first diplomatic post
as Embassy Secretary on my passing into the service, to my Chancellorship. For nearly a quarter of a century—from 1875 to 1900—
he had rejoiced in each of my successes, but the sight of me in his

father's chair was painful to him. I never was resentful of this feeling. He had hoped so long to succeed to the post of his incomparable father, whose natural successor he considered himself, that he could only, naturally, be chagrined at the sight of even his best friend, in the very palace in the Wilhelmstrasse, in which he himself had lived as a child. He dined with us there one evening, in the second or third year of my Chancellorship. My wife escorted him through the various apartments of the palace, all of which he knew so well, and took him at last into what we called the Bismarck room, where we had placed all souvenirs of the Prince, and which we consecrated entirely to his memory. Herbert was deeply moved: he kissed my wife's hand with real emotion. Next day he described the evening to a mutual friend, but added: " All the same I still hate the thought of Bernhard's being in our shoes. I can't help it." His ambition to succeed his father was both Herbert's strength and his misfortune: his strength because his goal was an inspiration to unflagging zeal in politics; his misfortune because, from the very beginning, it placed him in a false position, and embittered him more and more, as he watched the non-fulfilment of his hopes. Lieutenant-Colonel von Plessen once told me how, one day in 1887 or '8, shortly before the death of the old Emperor Wilhelm I— at the time when he was acting as his adjutant—he entered His Majesty's apartments just after Herbert had been received in audience. He found the Kaiser exhausted—almost in a state of collapse. The old gentleman said to Plessen: " These audiences with young Bismarck always take it out of me so. He's so stormy— worse even than his father. He has not a grain of tact. I do so miss the Secretary of State von Bülow with whom I always got on so well. And I miss Count Paul Hatzfeldt too, though some things about him didn't please me. But he was a man of the world, and had such good manners . . . and so was Radowitz, even if he did talk a bit too much sometimes."

The old Kaiser was silent a moment, then he added: " Lately, it almost appears to me that the Prince would like to see Herbert take his place one day. That is quite impossible. As long as I live I will never part from the Prince who will most probably, and as I hope, survive me. He is eighteen years younger than I. Nor will my successors wish to make the Chancellor's office an hereditary one. That won't do." Count Stirum, a loyal Bismarckian, said to me once that Herbert's desire to succeed the Prince was bad for both father and son. Stirum added: " It would have been impossible for anyone but his wife to dissuade the Prince from this idea, and she adored Herbert too much to have attempted it." It is characteristic of the complete impartiality of the great Chancellor that in spite of his wish to leave the Chancellorship to Herbert, he had no illusions about his faults and weaknesses. I have heard him say myself: " Herbert, who is not yet forty, is more unteachable and conceited than I, and I am over seventy. I have had a few successes." He said, too, to Busch, the Under-Secretary of State, who praised the industry of the new Secretary of State Herbert: " You need not praise him to me. I would have made him Secretary of State, even if he had not possessed all those qualities for which you praise him, since I want at my side a man in whom I can have complete confidence, and whom it is easy for me to deal with. At my great age, when I have used up all my energies in the royal service, I think I have the right to ask that." After his fall he said something of the same kind to his friend Wilhelm von Kardorff, the conservative deputy.

Considering the exceptional delicacy of the affairs with which he had to deal, both as Foreign Secretary and Chancellor it would have been quite natural for Bismarck to have used no other help than his son. The thought of making Herbert his successor only entered the mind of the great Prince in the very last years before his dismissal. Would Herbert have made the right Chancellor for William II ? In spite of all our friendship I cannot think so. I believe that the conjunction William II—Herbert Bismarck would have been perilous. Herbert certainly possessed more political method and far higher gifts than Caprivi, or even Bethmann and Michaelis. But, although more serious in the conduct of affairs of state, and superior both in industry and political acumen to the Kaiser he had many of the latter's faults. He had more energy and courage than William II, but was even more inclined to run his head against a brick wall. He did not understand how to avoid an obstacle; he could not catch himself on the rebound, to use the *terminus technicus* of his father. He was often too violent, sometimes obstinate, occasionally brutal. And yet I shall never forget the hour when I accompanied the mortal remains of Herbert Bismarck past the balcony of the simple house in the Sachsenwald from which Prince Bismarck had often addressed his admirers, and speaking to an unseen audience beyond them, the whole nation; past the stag who charged the big dogs with his mighty horns, to the mausoleum where lay his great father. Herbert, with his vices and his virtues " take him for all in all," was a man. His was an Achilles' nature, and like Achilles, a long life was not vouchsafed him. On his death Philip Eulenburg wrote me:

For me also Herbert Bismarck's death called up a world of

memories. What a sad creature! His inner life atrophied to bitterness and unfulfilled hopes. How little love he gave, how little he received. Once I was very fond of him. His life was like a coruscating rocket that we see rise swiftly and then suddenly fall into individual glimmering particles before our eyes in the dark. I should never have thought that I would outlive him. You have gained by the death of this unsatisfied mortal, who fought for his dreams with ever-growing passionate energy, more fiercely than ever as he found himself passing his prime. You regret his death because you are a good man.

While the death of Prince Herbert Bismarck called up again before the eyes of the nation the powerful figure of his father, the question of the regency and inheritance in Lippe-Detmold, in itself an insignificant matter, had been re-opened by the death of the Regent of Lippe—Count Ernest zu Lippe-Biesterfeld. From Rominten the Kaiser sent the following telegram to Count Leopold von Lippe who most ceremoniously had announced the demise of his father: " I send you my sympathy on the occasion of your father's death. Since the juridical aspect is in no wise clear I cannot acknowledge your taking over the regency. I shall not have the troops sworn." The Kaiser, without asking my opinion, had sent this telegram immediately after receiving the news from Count Leopold, although I had always urged him not to treat this petty matter in such a way as to cause unrest in the Reich. The imperious telegram to the son at the moment he was mourning his father made a very unfavourable impression, not only at most of the German Courts but in the widest circles of the German populace as well. The little federal state supported Count Leopold. The vice-president of the Lippe Diet, Hoffmann, came to me at Homburg where I happened to be staying, to tell me of the agitation reigning in his home. The Kaiser replied to the telegrams in which I advised greater circumspection with his constant argument of the equality of birth as the basis of German dynasties and imperial splendour. I cut out and sent him newspaper articles violently criticizing his Rominten telegram, and on the margins of these he scribbled little jokes. He had a preference for such jocular comments as: " In Lippe, Everyone's dippy."

In view of this I wrote to Vice-President Hoffmann without previously consulting His Majesty:

You asked me personally for an authentic interpretation of the telegram of His Majesty the King and Emperor of the 26th instant. I am very willing to confirm my answer in writing and empower you to declare publicly that His Majesty's communication was intended only to prevent the premature swearing in of the troops, and to give a reason for his action. His Majesty could not oppose Federal Diet's opinion, which was that the juridical position was not yet clear. His Majesty had no intention whatsoever of interfering with the Constitutional rights of the Principality, or of placing of any obstacle in the way of Count Leopold zu Lippe's taking over the Regency. In this case, as always in the Reich, the constitution will not be departed from, and the Lippe question will be settled by legal methods only. I trust that methods of arbitration under the auspices of the Federal Diet will speedily solve the problem to the best interests of Lippe, and I will do my best to hasten this end.

Obediently,

COUNT VON BÜLOW, Imperial Chancellor.

I at once had this communication officially circulated by Wolff and sent it without further commentary to His Majesty. The Kaiser had telegraphed me immediately after the death of Count Ernest shortly and crisply: " Biesterfelder is dead. Of course I do not recognize his son." On receiving word of my communication to Hoffmann, His Majesty wired me in direct contrast to his former opinion: " Agree with everything. Am astounded at the extraordinarily malicious and intentional twist given to my perfectly harmless and strictly business telegram against better knowledge. Your reply to Hoffmann is entirely in accordance with my views, which can really be read quite clearly into it. I call this kind of thing *chercher midi à quatorze heures*." Returned to Berlin I convoked a session of the Federal Diet in which I was able to inform the Assembly that the Lippe question had now been finally settled. The representatives of the German Federal States have seldom thanked me with more warmth than upon this occasion. The various sovereigns and ministers were touched in their tenderest spot—namely, their more or less formal but decided sense of justice and their feeling of independence.

Next day I had a final conversation on the whole Lippe affair with the Kaiser in the garden of castle Bellevue. I thanked him for his retraction, but could not refrain from saying that there were imponderabilia in this case which could not be ignored without punishment. I said: " There is a danger in the fact that Your Majesty is swayed too greatly by personal sympathies and antipathies in such matters instead of by cool reflection and the consideration of reasons of state." As we walked on the lawn where

Mme. de Staël's friend, brave Prince August of Prussia, who acted so boldly at Kulm, has erected modest memorials to his relatives who died as children, the Kaiser listened to me very graciously. He seemed really convinced that I not only meant well with him but had right on my side in this affair. Unhappily there were always Byzantines to be found in the persons of Adolf Harnack and Theodor Schiemann who assured him that moods like his own had been characteristic of Frederick the Great and were indeed an attribute of really great princes. Good-humoured as the Kaiser was at heart he bore no grudge against the house of Biesterfeld, once he had made his peace with it. Later he awarded the bitterly attacked Count Leopold the Order of the Black Eagle, and much enjoyed shooting fat stags in the Lippe woods.

Count (afterwards Prince) Leopold was one of the not very numerous people who were grateful to me for services received. I need scarcely add that my settlement of the Lippe succession was less for the *beaux yeux* of the house of Biesterfeld than in the interests of the consolidation of the Reich. As ruler of the Federal State— after the Diet of November 18th, when the Arbitration Agreement of November 5th had been juridically confirmed—Lippe wrote me:

It is thanks to Your Excellency's own sense of justice and wisdom that this whole question has been settled in a manner so generally acknowledged just. I feel impelled to express the wide recognition felt for Your Excellency's brilliant conduct of this affair and, at the same time, my warmest thanks. Your Excellency's ever grateful and devoted

LEOPOLD, COUNT-REGENT VON LIPPE.

Not long after this, I was spending the summer at Norderney. Count Leopold, in the meantime (in 1905) advanced to the rank of " Prince " and " Serene Highness," paid me a very friendly visit. When my Italian valet Augusto, who had been in my service for many years saw the exalted gentleman arriving in a hired carriage at our house, he said in surprise: "*E questo si chiama in Germania un sovrano!*" The whole difference between Italian and German unity, Italian and German mentality lies in this little remark. And yet the Lippe quarrel which, in Germany, could arouse such exaggerated excitement in courts, governments, and people, was a storm-signal of what was to follow in November 1908.

In the very days when the death of Count-Regent Ernest of Lippe and the question of the inheritance of that little state were occupying the Germans, I received a visit in Homburg from the

Italian Premier Giolitti, with whom I had established good relations during the Kaiser's visit to Rome.   Giovanni Giolitti may be
ranked as one of the finest statesmen that modern Italy, never poor
in political genius, has produced since the Risorgimento.   A
Piedmontese, he possessed the good qualities of his race.   He had
already worked in the Finance Ministry under Marco Minghetti,
had become during that premiership Inspector-General of Taxes,
and later Director-General of the Court of Accounts.   Not till 1882,
at the age of forty, did he stand as a deputy.   It has always been of
value to Giolitti that as a civil servant he worked his way up from
the very bottom, and knew the business of administration in all its
branches.   As a member he soon displayed unusual qualities: unshakeable calm in the face of parliamentary storms, firmness where
necessary, a flexible hand when this was needed.   He lost neither
his calm nor his good-humour, was capable of tackling two dozen
deputies one after the other, in the lobbies of the Chamber, and
satisfying each in turn.   He possessed sufficient physical elasticity
to give interviews for hours together in his room in the Palazzo
Braschi, in front of which stands the bronze statue of Marco
Minghetti, without once seeming ruffled by the never ending streams
of applicants who fill the antechambers of all Italian cabinet ministers, and whose importunities could drive the sickly Rudini, the
stormy Crispi, and the shy Sonnino to desperation.   In bearing and
manners Giolitti is, like most of his countrymen, simple and natural,
without pose or pretention.   The affectation displayed by some
Germans, as soon as they have attained a certain official rank, and
which makes them either unpleasing or absurd is far removed from
him.   Giolitti first became Minister in 1889, as Chancellor of the
Exchequer: a year later he was Minister of Finance and, in 1892,
Premier.   He was overthrown in November 1893, as I related elsewhere, on the occasion of the Sicilian and Lunigian revolts.   When
I first arrived in Rome, in December 1893, Giolitti was considered
done for.   In a Roman salon the witty Duca Onorato Sermoneta
characterized him amid universal applause as a " *Una mortadella di
Bologna, mezzo asino, mezzo porco.*"   That very tasty sausage called
in Italy " *Mortadella di Bologna* " is made of equal parts of pork
and asses' meat.   Pursued by Crispi, Giolitti spent the winter
1893-94 in Charlottenburg.   But this tall man with the big shoulders
and the heavy gait possessed such statesmanlike qualities as made
his recall inevitable.   From 1901 to 1903 he was again Minister of
the Interior, in March 1905 and often since he has been Prime
Minister.   Scarcely any other statesman, even in Italy, had so often
passed from Capitol to Tarpeian Rock and back again.   In May 1915

bands of roughs, paid by the French Embassy and the then Premier
Salandra, marched through the streets of Rome to the cry of
" *Morte a Giolitti*! " All Italy a few years later was clamouring for
this same Giolitti, and when he entered the senate in 1921 as
Premier, all the deputies, many of them his former antagonists, rose
and bowed to him in silence.

Giolitti is a great walker. On our walks together, through the
woods surrounding Homburg, in the autumn of 1904, our conversation turned on the weakest point in the Triple Alliance and the
most difficult problem of Italy's foreign policy—her relations with
Austria. The Zanardelli Cabinet had permitted irredentism to grow
too strong. On the other hand, Giolitti suggested, the Austrian
Government would do well to pursue a less biased and more intelligent policy towards its Italian subjects. Cis-Alpine Italians were
too small a minority to be of any real danger to Austria. Why
drive them into opposition against the Austrian state and the
German element in the population? The natural thing would be
for Italians and Germans to stand together against the Slavs.
Italy desired no personal entanglements in Albania but this must be
a *Noli me tangere* for Austria as well. To keep the Adriatic open
was a vital question for Italy, who certainly did not wish to supplant
Austria in the Balkan Peninsular—but at the same time she would
not tolerate either Austrian supremacy or aggression against
Rumania or Serbia. In this respect both Austria and Italy must
remain true not only to the letter but to the spirit of the Triple
Alliance. " *Patti chiari, lunga amicizia*." With quiet decision but
without unnecessary emphasis which was never his method, Giolitti
declared that Italy would refuse to be enticed out of the Triple
Alliance by France. It was not in Italy's interests to be on such
strained terms with France, as had occurred for a time in the
'nineties. Loubet's return visit to Rome after King Victor
Emanuel's visit to Paris had been very useful to Italy, because as a
result of this, the question of the Pope's temporal power had been
disposed of for good and all. There had been only one Power which
might have welcomed the re-establishment of the Papal State—
France. Now that the head of the French Republic had visited
Rome without taking any notice of the Pope this question was
finally settled and Rome had become, indeed, the " *capitale intangi-
bile* " of the *Regno d'Italia*. That was what Italy needed most in the
way of assurance from France. But the Italian Government did not
dream of supplanting the alliance with Germany by any agreement
with France. The majority of the Italian people, radical extremists
included, were too intelligent not to endorse their Government's

policy in this respect.   King Victor Emanuel was more convinced
than ever, to-day, of the necessity of co-operation with Germany.

As we emerged from the woods we saw spread out beneath our
feet a number of tiny villages, each with its charming village church.
I pointed out to my companion that, here in this Taunus countryside,
Protestants and Catholics were so intermingled that often a Catholic
village was situated next to a Protestant one.   From this we came
to the subject of the Italian Monarchy's relationship to the Holy
See.   Giolitti was delighted with Pius X—a simple country priest,
unversed in all political combinations.   Leo XIII and Rampolla
had pursued a policy of undermining the Italian Monarchy, in the
hope of establishing an Italian Federal Republic, under French protection, and with the Pope at its head, on the plan that had been in
the mind of Napoleon III in the days of the Peace of Villafranca.
Since the good Pius X had held the keys there had been no further
talk of this.   Of course the Pope could not, *pro foro externo*, cede the
principle of the Italian Church.   No Italian would desire that he
should.   In reality Pius X—a patriotic Italian—was doing his best
to consolidate and support the Italian Monarchy.   Giolitti felt a
pardonable satisfaction at the religious storms raging at that time
in France, but added that he would not be fool enough to set anything of that kind going in Italy.   The Italians were a sceptical
people, and did not understand how one could get so agitated over
religious questions.   I could only explain to him with difficulty why
a great part of Germany had been in ferment over the abrogation of
paragraph 2 of the Jesuit Bill.   When Giolitti at last grasped the
matter he exclaimed that the German doctrinaire mind was " un-
fathomable."   In Italy, since 1848, a number of laws had been
enacted against the Jesuits, but there had been no need to enforce
them.   The Jesuits knew that if they acted either directly or indirectly against the Italian national idea they would be expatriated
forthwith.   They therefore behaved quietly and very correctly.
Giolitti feared that M. Combes through his exaggerated anti-
clerical policy might bring about a clerical reaction in France which
would of course be undesirable for Italy.   President Loubet and
Delcassé, the Foreign Secretary, had told Signor Giolitti during
their visit to Rome that they found the anti-clericalism of Combes
" very overdone."   Both had said much the same to the piously
Catholic Queen-Mother, Margherita.   With regard to his internal
policy Giolitti repeated what he had often said to me, namely, that
order must be maintained with a firm, a very firm hand, but that
with the burden then pressing on the agricultural labourer in the
country, monarchist government in Italy dare not altogether

identify itself with the estate owners, the " Signori." But the Monarchy was much more firmly seated than was thought abroad. If the dispatches of foreign ambassadors in the 'sixties of the nineteenth century were ever published it would be seen that every one of these gentlemen, with the possible exception of the quietly observant English Ambassador, had prophesied the fall of the House of Savoy. Just as the prophets of those days had erred so would these to-day be mistaken who regarded Italian conditions too pessimistically. The Monarchy would continue to exist in Italy, and Italy, led by a sensible, calm and tactful policy would continue to remain on Germany's side.

No idea, throughout his reign, obsessed Kaiser William II so intensely as his desire for an alliance between the Houses of Hohenzollern and Romanov—between the Prusso-German and the Russian monarchies. This, like almost all His Majesty's projects, had arisen from personal feelings. William II knew quite well, even if he refused to admit it, that he himself was mainly, if not entirely responsible for the denunciation of the Re-Insurance Treaty with Russia, which, *ipso facto*, had led on to the Franco-Russian alliance. Indeed, according to his own all too frequently proclaimed theory of a monarch's sole responsibility to his God, his people, and posterity, he was himself alone to blame for this incomparable blunder. In the first years after Prince Bismarck's dismissal the Kaiser defended, on ethical grounds, the severance of the Russian ties. The treaty had been " treachery to the Hapsburgs." Since this explanation, suggested by Holstein and Philip Eulenburg, ceased, in the long run to convince people, the Kaiser maintained that he had been forced to turn away from Russia in order to keep on really good terms with England. But after the Krüger telegram this argument also lost weight. So there remained no alternative for the Kaiser but to show that even after Bismarck, without Bismarck, and in spite of him, he too could re-establish *rapprochement* on a treaty basis with Russia. I had informed the Kaiser when I was summoned from Rome to Berlin in 1897, that since under somewhat unpleasant circumstances we ourselves had broken off the Russo-German Treaty, the Russian Government, in view of the feeling in the country, would not be ready, or even able, to sever the ceremoniously proclaimed alliance with France, and once more, ally herself with us. That which we ourselves had broken in 1890 could not be put together again. But it should be quite possible to foster not only peace but friendship with Russia by means of a steady and skilful policy. The Kaiser, however, did not give up the hope of attaining his goal by personal influence on the Tsar. It was part

of his temperament and the false idea he had of his position as
ruler to want to arrange foreign policy by influencing other sovereigns, or conferring with them.   He had awaited the outbreak of the
Russo-Japanese war with an impatience I found difficult to curb,
because above all else he had hoped that the stress of a great conflict
abroad would force Tsar Nicholas to seek support and above all,
good advice, from his German " colleague."   When the Kaiser
received a telegram from the Tsar on 21st January 1904, that is to
say more than a fortnight before the outbreak of hostilities, expressing the hope that peace would not be jeopardized His Majesty was
much cast down.   He feared that the Tsar would never let it come
to a war with Japan.   That would, he considered, mean an Anglo-
French intervention, which could lead on to an Anglo-French-
Russian coalition against us.   The anxiety which Japan, America,
and, in particular, England, had caused the Tsar, would lead him to
a *rapprochement* with these Powers and probably also to a tightening
of the knot of alliance with France.   Above all, there was danger
that through the feeble policy of Russia, the Japanese would grow
obstreperous.   We were not yet the equals of Japan at sea.   Kiaochow seemed to His Majesty as good as lost.   I replied that we
must above all else avoid arousing the Tsar's suspicion that we
desired, for obvious reasons, to drive him and his ministers into a
war for which they felt no inclination.   For the moment the less we
showed our hand, the quieter we kept, the better.   If we did not
arouse the Tsar's mistrust, and particularly, if we did not seem to
him false friends and at the same time could prevent ourselves from
offending Japan or from being forced into hostility to England by
other Powers, we might await further developments calmly.   I
hoped I had quietened the Kaiser somewhat; but this was not the
case for long.   On 14th February he appeared at a very early hour
in the morning in my room.   He seemed worried, almost unnerved.
The dialogue between us I noted down that same day and have kept
among my archives, as I append it.

THE KAISER: I hoped the warmth of my last letters would have
persuaded the Tsar to proceed with full strength against Japan.
Instead of that his attitude is as spineless as ever.   He does not
seem to want to fight.   He is capable even of letting Japan have
Manchuria without one blow of the sword, or at least without serious
opposition.   Such a turn of events must be avoided *à tout prix*.

MYSELF: The surest way to make Russia conclude a premature
and bad peace with Japan would be careless German encouragement
to the Tsar.   If the Tsar notices that Your Majesty would like to

see him get his teeth fixed firmly into Japan, it will make him let go at once.

THE KAISER: From the statesman's standpoint you may be right. But my sentiments are those of a sovereign and as such I feel the cowardly bearing of Tsar Nicholas as a disgrace to all monarchs, and especially to myself. The Tsar compromises all great rulers by it. In the interests of monarchical dignity, something must be done to make Tsar Nicholas act more boldly.

MYSELF: Your Majesty's only duty is to watch over your own honour and that of the Prussian and the German peoples. For other rulers and other nations the German Kaiser is not responsible. Kaiser William I and Frederick the Great never troubled their heads about others. It was all the same to that great sovereign how Louis XV and Peter III were governing, provided he watched his own interests.

THE KAISER: Times are different to-day. In those days there were no Socialists and no Nihilists to take advantage of the mistakes of Kings. The Tsar is damaging the monarchical principle through his shilly-shallying. He must go to Moscow, call Holy Russia to war, and mobilize his whole army, bearing the Cross at the head of it!

MYSELF: I advise Your Majesty to let the Tsar decide that for himself. Princes like to be told what to do even less than other people. You yourself don't like it. (His Majesty smiled.) Too much advice would in any case not incline Tsar Nicholas to take the right path but will rather annoy him and make him suspicious.

THE KAISER: Your arguments may be correct from the political point of view. But you overlook one enormous danger. I, as a sovereign, understand this better than diplomats, who usually consider only the present. This is the yellow peril, the greatest danger threatening the white race, Christianity, and our entire culture. If the Russians run away from the Japanese now, the yellow race will be in Moscow and Posen within twenty years.

MYSELF: Your Majesty has long been aware that I do not believe in any yellow peril. In any case it touches other great powers, Russia and England, America and France, more closely than ourselves. You overestimate this danger. Your Majesty is too much inclined to see political events through a magnifying glass. Just as you exaggerate the yellow peril in the Far East, so do you overestimate in the Near East the power and significance of the green banners of the Prophet—I mean the power and significance of Islam—the Sultan and the Turks.

THE KAISER: I still stick to my opinion. In any case put down everything I have just said to you on paper, and place the memorandum among the archives so that posterity can see how rightly I judged the situation. It is a perfect scandal that France should leave her Russian allies in the lurch and that England and the United States should sympathize with Japan. We must open the Tsar's eyes to the yellow peril which the poor man has not yet realized.

MYSELF: The only result of that would be a suggestion from the Tsar that we send armed help to assist him against what seems to us so great a menace. That would imply a war between ourselves and England. I have tried to avoid it for years past, and you yourself do not desire it. Unfortunately you do not see the state of the outside world correctly. May I be quite frank? Your Majesty has *l'esprit batailleur*. But you have not, like Napoleon I, Charles XII of Sweden, or Frederick the Great, *une âme guerrière*. You do not really want a war! You never have wanted it and never will. You have often said yourself that your ideal would be, like that of Frederick William I, to forge the weapon which your son, or still better, your grandson will one day use. But why, if you are quite peacefully disposed at heart, either incite other nations or arouse their suspicions?

THE KAISER (sobered by the last words which were spoken with emphasis): Dear Bernhard, can you suggest any way out of this situation, so terribly complicated by the weakness of the Tsar, the perfidy of the English, and the egotism of the French?

MYSELF: Two things must be avoided. First, our relations with Russia must not be damaged by the war. To this end we must avoid everything that might make us appear uncertain, and more especially, quietly malicious or wily neighbours. On the other hand, it would be a great mistake to let the Russians push us into the foreground as their buffer against Japan or even against England. We shall steer round both cliffs the more safely, the more cautiously we behave.

Not long after this dialogue, news arrived which looked bad for Russian arms. I had succeeded during the whole of 1904 in keeping the Kaiser outwardly quiet with regard to the Far Eastern conflict, despite his internal agitation. While, in the late autumn of 1904 the Kaiser was, as usual, in Silesia, where he always liked to attend the hunting expeditions of the magnates, my exalted master was subjected to every kind of extraneous influence. Anti-German feeling in England, more visibly manifest every day, on the part, not of the English Government but of increasing sections of the nation, also contributed to his state of mind. All Russian operations in the Far East were under an unlucky star. This was chiefly the case during the transfer of the Russian Baltic fleet to Eastern Asia upon which the Tsar and the court had placed great hopes. The command of the fleet was unskilful from the beginning. While passing the Dogger Bank, the Russians opened sharp fire upon craft whose construction was unknown to them, and which they took to be Japanese torpedo boats. In reality they were harmless English fishing smacks. Several were sunk. The English press made a great commotion, attacked the Russian admiral, Roshdest-vensky severely, demanded satisfaction of the most exaggerated kind, and declared that war would be difficult to avoid. But at the same time the English Government was quietly endeavouring not to let it come to war with Russia. Still more zealous in this respect were the two Danish sisters, the Dowager Tsarina Maria Feodorovna and Queen Alexandra of England who, it will be remembered, had already in 1885, at the time of the Afghan crisis, done much to bring about an understanding between the Whale and the Bear. Our Ambassador, Count Metternich, had written to me on November 6th 1904:

> I do not lay much stress upon the North Sea incident in so far as England is concerned. Soon there will be the same endeavours as before on the part of the English to come to an understanding with Russia. France will never lose sight of this aim as long as it is within reach, and will try to act in a mediatory spirit on both sides. I do not consider any Anglo-German combination as practical politics. On the contrary, dislike of us is growing here, although for a long time past we have given no grounds for it.

I had done my best to prevent our press from playing its customary evil rôle of *tertius gaudens* in the Dogger Bank incident, and to make it maintain a tactful reserve. The lesson to be drawn from this incident was that all differences between the powers surrounding us—Russia, England, and France—would be comparatively easily disposed of since, for various reasons, none of them wished to fight the others. In our central position, therefore, and considering the envy our brilliant economic development, and the fears our sudden rise to power in the world were causing, it behoved us to avoid with redoubled care every danger of giving these powers their chance to attack us.

The various states of mind of the Emperor were reflected in a secret dispatch, addressed to me, on December 2nd 1904 by Herr von Schön, later Ambassador to Paris and Petersburg, who had been deputed by the Foreign Office to accompany William II on his travels. He wrote as follows:

In the course of his journey in Silesia His Majesty the King and Emperor had, of his own exalted initiative, the graciousness to inform me at great length—having warned me first that the matter in question was most secret—of the decisions which he might feel it incumbent to take should England's hostility against us, and her more and more evident intention of opposing the full development of our fleet, ever culminate in concrete acts which we should be forced to consider as inimical. His Majesty would feel it necessary to check with the mailed fist this British arrogance and to forestall any hostile action against our North Sea and Baltic coasts, by speedy and comprehensive military measures. His Majesty would moreover be impelled to depart from the considerate attitude he has displayed for so long towards his neighbours, great and small—an attitude which has not always been appreciated—and to enquire of them whether they intend to remain our friends and participate in this conflict as our allies, or become our enemies. Such enquiries would be handed in at Paris, Brussels, the Hague and Copenhagen concurrently, in the last instance with the occupation of various strategic points in and on the Danish waterways. Denmark would of course point to her neutrality. But such arguments would be worthless, since the Danish means of self-defence and preservation of this neutrality are pitifully inadequate. Moreover—His Majesty stressed this point especially—they are becoming entirely fictitious since Denmark permits foreign warships to take pilots, and grants the passage through the straits. My objection that Denmark based this principle of pilots on international agreements, on time-honoured tradition, and on practical necessity, was met by His Majesty with the remark that one must put such things aside at crucial moments. Against each of the neighbouring countries mentioned, continued His Majesty, which did not decide immediately and irrevocably for us, military measures would be taken without delay. The time when an inimical action on England's part might be expected would be when the British fleet was withdrawn from Mediterranean waters. To my careful enquiry as to whether we must not reckon with the possibility that our occupation of Danish territory and waters would make Russia uneasy and drive her away from us into England's arms, His Majesty said that this period had not yet come, since the war in the Far East was in full swing and might last for years. Moreover the old differences between Russia and England had been accentuated by the latter's wily machinations in Tibet as well as by the way in which the Dogger Bank incident had been treated. Later on His Majesty returned to the Danish question with the observation that Denmark would have to decide one way or other to place herself under Germany's protection, at first in the form of a customs union and then with military concessions, in return for which her *status quo* would be guaranteed. During the lifetime of King Christian the King and Kaiser would be as considerate as possible, but later on he would drop these scruples. In the same spirit as His Majesty, General Adjutant von Plessen spoke to me of Denmark during conversation at dinner. The General remarked that it was not only highly desirable for us to get Denmark into our hands but also Holland and her colonies if only on account of the coaling bases. He owned, in response to my objections, that such plans could not be accomplished without bloody conflicts with nearly all the Powers, America included, and that their realization must perhaps be postponed to a period far ahead.

Philip Eulenburg who had seen the Kaiser after his return from shooting in Silesia wrote me not without uneasiness on 19th December:

I am following your career with genuine affection and sympathy in these complicated times. Great political achievement is only possible in an atmosphere of deep secrecy and calm. To take all the guns out of one's own cupboard in order to arm one's enemies with them would be absurd. This is not the place to discuss such serious matters. I will wait till we meet again. Perhaps that can be managed during Christmas week.

Your old, grateful and true
PHILIP.

The Kaiserin wrote me after the Silesian trip:

The Kaiser seems to be very satisfied with the hunting and society offered him in the various houses he visited. I am glad he has had this change as he was becoming so very worried about the present political situation. I have tried to make him more cheerful by saying that even if our navy is weaker, our men are better trained and more dependable, and I told the Kaiser to remember the case of David and Goliath—how strength was on David's side because the Lord was with him. And that is what

II.   F

I hope in our case. Of course we must not cease our work, and of that you and the Kaiser will take good care. I should be grateful though, if you would send me a word telling me if things seem black to you also. I saw the little Altenburg the other day, but am very thankful that I have another daughter-in-law. This little Altenburg looks dreadfully delicate and boring.

With hearty greetings, your

VICTORIA.

In spite of all the excellent Kaiserin's efforts, His Majesty grew more and more pessimistic, and also more and more excitable. During the last months from his Silesian hunting grounds he had bombarded the Tsar with letters in which, contravening all I had advised him, he tried to draw him away from France. The result of these letters, of course, was the exact opposite of the success His Majesty expected. On 28th December 1904, three days before the New Year, the Kaiser wrote me that the Tsar had given him " a decided refusal to enter into any agreement without the knowledge of Gaul," which was " an entirely negative result after two months' honest work." This was " the first failure " which he had " personally " experienced since ascending the throne. It was to be hoped that no more were to follow. We must now cultivate Japan and " give Paris one in the eye." Delcassé, who was " damnably skilful and very strong " had spoiled His Majesty's plans. In a long conversation I had with him on New Year's day 1904, the Kaiser gave vehement expression to his low spirits. The gloom which had settled upon him was uncommon even for his volatile nature, with its oscillation from one extreme to another. " I understand Your Majesty's fears," I replied, " and your anxieties which I myself have long shared. But we must not lose courage. I must remind Your Majesty of Goethe's words:

'*Nur heute, heute nur lass dich nicht fangen,
So bist du hundertmal entgangen.*' [1]

Translated into politics this means that one must not lose one's nerve at every danger, and obstacle, but that these must be skilfully overcome with courage, patience, and tenacity. I must also remind Your Majesty of the words I spoke in Your presence at the launching of the ship of the line 'Preussen.'" "The State," I said, " whose name this ship is to bear was menaced from the beginning, feared and hated by its enemies but loved and esteemed by its sons

---

[1] Don't let yourself be caught to-day—
You've escaped a hundred times this way.

with such deep, concentrated love as is not to be found elsewhere. Often exposed to storms, it withstood every one victoriously by God's help. Again and again, from our youth up, they have threatened but never overcome us. To-day, the last of the troubled year 1904, I say to the King of Prussia and the German Emperor: Our enemies and those who envy us will not be able to defeat us in the future any more than in the past if we remain true to the spirit of Prussian history. With firm courage, cool heads, and flexible hands we shall weather this present storm with honour."

CHAPTER V

New Year 1905—*Note of the English Admiralty on Naval questions—Port Arthur—Renewed symptoms of anxiety in William II—Belgian neutrality—Visit of King Leopold to Berlin one year previously—His conference with Bülow, his tête-à-tête with William II—Bismarck's guiding principle for our attitude towards Belgian neutrality—Count Alfred Schlieffen on the Belgian problem—Article in the " Deutsche Revue "—Alleged differences of opinion between Foreign Office and General Staff on question of march through Belgium as laid down by Foreign Office on 6th July* 1920—*General Moltke on the Belgian question—Desire of William II for an alliance with Denmark—Reflections on the internal and foreign political situation in* 1905—*The English Ambassador, Lascelles, on William II—Kaiser's attitude regarding Japan.*

ALL nations, but especially the Germans, had a premonition that the year 1905 would be an eventful one, with more blanks than prizes in the lottery of Fortune. For me it opened, as usual, in the Chapel of the Royal Palace. The Cabinet Ministers sat on the right of the altar, the Knights of the Black Eagle on the left. I had my choice of taking my place with either, but, on principle, I remained with the Ministers, the solid pillars of the throne destined to support the Prussian State—whereas the Knights, in the blue-lined red velvet cloaks of their Order, served it as mere decorative ornaments.

The Kaiser and Kaiserin sat facing the altar, surrounded by the Princes of the Royal House, and the princely guests then in Berlin for the New Year's Court. There was no more attentive listener than William II. He who was so mercurial on other occasions could listen to the longest sermon and the most boring address with close attention, and that same immovable bearing he always displayed at court ceremonies and on parade. In this as in many other things, the Kaiser was my superior. From my youth I found it difficult to follow a sermon or a lecture. Even in the Reichstag I only listened to the speakers when I knew that I should have to reply to their statements immediately afterwards. During the sermon in the Palace Chapel, I used to look at the pictures of the kings with which Frederick William IV's romantic imagination had ornamented the chapel walls. There one could see the commonplace, sober, and sensible Frederick William III next door to the wild and violent Chlodwig, King of the Franks; next to David with his harp was Frederick Barbarossa with flowing beard and the rigid sword of the realm, and side by side, the devout believer Gustavus Adolphus and the rationalistic Frederick the Great.

After the service in the chapel there followed the court presentations. I noticed that the Kaiser looked pale. After the court I heard from Tirpitz that a memorandum for the end of the year, which the First Lord of the Admiralty, the Earl of Selborne, had laid before the House of Commons, had made a deep impression on His Majesty. In this it appeared that it was the aim of the British Admiralty to maintain the whole English navy in a position of readiness to wage war at a moment's notice. The Home Fleet would be called in future the "Channel Fleet," and the present Channel Fleet the Atlantic Fleet. It was clear that this change was a concession to English public opinion, more and more agitated because of our own ship building. It was also quite possible that the formation of a specified Atlantic Fleet was the English reply to the Kaiser's rather unfortunate notion of calling himself "Admiral of the Atlantic." The publication of the Earl of Selborne's memorandum had been preceded by an article in the *Army and Navy Gazette*, which said: "Formerly England would simply have destroyed a navy of which it was said that there was reason to believe it might be used against us. We should like to say that the present moment is a most propitious one to declare that this navy must not be increased any further. Other Powers would probably regard such a step with barely concealed pleasure, if not with open approval." Not long afterwards the Civil Lord of the English Admiralty, Mr. Lee, made a speech in which he declared that England must forbid Germany any increase in her navy. The leader of the Opposition, Mr. Campbell-Bannerman, expressed in the Commons his regret that Lee had provoked Germany without reason. Whereupon the Premier, Mr. Balfour, supported the belligerent Civil Lord, declaring the reproof of the Opposition leader to be ignoble, and praising the industry and great efficiency of Lee.

It was not to be denied that, at the beginning of the year 1905, much occurred to affect the nerves of the highly strung and emotional Kaiser. On 2nd January, Port Arthur capitulated, with 8 Generals, 4 Admirals, 57 staff officers, over 30,000 men, more than 50 guns and 4 battleships, which increased the excitement and (feeling as he did) the wrath of the Kaiser against the "Japs." William II had miscalculated the chances and had counted just as certainly on a Russian victory as seven years earlier, during the

Spanish-American War, he had counted on the triumph of the Spaniards. He had backed the wrong horse again. In his desire to have his finger in every pie and himself always in the limelight, he hit upon the compromise of bestowing upon victor and vanquished alike—on the defender of Port Arthur, General Stössel, and its conqueror, General Nogi—the highest Prussian military distinction, the Order, "*Pour le Mérite*," created by Frederick the Great. When he informed me of this, *post festum*, I did not conceal from His Majesty that ill-wishers abroad might see in this another example of his desire to distribute laurel wreaths right and left, and thus act as *arbiter mundi*. "Your Majesty," I added, "is the head of a great, a powerful and a prosperous realm which is, however, surrounded by hostile and envious neighbours. You are not a Roman Caesar-Imperator who either nods to the gladiators or condemns them to death, *pollice verso*." The Kaiser was silent. But in a long conversation with which he honoured me at a Court ball not long afterwards he revealed his inner agitation in a manner unusually tempestuous even for him. He repeated to me everything he had said to the Ambassador von Schön a few weeks previously in Silesia about the measures he would "irrevocably" adopt should England dare to impede the expansion of his fleet.

I must here recall an event which, although it occurred nearly a year earlier, only reveals its true importance when seen in connection with the state of mind in which I found the Kaiser on this unforgettable January day in 1905. I have kept notes of this event which took place in that same venerable palace to which my heart is still so deeply attached.

In January 1904 to my surprise the Kaiser informed me that King Leopold of Belgium had expressed the wish to pay him a visit in Berlin. He was convinced that this opportunity should be made use of, and Belgium drawn closer to us in consequence. "The Belgian King," the Kaiser explained to me, "is a minus quantity, a Mr. Nobody, among the great princes. Nobody bothers about him and yet Belgium has a glorious past. We must remind King Leopold of the magnificence of Philip the Good, and Charles the Bold, and the splendour of old Burgundy. If we open to him the prospect of rising to as great a height again through an alliance with ourselves, Leopold will be ready for anything." Of course I advised against this. The Belgians were not ambitious. They did not sing:

"*O nein, nein, nein!*
Mein Vaterland muss grösser sein!" [1]

[1] Oh, no, no, no,
My Fatherland must grow—

They were only concerned about their neutrality and independence, but on these they felt intensely. The Kaiser promised me that he would renounce the rôle of tempter for which he had already cast himself. I will not conceal my doubts even to-day as to whether King Leopold had really invited himself to Berlin of his own accord, had been summoned directly by the Kaiser, or whether the Military Attaché in Brussels had given the incentive. The King reached Berlin on 26th January 1904. On the following day, His Majesty's birthday, he honoured me with a long visit. We dealt with a number of problems in the Colonial question by means of a large map of Central Africa spread out on my writing table. I had studied these beforehand from information supplied by the Colonial Department of the Foreign Office. The King was a good business man. His clarity, practical common sense and decision made a favourable impression on me. From our own little colonial differences we proceeded to a discussion of the general situation in Europe, and following upon this, to the relations between Belgium and Germany. The King stressed the desire for peace, not only as his own personal wish but as that of all Belgians, without difference of party. Peace seemed to him perfectly feasible, if Berlin, London, and St. Petersburg would pursue a calm policy. Relations between Belgium and Germany were as good as they possibly could be. French was the mother tongue of the Walloons; all Belgium was under the influence of French civilization. Brussels, in point of mental, literary, and artistic culture, was a "*faubourg de Paris.*" But the Belgians were much too sober-minded and sensible to let themselves be influenced politically by this fact. They had, politically, more confidence in Germany than in France. The old fear of being overrun by France, or even entirely swallowed by her, was widespread in Belgium, and had been reinforced of late in this soundly Catholic country by the anti-clerical attitude of the French Republic. As to Germany, explained the King, every Belgian knew from the pronouncements of Bismarck before the outbreak of the Franco-German War of 1870, that this country was the defender and loyal guard of Belgian neutrality and independence. The King praised the German Ambassador in Brussels at that time, Count Nicholas Wallwitz, husband of my step-daughter Countess Eugenie Dönhoff. "*On m'a dit,*" said the King, "*que vous destinez Wallwitz à une ambassade. Si tel était le cas, je ne voudrais pas entraver la carrière de ce diplomate très distingué. Mais personnellement je serais heureux de garder le comte Wallwitz à Bruxelles, où il jouit de beaucoup de considération et de la confiance générale.*" I replied that I did not intend to suggest Count Wallwitz to his Majesty as Embassy candidate just yet, and that for the present he would remain in Brussels, which visibly pleased the King. The Flemish movement, the King said, was gaining ground though, of course, only within the scope permitted by the Belgian state, and in perfect loyalty to the common Fatherland of Flemings and Walloons. The Flemings were just as good Belgians as were the Walloons. If the German Press did not make too much of the justifiable efforts of the Flemish to cultivate their rich and beautiful language and to maintain their cultural individuality, the movement would be all the more acceptable to the Walloons. His Majesty wished to meet my wife, to whom he spoke in high terms of her daughter and son-in-law. He presented me with a magnificent tobacco jar bearing his portrait surrounded by diamonds. This still stands on a bureau in the Villa Malta, next to busts of King Edward and Queen Alexandra of England, to a portrait of Queen Alexandra with her grandson, the young Prince of Wales in her arms, two portraits of the Tsar, pictures of the Grand Duchess Maria Pavlovna, Queen Olga of Greece, the King and Queen of Rumania, the Empress of China and many other Royalties. A witty German friend visited me in the Villa Malta during the winter of 1914-1915 when, constantly crossed by Vienna and none too loyally supported from Berlin, I was trying to avert the outbreak of war between Italy and the Central Powers. He looked at these souvenirs of a happier period and said: " I find you surrounded by the ruins of the Bethmann-Hollweg policy."

When that melancholy phrase was uttered, in January 1915, more than a decade had elapsed since the visit of Leopold II. The first days of that visit passed off most harmoniously. Then came 28th January, the day of the Belgian King's departure. Dinner was fixed for eight o'clock and he was to leave immediately afterwards. All the guests were assembled; the Kaiserin had been waiting some time; only the Kaiser and his Belgian guest were missing. At last they arrived together. I noticed at once that the Kaiser looked angry, the King disturbed. I also observed that, contrary to his custom at table, Leopold barely spoke to his neighbour, the Kaiserin. As soon as dinner was over he left the Palace with the Kaiser to drive to the station. In passing me, the King pressed my hand, and said in a low voice but with deeply serious emphasis: "*L'empereur m'a dit des choses épouvantables. Je compte sur votre bonne influence, sur votre sagesse et sur votre savoir-faire pour éviter de grands malheurs.*" When the Kaiser came back from the station, one of the adjutants who had accompanied him asked me, with evident anxiety: " What was the matter with the Belgian King? There seems to have been a quarrel. The King looked as

though he'd had a shock of some kind. The old gentleman was so
upset that he put on his Prussian Dragoon's helmet back to front!"
Just then the Kaiser came up and drew me away from the assembled
company, which he dismissed quickly and absent-mindedly. When
we were in his vast study, where, side by side on the wall, portraits
of his father and grandfather, the great Prince Bismarck and the
great master of Bayreuth, the Tsar, and Queen Victoria hung peacefully, the Kaiser broke out in a rage about the " feebleness " of his
" colleagues." He had spoken to the Belgian King, in the kindest
way in the world, about his proud forefathers, the Dukes of Burgundy, and added that if he wished, he could reconstruct that old
realm, and stretch his sceptre over French Flanders, Artois, and the
Ardennes. The King gazed at him at first, open-mouthed, and then
said, " with a grin," that neither the Belgian Ministers, nor the
Belgian Chambers would listen to any such high-flown plans.
" Then I lost patience," said the Kaiser, " I told the King I could
not respect a Monarch who felt responsible to his Deputies and his
Ministers instead of to our God in Heaven alone. I told him, too,
that I could not be played with. Whoever, in the case of a European
war, was not for me, was against me. As a soldier I belonged to
the school of Frederick the Great, the school of Napoleon the First.
As, for the one, the Seven Years' War had begun with the invasion
of Saxony, and as the other had always with lightning speed fore-
stalled his enemies, so should I, in the event of Belgium's not being
on my side, be actuated by strategical considerations only." There
was a long pause. " I hoped," continued the Kaiser, visibly
annoyed, " to find that you understood and approved, but this unhappily does not appear to be the case. That is the most bitter
disappointment to-day has brought me." Whereupon, in as calm
and precise a form as possible I laid before His Majesty the common
sense political view. I told him my endeavours were all concentrated
upon peace, a peace upheld in dignity and honour. That was his
objective too. An honourable peace, since time was on our side,
would be in the interests of Germany. Should we be attacked—
should our enemies, French or English, enter Belgium and set
troops on that soil, we also should be justified in invading it. But
until our enemies had violated Belgian neutrality, we ourselves could
not disregard agreements we had solemnly sworn to uphold. I
would never countenance any such terrible mistake since, in
Bismarck's words, it would place too many "imponderabilia" against
us; those spiritual values that outweigh material factors. Again I
repeated that in the case of war, we must certainly not be the first
to violate the neutrality of Belgium, which had been guaranteed by

international justice. Wars were not won in the long run by military measures alone, but also by political considerations. Napoleon ended as a prisoner in spite of his military genius, while Frederick the Great, who was not only a general but a statesman, died on the throne. Our conversation lasted till midnight. In the course of it, the Kaiser grew more emotional and violent than he usually did with me. He said, half under his breath, "If that's how you really think, in the case of a war I should have to look out for another Chancellor." I left him feeling that I had not quite convinced him. But I felt that, as long as I remained in office, he would follow me in any crisis, less perhaps from conviction than from caution. He still felt, in those days, that he was safest with me.

I will not conclude this long parenthesis without adding that both Count Alfred Schlieffen, and his successor, Hellmuth von Moltke, had in the course of conversations with me touched upon the question of a possible march through Belgium. My personal relations with both were of the best. Moltke was a loyal old friend of my youth, and remained so until his death. Schlieffen had been Commander of the First Guards Lancers Regiment, one of the finest regiments in the Army. In front of his old barracks in Potsdam there now stands the memorial of the dying horseman—at which no good Prussian can look without feelings of deep emotion and melancholy. Two of my brothers, the future Generals Adolf and Karl Ulrich Bülow, had served in this Regiment under Schlieffen. I remember that Schlieffen, some time before my resignation, in 1904 or 1905, had discussed with me the chances of an eventual war. He felt that in the case of a war with France and Russia, we must first try to overthrow France. The surest way to do this was by way of Belgium. I said that I was well aware of that. Already, as a Bonn Hussar, I had studied Clausewitz under the influence of my Commander, the future Field-Marshal Loë, and learnt the phrase, "the heart of France lies between Brussels and Paris." But, I added, we could only pursue this course for the gravest political reasons and then only if Belgian neutrality had already been violated by our enemies. I reminded this master of strategy of an event in the winter 1887-1888, which had remained indelibly imprinted in my memory. At that time there was serious tension between France and Germany: as in 1875, 1879, and 1885, war was in the air. In those days English sympathies were with Germany, and an important English paper, the *Standard* if I remember rightly, wrote somewhat as follows: It is true that England has guaranteed Belgium's neutrality. But that does not imply that she will be forced to defend this under all circumstances, by taking up arms for France against

Germany. Prince Bismarck answered this tempting supposition in an article he dictated himself and which I remember exactly. In those critical days I was Attaché in St. Petersburg, and so had read the article of my great chief with considerable attention and reflection.

In that article, which appeared in a semi-official paper, the *Berlin Post*, Prince Bismarck laid down the following general rules which for me had remained decisive:

(1) Germany would never begin a war because she feared that otherwise war might be forced upon her.

(2) Germany would, above all, never begin a war with the violation of another European Treaty.

(3) If England imagined that the Franco-German frontier was closed against German offensive by the French forts, and that, because of this, the German General Staff would contemplate a march through Belgium, Berlin was of the opinion that the inventiveness of the German General Staff would not be so easily exhausted. In any case it was a mistake to believe that political leadership in Germany was subservient to the standpoint of the General Staff.

(4) Germany was no more likely to violate the neutrality of Belgium than that of Switzerland.

(5) The German statesmen at the head of affairs particularly stressed their intention to remain, as ever, strict observers of the Treaty concluded in Europe for the preservation of peace. Moreover, plain common sense taught that it would not be wise to force Belgium or Switzerland into military co-operation with France.

Count Alfred Schlieffen, with whom both before and after this conversation I was on the best of terms, twisted his monocle several times in his eye, as his habit was, and then answered: "Of course. It's still the same to-day. We haven't grown stupider since then." He said, however, that he was inclined to believe that, in case of war, Holland would regard us as her natural ally against England. With regard to Belgium, she would scarcely resist a German invasion by force of arms but would remain satisfied with a protest. He also believed that in the case of a big war, the French, and eventually the English, would march into Belgium. Then our hands would no longer be tied. I wish to emphasize the fact that, to my own knowledge, there were General Staff officers who, up to the beginning of the Great War, held the belief that if France were to be beaten in a war between France and Germany, the way through Belgium was not the right, and, in any case, not the only means of achieving that end. Even after the war, one of our best-known Generals told me that we should have done better to have decided upon another plan of attack rather than to have chosen the way through Belgium, with all its dreadful political consequences.

I will take this opportunity to hasten events and mention that a few months before my resignation, Count Alfred Schlieffen published a rather alarming essay in the *Deutsche Revue*, concerning the chances of a world-war. This essay contained some expressions which caused anxiety in Belgium. I sent a dispatch of Count Wallwitz's upon this subject—at this time he was still representing the Empire in Brussels—to the Chief of the Army General Staff, General von Moltke, who replied as follows on 19th January 1909:

> It is incomprehensible to me how anybody who reads Count Schlieffen's words can believe that the idea of a march through Belgium is entertained as probable or inevitable in any authoritative quarter. It should not be difficult for Count Wallwitz, who was not in possession of the original text of the essay at the time, to dispel any misgivings which have arisen.

I should like to state here that on 1st July 1920, I asked the Foreign Office to state definitely whether, after the resignation of Prince Bismarck, under the Chancellorship either of Count Caprivi, Prince Hohenlohe, or during my own term as Chancellor, any discussion had taken place between the Foreign Office and the Military General Staff, concerning the possibility of an eventual invasion of Luxemburg, Belgium, or Holland. On 6th July 1920 I received the following official reply from the Secretary of State of the Foreign Office, Herr von Haniel:

> ESTEEMED PRINCE,
> To your question of the 1st inst. whether, during the years 1890 to 1909, a discussion had ever taken place between the Foreign Office and the General Staff regarding an eventual invasion of Luxemburg, Belgium, or Holland, I have the honour to inform Your Excellency, that the archives of the Foreign Office contain nothing relative to such a suggestion.
> Your obedient servant,
> E. HANIEL.

Kaiser William II never, during the remaining years of my Chancellorship—from 1904 to 1909—returned to the subject of an invasion of Belgium. All the more zealously did he devote himself to the furthering of closer relations with Denmark. This desire was widespread in our naval circles. To obtain an alliance with Denmark, Tirpitz would have gladly given back North Schleswig to the Danes. Others among our seamen were rather more inclined to the Erlkönig principle, " *Und bist du nicht willig, so brauch' ich Gewalt* " (" And if you're unwilling, I shall use force "). I was never in doubt that any attempt to draw closer to Denmark or to force her to draw closer to us would bring down on us the wrath of England, and probably that of France and Russia also. After receiving two telegrams from the Kaiser, *ex abrupto*, in February 1905: " We must bring about closer relations with Denmark," I wrote to him that any diplomatic movement towards an alliance with Denmark on the part of Germany would considerably increase the already troubled condition of the world. An alliance between the powerful German Empire and little Denmark would be regarded, universally, as a repudiation by Denmark of her independence and as an annexation on Germany's part. Old King Christian IX still cherished, perhaps, that " paternal affection " for the German Kaiser of which the latter had often spoken to me. But the King could not conclude an alliance without the participation of the constitutional organs of State, and these last were dependent upon the popular vote. There was, certainly, an anti-German feeling in Denmark, but during the course of forty years, thanks to the healing influence of time and a sensible policy on Germany's part, this feeling had calmed down. But any suspicion that Denmark was to be made dependent upon Germany, would immediately arouse instincts which were beyond the scope of diplomatic influence. Not only the Danish Press and the Danish people, but the Government and the Court would turn for help to England and Russia. Any Danish Government which did not study national feelings at such a moment would be overthrown, and even the Danish dynasty, whose German origin had not been entirely forgotten, might then be endangered. This would give England an opportunity to " defend " the little country and its independence against a " forced " German alliance. " Many English circles are only waiting for a chance to play the pleasing rôle of protector of innocence." Delcassé would welcome the opportunity to prove to Russia and England that there were no differences between them which need prevent an Anglo-Russian-French understanding for the protection of Danish independence. The dream of incorporating Denmark into the Federation of the German Empire was a very dangerous one. Its realization would only be possible if the English navy were engaged elsewhere. Or if Germany, alone or in conjunction with an ally, could become England's equal on the sea. At present, both alternatives were out of the question. Any rash attempt by us to attach Denmark to Germany would give our enemies in Paris, London, and St. Petersburg the opportunity they needed to further a Franco-Russian-

English Triple Alliance. The question of the division of China was preventing this Alliance for the moment, but once such an Alliance had been formed to " protect " the independence of Denmark, new tasks would undoubtedly be found for it to accomplish.

That long and serious conversation with the Kaiser about Belgium was so firmly imprinted on my memory, that I remember every phrase, almost every gesture, and word he spoke. I warned His Majesty at the time against misuse of the so-called Hostage-Theory. This theory was a discovery of Professor Theodor Schiemann. Or, to express it truly, this tactless and conceited babbler had embellished a remark made by Holstein which suggested that if England should attack us, we ought to attack France. When a French newspaper used the word " Schiemanisme " to designate the doctrine alleged to flourish in Berlin, according to which the Germans, unable to withstand England at sea, would therefore invade France on land, Schiemann felt himself a European celebrity, and mouthed such careless phrases and constantly reiterated threats that I sent him a sharp warning by the Under-Secretary of State von Mühlberg. Whereupon he wrote me a humble letter in which he swore by all that was holy that he made a special effort in his " modest activity as publicist " not to conflict with the best interests of the State, but that in future he would speak and write even more carefully. The letter closed with the words: " But if, in spite of this, I should still say too much, please attribute it to my awkwardness and not to my lack of good will. In constantly grateful devotion, Your Excellency's humbly obedient Theodor Schiemann." Unfortunately this declaration did not prevent Herr Schiemann from repeatedly approaching the impressionable and highly-imaginative Kaiser with nonsensical theories and projects. Now would come the suggestion that, even in a period of peace, we were to occupy Libau and Riga in order that we should have a pledge in hand against Russia; next, that an ultimatum should go to England to the effect that either the threats concerning our naval expansion must cease, or that " an honest and chivalrous crossing of arms " at sea would ensue. With regard to the dangers menacing us at home and abroad, Schiemann assured the Kaiser that a " brisk and bright little war " would be " the best way out." He advocated the methods of the mediaeval tournament for a war with England, namely, that meeting place and choice of weapons should be decided beforehand, and, in this case, the number of ships to be put into action. My patience was sorely tried and the nervous energy needed for serious affairs exhausted, by refuting these childish suggestions to the Kaiser, who, unfortunately, in such matters displayed a peculiar *naïveté*. With all the exalted ideas of the dignity and sacredness of his Imperial calling, William II failed to understand that, more than any other, this very calling demanded hard work, concentration, and seriousness. He had never understood the deep truth of the advice which in the *Elective Affinities* our greatest poet puts into the mouth of his clever Captain. " Let us note one thing and act upon it," says the Captain to his friend Edward, ' Let us separate whatever is simply business from life itself! Business demands seriousness and severity, life needs free will; business means consistent action, life is often improved by being inconsequential; that, indeed, is what makes it amusing and worth living." Kaiser William II was more akin to the Edward of the story who could never manage to arrange his papers in their proper pigeon-holes, or separate business and pleasure, vocation and avocation.

It was my practice from time to time during my whole term of office, to think over, in the quiet of my study, our internal problems and the whole international situation. If ever a year gave food for such reflection, and made it necessary, it was the year 1905, which began so inauspiciously for the character of William II. Often, while anxiously meditating the safety and future of the Fatherland, I would look out at the beautiful old trees in the garden of the Chancellor's palace, under whose branches Princess Elizabeth Radziwill, the first love of our good old Kaiser, dreamed and suffered, and upon which the eyes of Prince Bismarck had often rested. In common with every man who has lived in the limelight of politics, I have made mistakes. When wise King Solomon, he who was so deeply versed in the ways of mankind, consecrated the Temple in Jerusalem, he turned his face to the whole congregation of Israel and said: " There is none who hath not sinned." This is truer to-day of Princes and statesmen than it was of the contemporaries of that monarch, whose wisdom was greater than all the wisdom of the Egyptians, he who made 3,000 proverbs, composed 1,005 songs, and who knew all trees, from the cedar of Lebanon to the hyssop which grows out of the wall. But if I do not wish to hide my errors and failings in any way whatsoever, there is one reproach which has been levelled at me which does me grave wrong—the rumour that I performed my duties in office with a perpetual smile on my lips, in a mood constantly and persistently gay. Caricatures which I have not underrated from the artistic point of view, have done much to belie the truth. Impressionistic to a degree attained by no other form of art these made me appear as the serenely smiling *bon viveur*, just as later they made of Bethmann-Hollweg the profound philo-

sopher. I was just as little an Epicurean as Bethmann was a
Kantian, a reputation he gained solely because our comic papers
repeatedly depicted him with *The Critique of Pure Reason* under his
arm. During my twelve years of office in Berlin, I rarely woke up
without serious worries, and too often at night lay down again in
the same mood. But I was certainly of opinion that the leading
statesman of a great country should not walk about steeped in gloom.
I thought it better to play Hector than Cassandra, believing that
the English " never say die " is a good phrase, and that, to quote
our greatest poet:

> " *Nimmer sich beugen,*
> *Kräftig sich zeigen,*
> *Allen Gewalten*
> *Zum Trotz sich erhalten.*" [1]

puts the gods upon one's side.

The foreign situation was indeed serious. The Indians say
that every human being bears his destiny written on his brow. So
do the nations. The destiny of the German people is to be found in
its geographical position, crushed in between Frenchmen and Slavs
in the middle of Europe. It was in this sense that, in my book
Deutsche Politik [2] I wrote that we had been encircled for more than a
thousand years, since the Treaty of Verdun. The difficulties of our
situation were increased by England's jealousy of our industrial
development, which was placing us in the forefront of the world's
markets. The democratic population of our great cities, the "pave-
ment-democracy " as I once called it, did not understand that it was
not only for reasons of internal political justice that I stood for the
protection of German agriculture. I saw in a flourishing agrarian
population the balance against a completely industrial development,
which would be as undesirable for our internal as for our foreign
policy. But Bismarck himself had said that our industrial progress
could not be forcibly held back. Since, I had often said in my public
speeches, and say again in these my memoirs, we were developing
along these lines, it was necessary for us to protect that part of our
national fortune entrusted by us to the sea—that is to say, to build
battleships. This statement of mine considerably increased England's enmity and so made our political situation more difficult.
When I accompanied His Majesty to Wilhelmshaven in 1904, for

---

[1] Never to give in,
To show oneself strong,
To defy
All the fates.
[2] *Deutsche Politik* (p. 293)

the purpose of swearing in the naval recruits, he suddenly laid his hand on my arm in the course of the dinner in the naval casino which followed those proceedings, and said in a low voice: " Is it not dreadful to think that these good boys in blue, whose oaths I have just received, may perhaps be lying at the bottom of the North Sea in a few weeks' time?" In his kind eyes as he said it there was such sadness, such melancholy anxiety, it touched my heart. But this human and simple sentiment could in no way influence my conviction which arose from a quiet study of the situation. In spite of all the menacing speeches of the English naval men, whose most important representative, Lord Fisher, was constantly telling King Edward that he should be allowed to "Copenhagen " the German fleet before it was too late—sink it, that is to say, without any declaration of war—England would only turn against us if, and after, we were involved in a war with Russia. On that account alone, then, we must remember Bismarck's warnings and keep peace with Russia. This would be possible if we did not oppose Russia in the Dardanelles, or make any concessions to pan-Polish propaganda in our Eastern provinces. We could not, of course, let Austria be crushed. But we must not allow the plans of excitable Austrian Generals, the well-known incompetence of Viennese diplomats, or the violence of the Magyars to reach the point where war between Austria and the Slavonic and orthodox Russia became unavoidable.

Delcassé, the French Foreign Secretary, was one sinister figure on the European chess-board. King Edward was not the man to fall upon us suddenly, as many Jingos, with and without a naval uniform, would have had us believe. He had replied to my New Year's greeting: " The Queen and I thank you for your good wishes and trust that the new year may bring peace and prosperity to the world at large. Edward R." It was a very different question whether the King might not view a French attack upon us with complacency. Delcassé manœuvred in accordance with the well-known phrase which Prince Felix Schwarzenberg is alleged to have uttered before Olmütz: " *Il faut avilir la Prusse et puis la démolir*." Delcassé wanted above all to give our prestige in the world a severe blow; everything else would follow of its own accord. He was not disturbed by the fact that Russia was momentarily occupied with the Japanese War. He had, like the rest of the world at the time, an enormous opinion of the illimitable resources of the gigantic Russian Empire, with its 130 million inhabitants. He also believed, that in the case of a Franco-German War, peace between Russia and Japan would be swiftly restored under English auspices.

Bismarck used to say that contrary to the well-known English maxim, " Measures not men," he was of the opinion that the men who had to put the measure through were more important than the measure itself. He also defined the words he wrote in the Golden Book of the Germanic Museum at Nuremberg, " *Unda fert nec regitur*," as meaning that the strength of the wave was destined by providence, but that the capacity of men for being borne on it, was dependent upon the strength and the skill of the swimmer. In view of the evil intentions and the intrigues of the French Foreign Secretary, hesitation seemed inadvisable; his overthrow was the right aim to pursue.

The pivotal point of my internal and foreign political troubles was now, as before, the personality of the Kaiser. Bismarck, fully conscious of what he did, had made of the King the representative of the Prussian, and along with it, the German constitution. After his resignation, Bismarck said more than once that he had helped the kingly rider to his saddle again and all too effectively. " *Troppo mi ha aiutato Sant' Antonio*," says the Neapolitan fisherman if St. Anthony sends him a storm when he prays for a wind. Long before the year of destiny and misfortune, 1890, my father, an orthodox believer, politically conservative, and entirely royalist in his views, had told Prince Bismarck that he had more than once associated the centre of constitutional gravity, the weal and woe of the Reich, too closely with the person of the monarch. Bismarck spoke openly with my father who was one of the few persons from whom he took advice. To my father's observation that it would be good for the State, as well as for the monarch's own position, to allow the people a greater share in the government, Bismarck replied: " You are right in the main, but nobody can jump over his own shadow. I am first and foremost a Royalist, and everything else is secondary to that. I grumble over the King, I can imagine that, as a Lord, one can rebel against the King, I take the King in my own fashion, I influence, I ' manage ' him, I lead him, but he is the central point of my whole thought and action, Archimedes' point from which I move the world." But, in the German Empire, as Bismarck had constructed and equipped it, the individuality of the King of Prussia and German Emperor was of the utmost significance both in foreign and in home politics. Bismarck himself was never in doubt about that. After the Nobiling attack of 1878 he said in my presence to his son Herbert, who was making gloomy prognostications about the future: " I am not anxious about the future of the German people; the clod is too big to be rubbed to powder. The various parts of it will always adhere together again in some form or other. But the Hohenzollerns might be sent flying if they should lose the qualities our old master possesses, the sober sense of human values, the modesty and the courage based on a calm and well-balanced nervous system."

These very qualities, to his own and to our misfortune, were lacking in the otherwise so brilliantly gifted William II. The words of one of the most distinguished statesmen of the Victorian era, the Earl of Granville, who died in 1891, to a relation of his by marriage, my mother-in-law, Donna Laura Minghetti, were more applicable to William II even than to his mother of whom they were spoken: " Our Princess Royal, the Crown Princess of Prussia, is very clever, but not wise."

After seventeen years on the throne, William II aroused opposition and dislike, but also much interest and curiosity in other nations. Courts and Governments had ceased to have much confidence in him. He had made many enemies among Royal personages and foreign statesmen because of the freedom he permitted his tongue. " The tongue," says the Apostle James, " is a small member but it doeth great things." In the case of William II it did much damage, and above all, to himself. He might have saved himself bitter hours, and his advisers heavy troubles, if he had remembered better the warning of the apostle Peter, which I once wrote out before a journey for him: " For he that will love life and see good days, let him refrain his tongue from evil " (1 Peter, 3, 10). The English Ambassador in Berlin, Sir Frank Lascelles, a friend of mine of many years' standing, told me in 1905 that King Edward's objection to his nephew gave him less uneasiness than the fact that the Kaiser was gradually losing the confidence of the leading English statesmen. Sir Frank based his statement on the fact that the Kaiser swore high and low to every Englishman that as Queen Victoria's grandson he was England's best friend, whereas, behind their backs, he stirred up strife against them. When I queried this, Lascelles told me the following tale: During the last Kiel Week, the Kaiser paid frequent visits to the American yachts which had arrived there. When I was there with him he spoke fairly sensibly, but when I was not, he grumbled about the English continually, and told the Americans to look to him for support against "*perfide Albion*." The Kaiser, said Lascelles, did not know that on one of the American yachts there was the English naval attaché in Washington who forwarded His Majesty's utterances to London. He, Lascelles, had read the dispatch in person. The feelings of the Tsar for the Kaiser had grown more and more cold because " Nicky " found altogether too superior the tone in which " Willy " often " talked at " and exhorted him. At a chance meeting the Grand Duke Vladimir said to me: "*Votre empereur commence à donner sur les nerfs à mon neveu, l'Empereur. Mon neveu le trouve trop outrecuidant et les conseils que votre Empereur lui donne, trop cousus de fil blanc, surtout quand dans ses lettres il lui dit du mal de l'Oncle Edouard et de la République française.*" In Italy, William II had long since personally offended King Victor Emanuel and Queen Elena. The only Court he influenced was that of Austria, and that was the least necessary of all, since Austria needed us more than we the Dual Monarchy.

The idiosyncrasy of the Kaiser, where the Japanese were in question, also disturbed our political circles. When the Russo-Japanese War was nearing its end, I wrote to His Majesty as follows:

We had no reason to fear, for the present, any resurrection of Tamerlane and Jhengis Khan. Moreover, a glance at the map shows that Russia, England and France would be called upon first to encounter any danger of that kind. It was for these countries to repel any eventual Yellow Peril. Of these three representatives of the white race, only Russia now appeared in the arena. France had withdrawn from the game quietly. England had allied with the Yellow race. In view of the present dislocation of the factors of power it behoved Germany, in my opinion, to be careful. There were signs enough that all would not go too well for Japan even without our interference.

I impressed it upon him that perhaps a more immediate danger was that one day we should have Japan against us as the ally of white enemies. We had therefore a distinct and definite political interest in utilizing the present crisis to improve our relations with Japan, which could be done without disloyalty to Russia, if we continued in our present unswerving pursuance of neutrality.

CHAPTER VI

Bülow's relations with William II—Miners' strike in the Ruhr—The debate on the question of the miners in the Prussian Diet—The new Commercial Treaties in the Reichstag—Congratulatory letters—The passing of the Canal Bill—Minister von Budde—William II's relations with the various Parties—Letters of Count Monts concerning the Centre and Catholicism—Baron von Hertling's mission to Rome— Resignation of the Lord Lieutenant of Silesia—Dr. Michaelis, the future Chancellor, is considered inadequate for post of Chief Commissioner in Breslau—William II's attitude to the Moroccan question.

IN our home politics Imperial blunders were as frequent as in the diplomatic treatment of our neighbours. They were, however, not so dangerous; the bill for damage done abroad was heavier. A disastrous war could only end in revolution—that, till the day of my retirement, was always my profoundest conviction.

Nevertheless, William II would have done well to have avoided outraging too profoundly, by display of autocratic *sans gêne*, our intellectual circles at home. In reality he was not in the least the type of monarch of whom Frederick William I or Nicholas I are the examples. He only liked to appear an autocrat. He had never seriously contemplated abolishing the Constitution. He had neither the firmness, callousness, energy nor unrelenting consistence of real autocracy. His conception of the duties of a sovereign never appeared to me more clearly than in the course of a short conversation which I had with him at the Neues Palais.

He had invited me there to dinner with my wife and mother-in-law. At the end of our meal, the Emperor very graciously conducted us through the apartments that had been used by Frederick the Great. On a table, framed under glass, lay spread a facsimile of that great sovereign's last will and testament, with an address to his successors and their children. It was written in French and began more or less as follows: "An accident of birth has decreed the future Frederick William II the heir to the Prussian Crown. He can only prove himself worthy of this great office by his own ability, strict probity and hard work." As I was reading this admirable sentiment the Kaiser came up to me and said, "You, I suppose, admire this theory, but I cannot altogether endorse it." And after a pause he added, "I agree with Maximilian I. During a hunting

85

expedition he was forced to pass the night in a little hut. While he was sleeping, several gentlemen of his suite, impudent *petite noblesse*, chalked up a sentence on the wall: 'Maximilian, Maximilian, you are only a man like all the others.' The Emperor wrote underneath, 'Certainly I am only a man, but a man to whom God has done great honour.' That was one in the eye for those gentry." Gregorovius, in his *History of Rome in the Middle Ages*, says of the Emperor Maximilian that though he was excitable and imaginative, his mind was superficial.

In spite of some unpleasant incidents, my relationship with the Emperor remained good. But even then I had begun to seem inconvenient. The following incident went to prove it. King George of Greece had announced his visit. He was not a favourite of the Kaiser's, who already while he was still a Danish Prince had treated him with scant courtesy on account of old quarrels between the houses of Glücksburg and Augustenburg. On the other hand, he was the brother of Queen Alexandra and the Dowager Empress Maria Feodorovna, and could do us considerable harm. I therefore urged the Kaiser to treat him prudently. He wired to me:

> Think it to say the least undignified that Your Excellency should mistake me for some scandal-mongering old apple-woman. Am usually far more discreet than your own officials at the Foreign Office.

I was not long in answering this. His Majesty replied from Castle Hohenzollern which he visited with pleasure from time to time:

> Heartiest greetings from this ancestral home of our family. The lovely weather affords me magnificent view, uplifting my spirit with thankfulness towards those blue heights from which God so prodigally blessed this castle and the dynasty born in it, blessings of which such loyal servants as yourself are not the least.

It was impossible to be annoyed for long with him. On calm consideration I decided to put through the bills, the drafts of which were awaiting parliamentary debate. Voltaire's immortal Candide replies to the metaphysical speech of his master Pangloss: "*Cela est bien dit, mais il faut cultiver votre jardin.*" And the old philosopher Martin, the friend of both personages, opines: "*Travailler sans raisonner, c'est le seul moyen de rendre la vie supportable.*"

The question in home politics which first of all needed my attention was the threatened miners' strike. In the Ruhr, discontent had been fermenting since the beginning of January 1905. The miners complained of the fall in wages during the past years, of the fact that the time spent in getting up and down the pits was not paid for as part of their working day, of high fines and harsh treatment by their overseers. On 14th January 1905, 60,000 men came out on strike; a week later, 200,000 out of a total of 270,000 were out. The Kaiser inclined to the opinion that we should not interfere and especially not mediate in the strike. The wilder the Ruhr showed itself to be the better. It would make the bourgeoisie more cautious and more alert in future. It would also show them how right he, their Emperor, had been when, in his Bielefeld speech he had demanded hard labour for every man who prevented a German worker from going to work. In one word His Majesty upheld the standpoint he had fought so bitterly when, not long before Bismarck's resignation, the Kaiser and the great Chancellor had held widely differing opinions on workers' questions in general and the Ruhr strike of those days in particular. With all my admiration for Prince Bismarck I still could not share the opinion he had maintained on industrial questions in 1890. *Amicus Plato amicior veritas.* In any case I considered the tactics with which, fifteen years previously, the founder of the Empire might have triumphed, unsuited to 1905. I sent von Velsen, the Chief Inspector of Mines, into the strike area to try to bring about an understanding. His suggestions met with a brusque refusal from the owners. They declared that under no circumstances would they negotiate with the miners as a whole but would only consider negotiations between individual owners and their men. Some of the great magnates ordered von Velsen, with whom formerly they had been very friendly, off their premises. This uncompromising attitude caused sympathies to turn more and more towards the miners. Archbishop Fischer of Cologne contributed a thousand marks to the funds of the Christian Unions; the Protestant Socialist Congress called for support of the men without actually endorsing all their demands. In the middle of January the question came before the Reichstag. I did not hesitate to express my point of view. When strikes occurred a government had a double duty. First it must see that peace and order are maintained and laws applied impartially and justly. But it should also, in the interests of social peace, industrial prosperity, and the protection of the workers themselves endeavour to bring about an understanding. I urged the workers to keep within the law and refrain from rioting, the owners to show a conciliatory spirit and do their best to meet the desires and understand the complaints of their men. In conclusion I associated myself most heartily with the hope ex-

pressed before my intervention by the Centre party deputy, Herold——
that quiet reflection on both sides might prevail over other sentiments. In the meantime with considerable difficulty I had prevailed
on the Prussian Cabinet to consider the draft of a Bill modifying
the former mining laws and which ensured that the interests of the
miners would be considered in any case of arbitrary lock-out. I felt
it my duty to defend this Bill personally in the Chamber. In any
case Möller, the Minister of Trade, was so sharply attacked by his
own party, the National Liberals, that I had to come to his rescue.
Möller before his nomination had been an universally respected and
very popular member of the Reichstag. I had suggested him to the
Kaiser for his post not only because he was qualified, but in
order to begin my new policy of filling ministerial posts with
parliamentarians. He had scarcely been appointed however when
parliamentarians themselves attacked him and sharply criticized
the appointment. Eugen Richter raised storms of hilarity in the
Reichstag by beginning his speech in the debate on the budget of
the Ministry of Commerce: " *Es wird immer döller, da kommt
der lange Möller.*" (" It's getting madder and madder now long
Möller's here.")

Möller was tall and well-built. His own party attacked him
most bitterly of all. Once when I asked him the reason he answered
with that equable good humour which never seemed to desert him,
" It's perfectly simple. There are at least three people in the party
who wanted to be ministers themselves." The member who
obstructed him most frequently was the National Liberal Heyl.
Herr Cornelius Heyl was a wealthy leather merchant from Worms.
He had bought the famous old estate, Herrnsheim, just outside
Worms, once the historic family seat of the Dalbergs, who as
hereditary Chamberlains of Worms Abbey had given several Arch-
bishops and Prince-Electors to the Empire. At every coronation,
it was the custom for the Imperial herald to ask, " Is no Dalberg
present? " If a Dalberg had attended it was his privilege to receive
the first accolade of knighthood from the new Roman Emperor of
the Germans. Karl Dalberg was the last Prince-Elector of Mainz
and Arch-Chancellor of the old Empire ; later he became Grand
Duke of Frankfurt. Wolfgang Dalberg did great honour to his
house when, as director of the National Theatre at Mannheim, he
produced Schiller's earliest dramas. Emmerich Dalberg first a
follower of Napoleon, went over to the Bourbons on his fall and,
later, was created a French duke. He was the last Dalberg of the
Herrnsheim branch of the family. His only daughter married an
English nobleman, Lord Acton, my wife's uncle. Then Herrn-

sheim passed to the rich Cornelius Heyl, whom the Grand Duke of
Hesse made a baron, and who caused an expensive brochure to be
written glorifying Herrnsheim and the Dalbergs. Ever since then
Cornelius Heyl had considered himself, by some form of auto-
suggestion, a Dalberg. Once in the course of a debate he managed
to provoke Eugen Richter to express the malicious opinion that
there were knights of the sword whom he respected, and knights of
the pen whom he could place equally high, but that for leather
knights he could feel nothing.

In contrast to Baron von Heyl, the Social-Democratic member for Bochum-Gelsenkirchen, Otto Hué, impressed me very
pleasantly. He was a miner's son who, as an apprentice locksmith,
on his travels through Germany, France, Belgium, and England,
had gained an unusual insight into working-class conditions as a
whole and those of the miners in particular. Later he became a
miner himself. In debate he kept to the point and spoke with
reflection. One only needed a glance at his honest face to see what
a decent fellow he was. During the Spa negotiations in 1920,
when the well-meaning, but somewhat *petit bourgeois* Chancellor,
Fehrenbach, more than once, by his sentimental appeals, drew down
on himself the sarcasm of the Allied politicians, Lloyd George
declared that, of the Germans, Hué had left the best impression on
him.

In 1905 Bebel used the strike and the situation it created
chiefly as an excuse for agitation. I was, of course, the principal
object of his wrath. He hurled reproaches at me for my lack of
sympathy with the needs and aspirations of the miners, my submissive attitude towards employers. These, on their side, accused
me of hostility towards themselves, of coquetting with Social-
Democracy. Once again with the Apostle Paul I might have
exclaimed, " *Judaeis scandalum, Graecis stultitia* ". I had at least one
consolation. The French Ambassador assured me that a strike of
200,000 miners which had lasted several weeks without rioting,
without a single shot being fired, was an admirable proof of the
order and social stability in Germany, and of the intelligence of our
government.

My amendment to the miners' bill made it possible for the
government to curtail working hours, which were far too long,
to reform the system of fines, and institute a number of sanitary
reforms. Above all it set up workers' committees to enable the
miners' wishes to be conveyed to their employers. In the Prussian
Diet it encountered a stubborn resistance, both at the hands of
Conservatives, and even more at those of the Right Wing National

Liberals, but a majority composed of Centre Party, Independent Conservatives and a section of the National Liberals accepted it. I have always held that employers and employed should co-operate in our economic development as a whole. It had been my hope that this great thought—of peaceful economic evolution—would materialize gradually without violence. May the realization of this need, after so much blood, so many tears, be born again in the German mind and help to cure the wounds of war and revolution!

On 1st February I introduced the new Commercial Treaties in the Reichstag in a speech[1] that lasted over two hours. The parties who in the former Reichstag had helped me to put through the tariff duties were loyal also on this occasion. When I stated that I and my colleagues had been successful in protecting both trade and industry in spite of considerably increased protection for agriculture, I reaffirmed my belief that Germany was both an agricultural and an industrial country. I was interrupted by shouts of protest from the Left. I have never heard that those who then protested acknowledged their error in the following decade during which both industry and commerce flourished more than ever before under the protection of those Commercial Treaties concluded by myself and my coadjutors. None the less I was right when I said at the end of my long speech, that no class of producer in Germany would find them completely satisfactory, but that they would increase the industrial welfare of the whole nation, that those who voted for them would be serving the interests of Germany both at home and abroad.

This conviction was shared by the rulers of the Federal States. Grand Duke Frederick of Baden wired to say that his feelings as a German impelled him to express to me his gratitude " for this great act of statesmanship." The King of Saxony wrote that this result, particularly gratifying for Saxons, was due to my foresight and intelligence. Von Brauer, the Premier of Baden, wrote as follows: " We all know that the conclusion of this important agreement is due first and foremost to the skilful manner in which you handled it." The eighty-four years old Prince Regent Luitpold wrote from Munich personally: " With the achievement of these new Commercial Treaties Your Excellency may congratulate yourself on the accomplishment of a most difficult political task to be ranked amongst the most arduous achievements of statesmanship. I confidently expect that these treaties, of such importance for the industrial development of the Empire, will benefit every class of

[1] Prince Bülow's *Speeches*. Complete edition, vol. ii, pp. 157-76. Compressed edition, vol. iii, pp. 212-38.

German producer. The honour of having brought this great work to its happy conclusion through the manifold difficulties besetting it, belongs exclusively to Your Excellency. It gives me genuine pleasure to tell you this and to congratulate you on this latest triumph of your unflagging and self-sacrificing activity." In addition to this letter the Bavarian Minister, von Podewils, wrote: "The Bavarian Cabinet feel compelled to express their conviction to Your Excellency that, without your wise leadership, vision and untiring energy, the advantage of this important piece of legislation, promising to Germany many years of peaceful steady development, would have been far harder to gain so successfully." Von Podewils added that the Bavarian Government as a whole felt it their duty to set on record their warmest thanks for my constant furtherance of the specific interests of Bavaria. In view of the attacks in Free Trade circles, especially those of Barth, the Member for Bremen, it was gratifying when the Presidents of the North German Lloyd, which equally with the Hamburg Hapag was an object of my particular interest, expressed the opinion that these new treaties, due mainly to the energy of the Chancellor would bring a rich harvest to German economic life. The most gratifying of all these tributes was, perhaps, the following telegram from my old friend the poet Adolf Wilbrandt. He wired from Rostock: "These last weeks and years have brought the achievement of a great part of your life's work. What you have done may not be perfect—nothing under Heaven ever is; it may not be acceptable to everybody—such an act still slumbers among the wildest of uncreated impossibilities—but a great achievement composed of patriotism, energy, ability. May God grant that this law becomes our point of departure for a glorious new release of energy. My dear friend, I congratulate you from the bottom of my heart." The Kaiser also sent me a personal letter:

I gladly acknowledge that your skill as a statesman, the unflagging zeal with which you conducted negotiations in the face of all the obstacles in your way, have achieved this wonderful success. My thanks must go to you first of all and I express them cordially. I beg you at the same time, as an outward token of this letter to accept with all good wishes a marble bust of myself. [His Majesty signed himself] Eternally cognizant of your loyalty and devotion, I remain

Your grateful King and Emperor,
WILLIAM I. R.

The word " eternally " had been heavily underlined by His Majesty.

The Kaiser at my suggestion awarded the Black Eagle to my invaluable supporter Count Posadowsky and named von Richthofen who had been helpful in drawing up the Commercial Treaties, a Prussian Minister.

For long the question of the canals had played an important part in our home politics. It had been the cause of much unpleasantness, contributing not a little to poison our political atmosphere. The Kaiser, as so often happened, had an excellent object in view, worthy of the noblest effort; this only made his tactics seem the clumsier; alternately he would threaten, storm, abandon hope. On 27th February 1905, I managed at last to put the Canals Bill through with 255 against 132 votes. A number of leading Conservatives had had the discernment to vote for it, among them the following: Wartensleben-Rogasen, Wartensleben-Schwirsen, Pappenheim, the editor of the *Kreuzzeitung*, Dr. Kropatschek, Arnim-Züsedom, Saldern-Plettenburg, Bülow-Bothkamp, Bülow-Bossee, Putlitz. The chief credit for the final realization of this great work must go to Budde, the Minister of Public Works. The old Prussian State with its bureaucracy and official class produced many distinguished officers and officials but scarcely one more capable than Hermann Budde.

Such a life as his deserves to be studied, particularly in the schools of the New Germany, where all too many " Republicans "— many of them superficial mediocrities—do their best to kill all memories of better times. It might show the coming generation what it really meant, in those days, to " be a man." Born at Bensberg near Cologne, and entered as a cadet, he fought through the Franco-Prussian War while still almost a boy, and was shot in the chest. After the war he remained on the active list, and in a few years was drafted to the General Staff where his superiors very soon realized his exceptional capacity in matters of railway transport. He retired in 1900 as Major-General. His value was so generally acknowledged that several big industrial enterprises strove to secure his services. He decided on a post at the Armaments Factory at Löwe, which offered him a very high salary for those days. When the government offered him the post of Minister of Public Works we travelled together from Berlin to the Neues Palais at Potsdam, where I was to present him to the Kaiser. During this journey he told me that, when he remembered his wife and children he found it hard to decide to give up the large salary and still larger perquisites of the Armaments Factory for the meagre appointments of a Minister. But he was always ready to sacrifice his interest to the State's. While still fighting for the Canals Bill he was seized with a grave illness, a cancer which rapidly developed, was pronounced from the start to be incurable, and caused him the severest physical pain. But he did his duty to the end.

The Kaiser granted my request very willingly, and sent the Black Eagle to the death-bed of this heroic servant. Frau Budde wrote on this occasion: " Your Excellency knows the dark hours through which we have passed, and that my husband achieved the task assigned him under the strain of never ceasing physical agony. Cares often fill my mind which the future seems unlikely to dissipate. But I am everlastingly grateful to Your Excellency for having given my husband the joy of receiving this honour. May God restore his old health; he will devote his last breath to the service of the Fatherland."

Budde died in the spring of 1906. His young and beautiful wife survived him by a few years only. One of his brothers was the well-known Protestant theologian, who published such notable works on ancient Hebrew literature and Biblical history.

On the passing of the Canal Bills Scheme the Kaiser thanked me " most warmly " for my " furtherance of the Canal Scheme, as able as it is energetic." Herr von Heydebrand-Nassadel, less gifted with persuasive eloquence than his cousin of Klein-Tschunkawe, but more reflective and intelligent, wrote:

> Will Your Excellency kindly permit me also to offer you my sincerest congratulations—not only on the honour bestowed on you by His Imperial Majesty, but especially on the " *monumentum aere perennius* " which you have erected to your own fame in restoring confidence to German agriculture, even without fulfilling all its wishes. Much will still depend on administration and management, but the speech at the banquet of the German Agrarian Council in which Your Excellency assessed the attitude of the various parties, especially the Conservatives, towards the Canal Bill, was warmly appreciated by myself and many others. It will be long before anyone else achieves such a masterpiece as these two bills.

My relationships with the bourgeois parties were on the whole satisfactory. None of them, however, was quite pleased with me, and that was a very good sign. In a country like Germany, where Party spirit unluckily far transcends the sense of the State and of its interests, it is always an ominous sign for any Minister if a party finds nothing to complain of in him.

Prince Bismarck in his *Thoughts and Memories*, exclaims with Shakespeare's *Coriolanus*, " Get home you fragments " to the party cliques he so thoroughly despised. But though it seemed to me my duty, as a conscientious Minister, never to yield to Party egotisms, I always endeavoured to keep the Kaiser out of these petty squabbles, and to prevent him from attacking the Parties or from grumbling too much about any one of them. In my opinion the Crown should be above Parties.

It was not always easy to persuade him to accept this view. Conservative opposition infuriated His Majesty most of all. It seemed to him just as despicable as would a mutiny in the 1st Guards Regiment. His especial dislike was for the Centre Party. On the occasion of an unimportant speech in the Munich Diet, on some minor question of Army discipline, the Kaiser, apparently still excited by my repeal of paragraph 2 of the Jesuit Law, wired me as follows:

" Those curs in Centre Party attempting to undermine military discipline, and with it the Hohenzollern Monarchy."

The case in debate was that of a one-year conscript who had been punished for having lodged a complaint in a manner not prescribed in regulations. This led to a conflict between the Bavarian Minister of Defence, Asch, and a Bavarian deputy, Pichler.

William II was tolerant, and just in thought, on all matters of religious belief. He had no hatred of Roman Catholicism; was never at all anti-Semitic. Yet when his sister Sophie, Crown Princess of Greece, was converted to the Orthodox Church, he raged and wrote her a letter " banishing her for ever from his domains." When the Landgravine Anne of Hesse, who had loved much in her youth, turned in later life for peace and comfort to the bosom of the Roman Church, he wrote furiously to the ageing apostate. He showed me the draft of his letter, and I had much difficulty in making him suppress the worst passages. One sentence he insisted on retaining: " The House of Hohenzollern from henceforth rejects Your Royal Highness and would prefer to forget your existence."

In vain did I remind His Majesty of the saying of his greatest predecessor—that in the Prussian State everyone had a right to his own way to heaven; in vain of the even greater word of the Saviour: " My Father's house has many mansions." His Majesty's taste for emphasis was engrained. It is true that such outbursts were very rarely followed by action. He was soon reconciled with his sister, and did not long keep up his quarrel with Anne.

But it never ceased to be difficult to reckon with his verbal impulsiveness. In the summer of 1905 I received another Imperial telegram *en clair*: " B.T. has had the insolence and obscenity to slander my mother and accuse her of the most horrible things. I have just sent Plessen and Löwenfeld with sabre and revolver to the editor to insist on immediate withdrawal and enforce a public apology. I leave it to Your Excellency's discretion to unmask and brand in the press this gang of newspaper freebooters."

The *Berliner Tageblatt* had, if I remember rightly, dished up the silly rumour that the Empress Frederick had married again after the death of her first husband. The whole thing was a piece of clumsy bad taste, without any deliberate wish to offend. The two " sabre and revolver " bearing generals had sensibly refrained from provoking a scandal, and the matter had been arranged in a conversation carried on with politeness on both sides.

In the spring of 1905, after a parade he had held in Strassburg, the Kaiser had called the Generals round him and addressed them, in his vivid and forceful but too often indiscreet fashion, on the subject of Russia and Japan. On both he had poured the vials of his wrath. He had it on direct information from his cousin, Prince Friedrich Leopold, that Russian generals possessed no Staff Maps, but had carried instead whole hampers of champagne into action. The whole Russian army at Mukden had been rotten with drink and debauch. Now it would be Germany's task to confront the Yellow Peril alone. Russia had unluckily failed us. Both officers and men in the German army must scrupulously fill up each hour of their time, so that they, unlike the Russians, might not find themselves the victims of drink and women. As to the Japanese they would never have won if the German Reichstag had granted its Emperor a navy earlier: he would soon have made them toe the line, etc.

His Majesty's sonorous voice enabled a reporter of the Strassburg *Bürgerzeitung*, who was posted a little way off, to take down this whole speech in shorthand. It was published in the evening edition. I protested against these remarks as insulting both to Russia and Japan. The Kaiser replied from Urville, whither he had gone in the meantime, that the press had been so intrusive as to leave him no chance of escape. He had, personally, in his own garden at Urville, arrested a notorious member of the staff of a Metz paper. " I nearly gave him a good sound thrashing with my own hands."

To pilot the ship of state through these shoals was a duty which demanded eternal vigilance, an unremitting strain on nerves and patience, when its captain was liable to play such tricks.

More than once during my term of office did I recall a saying I had heard, as a young Secretary of Embassy in Paris, from the lips of the brilliant *Times* correspondent there in those days, Herr Oppert-Blowitz. I had expressed my great and undying admiration for Bismarck. Blowitz answered: "*C'est bien, mais n'oubliez pas que Bismarck est une rose dont l'Empereur est la tige.*"

In a country whose monarch possessed all the power and influence which, since Bismarck's day, had been the prerogative of the King of Prussia and German Emperor, it was difficult to pursue any policy unless one could place constant reliance on the sovereign. Old Lucanus, the Cabinet Councillor, said to me once, soon after I became State Secretary: "All and none can influence our exalted master." This meant that William II, as I was to learn, would not permanently take anyone's advice, though, for a certain time, he would let himself be swayed by whoever offered. It was natural that every type of intriguer should make full use of the varying moods of His Majesty to play an ever changing party game.

Count Monts, our Ambassador to Rome, had scarcely heard that the Kaiser had begun to rail against the Centre Party than he began an ostentatious display of his old aversion from all things Catholic.

He wrote to my immediate assistant, Prince Lichnowsky, who happened to share his views on the subject, that my internal policy, because of its indulgence to Rome, was causing him the gravest perturbation. Monts, who as Ambassador to Rome, still made his customary display of profound admiration for me personally, wrote as follows:

"Bülow is so much cleverer than the rest of us, that it becomes from the outset very difficult to show him where he makes his mistake." Lichnowsky would be the only person likely to be able, now and then, to point out to me the reverse side of my home policy. He was broad-minded and without *parti-pris*, etc. It was necessary for him to suggest to me that even the wisest make mistakes, that I had failed to appreciate the dangers of Ultramontanism. If I sacrificed Schools to the "Romanizers" and allowed "Bavarian methods" to creep into the Universities, we might be lost and France surpass us intellectually. "The league with the priests means perdition." Monts who, when he composed this epistle, was in the Southern Tyrol, in Campiglio, pointed out how, in such a country, completely under clerical influence, one saw quite plainly whither such an influence tended.

"This fine country is going to ruin under its priests who stand in the way of all progressive methods of cultivation and forestry. Limitless poverty and stupidity prevail." Of the new pope, Pius X, Monts added:

I know nothing as yet of Pope Sarto. As an outsider he will have brought enormous winnings to the Rome totalisators. In my opinion the great problem at present confronting the Papacy is France. The Gallic province forms for the moment the chief source of material revenue for the firm Rome and Co. Will little Pius give way to them? It is to be feared that the French with their free-thinking schools may get one up on us, if we continue along the same path as now. There are clericals in Rome who see a French secession as the end of the universal spiritual ascendancy of the Papacy. That, in itself, would only be to the good as far as we are concerned, but as things are, it might have the unfortunate result of making us take France's unwelcome burden on our shoulders, and ourselves become protectors of the Pope. Such a policy could only lead to new concessions to the priesthood and to defeats in our foreign policy. I am always meeting with the same misconception in Rome. The Papacy as a whole sees Germany, with its Protestant Empire and its Lutheranism, as the source and origin of all evils. Yet we poor German idealists weave fantastic pictures for ourselves of spiritual re-union, the throne as the ally of the altar, Roman orthodoxy and loyalty to the Empire side by side which, seen from the standpoint of the Curia, are so much moonshine. . . . But you, my dear Lichnowsky, know all this far better than I do.

Monts would probably have inveighed still more pompously had he known how well-disposed towards me was the new Pope, Pius X. As early as the spring of 1904, Baron von Hertling, the Reichstag deputy (later Chancellor), had been sent to Rome at my behest. He wrote to me from Munich on his return:

" When at the close of my farewell audience I asked the Holy Father whether he had any message for Your Excellency, he emphasized his personal friendship for you, then added: ' *Il papa se gli raccomanda*,' a sentence he repeated with emphasis."

I sent Hertling twice to Rome—in 1904 and 1905. The ostensible purpose of these journeys was merely the institution of a chair of Catholic theology in Strassburg, a project which had encountered difficulties at the Vatican. But secretly I had instructed Hertling to make himself familiar with the state of affairs in Rome. I hoped, in time, to replace our representative at the Curia by a separate ambassador to the Vatican, and Hertling seemed to me the right man. Cardinal Kopp did not altogether approve of my sending Hertling. That great prince of the Church, who remained to the day of his death my staunch friend and well-wisher wrote to me:

Let us hope our worthy Hertling will be very careful in

Rome. There is a danger of his offending both sides by arousing the suspicion in Vatican circles that he wants to continue the policy of Kraus, and of his making our Liberals feel that he would like to take up a parallel position to that of our representative, Herr von Rotenhan. But no doubt Your Excellency, with your customary wisdom and breadth of vision, will have circumscribed his activities with precision.

I never, during my whole term of office, allowed my conviction to be shaken that in our Fatherland, with its division of faiths, justice towards both is a vital necessity, with full regard for the feelings of the Catholic minority. No changing mood in the most exalted quarter, nor public opinion which, in Germany, is mostly more a matter of emotional prejudice on this question than the result of any calm deliberation, have been able to shake my view. But my attitude to the Catholic Church, based on these principles, did not prevent my opposing the Centre Party nor taking up arms against it, if this seemed to me in the interests of the State.

In this review of my home policy, I should like to recall a matter which, although without importance in itself, I was to remember twelve years later at a tragic moment in our history. Prince Hermann Hatzfeldt, Duke of Trachenberg, for many years Lord Lieutenant of Silesia, had sent in his resignation. His ostensible reason was a sudden affection of his eyes; in reality he had resigned because of an unfortunate *affaire-de-cœur*. He came of an ancient and distinguished family of which, however, it might be said with justice, that it could show more liaisons, divorces, and abductions than any other noble house. The radiantly lovely Princess Elizabeth Carolath, whom Herbert Bismarck persuaded to a divorce from a husband she did not love, had been a Hatzfeldt. But when, the divorce accomplished, Herbert wanted to marry his mistress, he met with such violent opposition from his parents that poor Elizabeth suffered the fate of Ariadne and was left to languish on Naxos. Herbert deserted her, and eleven years later married Countess Marguerite Hoyos. I am still convinced that the struggle through which he had fought his way in those days left permanent traces upon Herbert, that the wound in his heart was never entirely healed. An intellectually distinguished daughter of this house was the Countess Sophie Hatzfeldt, the friend of Ferdinand Lassalle. She was the mother of Paul Hatzfeldt the Ambassador. In the case of the Lord Lieutenant of Silesia, Cupid manifested himself to the end. He was surprised, at an advanced age, by a railway guard, in the act of instructing a young Silesian Countess in the rudiments of the *ars amandi*, on a journey between Breslau and Berlin. The guard reprimanded the Duke sharply, but received too sharp a reply. When His Grace, who had a reputation for meanness, tried to placate the majesty of the law with a miserly tip, he threatened to report the whole matter. To avoid a scandal Hatzfeldt sent in his resignation. This was accepted and an Order conferred on him. Touched with gratitude, the noble Duke wrote me as follows: " Your Excellency's note of yesterday impels me once again to express my thanks. At the same time I beg Your Highness to assure yourself of my entire homage and fidelity. Your most obedient Hatzfeldt."

The Kaiser wished to appoint, in place of Hatzfeldt, Count Tiele-Winkler, of Moschen, one of the richest Silesian magnates and a friend of his, or alternatively, Prince Henry XXVIII of Reuss, who was what the English call " a good whip," that is to say, a man who can manage a four-in-hand adroitly. Lucanus asked me if I consented to either of these candidates. He hinted at the same time that if Tiele or Reuss became Lord Lieutenant, the first member of the staff, Dr. Michaelis would have to be replaced by a better man, since, in the most normal times, he was inadequate and would be impossible under an inexperienced aristocrat. I really never thought that twelve years later a civil servant who had been considered inefficient as a Presidential Councillor in Breslau, would be elected Chancellor of the Empire at the most fateful, critical moment of its history. I succeeded in 1905 in getting Count Robert of Zedlitz-Trützschler appointed in place of the Duke of Trachenberg. In 1892 he had resigned the Ministry of Education, and in '99 become Lord Lieutenant of Hesse-Nassau. He was one of the most notable and characteristic statesmen that Prussia has ever produced.

This same year, 1905, when I heard for the first time in my life of Michaelis, was the year in which I suggested to His Majesty that the then Lord Lieutenant of Brandenburg, Herr von Bethmann-Hollweg, should be appointed Minister of the Interior. In the previous year I had already considered him for this post since he had impressed me favourably by his efficiency as an administrative official, his modesty and simplicity of manner. He had begged me at the time not to suggest him until after the Canals Bill had been settled. As *homo novus*, he explained, a man of the new nobility " half commercial, half academic by extraction," it would be hard for him to struggle against the Conservatives ruled over by the old landed gentry. His wife came of this class, though he did not. " They would attack me savagely," he had said, and seemed really worried about it. But on the evening of the day in 1904 when he gave me this verbal refusal, he had written me a sentimental letter expressing a certain regret and recommending himself to my "gracious consideration" in the future. This unfortunate man already showed that:

> "*bängliche Schwanken, weibische Zagen*
> *ängstliche Klagen*" [1]

which, in Ballin's words, allowed him to "blunder us into the stupidest and most unnecessary of all wars" and then to lose it.

I have already mentioned that our foreign policy failed in an attempt at an English understanding on the Morocco question. Notwithstanding all my efforts and those of our Ambassador, Hatzfeldt, in spite of the good will of the British Ambassador in Berlin, Sir Frank Lascelles, Lord Salisbury's fear of European commitments and also, perhaps, his profound dislike of William II were responsible. When in 1902 he retired from the political stage, English envy and hostility towards Germany had become too pronounced for any Anglo-German convention on the Morocco question. But in spite of this mental attitude, the maintenance of peace with Great Britain had always appeared to me quite possible provided we were prudent in Russia. In Morocco the matter was different. On this subject there had existed from the beginning a difference of opinion between the Kaiser and myself. In His Majesty's opinion it was in Germany's interests for France to engage and commit herself in Morocco. This would turn the eyes of Frenchmen away from the Vosges, and they might, in time, forget and forgive Alsace-Lorraine. Moreover, this conquest would weaken them from a military point of view. The Kaiser, to my astonishment, found these views encouraged by his Generals. Indeed, with all my admiration for the science, hard work, loyalty, and patriotism of those excellent men, whose work in the now empty red brick building on the Königsplatz, was animated entirely by the spirit of our great Field-Marshal Moltke, I am forced to admit the fact that our General Staff failed to show immediate understanding and insight into new developments. Just as, later on, our Staff Officers underestimated the whole significance of the technical and mechanical side of modern warfare—the capacity of the English and Americans for suddenly improvising an army, their artillery, their tanks, the whole energetic conduct of the war by a lawyer, Poincaré, and a doctor, Clemenceau, the rivals of revolutionary leaders—so ten years earlier, had they failed to perceive the military significance of French conquests in North Africa. I have already pointed out,[2] in a study of German

---

[1] Anxious wavering, feminine hesitation, timid plaints.
[2] Prince von Bülow, *Deutsche Politik*, p. 84.

policy, made in 1913, how the full unlimited economic, military,
and political domination of Morocco might mean a considerable
increase of French strength. That was the impression I had gained
on a trip through Tunis and Algiers as long ago as the spring of '84.
And I never for one instant considered that France would regard
even this enormous colonial addition to her strength an equivalent
compensation for Alsace-Lorraine. Tunis and Fez, Käiruan and
Rabat, I felt certain, could never make the French forget the
Cathedral of Strassburg or the Promenade at Metz. I was always
laying these views before the Kaiser. But he stuck to his own
opinion. On 20th August 1904, he had told von Mühlberg, the
Under-Secretary of State, what a good thing he felt it to be that
France should have to pacify Morocco and work there to establish
law and order. This pioneer work of cultivation would cost heavily
in blood and money. When France had accomplished her task and
Morocco was opened up for civilization German commerce would
easily find a place there. Von Mühlberg tried in vain, by pointing
out the French protectionist policy, to combat this obsession of His
Majesty's. The Kaiser, even before this, at his meeting with King
Alfonso XIII of Spain at Vigo (16th March 1904), had tempestu-
ously urged that Sovereign to remain on good terms with France.
He had suggested that King Alfonso should make Paris the first
foreign capital he visited. He must be prudent with England;
with Portugal he could not be too careful. But Germany, the Kaiser
had emphasized, had no special interest in Morocco, no plan of
territorial aggrandizement, and would concentrate solely on the
furtherance of European civilization. Spain had her own particular
cultural mission in Morocco and to this she should devote all her
energies. She should seek an understanding with other powers
whose interests lay in Northern Africa, but first and foremost with
the French. Such love of France on the part of William II, such
a fund of disinterested benevolence, had almost stupefied the
King; more especially since Queen Christine had told me on our
Viennese visit (September 1903) what difficulties Spain had had
ever since the early '90's in resisting French offers of alliance. The
zeal with which His Majesty urged on Spain the necessity for
cordial relations with France sprang in part, no doubt, from the
hope that these remarks would reach Paris via Madrid and create
there a favourable impression. The wish to " be reconciled " with
France was a constant obsession with the Kaiser from the day he
ascended the throne to 1914. There were of course occasional fits
of bad temper when his advances did not meet with success, but
these were only *dépit amoureux*.

CHAPTER VII

William II's Mediterranean trip in March 1904—Development of the Morocco Question—State of same at the beginning of the Kaiser's trip—German Government programme—The actual juridical position—Our tactics—The Kaiser drops anchor at Tangier—The Kaiser's landing in Tangier—Kühlmann, secretary of Legation—Count Tattenbach's mission to Fez—Count Monts' endeavours to instigate a rescue attempt for Delcassé under the influence of his colleague Barrère—English efforts on behalf of Delcassé—Delcassé's fall.

ALREADY in 1898, on his return from the Palestine trip, the Kaiser had cherished the desire of passing through the Straits of Gibraltar. On this occasion he wanted to see Tangier. " Now I have been in Asia, I should much like to set my foot once upon African soil, particularly since I have had to give up Egypt," said the Kaiser at the time to me. This wish arose in the main from his love of travelling: there was no political reason for it. As I related at the time, the Kaiserin and I succeeded in 1898 in persuading the Kaiser to return to Germany from Malta by the shortest way, through the Adriatic Sea. The Kaiserin, like the good mother she was, was eager to see her children again: I felt it necessary after so long an absence to take into my hands again the reins of the Berlin Foreign Office. On his first Mediterranean trip, for which William II started from Bremerhaven on 12th March 1904 on board the Lloyd steamer " King Albert," he wished to visit Tangier too, again only as a tourist eager for new and interesting impressions. I was against a stay in Tangier at the time, as in the February of 1904 it did not seem to me advisable to attract attention in any way to this matter, and the Kaiser, immediately and willingly, gave up all idea of a landing at this African port. When he embarked on 28th March 1905 in Cuxhaven on board the Hapág steamer " Hamburg," for his second Mediterranean trip on which, as on the first occasion, he was accompanied not only by an imposing military following but by a large number of personal friends and acquaintances in all positions of life, there were rumours in the foreign press that he would visit Tangier. At the time His Majesty had no such intention. It may be that indiscreet gossip of Berlin courtiers as to the Kaiser's former desire to see Tangier and to walk on African soil, had found its way into the press. In any case, at the time he began this journey, in 1905, French papers were full of noisy threats, some of them very impertinent, should the German Kaiser dare to show himself in Tangier.

The attitude, not only of the Parisian press, but of the statesman who inspired it, the Foreign Secretary Delcassé, became as time went on, more and more bold. Three weeks before the conclusion of the Anglo-French Treaty of 1904, M. Delcassé had informed our Ambassador in Paris, Prince Radolin, of the chief clauses of the Agreement and assured him that the rights of third-party states, including Germany, would not be affected by them. I had immediately acknowledged this information in a polite manner by saying in the Reichstag on 12th April 1904 that we had no occasion to presume that the Anglo-French Colonial Agreement was pointedly directed against any other Power. It appeared to be only an attempt to remove a number of old differences between England and France through mutual understanding. German interests were not affected. I replied to opposition from the Pan-Germans two days later, by saying that we aspired neither to a whole nor to part of the Sherif's Empire. At the same time in April 1904 I had given it out to the press that Germany did not seek political influence in Morocco but wished only to preserve the interests of her trading circles. When it became known, in October 1904, that Paris had concluded an agreement with Madrid in regard to Morocco, I asked Paris for information, whereupon Delcassé assured me that this agreement would not affect German trade in Morocco, but actually further it, because of the improvement in the state of Moroccan national justice which was to be expected. Thereupon I instructed the Secretary of State, Richthofen, to tell the French Ambassador Bihourd, that this information satisfied us. But in the winter of 1904 to 1905, there was a change, and Delcassé again showed his claws. He not only circulated the words *pénétration pacifique* of Morocco in the press but the French newspapers demanded the " Tunisification " of the Moroccan Empire—that is to say its degradation to a vassal state after the fashion of Tunis. We were not asked our opinion. They did not even show us the consideration of informing Berlin and Vienna of the contents of the 1904 Treaty after it had been placed before the Parliaments of London and Paris.

In Morocco itself things came more and more to a head. On 21st February 1905 the French Ambassador, Saint-René Taillandier, arrived in Fez and demanded from the Sultan categorically, *en termes pressants*, that he should employ French officers to drill his troops and also place the customs duties under the supervision of French officials. The Sultan, who had been addressed by the

French delegate, *du haut en bas*, like a vassal, turned to the German government and asked whether the statement of Taillandier, that his demands were made, not only as France's ambassador, but in the name of Europe, were the real truth. In the face of this chain of French aggressions it seemed to me necessary to remind Paris again of the German Empire.

It was not only the extent of our economic and political interests in and about Morocco which decided me to advise the Kaiser to set his face against France, but also the conviction that in the interests of peace we must no longer permit such provocations. I did not desire war with France either then or later, because I knew that every serious conflict as things lay in Europe would lead to a world war. But I did not hesitate to confront France with the possibility of war, because I had confidence in my own skill and caution. I felt that I could prevent matters coming to a head, cause Delcassé's fall, break the continuity of aggressive French policy, knock the continental dagger out of the hands of Edward VII and the war group in England, and, simultaneously ensure peace, preserve German honour, and improve German prestige. I was strengthened in my determination by the letter of an old and trustworthy friend in Paris, the same who had informed me, seven years before, of the Windsor Treaty. He was Swiss by birth: we had met in Lausanne. Later on he settled in Paris. He cherished lively sympathies for both France and for England, which he frequently visited and where he moved in the best circles. But everything was subservient to his deep-rooted pacificism, born of conviction, and amounting almost to a passion. He was never tired of depicting the terrible consequences that a great war would entail. Such a war would arouse all the evil passions of mankind, hatred and revenge, cruelty and brutality: it would cost milliards, demand hecatombs of human lives, and ruin Europe for decades, perhaps for centuries. This worthy man who did not live to see the Great War had foreseen only too rightly. He was convinced, and that quite correctly, that I was honestly bent upon keeping peace. More from this reason even than from personal affection he gave me useful hints from time to time. I had given my word of honour that I would never name him as the source, and would destroy his letters as soon as I had read them, as he did not wish to share the fate of Captain Dreyfus.

This man, actuated only by the purest motives, and who pursued an idealistic goal, wrote me at almost the same moment as the Kaiser began his Mediterranean trip in 1905, that Delcassé was determined to let it come to war, convinced that King Edward would not desert him and that it would soon be possible to restore peace quickly between Russia and Japan. King Edward and the English ministers and statesmen influenced by him did not want to enter into a war with Germany at once, but would not permit a complete defeat of France, and in any case, as soon as the conflict began, would tell Germany categorically to cease increasing her navy. I was willing from the beginning to keep to the basis of the treaties on the Moroccan question. I knew very well that in vital matters affecting the honour and security of the country it was foolish to depend only upon treaties. The only real and permanent security for a great people lay in its own strength and, above all, in the national sentiments and patriotism of its citizens. But even from the standpoint of practical politics it is desirable in a high degree, to stand to the letter of treaties, to uphold these rights for oneself, and thus ensure the sympathies of those who think justly and ethically. It was an hour of disaster therefore for the German Empire, when Chancellor Bethmann-Hollweg in his interview with the English Ambassador Goschen, which has (unfortunately) not been forgotten, described agreements as "*chiffons de papier*" (scraps of paper). In 1905 we could base our actions on the result of the Morocco Conference held in 1880 at Madrid, at which the countries trading with Morocco (Germany, France, England, Austria-Hungary, Italy, Spain, the United States and Holland) had arranged that no preferential rights should be accorded the subjects of any foreign countries by the Empire of Sherif. If France wished to seize economic or political power in Morocco, the remaining signatories of that Madrid Conference of 1880 must be asked for their permission. Apart from this Madrid Agreement there had existed a commercial treaty between Germany and Morocco since 1890 which accorded us preferential treatment. We were, therefore, in the fortunate position of being able to base ourselves on international justice. As regards the tactics of our proceedings France had expressly promised us in the agreement of 8th April 1904 not to alter the political position in Morocco. It seemed to me indicated that we should first wait and see whether the French government fulfilled this promise, how it would put the agreement into practice, and particularly how it would arrange matters concerning our own judicial rights in Morocco and German interests there. Apart from this, diplomatic action, at its outset, always depends upon circumstances. It seemed to me advisable to answer the Anglo-French agreement neither by immediate threats nor by a display of nervousness. I did not want to show towards France in the Morocco question either distrust or spite. There was no reason to object to that part of the Anglo-French Agreement which was concerned with Egypt. By doing this we should only have complicated our already difficult relations with England still further, apart from the fact that we had traditionally never made difficulties for England in Egypt. All the more were we justified in taking up a defensive attitude against the violation of the existing state of things, and in defence of our economic interests in Morocco, if it should be apparent that France was not intending to respect them.

For this reason I showed at first neither surprise nor annoyance. But when Delcassé displayed that "malicious enmity" towards Germany for which Jaurès reproached him in the Chamber, when he showed it more and more boldly in his Press and in his remarks to the foreign diplomats in Paris, when even Lord Rosebery declared that it was wrong ostentatiously to thrust aside a great power like Germany in international trading circles, when Delcassé obstinately refused all compromise in spite of this, I advised the Kaiser by letter to land at Tangier. I recommended him at the same time to make no bombastic speech there, but to say only with the greatest possible simplicity that there was no reason why he should not pay a visit to the Sultan of Morocco, who was an independent sovereign, and that he hoped Morocco, which could depend upon the Madrid Treaty and international justice, would in future continue to be open to the peaceful competition of all nations. The Kaiser did not decide any too willingly upon this visit to Tangier, because he naturally felt immediately, and moreover gathered from my letter, that it was not mere tourist sight-seeing, but a very significant political action upon which he was about to embark. In addition to this, at the time when His Majesty proposed to follow my instructions, the sea was very stormy and the disembarking into small boats and subsequent landing was fraught with the possibility of a cold douche.

It was on this occasion that the chargé d'affaires in Tangier, Herr von Kühlmann, attracted the attention of His Majesty for the first time. Young Kühlmann, a son of the representative for many years of Hirsch—the so-called "Turkey-Hirsch" of Constantinople—came on board the Royal ship after the "Hamburg" had docked. The agility with which Kühlmann clambered up the rope ladder dangling from the heaving sides of the "Hamburg," clad in the smart uniform of the Bavarian Lancers, with the *tchapka* on his head and in high boots, helped to create the favourable impression he at once made upon His Majesty and which was maintained throughout the career which culminated in his Secretaryship of State. As Foreign Secretary he unhappily neither displayed the same agility nor the same security he had manifested in his gymnas-

tic feats on the Hapág steamer. Josef Joachim, the great violin
virtuoso and a delightful personality, told me once how he had tried to
skate one winter on the Rousseau islet in the Berlin Tiergarten.
When he had fallen flat on his face a few times the skating rink
attendant said with a good-humoured smile: " Well, well, Herr
Professor, skating isn't so easy, you see, as playing the fiddle."
With Kühlmann it was the other way round. He was to discover
by experience that, to use a Bismarckian phrase, it is more difficult
to keep one's balance on the tight-rope of high politics than to climb
up the rigging. Kühlmann failed signally as Secretary of State for
Foreign Affairs and afterwards disappeared from the political arena.
On that 31st March 1905, when the Kaiser landed in Tangier, he
reached solid ground safely enough physically, but he was inwardly
agitated by the risks of the whole enterprise. Added to this, the horses
which the Sultan had sent to escort him from the landing stage,
Barbary stallions, were difficult to manage, so that the Kaiser,
immediately after he had overcome the fear of taking a cold bath in
the Mediterranean, was in danger of being thrown from his steed
before the eyes of the astonished and staring Moors and Arabs.
Consequently the two addresses which the Kaiser made to the uncle
of the Sultan who greeted him, and to the German colony, took on a
sharper and more excited tone than had originally been his intention.

Holstein, at least as impressionable as the Kaiser, but older and
more worn out, was annoyed at this departure from the programme,
which he much desired should be regarded as his own, so much
annoyed indeed, that the following night he suffered a hæmorrhage
of the stomach. It was the first sign of a disease which was to cause
his death four years later. I wish to state, on this opportunity, that
the entire action, for which I undertook the whole responsibility
towards the Reichstag and the nation was done at my instigation.
Because Holstein kept as much as possible in the background and
in the dark, saw only a few people and lived in three small rooms in
the lonely Grossbeerenstrasse, which was a long way from the
Wilhelmstrasse, his personality and his political activity appeared to
most people in an almost romantic light, in any case in a very
exaggerated and often distorted light. During my term of office
his influence was not so great as during the preceding two decades.
Paradoxical as this may seem to many, Holstein never exerted
greater influence than during the second half of the Bismarckian
era. At that time his personal power was far-reaching and his
position almost unshakeable, because of the great confidence reposed
in him by the Chancellor, and the intimate friendship which had
united him to Herbert Bismarck from his earliest youth, when as

attaché of the Prussian Embassy in St. Petersburg he was a constant guest in the house of the Ambassador of those days, von Bismarck-Schönhausen. He came more and more into the foreground particularly after the death of my father in 1879, who as long as he presided over the Foreign Office formed a welcome contrast to Holstein by reason of his old and confidential relations with Prince Bismarck, and his calm and lucid manner. My father did not like Holstein; their natures were diametrically opposed. Holstein, who could cast up his eyes sentimentally when he chose, told me more than once that he well knew he had not been in my father's good graces; all the more touching was the loyal affection with which he supported and served me. After Prince Bismarck had been overthrown, certainly not without Holstein's co-operation, his successors Caprivi and Marshall, who lacked all knowledge of diplomatic routine and all insight into the international game, even as far as languages went, clung to Holstein like drowning men. But he was obliged to share the power he thus won with Kiderlen, who did not like others to skim the cream from his milk. At this time, too, he was the object of violent press attacks, in *Kladderadatsch* and Harden's *Zukunft*, which made him more of a recluse and therefore more strange to the ways of the world than ever. Under Hohenlohe he began to breathe freely again, for the press attacks which had injured his sensitive soul so deeply began gradually to lessen. Hohenlohe treated Holstein with the unvarying well-bred politeness peculiar to him, but had by no means the confidence in him displayed by Prince Bismarck. When I became Secretary of State, Hohenlohe warned me of Holstein in the words: "All doubtful and bad advice emanates in the main from Holstein." In direct contrast to this Prince Bismarck said to my father, who had made a disparaging remark about Holstein: "But he is very sensitive indeed. I owe him many a useful warning, many a clever idea, and many a piece of good advice."

I will return to the Morocco differences. On the day when the Kaiser landed in Tangier, Delcassé had made it clear in the French Chamber that he would not be deterred by German opposition from the path he had entered. There were always doubts as to whether it was advisable to let the Kaiser appear in the foreground at Tangier. After this had once occurred we had to continue in the same course. On 11th and 12th April, I sent a proclamation to our Embassies in London, St. Petersburg, Vienna, and in a number of other places, in which I set out that the Imperial Government could not recognize the right of France, England, and Spain to settle the Moroccan affair independently, and demanded the co-operation of the eight

countries which were signatories to the Madrid Treaty of 1880. I
repudiated the French statement that the Madrid enactments were
only intended to protect the private rights of foreigners in Morocco,
and placed the international juridical significance of the Treaty in
the foreground. German rights could not be disposed of to anyone
else by other powers, nor handed over from England to France. In
the edict I addressed to the Imperial Ambassador in London I
wrote: that we were upholding our interests of which nobody could
dispose without our agreement. The importance or otherwise of
the interests was non-essential. Whoever is to have money taken
from his pocket will defend himself as long as possible, no matter
whether the sum in question is 5 or 5,000 marks. If we were to
give up our not inconsiderable economic interests in Morocco without a word, we should be encouraging others to act against us in the
same way in matters of, perhaps, vital import. I sent Count Tattenbach, Minister hitherto in Lisbon, on a special mission to Fez
to fortify the Sultan in his refusal to countenance the breach of
contract entailed in these demands for the supervision of his army
and his finances, and to advise him to invite the cabinets associated
with the Madrid Treaty to a conference in which his rights should
be ascertained. I emphasized again particularly that Germany was
not seeking her own advantage in Morocco but desired, on the other
hand, the maintenance of a Treaty which had been violated in all
senses for all signatories. Our position in the struggle was strengthened by the fact that the Sultan of Morocco did not merely appeal to
us for aid. Tattenbach continued to keep firm hold of the Sherifian
majesty. Count Tattenbach was an Old-Bavarian and possessed
the indomitable courage and plucky tenacity which distinguish this
doughty race. He had been wounded as a Bavarian officer in the
Franco-German War and was a loyal, even a passionate patriot.

Meanwhile the position of Delcassé became difficult. In the
French Chamber on 19th April 1905, he was not only violently
attacked by the Socialists Jaurès and Pressensé, but by the preceding
and succeeding Presidents of the Chamber, the opportunist Des-
chanel, the handsomest and for many years to come the most fortunate
man in the French parliament, while the Premier, Rouvier, supported
him tepidly. The *Times* did not cease calling Delcassé the " great
Frenchman," at the same time as it insulted and threatened Germany.
The idea of a conference on the subject of Morocco was repudiated
by this paper as a humiliation, a capitulation. Other English newspapers raged in the same way: *Daily Chronicle, Standard*, above all
Lord Northcliffe's *Daily Mail*. King Edward himself appeared in the
French capital on 6th April 1905, and in a long conversation with

President Loubet, advised him to keep Delcassé. On 30th April 1905 the King stayed again in Paris on his return from Nice, and received Delcassé there, discussing matters with him thoroughly. Edward VII did all that was in his power to render the Franco-German conflict more bitter, just as three years later he was eagerly engaged in stirring up Russia against Germany in the Bosnian crisis. He was an adept at mixing venomous potions.

After King Edward, *proximus sed longo intervallo,* our Ambassador in Rome, Count Monts, attempted a timid but strange move to support Delcassé, who was already tottering. Bismarck had often complained that German diplomats were mostly enthusiasts for some other country; the German diplomat who lived for some time in England became pro-English and declared that only in England did one know how to dress, to hunt, to sail, to row, to fish and to behave oneself. Other German diplomats regarded Austria as the seat of true culture and distinguished tradition. Others again were impressed by Russia, the Russian Tsar, and Russian life, from bear hunts down to balls at the Winter Palace. For others the climate of Paris was the only one that suited them. Monts belonged to the last category. He boasted of being descended from a Languedoc dynasty. People better versed in genealogy than myself declared, however, that grandfather Monts was one of those French clerks of the financial department whom Frederick the Great imported from France, during the last years of his government, to collect the indirect taxes in Prussia with the same harshness and cupidity as they were collected in France. However that might be, Monts often used the alleged motto of his family, "*Fortis ut mons,*" and had three small mountain tops engraved on his cuff-links—the device, he gave people to understand, which his ancestors displayed on their shields when they rode in knightly tournaments at Toulouse. When he wished to become an Ambassador he said to me: "I do not want to praise myself, but I believe that I possess two qualities good for diplomacy, *un nom ronflant et un dévouement absolu* for yourself." In Rome, Monts soon came under the influence of his French colleague Barrère, who was more practised in diplomatic routine, in dealing with people, and above all in skill. Barrère was an intimate personal friend of Delcassé. He did everything in his power to maintain his chief in office. Luigi Luzzatti, a well known political economist, a good finance minister, an idealist, but French through and through in his convictions, worked along the same lines. Barrère and Luzzatti persuaded Monts, at the height of the Delcassé crisis, to send me a report intended as a life-belt for Delcassé, in which it was stated that

Luzzatti had gone to see Monts and had told him in moving language
of the anxiety Barrère felt for his chief and his friend Delcassé.
When Luzzatti pointed to the pronouncedly anti-German policy of
the French Foreign Secretary Barrère defended this, pointing out
that in principle the Republic could not give up the tradition of
Gambetta, who had in his heart always cherished the hope of a
reunion with Alsace-Lorraine, and that the French nation was not
yet prepared for a reconciliation with us. To these arguments he,
Luzzatti, had replied, that the question of "revenge" was one similar
to the miracle of St. Januarius' blood at Naples. Only when the
wire-pullers in Paris desired it, did the Alsatian wounds bleed. In
reality the great mass of the French people desired peace. That was
what Delcassé felt at present. It was understood in Paris that
Monts personally was free from all jingoism and inclined for a
compromise with France. The fact that he, Luzzatti, was equally
united to Barrère and Monts in friendship had first drawn the
attention of French statesmen to the two diplomats. They wished
to make use of it, so as to gain relief from the present tension.
France's position was now precarious. The nation longed to put
an end to an untenable and, in French opinion, threatening crisis,
but the government did not know how to emerge from the Moroccan
cul-de-sac. People were asking in Paris whether some striking act
showing appreciation of His Majesty the King and Emperor would
be pleasing to the exalted personage. The French Ambassador was
empowered by Delcassé to discuss the affair with his friend Monts.
M. Luzzatti had also said that England had bitterly disappointed
France's hopes. It had been declared in London that the Morocco
Agreement enjoined upon England the need of supporting France's
demands. Beyond this England could not go. Nor was it desired
on the Neva to jeopardize friendly relations with Germany on
account of Morocco. Luzzatti owned that Delcassé had been
planning to isolate Germany completely. But he had started from
a false premise. His plans had been overthrown, as Delcassé himself had written to Barrère, by the Japanese victories, after he had
refused the hand held out to him by Germany the year before.
M. Delcassé had refused a meeting of the French President with
the German Emperor, which was suggested to him at the time in
Rome, with the express statement that the wound of 1870 was
still so deep in French hearts, that France would not understand this
action of her statesmen and might even send them and the President
flying, if it should actually come to a meeting of the German Kaiser
and the head of the French state. There was now, negatively
speaking, a certain nervousness amongst the most far-reaching

French circles, and a positive will to force the government to an understanding with ourselves. The glowing patriots Delcassé and Barrère certainly did not decide with too light a heart upon a step which was humiliating in itself, but through Luzzatti they now asked Monts for a favourable turn of events. Luzzatti gave no clear reply to the question of the German Ambassador, whether the French government desired an honest peace with us—since the God of battles, not invoked by us in 1870, had decided in Germany's favour; the provinces had been bought with the blood of 100,000 good Germans, and we should not relinquish them so long as a German Empire existed. On the other hand he had seized with great enthusiasm upon the idea " suggested " by Monts of a big understanding, similar to the Anglo-French understanding between Germany and France which should include Morocco as well as other interests in the Near and Far East. Luzzatti had exclaimed that if such an arrangement were successful, history would engrave the name of Kaiser William II on its bronze tablets for all time as the great pacifist of the world, a second Titus. Here it was to be inferred that M. Delcassé had in mind proposals of a division, or was at least hinting at them. Monts had replied that Germany could not depart from the basis of the Madrid Treaty. She demanded for herself only the same rights as she demanded for everybody and because of this her position was unassailable. The whole Moroccan affair was moreover only the symptom of a deep-rooted disease. It was not our fault that Franco-German relations had not been normal for a long time past, as was fitting between two neighbours. But even the more than patient German Michel would not be treated as a *quantité négligeable* any longer.

Monts had added a private letter to this long dispatch in which he wrote to me:

> Without in any way precipitating Your Excellency's decision, I should like to add as my personal impression gained from the statements of Luzzatti and other symptoms:—Delcassé is probably seeking at the present moment, with a clever change of policy, support in the very place where all his former attacks were directed. The ambitious man feels that he is lost unless he can come to an agreement with us. Perhaps he would be easy to deal with for that reason. Added to this is the fact that Barrère, who has lost all interest in Rome long ago, sees that his getting the Berlin post for himself depends upon this affair. He would therefore work at top speed and add the weight of his authority whenever, as is to be expected, negotiations grow

difficult. He might, in future, really prove to be the right man to bring about permanently good relations between Berlin and Paris. Your Excellency would know how to keep him within bounds! The ambitious Barrère desires personal success above everything. He would work perhaps, still more avidly for his own glory than for France if his game were based on the first-rate German trump card. M. Barrère said to me two years ago in Camaldoli: "Why did you not enter into an alliance with us instead of renewing the Triple Entente?" The crux of the matter seems to me the changeableness of the French national temperament. Or has the bourgeois Republic really so changed that it is possible to reckon on its stability and on peace with France for a further number of years? However, Your Excellency's more subtle insight may judge, and however far you may be prepared to go eventually in your French policy, you will permit me to-day to congratulate you on the obviously great success in the Morocco affair, and to couple with this my warmest wishes for the *faustum eventum* of your birthday. The fruits of France's pilgrimage to Canossa will be doubly precious if His Majesty the Kaiser will now maintain the greatest reserve in all his remarks.

Fistula dulce canit, volucrem dum decipit auceps.

Ex post, I incline to-day still more than in 1905 to the view expressed by Holstein at the time, that Mont's desire to save Delcassé sprang from the wish to obtain the Ambassadorship at Paris with the help of Barrère and Delcassé. Monts had not been comfortable in Rome for some time past, having made himself unpopular both in Italian society and in the German colony. The goal of his ambitions was in the first instance Paris, in the second, Vienna. Holstein had a suspicious nature. He was often indeed, as is undeniable, filled with morbid suspicion. But if Robespierre is reported to have said that suspicion is the basis of all Republican virtues, it is not to be denied that a good dose of this quality is to be recommended to diplomats.

"Be sober, remember suspicion, this keeps the mind agile," says Aristophanes somewhere, whose soul, according to Plato, was not only the favourite resting place of grace but was also that of crystallized common sense. Whatever the motives of Monts actually were his plans were destined to fail. I recall *en passant* a suggestion of Eckardstein, who had insinuated to the Kaiser in a roundabout way that in one of his "great" speeches His Majesty should explain that he wished to uphold his rights, but that a disturbance of the peace was far removed from his desires or those of his government. I nipped this suggestion in the bud since I soon gathered that Eckardstein's propositions could be traced to a Stock Exchange operation on a large scale, in which he did not gamble *à la baisse*, as usual, but *à la hausse*. As a curiosity I must still mention that the " striking act of appreciation " in the minds of Barrère and his friend Delcassé for Kaiser William II was, I discovered later, either the Grand Cross of the Legion of Honour, or the promise of President Loubet to consent to a meeting with him somewhere, next year.

In my conversations with the French Ambassador Bihourd, a very polite and cultured, if somewhat shy diplomat, whom Delcassé had probably sent to Berlin for the purpose of concealing his iron fist under this velvet glove, I avoided all threats and any appearance of impoliteness. In a friendly manner I told the Ambassador that if he were convinced that England would come to France's aid I did not wish to question this surmise at the outset. I also acknowledged that England could deal our industry a heavy blow and could also destroy the fleet that was in course of construction. But as things stood, in a war which I desired to avoid as much as Bihourd himself, France would be the unfortunate who would suffer most. " *C'est vous, je le constate avec tristesse, qui payerez les pots cassés, non par notre méchanceté, mais par la force des choses.*"

The more acute the situation became, the more eager was England to uphold her favourite, Delcassé. The English government informed him that it would not desert him. France was to refuse the conference and to wait and see whether we would venture to adopt the offensive attitude. Delcassé assured his colleagues in office, again and again, that England was willing to send 150,000 men to Holstein, which action would divert a great part of Germany's land army from the western frontier of the country. On 6th June the decisive Cabinet meeting took place in Paris. Delcassé upheld the opinion that if France persisted in her refusal of the conference, Germany would draw back, *i.e.*, prefer humiliation to a war. The Minister of Defence, Bertaux, was less confident of this. The Premier, Rouvier, gave the casting vote when he expressed his conviction that Delcassé was mistaken if he thought that Germany was merely bluffing. The Cabinet Council decided, against Delcassé, to send delegates to the conference. The latter rose, declared he resigned from the government, and left the conference-room in deep dudgeon. It was eight years later, four years after my resignation, before he appeared in the political arena again, when the Ambassadorship in St. Petersburg was offered him in 1913. Here he used every possible lever to win Russia for a war against

Germany and to drive Germany herself into war. If in 1905 he had tried in vain to bring about either a war of revenge or a deep humiliation of Germany, he was in 1913 the stormy petrel which swept ahead of the tempest that broke a year later. The deliverance from Delcassé kept the peace for us for many years. A newspaper which in 1905 had criticized my policy severely, the *Berliner Tageblatt*, wrote after the death of Delcassé, in 1923, an article entitled "The Death of an Incendiary." It set forth that the career of this incendiary had begun with the conclusion of the Entente Cordiale, but was interrupted when Delcassé, inflamed with hatred and ambition and with all his energy heading for a war with Germany, was overthrown in 1905. Nine years afterwards, Delcassé, after preparing the World War in St. Petersburg as envoy of his friend Poincaré, saw his dream of an international conflagration come true.

CHAPTER VIII

The marriage of the Crown Prince (6.vi.1905). Elevation to princely rank—William II and the French general, Lacroix—Consequences of Delcassé's fall—Rouvier—French patriotism—Metternich's letter on the situation—Edward VII invites the German Crown Prince for a hunting expedition—William II against this trip—The situation in Russia—Letter of the Grand Duchess Maria Pavlovna to her uncle Prince Henry VII of Reuss—Relations between William II and Nicholas II—Prince Henry of Prussia—Draft of a German-Russian Re-Insurance Treaty—Correspondence between William II and Nicholas II.

ON 6th June 1905, the day when Delcassé fell, the marriage of the German Crown Prince to the Duchess Cecilie of Mecklenburg-Schwerin took place in Berlin. In the morning the Kaiser called at the Chancellor's palace to tell me that he had elevated me to the dignity of Prince. With the delightful naturalness that was and remained his greatest charm he said: "You can't escape me this time. The patent has been signed, Wolff's news agency is already publishing it. Lucanus has attended to everything." In a very kindly and warm-hearted manner the Kaiser added that he was glad to be able to award this honour to one of his most excellent servants on the actual wedding-day of his eldest son, the future King and Emperor. I should like to mention here that my elevation to the rank of prince had nothing whatever to do with the resignation of M. Delcassé, which was not known in Berlin until the evening of 6th June. During Kaiser William's reign he raised seven people to the rank of prince. Before me there were the Ambassador Count Münster-Derneburg in 1899, the Ambassador Count Philip Eulenburg, Count Richard zu Dohna-Schlobitten, and Count Edzard Kyphausen in 1900, and Count Guido Henckel-Donnersmarck in 1901. After me the Governor of Alsace-Lorraine, Count Karl Wedel, was made a Prince in 1913. Prince Hermann Hatzfeldt had received the rank of Duke in 1900.

The marriage of the Crown Prince was celebrated with great pomp. The Crown Prince looked happy, his young wife charming. In the evening, according to time-honoured tradition in the royal house, the torch dance was performed. Originally the torches at this old German wedding dance were carried by the Ministers. William II thought however that the sight of elderly, stout, decrepit statesmen, holding torches which dripped wax on their richly emblazoned uniforms, and gyrating painfully on the slippery floor of the White Hall, was not aesthetic. He commanded that young and smart pages should in future act as torch bearers, which certainly made a more pleasing impression. Each prince and princess was obliged to make a circular tour of the Hall behind the pages who walked by twos. At their head marched Prince Max Fürstenberg. Formerly the Lord Marshal and Grand Master of Ceremonies, Count August Eulenburg had led the Torch Dance with incomparable assurance, dignity, and distinction. He looked as though he had stepped out of some handsome engraving of the Grand Siècle. But Max Fürstenberg too, although less distinguished made an imposing impression in the red gala uniform of the Life Guards. During the ceremony I stood next to the French Ambassador who, with mingled melancholy and envy made the remark: "*Et nous aussi, nous avons vu et connu tout cela lorsque le Roi-Soleil trônait à Versailles et attirait tous les regards. Enfin, chacun son tour, comme disait en mourant ce bon Benjamin Constant.*" The wedding festivities of the Crown Prince were brilliant, and must have rejoiced every cultured European who did not cherish Boetian sentiments. And yet the most dazzling Court functions generally left me with an impression of melancholy. I remember once a gala banquet, after parade on September the 2nd, anniversary of the Battle of Sedan, at the end of which Posadowsky and I looked down out of a window of the castle upon Berlin, glowing red in the light of the setting sun. With the deep seriousness that was peculiar to him, Posadowsky said to me, pointing to the glowing sky: "If the Kaiser continues in his present arrogant ways and if he remains as thoughtless as he is now, sooner or later, this castle will be threatened by the masses, perhaps even stormed by them."

On 6th June 1905, somewhat wearied by the lengthy wedding ceremonies and still more by the great heat that had prevailed in Berlin all day, I was sitting on the cool terrace outside my study about midnight when the Kaiser had me informed by telephone that he had just received news from Wolff's agency of Delcassé's fall. I had expected this resignation, which pleased without surprising or, in any way, exciting me. But I made a mistake by not at once saying to myself that the Kaiser, with his volatile nature and temperament, and freed from the oppressive worries which tension with France had brought him, would now fall into the other extreme—into extravagant rejoicing, exaggerated hopes, and particularly into too accommodating an attitude towards France. He had no comprehension of the necessity for Horace's

> " *Aequem memento rebus in arduis*
> *Servare mentem, non secus in bonis*
> *Ab insolenti temperatam laetitia, moriture Delli.*"

Count Kuno Moltke, who was fairly well-versed in political matters, had the same feelings as myself. He was a school-friend of mine from Neustrelitz, and wrote to me that night that the Kaiser would meet the French General Lacroix, who had attended the wedding ceremonies, at the field exercises arranged for the next day: " I let you know this so that you can pour something into the foaming wine-cup of the royal pleasure—I won't say bitter-water, but *aqua destillata.*" Unfortunately, through an oversight or slackness on the part of the lackey deputed to bring me this message, I only received the letter the following midday. Meanwhile the Kaiser, in an excited flood of sentiment had poured out his enthusiastic delight over Delcassé's resignation to General Lacroix and, at the same time, expressed his firm conviction that now everything was in the best of order. He had never attached any value to Morocco, he gladly gave it to the French! This spontaneous, well-meant but undiplomatic and unpolitical effusion of the Kaiser greatly increased the difficulties of our negotiations with France up to the conference of Algeciras. Holstein was not so wrong when he wrote to me before the Algeciras Conference in the autumn of 1905: " While we were working in the sweat of our brows to bring the Morocco struggle to an end which should satisfy both our economic and our political interests, His Majesty had given things up long ago. The French knew this, but our people did not, and so were without any solution to the riddle of why the French Government was soft and yielding before the return of General Lacroix, but tough and tena-cious after it. The French had had the direct acceptance of their Moroccan demand from the Kaiser."

The fall of Delcassé was no mere momentary success for us. His overthrow impeded French chauvinism as much as it did English jingoism, and the continuance of our naval policy was made considerably easier. Delcassé was the instrument chosen by our enemies in order to destroy us. Those in England who wished to prevent the completion of our naval programme, had hoped to persuade France, through Delcassé, into a military alliance with England, and to fall upon us afterwards with the British fleet. So Karl Peters wrote at the time from London. This catastrophe was averted, and we were able to continue work upon our fleet-

building programme. Rouvier, who took Delcassé's place, was a
thorough patriot, like all the French Ministers who, since 1871 and
the Peace of Frankfort, have ruled in the fine Palace on the Quai
d'Orsay. He had been a close friend of Gambetta's. The story
of his rise to power contains the dramatic element which makes
French history and French politics so attractive. A few days after
the French National Assembly at Bordeaux had concluded the
preliminary peace with Germany, two young Frenchmen from the
South, Crémieux and Rouvier, met in the capital of the Gironde.
They had been friends for a long time, and discussed together what
they should now do under existing circumstances. Crémieux
suggested going to Marseilles, where the Radical party, to which
they both belonged, had seized the reins. As political agent of
Gambetta, Crémieux had good connections and influence in Marseilles. Rouvier thought it would be more advisable to go to Versailles with Thiers. When Crémieux arrived at Marseilles, he was
received by his friends, and conducted to the City Hall, where he
proclaimed the Commune of Marseilles and nominated himself its
chief. In the course of the same afternoon, he was arrested by the
General in command of Marseilles, and shot on the following night.
In accordance with French tradition, approved in all French
revolutions, Gambetta, even after he had become the most powerful
man in France, never came to Marseilles without paying a visit to
Crémieux's widow. Rouvier, more cautious, withstood the danger
in the Commune by standing in Thiers' shadow, was elected to the
Chamber of Deputies in 1876, became Minister of Trade in 1881,
and Prime Minister in 1887 and again in 1905. By degrees he
acquired, not only considerable political influence but also, by
skilful investments, a not insignificant fortune. He had good connections with Parisian high finance, the house of Rothschild in
particular. In the situation created by Delcassé's resignation, he
was the right man, since with regard to French finances, he desired
peace above everything.

Even before Delcassé's resignation, von Mühlberg, Under-
Secretary of State, whose calm and measured judgment was making
itself felt increasingly, had written:

> All suggestions emanating from Delcassé I feel inclined to
> regard as attempts to oust us from our present position, without
> offering us anything seriously in exchange. This is not the case
> with Rouvier, who is a man of finance above everything. Like
> everybody in this category, his principal quality is the desire for
> peace. He wants no complications with us. I should therefore

like to think that his attempts at reconciliation are genuine. They will be put to the test if Radolin challenges his desire for peace, and says to him at the given moment—not brought about by himself: " If you are really so conciliatory and pro-German, then a conference would be the best way to settle matters." We shall then hear whether Rouvier continues to blow the peace-pipes. The Conference would not only be an outward triumph for us, giving us prestige both at home and abroad; it could also be utilized very well in a material sense.

The Envoy, Count Tattenbach, after he had convinced himself in Fez of the disintegration and decay in the Sherifian Empire, the *Maghreb el Aksa*, made the suggestion that France and Spain should divide Morocco according to the different spheres of interests, with ourselves. This thought would certainly have met at first with the tumultuous applause of the Pan-Germans, but I still think to-day that Herr von Mühlberg was not wrong when, in his report of 30th April, he said:

If after many decades, an historian digs up telegram number 1084 in our archives, he will probably say: The Minister was right. Why should Germany attempt the rôle of protector over countries which, like Turkey and Morocco, are destined by the process of history to decay? We poor contemporaries must reckon with things as they are. The policy which Count Tattenbach wishes to see inaugurated meets first of all with the opposition of His Majesty, who desires no military agreement over Morocco, and this would have to be considered as soon as we annex a sphere of interest there. Such tactics would be a contradiction of our former declarations and assurances that we desired only to maintain the *status quo* and to fight for the " open door."

Positive suggestions regarding an agreement over Morocco were never made to us from a French quarter in 1905. This was stated six years later in the session of the Budget Commission in the Reichstag of 11th November by the Secretary of State, Kiderlen-Wächter, who said: "After the German Kaiser's Tangier trip, Delcassé made an attempt to negotiate with us directly, but this attempt failed owing to a lack of positive suggestions on the French side. After Delcassé's resignation, Rouvier expressed a wish to come to an understanding with us, both officially and semi-officially, and the word ' Congo ' was heard in this connection for the first time. We had asked for concrete suggestions without obtaining any result." " Meanwhile," said Kiderlen, concluding his statement at the time, " we had committed ourselves to the point of view that changes in Morocco could only take place with the permission of the signatory powers of the Madrid Conference. For this reason Prince Bülow could no longer entertain the French desires for an understanding, since they were never accompanied by concrete proposals." Public opinion in our country was often incorrect in its judgment of the whole Morocco conflict because it failed to estimate the undercurrents in France and the passion and intensity of French patriotism. Peaceful, good-humoured, rather naïve, with little political insight, in spite of otherwise great and splendid qualities, the German judges the Frenchman too much according to his own lights, and underestimates the burning French ambition, the boundless French vanity, the French hardness and cruelty. At the same time he can never truly value French flexibility and buoyancy and the admirable patriotism of all Frenchmen. Before the Great War I had called attention to the still unequalled description of the French character by Alexis de Tocqueville, who, in the middle of the nineteenth century, wrote in his masterly work, *L'Ancien Régime et la Révolution*: " *Quand je considère cette nation, je la trouve plus extraordinaire qu'aucun des événements de son histoire, faisant toujours plus mal ou mieux qu'on ne s'y attendait. La plus brillante et la plus dangereuse des nations de l'Europe et la mieux faite pour y devenir tour à tour un objet d'admiration, de haine, de pitié, de terreur, mais jamais d'indifférence.*"

There was great rage in London over the fall of Delcassé, who had seemed to incorporate the whole idea of revenge on Germany in his own deep and fervid hatred. He was supported by all— loudly and impudently by the English Press, more subtly by King Edward and the Tory Cabinet which was under the King's influence.

On 25th July 1905 our Ambassador, Paul Metternich, wrote me from London:

Their Royal Highnesses the Crown Prince and Crown Princess of Greece and Princess Frederick Charles of Hesse, who have been staying at Seaford, a small seaside resort, and have been at Buckingham Palace for the past week, came to lunch with me to-day. The Crown Princess told me how deeply alarmed and sad she was at the anti-German sentiments that prevailed at Court. She had dropped into this embittered milieu without the slightest idea of it. This was very sad, as England and Germany were really destined to co-operate together. King Edward wished at the bottom of his heart to have good relations with us, in spite of his momentary annoyance. This was due, in great measure,

to his jealousy of his Imperial nephew's greater talents. Morocco
also played a part. A meeting between our exalted master and
King Edward would certainly do much to blow away the clouds
on both sides. King Edward belonged to the old school, he had
a good disposition, was benevolent and easy to win, *avec de
petits égards*. The Crown Princess of Greece who, as you know,
sincerely admires her imperial brother, but at the same time has
many feelings for England regrets the irritability displayed here,
and agreed with me that there was really no reason for it, as we
had done nothing against the English. Princess Frederick Karl
of Hesse confirmed the existence of an anti-German spirit which
verged on foolishness. I do not know what Count Seckendorff
says to you. As his remarks are not free from personal motives,
I do not attach all too great weight to them. He tried to work
for a better understanding, but without any special success. He
explained that we were building our fleet so that we might be a
valuable ally to England. The English, of course, laugh at such
suggestions at the present moment. I am informed, on good
authority, that King Edward was particularly annoyed at the
widespread German belief that England only wanted to drive
the French into the Morocco conflict in order to embroil them
with us, and then to leave them in the lurch. Efforts are being
made at Court here, particularly by compatriots passing through,
to blacken my character, accusing me of a strong anti-English
policy. These attempts have, however, met with no success up
to now, least of all with King Edward. I imagine that the same
visitors accuse me in Berlin or Norderney of a pro-English
policy.

King Edward's annoyance at the German press was in this case
not quite without foundation. Many German papers published
crude insinuations regarding *perfide Albion*, who had enticed
the " poor " French into the Moroccan morass, there to leave them
cold-bloodedly to their fate. Not only the English king, but wide
circles of the English people were angered by this. The intention
of such insinuations was only too clear. The former Marshal of
the Empress Frederick, Count Götz Seckendorff, was not the only
courtier who considered himself especially suitable for the London
Embassy. Others, such as the Marshal Reischach and the Master
of Ceremonies, Eugen Röder, were affected by the same delusion.
The former based his aspirations on the distant relationship of his
wife, who was a Hohenlohe, to the English Royal House; the latter
founded his on the fact that his wife was actually English by birth.

The enmity between Germany and England was increased by the unfriendly relations existing between the uncle in London and the nephew in Berlin, and I endeavoured to improve matters, at least as far as these personal relations were concerned. Our Crown Prince was more pleasing to King Edward personally than was the Kaiser. The Crown Prince was less brilliant and versatile than his father, but he was more modest, and had more tact, a quality which is inherent, and can neither be acquired nor taught. Above all, between the King and his grand-nephew there were none of those evil memories which, since San Remo and the ninety-nine days, had envenomed the relations between uncle and nephew. King Edward had repeatedly invited his grand-nephew to visit him in London. I wanted the young Prince, who was barely twenty-three years old, to accept the invitation, but I met with stubborn opposition from both the Kaiser and the Kaiserin. The Kaiser would have liked to visit England frequently. If that were not possible, then " the boy," as he called his eldest son, should not enjoy the pleasures of English hospitality and the splendid English life. It was the same thing with the Life Guards uniform. On his repeated request, the Crown Prince was given a squadron in this crack regiment, but not its uniform. He had to wear that of a Cuirassiers' regiment of the line. There were rights and privileges which William II was not prepared to share with anybody, not even his eldest son. Among them was the right of shooting the finest stags in Rominten, the monopoly of the most magnificent uniforms, and the privilege of travelling in England. The Kaiserin was particularly opposed to this trip of her eldest son, fearing that the virtue of the Crown Prince might be endangered in the land of lovely women and charming girls.

The more inimical to Germany was the feeling in England, the more did the Kaiser lean towards Russia. As a final goal he had a formal German-Russian alliance in view. I had, however, repeatedly explained to him, since I took office, that his refusal, in the spring of 1890, to renew the Bismarckian Re-Insurance Treaty, and the effects of the Franco-Russian Alliance, had made it difficult to reinstate the old conditions that had existed between Germany and Russia. I repeatedly pointed out that a clever German policy would make friendly relations with Russia possible without a state treaty. The urgent desire to bring about a formal agreement with Russia arose once more in William II, when the Tsar appeared in need of support after the Russo-Japanese War which ended so unfortunately for his country.

It was not alone the success of the long-despised Japanese

which caused anxiety to the Tsar. In Russia also the situation was growing critical. Prince Henry VII of Reuss, our former Ambassador in St. Petersburg, Constantinople, and Vienna, gave me a confidential account of a letter he had received from his niece, the Grand Duchess Maria Pavlovna. The revolts of the working classes had been mastered by the troops. But the people had not been calmed. On the contrary, a kind of fever had seized upon all classes and all circles, and everyone felt himself called upon to rescue and lead the Fatherland. This universal state of things was only too fertile a field for serious revolutionary plans, and *il y a des gene pour exploiter et diriger le mouvement*. The letter continued:

> The saddest thing of all is the absolute lack of a *ligne de conduite* from above. One oscillates from one system to another, often from one day to another and you can imagine the effect of this. There is therefore neither hope nor safety, and the apparent reforms achieve nothing because they are given no time. They are scarcely proclaimed before they are supplanted by others. Either those in command can't or they won't see, and warning voices such as Vladimir's, are unheard. I am afraid we shall soon have the added terror of outrages to increase the general confusion. If only a fairly decent peace would come soon, things might be staved off. A firm and energetic lead could still save everything. Well, that lies in God's hand!
>
> With fond love,
>   MARIA.

The Russian Ambassador, Osten-Sacken, told me a similar story. The principal danger sprang from a general sense of insecurity. Almost weeping, the old diplomat summed up his views in the words: "*Un peu d'énergie pourrait nous sauver, mais on ne la voit paraître nulle part.*" For Osten-Sacken, with his mentality and the tradition of his family, the rescue of the Russian dynasty was the principal object. Consequently he was against peace at any price with Japan. This was desired, he said, by Liberals and Revolutionaries, who, in Russia, were sometimes difficult to distinguish from one another. Witte, too, recommended it, out of spite against Nicholas II. Of course, said the Russian Ambassador, a peace concluded at this moment would be welcomed momentarily by the Russian Press and Stock Exchange circles the world over, but would be felt by the entire Russian people as a terrible humiliation, and the Tsar would be made personally and directly responsible for it. "*Ça pourrait être la fin.*" But if the Tsar held out, the situation might improve for him and worsen for the Japanese. The German

General Staff regarded the military position in the Far East in a similiar fashion. The Japanese could not force Russia to make peace by gaining further victories on land or sea. Japan could take Sachalin, and Vladivostock, but somewhere in the Siberian Steppes she would be forced to stop, and to wait, with guns at attention, at a terrific pecuniary sacrifice, until the Russian Army should be ready to fight again. General Kuropatkin had made some big mistakes, but he had developed extraordinary energy in retaliation. The Russian soldier, too, had displayed in misfortune a quite exceptional toughness and resilience. Our General Staff regarded tenacity as the decisive factor for Russia. At that time, in my judgment, there were two reasons why Russia should continue to resist Japan. There was, firstly, the danger that a precipitate and unfavourable peace might imperil the Tsar's throne. I agreed with my great predecessor that a Tsarist Russia was more useful to international peace and to Germany's interests than would be a parliamentary or Republican Russia, in which the Pan-Slavonic elements, passionately anti-German, would attain to greater influence. Secondly, it was in our interests that Russia should be as heavily engaged as possible in Eastern Asia, in order to distract her attention from the Balkans, and to keep the Russian armies from the Austrian and German frontiers.

Tsar Nicholas, from the beginning of his reign, regarded our Kaiser with mixed feelings; at one time he was friendly and confidential, at another irritable and ill-humoured. The Kaiser had upset the Tsar, as I have hinted several times already, by too frequent and unasked advice and visits, and by his almost naïvely displayed superiority, which particularly annoyed the two Russian Empresses. This superiority was not only expressed in the Kaiser's letters, but also in the pictures painted according to his directions by his pet artist Knackfuss, which he presented to the Tsar at Christmas and on his birthday, as his own works. The first of these pictures was painted after the taking of Kiaochow, and showed William II glorified allegorically as an Archangel, with a fiery sword, exhorting the Great Powers to fight against the unholy Buddha. In discussing our economic and political relations with Japan, I have mentioned how much damage the bad taste of this allegory did in the eyes of millions of Buddhists, and how it increased our difficulties with Japan. Perhaps it pleased the Tsar!

The second picture in which Saint Michael, the Iron Cross on his breast and many Imperial eagles on his armour, drives off the demons of hell, who are storming the temple of peace and order, might have displeased revolutionary spirits, but not the Russian Tsar. The third picture was the worst. Kaiser William, in magnificent attitude and shining armour, was standing in front of the Tsar, with a huge crucifix in his raised right hand, while the Tsar looked up admiringly at him in a humble, almost ridiculous position, clad in a Byzantine garment, rather like a dressing-gown. In the background, German and Russian battleships were cruising.

But if the feelings of Tsar Nicholas for Kaiser William were mixed, the Tsar felt only those of friendship and confidence for his brother-in-law, the Kaiser's brother, Prince Henry of Prussia. This led me, in April 1905, to ask the Prince to pay the Tsar a visit in order to gather information *de visu et auditu* as to his personal feelings, and to give him courage and the will to persevere. The Prince was always ready to make himself useful to his brother the Kaiser, and to his country. He wrote to me that his private news from St. Petersburg was disquieting. At Court the revenge of Witte was feared. He was on the best of terms with the Dowager Empress, but on very bad terms with the present Tsarina, who believed that he would stop at nothing to gain his own ends. The letter ran further:

On the trip from Bremen to Cuxhaven I had, unfortunately, a not very helpful conversation with our Kaiser about the Tsar, as usual in a large circle of listeners. I was forced into the rôle of defending the Tsar from accusations and expressions of the severest sort. His Majesty urged that it was necessary for the Tsar to visit his troops at the Front. That the House of Romanov is fighting for its Crown and for its very existence, is quite apparent. . . . The part you think I ought to play will be best arranged, if I accompany my wife to Tsarskoe-Selo, where she will meet her sister Elisabeth, and go with her to Moscow for a few weeks. I thought of limiting my own stay in Tsarskoe to two or three days. I am sincerely grateful for the confidence you have often displayed in me of late, and I will try and prove myself worthy of it. I am sending these lines by the courier who brought me your letter in code, and send you at the same time very hearty greetings, from your always grateful and just as loyal and sincerely devoted,

HENRY PRINCE OF PRUSSIA.

After a few days' stay in Tsarskoe-Selo, Prince Henry wired me: " Tsar determined at present continue war in spite of strong agitation for peace. He pins his whole hopes on Roshdestvensky who will arrive shortly in the Sunda Archipelago. Tsar in calm and normal spirits." In spite of serious misgivings on my part, the Kaiser insisted that the Russian fleet, under Admiral Roshdest-vensky, should be aided by German coal supplies. His Majesty was inspired in part by the wish that his beloved Hapag, the Hamburg-American Packet Boat line, should do a business deal that was strongly recommended by Albert Ballin and one which proved indeed of great value. His Majesty longed so violently for the Russian fleet to deal the hated Japanese a crushing blow, that, when I advised care in regard to Japan and England, he wrote with his customary hot-headed exaggeration: He himself, personally, could reconcile it neither with his friendship for the Tsar, nor with his Christian conscience, to leave the Russian fleet alone in its fight for the Cross. As, however, in the difficult international situation, I was more necessary for the guidance of our foreign policy than he was, he would, if I insisted upon upholding my objections to the German coal supplies, lay down the Crown, and ask his son to reign, with my support, on the lines which appeared right to me. Of course, I regarded this odd idea no more seriously than the numerous similar eccentric marginal notes.

The Dogger Bank incident shook the Tsar temporarily out of his customary apathy, and, in a moment of discouragement and anger against the perfidious English, he suggested an Alliance to the Kaiser. I drew up the draft of an agreement according to the Kaiser's wishes. This was in three paragraphs, and might perhaps meet with Russian approval in spite of the existing Franco-Russian Treaty. The preamble of this draft-agreement expressed a desire to localize the Russo-Japanese War. The defensive character of the alliance was placed in the foreground. Article I stated that if one of the two Empires should be attacked its ally must support it with all its means of defence on land and on sea. Should occasion arise both allies would make common cause to demand recognition from France of obligations taken over literally from the Franco-Russian Treaty of Alliance. In Article II, both exalted parties bound themselves not to conclude a separate peace with any common enemy. Article III laid down the obligation to mutual aid in the case of any action carried out by one of the signatories of the alliance during the war such as, e.g., the delivery of coals to one of the inimical parties, giving rise to complaints on the part of a third Power of an alleged infringement of the rights of neutrality. I had suggested to His Majesty a letter to the Tsar, short and concise, dictated by myself, which should accompany this draft. But the Kaiser enlarged the rough draft I gave him, into a long letter, which the world read fifteen years later when the Bolshevists published the Kaiser's letters to the Tsar. If this communication stated that the German Foreign Office knew nothing of the Kaiser's answer, this assurance did not accord with the facts. The somewhat sentimental blessing which I was said to have pronounced over the conclusion of this draft ("May God's blessing rest over both rulers, and the mighty triple group, Russia, Germany, and France, for ever preserve peace in Europe: so may God will!"), was only the picturesque embellishment, such as the Kaiser delighted in, of a bald matter of fact statement.

As I had foreseen and prophesied to His Majesty, our plans for an alliance were shattered by the opposition of Lambsdorff. He succeeded in persuading his sovereign that the German proposal was contrary to the terms of the Franco-Russian Treaty, that *Héritage sacré de feu l'Empereur Alexandre III d'impérissable mémoire*, although in a second draft I had paid special attention to the misgivings of the wavering Tsar. Would the opposition of Count Lambsdorff have been so tenacious, if he had not been offended by William II earlier in his career? Perhaps a Lambsdorff who had been treated with an unchanging kindliness by the German Kaiser, would have seen at last that the Franco-Russian Alliance and the carefully drawn-up German-Russian defensive agreement, could exist side by side. Conditions at this time were something like those prevailing when Anglo-German alliance possibilities were discussed at about the turn of the century, when the obstinate opposition of the English Premier, Salisbury, was also due in measure to his personal rancour against the Kaiser. Only after I had emphatically declared, in a conversation with Count Osten-Sacken, that I would not play the *dindon de la farce*, and would only permit German coal supplies to Russia, if Russia gave us binding assurances should these supplies involve us in a conflict with Japan or England, did the St. Petersburg Cabinet condescend to a written reply.

William II persisted in his rôle of mentor to the weak and touchy Tsar, despite Grand Duke Vladimir's warning. Already, in February 1905, the Kaiser had told one of his intimates, Professor Theodor Schiemann, that he was working at a "splendid" letter in which he was giving the Tsar "good advice." The Tsar must issue an edict from Moscow, introduce aristocratic representation, and crush out the anarchistic movement by force. After a while, the Kaiser became still less reserved. As his letters to the Tsar revealed, when published by the Bolshevists, he advised the Tsar to place himself at the head of a Black Sea Fleet, to force his own way through the Straits and join, with his proud ships, in the fray. He should summon delegates from every province to the Kremlin in

Moscow, so as to inflame the people; he should arouse their enthusiasm for the war in a fervid address, and so gain national support for the national cause and public welfare. This same monarch who was so free with his bold and dauntless advice to others, let the political reins drag along the ground in a much more serious war, ten years later. After so often describing his position, as chief War Lord, as the *rocher de bronze* of his throne, he played the part of passive observer in the Great War. He was more passive in every way than the Monarchs of Belgium and Italy, Rumania and Greece, whom he had so mocked because of their modesty—more passive even than the Presidents of France and the United States. True indeed is the phrase coined by old Destouches: " *La critique est aisee et l'art est difficile.*" Destouches was a favourite of the French Regent, Duke Philip of Orléans. He wrote a comedy famous during its day, " *Le Glorieux.*" This was produced in Paris on 18th January 1732, just thirty-one years after the coronation of the first King of Prussia. His trenchant remark concerning criticism and art is to be found in this work.

CHAPTER IX

*Meeting of the German and Russian Emperors in Björkö—Enthusiastic
telegram of the Kaiser over his triumph in Björkö—My Immediate report to the Kaiser (3.viii.1905)—I send in my resignation—
Refusal of the Kaiser to accept it—The Imperial communication;
My answer—William II " as though reborn "—End of the Björkö
affair.*

WHEN Kaiser William II told me in June 1905 that, in
view of the conflict between Norway and Sweden, he did
not intend to visit the Norwegian fjords on his usual
summer cruise, but would remain in the Baltic, I could only approve
this decision. I soon saw that the Kaiser wished to meet the Tsar
in the Baltic, and His Majesty and I discussed the advisability of
this meeting in several conversations. I agreed with the Kaiser
that it might be possible for him now, through a display of sympathy, to win the friendship of the much-tried Russian monarch,
just as had happened once with Alexander I of Russia, and Frederick
William and Queen Louise at their first meeting after the dark days
of Jena and Tilsit. But I told him at the same time that it was
possible that the Tsar, feeling conquered and more or less shamed,
would find such a meeting with his " brother " painful. To His
Majesty's great astonishment, I suggested that it would be better
if Count Lambsdorff were present at the meeting, where he must
express his views and counter-views openly, instead of playing the
part of Penelope, who worked by day and unravelled her thread by
night, after the return of the Tsar to St. Petersburg. The Kaiser
must not forget that without the consent of the Russian Foreign
Secretary, it would be difficult to attain anything of permanency.
Therefore it was advisable to obtain only the Tsar's promise, but this
in the most binding form, that he would recommend the conclusion
of a defensive agreement with Germany seriously to his Foreign
Secretary, and insist upon such a serious and unmistakable order
being carried out. I enjoined upon the Kaiser particularly, in the
last talk I had with him, before he left for Swinemünde on 10th
July 1905, to make no unconsidered agreement about Denmark
and the Baltic, as, according to my opinion of the general situation
at present, this might lead to an English attack, or at least to a
humiliation brought about by England. I left His Majesty in no

doubt that in my opinion it would be advisable to get from the Tsar only the promise mentioned above, that he would recommend to Lambsdorff the conclusion of a German-Russian peace and defensive treaty *qui serait une infraction ni aux stipulations Austro-Allemands ni au traité Rrusso-Français, mais qui garantirait et assurerait le repos et la paix de monde*, and that he should leave everything concerning the working out of this to Lambsdorff and myself. To accomplish this we could meet either in Baden-Baden, or Lambsdorff might come for a few days to Berlin during his annual autumn trip to Paris, or I would go to St. Petersburg where I had good connections and was familiar with conditions. A slight shadow crossed the alert, volatile countenance of His Majesty and showed me that the exalted gentleman was this time particularly confident of achieving everything through the compelling power of his own personality. When I asked whether I was to accompany him, the Kaiser replied with the greatest affability, that although my society was always and everywhere most desirable and pleasant, yet this time he felt he could accomplish more if he were face to face with the Tsar of all the Russias. Only the " loyal " Tschirschky was to go with him.

On 22nd July I received a telegram from the Kaiser in which he informed me that the Tsar had asked him to meet him in Björkö, a small island in the Finnish Schären of the Baltic. On the next day a still more delighted telegram from His Majesty reached me in Norderney, where I was staying, telling me that the Tsar was deeply moved and highly delighted at the reunion. He had acquiesced in all the German Kaiser's wishes; the Russo-German Treaty was an accomplished fact. I have had many strange telegrams from the Kaiser, but never one so filled with enthusiasm as this one from Björkö. With excessive rapture William II described the moment of signing the agreement. When he laid down the pen with which he had signed this act of historical importance, a ray of sunlight gleamed through the cabin window on to the table. He had looked up. It was as though his grandfather William I and Tsar Nicholas I had clasped hands in Heaven, and were looking down with satisfaction upon their grandsons.

When soon afterwards the Ambassador, von Tschirschky, who had accompanied the Kaiser as representative of the Foreign Office, sent me the text of the agreement, I was struck by the addition in the first article, " en Europe." The Russo-German Treaty was confined to Europe. I recognized at once, of course, that through this limitation the agreement lost the greater part of its value to us, because Russia could not be of service to us against England in

Europe. Only if India were threatened would the English be hit in a sensitive spot. I regarded as still more grave the intention of the Kaiser to include Denmark in the Russo-German Alliance. It was intended that Denmark, if need arose, should make the incursion of a British Fleet into the Baltic impossible by closing the Sund. Matters were made worse by the fact that the Kaiser had gone to Copenhagen, in the meantime, to obtain from old King Christian IX himself the inclusion of Denmark in the Russo-German agreement, and the danger threatened from this side was increased. I was displeased, moreover, in the highest degree, that the treaty drawn up by the Kaiser, had not been signed by the Foreign Secretaries of both countries, but on our part by the Minister in Hamburg, Herr von Tschirschky, and for the Russians by Birilev, the Naval Minister. Nominated barely a fortnight beforehand to the post of Naval Minister, Admiral Birilev, a worthy seaman, had no idea of politics, and indeed declared afterwards that he had not even read the Treaty of Björkö, which he had countersigned, since the German Kaiser had held his hand over the document. When the Tsar told him to countersign the Treaty, he had replied as in duty bound: "*Slushaius*!" that is to say, "I obey!", the formula used by the Russian soldier when he receives a command.

After a long and careful consideration of the situation created by the Kaiser's action, I wrote to Holstein who, through fear of responsibility, as often in a crisis, could come to no clear decision in the matter:

There is a discrepancy between the manner in which you judge the Treaty from Björkö in the letter just received, and in your last telegrams. In telegram No. 51 you said: "The Treaty in its present form is still decidedly favourable for us." In telegram No. 57 you still said: "The Treaty has been impaired by the two additions, but is still worth preserving. I should consider a refusal of your counter-signature to be very unwise." Whereas you now write me: "Public opinion will adjudge the Treaty, as it now stands, to be a diplomatic trap for Germany." If the last opinion is correct, I shall not dream of counter-signing the Treaty but shall either annul it by refusing my signature or resign. I do not think I am mistaken if I consider your suggestion, that the Tsar laid the draft before His Majesty, to be incorrect. I do not even think that the Tsar brought a draft of the Treaty with him. I almost believe that when the Tsar arrived in Björkö he did not even think of the Treaty. I believe that the whole initiative emanated from His

Majesty—but all this *sauf erreur*. Where I surely am not mistaken is in thinking that the words " en Europe " were not inspired by Tschirschky. Both additions certainly came from His Majesty. Blame is attached to Tschirschky, only because he did not prevent that " en Europe." It is therefore impossible to tell His Majesty that the impairment of the Treaty is due to Tschirschky. His Majesty is too upright to accept this statement if it is not true. We must not forget either, that the merit of achieving the Treaty—*si mérite il y a*—is due in the main to His Majesty. But all this does not alter the fact that I do not accept it and would prefer to resign if, after mature consideration, I feel it does not make for the good of the country. I am curious to see whether my supposition, that Lambsdorff was just as surprised by the conclusion of the Treaty as I was, will be confirmed. The following point appears to me very important: If we wish to uphold this treaty with Russia, it is my firm opinion that we must have no double-crossing with France in the period looming ahead—particularly not on the Morocco question. That we have agreed with France on the main points was doubtless the only premise which led the Tsar to enter upon the agreement.

On 3rd August I handed to the Kaiser, who had just returned from the Baltic to Wilhelmshöhe, the following report. I criticized first a few ungracious marginal notes His Majesty had made to two telegrams I had sent him just before his arrival in Björkö, on 22nd July, and then before his arrival in Copenhagen on 28th July. I continued:

I have had the honour of receiving your royal and Imperial Majesty's most exalted marginal notes to my humble telegrams of the 22nd and 28th instant. In a question as serious and important to your Majesty and the country as the agreement concluded between Your Majesty and His Majesty the Tsar of Russia, I must be completely sincere towards Your Majesty. When I received the news through Your Majesty's gracious telegram of the 24th inst., I was most pleased. When the text of the Treaty was wired to me in cipher and I saw the addition, " en Europe," I believed at first a mistake had been made in code. When it was confirmed that it was not a mistake, I presumed that this addition had been made after strong pressure from His Majesty Tsar Nicholas, or the flat refusal of His Majesty to accept the Treaty in its original wording. Since I discovered that that addition was made on our side, I have been sincere in my endeavours to regard it favourably. Your Majesty knows that

I am not one who insists upon having his own way. But the longer I ponder the subject, the more convinced I am in my belief that the addition "en Europe" implies a distinct and fateful change for the worse. Through this addition, the relationship between the German and the Russian States in the case of a war provoked by an attack upon Germany, would be in our disfavour. What has Germany at stake? A fine navy, flourishing trade, rich coastal cities, her colonies. And what, after Asia is once out of the question, does Russia offer? A navy that scarcely any longer exists, very little commerce, insignificant towns on the coast, no colonial possessions. With the reservation "en Europe," the risk has become disproportionate. With these limitations the demands made, if a concrete case arose, would be very unequal. In Europe, Russia can help us little with her navy, and nothing at all with her army against England. Just the very point on which England fears Russia, namely a menace against India and Persia, has been *expressis verbis* ruled out through the addition "en Europe." The argument that a Russian attack on India would be difficult or impracticable is, in my humble opinion, not sound. I should think that the opinions which prevail in England on the subject are those to be considered, not those of our General Staff on the prospects of a Russian enterprise in Central Asia. Why should the English spend million after million in fortifying the Indian frontiers and reinforcing the Indian Army? Why should they send their best generals to India, if they did not fear a Russian invasion? The entire Anglo-Indian literature, the English Press, the English political world, and the masses of the English population all share this apprehension. At the present time, the English are endeavouring, with the renewal of the Anglo-Japanese Alliance, to obtain binding assurances from Japan in the event of a Russian attack upon India. According to English ideas, India and Canada are the only two vulnerable points of the British Empire. The fear that, in the event of an English attack upon Germany, India might be menaced by the Russians, would make the English more wary in dealing with us. Now that this danger seems to have been averted through the addition of the words "en Europe," it is to be feared that such an agreement would only incite the English. A strong bullet stops a man; a small bullet irritates him. The Treaty in its original form was a strong bullet; with the words "en Europe" added it becomes, I both believe and fear, a small bullet. Your Majesty thinks, according to the marginal notes to my telegram of 28th inst., that the Russians might attack India without an agreement with ourselves, and that we might advise them to attack India in the case of a war with England. But here it is wise to quote the proverb: "What one has got in black and white can be carried home safely." If the Russians had not been expressly freed from an obligation to attack India, they would at least have made military demonstrations on the Indian frontier in the case of a war with England, which would have diverted a part of the English military forces from Europe towards Asia. They will scarcely do that of their own free will. There is even the possibility that Russia will make an agreement with England sooner or later, which excludes a war on the Indian frontier and therefore limits the brunt of warfare to Europe and creates a situation in which Russia does not come to our aid at all against England. The Tsar's state of mind may change. *E mobile.* The ladies of the Russian Court, in so far as they have influence, lean more to England than to Germany. Whether, in the case of a war with England, Your Majesty's advice would persuade the Tsar to proceed against India of his own accord is, in my most humble opinion, very doubtful. For ten years past we have often experienced the fact that Your Majesty can exert personal influence on the Tsar, but that written communications were of little effect. In such a case, even personal pressure would be far more difficult, since the Tsar would not be, as he was this time in Björkö, the weaker and more suppliant party, but in the event of a war between England, Germany and Russia, in a stronger and more favourable position than ourselves. The principal fact, however, remains, that through the reservation "en Europe," English military intentions against ourselves, which are the concrete danger of the moment and, according to human calculation, will so remain in the near future, will not be lessened but increased. The rumour that we are trying to bring about the neutralization of the Baltic has added new fuel to English suspicions. The English, who know well enough that Denmark, in particular, will never entertain any proposition which might bring her into conflict with England, would go against us if any such intention to exclude the English from the Baltic took on a concrete form. The danger of war is more imminent than it has been for years past. I have asked myself whether Your Majesty in adding the words "en Europe" only had in mind the case of England attacking Russia and our having to come to Russia's aid. In this case the German navy, the little there is of Russia's navy, and small portions of the German and Russian army would be necessary for offensive and defensive on the coast. There would remain nearly the entire German and Russian armies, which would be needed to concentrate on the only seat of war which still seemed vulnerable—the Indian frontier. The possibility of England attacking Russia is, however, far more unlikely than that of England attacking us. That was already seen in 1885, twenty years ago, during the Afghan War; it showed itself again a year ago when English ships were confiscated by Russian cruisers, and in the incident of the Dogger Bank. It is visible in the whole tendency of present English policy, just as it is in the personal attitude of His Majesty King Edward. And if it ever came to such an English attack upon Russia, an attack by the English fleet on the European coast of Russia would be more probable than an English advance in Asia. Here, too, it is clear that the fulfilment of an obligation to send troops to Asia could be refused by us, at any time, in view of the necessity to concentrate our military forces against France. As far as I am able to foresee, the Treaty in its present form with the addition of " en Europe," will, if it becomes known, bring a great sense of relief in England. But the Treaty will appear to the German population as a *societas leonina*, in which we give and risk incomparably more than the other party. In regard to France, through the Treaty, with or without " en Europe," we are safeguarded on our Eastern frontier should France attack us or remain neutral. The first case is not very probable. The latter would be the most unfortunate thing that could happen to us, for France would only remain neutral until we had been so weakened by England, that she would have an easier task. The event of our attacking France is not covered by the Treaty, but by the Franco-Russian Commercial Treaty. The Russo-German Treaty in its original form, without the addition " en Europe," would, in a conflict with England, have so divided the chances, that a co-operation of France with Germany and Russia did not appear impossible even in the case of an English attack upon Germany. Through the express exclusion of Asia, the chances in a war between the two Empires and England seem so unfavourable for ourselves, that France will not join us. The possibility, too, of a Russian-English-French understanding concerning Asia is enhanced. This addition takes away our chief trump card, leaving Russia her tricks, and an ace in the hands of the enemy that England need no longer fear. I owe it to my Imperial master to say openly that, after calm and sober consideration before God and my own conscience, I regard the addition " en Europe," as harmful and dangerous. On the other hand I can see that Your Majesty

cannot well ask that His Majesty Tsar Nicholas should modify
the Treaty Your Majesty himself suggested and signed. His
Majesty Tsar Nicholas will not easily relinquish an addition
which implies an easier situation for Russia. Alvensleben, who
is not initiated into the secret, announces that Lambsdorff, who
during the winter did not want to hear anything about the Treaty,
is in the best of spirits since Björkö. Will the Russians give up
the advantage that has been presented to them? Will it be
possible to make them accept the subsequent elimination of the
words " en Europe "? The Tsar will only be won over with
difficulty for an alteration of the Treaty which would oblige
Russia, in the case of an attack upon Germany, to declare
a state of war throughout the extent of the entire Russian realm,
or according to whose terms, both powers engage to declare war
in the case of any hostilities arising out of the Treaty. Would
not any such suggestion fall like frost upon the Tsar's present
good humour? I do not deny that any such initiative would be
highly dangerous, since it offers the Russians the possibility of
repudiating the whole Treaty. Should this happen, a situation
would ensue which would be worse than that existing before the
Treaty was concluded. Therefore, I beg Your Majesty, in deepest
devotion, to place the leadership of our foreign policy in other
hands. It is possible that another person once initiated in the
matter would adjudge it differently to myself. He might be
able, with a good conscience, to share Your Majesty's point of
view and operate further on the basis of the Treaty. I need not
say that I shall, of course, substantiate my resignation by reasons
of health. I need say still less, that my most loyal, grateful, and
warmest wishes will always accompany my Imperial master, and
that to my last breath my whole heart will beat for the happiness
and the fame of Your Majesty.

(Signed) Bülow.

In this dispatch I had refrained purposely from expressing the
suspicion I had immediately felt when I received the Kaiser's telegram
telling of the triumph he had had in Björkö—namely, that Count
Lambsdorff would succeed, after the return of his sovereign to
St. Petersburg, in persuading the Tsar to disown the Treaty over
which Kaiser William had taken him by storm, and to withdraw his
signature. In dealing with the Kaiser, the Tsar had shown himself
to be weak, vacillating and simple-minded. Towards his ministers
he was not only just as weak, just as vacillating, but also perfidious.
When Tsar Nicholas again saw Count Lambsdorff, who pleased

him by his obsequious bearing and quiet manners, which were a pleasant contrast to those of Finance Minister Witte with his loud voice and masterful demeanour, he found his Foreign Secretary in very low spirits. Vladimir Nikolaievitch showed that he was very pained at not being consulted when the " *traité ou soi-disant traité de Björkö* " was drawn up. He implied that the Tsar, an autocrat, had been the tool of the Kaiser. The latter had availed himself of the too great courtesy, perhaps even of a momentary " distraction " of the Tsar, to palm off a deception upon him. That is how von Witte and Isvolski described to me the scene that took place between the Tsar when he came home from Björkö, and his Foreign Secretary. In any case it was not difficult for Lambsdorff to convince his monarch that the Treaty he had signed in Björkö did not tally with the Franco-Russian alliance. To the German Ambassador Count Lambsdorff said it was a pity that he, the proper Minister for the occasion, was not present in Björkö. He would have warned the monarchs against cherishing too sanguine hopes, and prevented them from signing a pact which was impossible to put into practice. It is only too probable that Lambsdorff expressed himself along these lines to the French, and, perhaps also, the English Ambassador. In any case, the St. Petersburg correspondent of the *Daily Telegraph*, Mr. Dillon, was empowered from a Russian quarter, to give the English Government Count Lambsdorff's version of the Björkö meeting.

Kaiser William's visit to Copenhagen had been completely unsuccessful. King Christian IX, already eighty-seven years old, whose long life had brought him many changes but much experience, was able to parry the stormy wooing of the German Kaiser by a polite but decided refusal. He even sent his Foreign Secretary, Count Raben, to London, to assure them there that Denmark would maintain the strictest neutrality under all circumstances. Count Raben, to whom I was attached by old connections and a distant relationship, told me later that King Christian was moved to this step by a letter from his daughter Queen Alexandra of England, who had asked him, " quite horrified," if he were going to " betray " England. The English press spread the news that the Kaiser not only coveted the Norwegian crown for a prince of his house, but that he also wanted to force Denmark to close the Baltic to all ships, save those of the Baltic nations. At the same time the impending visit of an English squadron to the Baltic was announced.

This was the situation, in broad outline, when Kaiser William received my request for resignation in Castle Wilhelmshöhe, whither he had repaired on his return from his Baltic trip. His reply was the following letter:

My dear Bülow,

Your letter just received per messenger. After long reflection I am utterly incapable of seeing why the situation for us through " en Europe " has become so much more serious or dangerous than it was before, that you feel it necessary to offer me your resignation. You have been informed by me of two facts which alone imply such enormous progress that they must be highly esteemed. (1) That His Majesty the Tsar solemnly declared to me that, for Russia, the Alsace-Lorraine question was " un incident clos "; (2) that he gave me his hand upon the promise never to enter into an agreement or alliance with England against us. If Bismarck had succeeded in obtaining either of these two points from Alexander II or III, he would have been beside himself with joy and would have permitted himself to be fêted by everybody as though he had won a great victory. These are such significant facts, that I believe they, alone, mean for our Fatherland a safer guarantee than all treaties and other reassurances. From my private letters you will have gathered how highly serious, yes and even holy, my country's welfare was to me, how convinced I was that I was capable of greatly lightening your heavy burdens—of this I am still convinced even now—and that above everything I had as a goal the intention of preparing your path and helping you. Think of your farewell words to me in Sassnitz: " Oh, if it were only possible that you could meet the Tsar, I should be pleased beyond measure; it would be, both for the nation and for the world, a great blessing, but we cannot initiate it in Berlin; should he suggest, or ask it, go to him, and God's blessing be with you." So it happened that I believed I was working for you, and had achieved something special, and now you send me a few cool words and your resignation!!! You will spare me a description of my present spiritual state, I am sure, dear Bülow. To be treated like this by the best and most intimate friend that I have had since my poor Adolf died, without any reasonable ground being given, has dealt me such a terrible blow that I have completely collapsed, and fear that a serious nervous trouble may result from it. You say the situation since the addition of " en Europe " to the Treaty has become so serious that you cannot take the responsibility. Serious to whom? And in the same breath you believe you can be responsible to God for leaving in the lurch, in a situation you, yourself, describe as peculiarly serious, your Emperor and Master, to whom you **have** sworn fealty, who has showered affection and distinctions upon you, your, as I believe most faithful friend, and your Fatherland? My dear Bülow, you can't do that to either of us! We have both been called by God and made for one another to work and to achieve for our German Fatherland! If it is true—which I do not think possible—that through a fault of mine, according to your opinion, a still more serious situation has been brought about, that happened in the best of intentions! You know me well enough to believe that! Your personality is worth, both to me and to our Fatherland, 100,000 times more than all the treaties in the world. I have taken immediate steps with the Tsar, either to weaken the significance of these two words, or to eliminate them! Remember that you, personally, placed me in **the** foreground in Tangier against my will, to win a success in your Moroccan policy. Read through my telegrams before the Tangier visit. You owned to me yourself that you had such fears that when you received the news that I had left again, you burst into tears. I landed because you wanted me to, in the interests of the Fatherland, mounted a strange horse in spite of the impediment that my crippled left arm caused to my riding, and the horse was within an inch of costing me my life, which was your stake in the game! I had to ride between Spanish anarchists because you wished it, and your policy was to profit by it! And now, after I have done all this, and as I believe, much more, for you, you want to desert me simply because a situation appears to you to be serious! But Bülow, I never deserved that of you! No, my friend, you will remain in office and continue to co-operate with me *ad majorem Germaniae Gloriam*. You actually owe it to me, seeing the part I have played in interceding this year. You cannot and must not repudiate me; it would be a confession of failure of your own policy this year and I should be ashamed for evermore. This I cannot survive. Let me have a few days' rest and concentration before you come, because the agitation your letters have caused me is too great; I am incapable of any calm discussion at present.

Your faithful friend,

WILLIAM I.R.

P.S. I appeal to your friendship for me, and do not let me hear any more of your intention to retire. Wire me after this letter the word " All right " and I shall know you will stay! For the morning after your request for resignation had been received, would find your Emperor alive no longer. Think of my poor wife and children. W.

P.S. Have prepared a code telegram for the Tsar in which alteration is suggested along your lines. Since Björkö, I am on such good terms with him that I hope to achieve it. Shall I mention you and constitutional grounds? Or only our direct proposals? Please wire answer W.

When I read this letter I was deeply moved. There was no lack of exaggeration in His Majesty's communication. Some things were a pure invention. The words he placed in my mouth regarding a solemn farewell on the chalk cliffs of Sassnitz I never said. I had only advised the Kaiser, in the case of his meeting the Tsar, an eventuality I regarded *rebus sic stantibus*, soberly, even sceptically, to keep calm and clear-headed. The dangers of landing in Tangier which I had not properly foreseen, I regretted myself very deeply. The statement that I had told the Kaiser that I had burst into tears when he left Tangier was untrue. *Je n'ai pas la larme aussi facile*: my tears do not flow so easily. These tears are the same as those others which William II ascribed to his great Chancellor in the letter which he wrote to the Emperor Francis Joseph after Prince Bismarck's dismissal.

But in spite of such small blemishes this Imperial letter overwhelmed me. I was particularly touched by the reference to his withered arm. Among the many lovable human qualities of the Kaiser, scarcely one was more appealing than the truly stoical manner in which he bore and overcame the paralysis of his left arm. Without in any way concealing this physical defect, he had by iron determination developed into a bold rider, a brilliant shot and a skilful tennis-player. After working eight years with the Kaiser, I was obliged to recognize that he lacked many qualities which the head of a state should possess if he is to govern with success. There had been many conflicts of opinion between us; we had had many skirmishes. I had sometimes even been annoyed with him. But in spite of that I loved him with my whole heart, not only for all the goodness and kindliness which he had shown me almost too profusely, but for the sake of the gifted, nobly-endowed character he possessed; so lovable and so amiable, so natural and so simple, so large-hearted and so broad-minded. I am not ashamed to confess that I had fallen completely under his spell. Although I was barely ten years older than the Kaiser I was more mature than he. Those born in the purple, the *porphyrogeniti*, generally remain immature for a long period; at forty they are often younger than other mortals

of twenty-five.   Years of discretion begin for princes later than for
most people.   The feelings I cherished for the Kaiser were those of
a father for his son, who often worries him, still more often causes
him sorrow, but whose brilliant talents, and great gifts of heart and
mind and many fine qualities attract and rejoice him again and
again.   In later years too, when I had no longer any illusions concerning the superficiality and vanity, the unreliability, and, particularly, the untruthfulness, of the Kaiser; even after he had fled
abroad, leaving a ruin behind him, I could not bring myself to
hate him.   In the November days of 1908, too, I felt no dislike,
irritation, or even impatience with him.   My sentiments at the time,
if I can use the simile, were those of a conscientious doctor who has,
at a given moment, to carry out a painful but healing operation on
a patient, however dear he may be to him.   Above all, I saw in the
Kaiser from the first to the last day of my term of office, the son of
his splendid father, the grandson of the victor of Sadowa and Sedan,
the successor of the great King and the Great Prince Elector, the
King of Prussia and the German Emperor, representative of the
most famous dynasty Germany has seen since the Hohenstaufen,
the dynasty for whom, and with whom, Bismarck unified Germany,
the ruling family upon whose shoulders the future of the German
Empire rested.

   The Kaiser's letter was brought me by Adjutant von Moltke,
who told me that the Kaiser had been completely upset by my
request for resignation.   He now not only feared that Russia would
withdraw, but also that England might attack.   General Moltke
gave me a touching description of how the Kaiser was at first
agitated, and of how a deep depression quickly followed.   He spoke
too of his physical exhaustion, brought about by the " eternal
running to and fro," and which was increased by the August heat.
He was sitting at his writing table with an unhappy expression on
his face, drops of sweat on his brow; he was looking very pale.
Moltke begged me insistently to write warmly to the Kaiser as soon
as possible in order to calm him.   Otherwise a " complete collapse "
might be expected.   My heart as well as my head urged me to
write at once.   I wrote that his words had deeply moved me.   It
was painful for me to have caused him anxiety and grief.   I would
give my life to make everything smooth for my King and Emperor,
to remove obstacles from his path, to render possible the achievement of his great aims for the welfare of the Fatherland.   The
Kaiser's genuine successes did not make me jealous; they made me
proud.   Nor was I ungrateful, and I bore constantly in mind the
great goodness he had displayed towards me for so many years, the

many distinctions he had showered upon me. I should be the most
petty-minded of all people if I cherished the slightest sentiment of
pitiful self-assertiveness or vanity towards my King and Emperor.
But it was just the goodness he had shown me which made complete
candour on my part towards His Majesty imperative, even where it
was difficult for me. It was because I not only loved the Kaiser as
my sovereign and master, as the upholder of the national idea, but
also as the human being, excelling in mind and character, that it was
incumbent upon me to be open and candid. I should not deserve
His Majesty's confidence if I did not have the courage and honesty
to act under all circumstances and *coûte que coûte*, as my conscience
dictated. If I had requested that foreign affairs be placed in other
hands it was because I was under the impression that another might
adjudge the situation differently, possibly more correctly than I did,
and might, under given circumstances, accord better with His
Majesty's intentions. If even after I had openly expressed my
misgivings the Kaiser still wished to keep me, my endeavours would
be directed towards doing all that was possible so that what the
Kaiser believed he had achieved in Björkö should really work out
to the advantage of the Fatherland and of our policy. In the face
of his anxieties, I reminded him of the motto of the first and greatest
prince of Orange: " *Saevis tranquillus in undis.*" That had been
his emblem, written under a stormy petrel which was poised calmly
over a stormy sea. The brave Orange prince had been hard pressed
by those who both envied and hated him, but with calmness and
tenacity he had withstood them. The Kaiser could take courage
from this example. If he wished to make further use of me I should
serve him in gratitude and humility, directing all my thoughts and
desires towards this end, as was becoming to my duty and my love
for him and for our country. I closed with the request that he
should let me know when I might be received in audience to speak
of the general situation and of an eventual letter to the Tsar. His
Majesty replied at once by wire: " Warmest thanks, I feel reborn."

I had still before me the delicate task of so squaring the Björkö
episode, that it left no deep scar behind in the mind of Tsar Nicholas.
For a long time Kaiser William cherished the illusion that the Tsar
would remain true to the treaty that had been wrested from him
à la hussarde in Björkö. In September he had suggested to the
Tsar that he might instruct his representatives abroad to co-operate
with their German colleagues in all questions of mutual policy
and to inform them of their plans and intentions. But when Lambsdorff instructed the Russian Ambassador in Berlin to inform me
confidentially that the Tsar felt himself obliged, for pressing reasons,

to withdraw from the Björkö agreement, William II was obliged to recognize that a grouping which had existed for fifteen years cannot be changed in a moment. Count Osten-Sacken had informed me at the Tsar's express desire, and on behalf of Count Lambsdorff, that both not only had complete confidence in me, but that it was the sincere wish of the Tsar and the St. Petersburg Cabinet to continue as before the peaceful, neighbourly, and steady relation which had existed for the past hundred and fifty years between Russia and Prussian-Germany. Kaiser William, with my co-operation, which, under one pretext or another, he had managed to evade for some time when writing letters to the Tsar, sent him a dignified communication in December 1905, in which he told the Russian ruler that it was not his intention to force a solution upon him which Russia regarded as undesirable. He added: " Under all circumstances we shall remain faithful and loyal friends."

The first serious test to which for the welfare of the Empire I had to submit my personal relations to William II had passed off satisfactorily, with reasons of state prevailing over other sentiments. Whether our relations could sustain a second such trial appeared to me even then doubtful. The year 1908 confirmed my supposition.

CHAPTER X

THE news of the meeting of the Emperors at Björkö reached London from St. Petersburg with a malicious distortion of the facts, in so far as they went through Court or Diplomatic channels. The effect in English government circles was just what might have been expected, and this effect was increased by the hasty and demonstrative visit which William II had paid to Copenhagen, a visit that was the subject of the wildest surmise in that part of the European press that was hostile to ourselves. Towards the end of August English ships appeared in the Baltic where the navy of Great Britain had not been seen for a long time.

On the 22nd August 1905, the representative of the Foreign Office at His Majesty's Court, Ambassador von Tschirschky, wrote to me of the impression made by this English demonstration on William II, and of his attitude towards the English Court.

I feel [he wrote] that I should inform your Serene Highness with regard to the following: H.M. showed me a telegram from H.R.H. the Crown Prince this afternoon. The latter announced that he had received a letter from uncle Bertie, in which he and Cecilie are invited to take part in the hunt at Windsor early in November. The Crown Prince added that the King seemed to set much store by having this invitation accepted, for he put the Royal yacht " Victoria and Albert " at the disposal of the guests. The Crown Prince asks that he may be permitted to accept the invitation. H.M. was very much excited and annoyed about this new " trick " of his uncle's. In the previous year, so H.M. thought, King Edward had also invited the Crown Prince without informing him, the Kaiser, as he should have done. The King had even gone so far as to tell the Crown Prince (when he should have known better) that he had assured himself of the Kaiser's consent in advance and the Crown Prince had accepted the invitation on the strength of this assurance. He, the Kaiser, had then been compelled to explain to the Crown Prince that, as he was engaged to be married, he could not possibly allow himself to be courted in England by all the ladies. Now that the King had so ostentatiously avoided him, the father, he was again beginning to invite his son "behind his back." The King was pursuing a double purpose: first, to divide father and son, second, to secure (according to an old English recipe) a member of the family here, who would serve him as spy and observer and whom he could use in his own interests just as he thought fit. His uncle had skilfully selected just that one of his sons who was most easily entangled, for such plans. The Crown Prince was a blind admirer of England and could not resist the charms of life in general nor of the beautiful women in particular of that country. The invitation extended to the Crown Prince was a " public insult " for him, the Kaiser, after all that had gone before. Her Majesty fully shared the Kaiser's opinion. The Crown Prince was to wire in reply that he was unfortunately unable to accept the invitation because of the visit of the King of Spain, who is to come to Berlin in the week between the 5th and 12th of November. General von Plessen was let into the secret later on and expressed the view that, considering the Crown Prince's character, he would be completely " taken in " by King Edward and by the English ladies. General von Plessen told me this very evening, that the Kaiser had given orders that he and General Löwenfeld were to stand by inconspicuously during the visit of the British Fleet to Swinemünde, in order to observe the course of events on the spot, and then to report. I have talked to General von Plessen and impressed upon him that his presence at Swinemünde would not remain secret and that it would make a very bad impression if he, with his intimate relationship with H.M., were to turn up there as the Kaiser's secret agent. In accordance with my instructions, despatched in cypher through the F.O., General von Löwenfeld has been advised to proceed to Swinemünde in civilian dress. Plessen will ask H.M. to refrain from sending him. During the last day of his sojourn at Wilhelmshöhe, Max Fürstenberg came to me and told me, in considerable excitement, that H.M. had spoken to him about King Edward in such terms that he was still quite mystified. He simply could not

repeat what the Kaiser had said. And H.M. seemed to have a
very low opinion also of the Austrian Ambassador in London,
Count Mensdorff. I told Prince Max Fürstenberg that the
Kaiser had apparently talked with him as though with a personal
friend and I hoped that, as such, he would keep H.M.'s words to
himself. In the evening, when we were alone, I told H.M. what
Fürstenberg had told me, and I implored H.M. to be careful.
The personal conflict between him and King Edward, I said,
could have the most far-reaching and disastrous consequences—
all the English were waiting for was that he should expose some
weak spot. And now, on the top of everything, there was this
unfortunate affair with the Crown Prince! Both their Majesties
are impressed by the Crown Prince's immaturity. The other day
I had a long talk with the Empress about it, and I told her that
as far back as two years ago, I had given the advice that the Crown
Prince should work with a Landrat or with the Oberpräsident
and work seriously, for hitherto he had only been playing, not
working, even in military matters. The Empress found all sorts
of reasons why it had not been possible hitherto, but she will now
do all that can be done to secure a decision of this kind in the
autumn. Your Serene Highness's support of this plan would
certainly have the best effect, and would secure the realization of
their Majesties' good intentions. With the highest esteem and
deepest respect your Serene Highnesses most obedient

Von Tschirschky.

The idea of sending two Adjutant-Generals to Swinemünde in
order to observe the behaviour of the English fleet there was indeed
not a happy one. Almost more childish, not to say infantile, was the
letter which Kaiser William wrote to his friend Nicky at the same
time, on the 25th August 1905: " I have ordered my fleet to
follow the British fleet like a shadow in the Baltic and, when it has
come to anchor at Swinemünde, to moor in the neighbourhood of
the British Fleet, to give them a dinner, and to make them as
drunk as possible, so as to get out of them what their intentions
are, and then to sail away again."

As a matter of fact, the English fleet was welcomed quietly and
politely in the usual manner by all the authorities at Swinemünde.
All the officers of our navy with whom I came in touch during my
life, distinguished themselves by their good manners and their
attractive personality and won everybody's affection.

The Austrian Ambassador in London, Count Albert Mensdorff, who is mentioned in our Ambassador, Tschirschky's letter, was

persona ingratissima with His Majesty. The Mensdorffs came of a little Lorraine family who were originally named Pouilly. During the French Revolution a Pouilly emigrated to Coblence, and from there drifted to Austria, where he succeeded in conquering the heart of Princess Sofie of Saxony-Saalfeld-Coburg. He was raised to the rank of Count so as to make the marriage possible, and received the name of the village of Mensdorff where he was born. Queen Victoria extended the unbounded love which she felt for her husband to all his relatives, to all who were in any way connected with the House of Coburg, and therefore also to the Mensdorff family. If a Mensdorff was invited by the Queen he received a special and very high rank. In this respect Edward imitated his mother. The Archduke Francis Ferdinand once told me, angrily, that on some festive occasion he had been placed in the same rank as an Austrian subject, the Ambassador Mensdorff, in England. The Queen and her son proceeded on the assumption that rank went according to the degree of relationship with the English Royal family. In England everybody, with true English self-assurance and English arrogance, considered this fully in order, Tories and Whigs, aristocrats and democrats. Kaiser William, although he was the most nearly related to the English Royal family of all non-English Princes, so that for this reason alone his rank could not suffer, was nevertheless annoyed that Albert Mensdorff was so very much fêted. Mensdorff, who, incidentally, was quite skilful and somewhat of an intriguer, naturally did not mind seeing "nice" Austrians preferred to the "wicked" Germans in English society. On the 8th of September, Tschirschky reported to me further:

I take the liberty of informing you of the following. His Majesty has just graciously condescended to tell me that H.R.H., the Crown Prince, has received a letter from King Edward in which the King complains that His Majesty had this year again hindered the Crown Prince's visit to England, thus making it clear that the Kaiser simply does not want the Crown Prince to come to England. The tone of the letter was not at all friendly. H.M. added that the Crown Prince had unfortunately not followed his instructions to mention the King of Spain's visit as a reason for declining the invitation, but, petulant because the pleasures in England had been denied him, had only mentioned the Imperial veto. H.M. now wants to write to the King direct, and to tell him quietly that the usage prevailing in all Courts, when Princes are invited, is to ask the consent of the head of the family beforehand. [*The publishers wish to dissociate themselves from the following observation which is included in order to preserve for English readers the full text already available in the German edition. This passage has historical value, not as a comment on the distinguished Englishman concerned, but as an indication of the Imperial Chancellor's point of view.*] Lord Lonsdale as usual, does all he can to kindle the antagonism between the two monarchs. H.M. tells me that Lord Lonsdale has complained to him that the King will no longer receive him at all because he is a friend of the German Kaiser's! Lord Lonsdale, so he says, has also confirmed the fact that the press campaign against us in England is led by the King in person. He, Lonsdale, had placed a number of articles, friendly to Germany, in the English press during the summer and had, for this reason, been called to account by third parties acting on behalf of the King. But he had firmly refused to put up with this action of the King's, and had let him know that if the King wanted anything from him, he could send for him as a Peer of the Realm and Member of the House of Lords. The German Embassy had not been skilful in handling the English Press. Count Bernstorff had worked with subordinate pressmen, and all he had achieved thereby was to hurt the feelings of the real newspaper chiefs. The Embassy had also wanted to place anti-French articles in English newspapers, but this had, of course, become known at once and had had exactly the opposite effect. Lord Lonsdale had further told H.M. that, together with a minority in the House of Lords, he was against the conclusion of the new Japanese Treaty, but that the Government had forbidden every demonstration in this direction. The treaty would be disastrous for England! Lord Lonsdale had spoken of the " Asiatic " and the " Yellow Peril " in this connection.

The pretentious boastfulness of the Earl of Lonsdale showed that King Edward was not wrong in calling this bankrupt nobleman and personal friend of the Kaiser's, " a great liar." The insinuation against Bernstorff was unfounded. Count Bernstorff, who was then Chancellor of the Embassy in London, and, later on, Ambassador in Washington, had, unlike Eckardstein, promoted the difficult relationship between the German Embassy and the English press with as much dignity as skill.

In June 1905 the long expected dissolution of the union between Sweden and Norway was announced by Norway. Relations between the two countries had never been really friendly since the Vienna Congress had soldered them together. Their relationship resembled one of those hopeless marriages such as are described by

Strindberg. It is difficult to say whether English policy helped to
bring about the final separation. In any case it was in England's
interest. During the eighteenth century, Sweden had inclined now
to Russia, now to France. In the nineteenth century she had
come under the influence of a dynasty of French origin and had
tended towards France right into the 'eighties. But since then,
strong pro-German sympathies showed themselves amongst the
chivalrous Swedish people. William II had taken great pains to
win Norway over. Like so many Germans, he visited that glorious
country every year. The song, *Aegir*, which, as a matter of fact, had
been written and composed by Phili Eulenburg, appeared under the
Kaiser's name. The Kaiser had erected a magnificent statue on the
Norwegian shore to the hero of the Norwegian Saga, Frithjof, who,
after overcoming endless dangers and difficulties, and despite the
resistance of her wicked brothers, Helgi and Halfdan, wins as his
wife the beautiful Ingibjorg, the daughter of King Belli. But the
political sympathies of the Norwegians, like their trade and shipping,
tended overwhelmingly towards England. The erection of a monument to the sturdy Frithjof has had just as little lasting effect as had
the present of a statue of the Great Prussian King to the United
States, the erection of a Goethe statue in Rome, and the erection of
a statue to King William III of England in London. When the
last mentioned monument was on its way to England, I showed the
Kaiser a cutting from the *Times*, according to which a question had
been asked in the English Parliament as to what the English
Government intended to do with this strange present. A quick-
witted representative of the Foreign Office on the Government
benches had replied, that the Government intended erecting the
statue of King William III, who had been a member of the House
of Orange, in front of an orangery. The Parliamentary report added
to this remark, " loud and general laughter." But even this did not
deter the Kaiser from his fondness for gratifying other peoples, and
states, by presents. The English expression, " to enjoy oneself,"
fitted William II, showing his amiable disposition. To be attentive
to others, to show himself generous and magnanimous towards
others, gave him the greatest pleasure. King Edward succeeded
in making Prince Charles of Denmark, the second son of King
Frederick VII of Denmark, and the husband of his third daughter,
Princess Maud, acceptable to the Norwegians, as King of an
independent Norway. The young Princess, who until then had
inhabited a charming cottage near Sandringham, felt no desire to
exchange her splendid and comfortable life in England for a much
less brilliant existence in melancholy Christiania (now called Oslo).

She told her father she would rather live on the smallest English, or even Irish farm, than sit on the Norwegian throne. King Edward, who with all his good-nature tolerated no contradiction from his family, replied to his daughter's prayers and lamentations: " Princesses have duties and not hobbies."

Prince Charles adopted the truly Norwegian name of Haakon with the number VII, for in legendary ages there had already been six Norwegian Kings named Haakon, amongst them Haakon the Old, who subjugated Iceland and Greenland in the thirteenth century. The young King Haakon's little son who was not two years old when his father was raised to the Royal throne in 1905 and who had till then been called Alexander, was re-christened Olav. King Oscar of Sweden felt the secession of the Norwegians very strongly, although he had striven after the laurels of a poet rather than those of a monarch during his long reign. When he spoke to me about it on his journey through Berlin, he was overcome by convulsive weeping and flung his arms round my neck and sobbed. I saw no reason for taking sides in this Scandinavian conflict after the separation was complete. When King Haakon landed in Christiania on the 25th November 1905, he was, at my suggestion, accompanied not only by English, but also by German battleships, and Prince Henry of Prussia, the brother of his Majesty, attended the coronation festivities.

Although the tone of the English press during the whole of the year 1905 had been rather hostile, and although King Edward's attitude had, to put it mildly, been somewhat impenetrable and malicious, nevertheless sensible opinions were also held on the other side of the channel. When an English naval officer gone mad, ex-Vice-Admiral Fitz-Gerald, explained in the *German Review* (of all papers), that a war between England and Germany would come soon and inevitably if Germany increased her fleet any further, this lapse was repudiated by most English papers, by some of them sharply. What was gratifying and what did create hopes for the future, was the quiet language and attitude of the Prince of Wales, who afterwards became King George V. The Ambassador Metternich wrote to me in this connection:

> I dined with King Edward yesterday and sat next to the Prince of Wales. The Prince talked to me about Arthur Lee's speech, which he described as a piece of clumsiness without evil intention. He relegated the idea of warlike intentions on the part of England against Germany to the realm of legend, and expressed himself quite vehemently against newspapers in

general, and against the *Times* in particular. The agitation
carried on by this paper, he said, was disgraceful, but the British
Government was powerless to do anything against such conduct.
He could not understand how people in Germany could believe
in England's warlike intention. A "rotten paper"[1] like the
Army and Navy Gazette was of no consequence whatever, just as
little as the *Court Journal* which, except for its self-bestowed,
portentous name had no more to do with the Court than the
Daily Mail. Warlike entanglements between England and
Germany were so opposed to the interests of the two peoples and
so contrary to common-sense that he, for his part, thought it out
of the question that there could ever be a war between them.
The biggest misfortune the world could suffer was, in his opinion,
a war between England and France, or between England and
Germany, or Germany and France. King Edward also had a
long talk with me, but without referring to anything of political
importance.

The fact that the Prince of Wales was more open-minded than
his father in his judgment of Germany and the German Kaiser, forti-
fied me in my policy towards the maintenance of peace. Time was
on our side. What mattered was to avoid reefs and sandbanks until
there was a change in the whole world situation, such as always
comes about from time to time, for πάντα εἶ everything changes,
and we were vouchsafed an easier and calmer passage.

Whether an autocratically governed or a revolutionary Russia
would be more useful to us might seem doubtful. Prince Bismarck
thought the former. Herbert Bismarck told me in 1884, when I
was sent to St. Petersburg as Councillor of Legation, that his
father had always adapted his Russian policy to the person of the
Tsar who happened to be governing. On the other hand it was
clear that whereas it was easier for us to be on good terms with a
Tsarist than with a republican Russia, because many more ties,
much more understanding and fellow feeling existed at the Russian
Court, in Russian society, and in the Russian bureaucracy than
amongst those elements who were fighting the autocracy, the rise
of these elements must nevertheless weaken the power of Russia.
In any case, Prince Bismarck was right in his prophecy that any war
between the three Empires would gravely endanger the three
Emperors. He would never have given a war against Russia so
anti-Tsarist a twist as Bethmann did. And he would hardly have
conducted the Bolshevik leaders from Switzerland back to Russia.

---

[1] English in the original.

That Russia's internal situation became the more threatening the longer the war against Japan lasted was beyond doubt.

The Russian Ambassador in London, Count Benckendorff, talked with great anxiety to his German colleagues about the further development of the Russian internal situation. He had told Count Metternich, amongst other things, that the Emperor Nicholas was, for the time being, still resolved to prosecute the war with Japan with all the means at his disposal. But this idea might be subject to sudden change because the most diverse influences were working upon the Tsar. It used to be quite different and the Tsar used to remain secluded, but now anyone who had a plan for the salvation of Russia could approach him personally. Representatives of the zemstvos and others, came with proposals and petitions to the Tsar all day. In reply to a question of Count Metternich's about the position of Count Witte, the Russian Ambassador replied, that now as before, the Tsar could not endure Witte, whose power, in view of his considerable personality, was nevertheless not to be underrated.

For Russia the year 1905 had opened with the step taken by the President of the Moscow zemstvos, Prince Trubetzkoi, who wrote an open letter to the Minister of Interior, the liberally inclined Prince Mirski, emphasizing the necessity of reforms " so as to avoid a revolution." Numerous demonstrations both by workmen and by the " intelligentsia " in favour of constitutional and administrative reform followed. The police tried in vain to stop them.

Every year at Epiphany the festival of the Blessing of the Waters was held by the St. Petersburg court with a special brilliance. What made an even deeper impression on the Tsar than the demonstrations was an incident that took place during this festival. When the salute was fired, several balls of grapeshot struck the tent in which the Tsar and his Court had gathered on the ice of the Neva. It has never been established how it was possible that this live charge could have been fired. Three days later there was a sanguinary collision between soldiers and a mass-deputation of strikers who were led by Father Gapon, an eccentric priest. The workmen, headed by Gapon who held the orthodox cross in one hand and a picture of the Tsar in the other, wanted to hand in a petition at the Winter Palace, with a list of all the demands and fundamental rights which Western democracy had long achieved, but which had never been publicly demanded in Russia (and were, incidentally, trodden under foot after the collapse, by the victorious revolution): freedom of speech, freedom of conscience, freedom of assembly, guarantees for personal liberty, popular representation, equality before the law, responsibility of ministers, compulsory education at State expense, income tax, etc. New socialist demands were also made, such as the eight hour day, the right to strike, measures against the oppression of labour by capital. A regiment of guards, rapidly summoned, prevented the demonstrators from reaching the Winter Palace. There were several thousands of dead. Amongst those arrested was the talented writer, Maxim Gorki, whose *Night Shelter* has aroused much interest in Germany too, where it was produced in a masterly manner.

Forty-eight hours after the clash, a military dictatorship was proclaimed in St. Petersburg under General Dmitri Feodorovitch Trepov. He was truly Russian to look at. His father had been a foundling child, discovered on the doorstep of a rich German merchant's house at Vassili-Ostrov, and had received the name Trepov (treppauf).[1] When old enough, he joined the Cadet Corps, rose to the rank of Colonel in the Army and, under the Tsar Alexander II, became chief of the St. Petersburg Police when he was still a Colonel. Vera Sassulitch's attempt to assassinate him in 1875 marks the beginning of the modern Russian revolutionary movement which emerges from below. Until then Russia had only known palace revolutions and aristocratic conspiracies. A Russian peasant once expressed it in this way to my friend Count Levashov, after the assassination of Tsar Alexander II. " In olden days only gentlemen were allowed to kill Tsars, but nowadays the smaller fry are fond of doing it, too." The speeches which the poor young Emperor Nicholas II addressed from time to time to deputations of workmen or peasants, were feeble and made no impression. Further outrages followed in rapid succession. It was only with difficulty that the Grand Duke Vladimir, the new Minister of the Interior, Bulygin, who was accounted energetic, and the Governor-General Trepov, escaped the bullets intended for them. Most of the big towns were the scenes of sanguinary street fights. In Russian Poland there were national Polish riots, as well as socialist disturbances.

The Grand Duke Sergei, brother-in-law and uncle of the Tsar, was murdered at the time when Prince Frederick Leopold of Prussia was staying at the Russian Court. After his return, the Prince told me that the news of the crime committed in Moscow, reached Peterhof, where the Tsar was staying, two hours before the evening meal. The Prince inquired whether dinner would be served, or whether

---

[1] *I.e.* " up the stairs."

the Tsar preferred being alone after such a blow of destiny. He received the reply that he should come for dinner in the ordinary way. The Tsarina, it is true, did not appear, but the Tsar and his brother-in-law, Grand Duke Alexander Mikhailovitch, were in the best of humours. Not a word was said about the murder of the Grand Duke. After dinner, the Tsar and his brother-in-law amused themselves by trying to edge one another down from the long narrow sofa, before the eyes of the astonished German guest. In the same hour the Grand Duchess Sergei, a Princess of Hesse-Darmstadt, entered the prison alone, in which the man who had murdered her husband was confined until his execution, which had been fixed for the following day. She asked him why he had robbed her of her husband in such a cruel manner. The murderer replied that he had nothing personal against the Grand Duke, and that he was grieved to have inflicted sorrow upon the Grand Duchess, but his principles made his deed a duty. When the Grand Duchess left the cell he bowed low before her, and kissed the hem of her dress. As is well-known, the Grand Duchess Elizabeth Feodorovna was thrown down a deep shaft by Bolsheviks at Alayagavesk, a little town in the Urals, in June 1918. Quicklime was thrown upon the still living, but broken and gasping body. The sister of the Grand Duchess, Princess Victoria of Battenberg, who was living in England, was able to secure the dead body through an intermediary. She had it buried in consecrated soil at the foot of the Mount of Olives in Jerusalem. George Sand rightly observed: " *Que la vie ressemble plus au roman que le roman à la vie.*" History records tragedies even more terrible than those created by the imagination of the greatest poets, Aeschylus or Shakespeare.

The drama of Björkö was to receive a satirical touch to its tragic elements. In the middle of August, I received a longish letter of apology from von Tschirschky, who accompanied the Kaiser on his journeys as representative of the Foreign Office. He naturally felt that he had been a complete failure during the Björkö meeting, since, being extremely afraid of displeasing the Kaiser, he had merely tried to say the things expected of him by his exalted Majesty. He had neither pointed out the harm that might be done by the addition of the words " en Europe," nor had he given any sort of warning against concluding a treaty between two states with such haste as would even appear absurd in a young lover, and, to add to this, he had not urged the collaboration of the German Imperial Chancellor and the Russian Minister of Foreign Affairs. In a letter marked " Private " and " Very confidential," he wrote to me that " in consequence of an urgent inner need " he must submit a few reflections, not having the courage to tell them to me by word of mouth. He owed me an answer, he said, to the question I had addressed to him, namely, why he had not kept me better informed about all that happened at Björkö before? He had omitted to do so because all his attempts to approach me in a non-official capacity (attempts that had sprung " out of his innermost heart ") had met with what seemed to him cool reserve on my part; in particular, neither he nor his wife had been honoured with an invitation to my " otherwise so hospitable house " of late, although they had regularly left their cards. In the winter 1903-4 he continued, he had spent almost the whole week in Berlin, without being invited to dinner by the Imperial Chancellor; this had doubled his pain, for he had hoped to hear some comforting words from me, after he had been " passed over " (to his deep regret) during one of His Majesty's shorter journeys. He disliked nothing more than the idea of inflicting himself upon me, nor would he ever dare to give the Chancellor advice, but his despondent mood and the reticence resulting from it were surely understandable. Two years ago, he said, I had reprimanded him officially because of a mistake he had made, and this reprimand had wounded him deeply, all the more so as he felt himself to be " a German nobleman and a Saxon Chamberlain " rather than an official. He would not, he said, venture to criticize me, but he did think that his " loyalty " and his " qualities as a nobleman " were insufficiently appreciated by me.

Then he went on to say: " I shall not mention how I have done everything in my power to maintain good relations between His Majesty and your Highness, especially in the last few weeks. It was no more than my duty. I want nothing for myself, I am not a climber, not, perhaps, through deliberate virtuousness, but it is not in my character. I have been with His Majesty close on six years and, as far as I am aware, I have never during the whole of that time said one word about myself or tried to secure any personal advantage. I do not want to oust anybody and have no ambitions to play a public part. If I harbour the hope that an Ambassadorship may be entrusted to me sometime, this is only natural, and I would desire it principally for my wife who is really born to something better than to spend her best years in Hamburg, where, as your Highness knows, life is devoid of charm unless one is a Hamburg merchant or a shipowner." At the end of his letter, Tschirschky begged me to consider his letter a " monologue " that surged up from the depths of his soul (he had once before, after sending the Kaiser's Swinemünde telegram to the Prince Regent of Bavaria, indulged in similar fussy and tearful complaints). He assured me that he would always, and with due respect, accept everything his superiors might decide with regard to himself, and closed with the words: " May your Highness forgive the length of this letter, but I hope it will seem but short compared with the length of the time during which I may be allowed to place my humble services entirely at the disposal of your Highness in your exalted office."

This petitioner's statement, that he did not strive for any better post than Hamburg, which he, " as a nobleman," despised so much, was of course not true. It was surely not on his own initiative that the Kaiser had repeatedly asked me whether Tschirschky would not be suitable for the London or the Roman Embassy. This little example shows how very difficult the conduct of affairs was made by officials, whose petty personal sensibilities and ambitions so greatly outbalanced practical considerations and proper regard for the greater interests of the Fatherland. And this evil, too, was doubtless a consequence of the personal policy that was carried out in so exaggerated a manner by William II. Not only did all officials who were devoid of character—and such exist in every land and under every regime—turn towards the Imperial throne as sunflowers turn to the sun, but all too many of them subordinated every other consideration to the burning desire to use the time they were allowed to spend near His Majesty to "stuff their own mattresses," to use an expression of Bismarck's, that is to say, to further their own careers.

Count Paul Metternich, who was afterwards Ambassador in London, was quite free from such tendencies when he accompanied the Emperor. He never moved a finger to oust Count Paul Hatzfeldt, who was Ambassador in London at the time, although he was himself eminently suited for the London post and although Hatzfeldt, being in a sad state of health, could be " demolished," to use a technical diplomatic term. Holstein and Kiderlen certainly had their great faults, but they differed from Tschirschky, Schön, Flotow, Jagow, *e tutti quanti* in that their purely political aspirations and energies were more strongly developed than their personal ambitions.

Another fault which I encountered only too often in reports of our representatives abroad, was the inclination to criticize foreign countries, foreign conditions, and leading personalities abroad, with exaggerated sharpness and, particularly, to be ironical at their expense with more complacency than wit. But this bad habit was, ultimately, also attributable to certain weaknesses of His Majesty's. Our representatives when writing their reports knew that a certain arrogant belittling of everything foreign, a certain, *sit venia verbo*, did not displease His Majesty, and that he was fond of laughing at bad jokes, particularly jokes against Princes, Ministers or even Members of Parliament who were antipathetic to him. I therefore found myself obliged to address the following circular to our missions abroad on the 20th May 1905:

> A report which I have before me, gives me occasion to remark that one-sided criticism of public life in foreign countries is a mistake which our diplomats, to my regret, make too often. Destructive criticism has no practical value. Positive work is the first duty of His Majesty's representatives abroad. Many an official in the foreign service of other countries showed what could be achieved by purposeful, unprejudiced, intense, and positive work. We too must endeavour to derive every possible advantage from conditions as they are. Thus, to give only one example, German exports should be adapted to the customs and wishes of foreign importing countries but without attempting to impose our own taste upon those countries. Frequent journeys over the country, personal activity on the spot, and frequent intercourse with the people of the country will help Imperial representatives to acquire a knowledge of the special conditions that exist abroad. They must do unbiased justice to varying opinions and usages and they must avoid making the standards of their own home, abstract principles, or subjective preferences, the measure of their verdict. To promote German economic and political interest must be the only aim. Lamentations about the faults of foreign countries and more or less successful ironical descriptions of foreign conditions are worthless. These directions will serve not only in drawing up reports, but also for general guidance.

Meanwhile the preparations for the Morocco Conference were well advanced. Agreements about the programme were reached on the 8th of July and the 28th of September 1905, between ourselves and France. These agreements showed that it was easier to come to an understanding with M. Rouvier than with his predecessor. An improvement in the atmosphere was also noticeable in French parliamentary circles. The undercurrent which existed since the Peace of Frankfurt naturally remained unchanged, but the surface had grown considerably smoother since Delcassé's retirement. In the autumn of 1905 the Deputy Millerand, who in those days was the leader of the French socialists and later on became a very nationalist Minister of War, Premier, and President of the French Republic, visited the German Imperial capital.

The Secretary of State, von Richthofen, reported to me as follows on his meeting with Millerand:

> M. Millerand paid me a visit to-day. He looks middle-class, not tall, plumpish, with good manners and very polite. He is on the way to a Workmen's Insurance Congress at Vienna with his wife; he is staying here for two days, leaves this evening, and is going to view the Dresden museums for a few hours to-morrow. It is his first visit here and he seems to like Berlin very much. He says he is very satisfied with the way he has been received here, and the way so many things have been shown to him, particularly by Herr Bödecker and Herr Freund. All official matters, he says, seem to him excellently organized. Politically, Millerand spoke of Delcassé with disapproval. After he had been sacrificed to Germany more concessions had been expected in the Morocco question and there had been some disillusionment. I replied that, essentially, only trivialities were involved, and I did not understand why there was so much difficulty about them in Paris; but that everything was, apparently, being arranged now. Millerand also remarked that it was a mistake if they believed in Germany that France and England intended to conclude an alliance. England had found it in her interest to present the matter as follows: " *L'alliance avec la Russie et bon amie avec l'Angleterre et avec L'Allemagne si elle veut.*" The better relations with Germany become, he said, the more will they be satisfied in France, and we hope—and I share this hope—that the Morocco discussions will, in the end, develop in a better atmosphere between the two neighbours. He said he had just been to Hamburg, and admired what German energy and activity had achieved here, and there. Germany seemed a particularly fortunate country to him for, merely by its weight and the plenitude of its power, as well as by the industry of Germans, it was exercising an influence everywhere abroad. In no utterance of Millerand's was even the hint of socialist opinions betrayed. His endeavour to remain a candidate for ministerial rank is obvious! I told M. Millerand that if your Highness had been here you would gladly have taken the opportunity of making his acquaintance.

CHAPTER XI

Delcassé's indiscretions—Preparatory work for the Morocco Conference—Russo-Japanese Peace negotiations—Witte's success at Portsmouth—Witte in Berlin and Rominten—during his return journey—Philip Eulenburg's letter about Rominten (September 1905)—Countess Witte's letter to Herr von Mendelssohn—The Grand Duchess Vladimir's letter to her uncle, Prince Henry VII of Reuss, on Russian conditions—The Grand Duke Cyril's marriage—Military manœuvres under the Kaiser in Rhenish Prussia—I am appointed Major-General à la suite with the uniform of the King's Hussar Regiment—Herr von Bethmann-Hollweg becomes Minister of the Interior.

DELCASSÉ, who had been judged so unfavourably by M. Millerand, was not to be consoled for his fall and the failure of his warlike plans. Hardly a month after his resignation, he informed one of the editors of the *Gaulois* that, at the last Cabinet Council he had attended before he resigned, he had urged his colleagues to place every confidence in England, and venture anything. Nothing, now that France had decided to abandon all naval competition with England, and never again to challenge her supremacy at sea, would prevent an Anglo-French alliance; this in its turn, automatically, would lead to improved relations between England and Russia. To these courageous words, so he stated, his colleagues had returned a timid echo: "But suppose Germany attacks us?" Whereupon he, Delcassé, had bluntly answered the timid Cabinet: "Let her attack us! We shall be in a position to strike back!" Delcassé closed his speech as follows: "France is making a mistake—and what a mistake!—in going to this conference."

Three months later Delcassé's indiscretions grew bolder. He announced in the columns of the *Matin* that, during the Morocco crisis, he had been in a position to declare in the Cabinet Council that England had promised, in case of an attack, to mobilize her fleet, occupy the Kaiser-Wilhelm Canal, and land 100,000 men in Schleswig-Holstein. That had been the reason for all his opposition at the Council. A few days later, Jaurès, the French Socialist leader, replied to this "revelation" that Delcassé had given the British Government the impression that he would go to any lengths. England had played a tempter's part in its dealings with this vain ex-minister.

Most French newspapers blamed Delcassé for having revealed state secrets. The semi-official Havas Agency declared itself authorized to describe as inaccurate the stories spread by the *Gaulois* and the *Matin* concerning incidents that had led up to Delcassé's fall. It also denied the details he had given of the Cabinet Council. At the same time, Reuter's Agency contradicted the *Matin's* statements about England's military promise to France.

The English Ambassador called on me to deny, on behalf of his Government, the truth of Delcassé's assertion. The English had not held out the prospect of military assistance, nor were they willing to land 100,000 men in Schleswig-Holstein. I replied to my friend, Lascelles, that I clung to the hope that neither England nor Germany would be led astray by French machinations into starting a quarrel "*pour les beaux yeux de la belle France*." An European war would be an unspeakable calamity. The semi-official *Norddeutsche Allgemeine Zeitung* published at my orders an article denying any influence on the improved Franco-German relations, which the last few months had achieved, to the *Matin* and *Gaulois* articles. But the semi-official *Kölnische-Zeitung* declared that the *Matin's* story could not be dismissed as ridiculous. The passionate sentimentality of M. Delcassé's foreign policy had almost plunged Europe into the most terrible of wars.

While the Algeciras Conference was in preparation, the political department of the Foreign Office became afflicted with petty jealousies and disputes. Most of them arose from Geheimrat von Holstein's inability to work with anybody else. At one time he had managed to get on fairly well with the Secretary of State, Richthofen, but at present he was making his life a burden. At the same time— Heaven knows why!—he had taken one of the best informed, most talented officials of the Foreign Office, Rosen, "*en grippe*." Rosen was then Secretary of Legation, later Ambassador, and finally after the upheaval, for a short while, Foreign Minister. Radolin, our Ambassador in Paris, imagined without any reason that I had intended Rosen to succeed him, and therefore, when the latter was sent for a few weeks to Paris to clear up a number of special problems, he did his best in small ways to make his life as difficult as possible. Geheimrat Kriege was Holstein's bosom friend at the time—too efficient a jurist to be a first-rate diplomat. The Secretary of Embassy in Paris, Hans von Flotow, whose official and political abilities were not on a level with his love of intrigue, did his best to add fuel to the flames of Radolin's anxious jealousy. There resulted a deplorable confusion among the *dii minores gentium* in all their handling of the eminently important Morocco question. I wrote as follows to the Secretary of State on this subject:

> My thanks for your news on the progress of the Morocco affair. It will be of decisive importance, both for our position in the world and for public opinion at home, if we come out of this question decently. This we can only do on condition that every official dealing with it—Rosen and Kriege—Radolin and the whole Foreign Office—put the Fatherland and its well-being first, and push all petty personal rivalries into the background. You must help to see that they do this and if necessary I will always support you with ruthless determination, without sparing anyone, whatsoever his official position may be. I will tolerate neither intrigue nor personal vanity.

Russia meanwhile, in her struggle against Japan, was nearing the end of her strength. The internal situation was becoming more threatening every day. The Tsar decided to make peace, against the advice of his councillors and of many generals, in particular, the Grand Duke Nicholas. After a fight in Moscow streets, which had lasted for several days, the authorities had succeeded, though with difficulty, in quelling what was no longer a revolt, but an actual socialist revolution. The police attempted to divert the excitement of the masses against the Jews, and terrible pogroms were the result. This only damaged Tsarism still further in the eyes of all humane and educated people, without achieving anything more decisive than a temporary relief for autocracy. In a Crown Council specially convoked, the Tsar decided for the peace party. He determined moreover to entrust negotiations to Witte, although he disliked him personally. These were held, under American auspices, at Portsmouth, a little American town north of Boston in the State of New Hampshire. Witte proved himself a first-class mediator. He spoke very bad English but succeeded, none the less, by means of his impressive personality, the Slav dexterity with which he handled his opponent, his untiring readiness to shake hands at any moment with all and sundry, in winning American sympathies. Later he told me how, through the whole of a certain afternoon, he had gone on shaking hands for hours, till his right hand ached the whole night long. He had, he said, rubbed it with opodeldok and begun again the next day. His success showed the truth of Talleyrand's saying, "*qu'avec un front d'airain et le sourire sur les lèvres un diplomate de race passe partout.*"

What helped Witte most was his great name. It is intolerable

THE TREATY OF PORTSMOUTH

The representatives of Russia and Japan as guests of Roosevelt on board the
President's yacht *Mayflower*, 5th August 1905
From left to right: Witte (the Russian Ambassador at Washington),
Baron Rosen, Roosevelt, Baron Komura, Takahira

to think that when Germany was forced to sue for peace we had no better negotiator to send to the victorious French in the Forest of Compiègne than poor Mathias Erzberger, of whom Pope Benedict XV (after several interviews with him in the spring of 1915) said to a gentleman of his entourage: " *Pare che questo famoso Erzberger sia molto bravo nel parlamento. Ma come, per Bacco, si mescola nella diplomazia per la quale mir pare non sia adatto a fatto?* "

At the Portsmouth negotiations the English did their best to help the Russians and deter the Japanese from presenting extravagant demands. Witte obtained far more in Portsmouth than anyone in Russia had hoped. I received a report from St. Petersburg that, thanks to his diplomatic skill, Russia had avoided a defeat after a lost campaign. The Tsar sent a most dignified telegram to General Linevitch, who had taken command of the Russian troops in Eastern Asia on the recall of the unfortunate Kuropatkin, thanking the Russian soldiers for their repeated bravery and self-sacrifice. This telegram read in old-style Russian, the style of Tsar Nicholas I: " Let the army be assured that I and Russia can appreciate the heavy losses it has sustained in this disastrous war." It was to be expected that, after this reverse, the Near East, the Balkan Peninsula, would become again as they were in the '70's and '80's the centre of Russian intrigues and aspirations, and that Anglo-Russian relations would therefore be much improved.

Witte on his return from America asked me for a private interview. I invited him to dine with me at Borchardt's, the old and famous Berlin restaurant, and there, from eight o'clock till after midnight, we thrashed out all the questions that concerned us. Witte's ideal was still a German-Russian-French alliance against the English. He tried to convince me that if we restored Lorraine to France, a grouping of this kind would not be impossible. He added that in such a case the French would quite possibly be willing to dismantle the fortifications of Metz. I replied that it would be almost impossible for any German Chancellor, any Emperor even— no matter who—to surrender Metz, which had cost so much German blood, and which had now been ours for a generation. I proceeded to ask him point blank if really he were so sure that the French, even should Metz be restored to them, would frankly and sincerely renounce all claims to Strasbourg. Witte, who like all serious statesmen despised petty evasions and half-truths, replied after a moment's reflection: " *Non! ils déposeront dès le lendemain des couronnes aux pieds de la statue de Strasbourg sur la place de la Concorde, en criant: Et Strasbourg? Et Strasbourg?* "

He tried to convince me after that, that a continental league

against England would not have been bought too dearly with the
sacrifice of Alsace-Lorraine.   I had to explain to him that the
German renunciation of Alsace-Lorraine would not be so easy to
arrange as the sacrifice of Sakhalin or even Korea.   It was possible,
after the event, to ask oneself whether in '71 Bismarck had foreseen
all the consequences of annexing Alsace-Lorraine.   Perhaps he had
underrated the passionate tenacity of French patriotism, the force
of the *idée unitaire*, the importance of the spiritual ties and memories,
which since the revolution had bound Alsace-Lorraine to the
French.   But however that might be, the thing had been done for
a generation, a German flag waved over Strasbourg Cathedral and
on the ramparts of Metz, and no revision of the Peace of Frankfurt
seemed possible.

From Berlin Witte went to Rominten where the Kaiser, who
relished nothing better than meetings and talks with eminent
foreigners, awaited him impatiently.   Philip Eulenburg, who had
arrived there some days previously, gave me his impressions in a
letter (24th September 1905) written on the eve of Witte's visit.
He could not, he wrote, conceal the fact that to him, who had said
his good-byes to diplomacy, the stagnant Court—stagnant in spite
of all its superficial movement and unrest—the intrigues, the smiling
masks of human marionettes puffed up with ambition and hope,
seemed strange.   He had to control himself the whole time so as not to
speak the truth quite dispassionately, without either rancour or design,
but in a way which nevertheless would have wounded and astonished
all the people in this environment.   " And yet," Eulenburg continued, " it is really very difficult to keep silence when His Majesty,
confidential as ever, explains to me the whole course of politics,
embellishing with a hundred details in each of which I can see
precisely where truth ends and fantasy begins.   At times he seeks
to impress, at times even to amuse me.   Sometimes it is altogether
purposeless, a habit like any other.   When we meet again, you and
I, we will check these little stories together and pass in review the
various incidents—Monaco, Bourgeois, Rouvier, the meeting with
the Tsar, etc.   Of them all the old antagonism between ' Uncle
Bertie ' and his nephew seems to me the most authentic, and at the
same time noteworthy, since the strongest spring of future action
—even political action—is always personal.   In some natures envy
is the touchstone, others are guided by revenge.   Both are most
probably active in ' Uncle Bertie ' who I do not think will ever have
forgotten his nephew's moral indignation over his ' gambling
Uncle.'   Besides, as the ruler of mighty England, he wants the
world to hear more of him than of his nephew.   Formerly his sport

was women, at present he plays at politics, and since, his whole life
long, sport has been his chief preoccupation, his enemies have every
reason to fear the mixture of sport and personal passion. Witte's
visit interests me much. I will describe it to you as soon as it
happens but I fear His Majesty will once again be too frank—and
that after all is not in my control."

Two days later I had another letter from Eulenburg (26th
September 1905):

> Witte arrived to-day (Wednesday), reaching the station at
> 12.30. I met him in a closed car, which disastrous vehicle was
> so noisy that an effort on my part was needed to hear Witte's
> mumbling voice. We were soon *in medias res* and it was really
> a pleasure to ascertain how precisely his ideas went with ours.
> Indeed he feels great solidarity with our interests. But what use
> is that unless Tsar Nicholas puts him in charge of affairs? We
> reached the hunting lodge by 1 o'clock. The Kaiser was pacing
> up and down in front of the door where he welcomed Witte.
> He showed him to his room with August Eulenburg. Dinner
> at 1.45. Witte on the right of the Empress. The conversation
> (on American manners and customs) flowed without being
> particularly enlivening. When the meal was over things were
> better. The Kaiser, Witte and I chatted and laughed most
> innocently. Then the Empress retired. At a quarter to three
> the Kaiser wandered up with Witte to his room and now (it is
> 4.30) I, in my room next door to them, hear the sound of their
> conversation growing loud and softer again by turns.... At about
> 4.45 the carriage was announced, and after a talk that had lasted
> nearly two and a quarter hours the Kaiser came out of his room
> with Witte. His Majesty whispered as he passed me, " He's
> been splendid," and I accompanied Witte to his own room. He
> seemed quite fascinated by the charm of the Kaiser's personality,
> and said to me with as much emotion as it lies in his nature to
> display: " *Björkö est le plus grand soulagement de ma vie!—le
> seul moyen d'arriver à une politique stable.*" (His Majesty had told
> him I was informed.) Naturally this led on to a discussion of
> the best way of handling the matter. I repeatedly urged that
> absolute silence was the first and most important necessity. The
> position of France would be most difficult, and unless absolute
> silence were preserved King Edward would exploit this difficulty.
> Witte spoke with peculiar vehemence against Benckendorff and
> Nelidov. To what extent will his influence serve to bring about
> a change? That must remain an open question. He seems to

think his visit to Rominten and talk with H.M. will be of use—
all the more so since he is in the position to lay all kinds of details
before his sovereign in the matter of English intrigue. Surely
these will affect the Tsar unpleasantly. Let us hope for the best.
His Majesty will communicate to you the substance of his talk
with Witte. It would take me too far afield to do so myself—
I have already done more than my wretched health really allows.

On 27th September 1905, Eulenburg reported further.

Last night at supper Witte had thawed completely, and
seemed to be quite at home; but I very much doubt whether
Hollman's endless story afterwards about a ship's chronometer
that had not been properly wound up, or the Kaiser's (equally
endless) about a buoy that ought not to have been the buoy it was,
can have served to amuse him very much. When on the top of
everything Richard Dohna began a solemn tale about an earthquake in which nothing happened, I remarked that there was
once a lady who had had such a shock in an earthquake (*erdbeben*)
and remained so sensitive all her life, that she fainted in a
station restaurant on hearing a waiter shout " strawberries "
(*erdbeeren*) at the top of his voice. This silly story caused so
much amusement that Their Majesties rose and, to Witte's relief,
went to bed—it had acted in a rush like a pill! Breakfast early
this morning at 8.45 at which Witte, with sleep still in his eyes,
had to be present. At 9 o'clock the Kaiser drove us both to the
station. Conversation mostly about France and how difficult it
is to set a bait tempting enough to entice that country. On our
way back, His Majesty went through it all again with me. As
always on such occasions he set too high a value on anything
that had any value at all.

To me also Witte had spoken very disparagingly about the
Russian Ambassadors to London and Paris, Count Alexander
Benckendorff and Alexander Ivanovitch Nelidov. He had said
that he thought the latter—at one time a pronounced supporter of
good relations with Germany—saw everything now with French
eyes, under the magic influence of Parisian *grandes cocottes* in whose
arms the seventy-year old Nelidov forfeited not only his health
but his former political acumen. Matters stood even worse as far
as Benckendorff was concerned. He was in constant financial
difficulties in spite of his rich wife, and Witte declared that, when
he was Minister of Finance, he had often had to pay his debts at
the request of the Empress-Mother, whose good will Benckendorff

had gained as a mazurka dancer. But now, he said, it was the English Government which had taken over the task of keeping Benckendorff's head above water. " *Il se fait payer par l'Angleterre.*"

Eulenburg's remark that the Kaiser set too high a value on anything that had any value at all was justified, though in the present instance, Eulenburg had himself made this mistake. Witte in his *Memoirs* relates (in direct contradiction to His Majesty's statement and Eulenburg's information) that William II had wanted to show him the text of the Björkö Treaty, but that he had declined, and only told the Kaiser that his words " filled him with gratification." Later when he learned from Lambsdorff the exact wording of the Treaty he was, according to his *Memoirs*, horrified. There is little doubt that Witte also, in spite of his wish for a possible continental alliance between Germany, Russia, and France, and in any case the maintenance of peace with Germany, disapproved of the surprise attack made at Björkö, which he regretted. He, like Lambsdorff, did his best to persuade the Tsar to abandon this Treaty. But Lambsdorff's methods were more insidious.

A letter which Countess Witte wrote at about this time to Herr Ernst Mendelssohn threw singular light on the state of affairs in Russia; the Countess begged us to intervene to obtain for her husband the post of Ambassador in Paris. She wrote with a certain *naïveté*, curious spelling, and in a French peculiar to herself, to the great banker who floated the Russian loans.

Cher Monsieur Mendelsohn,

Voilà je m'adresse à Vous de nouveau avec une grande prière, voilà en quoi elle consiste. Maintenant dans quelques semaines viendra le jour où on proposera à mon mari toute sorte des postes en Russie. Vue la santé de mon mari et la position intérieure de la Russie pour lui ce serait tout bonnement un malheur de se fourrer dans toute cette affaire. D'un autre côte vu que maintenant le poste d'ambassadeur en France devient non seulement pour la Russie mais au plus forte raison très grave aussi pour l'Allemagne, ce serait un vrai bonheur pour nous si l'Empereur nomme mon marie Ambassadeur à Paris. Je sais que l'Empereur est mécontent de Nélidoff et Sa Majesté trouve lui-même, vu les circonstances, qu'il faut nommer une personne qui a des autres vues. Vous nous ferez, cher Monsieur Mendelsohn, un veritable service d'ami si vous insinuerez cette idée à sa Majesté Votre Empereur. Nous sommes sûr que Votre Empereur trouvera cette idée magnifique et si Il insiste sur cette idée chez notre Empereur, notre Empereur consentira, mais seulement il ne faut pas perdre du temps. Je vous serai très reconnaissant si vous trouvez

le moyen de me faire savoir le résultat de Vos démarches. J'éspere
que vous ne m'en voudrez pas pour les ennuis que je vous cause, mais
votre amitié me donne le courage de vous déranger avec ma lettre.
Mes compliments les plus amicales à Madame Mendelsohn, Je me
dis Votre très dévouée,

Comtesse Witte.

This faithful wife was quite justified in thinking that it would
have been better for Sergei Yulevitch to be Russian Ambassador
in Paris than to waste his strength on Russian domestic policy; but,
as things were at the time, we were unable to satisfy her wish.

The last time that I dined with Witte at Borchardt's I told him
that he had been a good Minister under Alexander III, that he
would probably have been even more in his right place under
Nicholas I; but that though under the weaker Nicholas II he had
achieved considerable things as long as the Tsar remained, at least
in name, an autocrat, he lacked almost every quality necessary for a
parliamentary Premier. When Witte, not without pique, replied
that he was a convinced Liberal who looked forward to co-operation
with parliament and would know how to lead and manage the Duma,
I did not conceal from him my scepticism. It is true that on the
surface he was a Liberal; he possessed a remarkable European
culture; but his whole way of thinking was not only purely Russian
but old-style Russian. Fundamentally he agreed with the maxim
of Nicholas I, "unwilling bees must be forced." I added that,
once the sluice gates of the parliamentary system were opened, he
would soon be obliged to admit that a parliamentary Russia was not
for him. In any case he would do better to leave collaboration with
the Duma to some other politician. He was not a parliamentary
minister, still less a parliamentary chancellor; he lacked the cleverness, the *souplesse*. Witte's expression clouded. He was not
without vanity, but events were to show that I was right. To spare
his *amour propre* I had not told him how at Norderney I had judged
that his brutalities were all entirely on the surface; there was no
real energy, no iron inflexible will beneath.

A few weeks before Sergei Yulevitch was appointed the first
constitutional Russian Premier, the Grand Duchess Vladimir had
written to Prince Henry VII of Reuss, her uncle (who showed me
the letter in confidence), on Russian domestic, and in particular
Court, affairs, which were daily going from bad to worse.

MY DEAR UNCLE,

On Sunday 8th October (new style) Cyril got married to
Victoria Melitta von Coburg. The wedding took place at

Tegernsee and was celebrated by my sister-in-law's priest. The situation had become impossible and, since peace has come at last, Cyril was keeping his promise to wait till then. We have done all we could these last four years to hinder this marriage; but their love refused to be separated and so finally we considered it better both for Cyril's name and honour that the business should end with a wedding. We knew that the matter would not pass off very smoothly here, and were ready for some passing unpleasantness. But the blind vindictiveness and rage of the young Tsarina has, for sheer malice, exceeded everything the wildest imagination could conceive. She stormed and raged like a lunatic, dragging her weak husband along with her until he lent her his power and so made it possible for her to revenge herself on her ex-sister-in-law for marrying the man of her choice. The matter has been dealt with as though some terrible crime had been committed and judgment has been passed in this sense. Yet all these storms are directed against a Grand Duke, a war victim, a man who made a name for himself at Port Arthur, who has chosen an equal for his wife, and who, instead of deserting like the others, came here at once to take his punishment from the Tsar. It is too much that the son of the eldest uncle, of the man who, for the last twenty-five years has been the true and indefatigable head of the Army, who has saved the Tsar a hundred times, should be treated in this way at such a moment. One unanimous cry of indignation has been raised by all classes of the people. Vladimir has resigned as a protest at the indignity of the treatment meted out to his son. Even he, the truest of the true, says that he can no longer serve the Tsar with such anger against him in his heart. The troops are in a state of ferment at the loss of their beloved Chief, and I know the Tsar is being warned on all sides how dangerous it is to let his uncle go. That is why his answer has been delayed six days. But I do not think that Vladimir will consent to stay, even at the Tsar's request, unless our son is rehabilitated. What puts the last straw upon our patience is that Cyril came here with the Tsar's sanction to announce his marriage, and yet this very appearance here has now been made his chief offence. You, my dear uncle, will find this hard to believe; but, alas, here everything is possible; and when I add that this permission was given without the knowledge of the Empress you will be able perhaps to form a just idea of the position here. This is how it was done: scarcely had Cyril arrived when the House Minister came with an order that he must leave Russia at once. The Tsarina wanted him to go that very night but that would only have been possible in a balloon! Then he was dismissed the Fleet and the Army, he was to lose all uniforms and rank, to lose his regiment which was conferred on him at birth by his grandfather, to lose his appanage, his name, his title. He was to go into perpetual banishment. As far as his name was concerned the Tsar had to retract a few days later, since all the Ministers declared to him that this could simply not be done. And why all this? Because the Tsarina does not want her hated ex-sister-in-law in the family. All the other reasons given are mere formalities which could easily all have been arranged, since even if we did not desire this marriage there is nothing dishonourable about it. We have suffered much and still suffer, and in addition to it all I am worried about Vladimir's health. The Tsar knows that strong emotions are a danger to him. What does he care about that? Think of us.

Your MARIA.

I have previously mentioned the fact that the Grand Duchess Victoria Melitta of Hesse, a daughter of Duke Alfred of Coburg, and of the only daughter of Tsar Alexander II, had got a divorce in 1901, and four years later married her cousin, the Grand Duke Cyril Vladimirovitch. From that day onwards the Tsarina Alexandra, who was deeply attached to her brother, the Grand Duke Ernst Ludwig, began to detest her former sister-in-law. Left to himself the feeble Nicholas II would probably not have troubled to do anything against Cyril and his wife. But the strong will of the Empress would not rest till the young Grand Duke had been deprived of his regiment, his uniform and his appanage, in a manner most wounding to his parents, and sent into perpetual exile. The affair made a scandal in St. Petersburg and contributed in singular fashion towards making the Tsar appear a weakling, a man under his wife's thumb. The Tsarina, who, in some respects, possessed nobility of character, but whose disposition was unfortunate, passed for an hysterical fool and was thus described by the young Grand Dukes amongst themselves. From that time onwards the Grand Duchess Vladimir and her sons entertained towards the whole Court, the Tsarina, the Tsar, the sickly heir-apparent, those feelings which, from Phillipe Egalité to Louis Phillipe, the House of Orleans had harboured towards the elder Bourbon line. It is difficult to determine to what extent the "Vladimirovitch" contributed to the fall of Tsar Nicholas. On the latter's abdication the young Grand Dukes issued several public statements repudiating the Tsar and insulting his unhappy consort in a brutal and vindictive manner. This treachery did them little good. The monstrous wave of Bolshevism soon swept them, too, into the rubbish heap.

Looking back on this eventful year 1905 I must also recall the Imperial manœuvres in the Rhineland; my old regiment was quartered at Coblentz in the first half of September. A former comrade and friend, Adolph von Deines, in those days commanded the 8th Army Corps. He was one of the few really good men I have ever met. His sole fault was an excessive idealism, proceeding from his own goodness of heart and spiritual purity, and which assumed the like in other people. He was the son of a Hessian official, much attached to his Electoral dynasty in spite of its notorious sins and stupidities. His loyalty was truly Germanic. The father at first refused to allow his son, whose inclination and ability equally drew him to the Army to serve the Prussians as a regular. Not till Adolph became an officer of the Reserve did his father allow him to join the standing army. Though Deines' Christian name was really Adolph, his friends and all his mess-mates knew him as " Anton." He made an excellent officer who did equally well as Lieutenant of the King's Hussars and later, as Captain of the Zieten Hussars, renowned for the boldness of their horsemanship. Finally he was gazetted to the General Staff. Ever since we had been soldiers together "Anton" and I had remained close friends, though he could not conceal his dislike of diplomats, whom with a few exceptions, he considered either soft or treacherous. Deines was the favourite of Waldersee who liked his open manner, and may perhaps have felt that " Anton " was by nature inclined to be the easy instrument of those more cunning than himself. This brought Deines into conflict with Prince Bismarck while he was Military Plenipotentiary in Vienna. A conflict characteristic of both parties.

In December 1887 Major von Deines had sent in a report of a talk with the Emperor Francis Joseph, together with his own comments on the public opinion in Austria-Hungary, and its prevalent enthusiasm for a war of the Central Powers against Russia. Austrians firmly believed in an eventual victory shoulder to shoulder with Germany. The Austrian army without any German assistance would embark on a war with Russia only with the greatest anxiety and with the bitter feeling of having been betrayed by us. The mass of the people saw in a German-Austrian alliance a league of defence and offence for any eventuality. This feeling had not been artificially stimulated; it had come into being of itself—would have to be reckoned with. The whole Officers' Corps of the Dual Monarchy saw in us a rock of safety since our banners were accustomed to victory. Should we attack at once all doubts would vanish and in their place, enthusiasm and healthy ambition to emulate the Germans, would prevail. In answer to this report my friend Anton received an instruction from Prince Bismarck. The closing words of this instruction are so characteristic of the great Chancellor's manner that I reproduce them. " My reason for having laid before you briefly such considerations as guide me in my capacity as political adviser to His Imperial Majesty, are not the desire to convince you that they are right, but the wish to avoid the disagreeable necessity of asking His Majesty to break off official relations between the Foreign Office and yourself. I, not the General Staff, am His Majesty's sole adviser on Foreign Affairs." Bismarck had preceded the above with the following monumental sentence: " The most important question that can be asked on the policy of the German Empire is; are we, deliberately and consciously, to entangle Austria, and so Germany in an offensive war against Russia —a war that would lead at once to another, of defence, against France—that is to say the most extensive war at present possible on two fronts; a war which, even if we are victorious on them both, will bring us no appreciable gain and lead to no predictable consequence, except that the French desire for revenge might permanently be shared by the Russians? "

Honest " Anton " Deines could feel the breath of genius in these words. In the fullness of his heart he wrote to Bismarck, thanking him for his warning, and the guidance so graciously given, and promising faithfully that henceforth he would only act in accordance with His Highness's instructions. Deines told me of these words received in '87 from the Prince at the time when he was still Military Attaché, during my stay in Coblentz for the September manœuvres of 1905. They left so deep an impression on me that three years later, during the Bosnian crisis, they became an admonition and a directive.

My brother Adolph had recommended Deines to the Kaiser as a possible tutor for the Crown Prince. In a letter which my brother wrote to Deines in November 1894 explaining why he considered him the right man to educate the Crown Prince, he said:

What makes me think you suitable? You are, as King Philip said of Posa, one of the few who are good and cheerful and yet know all men. There is no danger of your taking your duties lightly, or becoming mechanical and blasé in the course of time; no danger of your turning the future Kaiser's head with parades, uniforms, and guard-rooms; no danger of your stimulating his memory and polishing the surface of his mind while you neglect the deeper traits of his character. I am confident that if the future Kaiser has the benefit of a few years of your example he will become what the Fatherland needs.

It would indeed have been hard to make a better choice than Deines—the pattern of a Prussian officer, brave and highly cultivated, strict with himself and kind to others, and what Goethe called, a true German. " Anton " died not long before the beginning of the World War, in great pain from the results of a dangerous operation. He said to the nurse who was attending him: " I do not complain about this suffering, but, dear sister, to die on the battle-field is more beautiful."

To my joy, in the course of these manœuvres, the Kaiser permitted me twice to lead my old regiment past the flag—at the trot and the gallop. When after the march past I pulled up left of His Majesty with the regulation volt, Deines who stood next the Kaiser said to me: " Your beautiful volt gives the Kaiser far greater pleasure than the longest memorandum you could draw up for him." Later I greeted the officers of my regiment, many of whom, within ten years, were to seal with their blood their loyalty to King and Country. The King's Hussars, commanded in the last century by Count Karl Lazarus Henckel von Donnersmarck, Count Edward von Oriola, Count Karl von der Goltz, the Freiherr Walter von Loë, Prince Henry XIII of Reuss, Karl von Colomb, Richard von Winterfeld, and Friedrich von Hertzberg, maintained its reputation in the World War and covered its proud flag with fresh laurels. At the end of these manœuvres, immediately after the defile, the Emperor handed me my brevet as *General à la suite*, with uniform of the Royal Hussars. Here is the text:

My DEAR PRINCE,
It is particularly agreeable to me to give you to-day a fresh proof of the benevolence of my feelings towards you by conferring upon you the rank of Major-General with leave to wear the uniform of King William I's Hussar Regiment (1st Rhenish, No. 7).
I remain, with special esteem,
Your Highness's benevolent and always grateful,
WILLIAM R.

The closing words " and always grateful " had been personally underlined by His Majesty, and the word " always " doubly underlined.

In March 1905 the worthy Freiherr Hans von Hammerstein, the Minister of the Interior, died of heart failure. Overwork was the real cause of his death, as of Richthofen's a year later. Hammerstein was so poor when he died, and widows' pensions were so modest in those days, that the dependants of this Minister of State had hardly enough to pay for the funeral and their removal to a little house at Lüneburg. When I compare this simplicity and frugality with the economic disorders and extravagance which began with the birth of our Republic, I should like to cry aloud to those now in power in Germany the words that King Evander addressed to Virgil's pious Aeneas as he conducts him beneath his narrow gables:

> " *Aude, hospes, contemnere opes, et te quoque dignum*
> *Finge Deo, rebusque veni non asper egenis.*"

I named Herr von Bethmann-Hollweg Hammerstein's successor. He had done well as " Regierungs-Praesident " in Bromberg and " Ober-Praesident " in Brandenburg. The Kaiser liked this appointment. Bethmann's honest, although it must be admitted, obsequious manner, pleased him. Less satisfied was Herr von Heydebrand, the Conservative leader in the Diet, who said to me: " We need a man of some strength and determination as Minister of the Interior—a man like Fritz or Botho Eulenburg, Puttkammer, von Köller. You've given us a philosopher, not a real man."

Bethmann-Hollweg was above all a doctrinaire; even as Minister of the Interior he would encroach upon my precious time far more than was necessary, with interminable memoranda in which, more academic than realistic, he set forth his plans for " idealizing " the Prussian State—for " strengthening the German *morale* " by an infusion of the Prussian spirit.

CHAPTER XII

The successor to Count Schlieffen, Chief of the General Staff—My talk with General Hellmuth von Moltke as we rode round the Water Tower in the Berlin Hippodrome—Count Hülsen, the Chief of the Military Cabinet, on Count Schlieffen's successor—The Kaiser insists on von Moltke's appointment—Hereditary Prince von Hohenlohe-Langenburg—Director of the Colonies—Erzberger's first appearance—The growing tension between William II and Edward VII—William II's letter on the subject of his talk with the English financier, Beit (30th December 1905).

ON a lovely autumn morning in 1905 I was taking my morning ride in the Berlin Hippodrome when I met my old friend the Adjutant General Hellmuth von Moltke. I was struck with the anxiety in his face. When we had galloped for a certain time side by side Moltke said that he would like to talk over a very serious matter with me quietly, and suggested that we had better slow down. We turned our horses' heads towards the " Water Tower " near to the entrance of the Hippodrome, and began to canter round and round it. Then Moltke told me that the Kaiser had decided to retire the Chief of Staff. His Majesty fully appreciated Count Schlieffen's ability, but thought that, at seventy-three, he had grown too old for his post which demanded not only great industry but undiminished physical energy. Count Schlieffen himself wished to retire. " But," continued Moltke, " His Majesty insists on making me his successor and everything in me dislikes the thought of this appointment." He explained to me quite clearly and lucidly that he had no desire for self-abasement but knew exactly how much he could do. He would always conscientiously discharge his allotted share of work on the General Staff and was, as he believed, efficient; nor would he hesitate for one moment to tell His Majesty that there could be no more " playing at manœuvres "—a source of so many well-founded complaints. After all, he said, as a young officer he had led a charge at Saint Privat in the van of the Alexander Regiment and proved that he did not lack courage. But an inner voice of warning told him plainly that he was not the right man for the task which a Chief of the General Staff must perform in war-time. He continued in his accustomed simple manner stressing every word he said: " I lack

the power of rapid decision; I am too reflective, too scrupulous, or
if you like, conscientious for such a post. I lack the capacity for
risking all on a single throw, that capacity which made the greatness
of such born commanders as Napoleon, our own Frederick II, or
my uncle. That master of theoretical strategy Clausewitz calls
Napoleon 'a passionate gamester'; he also says, and lately his
words have often been in my mind, that war has always something
of gambling in it, and that consequently a commander who cannot
gamble will probably lose the great game 'Victory.' Now in me
this taste is utterly lacking. I have not the temperament which can
risk all on a single throw."

Moltke seemed terrified at the idea of such a responsible post,
conscious as he was of his inadequacy, and aware of the danger it
might entail of ruining the Army and the Empire and tarnishing
his uncle's glorious name. He begged me most earnestly to use all
my influence with the Kaiser to make him abandon the idea. I
answered that, though I found it painful to refuse any request of
his, I had made it a rule never to interfere with the Army and
especially not in any question of personnel. No one was allowed to
interfere in any business of mine and I had to stand well apart from
the rights and obligations of others. Moltke expressed his regrets
but understood and approved my motive. He left me with a
vigorous hand-shake.

On the afternoon of that same day I met Count Dietrich Hülsen,
the Chief of the Military Cabinet, in the Wilhelmstrasse. Like
Moltke, he was an old friend. I told him of our morning's talk.
Hülsen answered in his quaint Berlin accent: "It only shows how
sensible ' Julius ' is." (For some reason or other, Moltke was
called " Julius " by his friends.) " He would never fit into the
Red box on the Königsplatz. It's a mad idea of H.M.'s." Suddenly he became very serious. " It will be very difficult to get it out
of his head though. Whenever I suggest a new General, even for
the most important Army Corps—for Metz or Posen—and it
happens that the Corps in question is not engaged in Imperial
manœuvres, His Majesty agrees right away. But if it's a case of
Commanders whose posts bring them into frequent personal contact with him—Bodyguards, for instance, or Commandant to
General Headquarters, or Chief of the General Staff, His Majesty
is apt to be touchy. He seems to find it almost intolerable to have
any but his personal friends, or people he specially favours, in such
positions."

I replied to Hülsen that in his choice of military chiefs the
Kaiser unfortunately behaved very differently from his grandfather.

COUNT ALFRED SCHLIEFFEN

Chief of the Great General Staff from 1891 to 1905

The latter when he ascended the throne had made Manteuffel, who later became Field Marshal, the chief of his military Cabinet, in spite of their violent and frequent clashes of opinion in the days when Manteuffel was aide-de-camp to Frederick William IV. When Manteuffel heard of his impending promotion and reminded the old king of these, William I replied: " It is because you served my brother so faithfully that I have chosen you for such an important post." In just the same fashion the celebrated General von Voigts-Rhetz, one of the few Commanders the old gentleman really disliked, enjoyed a speedy promotion, was appointed Chief of Staff in the first Prussian Army in 1866, became Governor-General of Hanover, and in 1870, Commandant of the 10th Army Corps. I asked Hülsen who, in his opinion, besides Moltke would be suitable for the post of Chief of Staff. He particularly mentioned Karl Bülow, the General in command of the 3rd Army Corps, who subsequently became Field Marshal, but added at once: " The Emperor won't have him, he says he's stubborn." He then mentioned two other Generals—Bock von Polach who commanded the 9th, and von Falkenhausen who commanded the 14th Army Corps. He also suggested Colmar von der Goltz, General Hindenburg, General Eichorn, and General von Voyrsch, but added, with every name, that for this, that, or the other reason the general in question would never suit His Majesty. The Kaiser called the one a drawing-room strategist, the other a *raisonneur*, the third a visionary. This, by the way, was the first time I heard the name of the great victor of Tannenburg, the subsequent Field Marshal, General von Hindenburg. In the end Hülsen told me he had no objection, would indeed be glad, if I tried to dissuade His Majesty from appointing von Moltke.

The same day I wrote the Kaiser a letter more or less to the following effect: he knew from long collaboration with myself how far I was from wishing to interfere with military and personal matters; but General Moltke had told me categorically and with the utmost candour his excellent reasons for not feeling himself equal to this post, whose importance for the Army and the safety of the country was supreme; I therefore begged His Majesty, most urgently, to reflect again and if possible make another choice.

The Kaiser replied with a brief letter, followed by a long and most gracious conversation. My suggestion, he said, had in no way given him offence; he saw in it only a fresh proof of my zeal and devotion to duty. He also realized that Moltke was unwilling. His refusal did honour to his modesty but could in no way change His Majesty's decision which was well-considered and irrevocable, and would therefore not lack the divine blessing. The Kaiser reminded me that I too had declared myself, at first, most unwilling to take over the post of Secretary of State at the Foreign Office, which I had only accepted in the end after having overcome many scruples. Nevertheless I had filled it very well. He was convinced Moltke was equally capable. It is known that in Prussia all military appointments were made by the Emperor in his quality of Supreme War Lord, without needing to be countersigned by the Minister of War, and mainly at the suggestion of the Military Cabinet. This principle, under so wise and experienced a sovereign as William I, had very much in its favour; it had even contributed towards producing in the Prussian Officers' Corps that spirit which had won us three wars. Under William II, who was often just the opposite of his grandfather, the drawbacks of the system became apparent.

In November 1905 the Director of Colonies, Stübel, resigned. The Kaiser suggested as his successor the Hereditary Prince Hohenlohe-Langenburg, with the proviso that he would be particularly pleased if I could express my agreement with his choice. I have never been able to find out who put the idea into the Kaiser's head of proposing Ernie Hohenlohe for such a post. This worthy man, whose sole recommendation was the fact that he was very well connected, had ruled the Duchies of Coburg and Gotha as Regent from 1900 to 1905 on the death of Duke Alfred of Coburg. He had no idea that in these days it is easier to "rule" a Thuringian petty State than administer a rather difficult Government Department, demanding industry, administrative experience and a capacity to answer questions in parliament, some of them very inconvenient ones. Ernie Hohenlohe had not only married an English Princess, the daughter of the late Duke of Edinburgh, the second son of Queen Victoria, but was himself the son of a Baden Princess and the cousin-german of the Kaiserin, whose mother had been a Hohenlohe-Langenburg. All this did not prevent the Kaiserin, who was always dutiful and amiably disposed towards myself, from giving me a gentle hint in her own prudent fashion. She suspected that Ernie wanted to treat a Colonial Department as a jumping-off place for eventual promotion to the Chancellorship. "But poor little Ernie," she added smiling, "would never be equal to that." I still consider this suspicion of Her Majesty justified. I consider it even quite possible that Holstein was involved in this intrigue, since he knew the political helplessness of the Hereditary Prince of Langenburg, and hoped he would be as wax in the hands of an old and experienced diplomat with whom he had been intimate for years. But whatever the truth may have been, though I accepted the Hereditary Prince as head of the Colonial Department, I refused in this, as in so many other manœuvres of the kind, to allow my judgment to be affected. I only made one stipulation. Ernie, like his father, the Statholder of Alsace-Lorraine, was a very zealous Protestant, and I impressed upon him the necessity of performing his official duties, which brought him into close contact with the Catholic Mission, without sectarian bias.

A few weeks later I had an opportunity of practising what I had preached. The principle of complete religious tolerance is one from which I have never departed. Schönstedt, the Minister of Justice, had resigned for reasons of health. He was succeeded by Dr. Beseler, the President of the Oberlandesgericht at Breslau, a capable jurist. Beseler came of a well-known Holstein family of savants, whose most famous member was William Hartwig Beseler—President of the Schleswig Diet in 1844, of the Schleswig-Holstein Provisional Government in 1848, member of the Assembly of Statholders and of the German National Assembly. The President of the Oberlandesgericht in Kiel, Dr. Vierhaus, was transferred to Breslau. As Dr. Vierhaus' successor I suggested Peter Spahn, the Reichstag Deputy to the Royal Ministry of State. At first I encountered strong resistance. Most of my colleagues had doubts about entrusting that responsible position in an entirely Protestant Province to a member of the Catholic Centre Party. I resisted these objections, on the principle that if the Ministry of State thought nothing of sending Protestants to the Rhenish Province, Westphalia, and Upper Silesia, there seemed to me no reason why a Catholic should be found unable to work successfully in a district with a Protestant majority.

I should also like to mention the fact that in the same year, 1905, the Deputy Mathias Erzberger became publicly known for the first time. The *Kölnische Volkszeitung* had published a series of attacks on our whole colonial administration, which it accused of having given false information on the Cameroon Railway, and of using Government funds for private literary publications. The administration denied this statement as "empty gossip" and convincingly disproved it with documentary evidence. The *Kölnische Volkszeitung* had to admit that its informant's statement had been untenable. It transpired that the libel had originated with the Deputy Mathias Erzberger. This wretched man, who came to such an evil end, after having done so much damage, began his political career with muck-raking.

In the late autumn of 1905 I got several letters from Metternich in London dealing with the personal relations between our

Kaiser and his uncle, King Edward VII. These were, unfortunately, not at all cordial. Already on the 2nd of October, Metternich had written as follows during his autumn leave:

Lascelles, as you know, has reported to His Majesty King Edward a conversation which he had with His Imperial Majesty, the Kaiser at Homburg, on the personal feeling between the monarchs. A few days ago the Ambassador received the King's reply through Lord Knollys. I have just seen Lascelles in Berlin, and he communicated parts of the reply to me in confidence. King Edward begins by declaring that he has no quarrel with H.I.M. and no desire to have any. It was impossible to arrange a meeting at the time of his visit to Marienbad because every day his programme had been fixed for his cure. The King considered every point about which H.I.M. complained to be without foundation. He, on his side, asserts that everywhere His Majesty the Kaiser is trying to make his influence felt against him. This brief resumé will show you that the time is not yet ripe for any really effective talk of reconciliation between the monarchs. The more calmly H.I.M. behaves in face of his royal uncle's displeasure the more he will put the latter in the wrong, and the sooner will a more cordial relationship be possible between these two royal gentlemen. I know for a fact that, even now, leading English statesmen deplore, for political reasons, the personal discord between King Edward and the Emperor. The sooner they can be made to realize that our Kaiser is not at fault, and that political difficulties may arise out of the present strained situation, the sooner they will try to intervene and approach King Edward themselves. King Edward's subjects have not the slightest desire to crack their skulls in a quarrel with the Germans merely because an uncle dislikes his nephew. His Majesty King Edward is intelligent enough to give way as soon as he feels that things have gone too far. But the English must discover it for themselves. Should we take any steps that could be interpreted as an attempt to prejudice the English against their King, he would have the whole nation at his back against us. It seems to me altogether out of place to drag these personal differences into the newspapers. In the present instance it would be little short of disaster. Now as before, I shall continue to act here without partisanship and take every chance of pouring oil on troubled waters. Should His Majesty King Edward approach me on the matter of inviting the Crown Prince, I shall most tactfully give him to understand that it is not a very friendly proceeding to invite a son behind his father's back, while at the same time avoiding a meeting with the latter. More especially when the father has been informed that dealings of any kind with him are not wanted. I cannot however use the argument that it is just as necessary for the Crown Prince to remain in Berlin at the time of the King of Spain's visit as for the Prince of Wales to be present for the Spanish King's reception in London, since King Edward, before inviting the Crown Prince, had already informed himself in Madrid as to the date of the Spanish visit to Berlin, and invited the Crown Prince to come to England after it was over.

I deplore the hostile attitude of an influential section of our press towards the Anglo-Japanese Agreement. The wording of this Agreement exactly corresponds with our declared policy: integrity of China, maintenance of the *status quo*, guarantee of the present possessions of separate Powers in the Far East, equal trade facilities for all. We must wait and see if the spirit of this new Agreement is directed against our interests. It is, from our point of view, both useless and dangerous to set up German-Russian opposition to this English-Japanese Agreement. We should be forced in any Russian-English war, to play the same part as would France if England declared war against us—*i.e.* we should pay for the broken crockery. A German-Russian *rapprochement* ought to consider France not England. It should decide either to leave France out in the cold or induce a more cordial relationship with her, though in spite of all, it is never out of the question that she would turn completely to the English. We have nothing to hope from any *rapprochement* with Russia at England's expense. That could only be dangerous and harmful, for the simple reason that, as I permitted myself to say some time ago, no Russian help against England would be worth more than the help of the man in the moon. Russia has no Fleet, she cannot protect our harbours and our trade; her Army would be of no use to us against England, and we might, under certain circumstances, turn the Japanese against us and lose Kiaochow. We ought, therefore, to leave the Anglo-Japanese Agreement alone as far as possible. Let the Russians get excited about it—they have good reason to be!"

Metternich was only too right in censuring the continual tactlessness of German newspapers about the English. It was inexcusable to drag into public discussion the differences between uncle and nephew. It was clumsy to open a press campaign against the Anglo-Japanese Agreement as such, and with arguments that were anything but felicitous.

On 19th October I received further news from Metternich on the same unsatisfactory theme. This time his letter was marked " Very confidential."

> From certain hints dropped in Court circles since my return, I conclude that King Edward's displeasure with His Majesty can be attributed to more than politics. A greater part of it arises from some expressions which our Imperial master seems to have used this year at Kiel in the company of foreign— particularly American—visitors. This kind of remark is sure always to come back here to roost, and as a rule it returns much exaggerated. It is said that the Emperor talked freely in yachting circles about the " looseness " of English Society, and in particular, about King Edward's relations with Mrs. Keppel. King Edward is very touchy on this subject and this seems to have annoyed him especially. I am not writing this as mere gossip but to keep you as closely informed as possible about this most regrettable estrangement between two closely related sovereigns. I do not think that for the time being anything very useful can be done to reconcile these two exalted personages. Some time ago Count Seckendorff wrote to the King that it was his duty to make peace with the Emperor. The King, when he received this letter remarked that it was a piece of impertinence to try to tell him what his duty was. So much for this unpleasant subject. Let us hope there will be no German press campaign against Lord Lansdowne as a result of the article in the *Neue Freie Presse*. It could not only fortify the Minister's position here, but would help his party as a whole and injure the Liberals, who are publicly working for better relationships with Germany.

On the 3rd of November 1905 I received the following lines from Metternich: " I know positively, from the most reliable source that King Edward desires a meeting with the Emperor at the beginning of next year ' unless anything should happen to prevent it.' I suppose—but only suppose—that he intends to invite him to England. Of course it may also be possible that King Edward will propose the Mediterranean. I would most urgently advise you not to mention this to anyone, not even to Lascelles." Metternich added the following in regard to the situation in Russia: " I do not know whether your information tallies with mine—that Russian autocracy is in danger. I am convinced that autocracy is lost. Even if once again revolution could be violently repressed—

though it does not look as though it will be—it will only have
broken out with fresh armed violence within six months. The
unrest is too general, the discontent too widespread, to make it
possible to restore order on the old lines."

At about the same time I wrote to Richthofen on our strained
dynastic relationship with London.

> When I left His Majesty at Coblentz he no longer seemed to
> have the intention of writing to King Edward directly, especially
> in view of the fact that he had talked quite frankly to the Am-
> bassador, and even, to a certain extent, to the English military
> attaché. Tell Lascelles that I share his view that the unreasonable
> hostility between the two peoples is diminishing little by little.
> It must, just because it is so entirely unreasonable. All the more
> necessary therefore to do everything in our power to allay any
> personal difference between the two sovereigns. I would do
> anything I could to bring this about, and I hope that my task will
> be made easier by my old and sincere personal attachment to
> King Edward. I am convinced that Lascelles, who is as aware
> as I am of the finer side of our Emperor, will do his best to assist
> me. The chief thing is that there shall be no further pin-pricks
> on either side. Let there at least be mutual reserve, not irrita-
> bility and provocation.

On the 30th December 1905 I received a long letter from
William II dated from the Neues Palais. In it he reported a conversation he had had with the London financier, Beit. Beit, a
native of Hamburg, had acquired a gigantic fortune in South
Africa. King Edward, who had a marked predilection for very
rich people, had admitted Beit into the circle of " his personal
friends." Beit was a fellow-townsman and friend of my old friend
Albert Ballin, who had often described to me this original, and, in
his way, important man. Beit, for all his millions, lived in a comparatively small house, every room of which was filled with Old
Masters. There were Titians, Rembrandts and other masterpieces
in his bedroom. His Majesty wrote to me as follows:

MY DEAR BÜLOW,
Yesterday the notorious Stock Exchange crony and specu-
lator of H.M.E. VII, Mr. Beit, paid me a visit. His ostensible
object was to present me with the illustrated catalogue of his
Art treasures—the catalogue, incidentally, was made by the
good Bode. After I had duly admired everything and shown
him the apartments of Frederick the Great, the conversation

turned to Morocco, and relations between England and Germany. When I remarked that it was very gratifying to see how, both here and in England, people were busy holding meetings, striving to diminish the friction, etc., he agreed with his usual vehemence, adding that it seemed all the more satisfactory since England wanted nothing of us, except that we should live on good terms. The only black spot was Morocco. When I asked him why, he replied because the view prevailed in England that we wished to go to war with the French for having signed an Anglo-French agreement and concluded the Entente Cordiale. I said that was utter nonsense, that the English could conclude as many Entente Cordiales as they liked, it would be as great a matter of indifference to us as the Franco-Russian Alliance, which had not upset us in the least. As for the Agreement, England had ceded her interests to France at the expense of other states and of their interests, thus inadmissibly violating the Madrid Convention. This would not do. Tunis and Algeria showed how other states were faring under French protectorate. ("And so," added Beit, " did Madagascar.") That threatened us all in Morocco and we could not admit it. Besides, it was really rather ill-mannered that no one had considered it correct to give us even the barest information about an Agreement in which our rights were ignored. Finally, there were the English intrigues in Paris revealed by Delcassé. These, in themselves, were enough to spoil our temper. We felt as though in the presence of two foot-pads who had agreed to garrotte us in the midst of a peaceful walk. What could we do but feel for our revolvers? Here Mr. Beit interrupted me excitedly, declaring that as far as the offer mentioned in Delcassé's revelations went—the offer, that is to say, of armed assistance—" it would only apply in the case of an unjust German attack on France." England, by the Entente Cordiale, considered herself bound to France in the Moroccan question and would support French claims, as she was pledged to do in the Agreement, since this was one of its conditions and she wanted above all else to keep French good-will. In the case of a Franco-German war, England would consider herself pledged to help the French at once and would certainly do so. But no one in England, said Mr. Beit, would ever dream of going to war with Germany and certainly not of attacking us *à l'impro-viste*. The whole nation was opposed to that, and would insist on good relations with Germany. He added that the Government also, whose members were his personal friends, was entirely of the same opinion, and would do its very best to promote a

friendship.   But it was extremely important that the Moroccan
question should be shelved.   It weighed on the English like a
nightmare, because it might so easily be the cause of a war between France and Germany.   When I repeated that there could
be no question of such a war; that we could easily come to terms
with the French if only London would leave them alone, Beit
replied that in France they were almost equally convinced that
England was on the eve of a war with Germany.   Rouvier, whom
he had visited a few days before, had said the same; in his
opinion the Conference would run its normal course but he
feared surprises " *car il est incontestable qu'il y a quelque chose dans
l'air.*"

Beit had ascertained that in Paris they were secretly preparing
for war.   And not only this—even the officers of the Reserve had
received their marching orders for the end of February, at which
date they supposed the war would break out.   Everywhere preparations had gone as far as they could go, without downright
mobilization.   The feeling in Paris had been grave, restless, but
firm and resolved.   The panic of last spring had passed and the
certainty of English aid is inspiring confidence.   I replied as
follows: " Delcassé's revelations have left no doubt in our
minds that England is on the side of France.   We know that
England will always be found at the side of our opponent, whoever that opponent may be, but this whole French war scare is
absurd, bordering on lunacy.   If the French have made up their
minds to behave decently and ' like gentlemen ' at the Conference,
they will meet the same behaviour from us."   I further expressed
the hope that we should reach " a good understanding."   There
was no reason at all for a war or any fear of sudden attack on our
part.   But the cause of all this trouble was not to be sought in
France but in London.   It was this accursed English system of
deliberate, organized agitation—the lies, the calumny, spread by
England throughout the press of every country—by means of
which she tries to incite the whole world against us.   " Do you
really think the English Government does that? " asked Beit.
" No," I answered, " but English capital, in the hands of rich
individuals, who in this way do an indirect service to their
Government.   I knew from a French source that the English
had spent 300,000 francs in a single year in the Paris press for
anti-German articles."   Beit admitted this to be a fact though he
had not heard the sum I mentioned.   I added that the Russians
had done the same, and that they kept at Paris a special secret
fund for use against us, and I gave him the exact figures—

360,000 francs—to which Beit added, "Monthly!" I said I knew that the same was being done in Belgium, where the Liberal Party chiefs, who would have liked to be on friendly terms with us, complained that they could not guide their press, which was "bought" *en bloc* by the English, and spoon-fed with anti-German propaganda. The same might be said of Russia, where influential papers were "bought" and supplied with poison against us. Besides these operations abroad, there was a continual and systematic poisoning of the well-springs, in countless English reviews, where people who signed themselves, "Calchas," "Diplomaticus," "One Who Knows," "Vates," etc., served their English readers with the most unheard-of, shameless lies about Germany, and calumnies against myself. None of all this got contradicted and therefore it was easily believed. "Yes," Mr. Beit exclaimed, "Now, if only one could pin them down— find out who these scoundrels really are. It has often infuriated me too." When I replied that we had long known these gentlemen's names, he looked astonished; but his eyes grew even rounder with surprise when I mentioned Vesselitsky, Toklevski, Tatischeff, and Delcassé's private Secretary. "Goodness gracious! But I assure you, they know nothing of this in England," he replied. Then he added that I had every reason to complain, that the press was behaving itself unwarrantably and was really mainly responsible for the state of things to-day. *Peccatur extra et intra.* Unfortunately it was only too true that much English money also had been spent in the foreign press on low and evil purposes. But he hoped that, now, we were at the beginning of a sincere *rapprochement*, and promised to use all his influence to put an end to press incitement and calumny. He would have all the more pleasure in doing this because what I had said had shown him how sincerely I wanted peace, and that I had no intention of attacking France, as they had persuaded him I had in London and Paris. H.M.E. VII was also a determined peace-maker. Only a short while ago an officer addressing His Majesty on the subject of the South African War had said that the next war would be a better one because England was so much better prepared. Whereupon H.M. had cried out:[1] "There shan't be any more war. I won't have any more war. Peace, peace, peace!" That was the feeling that inspired the whole British Government, the Stock Exchange, the City, and British business men in general. Nobody wanted war. They were only a little anxious because of Morocco, for if the French should

[1] English in the original.

happen to be attacked there, they would be compelled to rush to their assistance. Beit assured me that he would allay this anxiety in London. I added the request that he should hasten to take some steps to calm the excitement in Paris also. In spite of all our good intentions, our sincerity, our love of peace, the danger would persist there too, if the French, counting on English help, went on letting themselves be excited by London. They might adopt such an obstinate, reprehensible and provocative anti-German attitude that in the end national honour would be involved, and for honour's sake there could be no appeal save to arms. Then if we drew our sword, England would have her chance of intervening on the pretext of a " sudden unlawful attack." It would be monstrous treachery for anyone to work to bring this about. Mr. Beit declared at once, " That must never be allowed to happen. I shall say in England that in Berlin they only ask that London should leave Paris alone, so that the French may make an agreement with the Germans and discover a *modus vivendi*. England had made her Entente Cordiale without being disturbed by Berlin, and she ought, in the name of common decency, not to raise any difficulties for Germany if Germany wants a similar agreement with France. Indeed, London ought to be helping Berlin in Paris." To what he had already said on the English Government's wish for peace, Beit added that there was one person who did want war and was doing his best to prepare for it down to the last detail—Admiral Sir John Fisher. He had said only the other day,[1] " We are now quite ready and as powerful as possible, the Germans are not yet ready and are weak, now is the time for us, let us hit them on the head." I replied that that was just what I should have expected from Sir John Fisher, and that I had taken the necessary precautions. Since November 1904 I had regarded all orders to the British Fleet as preparations for mobilization. " Well," answered Mr. Beit, " you mustn't take it too much to heart, you know. Fisher is a firebrand but he doesn't count for anything in politics. He's got to obey the Government. Even if these Admirals do make such speeches after dinner, it's better not to take them too seriously. For example, there was that absurd threat of landing 100,000 men in your country. It's perfect nonsense." I replied that it was not nonsense at all but, given the colossal numerical superiority of the English Fleet, quite feasible along the Danish coast, where that Fleet had reconnoitred this summer. " Indeed," Mr. Beit exclaimed, " is that possible? Yes, but if they

[1] English in the original.

land, you'll kill them all." "That's another matter," I answered, "and essentially our own affair." He exploded with laughter. "Well," he said to me at parting, "you try and arrange this Morocco business with the French, and you won't have any trouble with England. You leave it to me and I'll see that people get the truth in London." "Go for our chief opponents there," I told him—" Mr. Moberly-Bell and Mr. Harmsworth, whom His Majesty is just making a Lord." "That's it," replied Mr. Beit, "and there's another who's even worse—Mr. Saunders, the *Times* correspondent in Berlin. Why, only the other day he wired to London that he had heard from an unimpeachable source how within two months—that is, by the end of February— Germany would have declared war on England. That is a fat lie and a good one." [1]

This interview with Mr. Beit has given us some very import- ant facts. In the first place we know that England and France will be sure to act together in Morocco. Then that Fisher is burning for a chance of destroying our Fleet and Merchant Service. We know that English private capital is being poured into the Paris press for the purpose of working up the French to provoke, and so provide a *casus foederis*. Our Naval Chief of Staff was quite right then, in estimating the naval changes begun last November [2] as preparations for war, and not as ordinary re- shufflings. The reports on the state of public opinion in Paris are also correct: the French are resolved on war, even though it goes against the grain, they are united, and stand behind their Government. They have made a number of preparations and continue to make them, and this would prevent a surprise attack, and render an invasion more difficult. It is evident that the date telegraphed by Saunders to London is considered exact in London and in Paris, since England has sent a cruiser to Kiel to find out how far our secret mobilization has proceeded. There has also been a French cruiser at Copenhagen, observing whether defensive measures in Denmark are being taken by the Danes themselves or by us. All this is confirmed by the recently com- pleted new formations—of the English North Sea Squadron (" Eastern Squadron "): six ships of the line, five cruisers, and by the concentration along the Portuguese coast of the entire English Naval forces (thirty-three ships of the line, twenty-five armoured cruisers) ordered for the beginning of February, *i.e.*,

1. Channel Fleet, eleven ships of the line and a cruiser division.
2. Atlantic Fleet with eight ships of the line and a cruiser division.

[1] English in the original. [2] In 1904.

3. North Sea Squadron with six ships of the line and a cruiser division. 4. Mediterranean Fleet with eight ships of the line and a cruiser division.

The date in February has been separately confirmed in another quarter by Her Majesty's chamberlain, Mirbach, who has just been spending a month in Belgium with his wife. More than a dozen mothers and mothers-in-law of French Reservist Officers from amongst his wife's relatives and acquaintance have rushed to him in tears to find out if it were true that war would be declared in two months. He nearly died of laughing, and the ladies became quite angry and told him that their relations had informed them that they all had instructions to be ready to join the colours in February, when Germany would declare war. They had all been making their wills. Mirbach talked most seriously to these ladies, begging them not to believe such nonsense and authorizing them to write to Paris contradicting this absurd rumour. The poor ladies breathed more freely and went off to write as he had told them.

On the other hand only co-operation with Paris on the Morocco question would be likely to make England declare war, since, unless France attacks us directly, England would not embark single-handed on a war which would be disliked by a large section of her population. H.M.E. VII has grown more peaceable, and no longer wants war for its own sake. Mr. Beit came here from Paris to get the material for spreading his denials. These will no doubt have a calming effect everywhere. That Saunders is a first class scoundrel! Most important of all, however, is the fact that England has, in effect, made an offer of armed support to France—Mr. Beit made no secret of this; he only suggested certain limits—and that this offer continues as before. Lansdowne therefore lied to Metternich (we always thought that he was lying) and so could not issue a denial. The reports from our people in Paris were exact. They were perfectly right when they suggested that recent French military publications proved that the French no longer fear us as they did. A further hint of Beit's makes me suppose that the next Conservative Government will, under Chamberlain's aegis, introduce Protection, to which Mr. Beit seems very partial.

With best greetings,

Yours,

WILLIAM, I. R.

CHAPTER XIII

*William II's excited letter (New Year's Eve, 1905)—His fear of war—
The Algeciras Conference—Herr von Radowitz and Count Tattenbach
—Count Metternich on the Algeciras situation—The English Elections
in January 1906—Defeat of the Unionists and its significance for
the improvement of Anglo-German relations—Further news from St.
Petersburg—Count Udo Stolberg on Moroccan policy—William II's
speech on the 1st January 1906—Grand Duke Frederick of Baden's
letter to William II—Another conversation with the Kaiser.*

THE contradictions in William II's nature—his uncertain and
mercurial temperament—came out in his correspondence as
clearly as in his speeches and conversation. My editor in his
preface to these Memoirs will have stated that I possess very few
autographed letters from the Kaiser. When I resigned I handed
back to Herr von Valentini, the Head of the Privy Council, everything His Majesty had written to me; his letters, telegrams, loose
notes. I did this without having been asked to do so. I had only
made extracts from a few of these communications as *aides-memoire*
at the time; others happened to remain amongst my papers.

Of these I discovered the letter addressed to me by William II
twenty-four hours after his conversation with Beit on New Year's
Eve, 1905. Every impartial reader will admit that, apart from a
few expressions which might have been less forceful than they are,
the Kaiser conducted this conversation not only with remarkable
adroitness, but with foresight, and above all, with dignity. Alas,
His Majesty's moods were more variable than April weather or the
chameleon. Few monarchs have had more need than he of a level-
headed, prudent, but above all, courageous adviser.

The same sovereign who, in his talk with Beit, had shown such
clear-headed self-possession, and so much common-sense in his report of it, wrote to me how, as the year ended, he had reflected on
the world situation beneath the re-lighted candles of a Christmas tree.
He did not, he said, want a war till he had concluded a formal
alliance with Turkey, and this must be brought about at all costs.
We must strive to ally ourselves with " all Arabian and Moorish
rulers." We could not begin a war till some pact of this kind with
Islam had been sealed. Neither, he continued, could we conduct a
war against France and England single-handed, " at least not on the

sea "—these last six words had been thickly underlined by His Majesty—and, besides, the year 1906 would be particularly un-favourable for a war, since we were in process of renewing our artillery and this would take us at least a year. The Infantry also were being newly armed, and there were many incomplete fortifica-tions and batteries at Metz. But the greatest obstacle to a war was that we could not take a single man out of the country because of the Socialist menace. To do so would be to jeopardize the property and lives of our citizens. " Shoot down the Socialists first, behead them, put them out of action, if necessary, massacre the lot—and then war abroad! But not before, and not *a tempo*! "

This letter closed with the demand that I should direct our foreign policy in such a manner as to avoid any warlike decision, " for the time being at any rate and as far as you consider this possible. But don't back out as the French did at Fashoda!" The Kaiser's fear of war was expressed in every line of this letter. By itself it would be enough to refute the lie, spread by our enemies in 1914 and even after the World War, that William II, deliberately brought the war about. In one sense he was almost too pacific. He revealed his aversion to serious conflict too transparently to any keen observer, and sometimes immediately after he had excited public opinion in all countries by boastful speeches or misplaced and tactless remarks. When, at an Official Reception on the 1st of January 1906, he asked me anxiously what I thought of his New Year's letter, I replied that I was extremely sorry that he had taken no part, on 9th May, in the Berlin celebrations of the Schiller Centenary. After an admirable speech by Erich Schmidt, the Song of the Horseman in Wallenstein's Camp had been sung at this festival:

> " *Und setzet ihr nicht das Leben ein*
> *Nie wird euch das Leben gewonnen sein.*" [1]

If we, I said, were filled with Schiller's spirit, the true spirit of German idealism—if, with the sense of realities necessary in politics, we avoided the snares of our adversaries, we should have no reason to be discouraged, much less despairing; certainly we must not hide our heads in the sand, but still less must we bow them or lose them in a moment of crisis.

On 16th January 1906 the Morocco Conference opened at Algeciras, the little Spanish port in the Province of Cadiz not far from Gibraltar, opposite Ceuta. One hundred and five years previously

---

[1] Unless you risk your life entire
Life will ne'er answer your desire.

a Spanish-French fleet had defeated the English there, though, a few days later, the English took spectacular revenge. This time the two great Western Powers appeared there in close alliance, and Spain strove hard to reconcile that alliance with ourselves. Besides Germany, France, and England, Russia, Italy, Austria-Hungary, Spain, the U.S.A., the Netherlands, Sweden, Belgium, Portugal, were all represented at the Conference, and of course Maghreb el Aksa, the Sherif. When we went to Algeciras I was in no doubt that we should have a hard task diplomatically. Russia had now been France's ally for fifteen years; England was bound to France in the Moroccan question by the Treaty of 8th April 1904. Italy, as her Foreign Minister, the Marchese Guicciardini, had explained in the Italian Senate, was in a particularly delicate position. The Conference had, in effect, to settle a difference between a country allied to Italy and another with whom, for a long time past, she had had a particular convention on the subject of Mediterranean Africa. In the May of 1905 Tittoni, the then Foreign Minister, had declared in the Italian Chamber, that Italy had obtained guarantees for certain " most favoured nation " clauses in Tripoli; but, he continued, she intended to leave them in abeyance and would only occupy Tripoli as a matter of absolute necessity. Italy could not think of occupying Tripoli so long as she was on friendly terms with Turkey. Such a step would only encourage those who wished to hasten the dissolution of the Turkish State, whose integrity was one of the foundations of the whole Italian foreign policy.

Tittoni's statement had met with unanimous approval. Not till 1911 did Italy decide on her invasion of Tripoli, since then there were no doubts left that Germany, by the Congo Treaty, arranged by Kiderlen and Jules Cambon, had completely sacrificed Morocco to the French. At Algeciras in 1906 circumstances would have led one to expect Italy to follow a careful, opportunistic and conciliatory policy, and one that would lead to no breach with any of the contending Powers. Such tactics, by the way, were in keeping with the established traditions of Italian diplomacy which have always excelled in the faculty of fitting into every situation, while leaving a loop-hole for escape. A similar policy to this made it possible for the Holy See to survive the tempest of the World War unscathed, and had helped the Italian National State to overcome the failures and reverses of a century, until all the aspirations of its patriots, from Azeglio, Gioberti and Mazzini to Cavour, Crispi and Giolitti, were achieved.

I had no illusions about the considerable difficulties that stood before us at Algeciras. I was well aware that German public opinion would be dissatisfied even with a relatively favourable result. Our public opinion swayed impulsively between noisy imperialist demands and a vague and sentimental pacifism, and usually looked at everything in an absurdly childish way. If in spite of all this I went to Algeciras, it was because I considered it useful to show some proof that even so complicated, grave and dangerous a conflict as the Moroccan, could undoubtedly be settled without war, in friendly discussion across the Conference table. Nine years later, in that disastrous summer of 1914, if the diplomats of all the great powers had kept their heads—the Germans, alas, lost theirs even worse than the others—if, in that fateful second half of July a conference of the Powers had been summoned to settle the Serbian-Austrian conflict, the most terrible catastrophe the world has seen for centuries could have been averted.

At the suggestion of the German delegates, the Algeciras Conference elected the Spanish representative, the Duke of Almodovar as its Chairman. I had suggested to His Majesty that we should be represented by our Ambassador in Madrid, Herr von Radowitz, and our Ambassador in Morocco, Count Tattenbach.

Radowitz was one of those statesmen of whom Thiers used to say that they had a great future behind them. When he was thirty years old, people saw in him the coming man, a rising German diplomat of outstanding gifts, who talked copiously and intelligently and could write well and quickly. Radowitz was disliked by Holstein, perhaps because my father esteemed him so highly. During the Berlin Congress, the Secretariat of which was under Radowitz, Holstein did his best to blacken him in Bismarck's eyes. He was one of the numerous victims of Holstein's mistrust and persecution mania. Finally, in 1882, while still a comparatively young man, he became Ambassador in Constantinople, but his earlier fame had dimmed already, and Cosima Wagner, one of the most remarkable women I have met, said of him in those days, after a visit he had paid her in Bayreuth: " *Il n'a pas assez d'ésprit pour celui qu'il veut faire.*" Nevertheless he remained a man of wit and intelligence who could tell very interesting stories about his father. As a contribution towards the study of the psychology of Princes, he was fond of relating how Frederick William IV had parted from his dearest friend. When the latter ended his report as Minister of Foreign Affairs a few days before the Olmütz Convention, in November 1850, the King, with tears in his eyes, embraced him and assured him that nothing in the world could ever part them. He accompanied his favourite into the antechamber and watched him descend the Castle stairs. But when the Minister reached home he found a

letter from his sovereign; its contents more or less as follows:
When His Majesty embraced his Minister his tears had flowed all
the more abundantly since he knew that they would long be parted.
Reasons of State compelled him to sacrifice his dearest friend. A
sinecure at Erfurt was conferred upon the fallen minister, with instructions not to leave this place except by special permission of
His Majesty. The Minister only survived his fall two years; his
son was put on the shelf at Holstein's suggestion, and left in Madrid
after ten years' meritorious service at Constantinople.

It was a pleasure to me, after his many disappointments, to give
Radowitz a chance, at the end of his political career, of being in the
foreground of politics.

As the Algeciras Conference began I received an interesting
letter from Metternich on the general European situation, with
particular reference to England. In the summer of 1905, he had
discussed with the Liberal Party chiefs the anti-German propaganda
in England, of which he had pointed out the dangers. Lord
Spencer, one of the most respected Liberal leaders (soon after this,
an apoplectic stroke was, unfortunately, to end his career in politics),
energetically and publicly intervened in favour of a conciliation
policy. The English press, especially the Liberal newspapers, took
a calmer and, to some extent, even a friendly tone towards us. The
November issues of a number of English reviews contained quite
sensible articles about Anglo-German relations. Metternich continued:

All this shows that people are coming to their senses here and
considering a change of attitude. Unfortunately the *Matin* has
butted in with its " revelations " and this has filled our people
at home with excusable bitterness against England. This is not
the first time that I have noticed how, as soon as, in Germany,
people tend to become less anti-English, England rejects their
advances, and *vice versa*. The instruments are never simultaneously in key with one another, the harmony of the one is
answered by the other's discord. England and Germany have
not the same sounding boards. Nevertheless I know you share
my view that I ought to support whoever favours a *rapprochement*.
I should like to call your particular attention to a talk I recently
had with Mr. Haldane. It is of far-reaching importance to our
relations with England and may even be the starting point for an
era of reconciliation. All the more influential Liberal leaders,
whose party it is generally believed will be in power by either
February or March, have been won over to this task. Mr.

Haldane, an ex-Liberal Minister, is destined for an important post in the forthcoming Liberal Cabinet and is highly esteemed by both parties. His education has been German, he speaks German and is friendly to Germany through and through. To use the current English expression he will be in the "inner circle of the Cabinet." He is a Liberal of the new Rosebery school with Imperialist tendencies but without the least touch of jingoism. Rosebery, Sir Edward Grey and Asquith follow the same trend and are personal friends of Haldane's. But Haldane has not, like Rosebery, broken with the radical and more doctrinaire wing of the Party—Sir Henry Campbell Bannerman, Mr. Morley, Mr. Bryce, etc., but has great influence on them also. In foreign affairs the English would rather listen to Rosebery than to Bryce. The doctrinaire radicals are suspected of being Little Englanders, but the Liberal Imperialists are not. I told Mr. Haldane that I was sorry to see from a speech of Sir Edward Grey, whose view on foreign affairs carries special weight with the Liberal party, that he too had made a *rapprochement* with Germany conditional on our swallowing France's policy in Morocco without a protest. We urgently wished, I said, to be peaceful and friendly with the French, but we could not allow our rights and interests to be trampled on, not even if England, who, no more than France, had any right to dispose of Morocco, offered the French her help. The fact that France, believing in English help, might brush aside our rights seemed to me a real danger to peace, since we could never let that happen. We might have our faults, but we were not cowards. We hoped and assumed that our agreement with France over the Conference programme would have removed the worst difficulties. Nevertheless I had to fear that the French, if they felt English encouragement, would go further than was right and reasonable. Moreover, Anglo-German relationships had not been exactly improved as the result of recent newspaper scares and feuds. People in London, I said, do not seem altogether to realize what a deep impression it must have made in Germany to learn that England had suddenly declared herself ready to fight at France's side against us—and that, on her own initiative, without any previous engagement! To see a people with whom we had never been at war, with whom we had no vital differences, coolly declare that it would fight us if necessary on the side of our traditional enemy, could only arouse in Germans, not fear, but inevitable bitterness. And even if all that were sensational, if the latest " revelations " were disregarded, the brutal fact remained that the English

Government had given the French to understand that they could
count on England's armed assistance in the case of any war with
Germany, and that English public opinion had endorsed this.
No one who had felt the atmosphere in England could retain any
illusions as to the special stipulations regarding aggression.
Should the French invade Germany to-morrow, everyone in
England, the day after, would be saying that they had been forced
into doing so by Germany's provocative attitude. Mr. Haldane
well knew the strained relationship between our Kaiser and the
King. If that also were taken into consideration it gave the
finishing touch to the picture. (Mr. Haldane had just been
spending a few days with King Edward at Balmoral and is well
aware how matters stand between their Majesties.)

I have touched on all these points in my report so as to make
Mr. Haldane's answer fully intelligible, and, for brevity's sake,
I pass over many other details, in particular much that I said to
him on the absurdity of Anglo-German antagonism, and on the
danger of feuds in the press. I purposely showed him the dark
side because I wanted to impress him and strengthen his desire
to modify the existing situation.

Mr. Haldane answered that Sir Edward Grey desires better
relations with Germany. The Conservatives, he told me, do
their best to make it appear that the Liberals are opposing
England's traditional foreign policy. But England's good relationship with America, the Entente Cordiale and the Japanese
Alliance, are the foundations of a foreign policy to which the
whole of England subscribes. Sir Edward Grey has wished to
make foreign policy re-enforce the policy at home. He has tried
to demonstrate the continuity of policy abroad in order to check
the election manœuvres of the Conservatives, and prevent them
from discrediting the foreign policy of his party. It is from that
angle that his speeches should be examined.

Grey and the other Liberal chiefs are all of opinion that the
poison distilled in the press on the subject of Germany must be
counteracted. Enthusiasm for France was so great here because
love of France was still so fresh and new. Things would quieten
down in time, he said, and he hoped the Morocco Conference
would end without any serious Franco-German differences. If,
a few months hence, the Liberals are in power that will be the
time for a *rapprochement*. The Liberal Party wants to keep on
the best of terms with France without running counter to
Germany.

Haldane and his Liberal friends want to bring about an

Anglo-German entente similar to the Entente Cordiale. If the Liberals get into power, they will go to work on this systematically.

It will, of course, be equally necessary to attempt to reconcile the two sovereigns. King Edward's offended mood may still very largely be connected with the treatment he received at the time when he was Prince of Wales. For the work of conciliation between the two countries to succeed, it will be necessary, since both these monarchs have so great a personal influence on policy, to induce them to forget their differences.

I assured Mr. Haldane that in this task both he and his colleagues might rely not only on my modest support but on the good will of the whole Imperial government. He seemed very pleased with this. A reconciliation with Germany seems already one of the planks of the Liberal programme, judging at least by the numerous verbal and written declarations of its members. The chiefs will embark on it once they are firmly in the saddle, but they do not wish to go too far at present, to avoid seeming to disturb the Entente Cordiale.

I have arranged, at the end of next week, to meet two or three of the party leaders, to discuss the whole position with them. But, even with a Liberal government, the French entente will, I think, remain the pivot of British Foreign policy. Nevertheless it is pleasant to have encountered this desire in England to relieve the tension with Germany.

Your very devoted,
PAUL METTERNICH.

On 6th November 1905 Lord Lansdowne, the English Minister of Foreign Affairs, declared that the understanding with France and Japan in no way signified estrangement from other Powers. England, he said, would uphold her entente with both these countries, but this did not mean that she was unwilling to offer other nations her friendship. A few days later the Premier, Balfour, said at the Lord Mayor's banquet: " I am sanguine enough to think that we shall see no war in future unless there arises a nation or a ruler incapable of carrying out a plan of national aggrandizement except by trampling the rights of neighbouring states under foot. But I have no reason for assuming that such a misfortune will befall Europe. As far as human foresight can tell, I believe I may prophesy a long peace."

Soon after this speech of Balfour's, on the occasion of the first Budget debate, I too, in the Reichstag, took occasion to deal with the state of English feeling against Germany. It was only recently that serious Englishmen had begun to oppose this sinister anti-German phobia. I added amidst the cheers of the Reichstag: " I sincerely welcome these signs of a better understanding. I would gladly see in them the beginning of a return to that former mutual understanding between two great and civilized peoples, which has been so unluckily disturbed."

On December the 4th the Balfour Ministry resigned. December the 10th saw the formation of the new Liberal Cabinet under Sir Henry Campbell-Bannerman, with Asquith as Chancellor of the Exchequer, Sir Edward Grey as Foreign Secretary, Haldane as Minister of War, Lord Tweedmouth at the Admiralty, Lloyd George at the Board of Trade, the Labour Member John Burns for Local Government, Bryce for Ireland. The Earl of Crewe, the Earl of Rosebery's son-in-law, became Chief of the Privy Council, the Marquis of Ripon Privy Seal.

With that feeling for the need of a settled Foreign Policy which characterizes all English governments, the new Prime Minister, Campbell-Bannerman, announced in his party programme, on 21st December 1905, that the whole British nation endorsed the agreement " so wisely " concluded by Lord Lansdowne with the French. " As far as Germany is concerned I do not see the slightest cause for estrangement in any interest of either people, and we welcome the unofficial demonstrations of friendship that have been exchanged by the two countries of late."

In January 1906 came the English General Election, leading to an overwhelming defeat of the Unionists, of the party, that is to say, which really represented British jingoism, and the hatred of Germany which proceeded from it.

Even Balfour, the former Premier, was not re-elected at first, but returned to Parliament through a bye-election. In this Parliament 400 Liberals, with 29 Labour members and 83 Irish, were faced by only 159 Unionists. But the causes of Anglo-German estrangement lay too deep, they were too firmly rooted in the nature of things, to be changed by a mere change of cabinets. Nevertheless the change of Government in England considerably lightened the burden of our foreign policy and was a guarantee of the further maintenance of peace.

A very intelligent Russian friend wrote me the following disquieting letter from St. Petersburg:

> Lors de ma dernière visite à Berlin, vous m'avez peut-être trouvée très pessimiste pour tout ce qui se passe chez nous ; hélas, mes

*impressions étaient d'un rose tendre en comparaison du noir que l'on
broie ici. J'ai tort de dire noir, c'est rouge qu'il faut dire, car l'horizon
est rouge du sang des assassinats, des exécutions et des incendies. Quel
chaos dans les idées. J'ai passé deux jours à la Douma et, quoique
j'aie vu plus d'une séance orageuse à Paris, Londres et Berlin, tout
çela est pâle en comparaison de ce qui s'est passé ici il y a quelque
jours. Vous avez lu les discours de ces forcenés, mais ce que vous
n'avez pas pu voir, ce sont les poings tendus avec des gestes insolents
vers les ministres qui avaient l'air non seulement d'accusés mais de
condamnés, les regards lançant la haine, les têtes de forçats. Si,
comme moi, vous aviez entendu les applaudissements frénétiques qui
saluaient l'apparition de ces quarts-d'intellectuels, vous vous seriez dit
que la révolution est là, et que peut-être elle nous balayera tous.
Quand je pense, qu'il y a un an et demi à peine, ces murs du palais de
la Tauride étaient couverts de splendide portraits du dix-huitième
siècle, qu'une foule élégante venait admirer, il me semble que ces
images du grand règne de Catherine avaient été évoquées exprès pour
faire ressortir encore davantage le contraste avec toute cette canaille
haineuse, crachant sur les beaux meubles Louis XVI et n'ayant en fait
d'opinion politique qu'une seule idée, la terre d'autrui.*

The shadow of the storm that twelve years later was to destroy
the whole Russian Empire could already be perceived by those
with sharper eyes.

Never, neither before nor during the Algeciras Conference, had
I any intention of allowing a war to break out over Morocco. I was
fully convinced that any serious European conflict would be almost
certain to involve the whole world, and that the maintenance of a
worthy peace would be, both then and in the future, a vital matter
for our people. William II entirely agreed with me in this. Nevertheless he increased the difficulties of my task by imprudent speech
and action or even, at any crisis in our foreign policy, by too frankly
showing his fear of war. An *agent de change* of German origin in
Paris, who gave me reliable news from time to time, reported that
Edward VII, whenever he talked to a Frenchman, abused his
Imperial nephew in every conceivable way. He had said again and
again: " *Croyez-moi, dans l'affaire marocaine, il ne bougera pas. Il
rentrera dans son coin.*" A certain number of our deputies also entertained unfounded fears on the situation. It is strange that the same
public opinion, the same deputies even, who at the Conference of
Algeciras and during the Bosnian crisis in 1910, considered war so
inevitable, should not have understood in 1914 that the wolf was
really at the door.

The following anecdote may serve to illustrate the hypocritical spirit with which, in wide and responsible German circles, the Algeciras Conference was judged. My chief of press, Dr. Hammann, was not always skilful, and sometimes tactless in his dealings with public opinion and its journalistic representatives, but he listened, and nosed about everywhere, and he would have made a very good detective. He reported the following conversation which he overheard in the Lobby:

" Count Udo Stolberg: Our Morocco policy grows more and more incomprehensible to me. How disgraceful it would be if we went to war with France because of the Jesuits." " How do you mean?" " Well, it's clear enough. We're being made a clerical cat's paw to revenge the Papacy on the anti-clerical French Republic." " Do you really mean that, or are you joking?" " No, I'm quite serious. Just look how Princess Bülow goes to Mass with Prince Arenberg every Sunday." Moral: if former Presidents in the foreign service are so childish, what is to be expected of narrow party journalists? So far Dr. Hammann. Count Udo Stolberg, formerly Oberpräsident in Königsberg, one of the leaders of the Conservatives, and a personal friend of mine, was quite a sensible man in other respects.

On the evening of New Year's Day in 1906, a rumour had spread through Berlin that the Emperor in an address given at the annual parade in the Grand Hall at the Arsenal had expressed himself very pessimistically on the European situation. The Bourse responded with a slump. A member of His Majesty's entourage told me in confidence that the Kaiser, after having evoked the memory of 1806, had added among other things: " I have an excellent Chancellor, whom I love and esteem, but sometimes he drives the cart too near the ditch." When I asked the Kaiser quite innocently to tell me what he had said at the Arsenal, he sent me the text of his speech which no doubt he had subsequently edited, but which anyway contained nothing dubious. It was couched in the style of most Imperial manifestoes: the words " supreme war lord " appeared five times in it; the Army was to be trained so that it should become " His Majesty's invincible instrument." All the efforts of the Officers' Corps were to be directed towards " perfecting the Army for its King " whose praise and satisfaction were the soldier's fairest reward. There followed advice to revert to the old Prussian thrift, to shun all luxury, to restore the old well-tried simplicity of our fathers, to exercise self-mastery, etc.—all of which was perfectly justified if only the Kaiser had proceeded in this direction himself. Unfortunately he never did. It was a very good tradition that officers should do more than die for their sovereign, that they should live a life different from that of ordinary citizens, that they were a caste apart submitted to a more ascetic rule than that of the ordinary bourgeois. In his words at least the Emperor insisted on this even more than Frederick the Great or William I.

His Majesty followed the course of the Algeciras negotiations with such exaggerated concern that I was glad to be able to write to him, soon after the Conference opened, that Lascelles, the English Ambassador, back from London, had told me in confidence his conviction that an improvement in Anglo-German relations under the new Liberal English Government was not only possible but likely, once the Morocco question had been settled. Let this be done and Franco-German tension eased a little and the English would begin to play a more friendly tune to us in public. A Liberal Cabinet, based on a strong majority, could pursue a different policy towards us from that of Lansdowne, Chamberlain, and Balfour. I added, not as part of my report, but simply *ad usum delphini*: " I have brought my whole pressure to bear on the press to prevent its either raising a howl of triumph, or going too far in friendliness to England. What matters now is that the English Liberals shall not be disconcerted by our forced and impetuous demonstrations, and that the English party of action shall have no chance to discredit the Liberals as pro-German." The longer the Conference lasted, the more nervous His Majesty became. His anxiety was further increased by a well-meant but, in the circumstances, rather unfortunate letter from the excellent Grand Duke Frederick of Baden, who amongst other things wrote as follows: " Surely it must be self-evident how harmful a war with France would be for us and how unpopular in Germany. Such a war could only be desired by those who wish to impede our exports and so ruin our highly developed industry, since that would be the result of any war, even if we were the victors on land. We should lose all our allies and could only recover them with difficulty. Thank God, Your Majesty's Government is peaceful. A conciliatory policy in the Moroccan question would be received with acclamation by the whole country and would mean renewed industrial prosperity. Once France knows that her Eastern frontier is secure and that Germany sincerely wishes peace, a policy of accommodation at Algeciras will be of the greatest benefit to ourselves in spite of Alsace-Lorraine."

I took it upon myself to assure the wise and patriotic Grand Duke (who had always been so friendly to me), by showing him confidential excerpts from documents, that his wishes were identical with my aims, aims that I hoped, by God's help, to achieve. I still maintained to the Kaiser that if only we could control our nerves we should reach an understanding even without "going to Olmütz."

We should I believe have obtained more than we did at Algeciras on a number of isolated points if we had closed our ears to the ranting of the French and English press and the rather undignified whines of certain German newspapers. We ought to have made it clear that we were no more afraid than the others of a Conference that led to no result. But the Emperor did not wish to run the risk of the Conference ending in stalemate. At the beginning of April we had a long talk in the garden of the Imperial Chancellery during which he expressed his firm conviction that, unless we made further concessions at Algeciras there would be a war, and our chances, for various technical and military reasons, were "at the moment," as unfavourable as they could be. He would not, he said, and could not risk such a war! He said that I must not abandon him now, but preserve him from war, "without dishonouring him"—from a war for which neither the German Princes, the Reichstag, nor our people were in the mood.

CHAPTER XIV

*The Algeciras Treaty—The American Ambassador, Charlemagne
Tower, on the Algeciras document—My speech in the Reichstag on
the 5th April 1906—My fainting fit—Herr von Holstein's resignation—My convalescence at Norderney—Friendly letters and demonstrations—William II's telegram to Count Goluchowski ("the
brilliant second")—The Kaiser visits me at Norderney—William II's
Cuxhaven speech on my recovery.*

THE Treaty of Algeciras was signed on the 7th April 1906.
It regulated the police organization in Morocco, suppressed
the illicit traffic in arms, provided for the erection of a State
Bank, the improvement of the Revenues and Customs Service, so
that although it may not have given us all we wished, it did represent
the essentials of what we had striven to attain. It reaffirmed the
sovereignty of the Sultan which remained an integral part of the
system of international law. France did not obtain the Protectorate
at which she had aimed, nor, above all, that command of all armed
forces in Morocco she had demanded in the spring of 1905. We
had made a victorious stand for commercial freedom in Morocco.
We had secured a definite right to co-operate in the future development of Moroccan affairs, a right we should henceforth not forego
except with adequate compensation. The attempt to exclude us
from a great international decision had been successfully thwarted.
As I put it eleven years later in my book on German policy,[1] the
decisions of the Algeciras Conference were a barrier set up against
France's attempt to extend her Tunis policy in Morocco. They
were also in the nature of an alarm signal there, ready for us to sound
at any time should France again reveal such tendencies. When,
after the Treaty had been published, complaints and recriminations
became audible in certain German circles, the American Ambassador, Charlemagne Tower, a man of insight and very well-disposed
towards us, said to me: " I really cannot understand what some of
your people here are shouting about. You have just about achieved
everything you could reasonably expect in Algeciras." Alas, there
was soon to come a time when the fools of those days who prated of
" German shame " and German inadequacy, were to realize what

[1] *Deutsche Politik* (popular edition), p. 91.

real shame and real defeat mean. When I announced the results
of the Algeciras Conference and the impending signature to His
Majesty I received from him a telegram expressing his lively satisfaction. "Peaceful end of these difficult negotiations comes as a real
relief." He was, so he wired, entirely satisfied. His telegram
ended in Latin: "*Hic optime manebimus.*"

On the 5th April I seized the first chance that offered of explaining to the Reichstag the origins, aims and results of the
Algeciras Conference.[1] We had no direct political interests in
Morocco and no political aspirations, but we did possess treaty
rights and economic interests there. The dignity of our Empire
could not allow these German rights to be ignored. We were not
to be treated as a *quantité négligeable*. It would, I said, have been
short-sighted to break up the Conference on account of subsidiary
questions; in politics one must not risk major interests to secure a
triumph in detail. We had stood unshakably by the great principle of the Open Door which had never ceased to guide us since
the beginning of the Morocco affair. I closed with the words:
"Gentlemen, we have had to climb a rather steep and dangerous
peak. A period of unrest and effort is behind us. I believe that
now we may look about us with greater calm. I am sure the Algeciras Conference has produced results satisfactory to Germany,
France, and every civilized people."

It is indeed a fact that never, since the Peace of Frankfurt, had
relations between Germany and France been so calm and relatively
friendly as they were during the five years from the Algeciras Treaty
to the sending of the "Panther" to Agadir. My comments on the
Treaty were approved by all the bourgeois parties, in particular by
Freiherr von Hertling, who, amidst applause, thanked me on behalf
of the Centre. Bebel succeeded him on the Tribune, where he
abandoned himself to the usual Socialist complaints about the
Government in general and our foreign policy in particular. Bismarck, he said, would never have allowed the Algeciras Conference
to take place (Bismarck was as a rule his *bête noir*, he would attack
him even more fiercely than me); but an even worse blunder than
my Moroccan policy was the friendly relationship I still maintained
with "barbarous Russia."

During Bebel's speech I fainted. Bebel, whom as a man I did
not dislike since I always considered him good-natured, sent me a
few days later a message through our mutual friend, August Stein,
the *Frankfurter Zeitung* correspondent, saying how much he re-

[1] Prince Bülow's *Speeches* (large edition), vol. ii, p. 303 *et seq*. Réclame ed.,
vol. iv, p. 92 *et seq*.

gretted that his violent attack had brought on my fainting fit. These heart-searchings were quite unfounded; in the last few years the good Bebel had been ageing perceptibly, he had worn himself out by his years of untiring agitation on behalf of the ideas he considered right. His speech on the 5th April had been a feeble one. My ill-health was essentially due to the fact that throughout the whole winter, and especially in the last few weeks, I had been overwhelmed with work and unable to get enough sleep. In the days which preceded this session of the Reichstag I had rarely been to bed before two, sometimes before three, in the morning, and to receive the Kaiser, whose habit it was to call on me very early, I had had to be up again at seven. It is true that the last thing I remember, before consciousness left me altogether, is the not unsympathetic face of Bebel, framed in its grey beard, with lively and intelligent eyes. I may add that notwithstanding this vision, my sensation as I fainted was a pleasant one.

> " *Des Geistes Flutstrom ebbet nach und nach*
> *Ins hohe Meer werd' ich hinaus gewiesen.*
> *Die Spiegelflut erglänzt zu meinen Füssen,*
> *Zu neuen Ufern lockt ein neuer Tag.*
> *Ein Feuerwagen schwebt auf leichten Schwingen*
> *An mich heran! Ich fühle mich bereit,*
> *Auf neuer Bahn den Äther zu durchdringen*
> *Zu neuen Sphären reiner Tätigkeit.*" [1]

When I came to myself I found they had carried me to the office reserved for the Imperial Chancellor; the room was full of people; somebody was rubbing my hands, somebody else my feet, and they had taken off my boots and socks. Brandy was being poured down my throat and some abominable *tisane* of chicory. I could plainly hear my esteemed colleagues, the Ministers, discussing the question of my successor. Everyone seemed anxious to find out whether I were to go on long leave and, if so, who would take my place, and who would be the next Vice-Chancellor. Geheimrat Hammann seemed the only one who had not lost his head. I always remembered this, and got him out of a difficult situation not

---

[1] In slow degrees the tides of spirit ebb,
I am borne out alone on the high seas.
The mirror of the sea gleams under me
A new day draws me on to other shores,
A fiery light-winged chariot bears me up,
New trackless paths in the ether beckon me,
To other spheres' renewed activity.

long before I resigned the Chancellorship. Hammann chivied ministers, deputies and journalists out of the room and telephoned my wife and my excellent friend and doctor, Geheimrat Renvers, who soon arrived, sounded my heart, made me try to walk and said gravely and decisively: " I assure you, on my word of honour, that what you have just had was a simple fainting-fit and not a stroke. The only reason why you vomited as much as you did was the awful mixture which these fools have been pouring down your throat. You'll soon be as fit as a fiddle but you must rest, and above all, get plenty of sleep."

They had telephoned to the Kaiser of my mishap. He hurried off at once to the Reichstag where as a rule he never set foot. He expressed his sympathy with my wife in the sincerest and most touching manner and insisted how much he wanted to see me. But Renvers was a conscientious doctor. He said that this was absolutely impossible. My wife and Renvers drove me back to the Chancellor's Palace where I was put to bed and forbidden to do anything for a week except look at illustrated papers. After that I was allowed to read novels, and in subsequent weeks I got through a whole series of them. Some of them seemed very well written. My wife's maid, who had been in her service for many years—she still remains with us to-day and will soon be able to look back on fifty years spent in our family—tended me with the greatest devotion. Her care and self-sacrifice made me recover sooner than any trained nurse could have done. Frau Louise Cholin is more my wife's friend than her servant. Hers is a rare character. Her life has been one long fulfilment of duty, she represents the best type of German womanhood, a real daughter of Breisgau, and so she remained after having married M. Cholin who had been our *chef* for many years.

My fainting-fit was the involuntary occasion for the political demise of Geheimrat von Holstein, who till then had weathered so many storms, so many political shoals. His fall is a proof that the pitcher really does go to the well until it breaks. He could not, as I have said, in the long run, manage to get on with the Secretary of State, von Richthofen, any more than he could with other people. When, on 17th January 1906, death robbed me of the services of this excellent and faithful collaborator, it was not easy to find a successor, who should at the same time be equal to his duties, acceptable to the Kaiser, and not too inacceptable to Holstein. The Kaiser rejected Mühlberg and Kiderlen, nor did Holstein wish for either of these two. His Majesty wanted his faithful " Mimile " as, for some reason or other, he called Tschirschky. Holstein had enthusiastically seconded the Imperial wish, much to my surprise since, generally speaking, he was always in opposition to the Kaiser. His train of thought, intricate as usual, was as follows. Tschirschky, as Councillor of Legation in St. Petersburg, had grown very friendly with Prince Radolin. Frau von Tschirschky, in particular, gladly played the part of suivante to Princess Radolin. Holstein, intimate with the Radolins, thus thought himself quite certain of Tschirschky. This hope was deceived at the famous " connecting door " in the Foreign Office which led from the Bureau of the Secretary of State to von Holstein's private room. The latter used it on every occasion and would enter his Chief's room without having been previously announced. Marschall had put up with this and it did not worry me particularly since I have never been liable to " nerves." But Tschirschky kept the door locked. He was too emotional to be able to support with ease a continual threat of the sinister presence of Holstein discovered unexpectedly at his back. When, irritated by this exclusion, Holstein entered the room of the Secretary of State by the corridor, with a great bundle of documents under his arm, Tschirschky in a cold, discouraging voice, requested him to put them on the table and go outside to wait until he was called. With Holstein's warped and irritable nature this could only lead to a breach. He at once handed in his resignation but was convinced I would prevent its being accepted. On several separate occasions he had asked my permission to resign in letters addressed to me personally, and written in such elegiac accents as almost amounted to a kind of cosmic despair. He did not, he assured me, wish in any way to make my duties more difficult than they were; he only longed for peace and quiet.

Macchiavelli relates in his *Principe* how Cesare Borgia once said to him that he and his father, the cunning Alexander VI, had thought out all future contingencies except one—that they might die together or at least fall seriously ill at the same time. But unfortunately that was exactly what happened. Alexander wanted to get rid of certain inconvenient Cardinals. For this purpose he asked them to supper, when their favourite dishes, suitably prepared, were set before them. But the careless servants misplaced the platters and highly doctored food was eaten by the Pope and his son. His Holiness died the following night; the son with his gigantic physical energy managed to shake off the poison though he remained in bed for several weeks. But in the meantime the towns and castles of the Romagna which he had conquered revolted against him, and the House of Borgia fell. In much the same way Fritz von Holstein, though in the main his calculations were right, had forgotten one eventuality:—that I might be taken ill and, by doctor's orders, shut off from all enquiries and documents at the moment when his resignation was in the hands of the Secretary of State—that Tschirschky who was now his enemy.

Tschirschky used to the uttermost, and in the most cold-blooded manner, his chance of getting rid of Holstein. The Kaiser promptly accepted the resignation. Two years before when, tired of the incessant strife between Holstein and other Foreign Office officials, I had warned the old Privy Councillor that unless he could leave people in peace I should be forced, although with regret, in the interests of the Service, to part company with him, he had promptly, through his friend Radolin, brought my warning to the Kaiser's notice. The next time His Majesty met me (it was a gala banquet in the Schloss) he had darted towards me and exclaimed in a vigorous staccato: " Look here, Bernhard, you really must leave poor old Holstein alone. He was the only one who stood by me faithfully in my struggle with that devil Bismarck." Soon after Tschirschky's appointment to the post of Secretary of State, when it was clear that he was not up to his work, the Kaiser said with equal vivacity and conviction: " Look here, Bernhard, I must ask you one thing—I can't have Tschirschky interfered with. He was the only one who stood by me faithfully in my struggle with that brute of a Holstein."

As soon as I had begun to sleep fairly soundly again, Renvers packed me off to Norderney. I have rarely felt such *joie de vivre* as I experienced in the course of this convalescence in the May of 1906. I took long rides about the island, along the sands by the whispering sea, filling my lungs with the fresh sea air. Since my boyhood I have always loved riding. As Chancellor I never missed my daily gallop even when the weather was at its worst. I often think of those fine beasts on whose backs I cantered through the Tiergarten, round the Hippodrome, to the Norderney Lighthouse, and later, across the Roman Campagnia or down the sandy roads of Holstein. There was Rossbach the indefatigable, gallant Peter with his split ear, Senta the coquette, the elegant Torero, the fine dappled grey mare, Lena, the clever Hans. I have never yet sold a horse. When they got too old I pensioned them off and put them out to grass. Two of these fine beasts were killed in the World War. Rossbach was blown to bits in a munition dump explosion near Peronne, Torero killed by a bullet at the moment when his brave rider, the Battalion Adjutant of the 1st Foot Guards, Lieutenant von Oppen, died a hero's death with his regiment.

Joseph Vehres, my excellent servant, accompanied me on all

these rides. He remains in my service to-day, and his efficiency and affection make him my invaluable support. By birth a Rhinelander, he served in my regiment, the King's Hussars, and with this regiment did his part in the World War. He is a fine example of the valour, intelligence, and purposeful activity of our people. He has learnt Italian perfectly, and is as expert in technical matters, in electricity and mechanics, as he used to be in grooming the horses he tended with so much care. He was himself a smart horseman who had been through a very good school in the Suermondt stables at Aix, and at ten years old could take any obstacle, riding barebacked and without stirrups. If Fate had blessed his parents with greater fortune so that he himself could have studied, he would have been an excellent Civil Servant, a keen lawyer, an energetic Landrat. The numerous talks I had with this good fellow taught me that an open-minded man of the people can often grasp things far more clearly than many an " intellectual " politician.

The Berlin news which reached me at Norderney was by no means always very gratifying. Nevertheless the Reichstag voted in favour of Fiscal Reform. This gave His Majesty occasion to send me the following gracious letter, written in his own hand:

I am well aware how large a part in the drafting and success of this important measure is the result of your statesmanlike skill and the devotion with which you conducted and promoted this arduous task. With all my heart I congratulate you on another success which wins you again the thanks of your Kaiser and King, and of the Fatherland. May I also use this opportunity of conveying to you, my dear Prince, my heartfelt joy that your health, impaired by excessive work, is now by God's mercy fully restored. I harbour the confident hope that your valuable services may long be preserved for the further well-being of our people. With unchanging good-will and confidence,

I remain,

Your grateful Emperor and King.

The Military Pensions Laws, of so much importance to the Army, had finally been passed by the Reichstag. I had taken great pains to get them introduced and accepted. To his letter informing me that these laws had definitely been passed, von Einem, the War Minister added:

Without Your Highness's co-operation and the steps that you took to draft them, these measures would never have been possible. I feel that I owe Your Highness the expression of my

II.   P

warmest gratitude.   With sincere respect and devotion and in
the hope that Your Highness will speedily return to full health
and vigour,

I remain,
Your most obedient servant,
VON EINEM.

To this letter the Kaiser added a marginal note in " fullest agreement " with the War Minister.   The Reichstag, on the other hand,
rejected, to everyone's astonishment, at the third reading of the Bill
the appointment of the Secretary of State for the Colonial Office, by
a majority of 142 to 119 with 9 abstentions.   Soon after this, the
continuation of the Lüderitzbucht-Kubub Railway to Keetmans-
hoop was rejected by 186 votes to 95, although there was no doubt
that the line was really needed.   But the Government's standpoint
in both cases was very weakly defended by Tschirschky and Hohenlohe-Langenburg and by Posadowsky, who was offended because he
had not been appointed my successor.   It was indeed food for
thought that so relatively short an absence on my part should have
been sufficient to make the Governmental machinery creak.   It
certainly seemed not insignificant that my steady guidance and
surveillance of my colleagues was necessary to keep things running
smoothly.   Was not our whole Governmental machinery excessively
dependent on the Chancellor?   This, quite apart from the difficulties
and dangers of foreign policy which, in the international situation
of those days, demanded specialized experience, circumspection,
and a skilful hand.   But in contrast to the above the School Bill
passed the Prussian Diet on a compromise between Conservatives,
Centre, and National Liberals; a very significant victory in the
eyes of those who still remember how difficult it had always been to
handle educational questions in Prussia and to what violent struggles
and crises the school laws, more than any others, have always given
rise in the past.   At my request and to my delight, the Kaiser used
this occasion to confer the Black Eagle on Studt, the Minister of
Education, a tried and efficient Civil Servant, who had been a
Landrat in East Prussia, Under-Secretary of State in Alsace-
Lorraine, and Ober-präsident in Westphalia.

I must refrain from reproducing more than a few of the many
expressions of sympathy for my illness which reached me from all
over Germany.   The Kaiserin had telegraphed at once: " I pray
God to restore your health for the benefit of Kaiser and Fatherland.
Many heartfelt greetings to your wife."   The Crown Prince expressed his sympathy in a letter of hearty wishes for my quick and

complete recovery. He signed himself "Your ever devoted Crown Prince William." I received many hundreds of telegrams and letters, some from unknown admirers. I was most touched by a letter from Prince Henry XXXIII of Reuss. He told me of the death of his father, Prince Henry VII of Reuss, which had occurred on the day before my birthday, 2nd May 1906. Prince "Septi" Reuss, as he was called to distinguish him from his numerous namesakes, had been a kind chief to me in the winter of 1875-6 in Petersburg, at the time when I began my career as a twenty-six year old Secretary of Embassy. Ten years later he was my best man at my wedding in Vienna, where I found the truest happiness of my life. He always remained my friend and benefactor. His son wrote:

"These lines will bring Your Highness the last heartfelt greetings of my father, who passed away quietly early this morning. Yesterday evening, when he could no longer speak except with difficulty, Father reminded me on no account to forget to send you his best and warmest congratulations for your birthday. He kept on saying, 'I wish him a speedy recovery.' I hope Your Highness will allow me also to express my deepest thanks for your true friendship for my father, a friendship that brought him so much happiness. He had given standing orders that any passage in the newspapers relating to Your Highness' health should be read to him, and was really glad to hear that you were getting better."

A letter from Dr. Hinzpeter, His Majesty's tutor, received at Norderney, left a deep impression on my mind:

"May I too venture to take the liberty of writing you my best wishes, together with my relief that we received nothing worse than a shock. The shock was however a severe one, perhaps more so to me than to many others. My chief thought when I heard of the Chancellor's collapse was not 'poor Prince Bülow,' but 'poor Kaiser.' I cannot tell if your successes seem an adequate recompense for all the fatigues and heavy anxiety you have shouldered, or whether you think it desirable to continue in so arduous a life. But I certainly know that His Majesty's future activities would be considerably poorer and less fertile if it were not for his present Chancellor. Both as man and Sovereign he would have suffered an irreparable loss."

Few people knew William II's character so thoroughly as Hinzpeter. Moreover, since he had no cause to curry favour with me (he himself expected nothing more of life), his verdict was of particular value.

August Eulenburg, the Master of Ceremonies, who afterwards became Lord Chamberlain, wrote to Norderney:

Thank God that you have been restored in all your health and vitality to Kaiser, Fatherland, friends, admirers. Remember me, please, to the Princess, who will now begin to breathe more freely. With sincere and heartfelt respects,

Your devoted friend,
AUGUST EULENBURG.

Count Tattenbach, the Ambassador, whose successful activity at Algeciras had secured him a well-merited distinction, wrote with characteristic modesty: " It has been no merit of mine if I have been able to be of use at Algeciras. My knowledge of the land and its people, the fruit of my seven years' sojourn there, and a few useful administrative and juridical memories of my service in Alsace-Lorraine made matters easy for me. From numerous letters that have reached me, I conclude that those circles in Germany, including merchant circles in Hamburg, whose interests in the matter are practical, are satisfied with the result. . . . In my opinion the political value of the Agreement consists in the fact that, from now on, France will depend on our good-will in Morocco. We can, if we consider it necessary, close our eyes to what the French are doing. But we can also use the numerous reservations and guarantees in the Agreement to put serious difficulties in their way." Count Tattenbach judged the Algeciras Agreement exactly as did the *Revue des Deux Mondes* which wrote: " *On n'a vu nulle part une souveraineté aussi garottée par des liens multiples et assujettie à de si nombreuses servitudes. . . . Les puissances, ou plutôt la principale d'entre elles, l'Allemagne, ont consenti à ce que nous etablissons notre protectorat au Maroc à la condition de n'y jouir d'aucun avantage économique. . . . La France, c'est triste à dire, n'a obtenu aucune prime de gestion au Maroc.*"

The Speaker of the Reichstag, Count Ballestrem, who paid me a longish visit before my departure for Norderney, wrote that it had been a great pleasure to him to tell the Reichstag, at its next session, that he had found me in good health and looking none the worse for my illness. His statement, he said, was received with lively applause from all benches, which, in his opinion, showed that although I might have political opponents I had no personal enemies in Parliament. The leader of the Centre, Herr Spahn, wrote me a letter expressing the hope that it might yet be his privilege to co-operate with me for the welfare of the Fatherland. Herr von Hertling wrote to me to the same effect and that he hoped that he would soon see me back fully recovered. Herr von Heydebrand, whom I had thanked for his co-operation in getting the School Act passed, wrote to me:

In the arduous and thorny path of politics there is nothing more encouraging and refreshing to one, who is himself free from professional ambition and never quite satisfied with what he or others have achieved, than to be appreciated by our best statesman. Having said so much, I can do no more than express the hope, which all patriots share, that Your Highness's health will soon be fully restored.

Your most respectful and humble servant,
von Heydebrand.

The leader of the Imperial party, Count Hermann Hatzfeldt, Duke of Trachenberg, wrote:

Will Your Highness allow me the sincere joy of telling you how delighted I am that your indisposition has been a passing one, and that you have gathered up the reins of government once more in your resolute guiding hands.

I remain in deepest respect,
Your Highness's most obedient,
Hermann Hatzfeldt.

Hugo Jacobi, an old intimate of the House of Bismarck, wrote: " Through the rushing of the waves at Norderney there sounds the music of the Fatherland, an incessant appeal to you to get better, since on your health so much depends for Germany and for all of us."

His opponent, Theodore Curti, the editor of the *Frankfurter Zeitung* expressed his wish that I should soon be in full possession of all my powers and former robust health: " Next to the art of medicine, it is your own art, that wisdom with which you combine thought and action, philosophy with the cares of state, that will furnish the elixir potent to bestow on you further long years with joyful days."

Curti was right in assuming that my natural elasticity would overcome all personal trials and disappointments. My honoured teacher, Hermann Adalbert Daniel in Halle, had already observed this trait in me, and indeed that self-control which little by little I acquired in the course of my very varied life, came to my rescue at the time of my resignation, and protected me from the Kaiser's ingratitude as it revealed itself on that occasion, and from the pitiable behaviour of many, who for years had cringed whenever they met me. The friends of my Chancellorship abandoned me in craven fashion at a moment of crisis and difficulty, but for the pain that stabbed my heart when the Fatherland collapsed in shame and wretchedness I could find no healing herb.

Count Udo Stolberg wrote to my doctor, Renvers, after seeing me just before I left Norderney: "I confess that I breathe more freely now that I have been to see the Prince and convinced myself that his illness has left no traces. I simply could not conceive of a future in which he could be active with any of his faculties impaired, with his full power at all diminished. Of course in the end this may happen, but I shall not live to see it. You, my dear Renvers, might collaborate with Bülow in a hygienic reform of the upper classes and make it a punishable offence to invite people to dinner later than 7."

This last observation was quite just. The pernicious habit of prolonged and far too copious dinners was bad for the health of everybody and the purses of the poorer government officials. I suffered less than most of my colleagues from the unhygienic effects of Berlin dinners. Ever since I became a minister I had observed a strict regime, giving up tobacco, coffee, beer and liquors and limiting my evening consumption of alcohol to half a bottle of red wine. I combined this diet with a daily gymnastic exercise which lasted thirty-five minutes according to the rigorous methods of the worthy Dr. Schreber of Leipzig (Hygienic Home Exercises, Friedrich Fleischer). Even now in my old age I do Exercise 33, as recommended by Schreber (double knee-bend with closed heels on tiptoe with vertical body) twenty-five times every morning. This way of life, in conjunction with daily rides in fine weather and a tramp of several hours every Sunday afternoon, has, humanly speaking, saved me from the fate of Herbert Bismarck, Marschall, Richthofen, Kiderlen and many others, who departed this life before their time because they burnt the candle at both ends. It was not for nothing that Juvenal, who in decadent Imperial Rome must have been given ample opportunity to study the importance of hygiene, recommends *mens sana in corpore sano*. But of course this does not mean that the fiery soul and strong will cannot live in spite of a fragile body. Nevertheless, for those who serve the state as well as for those who lead it, physical health will generally guarantee the health of the soul and good nerves. I used often to wonder whether that excellent English institution, the week-end, might not be introduced into our country. But my efforts to import it came to nothing partly because of the unparalleled industry and devotion to duty of German officials under the old régime, who in company with the great Ionian painter, Apelles of Kolophon, arranged their lives on the principle *nulla dies sine linea*, and partly because of the exaggerated traditional German respect for writing,

that is to say, because of our *cacoethes scribendi*. It is in the
nature of things that the minister in a central position, whose time
is continuously occupied, who is often disturbed, is less able to
observe the many trifling, in themselves unimportant symptoms in
public life, than when he can read the events of the day in peace
during even the shortest holiday. I remember how painfully it
struck me when, soon after my arrival at Norderney I read that The
County Council of Waldshut in Baden had re-christened a local
square the Bismarckplatz, the St. Joseph's Platz. A clerical newspaper, the *Badische Landsmann* cried "Bravo! It is a sign of great
feebleness of character that we Badeners should so venerate Bismarck
amongst ourselves. We ought surely to show a little more independence, and not forget that it was Bismarck who *ad majorum gloriam
Borussiae*, forced on us the sanguinary war of 1866 and robbed us of
certain moneys. Let fire-eating pan-Germans build Bismarck
columns on which to burn their smoke-offerings to their idol
Bismarck on 1st April, the day on which nothing is taken seriously—
it would be quite in the nature of things if they were to roast an
ox, or better still, an ass (though a four-legged one)—but the
people of Baden have nothing to do with all that."

What dismal meanness, what stupidity, what lack of all patriotic
feeling, do effusions like the above reveal. Would such language be
possible in Italy about Cavour or Minghetti, of Thiers or Gambetta
in France, of Gladstone or Disraeli in England? Yes, Treitschke
was right. There are depths to which party hatred can descend in
Germany alone. As I dictate these lines there lies before me an
article by a German "intellectual," the art critic, Julius Meier-
Graefe, who writes in the *Neue Rundschau* for September 1922, on
his impressions during a recent trip to Paris.

> What could a world war do against this Paris? She is a
> hundred times more beautiful since we have grown proportion-
> ately uglier. And her people have not changed! How could
> they, even if they had wanted to themselves? Can the language
> of Racine, Stendhal, Flaubert, suddenly become a croaking
> noise? Can the girl, whose smile has been painted from Fouquet
> to Renoir, suddenly begin to grimace? Can the Place de la
> Concorde disappear? For me it was even delicious to eat real
> camembert again. I will confess that during the first three days
> I eat camembert morning, noon, and evening. And then the
> talk one hears at meals on a tone that exists only in Paris! To
> the Parisians pacifists in politics are something like the Cubists in
> art. They have long since been *vieux jeu*. Nor is there any talk

of the so-called German atrocities. Let us put away the war into the archives, let us pay our reparations, for Heaven's sake, and— *n'en parlons plus.* We sadly underrate the *rentier*-instinct of the French. That too, is a part of French culture. They do not care to slave as we do and they are right. This wish of theirs cannot be impressed with sufficient warmth on the German government. There is no more serious question on earth at the moment.

So writes a German aesthete while the French are on our German Rhine, while they squeeze the last farthing out of our people, while they torture us with sadistic cruelty and trample us under foot. Yes, there is a cringing spirit that is possible only in Germany. How different the Frenchman whose dash of vanity makes his patriotism all the more passionate. How different even the English with their self-seeking and often hypocritical but robust and unshakable love of country—the Italian with his " *slancio,*" his fiery devotion to his home.

But if in Germany the still persistent weakness of national sentiment, indifference to the national honour and lack of individual patriotic discipline, combined more often than not with an absence of elementary tact, were enough in 1906 to disturb any clear-sighted patriot, it was all the more desirable that the Kaiser should be a model of reason and dignity, that at least he should not lay himself open to criticism.

" *Il fallait à l'Allemagne un chef grave, silencieux, constant et mesuré,*" wrote Henri de Noussanne in a study of William II, to which other French writers who had made a special investigation of German conditions and personalities, also contributed, " *Mais,*" he continued, " *le Destin a donné aux Allemands un maître qui s'imagine encore que des paroles et des gestes suffisent à conduire les hommes. Encore faut-il approprier les paroles et les gestes à l'époque et aux circonstances. En réalité aucun chef d'Etat couronné n'a fait plus de mal à la monarchie que Guillaume II.*"

Scarcely twenty-four hours after my accident William II had wired to Count Goluchowski, the Austro-Hungarian Foreign Minister. His telegram ended as follows: " You have shown yourself to be a brilliant second, and may be assured that I shall return similar services in similar circumstances."

In this whole telegram the Emperor expressed himself like a school-boy; its substance even, only embarrassed Vienna, evoked protests in Budapest and laughter and sarcasm abroad, where people were not disposed in our favour. In the following autumn the Kaiser's so-called " gloomy prophecy " speech was an even more serious blunder. I wrote to the Kaiser calling his attention to the fact that, when the Reichstag met in the late autumn I should have difficulty in defending his telegram. I got no answer, but on 18th June he arrived unexpectedly at Norderney. He would have liked to take me completely by surprise since nothing gave His Majesty greater pleasure than unannounced descents and alarums; but one of his adjutants had been kind enough to warn me beforehand so that I could at least make suitable arrangements for the personal needs of the Emperor and his suite during their sojourn on the island.

His visit was characteristic of the strange mixture of amiability and roughness, of great kindness and lack of consideration that were William II's own. He began by sitting with me in a glass veranda under the blazing sun—in such a glare that the fact that I did not have another fainting-fit was at least a proof of my complete recovery. Having, in this way, investigated the state of my health in an animated conversation, lasting nearly two hours, he asked to be taken to see my wife who was really charmed by the cordiality with which he expressed his joy at seeing me well again. On the following evening at Cuxhaven he said, in the course of a speech at the North German Yacht Club: " God has preserved peace for us, peace with honour, and may He continue to bestow it on us. And he who did most work to maintain this peace, the First Counsellor of the Empire, whom for the last few weeks we have all accompanied with our prayers is now, to my joy, as I can inform you since I convinced myself in person of it yesterday, restored to the best of health, and will soon be back at his post, and helping, as my right hand, to guide the Empire."

The actual phrase used by His Majesty at the banquet had been " Guide of the Empire," and he had expressed his satisfaction that I should again be " governing " the Empire in the complete sense of the word. The Wolff Agency submitted his speech to me before publication and I naturally made the above modifications.

CHAPTER XV

My attitude as Vice-Chancellor towards the War Office—My letter to von Einem (1.vii.'06)—Military technique underrated by our army— My letter to my brother, Alfred von Bülow, in Berne on the home and foreign political situation—Congratulatory letter to the Emperor on the accouchement of the Crown Princess—Some advice to William II.

EVER since the beginning of my Chancellorship I had stuck to the principle of non-interference in military matters during peace time. On the other hand, should war be declared I was resolved to secure the supremacy of the civil power which, come what may, must never relinquish the reins of government to the army. Political leadership remains and must remain, the decisive factor. I had Bismarck's great example to guide me, who, with unbending energy, maintained this standpoint in all his dealings with Moltke, both in the critical days at the beginning of the war in '66, and throughout the whole Franco-Prussian campaign. But, in spite of myself, my deep concern at the whole world-situation from the beginning of 1906 forced me to break my general rule of never, for political reasons, disturbing the work of soldiers. On 1st July I wrote as follows to von Einem the Minister of War:

For some time past, in reading French newspapers, I have been struck with the increase in military preparation France seems to have been making all this year. There is talk of many hundreds of million francs spent by the French on armaments. God's help has enabled me to guide Germany safely through the danger in Morocco; I was able to keep the peace and, at the same time fully safeguard our rights, our interests, our dignity. According to all human computation we may expect several years of tranquillity. The world's need of peace and rest is very great. But I need scarcely say to you, my dear friend, that within a few years or even sooner, should things go counter to our hopes, the whole situation may have changed.

There is much enmity, hatred, and envy of us in the world nowadays. English dislike and jealousy have, it is true, diminished: but, even now, they have not been fully overcome. In France the idea of "*la revanche*"—the hope not only of reconquering Alsace-Lorraine but of revenge for the defeat of thirty-five years ago, and of the re-establishment of that hegemony in Europe which the French possessed from Henry IV to Napoleon III, is still very far from extinguished. Russian conditions are incalculable. The democratic, revolutionary tendency that appears to be rising higher and higher in Russia, is anti-German, partly because of its Pan-Slavist proclivities, partly because it sees in the German Empire and in Prussia a stronghold of the hated Monarchist and Conservative order, as contrasted with democratic France and Liberal, Constitutionalist England. Of our allies Italy represents a factor on which it is never safe to reckon; our other ally, Austria-Hungary will, at best, for some time ahead, be compelled to struggle with her own internal problems. In these circumstances it becomes our sacred duty to neglect no human preparation that may enable our Fatherland, should a storm sweep over us sooner or later, to receive and weather it in safety. The issues of the conflict, once war has been declared, are in God's hand. But to-day we ourselves are responsible before God and history for the technical equipment of our army, so that our people, if forced to take the field, may at least do so flawlessly equipped, and so with every chance of success.

I write as a layman, without knowledge of military technique, and can therefore only ask you to be indulgent if any of my questions sound absurd. What technical measures can we take as an off-set to these French preparations? Do we need more machine-guns? Is the more rapid conversion of our artillery a necessity? How far advanced is the training of the transport and supply columns? What about the traction of the field-army's heavy artillery? What about dirigible airships? What would be the most practical uniform, considered solely from the point of view of service in the field?

As your best method for getting an eventual bill through the Reichstag I should naturally recommend your avoiding anything that might arouse mistrust, or even too much attention abroad. In this respect we should imitate the French who are arming very quietly. No provocative speeches, no agitation in the Press against this or that foreign power, no discussions of international politics, no unnecessary noise. We must say as little as possible about eventual requirements either before or after the budget vote, and so avoid any agitation which the opposition might think fit to provoke. All your demands must be carefully considered in advance and backed up with technical arguments. Please

note that His Majesty the Emperor knows nothing about this
letter.

I had the above copied and sent to Moltke with whom I had
already talked over its contents several times. My urgent admoni-
tions were not simply the result of the feverish military preparations
of others, particularly the French. I could not avoid the impression
that, in our army, the importance of technical training was underestimated. Such an outlook in 1870, at Mars la Tour and Saint
Privat, had given the officers and men of the Prussian Guard their
chance for such a display of personal courage as the world had not
seen since Leuthen and Möckern, but it had also been the cause of
heavy, and in reality, unnecessary losses. During half a century of
peace which followed two victorious wars, an exaggerated conser-
vatism, too hide-bound a respect for tradition, an anxious mistrust
of all novelty, had prevented us from drawing the right lessons from
the experience of the Franco-Prussian War, although Count Alfred
Schlieffen had endeavoured to do so by speech and writing. Only
too often, at his manœuvres, the Kaiser had staged the ideal battle
based on a complete incomprehension of the limits which modern
technical development has set on the free advance, not merely of
cavalry, but of infantry. This same lack of technical insight was
equally visible in the artillery; I am speaking not only of tactics but
of the whole conception of the proper use of that arm. This led,
on the one hand, to an over-reliance on " furor Teutonicus," and on
the other to a wrong appreciation of the significance of technical
ability, and of the huge difference between the pretty pictures at
manœuvres and the stark reality of war. In no other army did so
fine a feeling of comradeship exist as in the German. But in many
cases it was hide-bound; a number of officers considered the
cavalry the only thing that mattered, the one branch of the service
" fit for a gentleman," the infantry a useful decisive weapon, the
artillery nowhere at all, in spite of the fact that Napoleon had begun
in it. The technical branches of the service were contrasted not
very flatteringly with the " fighting troops "; the real importance
of the supply corps was not appreciated as its services entitled it to
be, and the Technical Academy had been nicknamed " the black-
smith's school." Such cares and considerations as these had induced
me to meddle in military matters.

And besides I had one special reason. I had been a zealous
advocate both in the Prussian Cabinet and the Bundesrat of the full
development of our fleet. In parliament and in the country I had
successfully rallied opinion in favour of the Navy. No one admitted

this more warmly than Tirpitz. But I could not overlook the danger that the Admiral's boundless energy and dominating personality, which naturally made him a little one-sided in his views, might bring the army into neglect. That is why I had always assured the War Office from the very first day I became a minister, that I would be ready at any moment to endorse, before the country and the Reichstag, any necessary military requirement. I said I would even go *usque ad effusionem sanguinis*, that is to say to a dissolution of parliament, with all its consequences. It was my firm conviction that on the army the maintenance of the Empire and future of our people would depend, and that conviction enabled me to point out to a reluctant War Office and General Staff those prejudices and illusions which, together with much that was excellent, existed in our army, or rather in the mentality of the Prussian officer.

Some days after writing to the War Office I sent my brother Alfred the following letter, in which I expressed my view of the storm of criticism raised by the Pan-Germans in response to the Act of Algeciras. Alfred, after a short stay in Norderney, was on a visit to his mother-in-law, Countess Dillen-Spiering, in her castle of Dätzingen in the Böblingen district at the heart of Swabia:

My Dear Alfred,

First I must tell you how much I enjoyed your visit here. Our pleasant outings on sea and along the shore, our discussions on so many topics and problems have done me a lot of good. With whom could I speak so freely as with a brother whose age is so near my own? Since poor Adolf's death you have been the only one who shares the same memories of childhood. It was a delight to me to know that you, too, are convinced that we have gained by the Act of Algeciras all that we could reasonably ask or expect. Certainly on a number of minor points we might have obtained even more if His Majesty had not turned nervous at the end: but, on the whole we have upheld our standpoint, and upheld it in very difficult circumstances. Two distinct gains: We have proved that even thorny questions which concern the prestige of great powers can be settled by peaceful negotiation at a conference table. We have avoided a war in which, as the world-situation is at present, we should have risked much, could loose a great deal, but gain little. When I add that, by my handling of the Morocco question, I caused the fall of our most dangerous opponent Delcassé, who would have been only too glad to set a match to the powder magazine of Europe, I feel we may be content. It will interest you to know that, as long ago as

March, President Roosevelt said to our Ambassador, Speck von
Sternberg that, in his opinion, Germany, by means of the conference, had gained the object for which she intervened in the
Morocco business; that the agreement reached was a triumph
for German diplomacy. The president spoke from the point of
view of an observer friendly to both sides; of a looker-on, not
directly interested in the outcome in so far as the interests of
peace were not endangered. He said that he had good grounds for
believing that, had the conference failed because Germany wished
to extort any further concessions from France, both European
and American public opinion would have turned against us, and
German credit and influence have received a set-back in consequence. He added that, if that had happened, we should have
had to take far more than our share of blame for the evil consequences everywhere resulting from a disturbance of *status quo*.

All this was reported to me by Speck von Sternberg, on 7th
March, after a long conversation with the president. This
shrieking of Pan-Germans leaves me cold. What business have
these fools to reproach me with timid and unsuccessful advocacy
of Germany's rights and interests? I am as firm and conscientious
as any man where German rights and interests are at stake: in
that I will yield to nobody, and let myself be outdone by nobody!
Let these people who vaguely accuse me of tenderness to the
foreigner, make definite objections. Let them tell me just where I
failed worthily to uphold German rights, where I failed to maintain German dignity. Since no one seems able to give me a case
in point I can only conclude that they imagine the courtesy which
I always strive to show in my personal dealings with others to be
the sole characteristic of my policy. That is a profound mistake!
On my side I find it hard to believe that Liebermann, von Sonnenberg, Hasse, *e tutti quanti* do not go on the principle that politeness is a form of weakness—especially in foreign politics. What
they cannot see is that it is a matter of being firm or polite at the
right moment. A consistently overbearing, inconsiderate and
chauvinist tone, ill-manners and such violent provocation of the
foreigner as we see all too constantly in a certain section of our
press, work to our detriment. If I, in my responsible position,
were to adopt them, incalculable consequences would follow. I
am still resolved to abide by the motto emblazoned on an old
Bülow pedigree of 1650:

> " *Der ist nicht flugs ein Edelmann,*
> *Der geboren ist aus grossem Stamm*

> *Oder der Geld und Reichtum hat*
> *Und tut doch keine redliche Tat.*
> *Die Tugend und die Höflichkeit*
> *Adelt den Menschen allezeit."* [1]

If the Pan-Germans appeal to Bismarck, a careful study of the speeches and diplomacy of that greatest of German statesmen shows that his strength lay, not in sabre-rattling or spur-clanking, but in his just appreciation of men and circumstances. A minister, Bismarck once said in the Reichstag—or was it in the Prussian Chamber of Deputies?—cannot control the stream of time, nor can he turn it for a moment. He can only steer the ship of State to the best of his judgment and conviction. If fortune is with him he has done his country good service; if his luck is bad he passes into oblivion. The efforts of the Pan-Germans have this that is good about them—they seek to keep alive a vigorous national feeling, and to counteract the tendencies of the German philistines to a flaccid cosmopolitanism, and a narrow parish-pump view of politics. But in practical politics the head is of more importance than any blunt, warm-hearted, honesty. The worthy Professor Hasse would realize this if he were in my shoes. My patriotism is at least equally sensitive and quite as active as that of the most convinced Pan-German. The difference is that, with me, love of country is tempered by a greater measure of caution and self-control, of moderation and reflection. I know the situation more exactly than these well-meaning but unskilful people. My knowledge puts me in a position to see dangers of which they have no inkling, and prevents me from being ruled by purely subjective emotion. I can see better than they what consequences a policy of impulse might bring upon the country. So that therefore, and since mine is the responsibility for the whole course of events, I oppose both at Court and in the Reichstag, all efforts and tendencies which the exigencies of the moment make unsuitable. I oppose the application of that famous sabre-rattling policy, which Bismarck never applied at the wrong moment, to circumstances calling for a clear head and a wary hand. To those who can only din "national pride" into my ears I answer that true national

---

[1] To be born of a great house,
To possess gold and lands
And yet perhaps to do no deed of fame—
This does not, of itself, make a nobleman.
But courtesy and courage
Make a man noble at all times.

pride consists in keeping firmly in view in all circumstances, the real and abiding interests of the nation. The fate of the Second Empire and of Napoleon III, have shown us where a policy of romantic jingoism leads a country. That Emperor was neither ignoble nor ungifted and yet in the end he lost his throne. I do not want us, too, to end in a catastrophe.

You tell me that many people, even in Court circles and at the Foreign Office, feel that I have been lacking in resolution. I think that in China and Morocco, in Polynesia and South America in Venezuela and Haiti—not to mention the matter of Germany's creditors in Greece—I have always proved how seriously I take the insistence on our rights and interests abroad. Have I ever, in any crisis that occurred since I took over the control of foreign policy, in the spring, for instance, of '99 when the Samoa question became critical, or the January of 1900, when German mail-steamers were seized in the most brutal way by England—lacked what firmness the situation demanded? In each of these cases we had a choice of three courses; we might have declared war. No doubt! Either the Pan-German complaints of my alleged complaisance at these and similar incidents, are senseless, or they imply some kind of blame that we did not then appeal to the *ultiam ratio regum*. In foreign policy one has to realize clearly, and in good time, the consequence of all one says, advises, or censures. Nothing can be gained with half-truths, confused statements, a vaguely inflated tone. I say therefore that one possible course was to declare war.

I do not know whether Hasse and Liebermann, von Sonnenberg, and Jordan Kröcher, who also fails to find in me " the strong man," really do regret my having avoided war! I equally do not know whether these gentlemen themselves would have taken this path in my responsible position. I doubt it. In spite of all evidence to the contrary I still think too highly of their patriotism. If we had been attacked, no matter by whom, if in reality any interest vital to Germany had been injured—no matter by whom—while I remained in office, we should have defended ourselves, and fought to the bitter end. But to provoke without grounds amounting to compulsion, a war which would involve civilized nations in terrible conflict, among them nations who never before had faced each other in battle; a war whose consequences for the economic life of these nations, their national activity, their welfare (and with that the welfare of the world, the cultural progress of humanity!) I need scarcely indicate to you— that is something for which no one could be responsible whose love of his country did not merely consist in high-flown phrases but who seriously desired her happiness.

Prince Bismarck in his immortal speech on the market-place at Jena declared he had waged three necessary wars. After these, he continued, there was no need for us to wage any others. From future wars we had nothing to gain. It would be the result of incompetence or negligence if we let ourselves be drawn into war. I shall not raise the question whether there are people among us who have taken the chauvinists and jingoes of other lands as models. If many folk and some whole sections of opinion— even people at Court, even journalists, deputies, professors— want a Foreign Minister who will hurry Germany into war with what a French statesman has called *le cœur léger*, they had better look for a new Imperial Chancellor. I am not the man for that sort of thing. By misuse of the noble words " glory " and " honour " great nations have been led to the abyss.

As I have often told you I consider intelligent criticism of every government and Minister very desirable. Reasonable criticism is as necessary to the political health and intellectual balance of a minister as is salt for one's digestion and bodily health. Criticism has this advantage that it compels one to criticize oneself and puts an end to the great mistake of self-complacency. I consider that sort of criticism the very spice of my activities as a minister. That is why for the last nine years I have read both the *Berliner Tageblatt* and *Deutsche Tageszeitung* with my morning tea. If the one praises the other usually attacks me. Sometimes they both conduct a regular case against me, but so constructively that I can derive profit from the proceedings. In this way I take, each morning, the necessary pinch of critical salt my digestion demands.

But to put a spoke in the wheel of Foreign Policy, as so often happens, by some foolish propaganda article, full of hysterical venomous " criticism " without real insight into the actual foreign situation, or a due survey of the complicated international chessboard, is to cripple Germany's action abroad and weaken and discredit her with foreign powers. A country's foreign credit should be maintained—to discredit wantonly is thoughtless and may be criminal.

If therefore we did not wish to go to war over either of these two incidents—the Samoa or the East African coast—there remained a second course we might have pursued, though that also we refused to take. We might have let things slide and gone quietly home, confining ourselves, at best, to protests. But

II.   Q

Foreign Policy rarely scores a success with empty protests and never with mere verbal heroism, with windy expressions of "displeasure." But there was a third course—to maintain our point of view; get all we possibly could by means of diplomacy, stand fast to our rights, and see that our interests were ably defended.

That was my method and I am convinced that by my handling of these questions I not only pursued the ablest policy possible at the moment, but the only policy that took into account the permanent interests of the nation. By this method we reached a satisfactory result of the incident of the impounded ships. As for Samoa we acquired in the end Upolu and Apia and have therefore, in this matter also, successfully defended the real interests of Germany. No other star shall ever guide my policy than the permanent interests of the country. Consequently I am not disturbed by Pan-German reproaches and hysteria, since he who takes that star as guide will gain his victory in the end.

Now as to our relations with England, which once again are being much canvassed. The majority of the German people are cultured and civilized, they disapprove of the foolish, crude expressions of dislike, into which, alas, our sympathy for the Boers betrayed us. That majority is quite willing to admit that if the Boers fought bravely for hearth and home, the British army, officers and men, maintained, no less, its own reputation for courage and endurance, and that the English nation gave proof, throughout the whole South African War, of an energy, a resolution, a patriotism, such as it would be petty not to recognize, and which I hope our own countrymen would display if the need arose. Of course the latest attacks on us in the English press are just as silly and objectionable as earlier German press attacks on England. But above all, the majority of our people can recognize that it is not the Government's business to play that part of Providence in the world which the ruminating speculations of German doctrinaires are always assigning to it. Equally it cannot play the part of policeman, of guardian of international morals, which German public opinion, always too prone to take up a moralistic attitude, seems to expect. The business of the German Government is simply to look after the permanent interests of the Empire. That is what I have done, and I consider I have done my country good service. I may tell you quite categorically that any other policy would have jeopardized the safety of Germany. It might even have conjured up the spectre of a World War. I was not for me to expose the nation without cause to such a con tingency. So long as I remain a Chancellor I shall continue, undisturbed by aspersions and misrepresentation, careless alike of the *civium ardor prava jubentium* and of the *vultus instantis tyranni,* indifferent to unjust attacks, to pursue only such courses as will not endanger the future of the German people. I refuse to play *va banque* with the treasure of the national welfare, honour, and future well-being entrusted to me. I am too experienced and too patriotic for that. I am also a little too intelligent.

The policy of a great country cannot be conducted on sympathies and antipathies, but only after full consideration of the general international position. Our position in Europe and in the world is assuredly not so simple that we can indulge ourselves in the luxury of emotions which have nothing to do with politics. A foreign policy, dominated by the considerations of home policy—the sort of policy which many of our Conservative Agrarians, and even National-Liberal Industrialists would like to see us pursue towards England, which so many of our Democrats and Social-Democrats would like to see adopted towards Russia, is invariably a mistake. To steer the ship of state between the rocks which menace from all points of the compass, we must keep ourselves free from pre-conceptions, free from any considerations of sentiment. We need a clear head and a steady hand. I want to remain on good terms with England, but on a footing of complete equality, on a basis of complete independence. We must never let ourselves be misused—and least of all against Russia— as the sword of England on the Continent. Our relationship with a great Empire like the British must be maintained on our side with full national self-consciousness, but also with quiet foresight, and without those passions that obscure. It is not merely criminal, it is *stupid,* to embitter German feeling against England, always and everywhere to stir up hatred against England, to fan tiny sparks into a blaze. We have no need to bring ourselves into a position of hereditary hostility to England, to get into the kind of relationship in which we know in advance that, at every regrouping of the Powers, we shall find the English our enemies. If, in the course of world-history, historic necessity, what the Greeks used to call *ananke,* produces between two great nations such a relationship as at present exists between ourselves and France, it has to be reckoned with, just as everything fundamental has to be reckoned with. But, I repeat, it is infamous and stupid artificially to create a powerful opponent. We have numerous points of contact with England; she is our best customer; so far she has opened her ports and her trade to us as to her own subjects. In unison with her we struggle abroad for commercial liberty. Obviously there are points of friction, questions in which reciprocal concessions may be necessary; but not one in which, with calm, goodwill, and the requisite *doigté*, it is impossible to reach an understanding along peaceful lines in the interests of both countries. Such is my considered opinion.

So long as I remain at the helm I shall continue steadfastly to pursue the policy I have pursued till to-day. We must not awaken Russian mistrust by flirting with the Poles or opposing the Russians in the Dardanelles, the pivot of Bismarck's Re-Insurance Treaty. In the East we must prevent Austria from adventuring against the Balkan States (Rumania, Serbia, Montenegro) in the interests of ambitious Staff Officers and fiery Magyars. Neither the old Emperor, Francis Joseph, nor the anti-Magyar Slavophil Heir-Apparent, have any desire for such escapades. Let us prevent any action which Russia could not accept, and I do not see why peace should not be maintained.

" To keep the peace is our first task and is a necessity for us," said Bismarck fourteen years ago to the deputation of Swabians who came to Friedrichsruhe to do him honour. (Perhaps Dätzinger and Böblinger were among them.) His words remain true to-day.

One word more on the subject of this new " dislike of the Empire." I can understand the Socialists doing their best to stir up such dislike by word and pen. That is their *raison d'être*, their whole policy. Discontent is the fostering soil without which the Socialist baccillus could not develop. " This cursed contentment," said Ferdinand Lassalle long ago, and from his point of view he was right. But the jaundiced rage, the eagerness to befoul their own nest of our anti-Socialists and patriots *par excellence*, their ever-persistent painting of our circumstances, even the least significant incident, in colours of unrelieved despair, are something I find it harder to understand. I say with emphasis that such spiteful distortions by the Nationalists do Germany at least as much harm as Socialist hysteria and intrigue. The more confidence is destroyed from above, the more will be accomplished from below. How can we be respected abroad when those whom we consider our best patriots, those who have elected themselves the guardians of the sacred fire of the Fatherland, do all they can to embarrass our position, point out each failure, gleefully exaggerate each mistake, and distort everything *in peius*. This rage of self-depreciation and self-criticism is a disease, alas! confined to Germany. It is only the German eagle that constantly befouls its own nest. Where else will you find anything like it? Are there not everywhere innumerable imperfections, short-comings, abuses? But nowhere else are they so dragged into the light of day, so artificially exaggerated as in Germany.   I am sometimes reminded of Treitschke's saying that the German at home would do well to show a fraction of that intelligence in home affairs which he shows in the affairs of other people once he settles down outside his country.   Are things so much better abroad than here? I should like to see our Conservatives suddenly forced to live in the U.S.A.; our Centre Party in anti-Clerical France; our Socialists, I will not say in Russia, but simply in England or in Italy where no such thing as direct and universal suffrage with the secret ballot exists, in France, where there is still no income-tax, in America where they have little use for the disciples of Karl Marx. If the foreigner judges our country by the verdict we ourselves pass upon it he must have a fine picture of it.

What is one to think when great German newspapers (not to mention every beer-house politician) shout against German " militarism," whereas the French, whom I know almost as well as my own compatriots, are at bottom far more militarist than we? Why these invectives against German imperialism, so inoffensive in comparison with the imperialism, or rather " navalism," of the English? This continual crying of stinking fish forges excellent weapons for foreigners to use against us.

I have gone farther and said more than I intended when I began this letter. That's what comes of dictating. The man who dictates is always inclined to be long-winded. Perhaps, too, it may be a sign I am getting old; I have not, like Nestor, seen three generations, but almost two. I'm fifty-seven! In any case I think this habit of dictating, which I acquired at the Paris Embassy a quarter of a century ago, has something to be said for it. I even attribute to it my facility of improvization, of speaking without notes in public. Dictation forces a man to co-ordinate his thoughts, and cast his sentences rapidly, though it often leads into excessive verbiage. But now:

Claudite jam rivos, pueri, sat prata biberunt.

While I was in Rome, in my first winter there, a brilliant orator ended his speech with these words of the aged Palæmon in Virgil's *Eclogues*. The orator was Marco Minghetti, to whom I, a young attaché, listened in surprised admiration. The speech was made in the winter 1874-5. But when I myself began to speak in the Reichstag I had only, besides Minghetti, heard four parliamentary orators. I had listened on the 1st April 1867, to Bismarck's reply to Benningsen's interpolation on the Luxembourg. I was at the back of the Diplomatic box where father, who at the time was Minister for Mecklenburg in Berlin, had managed to smuggle me. In 1875, as I have said, it was Minghetti, Marie's step-father whom she loved and esteemed so highly. In 1879 at Paris, or rather, Versailles, since the French Parliament still sat there, I heard Gambetta, Leon Say, and Dufaure. When I spoke for the first time in the Reichstag it was Leon Say I remembered, with his calm and incisive eloquence.

Vale ac me ama,

BERNHARD.

When, to-day, I re-read this letter which contains a summary of ideas expressed in the Reichstag, and in numerous conversations with German politicians and publicists my report of the interview with Roosevelt, who at that time was still reckoned a friend of Germany, strikes me as really tragic. Eight years later Germany had to fight for her existence, and already she had turned the public opinion of the world against her. Germany, as Roosevelt had said, was made responsible beyond all justice, for the World War and for its consequences. And, with a brutal ruthlessness unknown till now in the history of the world, we are being bled white for reparations for which our signature was extorted.

The " brilliant second " dispatch to Goluchowski, had been, to say the least, clumsy. Other news of the same kind from Berlin seemed to show that in my absence the Emperor was letting his temperament run away with him. I therefore felt it to be necessary to read him a little lesson in political history. In any case another incident had given me food for thought. During the long and very gracious visit H.I.M. had paid me at Norderney one of his remarks had struck me especially. I had been praising the courage and intelligence of the new Russian Premier and President of the Council, Stolypin, and of the Minister of Finance, Witte, who, although they both fought the Revolution, did not wish a return to the old autocracy. The Emperor thought this over. Then he said: " Certainly Stolypin and Witte are clever and go-ahead, but it seems to me that they think more of Russia than they do of the Tsar, their master." A letter I addressed to His Majesty, to congratulate him on the successful accouchement of the Crown Princess, seemed to me a favourable opportunity for delivering my little lecture. It is dated 17th July 1906.

To begin with I advised His Majesty, on the occasion of his

grandson's christening, to address to the German people one of those messages which Lucanus knew so well how to phrase, expressing his thanks to all classes for the sympathy they had shown with the happy event.   I suggested that he should make as generous a gift as possible to the " League for the Prevention of Infant Mortality," which aimed at founding an Infants' Hospital and a special clinic for the study of infant diseases.

I then recommended him to invite King Edward to stand god-father to his grandson, the Crown Prince's first child.   The King, who, like all the Coburgs had a strong sense of family, would be sure to accept with pleasure.   " *Les petits cadeaux entretiennent l'amitié.*"

I added that, in my view, he would do well to make a similar request to the President of the U.S.A.   I seemed to remember how, in the eighteenth century, the magistrature of Berne and the States-General of Holland had stood godfathers at the baptism of Prussian princes, particularly of Frederick the Great.

In the more important part of my letter I dealt with the situation in Russia.   Actually it was very serious.   We were confronted with the breakdown of Russian autocracy, which for over a century, had been the hope and sometimes the buttress of Conservative and Monarchist Europe, just as it had been the bane, and sometimes the terror, of western democracy.   But this system, suitable enough to Slav and Tartar, to the Asiatic core of the Russian temperament, had always been against our ways of thinking.   The German is individualist and freedom-loving.   When the Germanic nations first appeared on the stage of history they already possessed conceptions of liberty and equality which recalled the tendencies of America to-day.   When, in the eighteenth century, absolutism momentarily won the upper hand (for the greater good of the State and our civilization), it imitated the Bourbons, whose châteaux and methods of government were alike copied by German princes.   And yet what a difference between Louis XIV and Frederick the Great! The one said, " *L'Etat, c'est moi,*" the other, " *Je ne suis que le premier serviteur de l'Etat.*"   The Germans have always felt the relationship between prince and people as a mutual obligation: trust for trust.

The Emperor himself, on the occasion when I had the honour to be present with him at a performance of " Tsar Feodor " by a really excellent Russian company, had pointed out how, with the Russians, servility was directed less to the person of the autocrat than to autocracy itself, as an institution.   In the same way the Turk bowed before the throne, and the Chinese was beheaded if he did not bare his head before a picture of the Son of Heaven. But such customs and ideas have never been understood by the Germans, who have no liking either for the Chinese kowtow or the Byzantine obeisance. What a difference between the proud bearing of the nobles of Brabant in the old German " Lohengrin " and the grovelling of the boyars in " Tsar Feodor " !

I urged that the Emperor would do well to maintain reserve with regard to internal events in Russia, and be careful not to become involved in them. He must not repeat the blunder of Frederick William II, who invaded France at the beginning of the French Revolution. Moreover the reigning Tsar and his late father were in no small measure responsible for present happenings in Russia. I proceeded:

> Neither were able to read the signs of the times. They imagined that without reforms, without any timely concession, a movement as widespread and deeply felt and, in spite of all its errors, as great, as the present Liberal movement in Russia, could be repressed with nothing better than Cossack knouts, the lances of the Uhlans, the muskets of the grenadiers. That has been a fatal mistake—the mistake not only of Plehve and Tcherevin, but of two Tsars. One disastrous war was enough to produce a débâcle, since defeat is what shakes autocracy most. The heavy hand of an Alexander III might conceivably have delayed, but could scarcely have avoided these events. In a certain measure events in Russia may improve the foreign political situation to our advantage. But on the other hand the Russian situation gives ocular proof to the peoples of the difference in development between Eastern autocracy and the Western European states. Constitutional and Liberal England is in a brilliant position; the French Republic whose Socialists take part in the Government, enjoys universal prestige, and all the kings of the world meet in its capital; parliamentary Italy is in a much better state than many people would have us suppose; the smaller democratic states, Denmark, Belgium, Holland, and Norway, are flourishing. But, on the other hand, that ancient citadel of monarchic and conservative principle, the Habsburg Monarchy, is crumbling, and in Russia, which appeared the impregnable fortress of extreme autocratic, militarist and orthodox ideas, foundations, roof, and pillars are shaking.

The whole position therefore had grown most difficult even for a powerful ruler. Though I was not on the whole more pessimistic I dealt with this topic on the assumption that in our internal policy we must combine great care and foresight with our firmness, that we must act with calm, with courage and intelligence.

Anyone who studies *à vol d'oiseau*, the developments of the last hundred years will be more than ever convinced that the course of events on earth never proceeds in a straight line, but oscillates, and is subject to ebb and flow. The French Revolution was an enormous push forward for democratic ideas and ideals. When Napoleon, the greatest soldier of modern times, the heir of the Revolution, had fallen, the old monarchies tried to re-establish the *status quo ante* 1789. But they based their action more on abstract principle than on skill and caution. The first reaction came in 1830. In 1848 their defeat was a greater and more serious one. Then, and through Bismarck, came the swing of the pendulum, in 1866 and 1870.

Since then the opinion has prevailed that a strong monarchy, with able ministers, is better than Liberal institutions, a democratic tendency, and petty parliamentary intrigue. But now by a sequence of blunders, of negligences and acts of rashness, the good old gentleman on the Danube and the amiable young sovereign on the Neva have succeeded in making people feel again that there is more hope from the left than from the right.

In that I saw no special danger so long as we continued to govern with calm and intelligence at home, with clear-headed dexterity abroad. Knowing William II's predilection for Latin quotations I ended with the recommendation given by the wise Horace to Calliope:

"*Vis consilii expers mole ruit sua!*"

But the Emperor neither understood the intention or *sous entendu* of this letter. To my cousin the Minister von Jenisch, who accompanied him on his Northern tour as representative of the Foreign Office, he said: " I've had a long letter from the Chancellor, but really I don't know what to make of it. He used to write brilliantly, wittily—it was a pleasure. Now he lectures. After he fell ill all the deputies made such a fuss of him. Is he letting himself be gulled by these . . . people in the Reichstag? "

CHAPTER XVI

Foreign problems—A report of Herr von Jenisch on the Kaiser's remarks about foreign policy—The fantastic ideas and plans of Professor Schiemann—Bethmann and the Polish question—A letter from the Kaiserin—Meeting of William II and Edward VII in Friedrichshof —Duke of Connaught in Kiel—Death of Prince Albrecht of Brunswick—The Brunswick Council of Regency—Amnesty on the occasion of the Crown Princess's accouchement—Prince Hohenlohe's Memoirs— William II's attitude to the Memoirs of ministers, etc.—Offshoots of the Hohenlohe family abroad—Podbielski and the Tippelskirch affair —A fresh enormity of Count Monts.

IN my conduct of Foreign Affairs the unstable, at times fantastic mind of His Majesty was a source of greater anxiety than in home policy, especially since there were always intriguers and dilettanti who sought to profit by this Imperial weakness. At the end of July Baron von Jenisch, who was attached to the Emperor as representative of the Foreign Office, wrote to me as follows from Drontheim:

To-day, after a long talk with Professor Schiemann, His Majesty spoke to me in more or less the following terms: " If, in the near future, things go to pieces in Russia; if, as Schoen seems to say in his report, they are preparing for the federation of a certain number of republics there, I will never consent to leave the Baltic Provinces in the lurch. I shall go to their assistance, and they must be incorporated in the German Empire. I shall not raise a finger to do this as long as the present Russian government maintains itself, but I could never leave the Balts to their fate. The Poles will naturally try to extend their territory northwards to the sea, and to that I will never consent. They can expand as much as they like eastwards and south-eastwards where they have economic interests. I have already settled with Bülow and Bethmann-Hollweg that in the event of catastrophe in Russia we shall put no obstacle in the way of the Polish programme (the restoration of the Kingdom of Poland). Then the hour will have arrived when all the great Polish landlords will have to take an oath of allegiance to me. Whoever refuses will

have to quit Prussian territory and so we shall be well rid of
inconvenient Polish elements.   In the near future our policy and
our diplomacy may find that they have to tackle very different
problems from those of to-day."

Baron von Jenisch added that he felt certain that this sequence
of ideas was the result of a talk which the Emperor had had with
Schiemann, who had previously spoken to Jenisch on very much the
same lines.   Jenisch had seriously warned him against making such
suggestions to the Emperor, and Schiemann had agreed but
broken his promise.   The report continued:

"Captain Hintze," I answered the Emperor, "assures me
that up to now there have been no signs of the German elements
in the Baltic Province gravitating towards us, and that Schiemann
appears to be very biased in his estimate of what is going on
there. Admiral von Müller informs me that the Emperor is
beginning to get impatient at not having received more certain
news as to the Tsar's intentions for a meeting with him.
His Majesty accordingly wants to make inquiries by telegram.   I
supported Müller in his suggestion that such a step would be
almost bound to create the impression at St. Petersburg that we
attached special importance to such a meeting, and that, at this
critical time, we wanted to induce the Tsar to quit his country.
That, as had happened before, might be used against us later,
politically.   Eventually the Emperor declared himself satisfied
that Captain Hintze, who is about to return to St. Petersburg,
should discreetly inform himself of the Tsar's intention.   Only
recently, at Kiel, Prince Henry begged me to ask you to do your
best to get Tirpitz kept in office. His Majesty is being influenced
against him by certain people, and has told Prince Henry repeatedly that Tirpitz was the cause of your illness.   Prince Henry
protested at once against this insinuation and against the suggestion that Tirpitz wants to become Imperial Chancellor. He knows
the latter far too well not to be certain that such ambitions are entirely foreign to his nature. Unfortunately Tirpitz is suspicious
and easily offended. The French yacht-owner Menier (the same
who, four years ago had Waldeck-Rousseau aboard his yacht) has
been chosen out for special attention by the Emperor. He was
accompanied by two charming young women and the usual
crowd.   Menier seemed strongly in favour of an agreement
between all the European Powers against America, and of the
Emperor's visiting Paris. His Majesty expressed a special wish

that all these guests (thirty-four altogether including the Embassy people) should be invited to a gala dinner at Drontheim."

Professor Schiemann, whose name I have mentioned several times before, was one of those Balts who see the world and every event from the narrow angle of local patriotism. This parish pump outlook has its touching side, no doubt, when one remembers the secular struggles of the Baltic peoples for Germanism. But this subordination of the interests of the whole Empire, the *salus publica*, to the woes and hopes of a small section of Germanism, was a matter for very grave objection. Moreover Schiemann was a dangerous flatterer for a sovereign whose reason did not always check his fantasy.

Hintze was our best naval attaché in St. Petersburg, where he had created a position for himself and set up some very useful connections. Tirpitz, though in every way exceptional, was what the French call " *un mauvais coucheur.*" It was never easy to get on with him. That His Majesty should have given out that he had converted me to his Polish programme gave me yet a further proof of how his loquacity and vivid imagination inclined him to put into others' mouths words which had as much to do with any reality as the exploits of the famous Münchhausen. He had rarely mentioned the Polish question, but I had never concealed from him my opinion that to re-establish an independent Poland would be the greatest blunder that Prussian and German policy could commit. A kingdom of Poland on our Eastern frontier would, as I often repeated to him, be the natural ally of our irreconcilable opponent in the West; a Polish army in Warsaw would be the equivalent of a French one on our Eastern frontier. Bethmann-Hollweg's enthusiasm for Polish ideals I ascribed to some hereditary influence. His grandfather, Professor Bethmann-Hollweg, had been to his dying day the deadly enemy of Bismarck. Between 1850 and 1860 he had striven with blind zeal, at the Prussian Court and in political circles, for a pro-Polish policy. One evening, after my return to Berlin at the end of the summer of 1906, at a dinner of the Ministers given in the Zoological Gardens, I asked Bethmann-Hollweg to his face to explain his attitude to the Polish problem. He answered with a certain embarrassment that all that he had said to the Emperor had been " purely academic—a mere toying with ideas." I left him in no doubt as to my own opposition to such puerilities, and he assured me that as a *Regierungspräsident* at Bromberg he had become too fully aware of the danger to the Empire latent in Polish

propaganda to think seriously of such a " folly " as any resurrection
of Poland.

And, indeed, from that day on, right up to the day of my retirement, Bethmann-Hollweg, as far as I was concerned, showed himself uncompromisingly anti-Polish. He even pleaded zealously the
cause of the Expropriation Law, about which I myself was very
doubtful. Soon after my retirement, Bethmann, now Imperial
Chancellor, answered an enquiry by the Eastern Marches League,
whether the old policy in the Eastern Marches would be maintained now that he was in power, with a pathetic " *nunquam retror-
sum.*" But, not long after that, he wavered in his Eastern policy
and, in spite of warnings and lively opposition in the Prussian
Ministry, began, little by little, to prepare the resurrection of
Poland, at first in secret, then in his speeches and negotiations in
Vienna. Next to the extravagant ultimatum to Serbia, the restoration of Poland is the gravest blunder in our history. To these two
errors the name Bethmann-Hollweg remains irrevocably attached.

I was destined to make the acquaintance of M. Menier, the
great French chocolate king, in the June of 1909; he had come on
his yacht to take part in the Regatta Week at Kiel. It was on this
same yacht, during a luncheon party given by the French on the
day when I resigned my Chancellorship, that for the last time I was
on board a ship with William II.

During my leave of absence in 1906 I did my best, by letters, to
improve the still very strained relations between the Emperor and
his uncle. Such an improvement seemed all the more desirable
since the political situation between their countries had taken a
decided turn for the better. Unfortunately my constant endeavours
were hindered rather than helped by the Kaiserin, as a rule so
kindly and so sensible. She wrote to me at Norderney, at the end
of July 1906.

DEAR PRINCE,
    Forgive me please if once again I disturb your rest at
Norderney, but to-day I received a telegram from the Emperor
informing me that the King of England intends to visit him at
Friedrichshof. Before his departure the Emperor said to me that
if the King wanted to see him he could come to him at Potsdam,
or Wilhelmshöhe or at Homburg. But now all of a sudden the
meeting is to be at Friedrichshof, in the Country house of the
Hessian Princess, and not even in one of the Emperor's own
Palaces. This idea seems to me rather unfortunate. What do
you think? It seems to me that after all the misunderstandings—

not to give them any worse name—between the two sovereigns and their countries, King Edward ought to visit the Emperor in one of his own Castles, at least, if not in his own capital. I don't want to interfere with things that are not my business, but I do want to prevent people from being given fresh food for gossip. Why can't the fat old gentleman manage to get as far as Wilhelmshöhe? Or couldn't the Emperor go to his Homburg Castle and meet his uncle there? I can't see why not!

With cordial greetings to your wife and best wishes for your recovery, I am,

Your most devoted,
A. VICTORIA.

I reassured the Empress; the interview took place at Friedrichshof. I had it "written up" in a friendly article by the *Norddeutsche Allgemeine Zeitung*, which met with a good reception in England.

This interview had been all the more desirable because of an incident that had occurred during the Regatta Week at Kiel. In itself it may be hardly worth mentioning, but it had very much upset the Duke of Connaught, who was so popular in England and so favourably disposed to Germany, as well as his wife, a Prussian Princess. The Duke and Duchess were returning from the baptism of their grandchild in Stockholm. The English yacht, "Enchantress," on which they sailed had been signalled to the officials of the Kaiser-Wilhelm Canal as desiring passage, and at the same time, an express request had been made that there should be no regulation honours rendered, and no official visits because of the lack of time. This had been announced to the Emperor. None the less, since he happened to be in Kiel for the Regatta, he could not refrain from going very early, in a pinnace to Holtenau, at the mouth of the Canal to see for himself whether his uncle would render honours to the Imperial flag over the port, and pay him a visit. The Emperor came alongside the "Enchantress" just as she was entering the locks, and promptly clambered aboard her. The Duke was shaving, the Duchess just beginning her toilet. When, their privacy thus invaded, they presented themselves before His Majesty he rated them soundly. The Duke replied that he had not had the least idea that his Imperial nephew was in Kiel, which only increased His Majesty's resentment. It is true that we no longer live in an age when a glass of water can decide for war or peace, but still it cannot be denied that by his constant display of a mixture of rudeness and touchiness, William II had succeeded in making himself

disliked in nearly every foreign court. This created constant difficulties for our policy and sometimes checked it altogether.

Before I pass to the most important event of the year 1906, the
dissolution of the Reichstag on 13th December, I should like first
to deal with some events which occurred in the latter half of this
year. On the 13th of September Prince Albert of Prussia, who
since 1885 had been Regent of Brunswick, died unexpectedly of a
stroke. A Council of Regency composed of the three leading members of the Ministry of State: the Minister Dr. von Otto, Privy
Councillor Hartwig, and Privy Councillor Trieps, was called at once
into being by the provisions of the Law of 1879. In addition there
sat on it the President of the last Diet and the President of the
Supreme Court of the Duchy. I was able at once to promise this
Council the Emperor's support. What a difference between this
provisional government, composed of responsible, serious men, and
that triumvirate of absurd rapscallions who seized power in the old
Guelph town after the November revolution! At the head of the
November Ministry in Brunswick there was a Herr Sepp Orter, a
Bavarian vagabond, who till then had picked up a living in Brunswick
by stuffing mattresses, whose preparation for government had been
several years' penal servitude. This worthy Prime Minister entrusted the Ministry of Education—that is to say the whole control
of primary and secondary education—to a midwife. This may perhaps have been an acknowledgment of the political equality of
women; or a delicate tribute to the *ars obstetricia*! In 1906 the
Premier of the Provisional Government, Herr von Otto, belonged
to that class of administrative official who, under the old régime,
was a credit and a blessing not only to Prussia but to every Federal
State. In an interview for which I had summoned Herr von Otto
to Berlin I asked him if Prince Albert's proper successor would not
be Prince Friedrich Heinrich, his son. Herr von Otto replied with
some reluctance that the eldest son of the dead regent would never
be acceptable to Brunswick because, in religion, his views and tendencies were too openly orthodox-pietist. When, a little later,
Prince Friedrich Heinrich was forced, because of grave moral
scandals, to retire into private life, I saw at once that Herr von Otto
had, even then, got wind of the Prince's backslidings, and so had
contrived another excuse for rejecting him. Prince Friedrich
Heinrich, who personally gave one an impression of modest industry,
was respected and liked, not only in the regiment he commanded
(the famous Schwedt Dragoons, raised in 1689 by the Margrave
Georg Friedrich), but in many intellectual and scholarly circles in
Berlin, and especially among ecclesiastics. When his delinquencies,

were revealed he was ordered to send in his papers, forbidden the Court, and deprived of the Black Eagle which, like all the Princes of Prussia, he had received at the age of ten. In 1914 the Prince begged to be reinstated in the army. He received permission to enlist as a private, but was never given any promotion in spite of all his bravery in the field. He took his duty so seriously that, in the presence of his former batman who, unlike himself, had been promoted lance-corporal at the front, he never failed to stand to attention. It cannot be denied that the old régime punished moral lapses with exemplary severity.

In the Brunswick question William II, whom Philip Eulenburg had some reason to call William Proteus, was constantly changing his mind. Before Prince Friedrich Heinrich's delinquencies became known the Emperor wanted him to succeed. Then he had some thoughts of creating a younger son's portion for his own son, Prince Eitel Friedrich. For a time he played with the idea of annexing Brunswick and uniting it with the province of Hanover. Finally, as is known, he married his only daughter to Prince Ernest Augustus of Cumberland and set the young couple on the throne of Henry the Lion. The wedding of the Emperor's daughter set the seal on the reconciliation of the Hohenzollerns with the Guelphs, who had so obstinately resisted the Hohenstaufens in early days. In 1906 such a reconciliation still seemed unlikely. At that time the Emperor was annoyed with the Duke of Cumberland, not merely because he stuck firmly to his claim to Hanover, but because he had refused rather stiffly to accede to His Majesty's (and still more the Kaiserin's) wish that he should consent to the marriage of one of his daughters with the Crown Prince of Prussia. In this connection Philip Eulenburg, who was again in the entourage of His Majesty, wrote to me as follows:

As you guessed, the Brunswick question has caused a certain amount of heart-burning. You can easily explain to yourself the annoyance now shown against the Duke of Cumberland by the failure of the Emperor's initiative in repaying the Guelph fund and the rejection of the suggested alliance. This excitement only lasted a short time since the stupidly passive attitude of the unfortunately disposed Duke produced calm. When yesterday the Emperor received a letter from the Duke announcing to His Majesty that he and his eldest son, Prince George William, had handed over their rights to rule the Duchy to the youngest son, Prince Ernest Augustus, who could now as Duke take over the government of Brunswick, the Emperor declared that there could be no question of that, and he added: " Well now, if Bülow manages to handle this matter energetically, he'll have a chance of showing that he's still his old self."

This did not prevent me from answering the letter which the Duke of Cumberland had addressed to the Kaiser and myself, *suaviter in modo*, even though *fortiter in re*, with all the courtesy due not only to the chief of one of the oldest and most distinguished princely houses, but to misfortune.

Soon after the accouchement of the Crown Princess, I had suggested an amnesty to the Emperor in an urgent report which was not only most carefully thought out, but signed by all the members of the Prussian Ministry. In this report I had said that the more generously the matter was handled the greater would be the political success. The Kaiser had rejected these proposals angrily and with very ungracious marginal notes. He had not the slightest intention of proclaiming an amnesty because of the birth of a grandchild. When *he* was born there hadn't been any amnesty, etc.! He was opposed in principle to all amnesties. On such a matter the State Ministry had no business to take a resolution behind his back; he ought to have been consulted beforehand. Constitutionally a minister ought to wait till the monarch condescends to make his wishes known to him. Besides, the time for such an amnesty had passed (that was a *contradictio in adjecto*). In the first place the Liberal press had " most impertinently " demanded an amnesty. Then, when it had abandoned all hope of getting one it had " shamelessly " attacked the person of the All-Highest. If now he gave way to Liberal demands the thing would be interpreted as weakness.

I, however, stuck to my guns, and at last, with the help of Lucanus, who, in this matter also, gave me the most loyal support, succeeded in getting an Imperial amnesty of wide scope proclaimed on 24th August. The Emperor made trouble only on the wording of the decree. He wanted it expressly stated that since, by God's grace, a grandchild had been born into his family who would, in a few days, receive the sacrament of baptism, and that since thus an occasion was offered him to pardon evil deeds and show clemency, he desired to pardon even those who had committed offences against his person. Condemnations for *lése majesté* had considerably increased under William II. Undoubtedly the reason for this was that the Emperor, as I often had occasion to notice, was apt to lay far more stress on the form than on the substance of the Imperial concept. To me, therefore, it seemed all the more necessary, once a suitable occasion presented itself, to apply the corrective of an amnesty, especially since such condemnations were not infrequently the result of spiteful denunciations, usually after previous attempts to blackmail, or from motives of personal revenge. But I ought not to omit to add that never, in all my term of office, did it enter my head to propose such a law in defence of Imperial prestige as that of 1922 which Herr Joseph Wirth had passed for the defence of the Republic, a Draconian, and at the same time, a petty measure, by which the Republican leaders confessed that they were almost as sensitive on the subject of their very questionable system and their own insignificant persons as the " re-action " had been at the time of the Carlsbad resolution. I may say, and not without satisfaction, that during my whole twelve years of office I never needed to invoke the shade of Prince Clemens Metternich. *Malo periculosam libertatem.*

At the beginning of October 1906 there appeared the Memoirs of my esteemed predecessor, Prince Chlodwig Hohenlohe, who had been for many years my chief in Paris. They contained much that was new on the subject of Prince Bismarck's dismissal, on German relations with Russia and Austria, on Bismarck's opinions of William II. Generally speaking, their tone was one of moderate and far-sighted caution, which always distinguished the old Prince. William II was very much perturbed by their publication. The book had been published at the instance of Prince Chlodwig's third son, Prince Alexander Hohenlohe, whom the Emperor had never liked, whom only at my urgent entreaty he had promoted to the important post of District President in Colmar. His Majesty sent off an angry telegram to Prince Alexander's eldest brother, Prince Philip Ernest, declaring that he had " taken cognizance of the publication " with " indignation " and " astonishment."

" How did it happen that such material had ever been given to the public without my Imperial permission? I must characterize what has been done as, in the highest degree, tactless, indiscreet, and completely inopportune." It was unheard of to publish things concerning a monarch without having first got his consent.

Poor Prince Alexander came to see me in Homburg, where the Kaiser very kindly had placed his Castle at my disposal in order to complete my recovery, and where I used to take daily rides through those woods and dales I have known so well since earliest childhood. The idyllic peace I had enjoyed there for several days was disturbed by Prince Alexander. He was very upset. He tried to throw all the blame on the editor of the Memoirs, Dr. Curtius, who excused himself by saying he had imagined that, in publishing matter relating to a breach between Prince Bismarck and the Emperor, he was doing the latter a service. I did my best to avoid disciplinary investigation, both for Prince Alexander's own sake and in tribute to the memory of his father.

But the Emperor was hard to pacify. Few things annoyed him more than any publication concerning a sovereign, more especially concerning himself, unless it were in the style of Schiemann or Harnack, that is to say, devotional, full of a Byzantine adulation which almost became an apotheosis. I have had several interesting talks on this subject with him. In his heart he would have liked a law forbidding ministers, generals, or court officials ever to prepare any memoirs, forbidding publishers ever to publish memoirs. This trait he had in common with Louis XIV, whom nothing irritated more than the thought that he—*le Roi Soleil*—should ever be represented otherwise than at the zenith of his power and infallibility. Eight years before I had already had an argument with His Majesty on the subject of Prince Bismarck's *Thoughts and Memories*. In 1906, as in '98, I observed to the Emperor that even Louis XIV, suspicious and severe though he was, had not, once he was dead, been able to prevent the appearance of Saint-Simon's *Memoirs* in which the great writer has fixed ineffaceably for all time, the image of that vain and all too egoistic monarch. I also quoted to His Majesty the fine saying of Chateaubriand who cries pathetically: " *Tandis que les Césars de la décadence romaine se livrent à leurs désordres, grandit déjà en silence le jeune Tacite qui transmettera leur véritable image à la posterité.*"

The only method, I told His Majesty, by which a sovereign can hope to obtain a favourable judgment from Clio, the severest of the Muses, is to govern wisely. Finally I managed to prevent any disciplinary measure against Prince Alexander. But he lost his post. He had confessed to me during his visit to Homburg that he had not even read his father's memoirs before publication. Prince Hohenlohe-Langenburg, the Statthalter of Alsace-Lorraine, to whom the whole business was very painful, if only on account of the relationship between his distinguished house and the Emperor, wrote to me that he was " most grateful " that I had spared him the unpleasant task of instituting a disciplinary enquiry against his nephew, whose conduct he characterized as " unpardonably indiscreet " and " most unfortunate." He had induced his nephew to ask to be retired for a time and had written at once, direct to His Majesty, in that sense.

The Langenburg branch of the House of Hohenlohe affords a good example of that cosmopolitan trait which for centuries has been a somewhat unfortunate characteristic of the higher German nobility. A brother of the head of this house went to England where he married an Englishwoman of no great family, a Miss Seymour. His son, who received the title Count of Gleichen, was as I soon perceived during King Edward's visit to Kiel, a true-blue Briton, very jingo and very anti-German. A second brother of Prince Hermann married a young Swabian girl, Marie Gratwohl, "whose cradle," as the pretty Socialist ditty has it, "had stood in a poor man's house." The son of this marriage was created Freiherr von Bronn by the King of Würtemburg: he went to Austria where he became adjutant to the Archduke Franz Ferdinand, married a Countess Czernin, became a Catholic and, last of all Prince of Weikersheim. He would talk like an out-and-out Austrian; all his ideas were exaggeratedly "black-yellow," and he was as anti-German as his English cousin. In every department of our national life the so-called "minor nobility," and especially the junkers, have done far more for the country than the noble and princely houses mentioned in the second and third parts of the *Almanach de Gotha*.

One of the most original figures of the old régime was Podbielski, commonly known as "Pod," the Minister of Agriculture. No one was fonder of cracking jokes about this nickname than he himself. Once he asked the somewhat prudish wife of a minister who was sitting next him at dinner if she knew why His Majesty had never given his name to an ironclad. When the worthy lady answered that she was very curious to hear why, he replied: "You could never expect one of His Majesty's ships to be called 'Pod.'" Podbielski had other characteristics besides the determination and resourcefulness I had described to His Majesty on my appointment as Imperial Chancellor—he possessed a conspicuous talent for organization. I emphasized this when he was appointed Minister of Agriculture. He had proved it as much in Rathenow on the Havel as in Hanover and Berlin. Before his appointment as Minister he had helped to organize the firm of Tippelskirch which soon became the chief contractor to the South West Africa force. After his appointment he was accused of having unduly favoured this firm, and of having made over his shares in it to his wife before he took office. Eulenburg wrote to me from Romintern that this was a "shock" to the Kaiser, since he could not overlook the significance of Podbielski's business methods. He had contented himself with remarking that though Podbielski did perhaps "take care of No. 1, he was extremely useful." Eulenburg added: "I really do not think that there is any wish of His Majesty, no matter how impossible it might be, that Podbielski would not perform; but I am sorry to have to see His Majesty not really dis-

"POD," GENERAL VICTOR VON PODBIELSKI

From 1897 to 1901 State Secretary of the Post Office,
1901 to 1906 Prussian Minister for Agriculture

inclined to consider, as suitable for a Minister, such a flabby personality as Pod has become—especially since he has control of the
woods, forests, and preserves. While he was here Podbielski, who
was hobbling with the gout, told me that the press campaign against
him is doing him no good." And indeed the stout Podbielski, who
not only had distinguished himself in peace-time in every office he
filled, but also, previously, on the battlefield, retired, of his own
free-will, in November 1906.

It is hard not to laugh ironically when I remember the sensation
—or to use a word much favoured before the Revolution, but which,
I think, has since gone out of fashion—the indignation (*Entrüstung*)
which the affaire Podbielski aroused in the whole opposition press.
Actually it was a question far more of rumours and gossip than of
any definite accusation. In any case, when all the charges against
Podbielski are put together, their total compared to the defalcations
of which, years later, Matthias Erzberger was accused, are as a
molehill to a mountain. And yet Erzberger after what, for him,
was the utterly damning result of his lawsuit against Helfferich, after
a verdict attesting his habitual unreliability, his corrupt practise of
mixing public interests with private affairs, was not only exculpated,
not only defended, but actually eulogized by two Socialists—the
president of the Reichstag and the then Imperial Chancellor!

At the time of the Erzberger-Helfferich case I asked a friend of
mine, the editor of a democratic newspaper: "Suppose that when
Podbielski was attacked because of some alleged trifling delinquencies in his relations with the firm of Tippelskirch I had stood up at
the ministerial benches of the Reichstag and delivered a panegyric
of him, what would you have said in your esteemed organ of public
opinion?" He replied with a grin: "I should have written that
since the decline of the Roman Empire, there has never been such
shameless cynicism, such utter lack of all moral sense." Other
times, other manners!

I was passing through Berlin and on the point of returning to
Norderney where I hoped to finish my convalescence, when Count
Monts, our Ambassador to Rome asked for an interview. An
annoying mishap had befallen him. There had been an exhibition
at Milan; it had been opened by the King of Italy, and the whole
Diplomatic Corps had been invited. At the moment when the
ceremony began a slight shower of rain came on. As etiquette
demands on such occasions, all the diplomatists were in uniform.
Now Monts was both famous as a hypochondriac, who could think
of nothing else but his health, and known to be notoriously stingy.
He was scared stiff that the rain would give him a cold and spoil

his uniform. At last he got into such a state of excitement that he began to shout across the show-ground, which the rain had made a little the worse for wear: " *Regardez-moi cette saleté!* " His French colleague, Barrère, was standing near him. I have already had occasion to show how Barrère—more skilful far, and better informed than Monts—could always play cat-and-mouse with him. He noticed Monts' agitation, and began, in the friendliest way, to excite him further: " *Cette pluie est vraiment désagréable, nous allons tous attraper un gros rhume, vous avez l'air bien pâle. Et puis nos uniformes seront abimés. Et ces uniformes, chamarrés d'or coutent très cher.*" Monts, who had completely lost his head, rushed up to Count Guicciardini, the Minister for Foreign Affairs, and shouted: " *Il n'y a ici que les diplomates et les domestiques qui soient en uniforme, je vous fais là une observation très sèrieuse!* " He ended by creating such a scene that Count Ponti, the Mayor of Milan, said to him, " If you used that tone to me as Count Monts I should be obliged to call you out; but since you are the German Ambassador I shall lodge a complaint with my government." Both Ponti and Guicciardini were justifiably considered friendly towards Germany. While this frenzy attacked Monts in the midst of a public ceremony, Barrère was saying with a smile to all the Italians who surrounded him: " *Comme les Allemands sont violents, comme ils sont mal èlevés, comme ils aiment à provoquer des rixes. On a bien raison de parler de querelles d'Allemand.*" As is well known the French call any quarrelling over nothing "*une querelle d'Allemand.*"

Next morning when his rage had cooled a little it began to dawn upon Monts that his ill-manners had gone too far. He applied for a few days leave, and asked me to see him and have a talk with him. He admitted, in my presence, that he knew his behaviour had been impossible. " I behaved incredibly," were his actual words to me. He added that he had only one excuse—his nerves had gone all to pieces through illness, and he asked me to grant him a long leave, to enable him to go to a sanatorium and get cured.

> " *Die von Irrtum zur Wahrheit reisen*
> *Das sind die Weisen.*
> *Die in Irrtum verharren*
> *Das sind die Narren!* [1]

In the case of Monts, alas! I was one of the fools. I did not use

---

[1] He who to truth from error flies
Goes with the wise.
He whose blood in error cools
Stays with the fools.

this lucky chance of getting him out of the service, but told him that I would settle the affair, and that, meanwhile, he was to go away and take a rest. " I never thought you'd have kept me on," he said, apparently very much moved. He grasped my hand, and told me that I had already done much for him, but that, never, never, would he forget this last proof of my " kindness and noble consideration."

> " *O Dankbarkeit, du süsse Pflicht,*
> *Du Himmelslust, du Himmelslicht.*
> *Wie hab' ich dich mir eingeprägt.*
> *Wie hab' ich stets dich heilig gehegt.*" [1]

[1] Oh gratitude, sweet duty, thou
Celestial, shining light.
Thee have I loved and cherished
And held with all my might.

CHAPTER XVII

*William II and the Centre Party—The Reichstag meets—Prince
Arenberg on the Centre's policy—A letter from Prince Lichnowsky—
Philip Eulenburg on William II's mood—Eulenburg's anxiety about
my health—A visit from Moltke the Chief of Staff—Reichstag's
session on 14th November 1906—Dernburg as Colonial Director—
His maiden speech in the Reichstag—I sponsor him—Erzberger's
attack on Colonial administration—I consider the dissolution of the
Reichstag—The decisive session (13th December 1906)—The dissolution—Cardinal Kopp's letter.*

AS early as the midsummer of 1906, while I was still in Norderney, a member of the Emperor's suite had told me that our
Imperial master was again in a state of great indignation with
the parties in general and with the Centre in particular. I was
already so used to these moods that the rumour did not especially
move me. The Emperor had no predilection for any party in itself,
and that I could well understand, but according to the political
constellation, he would take first one and then the other party *en
grippe*. At the time of the struggle for the canals his ire had been
turned against the Conservatives. Later it was the turn of the
National-Liberals. Even the Independents would sometimes fall
into disfavour, though there were men among them whom he held in
particular esteem. There were, for instance, Mommsen and Vir-
chow, whom he liked because they had been old foes of Bismarck;
there were Kämpf, Schrader, and Heckscher, whom he also found
fairly acceptable. Still influenced by Countess Anna's conversion,
though that had no political significance, and by all the turmoil
caused, in politically short-sighted circles, by the repeal of Paragraph 2 in the Jesuit law, his dislike of the Centre had increased.
It had become still more exacerbated by the clumsy and impossible
attitude which, influenced by the rising Erzberger, that party
adopted towards the Colonial Question.

On this topic I had already written from Norderney to Tschirschky, at the beginning of June 1906. The Secretary of State was
only too eager to adopt as his own any change of opinion in the
Emperor, whose faithful echo he now made himself. My letter was
as follows:

I should be most grateful to you, and you would be doing the country a real service if, without mentioning my name, you could make His Majesty aware that his continual attacks on the Centre lead him nowhere. I am most decidedly a good Protestant; but, in politics, bitterness, anger, and emotional diatribes are useless. You might point out to His Majesty that any party which can control a parliamentary majority tries to make itself a nuisance to the government, if only to show its electors its independence and not to lose ground in the country. That is one of the rules of German party politics. The Conservatives in the Prussian Chamber were far more recalcitrant on the question of the canals, and made far more serious strife, than the Centre on the less important Colonial question. When the National-Liberals controlled the majority in the 'seventies they always did their best to put obstacles in the way of Prince Bismarck. Any party which controls the majority, whether it is the result of universal suffrage, of indirect elections, or vote by classes, will try to impose its will on the government. If, therefore, irresponsible advisers excite His Majesty against the Centre, it must be because they fail to understand the results of such a way of going to work. Certainly any question of German unity, of national safety and defence, must be fought out at all costs. But such conflicts should never be lightly undertaken. In politics the first essential is *de donner aux choses leur juste valeur* and, above all, it is important to choose the right moment to act. One must never let oneself be influenced by ignorant and irresponsible prattlers.

But I had been influenced less by the changing humours of His Majesty than by a remark of my old friend, Prince Arenberg, the Centre deputy, who had come to see me at Norderney in the midsummer of 1906. We were strolling one day by the lighthouse when he suddenly told me that he did not intend to stand again for Parliament in 1908, at the next election. I answered that I was very sorry indeed. As reporter of the Foreign Office Budget he was performing most useful services. He was a link between me and the Centre and had always been a conciliatory factor; but, apart from that, it would be a real loss to me not to see him opposite me in his accustomed seat. I tried to appeal to him: " Stay by me Max," I said, " and don't desert me." He answered that it was precisely his affection for me that made him think of giving up politics. He could see that, within a given time, I should be in conflict with his party, and such a situation would be too painful for him. I saw no cause for such anxieties. I pointed out that, for almost ten years, I had been working in conjunction with the Centre, and that we had managed to get on very well together. Without wishing to boast I could recall that, shortly after the passing of the Education Act, the Prussian episcopate had expressed to me, through Cardinal Kopp, its gratitude and satisfaction; that it had only refrained from giving public expression to such feelings because it had not wished to expose me to attack or suspicion from the other side. " But now my party will turn insolent—just because it has all it wants," replied Arenberg. He did not wish to enter on a campaign against his best friend, as a member of a party to which he was bound by ties of the deepest sentiment and conviction, and so he proposed to get out of politics in time. Though I tried several times I could not make him alter his resolve. When he left I accompanied him to the landing-stage. That was the last time I ever saw my dear, kind François. He fell ill, not long afterwards, of a serious internal complaint, while on a visit to his brother Jean at the castle of Pesch in the Rhineland. A terrible pain drove him to his bed from which he was never to rise. May we be re-united some day, in a land where there is no mean spite, no malice or pettiness!

> " *Wenn ich einst von jenem Schlummer*
> *Welcher Tod heisst, aufersteh'*
> *Und, befreit von jedem Kummer,*
> *Jenen schönen Morgen seh'—*
> *Oh, dann wach ich anders auf,*
> *Schon am Ziel ist dann mein Lauf.*
> *Träume sind des Pilger's Sorgen*
> *Grosser Tag, an deinem Morgen.*" [1]

The Reichstag resumed its sittings on 13th November 1906. Next day an interpellation on Foreign Policy, tabled by the deputy Bassermann, was down for discussion. It was desirable that I should take this opportunity not merely of giving the Reichstag and the nation a general picture of our position but also of saying certain things that might bear fruit as much in Paris as in Vienna, in London as well as in St. Petersburg. From London Metternich had written to say that his Russian colleague, Count Benckendorff,

---

[1] When one day, I awake from that sleep
Which we call death,
Freed from every care
To that bright morning—
I shall not arise as now.
My journey's end will be reached
My pilgrim-cares will all be dreams
At your dawning—day of brightness.

had met Isvolski the Russian Foreign Minister, in Paris. Isvolski giving his reasons, had said, in the course of their conversation that Russia, after her defeat in the Far East, would have to come to an understanding with England on matters affecting Asia. He had added that he did not wish such an understanding to look as though it were aimed against Germany. From Berlin Isvolski had telegraphed to Benckendorff: " *Impressions de Berlin excellentes.*"

On the Polish Question Benckendorff had remarked that the complete agreement on this matter which existed between Isvolski and myself was well calculated to maintain confident and friendly relations between Germany and Russia. As regards the internal condition of Russia Benckendorff had heard from St. Petersburg that the honourable intentions of Stolypin were universally recognized by thinking people. But the Tsar must keep his constitutional promises, otherwise a permanent tranquillization of Russia would be impossible. An attempt to return to pure absolutism would be a blunder pregnant with consequences.

As to Anglo-Russian relations Benckendorff had declared that Afghanistan was a sphere in which, even with the best will in the world, an agreement would be difficult to reach. Afghanistan was under the exclusive protection of England and India. It received subsidies from Calcutta. It would never be easy for England to admit any permanent sharing of influence with Russia in Afghanistan. In Persia it might be quite possible for Russia and England to come to some feasible understanding but, on Afghanistan, it would always be hard to reach any lasting one.

From the Castle of Slawentzitz in Upper Silesia, where the Kaiser was staying with Prince Christian Krafft-Hohenlohe-Oehringen for the autumn hunting, Prince Lichnowsky, who was also a guest, and had been, till 1904, my personal representative at the Foreign Office, wrote to me in confidence: " To his astonishment, at the moment of his departure, His Majesty pressed into Gottfried Hohenlohe's hand a letter to the Tsar (!) with the superscription: ' Par le Prince Hohenlohe ' so that, as the Prince himself remarked with some embarrassment, it will be impossible for him to hand it over to General Jacobi the Prussian Military plenipotentiary at St. Petersburg. It goes, of course, without saying that, once again, in spite of his unfortunate experience last year, His Majesty has poured out his heart to the aforesaid Austrian military attaché. On the other hand Woyrsch, in front of all the guests, has had to jump over my cane, *à la Mohr.*"

Mohr was my faithful poodle whom the comic papers had made very popular. These confidences placed by the Emperor in the then

Austrian military attaché in St. Petersburg were fresh evidence of
His Majesty's political indiscretion. Prince Gottfried Hohenlohe
was anything but pro-German, and even passed for one of our enemies in St. Petersburg. Later, during the World War, as Austrian
Ambassador in Berlin, he furthered Austrian, at the expense of
German, interests, with reckless selfishness. General von Woyrsch
was one of our best officers who covered himself with glory by his
defence of Silesia during the war. In England, where such practical
jokes are popular, William II had learnt many queer bits of horse-
play like jumping over a cane held out to one. Over there they are
not taken amiss even on board a yacht or at a football match, but they
are not popular in Germany, and are considered especially unbe-
coming when the victim is a senior Prussian general.

I was looking forward to the reassembly of the Reichstag with
some impatience. During the autumn the air had been full of
rumours of war. There may have been intrigue on all sides. Philip
Eulenburg wrote to me from Rominten:

I feel I ought to keep you posted as to the attitude His
Majesty adopts whenever the talk turns on you. The Emperor
had found you perfectly well—as well as ever you were—in
Wilhelmshöhe, but just the opposite in Berlin. In August
Eulenburg's presence he raged about the African Railway. To
me he spoke quite sensibly, even prudently. It sounded as
though he put the blame for a certain lack of energy on your
illness from which you have not completely recovered. I got the
impression that "energy" is becoming a sort of obsession.
What is certain is that he simply knows of nobody to put in your
place. *That* I can feel from the way in which he always speaks of
you, in spite of an occasional fit of temper. This at least is useful,
and prevents him from being led astray. It is evident that the
thought of your actually being too ill to remain in office any
longer disturbs and frightens him. Such a contingency would
be fatal, he thinks. A few days ago, I happened to be talking to
the Empress about your health (H.M. was sitting beside us
reading) and I said: " Well, thank heavens everything's coming
all right now! It would have been too dreadful if Bülow had had
to resign." H.M. suddenly looked up from his newspaper and
interrupted: " Yes, certainly, that would have been the last
straw." This quite spontaneous remark is typical. It is also
significant, when one comes to consider his character, that he calls
any sort of action which runs counter to his own ideas " a lack of
energy," and is at present making your illness responsible. I am

giving you as precise an account as possible. Who else, I wonder, would do that for you, my dear, good, Bernhard?

But on the other hand my true friend Count Wedel sent me a message through my brother Karl Ulrich, the military attaché at Vienna, that a formidable intrigue was going on against me, and that Philip Eulenburg was in the centre of it, since he wanted Moltke, the Chief of the General Staff to become Imperial Chancellor. Eulenburg was persuading the Kaiser that my health was really much worse than he supposed. " It's touch and go with Bernhard," etc. He was also suggesting that, even without " dear Bernhard " things might still go quite smoothly. His Majesty (supported of course by Philip Eulenburg, and the loyal Tschirschky) should conduct foreign policy himself, while, as to home affairs, what was needed was a " strong man," preferably a general, who would sweep the land with an iron broom. I have never known how much truth there really was in this message, though I must say it did not entirely surprise me. Only one thing is certain: some little time after I left Norderney for Homburg, Eulenburg went to see Professor Renvers, to tell him that anyone who really wished me well ought to advise me to resign on grounds of health. Renvers, having replied that there was nothing at all the matter with me, Eulenburg declared that though to the cold eye of a physician, I might look well, an anxious friend could perceive how necessary it was for me to lay aside the crushing burden of the Chancellorship before it became too late.

It is not impossible that Eulenburg spoke as he did from a genuine feeling of friendship. He was a bundle of contradictions. Alfred Berger, the witty director of the Burg Theater in Vienna once compared him with an onion which has so many skins that it takes one a long time to get to its heart. And Eulenburg was not the only person who has found it convenient that I should be as ill as possible. When Bethmann-Hollweg began to get into difficulties as Chancellor, he went about saying unctuously to everybody that " unluckily " my wretched state of health made my return to power an impossibility. Yet Providence has allowed me to survive in perfect vigour both Eulenburg and Bethmann-Hollweg: " *Ironie délicieuse de la divine Providence*," as Monsignor Duchêne in Rome loved to express it.

A few days after receiving Wedel's letter I dined with the Emperor at his sister's, Princess Margaret of Prussia. I found him jovial and charming: nothing could have been pleasanter than the way in which he chatted with his youngest sister, and with my wife, who had been her friend for years. On 22nd October, during a *soirée* at the Neues Palais to celebrate the Kaiserin's birthday, I was asked by several different people if it were true that Moltke was going to replace me. I replied that, though I should be grateful to Moltke if he freed me from the cares of office, I very much doubted whether he wanted to.

Next morning one of the Berlin papers—I think it was the *Berliner Tageblatt*—announced, without any suggestion direct or indirect from me, that intrigues were afoot to put Moltke in my place. That same evening Moltke came to see me and, with his usual honourable frankness, told me how painful he found such rumours. He said he had no idea of becoming Chancellor, a post for which he considered himself entirely inadequate. I answered him in all sincerity that I had never for an instant doubted his loyal friendship.

I am still entirely convinced that this upright but unfortunate man was speaking the truth, as he always did. Nevertheless, considering the rather strained state of home politics I was glad when the re-opening of the Reichstag and the resumption of parliamentary debate brought a gust of fresh air into the stuffiness of Court intrigue and drawing-room gossip.

On 14th November, as I was strolling down to the Reichstag from the Imperial Chancellery I met, at the Brandenburger Tor, my old friend and medical advisor Renvers, who pretended that our meeting had been a chance one. He went with me as far as the Reichstag steps, where he felt my pulse and said: " It couldn't be beating more steadily. Now off you go." On that day, in answer to an interpellation of Bassermann on the state of our Foreign Policy, I delivered one of the longest speeches of my career.

I spoke extempore, without notes: first on our relations with France, saying that, when we bore in mind the traditional brilliance and *élan* of our very temperamental neighbours, their fervid patriotism and extreme susceptibility on the *point d'honneur*, we must be under no illusions with regard to them. To a Socialist interruption—" *Jaurès?* "—I replied: " Not even a red swallow makes a summer."

Next, on the Entente Cordiale, I said with emphasis that a policy intended to secure the encirclement of Germany, to surround us with Powers all working to isolate and paralyse us, was a danger to European peace. We had no thought, I insisted, of building a fleet as strong as the English fleet. But it was both our right and our duty to maintain a fleet equivalent to the magnitude of our commercial interests, whose only task would be to defend our coasts and our trade beyond the seas.

To King Edward VII I dedicated a few respectful and courteous words. I could legitimately declare that, with Russia, our
relations had not for long, been so normal, so tranquil and so correct.
I took occasion to protest against certain stupid mistakes and prejudices which cropped up again and again among ourselves. To
those gentlemen of the Press who reproached me with excessive
good temper I replied that the urbanity after which I strove as a
man, was far from being my guide in politics, but that good manners
do not spell weakness. It was a question of knowing when to be
firm, and of being suave at the proper time. It was in this speech
that I coined the phrase " the misunderstood Bismarck," which inspired Privy Councillor Hammann, the head of the press-bureau,
with the title for one of his political works which, though they may
not be very profound, and cannot always be called exact, are nevertheless, amusingly written, and interesting.

In this same speech I uttered a serious warning against " nerves."
" In Germany we are all becoming too nervous, both Right and
Left, above and below." Here the Socialists interrupted, and I
repeated: " Certainly—both above and below." I recalled that
last, immortal speech of Bismarck's, on 6th February 1888, in
which he had showed that, throughout the whole nineteenth century,
one coalition after another had threatened war, that the political
horizon had never once been free from clouds. I continued: " It
is good to observe any sign that foretells the weather, and certainly
every flash of summer lightning. But to tremble at each growl of
foreign thunder is unworthy of a great people."

I had spoken for over two hours and with much success; but
I had to speak again at the same sitting to parry attacks from every
side on the alleged " personal government " of the Kaiser, his
vagaries and extravagant language. I stressed the Kaiser's fine
qualities, his strong personality, clear head, uprightness, and sense
of duty. He had scrupulously respected the constitution. Surely
the German people did not really want a dummy Emperor, but an
Emperor in flesh and blood. It was a matter of political judgment
how far a Minister could endorse the personal expression of his
sovereign, his enunciation of ideas and sentiments; it was a matter
of doing one's duty to both crown and country—it lay in the
region of *imponderabilia*. " In my view," I added, " it is quite
possible for a Minister to feel that it is dangerous for the Sovereign to express himself too personally, to show himself too often
without what Bismarck, in his wisdom called ' the cloak of
Ministerial responsibility.' Such a course may be inconsistent
with the interests of the nation and of the Monarchy, and in that

case no Minister could take it upon himself to be responsible
for it."

After my breach with the Centre a few weeks later, that party's
newspapers published a rumour that I had arranged the interpellation with Bassermann, and had induced him to make his remarks on
" personal government." There was not a word of truth in this
assertion; neither directly nor indirectly had I had any communication with Bassermann before the debate, and I had not even seen
him.

On 15th November Hammann wrote to me, after an interview
with Stein, the representative of the *Frankfurter Zeitung,* that my
speech of the previous day had calmed the latter's " critical attitude,"
but that Stein, as a convinced democrat, was vexed at the difference
between my " brilliant eloquence and the clumsy speeches of the
deputies." That was very characteristic of the state of affairs in the
German Reichstag.

Stein was not the only person to be " vexed " by what I had
said. The Emperor filled the official report of the sitting with
irritable and mistrustful marginal notes. To these I answered that,
for weeks, I had had to make of myself a breakwater against much
criticism and numerous attacks on the throne, that I had turned these
attacks against myself, and had certainly succeeded in improving
the state of public opinion. I added that I would continue to do my
duty, would shield the throne, and endeavour, to the best of my
ability, to ward off everything which might seem painful or harmful
to His Majesty.

" As to the present discontent," I added, " whatever Your
Majesty may think, the best contrived press-campaign would never
have been able to produce it, if there had not been something there
to build from. The great majority of the German people is monarchist. At the last Socialist Congress one of the Social-Democratic
leaders admitted that, of the three million Socialist electors in 1903,
400,000, at most, had been organized and conscious Socialists.
And competent people have informed me that, even of these, there
are many who are not anti-monarchist at heart. But, on the other
hand, our people are extraordinarily sensitive to anything that
savours of absolutism. I have only told the truth in saying publicly
that Your Majesty had never violated the constitution, and never
would violate it. But certain of Your Majesty's speeches and telegrams have been exploited against you in that sense. The unease
and distrust which, as a result, has been evoked in all parties and
classes of the nation, though it in no way shakes my confidence in
God, in Your Majesty, and in Germany, compels me to use prudent

tactics. I beg you to believe that my speeches and suggestions are dictated by my deep solicitude and watchful care for Your Majesty." In the margin of this the Emperor wrote. "Agreed! Thanks very much. But I don't intend to change, and so they'll have to go on abusing me."

In his book *European Policy under Edward VII*, J. A. Farrer relates that Sir Charles Dilke, the well-known English politician, declared that Prince Bülow's speech on 14th December 1906 was one of the best that any statesman had pronounced.

At the beginning of September the attacks against the Colonial Section steadily increased, and I invited the head of the Colonial Office to a comprehensive discussion. The explanations of the Hereditary Prince of Hohenlohe-Langenburg were very meagre. All he could say in effect (though he said it very politely) was that he would be much obliged for my opinion on these difficult and involved questions. I saw at once that things could not go on as they were, and since, on the previous day, I had heard him regret that he would be unable to spend the winter at Nice with some English relations and good friends there, I suggested to him (also most politely) that he should go to the Côte d'Azur for a little holiday and leave politics to someone else.

But it was difficult to choose his successor. Apart from his incompetence Ernie Hohenlohe was a failure because his intimate connection with the Evangelical League made him an object of suspicion to the Centre. I suddenly remembered a witty remark, made in his own inimitable way, by the President of the Reichstag, Count Ballestrem. "We object to a Protestant Ecclesiastical Minister; as a minority we cannot insist on a Catholic. So why not give us a Jew?"

I thought at first of Rathenau. I did not know him personally as yet, but I had heard of his various talents and capacities. Finally, however, I decided on Bernhard Dernburg the Director of the Darmstadt Bank.

The Emperor approved the nomination; when I told him how Dernburg had come to visit me in an opulent-looking car he remarked with particular satisfaction: "That's right! That's right! I wish all my ministers would get cars." His Majesty and Dernburg always understood one another, though it took Dernburg some time to get used to Court etiquette. Once, at a dinner at my house, he forgot to stand up when the Emperor drank his health. Count Dietrich Hülsen, who was also present remarked. "Dernburg is too busy sitting on the rising in Africa to be able to get up himself." I insisted on the Centre receiving the new chief sympathetically, and made a point of saying to every Centre deputy I met that I counted on an end being made to the unfounded and pernicious opposition against our Colonial policy. On 28th November I gave the Reichstag my reasons for the change at the Colonial Office. I protested against the spiteful and dangerous methods by which every trifle had been exaggerated. Such polemics would depress our able and industrious officials and give the outside world an entirely false view of our position.

Dernburg introduced himself in a moderate and sensible speech. Next day Erzberger attacked him, just as he had attacked Prince Hohenlohe, but his attack was milder than that of the Centrist deputy Roeren, who followed him. Dernburg answered Roeren brilliantly, ending his speech as follows, amid the applause of the Right: "We shall support the mission to the Colonies because our State, by its very nature, is based on Christian foundations, and we live in a Christian civilization."

Earlier, in a *tête-à-tête*, Dernburg had told me with a certain pride that "the blood of parsons" flowed in his veins. In much the same fashion my old friend Paul Lindau, who was as witty and charming as he was good-hearted, once said to me: "If only I could tell where I get this accursed nose from—I who am the grandson of an ecclesiastical inspector."

Roeren the deputy, a thick-headed Westphalian Chancellor of the Court of Appeal at Cologne, who had always been the *enfant terrible* of the Centre Party, and continued to be so after my retirement, could only answer Dernburg with clumsy, boorish invective. Without the slightest reason he called Dernburg "a stock-market rigger and juggler," an uncivil and uncalled for allusion to the fact that, up to then, Dernburg had been a highly respected banker, and the director of one of our foremost banks. He referred to a junior official of the Colonial Office as a "jumped up bureaucrat," and closed his speech, amid an uproar, with the words: "No, Mr. Colonial Director, for all your past you aren't going to hoodwink me!"

Since the revolution and the Republic we have grown used to this sort of thing, and worse, in our national and local parliaments; but, in those days, such rudeness was very painful and was censured, not only by the Reichstag and by the spectators in the galleries, but by every educated person in the land. Dernburg replied that the Colonial Service deserved no blame, that none of the accusations against its officials were justified, but that Roeren and other Centre deputies were always meddling in the affairs of his department on behalf of Centre Party adherents or other protégés. This was a hit

COLONIAL DIRECTOR BERNHARD DERNBURG

In his house at Grunewald

at Erzberger who, owing to the disloyal conduct of two junior officials, Wistuba and Pöplau, had got private information of certain occurrences in the service which he, with equal disloyalty, had used to attack the department.   When Dernburg ended by saying that this festering abscess had needed lancing, that he had lanced it and was prepared to take the consequences, he was hissed by the Centre and Social-Democrats, loudly applauded by the Right, and clapped from the Ministerial benches.

Urgent official business had prevented me from attending the session on 3rd December, but on the 4th I ascended the tribune, and briefly stated that I entirely approved the speech of the new Colonial Minister.   In particular I mentioned his defence of officials unjustly attacked, and his refusal to let his department be meddled with.   I ended by regretting that Herr Roeren should have adopted the violent tone of Bebel, rather than the moderation of his colleague Erzberger, and that he should have alluded to facts some of which were still under investigation.

I was still persuaded that the Centre would not push things to a breach, which I myself wished to avoid.   I invited the two most influential Centrist leaders Herr Spahn and Herr Groeber, to come and see me.   In a long conversation, *à trois*, I reminded them how, for ten years, I had been fair and benevolent in my attitude towards the Centre Party, and towards the Catholic section of the nation. Never should I seek to attack the religious sentiments of Catholics, or of the Catholic Church.   But in any question of fundamental importance to the State, I refused to let myself be trifled with.   I expressed a hope that the Centre would understand this warning. These two gentlemen assured me that they disapproved of the recent opposition and would do all they could to avoid any conflict with the government.   Herr Spahn with all the honest dignity of a magistrate said to me: " Erzberger is to blame for the whole thing. He is a stupid and pushing young *arriviste* whom our friend Groeber most unluckily got into parliament.   He has an office at Lichterfeld where he writes parliamentary letters which make him the master of a good part of the Centrist press.   My time is fully occupied by my duties as a magistrate at Kiel, but *he* has nothing to do, and so it isn't easy for me to settle with him."   The eloquent Groeber expressed to me his deep regret at ever having sponsored such a fellow: " Certainly it would have been cleverer of me not to have brought that foul-mouthed Erzberger into the Reichstag.   Now we must try to freeze him out again."   But it was not so easy—as, twelve years later, and after the Erzberger-Hillferich case, Hertling and the whole Centre Party were to discover.   On that occasion

Spahn and Groeber left me with repeated promises to do all they could to prevent the Centre from going into opposition on the forthcoming vote for the supplementary estimates in South-West Africa.

I spoke on the same lines to Ballestrem, the President of the Reichstag, who declared that he would vote for the estimates and hoped his party would follow his example. While doing my best to calm the parties in this sense I still felt it advisable to keep my powder dry in case my warnings were not heeded. I wrote to the Emperor:

> The position is serious. After what has happened up to now in committee we must reckon on the possibility of a vote to strike off the estimates a considerable portion of those credits necessary for the maintenance of the troops in South-West Africa finally to quell the rising. Should the Committee come to such a decision and get it endorsed by the Reichstag I would be under the necessity of advising Your Majesty to dissolve parliament. A decision to dissolve the Reichstag is undoubtedly a very grave one. For reasons both of home and foreign policy any conflict within the Empire is more dangerous and difficult to resolve than, formerly, a conflict within Prussia. To render such a measure successful we must so arrange our tactics that, in the eyes of the Federated Princes, and of the nation, we have right and justice on our side. We must abstain from any sort of threat, any provocation of the Reichstag or the various parties, and in particular, avoid emotional demonstrations. Provocation, exaggeration, insults, must all be left to our opponents. Only calm and firm moderation on our side! Especially must we be careful, should we finally decide on dissolution, that no word is breathed of the matter until it is actually a fact.

His Majesty's temperament seemed to make it imperative to counsel prudence and reserve. In the margin of my letter the Emperor wrote. "Agreed. You have my full consent and authorization to proceed to any lengths you consider necessary." I was not surprised by His Majesty's conception of the situation, but I read this marginal note as all Imperial marginal notes *cum grano salis*. I knew that it was easy enough to make William II enthusiastic for any bold project or idea, but difficult to keep him resolutely to his course once he had committed himself to follow it. And moreover on the very day when I received this authorization to dissolve the Reichstag I received a letter from the Kaiserin, written in anxious care for His Majesty. It read as follows: "I should like to impress on you that the Emperor, although he looks healthy, must be protected against shocks. I am convinced that in a short time His Majesty will be as strong and well as ever, but for the moment, he must be treated gently. The Emperor is far more affected by any political disturbance, or any really wounding attack than the outside world imagines. I get no chance of seeing you nowadays, so forgive these hasty lines."

It was indeed necessary to spare the Emperor's nerves as much as possible. Consequently I was already taking pains to make certain that, in the battle which might soon be upon us, the Imperial person should be withdrawn from the firing line.

I wanted to be certain that, should the event prove unsuccessful, the Emperor, without loss of prestige, would still be able to part company with me and go on ruling with somebody else—Posadowsky for example. Of my colleagues Posadowsky and Tirpitz were opposed to a dissolution since they were both used to carry out their policy in co-operation with the Centre—the one his social programme, the other the development of the Fleet. Posadowsky raised every possible objection, and desired that, at least, the dissolution might be postponed until after Christmas. He looked forward to a General Election with misgivings.

Until my decision was taken Bethmann-Hollweg had maintained a prudent reserve. When I had decided he placed himself enthusiastically behind me. He wrote to me that he had " played the part of a simple politician who has no information and is not concerned " in front of two chiefs of the extreme Prussian Right Wing, Herr von Kröcher and Herr von Arnim-Züsedom, and that both, " spontaneously and naïvely " had declared themselves in favour of dissolution. Since he found such ideas prevalent among the junkers of the Marches he was more than ever convinced that my decision had not only been necessary from the point of view of the state but " corresponded with the general feeling of the nation which regards the sacrifices it has already made in men and money as of more importance than parliamentary rivalries." Here is the conclusion of his letter:

Your Excellency will pardon me for giving expression to this belief as it were *post festum*. I am simply actuated by the desire to state once again what your Excellency was already aware of.

Your Excellency's most obedient servant,

VON BETHMANN-HOLLWEG.

His gratitude for the good will I had often shown him was then unbounded. Shortly before the Reichstag was dissolved I wrote to congratulate him on some family anniversary or other and he re-

plied: " My most sincere thanks to Your Excellency for your good
wishes, with the assurance that Your Excellency's indulgent patron-
age gives me an indispensable support in all my activities."

December 13th saw the second reading of the bill for the
supplementary estimates in South-West Africa. I opened the
debate with a short and very moderate speech explaining the reasons
for our proposal to base our estimate for the financial year 1907 on
an undetermined garrison strength instead of on the present definite
and much reduced strength. I explained why this was inacceptable
to the Federal Governments, but added that I could not believe
that the Reichstag would take a decision so serious and regrettable
in its financial and military, its political and national aspects. But
should this prove my personal delusion I must refuse, as responsible
head of Imperial affairs, to sign such a capitulation before the German
people and before history. I could see, all the time I was speaking,
from the expressions on the faces of deputies, especially in the Centre
Party, that nobody took my declaration seriously. After a scene
between Roeren and Dernburg, followed by another between the
disgusting Ledebour, one of the most repulsive Socialists, and the
Conservative deputy von Richthofen, I intervened again for the last
time.

I spoke extempore, and not without agitation. What would
happen to us, I asked, if military measures in war-time, the life
and health of our troops, our national honour, were in future to
be made dependent on party politics? I recalled the obstinacy
and valour with which other nations, the English, the French,
the Dutch had waged their Colonial wars without once flinch-
ing. I declared that I had never uttered the stupid phrase
attributed to me, " above all, no internal crisis," and I added,
" there are situations in which, to shrink from a crisis would show
cowardice—the lack of any sense of duty. If you want a crisis, you
can have one." I raised my voice to affirm that if, in the Lobbies, it
was suggested that I was being manœuvred by the Emperor, that
was a " presumptuous mis-statement." I needed no direction in
this case to see that I was faced with a national necessity. I concluded: " What impression would be produced at home and
abroad if the Government capitulated on such an issue without
finding in itself the strength to do its duty to the nation? We will
do our duty and have faith in the German people."

The Socialists hissed; the majority of the Reichstag applauded.
In the ensuing division the Government Bill was rejected by 177
votes to 168. I at once asked for permission to speak, went to the
tribune and declared: " I have to communicate to the Reichstag a

rescript from the Emperor." While I was undoing the red envelope, wild applause broke from the Right; the National-Liberals and Independents clapped me vigorously; the Social-Democrats, confident of a great victory at the Election, shouted for joy. The Centrists sat in perplexed and angry silence. The general hubbub was drowned by a burst of applause from the Strangers' Gallery. I read out the Imperial decree by which the Reichstag was dissolved. It was dated from Bückeburg. Conservatives, Liberals, and the public welcomed it with prolonged applause. Count Ballestrem, true to his promise, had impulsively voted for the Government with three other Centrist deputies, among them von Savigny the son of the founder of the Party. As I left the Reichstag Ballestrem exclaimed very mournfully: " My successor in the Presidential chair will undoubtedly be the Socialist, Singer." Herr von Heydebrand who was much perplexed, muttered something about " a hussar's trick," on the part of the former Royal Hussar.

A few days later, without having paid any heed to the unjustifiable attitude of the Centre, I wrote as usual to the Prince-Bishop of Breslau, Cardinal Kopp, my sincerest Christmas wishes. He replied " with profound emotion," adding:

> There cannot be very many people who approve of the attitude of the Centre Party or find it a subject for rejoicing. I need not tell you that I am not one of them. At the Vatican it is severely censured and they are very disturbed over what has happened. They consider it, in exalted circles there, not only a serious breach of loyalty but a piece of base ingratitude towards Your Excellency who ought to have been spared the trials of such a situation. . . . But, come what may, as long as Your Excellency is at the helm, I can regard the confusion of parties with equanimity. All this has only strengthened my attachment, and my ardent desire to assist you, in so far as in me lies, to the solution of your difficulties and a full realization of peace at home. Your Excellency will permit me the expression of this assurance, which comes from the bottom of my heart, and at the same time allow me to present you and the Princess with my sincere good wishes for Christmas and the New Year.
>
> Your Excellency's ever devoted,
G. Card. Kopp.

A few weeks later the Cardinal informed me that he had heard, through the Cardinal Secretary of State, that Erzberger had got into touch with the Vatican, where he was spreading false rumours about me. At the same time Kopp wrote to his friend, Monsignor

Montel, who for many years had been German representative on the Rota Romana: " I am not at all pleased with the attitude of the Centre. I condemn it heartily and deplore its short-sightedness. The Centre has no leader in the Reichstag. Actually it is led by immature and undisciplined people such as Erzberger. It seems to me that the causes of its lack of morale go some way back, and were not immediately antecedent to this last unfortunate vote in the Reichstag. For several years the tactics of the Centre have been uncertain and, at times, merely provocative. Every scandal against the Government has been raked up and exaggerated under the pretext of championing justice, and dragged before the tribune of the Reichstag. Unfortunately the Centre as a whole is far too lacking in distinction and political tact."

CHAPTER XVIII

A letter from General von Deines on the dissolution of the Reichstag—
Other letters to me—My New Year's Eve letter—My election-slogan
as Imperial Chancellor—Election Day (25.i.1907)—Crushing defeat
of the Social Democrats—Letters of Congratulation—Opening of the
new Reichstag—The election of its President—My speech on the first
reading of the Budget Bill (February 1907)—I address the Agrarians
—Letters from leading intellectual circles of Germany—Gustav
Schmoller.

I THOUGHT it a good omen that the first message of sympathy to reach me after the Reichstag had been dissolved should have come from my old comrade of the days of the Franco-Prussian War, Deines, who had since reached the rank of general commanding the Eighth Army Corps. He wrote to me from Rome, where he and his young wife were spending the winter. His letter is dated December 14th, 1906:

" From the Eternal City, the place where first you were famous, let me most warmly congratulate you on the dissolution of this miserable parliament. It was an act, a decisive act, the first we have seen for many years. Every true German heart rejoices at it. When one is living abroad one is more conscious than ever of being a German. Bravo, bravissimo! I have read only extracts of your speech of yesterday in the *Popolo Romano*, and it has filled me with enthusiasm. There is wit and power in it, and you chose your moment admirably. I am sure you will direct this great wave of national feeling which seems to be sweeping over Germany, with force and understanding, and I hope that it will largely strengthen the National-Liberals and Conservatives."

From Rostock the poet, Adolf Wilbrandt, wrote:

Dear Chancellor and friend,

I am delighted! The root-cause of this crisis is so grave as to be almost tragic. We are resigned to that, since such has been our history for close on two thousand years. But what had to happen has happened, and it is entirely thanks to you that matters have been brought to a head. My personal affection for you makes me doubly glad that this is so. It is a victory— even if we only win a dozen seats. And you, as always, will have said and done what our national honour and future demanded. I say " amen " to every one of your words. Thank you with all my heart.

Ever your and Donna Maria's most devoted,
ADOLF WILBRANDT.

Lahusen, Schleiermacher's successor in the pulpit of Trinity Church, the parish church of the Imperial Chancellery, sent me a telegram. Thirty-two years before we had stood side by side under the Christmas tree in the Palazzo Caffarelli, when he was pastor of the little Evangelical Church in Rome, and I was an attaché. He wired: " Will your Excellency allow the German congregations to express their warmest thanks and jubilant approval of this act of liberation. May God give your Excellency strength for the heavy task which lies before you. May He, in the words of to-day's lesson, be ' a rock and fortress ' to you and to our people."

The passage (Ps. xviii, 3)—" The Lord is my rock and my fortress, and my deliverance; my God, my strength in whom I will trust; my buckler and the horn of my salvation and my high tower," had inspired me too with courage.

A powerful wave of feeling swept over the German people. It found its expression in hundreds of notes, telegrams, and addresses to me, and also in presents of flowers. Among the verses there were many which, though they may not have achieved the structural perfection of those of my poet friend, Adolf Wilbrandt, in his beautiful *Master of Palmyra*, were well put together, and certainly very well meant. I may quote the following, as characteristic of the spirit of that time:

> " *Das war mal recht! hör' ich's das Land durchdröhnen*
> *Wer fordert Frucht vom ungedüngten Feld?*
> *Ob Grimm, ob Hass, ob Neid ihn bitter höhnen*
> *So bleibt doch fest der sturmerprobte Held.*

> " *Erworbene Rechte werden wir uns wahren,*
> *Nie kann sich Licht dem Blinden offenbaren,*
> *So war es recht! Es sollen nicht verzagen*
> *Die Treuen, die voll Tapferkeit gekämpft.*

> " *Auch künftig soll der Feind es nimmer wagen,*
> *Die Flamm' zu schüren, die wir kaum gedämpft.*
> *Die Kolonien wollen wir behalten*
> *Und sie voll Lust nach unserm Sinn gestalten.*

" So war es recht! Wir lassen uns nicht rauben,
Was deutsche Kraft dem Vaterland erwarb.
Wir halten fest an unserm alten Glauben,
Dass deutscher Opfermut noch nicht erstarb." [1]

The following telegram in Low German, received from some Oldenburg admirers, rejoiced my heart as a son of the Lower Elbe:

" Wi Luet ut us butjenterland
Sünt van jo wohl red entflammt!
Us makt unmannig viel Vergnuegen
Dat rot und swart ehr fett hebt kreegen:
Drum ducht us dat just nich verkehrt
Wenn wie jo hartlich gratuleert! " [2]

It thereupon became my task to bring the powerful stream of national feeling and enthusiasm to the mill of politics. The election campaign began. My natural supporters in this struggle ought to have been the Minister of the Interior, Bethmann-Hollweg, and the Secretary of State for Home Affairs, Count Posadowsky. But, for reasons which I have explained above, the latter had been opposed to a dissolution. I felt that I was not wrong in presuming

---

[1] " Well done! Well done! The murmuring land rejoices
   Who asks for harvests from the untilled field ?
   Though envy, rancour, hate, with bitter voices
   Assail our storm-proved hero, he'll not yield.

" We will hold fast the rights for which we perished
   Blind eyes can never open to the light.
   It was well done: the heroes that we cherished
   We'll not betray—whose valour bought our might.

" No future foe shall ever dare re-kindle
   This blaze we scarce have trodden into earth
   The Colonies are ours, not strength must dwindle
   We'll use and shape them for our might and mirth.

" Well done, Well done!—they shall not snatch this token
   Our German strength won for the Fatherland.
   We'll keep our proud and ancient faith unbroken
   While German sacrifice and valour stand! "

[2] (Approximately) " Us folk out of the provinces
   Are all worked up like, with this 'ere news
   We feel no end bucked
   To think that Red and Black (*i.e.* Centre and Socialists)
   have got it in the neck at last.
   So don't you mind us Mr. Chancellor
   Sendin' you heartiest congrats."

that he would not be very upset if my electoral campaign ended in defeat. Bethmann, though by no means a deliberately conspiritorial figure, lived in the clouds, amid nebulous abstractions without content. He was, through and through, a doctrinaire, a martyr to shilly-shally, who reached a decision with difficulty, and was above all, very nervous. Consequently I was left to conduct the electoral campaign alone. But at my side I had the Head of the Imperial Chancellery, Privy Councillor (later Secretary of State) Loebell, the best of all possible collaborators. Loebell was that rare thing, a genuinely fine man, determined, but with a heart of gold. His character was loyalty itself, loyalty to Prussia and Germany, to King and Emperor, to me, his superior and friend. He was a zealous worker, and only too often was led to overtax his strength to the detriment of his health. A shrewd brain—though possibly, every now and then, he formed too good an opinion of other people, and certainly never did conscious harm to anyone. He spoke and wrote equally well. "*Fortes creantur fortibus et bonis*," says Horace. Loebell's father, who came originally from the Mark, was for many years with the Brandenburg Cuirassiers. He accompanied them to France in 1870, and after he had been retired as major, spent the evening of his life in his old garrison town, Brandenburg on the Havel, in a parsonage. Anyone who saw him, at almost ninety, sitting with his wife, who was only a year or two younger, beneath the old lime-tree in front of their little house, might have fancied he saw Philemon and Baucis. His son was my ever-loyal, diligent, and shrewd assistant. He advised me in approaching the party leaders and official bodies in the provinces, and shared my view that what mattered most was, not the placation of this or that party bonze on any minor issue, but the evocation throughout the land of a spirit that would compel the chiefs to sink their selfish aims in the national interest.

In my New Year's Eve letter against Social Democracy to General von Liebert, the president of the Empire League, I gave as my electoral slogan: "For the honour and welfare of the nation, against Social-Democrats, Poles, Guelphs, and Centrists." I intentionally made the action against Socialism the spear-head of our attack. I was not blind to the fact that even among the Socialists there were genuine idealists, men of real probity and value, and that their aims contained a certain element of goodness and justice. But I also knew that if ever they got power into their hands it would be a serious disaster for the Fatherland, in view of the stubborn doctrinairism, the bitter and fanatical party spirit, of German Social-Democracy, and above all, of the unpractical fashion in which, in contrast with all other Socialists, our Social-Democrats persisted in treating our Foreign Policy from the standpoint of party politics:—their complete illusion on the subject of foreign countries and foreign " comrades." I have never doubted that German Social-Democracy was not in a position and, in reality, had no serious wish, to put into practice the theories of Karl Marx. But I could also see that, if ever it came into power, it would disorganize the administration, endanger public security, unchain every base passion, arouse every unhealthy appetite. I could see that, once in the saddle, it would be forced, in order to maintain its own position, to the exercise of that " class justice " against which, when no such thing really existed, it had always ranted and raved: and especially in dealing with other countries, it would lack the necessary backbone and vision.

On 19th January 1907 there was a dinner, given at the Palace Hotel, at which were present many representatives of the parties in minority on 13th December, as well as a number of industrialists, professors, artists, and financiers. This was the audience I desired. As a gathering it was fully representative of the national culture and national effort. I addressed it in a speech in which I quoted Goethe's saying: " What is thy duty? The task of the hour," and I gave, as *mot d'ordre* for the elections: " A Reichstag whose majority shall not give way on any national question: that is the task of this hour." Two days later Singer, the Social-Democratic leader, declared to a correspondent of the Imperialist and frankly anti-German *Daily Mail* that German Socialism was marching, with full confidence, into the hottest battle in its history. It would raise the party strength in parliament from seventy-nine to at least ninety.

On the evening of Election Day (25th January) the first result was wired to me at about ten o'clock, to tell me that in my home constituency, Pinneberg, the Liberal, Carstens, had beaten the Social-Democrat. " Over Your Excellency's homeland," ran the telegram, " the national flag, black, white, and red, is waving again."

After that came a steady stream of good results. Saxony, in particular, which had sent practically only Socialists to the Reichstag, and had in consequence been nicknamed " The Red Kingdom," returned fifteen non-Socialist deputies.

When I went to bed, at nearly midnight, the whole situation was excellent. Some hours later my wife roused me to say she thought she heard singing in front of the palace. I laughed and said she must be dreaming, turned over, and went to sleep again. But soon there came a loud knock at the door. A Chancellery official reported that a huge crowd outside was clamouring for me. I dressed as quickly as possible and, infected by the excitement of the mass of people packed into the courtyard of the palace and across the Wilhelmstrasse, I delivered the following speech: " My friends— I thank you for having come to give me this friendly greeting, but, even more I thank you for the feeling of patriotism that brings you here. My great predecessor, before whom we all incline in reverence, said, nearly forty years ago: ' Let us help the German people into the saddle. It will ride all right.' I hope and believe that the German people has shown to-day that it still can ride! If each will do his duty at the second ballot the whole world will see that our people is firmly in the saddle, and ready to ride down whatever stands in the way of its prosperity and greatness. And now, my friends, let us all join in a cheer: ' Long live the nation! Long live the German people!' "

This speech was interrupted by several bursts of wild cheering, followed by a roar of enthusiasm.

Next morning a closer scrutiny of results brought the certainty that if all went well, the Conservatives, National-Liberals, and Liberals, would have a strong government majority in the Reichstag. The supplementary elections were due on 5th February. The weight of the nation's wrath had fallen so heavily on the Socialists that they lost thirty-six seats, their strength having been reduced from seventy-nine to forty-three. Had it not been for their electoral pact with the Centre, a pact disapproved by most of the bishops, as well as by Praschma, Hertling, and Ballestrem, they would have lost at least a dozen more seats, and have been reduced to only thirty members. The soul of our people had been moved, as never since the days of Bismarck. The big towns which for long had been Socialist strongholds—cities like Leipzig, Dresden, Magdeburg, Halle, Elberfeld, Frankfurt-am-Main, Darmstadt, Breslau, Königsberg, Bremen, Brunswick and Stettin—had been wrested, by the first results, from the Socialists. In the 1907 elections the Right Wing parties gained 113 seats in all: the Liberals 106. The Socialists had only forty-three seats left. It was the worst defeat the party had suffered since its creation. Right up to Election day the Left had been so sure of its victory that the *Wahre Jakob*, the Social-Democratic comic paper, had already prepared a cartoon, which it published on the morning of the elections, showing a victorious Bebel on horseback holding a red flag and riding over a prostrate Chancellor who held up his hands to beg for mercy. This was the first really funny joke which I, who have always enjoyed comic papers, ever found in the *Wahre Jakob*.

On the day following the election the royal princes, with the

THE REICHSTAG ELECTIONS, JANUARY 1907

Crowds cheering in front of the Berlin Castle

Painting by F. Skarbina

exception of the Crown Prince who happened to be out of town, were sent by the Kaiserin to my wife, with bouquets, to congratulate her on the result. The Emperor himself appeared that same afternoon in high glee. He declared next day that he had always been convinced that no Chancellor could help winning an election if he went to the country on a slogan concerning the army or the navy. On the third day, in the course of his morning visit, he expressed the opinion that, really, it was a matter of indifference to him how parties were grouped in the Reichstag, as far as respective numbers were concerned. The important thing was that the Reichstag should be kept in its place. On the evening of Supplementary Election Day His Majesty delivered an oration to a crowd, assembled in his honour, in front of the royal palace. Exaggerating, in his own peculiar fashion, all I had said on the evening of the first results, he quoted the *mot* of old Kottwitz in the " Prince of Homburg," who tells the Great Elector that there is only one way of beating an enemy, and that is by beating him, and exclaimed: " Well now we've learnt the art of thrashing, and we're itching to begin to practise it." It was necessary for me to speak again from the Chancellor's palace and assure thousands of patriotic burghers that what had triumphed, at the first as at the supplementary elections, had been the German spirit:

> " *Der gekämpft hat allerwegen,*
> *Der noch kämpft zu dieser Frist*
> *Und der darum nicht erlegen,*
> *Weil er ja unsterblich ist.*" [1]

I had been asked by many people, even by letter, who was the author of these lines, but could give no answer. I was therefore all the more pleased when Oberlandesgerichtsrat Creizenach wrote me from Frankfurt-am-Main to say that they were by his late father, the history master at the gymnasium there, Dr. Theodore Creizenach, whom I mention in my *Recollections of Youth*. As a fourth-form lad, in the winter of 1861-2, I had been his attentive pupil, and for six and forty years his fine poem on the immortal spirit of Germany had stuck in my memory.

The dark side of things at Court and the narrowness of the Court outlook were impressed upon me by an incident, in itself very trifling, which occurred at the conclusion of a service, on 27th

---

[1] " That has fought through all the ages
And still fights on at this hour.
That has never been brought low
Because it is immortal."

January, in honour of the Emperor's birthday. When service ended everyone except Their Majesties remained in chapel. My colleagues and the members of the Bundesrat thronged round me, all eager to hear more about the election results. One of the ladies of the Household, Countess Mathilde Keller, in other respects an admirable spinster of mature years, brushed us impatiently aside, with the words: " Stop your silly politics now, and let me pass. I must bring Her Majesty her cloak." But the Hereditary Prince Bernhard of Saxe-Meiningen, the husband of the Kaiser's eldest sister, Princess Charlotte of Prussia, as a rule very critical of me and my policy, honoured me with the following letter: " I should not like to be missing among the thousands who congratulate Your Excellency on this great victory. My congratulations to the brilliant organizer of the ' Sedan on the home front.' They are all the more sincere because I should never have believed in so complete a rout of anti-patriotic Socialism, and am therefore the more pleasantly proved wrong."

The Reichstag met again on 19th February. I had composed the speech from the Throne, it began as follows: " Called on to arbitrate a dispute between the Federal Governments and the majority in the last Reichstag, the German nation has shown itself resolved to safeguard the national honour and patrimony, without regard for petty party interests. The strength of this national resolve, welding together middle-class, peasants, and workers, is a sure guarantee of the future of the Empire and the Fatherland. As I am resolved to maintain conscientiously all constitutional rights and powers, so am I confident that this new Reichstag will see that its highest duty is to guard and strengthen, in full consciousness and readiness for action, our position among the civilized nations."

The election of a president was the first difficulty to present itself. The Centre wanted its leader, Herr Martin Spahn, to be elected. I had never had the intention of permanently excluding the Centre, and certainly had nothing against Herr Spahn personally. To my great regret the Centre had excluded itself. But I had never doubted the patriotism of the great majority of the party, though, throughout the elections, its Press had often reproached me for doing so. An American press-correspondent had inquired whether the victory of the Nationalist parties would not be likely to encourage the German Government to adopt an aggressive Foreign Policy. The Press Bureau of the Foreign Office answered the Publisher's Press Association in New York in the following terms: " It is entirely false to suppose that the result of the Reichstag elections will have as consequence the conduct of a policy of aggression. His Majesty the Emperor is no Chauvinist, nor can Prince Bülow be reproached with any taste for foreign adventure. It would be a grave error to conclude that the patriotic sentiment which resulted in the present Reichstag is ultra-nationalist or aggressive. This Reichstag has been elected in protest against the anti-national arrogance of a self-conflicting party alliance. Such arrogance stirred to its depths the national sentiment of the people. The same majority which intends to hold and subdue South-West Africa would be strongly opposed to any too ambitious suggestion."

The above was not submitted to me before dispatch or I should have suppressed the phrase " anti-national arrogance." But it needed a strong dose of susceptibility and ill-temper to discover in the form of this telegram, given out as it was by a junior official of our Foreign Office and inspired entirely in the interests of our Foreign Policy, an intention to attack the Centre Party. I could not in spite of all impartiality, when I viewed the situation as a whole, conceal from myself the fact that, if I chose as President of the Reichstag the leader of the Centre, immediately after such an election, the majority of the German people would be likely to mis-interpret my action and consider it as counter to their will. Such a spring frost might have shrivelled many flowers.

In consequence I approved the election of an entirely new president of the Reichstag. Count Ugo Stolberg was chosen; a conservative without narrow prejudice, equally amiable with all parties, on good terms with the Centre, and courteous with the Socialists. The first Vice-President was the Liberal, Kämpf, the close friend of Eugen Richter, a Berlin municipal councillor and senior alderman. He was a true child of Neu-Ruppen, objective, frigid, and scrupulously honest in outlook. The second Vice-President was, alas, Paasche, the " black sheep of the National-Liberals," as their leader Dr. Bassermann himself had called him. The relationship of Paasche to Bassermann was much the same as that of Erzberger to Spahn. But some profound spiritual kinship for years bound Erzberger to Paasche. The latter, in 1907, made a show of great enthusiasm for me, but his limitless affection inspired me with little confidence. I have already had to men-tion that Paasche was one of the very few deputies who, in the days before the 1918 revolution tried to turn to their personal advan-tage their status as national representatives. His son had first entered the Navy, but later had served in East Africa. His colonial adventures had inspired him to write a book brimming over with inflated enthusiasm for our Colonial and Foreign Policy. The father thought that his son had not been properly rewarded by the Order of the Prussian Crown (Fourth Class) which I had managed to secure for him. He was for ever pestering me to obtain another decoration, if possible a Mecklenburg, that is to say an entirely feudal Order. On the fall of the Monarchy this Order-coveting Hans Paasche, emulating the eldest son of Professor Harnack, went over promptly to the Socialists. On 9th November 1918 he distinguished himself by his brutal rudeness to the Empress, then very ill and broken by her grief. Later he became a Communist and was killed in a street fight. These matters, in themselves without interest, I mention for the light they throw on revolutionary times and personalities. They seem to me far more significant than elaborate psychological disquisitions on them.

On 25th February 1907 the Budget Bill was read for the first time. Bassermann welcomed the declarations made in the speech from the Throne, especially the clear and unreserved recognition of social obligations towards the working classes, and the promise that all constitutional rights and privileges, including that of universal suffrage, would be conscientiously maintained. The peculiar character and deep significance of these elections had been, he said, to dispel the legend of any " irresistible " Social-Democracy. In my reply [1] I first explained my slogan, which I had coined during the electoral campaign, on the desirability of uniting the conservative with the liberal spirit. Every truly fruitful epoch in our development had been due, I said, to the judicious mingling of the two. Yet on 13th December 1906 I had entirely opposed the Roeren-Singer coalition. I stressed the merits of the Centre Party with whose support I had governed for many years, but added that never would I submit to the tyranny of any single party. Spahn, who had spoken before me, had reproached me for treating the Centre as though it were Socialist. I answered that this would never have occurred to me if I had not, to my stupefaction, suddenly found the Centre in alliance with Social-Democracy, the party which, not two months previously, a great Catholic newspaper had denounced as the party of Anti-Christ. We cannot sin against the fundamental laws of ethics and hope to go unpunished. I sharply refuted the silly charge that I had improperly influenced the elections. In every country in the world the government claims the right to enlighten the electorate before an election takes place, as to its views and the views of its opponents. That right I claimed equally for myself. I added amid a storm of applause from the Right: " If at any future election I find myself still in this seat, I intend to use

[1] Prince Bülow's *Speeches*, complete edition, iii, 2. Compressed edition, iv, 202.

this right even more abundantly. I intend to sing quite another tune to the gentlemen of the Extreme Left Wing." The people, I continued, had emerged as the real victors in this struggle. I should not go back an inch on my programme: the protection of all national activities, an impartial defence of every economic interest, the protection of agriculture, the development of trade, and above all, care for the workers. This policy I considered my personal task and would not permit it to be tampered with. I would abide by it all the more rigidly since my policy had given its proofs, both economically and at the polls. Bebel asserted that nowhere was there any longer confidence in me; that even the Navy League would have none of me because they found me too weak, that Social Democracy alone represented the cause of progress; that, as a result I lost my nerve whenever I had to hear a Social-Democrat speak, whenever I was faced with a Bebel! To which I replied: " Good heavens. I certainly take the Socialist menace seriously, very seriously, but it doesn't make me nervous." I did not conceal the fact that, at one time, I had set great hopes on the Revisionists. But since recently I had seen the Revisionists grovel before the fanatical and terrorist majority of their party, I had given up any such hope. For as long as Socialism remained anti-patriotic, proclaiming itself, as it did in Germany, the public enemy of its country, which it would only defend in so far as its principles allowed, no compromise with it would be possible. I warned the majority not to do as the old Germanic tribes had done, who, after a victory, drunk with mead, would stretch themselves out on their bear-skins. " Then it was that the foe returned to fall upon them, and beat them utterly. We must remain on guard."

On 14th May 1907, at the banquet of the German Congress of Agriculture, I pointed out that my views on Agriculture had not changed. A day would come when I should retire from public life, though perhaps that day would not come so soon as certain individuals could desire. But I hoped that, when it came, they would inscribe on my political tombstone: " He was an agrarian Chancellor." No doubt that in the future there would be differences between myself and the Farmers' Union, since I could only know one line of policy—the interests of the nation as a whole. That was why I could never be entirely for one party. But I hoped that between the Union and myself there would be one of those happy associations in which, though people sometimes differed, until each had really got to know the other, they fitted in together in the end, and became the very closest friends. To these overwhelmingly Conservative, and in part ultra-Conservative farmers, I declared my intention of pursuing a policy of reform—of the laws of association and assembly, and of the penal code and criminal procedure. No real statesman had the right to refuse to modify, by a series of practical reforms, a state of things which no longer corresponded to reality. I intended also to tackle a reform of the Stock Exchange laws. It was not in the interests of agriculture that confidence in our commercial relations should be destroyed, as it had been by certain legislation introduced a few years previously. On the contrary farmers had every reason for wishing that the German Bourse should be as efficient an economic instrument as the Bourse of any other country. The high discount rate which was the result of our faulty exchange-policy should be lowered. It was against the interest of the farming industry if the Berlin Stock Exchange were handicapped as compared to those of London and of Paris, if our capital were forced abroad, if the little banks were all absorbed by the big ones. Agriculture had every reason to see to it that our Exchange should be kept as efficient as possible. We had in Germany still far too many prejudices in all classes, in all parties, in all camps. " We have too many preconceived notions, like blinkers, interfering with our vision." A Liberal professor, a very well-educated and competent man, had once said to me, " How is it that you, Mr. Chancellor, who are so cultured, can pursue a farmer's policy?" As though a man could not be both cultured and a farmer! At the same time there were Agrarians and Conservatives to whom commerce and the Bourse appeared an immoral and altogether pernicious element. Such are the blinkers of which we must rid our eyes, since in other countries this narrowness of vision is unknown. Abroad the sense of general solidarity between the different sides of economic life, the sense of their natural unity for the common good of the country, is far more developed than with ourselves.

I was approved not only in political circles but by the intellectual leaders of the nation with whom I had always striven to keep on the best of terms. I am well aware how much there is to criticize in the political activities of the average German professor. Neither in 1848, in St. Paul's church at Frankfurt, nor in his conflict with Bismarck, fourteen years later, did he cover himself with special glory. I equally admit that in the World-War the German professor, by his childish pacifism and equally childish sabre-rattling, his exhibitions of a purblind political stupidity, his monotonous, senseless reiteration of stale boasts about the " supreme glories " of German culture, our " unequalled " scientific method, etc.—in short by his utter lack of taste, insight, or tact—only too often gave our enemies their chance to discredit and slander, or at the very least, to pour out scorn on us. Professors like Lasson and Sombart, Hans Delbrück and Johannes Haller, Theodor Schiemann and Adolf Harnack, talked a lot of nonsense and did us a great deal of harm. The Socialist professor, Leo Arons, was not altogether wrong when he wrote that, after the foolish things he had said during the war, the German professor would do well to observe a prudent silence for evermore. Yet in spite of all this the German scholar, whose study lamp really has lit up the world, is worthy of the deepest respect. At present, in our hour of need, he preserves and fosters a true national spirit in German youth.

For Gustav Schmoller I had always had a special esteem. I saw him first when I was a sixth-form boy at the High School at Halle. In those days he was scarcely eight and twenty; his hair and beard were both jet black; his speeches to the boys were fiery, but they idolized him. I heard him once deliver such an address out of the window of a house in the market-place, before I had made his acquaintance. We grew in intellectual *rapport* in the days of my Paris activities, when I became an ardent reader of his *Year Book of Law, Administration and Economy*, which had just then appeared. I still remember how I read and meditated Schmoller all through a long summer day in the beautiful forest of Fontainebleau. His *Sketch of General Political Economy* became to me, as Thucydides puts it, a χτῆμα ἐς αἰεί—an eternal possession. His brilliant studies on the development of Prussian financial policy aroused or threw fresh light on many thoughts. Like Treitschke, the native of Saxony, like the Hanoverians, Scharnhorst and Hardenberg, like Freiherr vom und zum Stein, who was born on the Lahn, the Swabian, Schmoller, had penetrated more deeply into the spirit and forms of the Prussian State than many a born Prussian. His strength lay in this—that he had acquired an intimate personal knowledge of our political and party life, our economic circumstances, and, above all, of Prussian administration; that, apart from my humble self, he was in intimate touch with Miquel and Althoff, with Thiel and Lohmann, with Klemens Delbrück and Berlepsch, with Möller and Becker, the Oberbürgermeister of Cologne; that, both on the Staatsrat and on many preparatory legal and administrative commissions and committees of enquiry, and in the Upper House where he represented the University of Berlin, he could obtain direct insight into the workings of the State. An ounce of practice is worth a ton of theory. He wrote to me as follows on 10th February 1907, just after the election campaign:

Now that I have a minute to spare I hasten to congratulate you, and tell you how deeply convinced I am that the whole nation will thank Your Excellency. Your courage made the dissolution possible. While most patriotic people would scarcely have dared to take the risk you, in a flash of genius, foresaw the happy result. A just appreciation of those incalculable forces which make the future is the mark of a true statesman. This victory will also have vindicated an important part of your policy more decisively than we could ever have hoped—I mean the part for which I with every other believer in moderate and reasonable social reform, esteem you so highly. The present Socialist defeat has clearly shown to all the world the wisdom of your rejection of any provocative measure, or the passing of emergency laws. This rout of the Social Democrats may be the first step towards securing a transformation of that party from within. It may free the Trades Union movement from bondage to fanatical revolutionary leaders, give non-Socialist workers' organizations their chance to breathe and grow, and so make possible a more rational leadership for the working classes. It is all the more to your credit to have refrained from extreme measures since your assumption of office, in that you were obliged to win over the Conservatives once again to government policy, and yet not allow their chiefs to attain Cabinet rank. Since, with us, real parliamentary government is still impossible, and it is necessary to set a bureaucracy above the various classes and parties, you had to take account of many difficulties. To have overcome them will always be your sure title to fame. One day, a year ago, at Prince Knyphausen's, we discussed the reasons why to-day one has to govern along such lines, while all admitting that it was so. But in spite of that you have always retained your majority. You have created better conditions for the co-operation of Conservatives, National-Liberals, and Progressives than had ever before existed in Prussian political history. It will be your future task to maintain these conditions, and that will probably be more difficult than to bring them about in a general election. But your future will be made considerably easier by the fact that you now hold in your hands all the cards for obtaining an even more Conservative, ultramontane majority, if you wish it, though I hope you will be skilful enough to avoid the necessity. Such a solution could only rob you of the great popularity and power this election has brought you. "Bülow is so clever that he succeeds where anyone else would be sure to fail." That was what a member of the Bismarck family said to me, and surely, even now that the great

Chancellor is no more, the Bismarcks are still to be reckoned among the ablest and most far-seeing people, and are besides not over-inclined to admire and praise another Imperial Chancellor. Excuse me Excellency for having troubled you with these lines and please do not bother to answer them. You have other and better things to occupy you. I, along with millions of Germans, have as much reason to-day to be grateful to fate as we all had in the summer of 1906 to see you make so complete a recovery. May you remain as well for many a long year, for your happiness and the welfare of the Fatherland.

Your very devoted,
Gustav Schmoller.

Not all the hopes have been realized which this exceptional man had formed of the 1907 election. Had it been granted me to remain at the helm a few years longer, I think I might have come a good way nearer to my object of giving the workers what the nineteenth century gave both the industrial and professional sections of the middle class, that is to say, their rightful position in the State. I might have brought the proletariat into full, harmonious political equality with other interests and classes, have made the Fourth Estate a part of the commonwealth by the peaceful methods of evolution. That—both for the Empire and its subjects—would have been more profitable than any November Revolution, since, as so profound and penetrating a thinker as Hippolyte Taine has truly put it: " *En fait d'histoire il vaut mieux continuer que recommencer.*"

My friend the Ministerialdirektor Althoff, a man of great ability, for whom I had the deepest respect, wired me as follows: " Must let you know the heartfelt satisfaction which 25th January and the national re-awakening produced by Your Excellency, have caused me. Your very faithful and unbounded admirer, Althoff."

With that reverent devotion he always accorded the powerful, Harnack, the Court theologian, had written after the Reichstag was dissolved: " Come what may, you have done your duty, you have done what had to be done. And the fruits of such an action must be good though the harvest may not immediately be gathered. *Vexilla Regis prodeunt.*"

CHAPTER XIX

*The Kiel Week of 1907—Eulenburg quarrels with Holstein—The
attack by the " Zukunft "—The Kaiser's meeting with Nicholas II
at Swinemünde—the Russian Foreign Minister, Isvolski, on relations
between the two countries—Meeting of William II and Edward VII
at Wilhelmshöhe—Baron von Eckardstein—The Second Hague
Conference—England approves our attitude—Admiral Montagu's
letter to the Emperor—Bethmann-Hollweg replaces Count Posadowsky—Count Wedel made Statthalter for Alsace-Lorraine.*

THE Kiel Week of 1907 was an especially brilliant one. A
notable feature was the number of distinguished French
people who were present. The Emperor was overjoyed at
this, and fêted them in his most exuberant manner. Their
lively, witty conversation, and perfect courtesy, charmed His
Majesty. Among the French at Kiel there was a Rohan-Chabot;
when the Emperor asked him if he were connected with the Austrian
Rohans he answered that they were his cousins. Several members
of the family had been guillotined during the French Revolution,
and the remainder had fled to Austria. His Majesty, with his
usual spontaneity, answered that they had been perfectly right to
fly, since, otherwise, they, too, would have had their heads cut off.
Rohan-Chabot answered very seriously: " *Non, Sire, je ne suis pas
de votre avis! Quand on a l'honneur d'être Francais, on se laisse
plutôt trancher la tête que d'abondonner son pays.*" An answer worthy
of that ancient house which bears the motto: " *Prince ne daigne,
Roi ne puis, Rohan suis.*"

But the better his French guests at Kiel pleased the Emperor
the angrier he became that Jules Cambon, the French Ambassador
in Berlin, had not come with them. I wrote to His Majesty that
Cambon, who shortly after this had visited me (uninvited) at
Norderney, had pointed out to me that he had received no invitation
to Kiel. The Emperor scribbled in the margin: " That's no
excuse. He could have asked for one through Knesebeck or
Eulenburg." " If Cambon had been invited," my letter continued,
" I am sure he would have been very glad to come." A fresh
marginal note: " That's all nonsense. All he had to do was to
ask." I also informed the Emperor, as I was bound officially to do,
that Cambon, whom I had known for twenty years, had told me

several times quite frankly that, in the interests of Franco-German relations, no precipitate action ought to be taken. Exaggerated advances on our side would be as much out of place as threats and rudeness. French public opinion was not yet ripe for any closer Franco-German *rapprochement*: but still less did it desire conflict. What it needed most was calm, without any violent *soubresauts* in either direction. The Kaiser added in the margin: " Let Cambon keep his impertinence to himself. It is entirely my business how I choose to treat the French and, at Kiel, I have taken the necessary steps." Further on in my letter I reported that Cambon had spoken quite sensibly on Morocco, expressly declaring that France would abide by the Act of Algeciras. If, a few years hence, certain provisos in the Act should have been nullified, France and Germany would have had time in which to agree what was to be done. In France, he said, it was fully realized that all would depend on how Franco-German relations had modified in the interim. In spite of this very sensible declaration on the part of the French Ambassador the Emperor added the hasty and bad-tempered note: " Cambon has told you nothing new or interesting; all this is simply a *rechauffé*. He knows no more than Clemenceau or any other of their precious Cabinet what France will really do in Morocco. All this is simply on the level of the cheapest diplomatic drawing-room twaddle." What really alarmed me in these annotations of the All-Highest was, not the bad temper to which I was quite accustomed, and which as a rule was soon forgotten, but a manifest tendency in His Majesty to handle personally and *suo modo*, in accordance with his own whims and impressions, our future relationships with France—the wish to be his own Foreign Minister and attempt to shoulder a burden for which he was in no way equal.

The most depressing thing about politics is that the mean and common are always apparent, even at one's most inspiring and really encouraging moments. During my illness Holstein and Philip Eulenburg had quarrelled. " Which of the gods brought these two together to contend? " This the blind poet asks the Muse, at the beginning of the *Iliad*, before he goes on to tell the strife between the king of men, Agamemnon, and the swift-footed Achilles. Considering the morbid streak which ran through the character of the otherwise so highly gifted Eulenburg, and the fact that, despite his keen intelligence, Holstein only too frequently was a prey to pathological mistrust, the victim of false ideas which drove him on to a jackal-like pursuit of revenge, it would take a very experienced psychiatrist to determine the origin and justification of their breach. From the conflict between these two, each of whom for years had played a responsible part in public life, there arose a kind of dark miasma which little by little was to poison the whole official atmosphere of Germany, pervading it, in lurid contrast to that brilliant renewal of the national spirit that followed the dissolution of the Reichstag.

In the May of 1906 Eulenburg wrote to me in a panic that, shortly after his retirement, Holstein had suddenly sent him a letter, "insulting beyond belief," which began: "My Phili—you needn't take this beginning as a compliment, since nowadays to call a man 'Phili' means—well, nothing very flattering. You have now attained the object for which you had been intriguing for years—my retirement. And the general press attacks on me are also all that you can wish. . . ."

The rest of Holstein's letter Eulenburg refused to reveal; he said that it was all too horrible. He further wrote that it had had a deplorable effect on him, since before he received it he had already been feeling very ill. He had said to himself that bloodshed would be necessary if his children, whom he deeply loved, were still to have a father they could respect, the Emperor an honourable friend. Although opposed in principle to duelling, and conscious that to do so would be a concession to medievalism and against the practice of civilized nations, he had sent his seconds to Holstein. He forwarded me a long *compte rendu* which declared that Baron Axel Varnbüler, the Württemberg Minister who had acted for him in that capacity, had arranged the matter by Eulenburg declaring on his honour that he had had no share in Holstein's dismissal, nor any share in the press attacks against him. Holstein, on his part, had taken back the expressions he had used in his letter, and these were, in the highest degree, insulting.

Shortly after this, in the Berlin *Zukunft*, there appeared sharp attacks on Philip Eulenburg, whose friend, the Berlin Commandant, Count Kuno Moltke and the "Liebenberger set," were accused of harming the body politic by their intimate relations with the Kaiser. The *Zukunft* added, that in these circles, spiritualism, Christian Science, and "other decadent practices" were the rage.

I made Philip Eulenburg come and see me. I should like here to say that I was convinced that the accusations of unnatural practices brought against him were unfounded. His affectionate relations with wife and children, the deep and passionate love with which his charming and distinguished wife still clung to him, made such vile assertions appear monstrous. Moreover, when his only brother, the Cavalry Captain, Count Friedrich Eulenburg was convicted of them, Philip, with an abhorrence which in my opinion

was genuine, had refused to see or speak to his brother again.
This I have already mentioned. And Philip Eulenburg some little
time previously had confided to me that " a certain distinguished
lady," with whom he had had an intrigue some years before, had found
herself, as the result of it, in a very difficult position. Her husband,
a scoundrel and a gambler, had threatened her with divorce and
scandal, and it had needed a considerable sum to buy this black-
mailer's silence. Everything therefore seemed to show that this
charge of unnatural practices was unfounded. I retained my conviction right up to the lawsuit in Munich, at which the unlucky
Eulenburg broke down when confronted by the evidence of a
Starnberg fisherman. I have sometimes, since then, been told that
I was too credulous in my defence of Philip Eulenburg, or at any
rate, too rash. But I can answer this by pointing out that not I
alone but so unimpeachable and reliable a friend as Count Botho
Eulenburg, who had known his cousin Philip since childhood, also,
till after the Munich trial, considered him incapable of unnatural
practices. The often absurdly precious tone in which Philip
often wrote seemed to me to prove very little. What sentimental
letters, for example, the members of the Göttingen brotherhood
wrote to each other! Goethe himself, who was formal and even stiff
as a man, wrote, when he was nearly eighty to his equally aged
friend, the musician Zelter, that he could scarcely wait for the
minute when he would meet and embrace his beloved comrade.
But if, in the spring of 1907, I still entertained no doubts of Eulenburg's erotic integrity, I was only too well aware that he indulged in
spiritualist practices, against which I had often warned him. I
knew that he was a victim of neurasthenia and that already the suit
which, shortly before his retirement, Marschall had brought
against Tausch, in which Eulenburg had been called as a witness,
had left him very unstrung, and nearly driven him to a sick bed. I
therefore did all I could to prevent things coming to court. My
efforts were supported by Walther Rathenau, in those days an
intimate friend of Maximilian Harden—whom I did not, as yet,
know personally—and by another of Harden's friends, the clever,
and at the same time kind and helpful, Baron Alfred Berger, the
head of the Deutsches Schauspielhaus in Hamburg and the husband
of that talented actress Stella Hohenfels. In my next chapter I shall
have to relate how the Heads of His Majesty's Cabinets, Lucanus
and Hülsen, supported by General Plessen and the whole *maison
militaire*, disregarding my advice and warnings, and the able appeals
of Berger and Rathenau, not to mention those of Eulenburg himself,
who was most anxious to avoid a lawsuit, suddenly and against the

interests of the State, forced Kuno Moltke's hand to bring an action.

The splendid success of the government at the polls had strengthened our foreign position and raised our status in the world. Foreign nations had been convinced that the progress of Socialism in Germany betokened a weakening of the Empire. One might say that the outside world judged the strength of the body politic in Germany by the thermometer of the rise or fall of Socialism. The two meetings in the summer of 1907, between the Tsar and Kaiser on the one hand and the Kaiser and King Edward on the other—the one at Swinemünde, the other at Wilhelmshöhe—afforded opportunity for valuable observations in this direction. Both passed off very well. The Tsar, on 6th June 1907, at a farewell banquet on board the Russian yacht " Standard," proposed a toast the warmth of which contrasted with his usual laconic reserve. He insisted on the traditional ties of friendship and kinship which so closely united the two countries and dynasties. For the Emperor I had drafted a rather colourless speech, but one which could not possibly give offence, although it might have seemed somewhat lacking in point. But William II, encouraged by the Tsar's amiability, could not refrain from a trumpet blast. He boasted of his splendid fleet, and insisted on the pleasure it had given him to show it to his friend and brother, expressing the hope that it would not be so very long before the Tsar had just such another fleet to show, and offering his most cordial wishes for the speedy reconstruction of the Russian navy. I suppressed this oratorical exuberance, and ordered the correspondent of the Wolff Agency, on board the " Hohenzollern," to wire the speech I had drafted. Isvolski, the new Foreign Minister—he had replaced Lambsdorff, who retired for reasons of health in 1906, and died in 1907 at San Remo—was inclined to hesitate at first, but finally submitted with a smile: " *Certainement le discours de Sa Majesté l'Empereur était plus beau, mais le vôtre est plus sage. Publions le vôtre!* "

Next day, when the Emperor saw my speech in the papers he grumbled a little at first, but soon calmed down again. In those days it was still possible to guide him.

Alexander Petrovitch Isvolski was an old friend of mine. We had seen a good deal of one another in the course of my four years in St. Petersburg, both at the club and in society. I had also had the chance of being useful to him, thanks to my good relationship with Giers his Minister, with Vlangaly, Gier's assistant, and with Zinoviev, the influential Head of the Asiatic Department. In the Russia of those days, as in all autocracies, personal connections and influence, club

and society recommendations, carried great weight. Isvolski was a
snob first and foremost. Himself of very modest origins he was
anxious to marry well. At that time he was paying his court to the
beautiful widow of a certain General A.... who refused him again and
again. When later he became Ambassador and Minister for Foreign
Affairs, another lady asked Madame A. . . . if she did not regret
having missed so good a match. She replied: " *Je l'ai regretté
tous les jours, mais je m'en suis félicitée toutes les nuits.*"

   Isvolski was certainly not handsome. He looked like a Calmuck, but he was both intelligent and ambitious. He had known
many ups and downs. Entrusted originally with very minor posts
in the Balkans where, in the best tradition of Russia's Balkan
diplomacy, he threw himself into the thick of a hundred conspiracies
and complots, he was made Minister to the Holy See at the time
when I was Ambassador to the Quirinal. He was often my guest
in those days. He had married at last, a charming and most
elegant wife, who was also very well-born—Countess Toll, the
daughter of the Russian Minister to Weimar. By extraction and
upbringing she was at least half, if not three-quarters German, and
was moreover a Protestant. Her husband loved and admired her,
sans comparasion, very much as Bonaparte, in the days when he was
a young Republican general, had looked up to Josephine Beauhar-
nais, his social superior. Every Sunday he would go with her to
church, that is to say, to the Evangelical chapel in the Palazzo
Caffarelli. From Rome Isvolski was sent, to his great grief, to Japan.
He was afraid his career would be ruined there. Russo-Japanese
relations were already very strained, since many influential specula-
tors and Russian generals were beginning to shake the mailed fist,
though none of the diplomats wanted war. I tried to console him
with the assurance that his ability would carry him through. My
consolation comforted him, and he often reminded me gratefully of it.
He emerged unscathed from Japan and was appointed Minister to
Copenhagen which, to the Russian diplomat, is almost a family post
and is regarded as the stepping-stone to an Embassy. When
Isvolski learned that a great diplomatic change-over was due to take
place in St. Petersburg, he sent off his very intelligent German valet
with instructions to try and find out which Embassy he was going to
get. If it was to be Italy the valet was told to wire back " macaroni "
to his master; if Berlin, which Isvolski would have preferred,
" sauerkraut." The valet learned that his master would probably
be appointed Foreign Minister, and wired back the word " caviare."

   Isvolski was by no means anti-German, at any rate not to begin
with. But little by little he became so, after having on various

occasions been rudely treated by the Kaiser. And, naturally, his hostility increased as our excellent but often rather thick-witted German press made him a bogey with which to scare all good Germans. The case of Sir Edward Grey was precisely similar. Rahel once wrote that her lovers were but shadows given substance by her passion. Our heated political phantasy made our opponents, from Ignatiev and Isvolski to Grey and King Edward VII, seem more terrible than they really ever were, especially in the eyes of the Emperor. Mistrust is good and even essential, but it too should not be exaggerated. The conversation which I had with Isvolski at Swinemünde was not unsatisfactory. The Russian Minister seemed very much impressed by the progress of the revolutionary movement which continued to grow in Russia in spite of all repressions, and a number of concessions and reforms. In that I saw yet another reason for avoiding any conflict with Russia. I remember that Bismarck once explained to Count Kálnoky that, if we could wait, we should probably see Russia disintegrate from within and crumple up before she had managed to attack us. Such had been my opinion also, and in May 1914, I found it confirmed. In Rome I asked Kokovsev, the President of the Russian Council, who had just gone out of office, whether he believed in a war. He answered me calmly and decisively: "*A la guerre? Non. A moins d'y être forcés par vous, nous ne ferons pas la guerre. Mais je crois à la possibilité, et malheureusement, je crois même à la vraisemblance d'une révolution en Russie.*" On the subject of France Isvolski at Swinemünde repeated what Muraviev had said to me ten years previously —that Russia was France's ally and had to remain so but that she did not therefore want a strained relationship with us, not to speak of war. With England, he said, Russia, after her serious reverses in the Far East, would have to come to some kind of agreement; but that did not mean that with us she would play the part of "*lansquenet de l'Angleterre.*" Isvolski was convinced that tension between Russia and Germany would only profit the revolution. It was, he said, a capital error of certain Russian chauvinists to imagine that war abroad would serve as an outlet to revolutionary feeling at home. I replied: "*Vous parlez d'or, mon cher ami, se précipiter dans la guerre pour éviter la révolution serait imiter l'example de Guibollard, qui chez Rabelais se jette dans l'eau pour échapper à la pluie.*" He laughed, and quite agreed. If St. Petersburg could keep calm, if Berlin refrained from annoying Russia either on the Polish question or in the Balkans, neither of us would drown.

On 14th August, William II and King Edward met at Wilhelmshöhe. The King honoured me with a long conversation.

The idea on which he laid particular emphasis was that, in proportion as the Press on both sides of the Channel became more foolish,
and the two peoples, or at least a minority in either, more unreason-
able, the more it behoved the governments to keep a clear head.
He assured me once again of his entire and unchanging confidence,
adding that I could be certain that now, as always, his most fervent
wish was Anglo-German " peace and goodwill." [1]   In a cordial
toast, which he expressly desired should be published, he returned
thanks for the hearty welcome he had received, not only from the
authorities and the troops who had paid him official honours, but
also from the crowds in every street.   He continued: " While
wholeheartedly I express to you my gratitude, may I add that it is
my dearest wish to see only the friendliest relations between our
two countries. I am delighted that shortly your Majesty will visit
me in England. I am firmly convinced that not only my family but
the whole English nation will welcome Your Imperial Majesty, and
Her Majesty the Empress with the greatest joy."   Before dinner
the Emperor and the King had driven together round the outskirts
of Wilhelmshöhe, and into the pretty town of Cassel, whose burger-
meister in those days was, not Scheidemann, but a skilled jurist and
civil servant. The King had asked the Emperor to invite me to
accompany them, and H.I.M. had done so with pleasure. Our
conversation *à trois* was unconstrained and friendly throughout.
[*The publishers wish to dissociate themselves from the following statements which are included in order to preserve for English readers the
full text already available in the German edition.   This passage has
historical value, not as a comment on the person concerned, but as
an indication of the Imperial Chancellor's point of view.*]   I do
not know what put it into the Kaiser's head to ask the King
how things were going with Eckardstein. King Edward replied,
in somewhat contemptuous tones, and with a little gesture of re-
pugnance, that he did not know " what became of that fellow." [1]
The astonished Emperor inquired whether the King " did not
receive Eckardstein any more," [1] and His Majesty answered: " Oh,
good gracious. He is no more received anywhere." [1] He went on
to tell the Emperor that Eckardstein had behaved in " a most inconvenient, a most ungentlemanlike way," towards his wife. Her
father, the wealthy furniture dealer, Maple, had originally intended
to make Eckardstein his heir. When, in spite of all the warnings
of his worthy father-in-law, Eckardstein had continued to speculate
and lose huge sums in silly " flutters " on the Stock Exchange Maple
had left his money to his daughter with the stipulation that she

---

[1] English in the original.

should have the sole disposal of it. Eckardstein had proceeded to extort ever larger sums from his wife, with the natural result that their relationship had become very strained. When at last Baroness Eckardstein had declared that she would do no more to assist her husband, from whom she was *de facto* separated, either in speculation or with his debts, Eckardstein had threatened to make a scandal. Since she refused to let herself be blackmailed he had brought an action for divorce, citing her doctor as co-respondent. Baroness Eckardstein left the court with her reputation entirely unblemished, while Eckardstein had shown himself in such an unpleasant light that the public had hissed him and the crowd outside had threatened to give him a thrashing. Since then all decent people had considered him beyond the pale. The Emperor grew very annoyed and excited and declared at once with a certain pathos, as though anxious to prove to his uncle what a stout upholder he was of decorum and domestic morality, that Eckardstein should be " dismissed the service " in Prussia, and that a notice to that effect should be published in the *Reichsanzeiger*. This, like many other Imperial orders, I did not carry out to the letter, and the wretched Eckardstein, as later the unhappy Philip Eulenburg, was allowed to pass into retirement without undue fuss or scandal. I was not to hear of Eckardstein again till 1909 in the very last days of my Chancellorship, when he strove to create a " League of Loyalists " against me, in conjunction with Rudolf Martin the pamphleteer, who after the November Revolution went over to the Extreme Left Wing, and the Master of Ceremonies, Eugen Röder, the malicious brother of the intriguing Countess Paula Alvensleben.

From the 15th of June to the 15th of October 1907 the Second Peace Conference sat at the Hague. It was opened by M. Tets van Goudrian, the Dutch Foreign Minister, formerly Dutch Minister to Berlin, a well-intentioned and tactful diplomatist. The Presidency was taken by Nelidov, the Russian plenipotentiary. In the matter of international peace and disarmament and of the whole pacifist campaign I had, as in so many other questions, to steer a middle course between Scylla and Charybdis. I had, of course, never any thought of sacrificing the safety of the country to the sanctimonious assurances of our enemies and of those who coveted our good fortune; to the hollow phrase-mongering of unsophisticated, and occasionally dishonest, fanatics. That standpoint I need scarcely defend, now that the world has seen the victorious Allies, having got what they wanted by the use of Wilson's Fourteen Points, drawn up to deceive our silly German pacifists, throw off the pacifist mask to show the sneering, cruel face beneath. The Treaty

of Versailles is an outrage against all pacifist principles and ideas:
not only does it cut away the ground from beneath any further
attempt to reconcile and form a League of Nations but, alike in conception and execution, it is a travesty of justice and reason. It
proved beyond all doubt how mendacious the propaganda of our
enemies against us had always been, and still continues to be. It
is all the sadder therefore to think that through simplicity and
blindness, in some cases through mean party spite, or the shabbiest
of personal motives, many Germans have assisted our foes. That
brand of infamy and disgrace which history has set on the foreheads
of Ephialtes and Judas Iscariot is for ever attached to the names of
Eisner and Grelling, of Friedrich Wilhelm Förster and Fechenbach.

Since therefore, as a result of long and personal experience
abroad, I knew the mendacity of much anti-German propaganda,
I exerted myself to keep the Emperor from speeches or gestures
which might give him the slightest semblance of being a disturber
of the peace, a thing he assuredly never wanted to be and, equally
assuredly, never was. Ever since the May of 1899, at the time of
the Tsar's first peace proposals, I had begged him never to seem to
play the hateful part of a peace-breaker who, ruining the generous
projects of pacifists, would appear responsible for the woes of a world
crushed by its growing burden of armaments. For the same reason,
and in spite of his initial opposition, I made the Emperor give his
consent to our participation in this second Disarmament Conference.
I have often before insisted how sincere and true a friend of peace
the Emperor at bottom really was. His acts proclaimed him a truer
pacifist than many another sovereign, and certainly than most
rhetorical Socialists at home and, above all, abroad. Yet a fundamental lack of harmony in his character, his inability to separate
appearance and reality, made him love to oppose all pacifist mani-
festations, whether or not the moment were well chosen for doing
so. On every occasion, good or bad, he would pour his contempt
upon them.

As German representative at the Hague, I had selected our
Ambassador in Constantinople, Herr von Marschall. He was a
good jurist who, little by little, had acquired that mixture of dignity
and conciliation which is so desirable in a diplomat. He was soon
able to play a leading part at the Hague. Stead, the British apostle
of peace who, five years later, died so tragically in the wreck of the
" Titanic " declares in his book on the Hague Conference that the
German representative was not only the ablest speaker but that his
knowledge of affairs had enabled him, more than any other delegate,
to contribute to a positive result. Stead adds with real resentment:

" Instead of the English representatives taking over the leadership of the conference as they should have done, they remained in the background, and left the first place to Germany. I have rarely witnessed a more pitiable and shameful defeat." The establishment of a permanent court of arbitration was the work of the German delegate; later he was the spokesman for that minority which rejected compulsory arbitration and Belgium, Switzerland, and Turkey were among the states which supported Germany and Austria in rejecting it. This seems a characteristic indication on which side the honesty really lay, since nobody could doubt the sincere desire for peace of these little states, whereas compulsory arbitration was championed by the States of the Entente whose pacificism only the naïvest of politicians could take as genuine. When I explained our attitude to the Second Hague Conference in the Reichstag [1] I met with unanimous approbation and, to my great content, the applause of nearly the whole English press. The Liberal papers in England emphasized the honesty and dignity of the Reichstag debate and my declaration. The Unionist papers declared that the frankness with which I had stated Germany's position had obtained surprising success in England and had convinced " the party of all honest men." This good impression made on England—the praises even of the *Times*—delighted the Emperor. With many congratulations he sent me the following letter, from a leading English sailor, Admiral Montagu, who had written, à propos of my speech:

YOUR MAJESTY,

If anything in the world can conduce to peace and harmony, sound sense and great ability of statement, the speech of Prince Bülow on foreign policy in my humble opinion is the finest piece of rhetoric and absolutely sound judgment it is possible to conceive. I write as a humble individual but, I hope, I aspire to common sense. But as an Englishman all I say is, that his statement should be accepted throughout the world as a masterpiece of sound reasoning. He not only shows his patriotism as his first duty, but holds out the olive branch of peace to the world, in the most graceful manner. I hope that individuals of other countries besides my own will note the greatness of Your Majesty's Chancellor.

Your most obedient servant,

V. A. MONTAGU.[2]

---

[1] Prince Bülow, *German Policy*. Popular Edition, Hobbing, Berlin.
[2] English in the original.

The year 1907 brought two very important changes in Prussian and Imperial administration. I had decided for what others have called "a *bloc* policy." I myself should have preferred to call it the prudent and progressive transition to a more liberal internal administration, with the more frequent and fuller collaboration of parliamentary leaders in the government. Though I paid all due homage to the exceptional ability and attainments of Count Posadowsky I felt obliged to dispense with his further collaboration, since I found him entirely hostile to such a change. I replaced him by Bethmann-Hollweg who, in many respects, was far from the equal of his predecessor. But I was sure that so long as I remained at the helm he would "change front like a sergeant," to use an expression of Bismarck. Friedrich von Moltke, the Oberpräsident of East Prussia, was the new Prussian Minister of the Interior. He was the brother, and junior by four years, of Moltke the Chief of the General Staff whom he equalled in honesty and loyalty. I saw to it that His Majesty assured Count Posadowsky of his esteem by sending him a very graciously-worded autograph letter, and presenting him with his bust in marble. Studt, the excellent Minister of Public Worship and Instruction, also resigned less on account of the Liberal attacks against him than by reasons of age and ill-health. He too received an autograph letter from the Emperor, and was sent into the Upper House.

Anticipating a little I may add that 1907 also saw many important changes of personnel at the Foreign Office. Tschirschky, whom His Majesty had more or less forced on me as Secretary of State for Foreign Affairs, was entirely inadequate to his task, and quite unable to assist me in my relations with the diplomats. He was inherently proud; his manner with other people was wooden, sour, and pessimistic, always, to use La Fontaine's phrase, "*docteur tant pis*," very touchy, "an offended liver sausage," as the quaint Berlin expression puts it. In addition to these the Emperor was anxious to replace the Statthalter of Strassburg, Prince Hermann zu Hohenlohe-Langenburg, who at seventy-five had become unequal to his task though, at that time, it was a comparatively easy one.

All this made many changes necessary. From the very first one of the major difficulties of my function as Chancellor had been to prevent His Majesty's interference in questions of personnel. He interfered with the best will in the world, often from sheer good nature, but at times to the detriment of the Service. Given his particular love of Tschirschky he would never have allowed him to be replaced if I had not assured substantial compensation to this "ever loyal" Foreign Minister, who, indeed, never contradicted his

Emperor, but was quite incapable of making a speech in the Reichstag.

I am bound to admit that Tschirschky had accepted his office with reluctance. At the time when he was first appointed he had dolefully written to me as follows: " Your Excellency is not unaware that I have never had the inclination to play any sort of public part. All my instinct is for avoiding publicity." After having added with reason that his nervousness prevented his ever being effective in Parliament, and that his ideal was a modest obscurity rather than the most triumphant success as an orator, he had requested " that the Parliamentary side of my duties be lightened by assistance from others." I was far too overburdened with work to be able to answer every question put to the Secretary for Foreign Affairs, either in Committee, or in the Reichstag. In Germany we possessed no special spokesman of the kind that the Second Empire had in Rouher, so that Tschirschky's reluctance to go in quest of oratorical laurels had obliged me to change the Under-Secretary. As his successor the Emperor demanded a diplomat who would be " sympathetic " to him personally, a qualification which was, alas, no guarantee of ability in the chosen candidate. Moreover His Majesty wished to send to Strassburg a general, either Dietrich Hülsen, the Chief of the Military Cabinet, or von Plessen, the Commandant at General Headquarters. In the end I decided on a compromise: Tschirschky was sent to Vienna, Herr von Schön, then Ambassador in St. Petersburg, became Secretary of State for Foreign Affairs, and the Ambassador in Vienna, Count Karl Wedel, was made Statthalter of Alsace-Lorraine. The last selection was the only really good one. Tschirschky had nothing of an Ambassador in him, though at least he could do less harm in Vienna than in London, where the Emperor at first had wanted to send him. The inferiority of " baron de Schoen," as the new German Secretary of State described himself on his visiting cards, had already caused me occasional anxiety, but was destined to be revealed in all its seriousness only after his nomination to this keypost. I do not know if the notorious *Jew's Who's Who* is right in its assertion that Schön is descended from a " very ancient Jewish community at Worms," that he belonged to the highly esteemed tribe of Issachar, and that the Heyl family of Herrnsheim, a connection of the Schöns, is equally of Worms, Semitic in origin, and enriched by the leather trade. However all that may be I should not have allowed myself to be influenced by the fact that Schön was of Jewish extraction. But I feel bound to declare that he had neither the will nor the talent for good work, neither clearness, quickness of perception, nor the business ability and serious interest in his post which I have found in many other Israelites, and which as a rule even their enemies do not deny them. Madame de Schön, a Belgian, become "*par trop Parisienne*" as the result of a long sojourn amid the delights of the Babylon by the Seine, contributed in nothing to increase the very moderate value of her husband. But it was impossible to induce the Emperor to accept either Mühlberg or Kiderlen for the post of Secretary of State. Count Pourtalès was made Ambassador in St. Petersburg. He knew the *terrain* since he had been Councillor of Embassy there for some years. In the days of Bismarck, as Secretary to Herbert Bismarck, he had gained a certain insight into Affairs.

CHAPTER XX

William II's return visit to the Danish court—The Northern Marches— Attitude of the Kaiserin to Denmark—Prelude to the Emperor's visit to England—The Banquet at Windsor (12th Nov. 1907)—The Emperor's mood at Highcliffe—The Moltke-Harden case in the Reichstag—Prince Eulenburg's tragedy begins—The romantic marriage of Princess Augusta Eulenburg—Eulenburg's letter to the Kaiser—In spite of his friends' warnings Eulenburg goes to the Investiture—The Imperial rescript of 31st May 1907 on the settlement of the Eulenburg case—My action against the " author" Brand—Proceedings against Eulenburg for perjury.

IN June 1907 the Emperor and Empress went to stay with the new King of Denmark, Frederick VIII, who not long before had paid them a visit in Berlin. A few months previously I had concluded a treaty with Denmark, by which the children of Optants, until now without nationality, could at their own request, be nationalized in either of the two states. This " Optants' Treaty " was most favourably received by the Danes. The official organ of the Danish Government praised it as the most significant event since 1864 in the history of Danish-German relations, extolling the " desire for justice " of the German government, and expressing the hope that the treaty would mark the beginning of a new era. I had never shared the Emperor's constant illusion that Denmark could be won for a close union with us, and I certainly never hoped for any Danish alliance with Germany. Tirpitz also, in the interests of our naval policy, would have liked to attract Denmark as far as possible. But I did not conceal from him my view that correct relations, without any *arrière pensée*, were as much as we could ever hope from the Danes. These could be obtained by the reasonable and tactful handling of the Danish inhabitants of North-Schleswig.

I had always considered the nationality issue in North-Schleswig as being on a very different plane from the struggle in the Eastern Marches. " *Il faut donner à toute chose sa juste valeur* " was a favourite maxim of the wise Minghetti whom it is always a pleasure to quote. In the East it was a question of protecting the very foundations of the Prussian State, of maintaining the most vital possession of the German Empire. To allow the progress of Polish propaganda meant risking our whole security and future. Unworldly dreamers, without any sense of reality, were the only Germans who could advocate compromise with the Poles. On the other hand the Danes in North-Schleswig, who numbered scarcely 135,000, were no serious menace either to our State or culture. My policy would have been to get the Landtag to vote a sufficient sum for the gradual purchase of all Danish farms in Schleswig, and on these to settle South-Schleswigers or Holsteiners. I should have been willing to handle the language difficulty in a spirit of great accommodation, since for centuries in that region German has been gaining ground, whereas, alas, a long experience has shown us that both French and Italian easily triumph over our tongue; that, in their struggle against German, even the Slavonic languages have registered some deplorable successes. But unfortunately the Prussian Ministry had doubts about more money for North-Schleswig, and in the language question the Emperor, influenced by his very anti-Danish Augustenburg relatives, would not compromise. The Kaiserin had not concealed from my cousin Jenisch, who accompanied the Imperial couple to Copenhagen, that she found me " too pro-Danish." She wrote to him: " As Empress and as wife I have gone to Denmark; naturally I have been friendly and polite, because it was my duty to be so. But this is the first time that I, a daughter of the Northern Marches, have had to make friends with Danes. What use will it be? Who will thank me for it? You know that I never like to interfere in politics, but there is such a thing as local patriotism. All our family history has, in a sense, been the history of the struggle between Schleswig-Holstein and Denmark. My own father was one of the victims of this struggle, so you will understand that it cuts me to the heart when I see the Germans in North-Schleswig being penalized by too accommodating a spirit towards Denmark. The Danes have always spoken us fair, but they are false."

If the worthy Empress, true to a quite comprehensible family tradition, would have had no mercy on the Danes, the Emperor, on the other hand, was annoyed with me because the representative of our Foreign Office had been instructed to request him, in my name, not to make any too spectacular demonstrations of pro-Danish sympathies in Copenhagen. Herr von Jenisch wrote:

" I told His Majesty that, in your opinion, it was important to strike the right note at Copenhagen; that, since the King was a little timid, *il ne fallait pas être trop chaleureux*, and that you had instructed me in this sense before departure. The Emperor answered ' that it could be left to him; that he was quite capable of adopting the right tone, that he had been reigning for twenty years and ought to know something about it by this time.' After that it was naturally quite impossible to submit your draft-speech without risking a violent explosion."

On 9th November 1907 the Imperial couple were to start on their visit to England. The ancients believed that when peril and ill-success threatened the projects of a mortal the gods gave signs and portents in advance: eagles would fly left instead of right, the sacred fowls refuse their food, etc. From the classic point of view this Imperial visit started inauspiciously. All the preparations had been made when suddenly the Emperor telephoned to tell me that he had met with an accident. A sudden fit of giddiness had caused him to lie down on a sofa; there he had fainted, and rolled off his sofa on to the floor. " My head hit the ground so hard that my wife was alarmed by the noise, and came rushing in to me, quite terrified." At present, His Majesty added, he felt too ill to think of undertaking the exhausting journey to England, and had wired King Edward to that effect. A few minutes later the Marshal of the Court, Count August Eulenburg, arrived from the Empress to tell me that, after all, the accident had not really been so serious. The fainting fit and the bumping of the head against the floor had happened in His Majesty's fancy. Imploring me to preserve the strictest confidence, Count Eulenburg next confided the real meaning of the incident. The Emperor, in view of Harden's campaign in the *Zukunft* against Philip Eulenburg, Count Kuno Moltke, and others of his intimate friends, and the threat of an impending trial, had felt it would be too painful to go to England. In a few hours the English Ambassador came to see me in a state of agitation. He had received an urgent telegram from King Edward, sending him word that the Emperor was abandoning his English visit. So sudden and enigmatic a decision would be sure to entail the most serious political consequences, and could have no favourable effect on future Anglo-German relations, which of late had very happily improved. King Edward asked an immediate explanation of this mysterious *volte-face* of his nephew.

I promised the Ambassador to confer with the Emperor at once. He agreed that that was the right course, and added: " The worst of it is that about an hour ago I was in the Tiergarten, and met the Emperor, who is alleged to be so seriously ill, galloping down the Central Avenue, in very good spirits, surrounded by a troop of aides-de-camp."

I wrote off at once a most serious letter to His Majesty in which, not only for myself but to pacify the English Ambassador, I begged him to explain his conduct. It was, I urged, a matter of our relationship with England. An hour or two later the Emperor sent

me an invitation to spend the evening with him at the theatre, or, if I
were too busy for that, to present myself in the drawing-room behind
the Royal Box and talk things over during the long interval. I found
him very brisk and unembarrassed: his really was an exceptionally
mercurial nature! He declared that his indisposition had quite
passed off; he had been able to take a refreshing gallop and had
eaten a hearty meal, so that now he felt himself perfectly fit again—
ready for anything—to go anywhere I chose to send him in the
interests of our Foreign Policy. I was therefore able, that same
night, to inform my old friend Lascelles that His Imperial Majesty
had recovered, and felt himself sufficiently in health to undertake
the English visit.

On 10th November the Imperial couple arrived in London. On
the 12th the great banquet at Windsor took place. King Edward
could not quite resist the pleasure of putting into his speech the
somewhat malicious statement that he had feared that, at the last
minute, the Emperor's sudden indisposition might prevent this
visit to which he had looked forward for so long. "Happily Your
Majesties seem now in such splendid health that I have every reason
to hope that Your Majesties' stay in England can only be of benefit
to you both." Though the Emperor was by now forty-eight King
Edward was always rather inclined to adopt towards him the
jesting tone of a dignified and experienced uncle towards his
rather callow and scatter-brained nephew. The King added that,
as long as he lived, he would never forget the Emperor's kindness
and sympathy with him at the time of the Great Queen's death.
The Emperor could be certain that his visits to England always
gave the deepest pleasure to the Royal Family and the whole
nation. "I wish with all my heart," he concluded, "the prosperity and well-being of that great Empire over which Your Majesty
reigns, and above all, the maintenance of peace." Next day the
Lord Mayor and the Emperor exchanged very cordial toasts at the
Guildhall. Lord Curzon, one of the most eminent and influential
British statesmen, conferred on the Emperor the honorary degree
of Doctor of Civil Law of the University of Oxford. All the English
newspapers devoted most friendly articles to him, commenting on
the sensible improvement in Anglo-German relations, and asserting
that there was no real motive for tension between the two countries.
A few days later Sir Edward Grey, the Minister for Foreign Affairs,
in a speech at Berwick, stressed the fact that the Anglo-Japanese
Alliance was not directed against any other country. England was
always ready to sign analogous conventions with other nations on
matters directly concerning themselves and England. The con-

ventions with Russia had concerned the security of the Indian frontier, they were a guarantee of Anglo-Russian peace, and therefore a contribution to the peace of the whole world. The Eastern Question—in particular, the trouble in Macedonia—would never be allowed to disturb the concert of the European Powers. As for German naval construction he had no desire whatever to criticize it; if other Powers saw fit to increase their navies, Britain must increase her's as well; but that need not mean that she must ruin herself in armaments, nor need she feel disturbed by the naval budgets of any other land. A few days previously 136 Liberal members in the House of Commons had presented a memorandum to Campbell-Bannerman, the Prime Minister, in which they called for a reduction in the Army and Navy estimates.

The Imperial visit had therefore passed off smoothly enough and had given an opportunity for expressing the genuine desire for peace of the great majorities of the German and British peoples. But I was much less pleased when I learned of the mood and sayings of the Emperor during his stay at Highcliffe, in the Isle of Wight, the beautifully situated home of Colonel Stuart-Wortley.

While the Emperor was staying at Highcliffe, Spahn, the Centre Party leader, put several questions in the Reichstag on the revelations in the Moltke-Harden libel action which had brought to light offences against morality reminiscent of heathen Rome. He was highly indignant that two especially guilty officers, Count Lynar and Count Hohenau, should have been pensioned off and put on the retired list. Nevertheless he thanked the Emperor and the Crown Prince for having intervened so swiftly. I answered[1] that the offences against morality revealed by the Moltke-Harden case had filled me too with disgust and shame, but that I must protest against any suggestion that the German army—the German people—were rotten at heart. As no one for an instant could doubt the moral rectitude of the Imperial couple, whose family life gave so fair a model to the nation, so too it was infamous to suggest that Germany was a kind of Sodom. The state of the Imperial German Army had nothing in it to warrant comparison with Imperial Rome in its decadence. Our people's representative could depend on it that His Majesty would make a clean sweep of anything in any way offensive to the purity of his character and his house. As to the complaints about some *camarilla* it was clear that the first condition for the growth of such poisonous plants was the isolation and lack of personality of a monarch. Our Emperor might be

[1] Prince Bülow's *Speeches*. Complete Edition, ii, 250 *et seq.*; compressed Edition, iv, 30 *et seq.*

THE KAISER IN ENGLAND (NOVEMBER 1907)

King Edward, the Duke of Connaught, and Kaiser William II
at a hunting-party at Windsor

criticized for much, just as any other man might be criticized—but never accused of living in retirement, or of any lack of personal will. I added, amidst general hilarity, that up to now no deputy had ever complained of him for that! I went on to say that I thought it about time to put an end to all this stupid gossip and whispering about a *camarilla*. Bebel having remarked that only in monarchies were a *camarilla*, and other such phenomena, to be found, I replied that such things by no means only existed in courts. There was also a red *camarilla*. Incense was burned not only to princely vanity but also to the vanity of King Demos. "In the supple arts of belly crawling and cringing the favourites of King Demos are more pliant than those of any prince, and I speak as one who has had experience of both kinds." I concluded: "We live in an age when a Minister need no longer fear tyranny from above. What has any modern statesman to fear from such tyranny? At most he can be dismissed. Do you really think it is such a great pleasure to be a Minister? But what every Chancellor has really to fear to-day is tyranny from below, the worst and most oppressive of all tyrannies."

Extracts from this speech had been telegraphed in the usual manner to foreign countries, and therefore of course to England also. When, during dinner at Highcliffe, the Emperor amidst his German entourage read the Reuter report of it, his excitement and indignation knew no bounds. It was unheard of, His Majesty declared, that the Moltke case should even have been touched on by me in the Reichstag. I ought to have forbidden any public mention of the matter. There ought to have been no suggestion of any kind, in parliament, of *camarillas* or court intrigues. The Court ought not to have been mentioned at all. In this sense the Kaiser drafted a sharp telegram to me, conceived to the above effect, and which he read aloud to his fellow guests. All remained silent. Metternich alone observed to His Majesty that if I were to receive so rude a telegram I should in all probability resign, and that the Imperial Chancellor was most certainly doing his sovereign greater service by publicly defending him in the Reichstag than by preserving an embarrassed silence in the midst of events which had become common talk. The Emperor protested hotly, enlarging on his favourite theme that a Minister had no right to resign; his business was to wait until his resignation was demanded. But while he was arguing the point he gradually crumpled up the telegraph-form on which his angry effusion had been written, and when at last this masterpiece was reduced to a little ball, he flung it away into the corner with the exclamation: "Oh, all right!"

My poor master, even after the widest deviations, for long possessed the power of returning to the paths of common-sense.

But far worse than these incidents, *intra muros,* and in the privacy of an intimate German circle, were the conversations which William II held at Highcliffe with numerous English fellow-guests and visitors—conversations of which I had had no inkling till they were given to the public in the famous *Daily Telegraph* article.

Before, however, I proceed to relate the important political events of 1908 I must finish my account of the tragedy of Prince Philip Eulenburg, not only because, for several months, it was the chief topic of conversation in Berlin, but because to a serious extent it moved and affected the Emperor, and so produced political consequences. These very unpleasant happenings recall, *toute proportion gardée,* the sombre and mysterious excesses which two centuries before, under Louis XIV, had led to the setting up of the *Chambre Ardente.* Poor Eulenburg was assailed by every misfortune. During a holiday, in Territet on the Lake of Geneva with his family, his third daughter, Countess Augusta, a charming girl, eloped with her father's private secretary, Herr Jaroljmek. The parents at first thought their daughter had committed suicide on account of the father's refusal to consent to the marriage the young countess desired which was, to be quite frank, somewhat eccentric. For a whole night the lake at Territet was dragged but no trace was found of the missing girl—naturally enough, since by then she was married to her lover! I received from Eulenburg a copy of the desperate letter he had just written to the Emperor, which began with the words: " Your Majesty sees before you to-day a man stricken with boundless misfortune, misfortune before which he stands impotent, the worst misfortune which can befall a loving father, the head of a house." The whole incident was undoubtedly very painful. When I asked Eulenburg's intimate friend, the Minister to Württemberg, Axel Varnbüler, what sort of a fellow this Jaroljmek was, he answered: " Jaroljmek was the trusted secretary and special friend of our good Philip. He was a southern Slav, very handsome, very romantic. He had big eyes, and jet black hair, and when I last saw him he wore a straw hat garlanded with red rowanberries." Apparently Eulenburg was quite right when he described Jaroljmek to the Emperor as a young coxcomb who was no good for anything. But I felt that he exaggerated when he said that he repudiated his daughter for ever, that he refused to hear her name mentioned again in his house, that his family happiness had been for ever destroyed, that he would have preferred to see this unworthy daughter dead, that no one would ever again respect him or his, and that his agony was "inexpressible." This letter to the Emperor finished as follows: "When I am calmer, I will in person give your Majesty, at your convenience, full details. Now, wretched as I am, I must end." In a short accompanying letter Eulenburg wrote to me: "I suffer so terribly that every word is agony. There has been sunshine in my life, now comes the deepest darkness. It is time now to go home. God, in His mercy, give me a speedy end."

In a friendly letter to Eulenburg, which I wrote to steady and encourage him, I said that this was not the first time a young girl had kicked over the traces to run off with the man she loved. No intelligent person would ever cast a stone at him or his family because of that. At that time I was still convinced of the moral probity of Eulenburg, but the anxiety with which he followed the Moltke-Harden case began to disturb me, although I had always known how neurasthenic he was. He was for ever writing to beg me to see that his name did not appear, to use all my influence to keep him out of the case. "This case," he wrote, "although I myself have nothing to fear from it, terrifies me because I am so ill. My nerves are so shattered by the unspeakable physical and mental strain through which I have just had to pass, that the thought of being dragged through all the mud again so horrifies me that I feel I should never have the strength to survive the agony of it. Apart from that, I feel that any new edition of the Harden scandal would be a danger. Now that 'They,' by proceeding so hastily to general dismissals, have cringed before this Jew scribbler, any new scandal, which would of course be European in its effects, might constitute a danger to the State. But how the lawsuit and further scandals can be avoided I really cannot imagine. All my anxious thought on the matter leads me to this single conclusion, that the one possible thing would be to instruct the judge to refuse to let a word be breathed that is not directly concerned with the libelling of Kuno."

Naturally in my answer I had to tell him that, as the highest official in the Empire, I could not interfere with the action of an independent judiciary. In January 1907 I had advised Eulenburg, who had come to see me, still full of his daughter's escapade, to take the opportunity which an incident so painful in itself afforded, and spend some time abroad. Everybody would think that only natural. He could pass the winter with his family in Switzerland or Italy, escape from the gossip and rumours of Berlin, and at the same time restore his shattered nerves and forget the unpleasant impression of recent events. After what I had heard from Rathenau and Berger I hoped that, if Eulenburg left Berlin—and especially if he kept away from the Kaiser, both Harden and his enemies at Court would leave him in peace. But the poor devil seemed like a moth, which persists in flying back to the flame. He could not manage to live without the Emperor, without the Imperial favour and proximity. He had written to me: " I only ask to go far away with my family, and among my few remaining friends, and to sink back into the deepest obscurity. I am, in fact, too ill to do anything else. I have had enough of the torture of this world, and shall thank my God on my knees if only He will let me die in peace."

But that, in spite of all my warnings, did not prevent him from re-appearing in Berlin, in the January of 1907, for his investiture with the Order of the Black Eagle. The bestowal upon Eulenburg of this highest of all Prussian Orders aroused anger in many quarters at the time. His presence at the investiture—the accolade bestowed upon him with especial warmth by His Majesty—annoyed his opponents at Court, especially the Heads of the Cabinets, and embittered the Crown Prince. Again the hue and cry was raised against him on all sides. Suddenly, in the May of 1907, the Emperor also turned against him, as suddenly and completely as before, and for many years, he had favoured him. To my brother Karl Ulrich, then commanding the 2nd Uhlans of the Guard, he said at an inspection, that he thought I had been far too tender with Eulenburg, that I was not firm enough, that it was about time I pulled myself together. A few days later, on 31st May 1907, an Imperial rescript arrived, to the following effect: " His Majesty had learned that, for some months, Eulenburg had been attacked in the *Zukunft* and had taken no steps to defend himself: on the contrary he had got into secret touch with Harden and begged him to abstain from further attacks. In plain contradiction of obvious facts Eulenburg had, in several letters, assured His Majesty that he had no knowledge of the *Zukunft* articles, did not read the *Zukunft* and had no idea at all what it was saying. His Majesty could there-fore only conclude that Harden had in his possession letters, written by Eulenburg to Moltke, of an entirely compromising nature. Further His Majesty had heard that, during an Imperial visit to his castle of Liebenberg, Eulenburg had introduced disreputable people among the guests. That one of these had been a French diplomatist who had the worst of reputations and had for that reason never been received by the Prussian Minister in Munich. His Majesty was most displeased that Eulenburg should have allowed the All-Highest to be so compromised, in a fashion unheard of for a Monarch."

The " French diplomatist " to whom the Emperor here alludes

was a certain Lecomte, who was in every way an offensive person. The Bavarian Premier, Podewils, had already told me that Lecomte, as a member of the French Mission in Munich, had the reputation of indulging in unnatural vice, and had been under police surveillance on that account. Again and again I had seriously warned Eulenburg against him, yet in spite of that he had been so grossly tactless as to invite his friend Lecomte to Liebenberg at the same time as His Imperial Majesty. The rescript ended as follows: " I therefore insist that Philip Eulenburg shall at once ask to be retired. If this accusation against him of unnatural vice be unfounded, let him give me a plain declaration to that effect and take immediate steps against Harden. If not, then I expect him to return the Order of the Black Eagle, and avoid a scandal by forthwith leaving the country and going to reside abroad."

I learned from His Majesty's entourage that the impetus for this Imperial attack had been given by Prince Max Fürstenberg, who was Eulenburg's enemy and succeeded him in the enjoyment of Imperial favour.

I did my best to break the news as gently as possible to Eulenburg through the medium of his friend Varnbüler. On receiving the Imperial rescript Eulenburg wrote to me:

This ending is horribly brutal. It is not that I suffer at the loss of any brilliant outward distinction; on the contrary that only gives me a feeling of liberty. Nor was the loss of an old Imperial friendship the cruel deception which perhaps you expected it to be, since I know, only too well, the character of this pilot, who shouts " Abandon ship " in every case long before it is necessary. I am still objective enough to realize that a monarch must be rid as quickly as possible of any friend who has got into the horrible position in which, thanks to the efforts of the Harden-Holstein clique, I find myself. No! it is only the gross and brutal fashion in which I have received my *coup de grâce* which really cuts me to the heart. And I fear that in the Emperor's eyes I am made to appear as vile and sordid as possible. Here I ask for your protection and your friendship, in which I place the fullest confidence: I do not beg for myself—oh no— but for my wife, whom you have known for a long time, and for my children whom you know and love. Stand by me, if only for their sakes. I have no witness to fear at the enquiry: I can await the issue, since I know myself entirely innocent—but I fear false witnesses, since Holstein would not stop at having to spend ten thousand marks if he could buy some really damaging evidence.

It is incredible to what power Harden and Holstein have risen through securing these three dismissals (Kuno Moltke, and the two Hohenau's). All the same I think you have acted wisely in letting this monstrous thing be done, since, by it, you have avoided a crisis. If you had acted in any other way you would have strengthened the position of the generals permanently, and we might—since recent events have shown how strong their influence is even now—have ended by seeing Hülsen Imperial Chancellor. Your captaincy through this squall has been the only possible guidance and if you bring us through on these lines you will have done the Fatherland a service. You see, dear Bernhard, from this, what I really think of the situation, and how, far from bearing you a grudge for any share you had in my disaster, I thank you from the bottom of my heart for the constant use you made of my true friend Axel. Both Axel and my cousin August Eulenburg have told me how much you have done, and still are doing on my behalf, and that from sheer friendship, and in the most dangerous situation. I shall never forget it!

Some days after I had received his rescript I wrote to the Emperor that Philip Eulenburg was dangerously ill. I said that he had wired to tell me that he wished to leave the service entirely, since till then he had been on leave with pay. I added that " in these painful circumstances we must see to it that the crown is kept *ex nexu*, and completely removed from all connection with the affair," and that, " on the other hand, as far as the law permits, we must not allow too much scandal to be aired for the edification of foreigners."

Beyond all praise were the unshakable loyalty and boundless love with which Princess Augusta Eulenburg stood by her husband through the whole of his terrible ordeal. She never doubted him; she defended him always, against everyone, and, to the day of his death, shielded him with the tenderest care. It was not without justice that Eulenburg, in his earliest poems, had compared her to the still, clear lakes of her Swedish home. She was clear and unsullied through and through. Dishonour and injustice were not only foreign to her nature, they were things that she did not understand. When her husband died, in the autumn of 1921, she answered my wife who had written her a letter of condolence, that she had only one desire left in the world—to be reunited soon to her beloved " martyr," in a land where the flame of God's justice will make clear all that now is dark.

My brother Alfred, who from boyhood had been a close friend

of Philip Eulenburg, his fellow-student at Strassburg, and had read
law beside him at Neu Ruppin, wrote to me in the winter of 1907-8:
"Everything will depend on this—that Philip Eulenburg, no
matter how shattered he may be both physically and mentally,
should fight his way through this trial, which I see from the papers
is almost due, in a clear and unequivocal fashion. His answers must
be perfectly definite and straightforward. I hope that he realizes
his position, and is nursing no fatal illusions." That hit the nail
on the head. But Eulenburg, far from following this advice, sought
salvation in all kinds of phantasies, with an especial preference for
the assertion that the attacks against him were the work of the
Jesuits, who had never forgiven him for the anti-Catholic standpoint
which had determined his activities in Munich.

For the rest the wives of the other three unfortunates who
suffered the same exposure as Eulenburg—Countess Lynar, and the
two Countesses Hohenau—were equally faithful to their husbands
in the hour of disgrace. The former, by birth a Princess Solms, a
sister of the Grand-Duchess of Hesse-Darmstadt, accompanied her
husband who, since he had sinned with his subordinates was condemned to a longer term of imprisonment, to Leipzig, where he under-
went his punishment, in order to be as near him as possible. Such
loyalty was the only bright spot in this miserable and sordid business.
"The eternal feminine draws us on." Prince Eulenburg's sons
all followed their mother's example. The eldest remained loyal to
his parents, and I have never heard anything but good of him.
The second, Count Sigwart Eulenburg, was a very gifted musician.
He married that exquisite singer, Helene Staegemann, and in the
World-War died a hero's death on the Eastern Front. The youngest
son of Count Fritz Hohenau joined the Flying Squadron and was
killed in an aerial attack in the last year of the war, near Péronne.
Count Johannes Lynar's second son died in Galicia while serving
with the Uhlans of the Guard. Both, in knightly fashion, atoned
for the sins of their fathers.

To an assertion by the deputy Spahn that I should have informed
the Emperor earlier of the vices of some of his friends, I replied, in
my Reichstag speech of 28th November 1907, that no precise or
tangible information on the subject had come to my knowledge
before the previous spring. A responsible Minister, I continued,
could only make such serious accusations if prepared to substantiate
them in full. I added: "How much lying gossip do we not hear
on all sides to-day? Have I not myself been the subject of the basest
suspicion and stupid calumny?" The reference was to an action
I had taken against the "author" Adolf Brand. While staying in

II.   x

Flottenbeck it was reported to me that this Brand, the founder of a "Society of Unusual People," formed for the "Justification of homosexuality," had accused me of a similar *penchant*. I had been asked whether I should hesitate to take action, and had replied by taking immediate legal steps. The case was tried in the Moabit court. Philip Eulenburg was present, obviously in the hope of some evidence coming up in the course of it, which might later be of use in his own defence. The accused, a wretched disreputable looking creature, stood near the bench on which I as plaintiff would have to sit. In the course of my evidence I declared that I considered the practices in question loathsome in the highest degree, and quite incomprehensible; and, indeed, to me they were so. I added: "This my declaration on oath refers not only to contraventions of Article 175 of the Penal Code but to all and every unnatural, abnormal and perverse tendency, inclination, and passion, of every kind and in any degree." A wave of emotion went through the court as I said this. At the end of my evidence I added that this was the first action I had ever brought in my life and that I had brought it in the interests of public morals. Against such base and senseless calumnies I appealed to the protection of the court and the full rigour of the law. Brand received the severest legal sentence— eighteen months imprisonment. Before receiving it he formally recanted, and took back his libels against me, with an expression of regret at having been deceived. With a quite pathological solemnity he added that for him the only bright spot in an otherwise so sombre day had been the sight of that "noble prince" Philip Eulenburg! When I had finished my evidence and was allowed to leave the box the judges and all those present in court rose and bowed to me.

Some time after this the wretched Eulenburg, hard pressed by Harden and his opponents' counsel, denied on oath ever having indulged in unnatural practices. When, in the notorious Munich case in the spring of 1908, the evidence of a Starnberg fisherman showed that the Prince had been guilty of such practices with him, an action for perjury was brought against Eulenburg in Berlin. But, in view of his state of health, this was not proceeded with, and was never resumed, because Eulenburg steadily maintained that he felt too ill to go into the witness-box. Was he guilty in that particular instance? A few years later, in Berlin, I talked to one of the jury who had been called to act in the case. He said to me: "We were all convinced that Prince Eulenburg was guilty. But we should have let him off. After all, the thing had happened years before, and we were so sorry for the poor old gentleman!"

CHAPTER XXI

*Interview at Reval between Edward VII and Nicholas II (July 1908)
—Russian and English spheres of influence in Asia—The Kaiser's
speech at Döberitz—His fears of " encirclement "—Meeting of
William II and Edward VII at Homburg (11th August 1908)—
Count Metternich on German naval armaments—Conversation
between the Emperor and Sir Charles Hardinge—The Imperial
letter to Lord Tweedmouth—My circular to the Prussian envoys on
the Reval meeting—The Turkish revolution.*

LOOKING back on the political events of the year 1908, one
perceives that the central event was the meeting which took
place at Reval between King Edward and the Russian Imperial
couple on the 9th and 10th of July. I need scarcely say that I had
no doubts whatever on the political significance of this meeting, nor
of the political consequences that might follow it if our policy were
clumsy and incautious. The crushing defeats which the Russian
fleet and army had sustained in the war against Japan, so humiliating
to Russian pride, had again shifted the centre of Russian policy
from the Far to the Near East. The disappointment had been
too great to permit any Russian government to encourage Russians
in any further desire to burn their fingers again in the Far East.
But, in any case, in the soul of the Russian people there had never
been any real passion for Vladivostock and Harbin. All traditional
Russian hopes for centuries, had been set on Tsarigrad and the
Hagia Sophia. Out of that there was to be born a vehement
antagonism to Austria, and I could see that, unless our policy were
very skilfully conducted, this feeling would also be turned against
ourselves. Yet, even after her defeat, Russia still possessed a series
of strong points along the Pacific. In Siberia and in Central Asia
she possessed a formidable Empire, and this fact compelled Russian
policy to take account of Great Britain. About a year earlier, in
August 1907, a treaty on the partition of spheres of influence in
Asia had been arranged between Russia and England—between
the Bear and the Whale. North Persia was assigned to the Russians,
the Persian coast-lands to the British. Fundamentally the treaty
was more favourable to the Russians than to the English, and the
sense of satisfaction which the vain Isvolski showed immediately
after its signature was not without its justification. That such an

arrangement could be concluded proved, as I remarked at once to the Emperor, that we had now become the chief object of English anxieties and jealousy; that England was ready to make considerable sacrifices in order to be secure against us. Moreover all the Liberal elements in Russia set their hopes on the democratic Western Powers in the expectation that closer relationships with them would facilitate the victory of Russian Liberalism and Democracy.

This Reval meeting cast its shadow before for some weeks. In Berlin there were rumours of war. The newspapers babbled of " encirclement," mostly without seeming to realize that any display of unusual nervousness on our part was a proof of fear and weakness to the enemy, that it discouraged our friends, and so increased the danger of a conflict.

On 29th May 1908 the Kaiser delivered a speech on the parade-ground at Döberitz, alluding to the encirclement of Germany, and striking a war-like, threatening note. Russian and Japanese military attachés were present all the time he was speaking, and well within ear-shot. They naturally saw to it that this fiery inspiration was not lost. It looked, the Emperor declared, as though the tactics of an encirclement of Germany would continue. This created a very grave situation. We must be guided by the example of Frederick the Great who, when hemmed in on all sides by foes, had beaten them one after the other. When next I saw the Emperor I repeated what I had often already said to him: the very fact that a situation is strained and uncertain should make us doubly careful to take as our guide the motto, " *non cantu sed actu.*" But the Emperor never relished such criticism.

A few weeks later, having been welcomed with enthusiasm at Hamburg, he wrote, though in quite a friendly way, that never before throughout his whole reign had he been given so rousing a reception as in this greatest German trading port. The warmth and enthusiasm had far surpassed his every expectation. An immense crowd had thronged to greet him, their attitude and discipline had been admirable, the welcome on the Alster most affecting. And when, after it all, he had expressed to the Senate and Chamber of Shipping his surprised and gratified emotion at such an overwhelming cordiality, he had been answered: " This is our thanks for the Döberitz speech. It produced the effect of a fiery cross. The right word at the right time." Indignation against Edward VII and his machinations for the Entente were, His Majesty added, universal. The Hamburger's patience was exhausted. Then followed a long list of items of news from England which His Majesty declared he had had from Ballin, who had just returned from a visit to London. These last seemed to have been inspired by his own fecund creative brain rather than by the more objective intellect of the director of the Hamburg-America Line: King Edward's policy had been condemned on all sides in England; everywhere his anti-German attitude had met with the most trenchant criticism; in a distinguished London club Richard Henderson, the greatest English shipowner, had damned King Edward and his policy, in the midst of general clapping and applause. Sir Ernest Cassel, the well-known London banker, a native of Cologne and one of the King's most intimate friends, had given Ballin a message from King Edward that the Emperor might as well give up his naval construction. King Edward did not believe that the Emperor would attack him personally, but that, after his death he might fall on his son the Prince of Wales, and that was what he wanted to prevent! Ballin had, it seemed, replied to this, with spirit, that should England alone, or England, France, and Russia combined present so outrageous a demand, there could be only one answer for Germany— mobilization! The meeting at Reval, continued His Majesty in this letter, had been all arranged on a money basis. Cassel and his man of straw, Lord Revelstoke, had negotiated a Russian loan. In order to make it a success they had induced King Edward to go to Reval. The business had brought King Edward "colossal" profits. But now the City was up to the neck in this loan and since Japan was on the verge of bankruptcy, it did not know which way to turn. Cassel, as a finishing touch, had exclaimed: "Why on earth was the King so infernally stupid as to make this damned alliance with these loathsome Japs? He'll ruin the lot of us yet."

The King moreover was full of spite and envy of his Imperial nephew. Every morning at breakfast he had a habit of searching the newspapers to see what the Emperor had been doing and would then proceed to scheme how best to outdo him. His sole wish was that the newspapers should talk only about himself. *Au fond* King Edward was nothing but a "jobber in stocks and shares," principally on behalf of the French market.

This somewhat fantastic epistle gave me my chance to have with the Emperor the longest and most serious conversation I can remember. I explained to His Majesty in detail why this word "encirclement" which seemed to be becoming the fashion, did not alarm me in the least. We had been encircled, as I had already repeatedly explained, ever since the Treaty of Verdun—that is to say for one thousand and sixty-five years. We were always, as the result of our geographical position, exposed to the danger of coalitions. But difficulties are made to be overcome, with calm, with prudence and *common-sense*. I insisted on the last of these words. I mentioned each of our neighbours, reminding the Emperor of a long discussion we had had in the early summer of 1907 on the subject of our relations with France, and of his very ungracious marginal notes to my letter of 25th August 1907. Once again I stressed the conviction that, the Frenchman being what he was, Cambon's prescription on which we had quarrelled a year before, at the end of the Kiel week, was the right one for us: " Don't be in a hurry."

I wasted little time over Italy. The last meeting of the Emperor with King Victor Emanuel III—it had taken place at Venice on 25th March 1908—had not turned out well. When he had entered the gondola with the Emperor, the King had turned the conversation on the Balkans, which, given the state of agitation in Macedonia, was natural enough and certainly not a crime. The Emperor had curtly refused to discuss the subject. The King, who was very interested in history, had said, in the course of conversation, that Napoleon had been a man of genius, and had insisted on his Italian origin, and this had irritated the Emperor. When finally, to bring his Imperial guest into a better temper, the King had turned the talk on the splendours of the German fleet, he had drawn on himself the following remark: that during his long reign the Emperor had always noticed that his colleagues, the other European monarchs, had paid little or no attention to what he said; but that in future the strongest possible German fleet would contribute to secure more attention for the pronouncements of the German sovereign. In April 1908, I had stayed for a week in Rome, where I had had a fairly long talk with Tittoni, the Foreign Minister, and, later at Venice with Giolitti, the Prime Minister. In both cases I had tried as far as possible to remove the unpleasant effects of this interview.

But my chief aim, in this conversation of July 1908, was to try to persuade the Emperor to adopt a more cautious attitude towards England. Everything I heard from London pointed to this: that neither King Edward nor his Ministers wanted war with us. In July 1908, a well-informed English publicist had told me that, some little time before, the King had declared: " I shall never allow a rupture with Germany." [1] I explained to the Emperor that if, in exchange for a slowing down of our rate of naval construction, we could get the assurance from England that she would not support France, should the latter attack us, we should be doing a good bit of business. The Emperor contradicted my views with great vigour: he would take no advice from anyone on naval matters. I appealed

[1] English in text.

to the obvious fact, which I had already stressed in several conversations with Tirpitz, that I too had been in some degree responsible for popularizing the idea of a fleet and for getting the Reichstag's consent to the estimates necessary to build one. Consequently, I had the right to counsel moderation and prudence. *Est modus in rebus, sunt certi denique fines*, I quoted from Horace's *Satires*. I was as convinced as ever that we had both the right and the duty to build the fleet necessary for our defence. But I could not see why we should not attempt to negotiate with England for an understanding, on the basis of a slower rate of construction. There was scarcely any other question which I discussed so constantly, and on occasion so sharply, with the Emperor. With Tirpitz, I entered more into detail. While fully recognizing his talent for organization, his genius and ardent patriotism, I used to ask him why he kept our fleet in the North Sea, facing England, at full battle-strength and preparedness, instead of occasionally showing our flags in other seas—in the Mediterranean or the Pacific. I would further ask why he concentrated almost entirely on battleships, instead of paying more attention to coastal fortifications and torpedo craft and, above all, to the improvement and development of the submarine. Tirpitz answered that the Emperor was afraid that if he sent his beloved battleships out of home waters the English would " Copenhagen " them, to use an expression of Lord Fisher. But, for Tirpitz in any eventual war, the battleship, if not the only weapon, was at least essential and decisive. Clearly the fundamental thought in the mind of the creator of our fleet was, that, if it ever came to war, our navy must at once sally forth and compel the British to a naval action on the high seas. In such an engagement we should have a good chance of victory, and should probably end by so weakening the English fleet that there would come a moment when, by the use of the submarine, we could compel an Albion, no longer mistress of the seas, to sue for peace. I have not the necessary authority to judge of the rightness of this argument, but I think that, once the World War was upon us, William II would have been better advised to have entrusted the employment and command of our fleet to the man who had devised and created it. I am further convinced that, had he done so, we should not have witnessed the tragic end of the German navy at Scapa Flow. Those who, in 1914, took the power out of Tirpitz' hands and thrust him aside—Admiral Müller, the Head of the Marine Cabinet, Admiral Holtzendorff, and, above all, Bethmann-Hollweg and Jagow—the men who were afraid of " rousing " England, are responsible for the useless squandering of the work and effort of many years, for the waste of so much valuable blood and intellect. And William II, alas, who listened and let such " servants " have their way, must shoulder the same responsibility before his country, before history!

In 1908 His Majesty sacrificed everything to his desire to build more and more battleships in the shortest possible time. In the previous year, when I had gone to Swinemünde to be present at the meeting with the Tsar, the Minister von Treutler who had been in the Imperial suite, had begged me not to repeat my warnings to His Majesty about slowing down the pace of naval construction, because these " completely upset" the Emperor, and made him "very unhappy."

Thus for over a year this cloud had hung between His Majesty and myself, until the time when the Emperor met his uncle at Homburg. This short interview took place on 11th August 1908. Very urgent official business prevented my being present at it. The Emperor had had a talk with the Permanent Under-Secretary at the British Foreign Office, Sir Charles Hardinge, who had accompanied King Edward, and who in the course of it, while vigorously stressing the friendliness of the English government, had hinted that the rapidity with which German Naval construction was being pushed forward was causing real anxiety in England. Not long before this, our Ambassador in London, Count Metternich had reported: " No one will ever persuade the English that a German fleet of thirty-eight battleships, twenty armoured cruisers, and thirty-eight small armoured cruisers, with corresponding torpedo and submarine craft—the total of our units in commission for 1920, if the Navy Law is carried out—is a matter of indifference to England. All the technical arguments we adduce to justify this rate of construction only make the English more mistrustful."

But this report, which I proceeded to submit to His Majesty, was most ungraciously received. Naturally, therefore, Hardinge had displeased him even more. In retrospect the whole conversation which he had had with the English diplomatist became quite distorted in his mind, and still more fantastic and exaggerated his account of his declarations and attitude.

On the day following (12th August 1908) I had received a telegram from the Emperor—a very long telegram, relating in the most dramatic fashion all that had taken place at the interview. Hardinge had spoken of the " grave apprehensions " which filled every class of Englishman because of our naval construction. The whole nation was excited and strung up. But he, the Emperor, had replied: " That is sheer idiocy. Who has been pulling your leg?"

Sir Charles had then referred to authentic documents at the British Admiralty, whereupon His Majesty had declared: " Your documents are false. I too am an admiral of the British Fleet, and know it well—far better than you, since you are only a civilian, and know nothing at all about it." After which he had ordered the *Nauticus*, a technical handbook, published by the German Admiralty, to be brought, and made Sir Charles compare the tables printed in the *Nauticus* with the construction graphs, whereupon " a look of speechless astonishment " had appeared upon the Englishman's face. During the whole scene Sir Frank Lascelles, the English Ambassador in Berlin, had had difficulty in restraining his laughter. Sir Frank was enthusiastic over the *Nauticus* and fully shared its views. The conversation with Hardinge had continued. Hardinge had asked: " Can't you stop building. Or build less ships? "[1] Surely some arrangement could be made to slow down construction." To which the Emperor had replied: " Then we shall fight, for it is a question of national honour and dignity." [1] With that His Majesty had looked the English diplomat " fairly and squarely in the face." Sir Charles had flushed painfully, made a low bow, and apologized for his " ill-considered expressions," which he begged His Majesty to forget and forgive. In the evening Sir Charles had been quite a different person—amiable, cheerful, and had told more than one spicy story. When, finally, the Emperor had bestowed on him the Order of the Red Eagle (First Class), Sir Charles had " quite come to heel." " The frank conversation with me, in which I had shown him my teeth, had not failed to have its effect. That is always the way to treat Englishmen." At parting the Emperor had reminded the Under-Secretary of the last speech which he, William II, had made at the Guildhall. The English government could abide by it. He had added: " When the Emperor speaks it is not just phrases. He speaks what he means." [1]

I saw at once, without any difficulty, that this long telegraphic effusion was an attempt on the part of His Majesty to construct a scene *in majorem gloriam suam*, in the genre of that grand historic scene at Ems between William I and Benedetti, in July 1870. An interview which at the time he granted Stemrich, the Under-Secretary of State, was opened by His Majesty with the words: " Well, did you read my telegram to the Chancellor? Didn't I give it properly to Sir Charles? " Actually the conversation at Homburg, as I learned from some Germans who were present, had proceeded much more comfortably. Hardinge and the Emperor had sat side by side on a billiard table. Hardinge had spoken with British blunt-

<hr>

[1] English in text.

ness, but quite respectfully and calmly: the Emperor had been
good-humoured, and very gracious. Sir Charles, later Viceroy of
India, was held in great esteem by King Edward. In August 1907
he had accompanied the King to the meeting at Wilhelmshöhe,
where I was able to have a quiet and satisfying talk with him on the
whole political situation and the future of Anglo-German relations.
He occupied a very high position in London society, to which the
beauty, elegance and grace of his wife contributed. We had been
friends for over twenty years having got to know each other at
Bucharest, where he had been Secretary of Legation and I German
Envoy to the Court of King Carol.

But this conversation on the billiard table at Homburg, especially as reproduced in the imaginative mind of William II, had, alas,
this result—that the Emperor, as never before, was set against all
and every attempt at a naval understanding with England. When
once more, after Homburg, I recalled to him the prudence dictated
by the whole European situation, the indispensable caution which
in particular should govern our relations with Great Britain in the
matter of naval armament, he answered me, through Freiherr von
Jenisch, that he in no way shared my anxiety—that his talks, short
though they had been, with Hardinge, Lascelles, and King Edward,
had put everything straight again. Jenisch added to the Imperial
message a very confidential remark that His Majesty was most
displeased with me. My " chilly attitude " on receiving the account
of his Homburg " triumph " had bitterly disappointed the Emperor.
He had expected " thanks and congratulations "; had hoped that
I would have praised him for all that he had done with Hardinge,
would have understood and appreciated the service he had rendered
both me and his country. He, better than most other Germans, knew
how to manage an Englishman, how to tell them the truth without
offending them, how to give them food for thought and convince
them. He was quite confident that at Homburg, he had, in a trice,
won over to his standpoint not only Hardinge but also his uncle the
King. And the moment had been particularly favourable! That
enthusiastic Hamburg reception, when he, their Emperor, had laid
his finger on the pulse of the German people, our growing enthusiasm for Count Zeppelin—all had made John Bull pause and reflect,
had disposed him to caution. Moreover Moltke, the Chief of the
General Staff, assured him that we were absolutely prepared. We
had therefore no reason to be cautious, to slow down our rate of
naval construction, to yield an inch to Albion on the seas. All I
need do was to defer to him, my Emperor, and let him get things
straight " in his own way." With Englishmen the only thing that

worked was frankness; ruthless, even brutal frankness, that was the best method to use with them! One made no progress with diplomatic feints and finessing. He could understand the English, being " half an Englishman " himself.

As previously at Björkö, His Majesty was evidently tending once again to attempt the personal direction of Foreign Policy, cheerily following his " inner light," like the student in the second part of *Faust*. But with England that sort of thing was even more dangerous than with France, precisely because William II imagined himself a past-master in the art of handling the English. The conversations, so pregnant with fateful consequence, which His Majesty conducted at Highcliffe, were with English " friends," and were only one result of this, unfortunately quite unfounded, conviction.

It also led to that regrettable letter which, in March 1908, the Emperor, behind my back, wrote to Lord Tweedmouth, the First Lord of the British Admiralty, to convince that gentleman of the harmlessness of the German naval programme. Not long before that I had communicated to His Majesty a letter, received from our Ambassador Metternich, who repeated what he had so often said before—that every assurance that our naval construction was " harmless," provoked " an immediate, universal, and energetic denial," on the part of English public opinion. When it became known that once again the Kaiser had intervened in one of the thorniest questions of English administration and policy, such a storm of protest was aroused in the whole English press that His Majesty himself grew alarmed. Moreover King Edward had sarcastically asked in a letter if his Imperial nephew's direct correspondence with Lord Tweedmouth constituted "a new departure," [1] and would inaugurate a new era in international diplomatic usage. As an excuse for having written this letter, the Emperor reminded me that I had had a heavy cold at the time, and that, on account of his old ear trouble, he had not dared to run the risk of infection. But he was clearly indignant that his attempt once more to busy himself with the improvement of Anglo-German relations had proved unsuccessful; " a failure." [1] No one was more horrified than Tirpitz at the Imperial letter to Lord Tweedmouth. He complained most of all that the Emperor, in order to " smarm down " Lord Tweedmouth, had childishly sent him a whole set of false statistics, which the English promptly recognized as such. There were questions in the House of Commons, but English Ministers, especially Asquith and Grey, handled the whole painful business with tact,

[1] English in text.

in an obvious effort to calm the excitable. Count Metternich sent the following report: " English constitutional ideas do not admit that a foreign sovereign place himself in direct official contact with an English Minister. I have been made aware, not officially, but from a certain Ministerial quarter, of the very painful impression produced here by the recent letter from our august Sovereign to Lord Tweedmouth. I was asked how His Majesty the Emperor, and his Imperial government would take it if King Edward, without reference to his responsible Ministers, were to deal directly with the Secretary of State for the German Navy. I am well aware of the unpleasant nature of what I write, and know that my task is a most ungrateful one. But, since my position is responsible, it is necessary that I should have the courage to shoulder it."

It will be understood that this authoritarian attitude of His Majesty, which overstepped the limits of anything permissible, not only angered but filled me with the deepest anxiety, and strengthened my resolution to seize the first suitable moment for an energetic protest against these dangerous encroachments, so damaging to the welfare of our nation.

In the interviews at Reval, which took place on June the 9th and 10th, King Edward, thanks to the consummate skill with which he could always manage men, had succeeded in winning over the Tsar. In this he was helped by the Tsarina Alexandra Feodorovna, very English and anti-German in sentiment, although the daughter of an old German princely house. There seems to be no doubt that Isvolski, vain and for that reason malleable, was persuaded by the King into a programme which would solve the Macedonian problem by a serious curtailment of Turkish power. In view of the uneasiness—the positive fear—among the Austrians which this Anglo-Russian plan of action on an important Balkan question had aroused, it seemed an urgent matter to steady them. There was a danger that the Dual Monarchy, if tried too far, would lose its nerve and fall into the clutches of Russia, as the terrified dove falls to the snake. Our policy would have to put forth every effort to keep Austria faithful to ourselves and, in case of war—which, if we were skilful was avoidable, but which naturally remained a possibility—to be assured of the co-operation of the Imperial and Royal army, still formidable and efficient enough, in spite of the inner weakness of the Monarchy. On the other hand we must avoid letting Austria drag us, against our will, into a World-War. Consequently, on 25th July 1908 I addressed a circular letter to the Prussian Ministers in Munich, Dresden, Stuttgart, Karlsruhe, Darmstadt, Weimar, Hamburg, and Oldenburg, in which I declared that, though the

situation arising out of the Reval meeting was serious, we had no
need to lose our heads. We had very good reasons for supposing
that "till further orders" no "directly" hostile project against
Germany, and the Triple Alliance, had been conceived at Reval.
This belief we based, not merely on the general situation, on the
speeches—they had all been published—exchanged at the banquet
at Reval, but also on definite statements made by both the Russian
and British governments, not only to ourselves but to others, and
finally on a telegram from the Tsar, received by the Emperor at
Potsdam, on 11th June, immediately after the interview, assuring him
that the meeting had changed "absolutely nothing" in the political
situation as a whole. The Russian Foreign Minister had assured
the German Ambassador in St. Petersburg that no questions of
common policy had been negotiated other than those covered by the
Anglo-Russian Agreement of the previous year, and certainly no
questions of general policy. Least of all had anything been arranged, or even discussed, which in any way was directed against
Germany. Some time after this Isvolski sent a verbal assurance
by his confidential agent, the Chief of Section, Baron Taube, that
Reval had changed nothing whatsoever in Russo-German relations.
Sir Edward Grey confirmed him, in quite as positive a fashion, in a
talk with our London Ambassador: at Reval there had been no sort
of discussion of any projected action against Germany.

Here is the conclusion of my circular:

> We are therefore perfectly entitled not to consider the Reval
> interview as an immediate menace against ourselves and Austria-
> Hungary, even if we connect it with previous interviews and
> *ententes*. It would, however, be a fatal mistake to rely too
> absolutely on any assurance we have received; not to see that
> recent events might always—in a given set of circumstances—
> gravely hamper our political freedom of action. We have now
> the possibility to consider, that, in any case of a serious conflict of
> interest, between ourselves or Austria-Hungary and any of the
> Entente Powers, these ententes and understandings, vague to-
> day, may be changed into concrete alliances, so that we, with our
> ally, Austria-Hungary, might be faced with a powerful coalition.
> The real causes of the political dangers that surround us we cannot
> remove without self-abnegation. They spring, as far as Germany
> is concerned, from her continued increase in economic strength,
> ever since the creation of the Empire. It is the fear—the un-
> justified fear—of a possible misuse of the economic, and so of
> the political might of Germany, and Germany's closest ally,

which drives other States to make ententes against us. At first
these ententes are, on the whole, defensive. But conceivably
there would be no hesitation in taking the offensive against us,
and compelling us, where possible, to yield, if other Powers felt
themselves strong enough to do so. In like fashion our ally,
Austria-Hungary, is threatened by this new grouping of the
Powers, and moreover has to face the added danger that, in
hatreds and intrigues directed against the stability and future of
the Hapsburg Monarchy, third parties may see a chance to press
on the work of destruction inside her frontiers. Already the
dissolution of Austria—alleged to be close at hand—is a constant
and favourite theme in French and other foreign newspapers.
Moreover Austria, because of her extensive interests in the
Balkans, runs a greater risk than we in that region of conflict
with the Entente Powers. I would supplement the above by
adding the following comment on the subject of our relations with
neighbouring States—Russia, France, and England on the one
hand, and, on the other, the Powers of the Triple Alliance.

Russia, as a result of the war with Japan, will for some time
be incapable of much action. Her government, in view of her
weakened and dangerous position, in Asia especially, is now striving to come to an agreement with her former enemy, Great
Britain, yet at the same time to maintain her traditional friendship
with us. We, on our side, have still good reason not to sever
entirely the ties which bind us to St. Petersburg. England, un-
reasonably anxious at what she considers the threat of our
military and economic progress, seeks, if not yet alliances then
friendships, guided by her established policy of making other
nations her catspaw. With regard to England we must continue
our policy of patience and caution, of trying to remove these
groundless apprehensions as far as possible. France is still
decreasing in national and in military strength. She remains in
constant anxiety of a possible conflict with us, and, without
actually entertaining hostile designs on us, goes in quest of protective friends. Left to herself France will maintain correct
relations and a *modus vivendi* with us. Nevertheless her dreams
of " *la revanche*," her desire to recover the old hegemony which
she held for two centuries in Europe, and even to re-establish her
Rhine frontier, have not by any means disappeared. But time is
on our side, if only for the biological reason that the normal
increase of population has already practically ceased in France,
while our population goes on increasing. The longer we can put
off the day of conflict with our western neighbour the less inclined

will she be to take the risk, even with the support of others, of a war which, even to-day, would be numerically unequal. Our policy towards France will thus be obvious; it must be dilatory, and avoid all irritations. Yet any offer, direct or indirect, of friendship to France would probably still be misunderstood by our Western neighbour, and would work in an opposite direction to improvement of Franco-German relations.

The wishes, needs, and interests of Austria-Hungary, who is our closest ally, must decide our attitude to the Near East, especially in the Balkan Peninsular, where our interests are merely economic.

From this sketch of the general groupings of the Powers, which I do not hesitate to describe as equally serious to both the Central European Monarchies, the Imperial Government has drawn the following conclusions with regard to our political attitude: Our policy, while firmly resolute in protecting our legitimate rights and interests, must scrupulously avoid any action which might induce other States to form against us any too powerful coalition. In consequence the Imperial government must refrain utterly from yielding to pressure from chauvinists, Pan-German or other; must, above all, confine itself to the defence of our legitimate rights and interests, and hand over, at least for the time being, to private initiative any further development of our economic position. All State aid must be given as discreetly as possible. I should here like to draw your attention to the first speech I ever made in the Reichstag, on 6th December 1897, when I spoke as Secretary of State for the Foreign Office: " We have no need to stick our fingers into every pie: we do not think it a good thing to eliminate Germany, *a priori*, from competition with other peoples, in countries sure of a rich future." I am still of the same opinion.

But let us on the other hand admit that it is only their fear of our strength which prevents other nations from assailing us, and keep both our land and naval armaments in such a state that they inspire the uttermost respect. Whatever discontents such a policy may arouse in our neighbours we must recognize and encounter with calm. In no circumstance must we discuss any agreement which might tend to limit our armed strength. Any Power suggesting such a course must be clearly made to understand that that means war with Germany. And financial and economic strength must no more be neglected than military. Our actual state of public finance gives the foreigner some reason to doubt our economic force of resistance, and, as a consequence therefore, our political. It is thus indispensable, from the standpoint of our Foreign Policy, in the interests, that is to say, of the maintenance both of peace and our position in the world, that our finances should, for some time ahead, be established on a sound and sufficient basis, without delay or any regard for timid scruples or narrow and professional class interests. An abundant experience has shown that a very large part of that mistrust of us which the foreigner displays, and seeks to translate into political action, arises from demonstrations in our press, and of our public opinion, which will not take sufficient account of the habits of thought and feeling in other nations. It is therefore necessary that, in our pursuit of the aims and objects I have specified, we go quietly to work, with as little bluster as possible. A little less of that bragging which, in both our press and public meetings, often becomes a kind of challenge, and is unnecessarily wounding to other nations, is the first essential for carrying out such a calm, prudent, resolute policy as the present international situation imposes! If, however, we keep firmly before us for our guidance the view I have set forth above we can look serenely out into the future. So long as Germany stands firm, united, and courageous she can show to the world such military strength that other nations will not lightly provoke her. Germany and Austria-Hungary form a solid block which can withstand almost any tempest. The tie of solidarity of interests and of mutual resolve to uphold the principle of monarchy, common to both, is their best security against other nations, which are, for the most part, ravaged by revolutionary agitation, and by ideas hostile to the principle of authority. A loyal co-operation with Austria-Hungary must and shall remain the chief foundation of German Foreign Policy. I enclose copies of two reports on the situation from Count Pourtalès, of the 12th and 14th of this month, two reports from Count Metternich of the 5th and 15th, and a note by the Secretary of State, von Schön, on the above-mentioned conversation he has had with the Russian Chief of Section, Baron Taube.

I should like to add to this very confidential circular (25th June 1908), that, in refusing to admit any foreign interference with our armaments, I was simply defending our indisputable right, as a sovereign and independent State, to decide for ourselves the extent and character of our armaments, which were however intended to serve purely defensive ends. Naturally my statement in no way excluded the possibility that we might come to an arrangement with England on the rate of naval construction. The final passage was intended to keep a check upon Austria. I had never been in any doubt that, if we accept the comparison which that experienced diplomatist, Talleyrand, made between states in alliance and a horse and rider, we must play the part of rider in our alliance with the Danubian Monarchy. I had this circular brought to the direct notice of the Emperor Francis Joseph through Count Szögyényi. His Apostolic Majesty, who was then very graciously disposed to me, certainly owed to it his power of resistance to the blandishments of the tempter Edward VII, whom he withstood on 13th August at Ischl far more successfully than did our mother Eve the serpent.

The Turkish revolution purified, like a storm, the stifling atmosphere which hung over Europe through the midsummer of 1908. It had partly been provoked by the projects for reform in Macedonia, announced at Reval by Russia and England, plans to which, in the opinion of the Turkish patriots, the sultan Abdul Hamid, a master of finesse who always went in terror of his life, was not offering sufficient resistance. The Turkish revolution put a quick end to Anglo-Russian schemes for reform, since in England the Liberals were in power with a strong majority, and utterly refused to allow any coercion of those apostles of freedom, the Young Turks. In our official press I left no doubt that our attitude was friendly to the revolution. I was quite confident that our Ambassador, Baron von Marschall, who in eleven years had gained a position of great authority in Constantinople, would be as successful with the Young Turks as he had been with the Padishah, who now was sent into exile. I could therefore, without any fear of contradiction from Constantinople, allow an inspired declaration to appear in the *Wiener Politischen Korrespondenz*, to the effect that Turko-German relations had suffered no change: " The Turkish people is, now as always, assured that Germany is one of the few States which has never speculated on the often-prophesied dissolution of Turkey, but has on the contrary always done her best to contribute towards the economic and political strengthening of the Ottoman Empire."

CHAPTER XXII

Criticism of our propaganda in the World War—The beginnings of the Bosnian crisis—Meeting of Isvolski and Aehrenthal at Buchlau—Annexation of Bosnia and Herzegovina by Austria-Hungary on 5th October 1908—Preparatory work for the reform of Imperial finances—The Manuscript of the " Daily Telegraph " article—It is returned marked " No objections " from the Foreign Office, in spite of my strict instruction to examine it carefully—William II demands sudden, radical change in Foreign Policy—The speech from the Throne—The marriage of Prince August Wilhelm.

I ONCE heard Bismarck say that, in politics, it is more dangerous to be long-sighted than short-sighted. I share his opinion, and yet I can well understand that it is possible to hold the opposite view. But there can be no doubt that our besetting sin in the conduct of Foreign Policy is our tendency to refer the events and questions of the present to causes far too remote in the past. This is all of a piece with the German tendency to pedantry—to losing oneself in ever-receding depths of speculation.

> " *Der Philosoph, der tritt herein*
> *Und beweist euch, es müsst' so sein;*
> *Das Erst' wär' so, und das Zweite so,*
> *Und drum das Dritt' und Vierte so,*
> *Und wenn das Erst' und Zweit' nicht wär,*
> *Das Dritt' und Viert' wär nimmermehr,*
> *Das preisen die Schüler allerorten,*
> *Sind aber keine Weber geworden.*" [1]

This tendency did us much harm during the World-War. A French journalist at that time made quite good fun of our mania in

---

[1] " Then the philosopher learnedly
Shows you that so the thing must be.
The First was so, the Second so
Therefore the Third and Fourth are so;
And were not the First and Second, then
The Third and Fourth had never been.
All scholars praise it, but Lord love 'em
It hasn't yet made weavers of 'em! "

(Goethe's *Faust*, Part I, Act i, Sc. 5.
Latham's translation.)

this direction. He wrote as follows: "When Thiers after Sedan asked Leopold von Ranke, whose friend he had been for many years, whom the Germans were fighting, now that Napoleon III had fallen, the German historian wittily answered, against Louis XIV. Actually Le Roi Soleil had in his day taken advantage of the weakness of the German Empire to deprive the Germans of Alsace. But what had made the Germans so weak? The Thirty Years' War. And what caused the Thirty Years' War? The Reformation. And what was the Reformation? A phase in the history of Christianity. But why had Christ come on earth? To save mankind, in bondage since the Fall. Thus," the Frenchman concluded, " according to the latest German scientific method the World-War was really declared at the minute when our mother Eve got her teeth well fixed in the apple. *Sans Eve, et sans la pomme, point d'ultimatum, point de guerre.*"

During the whole war our effort at propaganda, the results of which were always very negative, diffused itself in long-winded dissertations on events which had happened in far too remote a past to interest anybody, either enemy or neutral. What we ought to have explained to the world was our attitude in the summer of 1914, which we should have tried, as far as possible, to justify. But such justification, especially after the disastrous finish of the war, when we had to answer the " war-guilt " lies of our enemies, was possible only if we admitted, and even emphasized, the clumsiness of those responsible in 1914 for the conduct of German Foreign Policy. Later I will go into this in detail, when I undertake the painful duty of explaining why our peaceable, solid, kindly and reasonable citizens, our Emperor who really wanted peace, and had indeed a genuine horror of war, were clumsy enough to get themselves involved in the stupidest, most horrible of all wars. But, for the moment, I will conclude this digression, which I began in order to criticize our mania for too much retrospective generalization, by admitting that there are sometimes events which form the last link of a long chain. To such a chain belonged the Bosnian Question which, in the autumn of 1908, caused serious tension between Austria and Russia, and brought Germany face to face with a fairly dangerous situation and one which certainly bristled with difficulties. The Bosnian Question, " *cette boite de Pandore pleine de surprises, de périls, et de graves possibiliti és,*" as a Rumanian diplomat once described it to me, had certainly its origins in the Russo-Turkish War of 1877. When in 1876 Alexander II determined, very much *à contre coeur,* in deference to the strong Slavophil feeling in Russia, and under the influence of old Tsarist sentiments and traditions, to draw

his sword in defence of Slav interests in the Balkans, whose Slavs were
attached to the Russians by common ties of faith and blood, his
Chancellor Gortshakov, remembered that Russia's final defeat in
the Crimea had really been due to the hostile attitude of Austria.
At the beginning of the Crimean War in 1854 when, after the occupation of Moldavia and Wallachia, the Emperor Nicholas I let his
armies advance into Bulgaria, he saw himself compelled to evacuate
the whole Balkan peninsula as soon as Austria had mobilized an army
in Galicia. Gortshakov, therefore, to avoid repeating the danger
of an Austrian army in the rear, decided in 1876, to abandon Bosnia
and Herzegovina to the Hapsburgs as the price of an Austrian
agreement to the Russian expedition against Turkey. I studied
minutely the whole connection of these events in my account of
what preceded the Congress of Berlin. " *Il faut faire la part du
feu* " as the old Chancellor had said in explanation of his motives
for this move, to his sovereign. As a youthful Secretary of Embassy
in Vienna I had witnessed the convention, concluded at the Royal
Castle at Budapest, by which Gortshakov left the time and method
of the military occupation of Bosnia and Herzegovina to the discretion of the Vienna government. As Secretary at the Congress of
Berlin I assisted at the public consecration, by the Treaty of Berlin
(Art. XXV) of the convention of Budapest, to which Russia gave so
joyful a consent: " *Les provinces de Bosnie et d'Herzégovine seront
occupées et administrées par l'Autriche-Hongrie.*" During the Congress of Berlin and six years later at Skierniewice, declarations, both
verbal and in the form of an *aide-mémoire*, had been exchanged
between Austria-Hungary and Russia, according to which Russia
would raise no objections if, in the interests of Balkan tranquillity
and European peace, Austria desired to make her occupation an
annexation. It was perfectly natural that Isvolski, soon after the
meeting at Reval, should have sent the Austrian Foreign Minister
a written proposal to start negotiations, firstly for changing the
occupation into an annexation, secondly for opening the Straits.
But what did surprise me was that Isvolski should have approached
his Vienna colleague in such a sense not long after the latter,
unexpectedly, had announced the Austro-Turkish Treaty relative
to the construction of the Sanjak railway—the stretch, that is
to say, between the Bosnian and Macedonian lines—a treaty
which caused a great sensation in Russia, and provoked a somewhat
lively exchange of notes between the Cabinets of Vienna and St.
Petersburg.

To understand Isvolski's proposal it must always be understood
that this ambitious and not very prudent Foreign Minister neglected

everything else for the secular aspirations of Russia in the Dardanelles, and had as his object the permanent conquest of a place in the hearts of all good Muscovites, and in Russian history, and also, perhaps, the title of Count, as well as the Order of St. Andrew. Aehrenthal, too, had spent almost his whole diplomatic career in St. Petersburg, as attaché, Secretary, then Councillor of Embassy, and finally as Ambassador. He thought he knew the Russians inside out, and was, indeed, very popular with the whole of St. Petersburg Society, among other reasons, because of his *liaison* with one of its most beautiful leaders. His position in St. Petersburg drawing-rooms was, indeed, better than Isvolski's, whom, socially, he considered his inferior. He thought himself quite certain of the Russians, and felt that, under any circumstances, he could get the better of the Minister. " *Je tiens les Russes dans ma poche*," he is said to have declared.

But Aehrenthal forgot that, in St. Petersburg, side by side with the fat and peace-loving General Adjutants and Ministers, the witty ladies, and charming Grand Duchesses, there had grown up a rough, and strongly nationalist opposition, fundamentally hostile to Austria, and which watched with jealousy and mistrust, over the interests of Slav and Orthodox " little brothers " inhabiting the Balkan peninsula. At first the Austrian had managed to induce his Russian colleague, Isvolski, to accept with grateful joy an invitation to meet him at the château of Buchlau, in Moravia, which belonged to Count Berchtold, the Austrian Ambassador in St. Petersburg, and later the most unfortunate Austrian Foreign Minister. Count, or rather before his success in the Bosnian affair, Baron von Aehrenthal was the grandson of the Jewish merchant Lexa of Prague who, at the beginning of the nineteenth century, in recognition of his business success in grain selling, had been ennobled under the appropriate title of Aehrenthal.[1] This minister's grandmother, a Countess Wilczek, and his mother, a Countess Thun, had come of the higher Austrian nobility. His sister had married a Count Bylandt, he himself a Countess Szechenyi, of that great Hungarian family. He united with the quick intelligence, the diligence and reflective caution of his ancestors on the paternal side, an innate arrogance— what the Viennese call the *Fumo* of the Austrian aristocracy. Tall, broad-shouldered, a little bowed, very short-sighted, sometimes almost blind, with eyelids that always drooped and a look of weariness, but with regular features and an aristocratic air; reserved, rather indolent, almost apathetic, Aehrenthal stood in utter contrast to the shorter, more restless and excitable, and

[1] *I.e.* Corn valley.

occasionally pushing Calmuck, Isvolski. With both Isvolski and Aehrenthal I had long been friendly, though I had never had the confidence in the latter which I had placed in his predecessor Golukhovski. When Golukhovski retired in October 1906 he wired in answer to my telegram of regret at his departure: " Deeply moved by the warm and friendly message which Your Excellency has been good enough to send me on the occasion of my retirement from office, I feel it a duty of affection to express to you my warmest thanks for the trust and co-operation which you have never refused me during the long years of our joint activity. At the same time I ask Your Excellency to accept the assurance that I reckon the friendly relations between us, which go back so far into the past, and which you always permitted me to enjoy, as among the pleasantest memories which I shall take with me into private life."

It was a peculiar fact that Golukhovski, who at first had much mistrust to encounter in St. Petersburg, should have been able, thanks to the agreement concluded in 1903 at Mürzsteg between Austria and Russia, to inaugurate a period of friendship between the ancient rivals in the Balkan peninsula, whereas Aehrenthal, who, in contrast to the Pole Golukhovski, had posed and been fêted by the whole of Russian Society as the true friend of Russia, was destined almost to provoke a breach with Russia. This confirms once again a remark made to me by a Rumanian Minister, M. Vernesco, when I, at the time a young and inexperienced Minister, recalled to his mind some promises he had made me, and then broken, after he came into power: " *Vous ne sauriez croire, mon cher monsieur, à quel point le gouvernment change les idées d'un homme.*"

It is impossible ever to judge of a politician's line of future conduct after achieving the control of affairs, by his antecedents, his sympathies and antipathies when out of office. " *Il faut le voir à l'oeuvre,*" one has to wait, to employ another expression of Bismarck, to see how he is going to " season."

Count Berchtold, in October 1908, caused a memorial tablet to be erected in his castle at Buchlau to inform posterity that here Aloys Aehrenthal and Alexander Isvolski had met, on 15th September 1908, to settle the affairs of Europe. I do not know if the tablet is still in existence or whether the government of that Czechoslovakian Republic, whose head—as of a dishevelled Caryatid—Frederick Hebbel once saw in a moment of prophetic horror, has since removed it as a monument of the " accursed past." Of the conversation between these two leading Ministers I subsequently received both Aehrenthal's version and Isvolski's. My first impression, confirmed by time and all that I have since seen and

COUNT ALOYS AEHRENTHAL

Austro-Hungarian Minister of Foreign Affairs

learned, is that Aehrenthal, who was also the cleverer player, had the formal right on his side, but that his conduct was not quite " fair," to use an English expression which meets the case.   Certainly Isvolski, having already assured Aehrenthal of his agreement in principle with the annexation proposed, seems to have acted stupidly and clumsily in not proceeding at once to inquire precisely when the Austrian Minister proposed to take the step he had announced.   Isvolski should have declared immediately that he must have time in which to prepare the Russian public for this act of the Austrian government, since Russians in general were ignorant of their government's arrangements with Austria and the Tsar himself knew very little about it.   But when Aehrenthal left Buchlau for Vienna, on the evening of 16th September, leaving his Russian colleague to spend another night in the château, Isvolski can certainly not have supposed that Austria, within scarcely three weeks, would have startled the world with the news of the annexation of Bosnia and Herzegovina.

The proclamation by the Emperor Francis Joseph, dated 5th October 1908, came like a bolt from the blue to Europe.   The Serbs were enraged, the Serbian Crown Prince placed himself at the head of the demonstrators, declaring that he was ready to die, with every other Serb, for Greater Serbia.   The crowds at Belgrade acclaimed the representatives of Russia, France, England, and Italy and tried to smash the windows of the Austrian Embassy.   At Constantinople Austrian subjects were mobbed, and all Austrian goods were boycotted.   The Russian press was passionately pro-Serbian.   It declared that, at the very least, the Serbs must demand a huge compensation from Austria.   And, to increase still further the confusion, Prince Ferdinand of Bulgaria declared his State to be an independent kingdom on the very day when the Emperor Francis Joseph, by autograph letter to Aehrenthal, extended his sovereignty over Bosnia and Herzegovina.   For many years Europe had not been so excited.

When all this happened I was at Norderney, at my desk, within sight of that sea which I, a son of the Lower Elbe, have known and loved all my life.   As may be imagined, I followed the Bosnian crisis with strained attention, as telegrams and reports poured in, one after the other, recording its development.   I had at the same time to pass the draft bills for the taxes on beer, wine, spirits, tobacco, electricity, gas, and advertisements, which, together with the Death Duties, and the taxes for armaments, were to help Imperial finances on to their feet.   In the justificatory preamble to this proposed Imperial reform there was the following: " The

, German Empire, as the result of the permanent want of proportion
between necessary expenditure and receipts, is burdened with a
heavy load of debt.   The ever-recurrent issue of promissory notes
and Treasury bonds, without prospect of redemption, has lowered
the market value of the loan to such an extent that the credit of the
Empire is threatened, even in peace time. . . .   The removal of this
deficiency is an indispensable necessity for the power and prosperity
of the Empire, and at the same time an essential preliminary to the
further favourable development of Germany's trade and industry.
Only through the unanimous co-operation in sacrifice of all classes
of the nation can Imperial finance be re-established on a basis of
permanent security."   With what feelings to-day do I remember
my justification of the financial reforms that I proposed—to-day,
when the abuses I then complained of, the taxes I then imposed,
seem so meagre, so moderate, so harmless!

In addition to the storm with which the Bosnian crisis seemed to
threaten us, and the difficult, thorny, yet supremely important task
politically, of financial and economic reform, the autumn of 1908
brought another painful Casablanca incident which re-opened the
whole Morocco quarrel and threatened with a new and heavy strain
our better understanding with France.   In this matter I obtained a
breathing space by proposing to the French government that this
obscure event, in which there were rights and wrongs on both sides,
should be submitted to the Hague Tribunal.   Nevertheless, I had
to attend to the reform of Imperial finances, and at the same time
prevent the Bosnian crisis from kindling a world-conflagration.

While overwhelmed with work, and absorbed from morning to
night in these difficult problems, I received, through Herr von
Jenisch, from the Imperial hunting-box at Rominten, to which he
had accompanied His Majesty, a bulky and almost illegible manuscript, written on bad typing paper, with a covering letter, asking
me if I saw any objection to its publication in the columns of an
English newspaper—a publication the Emperor very much desired.
By an extraordinary trick of fate the very same post which brought
me this ominous bundle from the Kaiser brought a letter from the
eighty-year-old Hinzpeter.   In it this aged mentor took the long-
desired occasion to express to the Imperial Chancellor his approval—
nay, his astonishment

". . . not at his brilliant conduct of the Foreign Policy of the
Reich, or masterly skill in handling the parties at home but,
above all, at the admirable pedagogic genius, whose effects are
constantly revealed in the moral development of the Emperor

under your guidance. With joy and astonishment I have watched
how self-control, the quality he most seriously needs, and which
is of all the most difficult to acquire, is becoming more and
more manifest in the thought, the words and actions of His
Majesty. There can be no doubt who is the author of this hap-
piest of all transformations, and I can only, with respect, acknowledge results, in a field in which perhaps I have some knowledge.
Age must be allowed its privileges, and at eighty, one may say
a great many things which, earlier, one would have kept to
oneself."

The writer of this letter, however, closely as he had studied the
Emperor's mind, had not yet managed to plumb its disconcerting
depths of incalculability. While I read these very amiable compliments on the success of my eleven years' labour as Imperial tutor,
there lay on my desk the little packet whose contents were to reveal
to the full, more than any previous manifestation of the kind, the
Emperor's intellectual extravagance, his incoherent disregard of
facts, his complete lack of political moderation and balance, combined with an excessive urge towards outward manifestation and
display. Without the slightest suspicion in my mind of the ominous
contents of the manuscript, which I could not find the time to read
myself, I sent it off at once to the Wilhelmstrasse, together with a
letter to Jenisch, adding to my note to the Foreign Office the
following instruction in my own hand: " Please read the enclosed
article carefully through, transcribe it in clear official script with a
wide margin (or better still let it be typewritten), duplicate it, and
enter, in the same hand, in the margin, such corrections, additions
or deletions as may seem suitable. Further, retain a copy of the
revised text for His Majesty. It is important that the utmost
secrecy be observed, and that this document be returned to me as
soon as possible."

The words " carefully " and " deletions " were both thickly
underlined. A few days later, back came the article from the
Foreign Office, with the remark that only a few unimportant corrections had been found necessary—such trifles, for instance, as the
correct name of the German consular official who had been sent to
Fez. Once again I had the article read, this time by the Minister
von Müller, in attendance on me as Foreign Office representative,
with instructions to examine it carefully since I, in those days of
crisis, could not spare the necessary time. When Herr von Müller
returned me the article next day I again asked, clearly and unmistakably, whether any possible objection could be raised against its

publication. He answered me quite definitely in the negative, and I authorized him to reply in that sense to the enquiry I had received from Rominten. I had no idea that this package, from the Imperial hunting-box, was a veritable charge of high explosive the detonation of which would shortly cause the most serious internal crisis I experienced during my whole term of office.

But before proceeding to that crisis I must relate an incident which occurred that same autumn at Norderney, the beautiful Frisian island, which I was destined not to see again till the time when I was no longer a Chancellor. It had become my habit every evening to walk with my wife for an hour by the sea, after dinner, when the beach was almost deserted. On several evenings she had thought she had noticed a man she did not recognize following at some distance behind us. In her constant anxiety for my safety she had offered, in order to protect me, to walk between the man and myself, and this caused me to chaff her a little. We had both of us long forgotten him when, one evening, I returned to Norderney after a short stay in Berlin where I went, from time to time, for reports and conferences. On the morning after my return the police reported that the body of a man had just been found on the beach. On it a crumpled piece of paper, scribbled with the following message in pencil:

To the Police!—If you find me dying let me die in peace. I am sick of life and have nothing to look forward to. I feel the deepest compassion for my victim, but really this is all I can do. I had to revenge myself on some beautiful woman whom I would very much rather have loved, but it is too late now for that, since I haven't a penny left, and I can't see any other way out. I therefore die in the knowledge that I have done my duty. As a matter of fact, I had chosen another victim— that notorious enemy of peoples' suffrage, Prince Bülow, who, at every opportunity, has insulted and oppressed the working class. But alas! I have not the means to wait until Prince Bülow returns from Berlin, otherwise he would certainly have had a bullet through him. That is why, as I said at the beginning, I am driven to my horrible deed.

(*Signed*) D. Braun.

Further police investigations revealed that this man had come from Stuttgart where he had been active as a Socialist. At the little Inn, at which he had stayed in Norderney, he had made repeated inquiries as to my habits, and the time and place of my walks. He had complained that he was without means of subsistence, that he had even had to pawn his overcoat—an unbearable loss for a man with lung trouble, amid the stormy winds of Norderney. And, indeed, as the inquest revealed, Comrade Braun had been tubercular. To his questions, the innkeepers had answered that the Chancellor had gone to Berlin and would not be returning to Norderney for some time. They had told him this without ulterior motive. Whereupon, that very same night, the fellow after shooting at a lady—a perfect stranger, whom he happened to see in the street—and wounding her somewhat seriously in the chin, had put a bullet through his ear. The lady he had wounded—she was the very respectable wife of a Bremen merchant—earnestly begged that her name might be kept out of the papers; otherwise she would be exposed to gossip and scandal. I gladly granted her request, all the more readily since I myself should not have disliked anything so much as unnecessary fuss about the business. I have never been subject to " nerves." From my youth up I have always felt the truth of the words which Caesar, in Shakespeare's play speaks to Calpurnia:

> " Of all the wonders that I yet have heard
> It seems to me most strange that men should fear
> Seeing that death, a necessary end,
> Will come—when it will come."

The incident, therefore, was not revealed to the public. A year before, some Galician Poles had been arrested at Norderney, who had also admitted their intention of coming there on purpose to assassinate me. I gave the same instruction to keep the matter out of the newspapers, and had these poor devils sent quietly back across the frontier.

When I got back to Berlin I found the Emperor as excited as I knew he would be over events in the Balkan peninsula. What stirred him most was the insult to the Turks, his favourites still, even after the proclamation of a democratic, parliamentary constitution in Constantinople, and the fall of his particular friend, the Sultan Abdul Hamid. He was also very angry at the fact that Prince Ferdinand of Bulgaria, whom he had always personally disliked, should have arrogated to himself the title of " Majesty " without having first consulted him. As we walked together in the garden of the Imperial Chancellery, where he and I had had so many arguments, His Majesty, in a perfect torrent of words, proposed a complete change in our Foreign Policy. He said we must make instant demands in Vienna for the immediate withdrawal of the Austrian Emperor's edict of annexation, and demand, at the same time, the retirement of Aehrenthal. Nor must we ever grant the presumptuous Bulgar a right to his usurped title of " Majesty." I answered that I had never exaggerated the value of the Austrian alliance, nor did I exaggerate it now; that I, too, was aware that Prince Ferdinand was an Ulysses, fertile in trickery. All the same, I said, there was no need to kick Austria straight over into the camp of our enemies—or even Bulgaria. We should be all the less justified in doing so because, in this Bosnian matter, the Hapsburgs had treaty rights on their side, and also, if the occasion arose, a formidable diplomatic weapon in the letter written to Aehrenthal by Isvolski in the previous June. But I would certainly not allow it to come to war. I was not disposed to allow the Austrians to take active measures against Serbia, still less against Russia, and naturally not against Italy. I would never abandon Austria; but I did not intend to allow her to involve us in an European war. The Emperor could leave me to act as signalman. I trusted my skill and strength to set the points so that the Austrian express should not collide with the Russian. The great example on which to base our action was one already given us by Bismarck in an earlier Balkan crisis. Our problem could be stated as follows: we must not risk the loss of Austria-Hungary, with her fifty million inhabitants, her strong and efficient army, but, still less must we let ourselves be dragged by her into the midst of an armed conflict which, I was convinced, would be very difficult to localize and might lead to a general war, in which we had certainly nothing to gain. I could not stop to ask permission in advance for every diplomatic move I should make, nor could I tell His Majesty at once just how I intended to act in detail: but I believed I could assure him that we should certainly come through unscathed, and, I hoped, with increased prestige at the end of this diplomatic campaign.

My influence over William II was then still strong. In an hour-and-a-half's discussion I had managed to convert him completely. He left the further handling of the Bosnian crisis to my discretion, and seemed to me entirely confident. He also, that same afternoon, agreed to the draft which I submitted for his speech from the Throne at the opening of the Prussian Diet, due on 20th October. I had worded the introduction as follows: " A century has elapsed since my ancestor, Frederick William III, now asleep in God, by promulgation of the Town's Ordinance, summoned all Prussian citizens to take their part in municipal government. Ever since this Constitution was promulgated the Nation too takes its share in the government of the State. It is my will that the prescriptions established on the basis of this Constitution, and relative to the election of deputies to the Diet, should receive further organic development corresponding to our economic progress, the improved education, political understanding, and general civic sense of our people. This, in my eyes, forms one of the most important tasks of the present."

The Emperor, *proprio motu*, expressed the desire to read this most significant speech himself. He wished there should be no doubt that, like myself, he believed a reform of the Prussian electoral system desirable and necessary in the interests both of the Throne and of the country. I could see, of course, that this speech would irritate the Conservatives, who till then had felt themselves to be masters in the Prussian House of Representatives, just as, under the same electoral system the Progressives, forty-five years earlier, had felt themselves to be omnipotent. " *Plus ça change, plus c'est la même chose,*" as they say in a French farce. But I hoped that the Conservatives would show more insight and statesmanship than their opposite numbers had displayed in the first half of the 'sixties. I hoped they would set the interests of the Prussian State above the interests of their party, which they themselves did not, really, fully understand. The Emperor, who had arrived with an anxious face, left me quite gaily, with the words: " Well now I can peacefully get my good Auwi married off to his adored Alix, and then go off myself to Wernigerode for the stag-shooting." " Auwi " was the pet name for the Emperor's fourth son, Prince August Wilhelm. Amiable, well brought up, but a little weak, artistically inclined, and fairly well-gifted intellectually, he seemed to his father better fitted for a civil career than for the rude and strenuous trade of a soldier. Having passed his legal finals he was to become, according to programme, first magistrate, then Regierungspräsident, Oberpräsident of Prussia, and finally Statthalter of Alsace-Lorraine. He had become engaged to his pretty cousin Alix, the second daughter of Duke Friedrich Ferdinand of Glücksburg, and Princess Caroline Mathilde of Augustenburg. The latter was the Kaiserin's eldest sister, and as good and honourable as she. Seldom has a marriage been concluded under what seemed to be happier auspices than this between Alix and Auwi.

At the wedding banquet, on 22nd October 1908, the Emperor delivered a moving speech, in praise of his dear Alix, the daughter of a sea-girt land, whom he welcomed with wide open arms as a true helper of her aunt, and her mother-in-law the Empress, in all their works of benevolence and mercy. He praised his son for having just brilliantly passed his examinations, thus bringing distinction on his family and opening for himself the way to a civil career.

The worthy Kaiserin, for whom there was nothing nobler or of more importance than such honourable, chaste, though at the same time profoundly tender attachments, as unite Hermann to his Dorothea, and later, Philemon to his Baucis, listened in rapture. *Quo promessa cadunt et somnia Pythagorea*! Twelve years later this marriage was to end in strident controversy, and with a divorce which still further embittered the last years of the Empress, so terribly shaken by the revolution. But a long and eventful decade separated the Imperial couple from these tragic events which were to overshadow the evening of their lives.

CHAPTER XXIII

Session, in Berlin, of the Inter-Parliamentary Conference—The unveiling of a bust of Bismarck in the Valhalla at Regensburg—The Empire and Bavaria—Without preliminary inquiry the Wolff Telegraphic Agency issues the " Daily Telegraph " article on William II's political conversations in England (29th October 1908)—My urgency report to His Majesty—The announcement in the " Norddeutsche Allgemeine Zeitung"—Conversation with the Emperor—The officials responsible.

THE autumn of 1908 brought two events, of no great importance in themselves, but which threw into relief our favourable international position, and moreover promoted between the Federal States, those sound and friendly relationships which guaranteed the solidity of the Empire founded by Bismarck. From the 17th to the 19th of September there sat in Berlin an inter-parliamentary conference, in which deputies from every country took part. It is to the excellent Liberal Reichstag deputy, Eickhoff, that must go the credit for this resolve that an inter-parliamentary conference should be held in the capital of the Reich. I was well aware that the dreams and illusions of most pacificists—in particular those of German pacificists—were objectively considered as foolish, and might become quite as perilous, as the blusterings and threats of the Pan-Germans. Nor have I ever over-estimated the real importance of such conferences. But such a reunion in Berlin afforded a good opportunity for destroying certain anti-German prejudices and for refuting many a false conception and misjudgment of conditions in Germany. All this was really useful and desirable, especially where it was a question of such distortions in our Left Wing press, as gave foreigners an entirely wrong picture of the great and flourishing Empire in Central Europe. The old German saying of the bird that befouls its own nest was, alas, never so ignored as in the old, happy, pre-war Germany.

It was above all the English and the French who came in the greatest numbers to the conference, 1908—to a Berlin still so flourishing and so brilliant, a Berlin whose streets were the best kept streets in the world. " *Berlin est propre comme un salon,*" used to say Laura Minghetti, who was equally at home in Rome and Paris, London and Vienna. And Berlin not only charmed, it surprised and en-

335

lightened all who had never visited it before. We had some right
to be proud of that Imperial Berlin, with its powerful pulsating life,
its masterly, disciplined organization, at once the greatest industrial
centre of the Continent and the seat of a brilliant court and a splendid garrison. But, beneath all this, for those strangers who could
see and think, more significant than all the surface splendour, was
the well-being both of our working and middle classes, our development of workman's insurance and social services, far superior to
anything that other countries had to show. It was about that time
that a delegation of English workers, having studied German social
organization and examined the conditions of our working-class,
asked of a German comrade, with all the ingenuous candour of the
English: " But what are you agitating for? You've got everything."

At the opening of this inter-parliamentary conference I delivered
a speech in which I protested at the scepticism, directed from so
many quarters against the efforts of all such gatherings. " You have
achieved," I told the members I was addressing, " far more than was
at first considered possible, and your success has increased from year
to year." I called as my witness the Nestor of such inter-parliamentary conferences, the venerable and honoured Frédéric Passy, whom
I beheld as young, as fresh, as enthusiastic at this session, as I had
seen him twenty-five years before in Paris. I recalled how, at the
Second Hague Conference, Germany had proposed and signed the
arbitration agreement, how she had supported a draft scheme for
the establishment of a permanent court whose acceptance was recommended to the Powers in the concluding protocol of the Conference. Since then, in various agreements, Germany had availed
herself of the methods of international arbitration. In a number of
our commercial treaties she had inserted an arbitration clause, either
obligatory, or at the very least, facultative. We were to join in the
Conference of Naval Powers due, in a few weeks, in London. Our
assent had been won in advance to all proposals in harmony with
the interests of lawful defence, with the unwritten law of humanity.
A remarkable proof of the interest taken in Germany in the work of
international understanding was the large number of German
deputies who had applied to take part in this inter-parliamentary
reunion. I protested against the idea that love of peace implied
less love of one's own country. " There are very good patriots," I
said, " whose aim is to keep out of war by making their own war on
ignorance, on blind hate and international rancour, on ambitions
which so often deceive." I concluded as follows: " A fairly long
experience tells me this: that nothing clears up all misunderstand-

ings so effectively as those personal encounters by which men come to know each other better. I know my own countrymen will all be with me when I say: ' May your labours be fruitful; may they be to the good of all the nations whose representatives have done us the great honour, and given us the great pleasure, of coming to Berlin.' "

My speech was frequently interrupted by signs of the most cordial approval and its conclusion received with loud applause. I had spoken in French, following Bismarck's example, since my great predecessor had used this language as his medium for all international gatherings, in particular for the Berlin Congress. From my earliest youth I have written and spoken both French and German equally well, and I do not consider this a misfortune. My long life has brought me many chances of proving that my patriotism has not suffered by it. To speak and write a second language fluently purges one's style and clarifies one's thought. Bismarck's oft-quoted remark that a gift for languages is an excellent thing for a head-waiter, even if Bismarck said it, was meant for a joke. I would prefer to say that a man who can express himself in several languages is like one who surveys the world from a house which has a different view from each of its windows. The French applauded loudest of all. The Frenchman, who like all Latins is born an orator and remains one by education and tradition, is far more sensitive to form than the average German. He is deeply aware of that truth emphasized long ago by Aeschines and Demosthenes, as well as by Quintilian and Cicero, that an orator should display both taste and pathos, that wit and a striking turn of phrase are never out of place in public speaking, that, in spite of all the grumblings of a Faust who toys with the idea of suicide, his ability to say a thing well is the chiefest joy and merit of a speaker—the only thing which can give his words their virtue of really rousing his listeners.

On 18th October 1908, the anniversary of the battle of Leipzig, and the birthday of the great Emperor Frederick, the unveiling of the bust of Prince Bismarck was to take place in the Valhalla at Regensburg. I had gladly accepted an invitation to be present because, on principle, I took every opportunity of strengthening and promoting good relationships between Berlin and Munich. I had never forgotten what Prince Bismarck had once said to me: " If our enemies ever try to disrupt Germany they will drive in their wedge in Munich." But I can affirm with pleasure that, during the whole of my Chancellorship, the firmest, best, most trustful understanding never ceased to exist between Bavaria and the Reich. In the speech which I delivered at Regensburg (18th October 1908)

I expressed my firm conviction as to the federal basis of Germany, on which, as on a rock of bronze, Prince Bismarck had shaped in concrete form the whole idea of German unity. The grandson of that great man whose bust we had gathered to unveil was also present at the ceremony—a delicate boy whose whole physique resembled that of his sickly Austro-English mother rather than of his burly father or the giant form of his grandfather. When the ceremony began I asked this youthful bearer of the great name, in whose honour we had assembled, to stand beside me. The Bavarian Premier, my old friend Podewils, welcomed me in a speech, both perfect in form and delivered with a noble passion, and full of loyalty to the Empire. My reply expressed my convictions as to the proper relationship between Prussia and the Federal States, between the whole Empire and Bavaria. They were formulated as follows: " No Chancellor of the German Empire can ever depart from the course prescribed in this sphere by Prince Bismarck. For myself I feel it necessary to insist that respect for the rights of German Princely Houses is of equal importance with the homage we all pay the Imperial constitution." While I was speaking the ten year old Prince Otto Bismarck gave a sudden howl, collapsed, and had to be carried out. After it had been ascertained that there was nothing really the matter with him more than a passing, and certainly not dangerous fit of giddiness, I finished my speech by praising the services which Louis I of Bavaria had rendered the cause of national feeling by his fostering of our German culture. I ended as follows: " The German dynasties and peoples welded in equal love of the Fatherland, indissolubly bound by their equal sense of common nationality, can be assured that the claims of united Germany will never mean that their separate individuality must be sacrificed. Were that to disappear the German Empire would be robbed of an essential possession, of that true individual spirit of each of its members which first secured its chance of proper development under the shelter, and in the peace of German unity. As the poet sings:

" *Eins nach aussen, schwertgewaltig*
Um ein hoch Panier geschart,
Doch im Innern vielgestaltig,
Jeder Stamm nach seiner Art." [1]

When I had finished my speech we all left the majestic Hall

[1] One outwardly, strong as a sword
Gathered in beneath a high banner.
Inwardly, many-faceted.
Each race after its kind.

of Fame, where Henry the Fowler looks across to the Emperor William I, Frederick Barbarossa to the great Frederick, Ulrich von Hutten to Baron von Stein, Georg von Frundsberg to Gerhard Lebrecht von Blücher, and the white marble busts of Johann Sebastian Bach and Richard Wagner, of Dr. Martin Luther and Emanuel Kant, of Goethe and Albrecht Dürer, stand side by side. Everything there recalls the manifold riches, the variety and magnificence of our history, summoning the German who is conscious of its inner oneness to patriotism and therefore to unity. Spread out before my eyes, in the mellow sunshine of October, lay the glorious country, the rich plain. That mightiest of German rivers, which had borne the ship of the Nibelungen, which still bears German men and German goods from the Black Forest as far as the Dobrudja, and the distant *Pontus Euxinus*, lay at my feet. The fruitful land stretched on and on to where the towering Bavarian Alps cast their shadows on it, and I saw the old town of Regensburg, the town of Barbara Blomberg, the fair mother of Don John of Austria, the town which under the might of the old Empire, had flowered and grown rich till, later, it met such sad decay, such bitterness of tragedy and decline.

Here Podewils presented his Chief of Cabinet, the Councillor of Embassy and Royal Bavarian Chamberlain Francis Xavier von Stockhammern. He praised him to me as a most distinguished official, his strong support in a very difficult office, in which his position was never safe from attack, and added that he had been mainly responsible for arranging the beautiful ceremony in the Valhalla. At that time I did not know I was meeting a man who, six years later when we grew to know each other in Rome, was destined to become a close friend. Herr von Stockhammern was the son of a brave soldier, a general distinguished in the Franco-Prussian War of 1870, whose family two hundred years earlier had migrated to Bavaria from the Archbishopric of Salzburg. His mother, distinguished for her intellect and strength of purpose, had come of the old Ulm family Kraft von Delmensingen, mentioned by Wilhelm Hauff in his *Lichtenstein* whose members include the builder of Ulm Cathedral, and which, in the World-War, gave the German army one of its best leaders. Francis Stockhammern had been educated at Augsburg, by the Benedictines, that noble order, compared by the Middle Ages to bees for their industry, and whose modesty and true humanity is well expressed in the glorious device of their founder: " *Spernere mundum, neminem spernere, spernere sperni, spernere se ipsum.*" After the model and under the instruction of the Benedictines of St. Stefan, Stockhammern, even as a boy, grew so versed in the Italian language that he wrote and spoke it nearly as well as

his native German. A longish stay in a Benedictine monastery in
Spain had given him his chance to become well acquainted with
Spanish, and the whole wealth of Spanish literature. He made
repeated journeys to Rome, where he attended lectures at the
Gregorian University, and these made of him a really accomplished
Latinist, that is to say, a man who speaks and writes Latin as one
speaks and writes a modern language, an accomplishment fairly
common in Italy but becoming ever rarer in Germany. To such
many-sided stores of knowledge, an iron industry, and keen intellectual curiosity, Stockhammern added real sincerity, idealism and
common-sense. A faithful, even devoted Catholic, yet without a
trace of bigotry or intolerance, Bavarian to his finger-tips, yet none
the less a patriotic German, Stockhammern united just those
characteristics which our nation needs if ever it is again to rise above
the tragic necessities of the present. Together with Friedrich
Wilhelm von Loebell, Francis Xavier von Stockhammern is one of
the few, the all too few, really good men I have met in my life.

The Valhalla ceremony concluded with a lunch in the Council
Chambers at which we were served with real Bavarian white sausage
and magnificent Franziskaner beer, of which I very seldom partake,
though I drank it now with the greatest pleasure. I had to speak
again in the Council Hall where one hundred and forty-three years
previously had assembled the Diet of the Empire, and to make a
third speech that evening at a banquet in the Government Palace.
That day at Regensburg which ended with a friendly " good-bye "
from the great crowd, gathered to see me off at the station, was the
last harmonious note before the discords of the *Daily Telegraph*
affair.

Back in Berlin I found a letter from von Jenisch containing the
report of a meeting between the Emperor and the Heir to the Austrian throne. This had taken place on one of His Majesty's many
autumn excursions, and seemed to have passed off very well. Jenisch
said that now the relations between these two exalted persons were
excellent, and that, in the opinion of His Majesty, was a good
guarantee for the future, considering the great age of Francis Joseph.
To the Emperor's lively satisfaction the Archduke had invited him
to Austria for the stag hunting. His Majesty's excursion into the
Austrian hunting district was to last several days, after which he
would go for a week to Donauschingen, to visit his best friend,
Prince Max Egon Fürstenberg. He looked forward to this, said
Jenisch, even more than to his stay with the Austrian Crown
Prince. There was much talk of magnificent preparations at
Donaueschingen, whose master not only intended to receive his

sovereign as became him, but to make his stay at the hereditary seat of the Fürstenbergs as amusing as it could possibly be made. The atmosphere around the All-Highest was once more *couleur de rose*.

The first days which followed my return were passed in conferences on the subject of fiscal reform, in meetings with foreign ambassadors to discuss with them the Bosnian crisis, and in interviews (usually painful) with the Chiefs of the political *bloc*. My friend Ballin once said to me that it is harder to get fleas back into a bag than to keep journalists on the rails, and prevent them from making themselves a nuisance. Our natural German obstinacy and dogmatism made it no easy task for me to get Liberals and Conservatives to work together in harness. Goethe's malicious saying on the Germans kept coming back into my mind: " As individuals very estimable, but a misery when taken in the mass."

On the morning of 29th October I went, as usual, to my big desk which, thirty years ago, was made for me in the Faubourg St. Antoine, the old " *quartier des ébenistes* " with the exquisite skill and care of Parisian craftsmanship, and which had since accompanied me everywhere—from the Seine to the Neva, from the Neva back to the Tiber, and so, at last, here beside the Spree. A heap of correspondence lay on this desk, at which I had read so many reports, drafted so many letters and instructions. To-day among the heap I noticed a long message from London through the Wolff Telegraphic Agency. I took it up without the least foreboding, and opened it with my usual calm. But my peace of mind quickly changed to startled amazement as I read it. The message was the summary of an article which had appeared in the London *Daily Telegraph* on a conversation with the German Emperor, announced as having recently taken place, and presented to English newspaper readers as coming from an unimpeachable source. It contained a series of distinctly unhappy observations, as for instance the Emperor's melancholy remark that he took, " as a personal insult " the " distortions and misinterpretations " of his " repeated offers of friendship to England " by a considerable section of the English press. Such an attitude on the part of the English press made his task as a ruler—never a light one at any time—almost unspeakably difficult. Worse, and far too characteristic and far too naïve, was the Emperor's assertion that, in wide sections of our lower and middle classes, the ruling feeling towards England was not a friendly one. He added that he himself was only speaking in the name of a minority of his countrymen—though a minority composed of the best elements—and added that such was the case in England also, with regard to the feeling towards Germany. That was another reason why he resented England's refusal to accept his pledged word that he was really England's best friend, a friend who nevertheless strove without ceasing, to improve relations with her.

Then came the three following enormities: 1. The Emperor had not only refused the request of the governments of France and Russia to join with them in saving the Boer Republics and, " humiliating England to the dust," replying to them that " Germany would always keep aloof from politics that could bring her into complications with a sea-power like England," but had at once sent the exact text of the confidential French and Russian notes, and his answer thereto, to Queen Victoria, who had deposited these documents in the archives at Windsor Castle. 2. In December 1899, in what was for England the darkest period of the Boer War, he had not only expressed his deep and heartfelt sympathy for his grandmamma but had, " bade one of my officers procure for me as exact an account as he could obtain of the numbers of combatants in South Africa on both sides, and of the actual position of the opposing forces." The Emperor, " with the figures before him," had " worked out what he considered to be the best plan of campaign (for England) under the circumstances," and " had submitted it to my General Staff for criticism." Then he had despatched it to England, and that document likewise, " is among the State Papers at Windsor Castle, awaiting the serenely impartial verdict of history." It was, he said, " a matter of curious coincidence " that the plan he had formulated ran on very much the same lines as the one actually adopted by Lord Roberts, and carried by him into successful operation. (In other words: in reality it was not, as had hitherto been believed, Lord Roberts who had defeated and crushed the Boers, but William II of Germany!) 3. Germany was not building a fleet against England but to be prepared for any eventualities in the Far East and the Pacific. (This of course was aimed at the Japanese, so as to give them fair warning that one fine day Germany and England might join together to fight them.)

As I read these sad effusions which could scarcely have been surpassed in tactless stupidity, I suspected in a flash that I had before me the article which, some time ago, I had received, via Herr von Jenisch, at His Majesty's request, from Rominten, and which I myself had not had time to read. I sent at once for the Councillor of Embassy, Klehmet, whose business, as reporter on duty, it had been to examine the manuscript. Having glanced through the Wolff telegram, he stammered out, in visible embarrassment, that this was the actual article that had been sent from Rominten to Norderney, and from there for examination to the Foreign Office. I asked him how he could ever have let pass such incredible expressions of opinion. He replied that he had received the definite impression that His Majesty was personally very anxious to have the whole article published, including even the passages to which I was taking objection.

When I first began to dictate my memoirs I swore to myself that all I wrote should be written as though I were under oath, just as a man in the witness-box swears he will tell the whole truth and nothing but the truth, implying also thereby that he will suppress nothing essential, will admit everything, however personally painful, not conceal any blunder or even fault, repeating even the actual words which later he may have regretted having uttered. That is why I will not conceal that when Klehmet, a Councillor of Embassy, attempted to excuse himself in that way I answered in a first burst of passion: " And haven't you learnt yet that His Majesty's personal wishes are often sheer nonsense? " I can honestly say that this was the only time in the whole of my official life when I lost my temper so completely as to forget all self-restraint. I next summoned the Head of the Imperial Chancellery, Herr von Loebell, and Hammann, the Head of the Press Bureau, to explain to them the whole situation. It was essential that we should none of us lose our heads. I suggested two possible lines of action. On the one hand we must tell the whole truth about the matter, even if I, and the whole Foreign Office, were compromised, and, on the other—this above all—we must keep the Crown well out of the coming clash of opinion. It was proved that the manuscript had been read by two other officials besides Klehmet, by the Secretary of State, von Schön, and by the Under-Secretary, Stemrich. The two latter had initialled Klehmet's report that there was nothing to object to in the article.

I then dictated this urgency report to His Majesty:

I enclose to Your Imperial and Royal Majesty a series of press-cuttings on the interview published by Colonel Stuart Wortley, and based on a conversation with Your Majesty. Almost the whole English press comments on this interview unfavourably, critically, and sceptically. Such important English personalities as Lord Roberts and Sir Edward Grey have refused to express an opinion on the subject. The French and Russian newspapers are taking the chance afforded them to publish violent attacks on Your Majesty and on German policy as a whole. But, above all, the German press, with only a few trifling exceptions, is unanimously of opinion that this interview has done grave damage to our policy and the status of our country. These attacks in the German press are unjust since Your Majesty deigned to send to me, by Baron von Jenisch, the notes of the English author for examination. I was then at Norderney, absorbed in two most serious questions (the Eastern crisis and the reform of Imperial finances) with other minor questions of home policy. For this reason I was unable personally to read this long document by Colonel Wortley, written almost illegibly on bad paper. I therefore sent it off to the Foreign Office with formal instructions that it should be most carefully examined from the point of view of its probable effect on opinion, and that I was to be sent a report of any such additions, corrections, or deletions as might seem suitable. The Foreign Office returned me the English manuscript with the remark that though certain minor changes might be made there was no valid objection to publication. It was in this sense that the Councillor of the Foreign Office, in attendance on me, wrote in answer to Baron von Jenisch. Had I myself examined the manuscript I should have begged Your Majesty on no account to authorize publication, especially not at the present juncture. If Your Majesty finds my action worthy of censure, in that, pressed as I was by other business, I did not personally read the English manuscript, and finds that I am responsible and to blame for the imprudence and lack of foresight shown by the Foreign Office, I beg to be relieved of my Chancellorship. If, however, I have not lost Your Majesty's confidence I feel I cannot remain at my post unless I am to be given the freest scope to defend Your Majesty, openly and vigorously, against every possible attack. Consequently I must beg Your Imperial and Royal Majesty for permission to state officially, in the *Norddeutsche Allgemeine Zeitung*, that the attacks against the person of the Monarch made in a large section of the press are entirely unjust, since Your Majesty had sent me the English author's manuscript, which I myself submitted to the Foreign Office, which proposed only trifling alterations.

In the margin of this urgency report the Emperor noted that I had not lost his confidence, that he would approve the publication of my statement in the *Norddeutsche Allgemeine Zeitung*. To my remarks on the deplorable effect produced by the article he wrote: " Quite right." At the end of my report he had added: " It can be added that the manuscript is a résumé of a number of conversations I had last autumn with various people in England, and that it was by their wish—since they seemed so confident of the English public—that the substance of what I said has been made available to as wide a section of their fellow-countrymen as possible. I consented to their entreaties in the fashion described above."

As to the effect produced in England I might have added to my emergency report that, as soon as the *Daily Telegraph* article became known, a member had asked in the House of Commons if it were true that the plan of campaign which ended the Boer War—a war which England had always imagined had really been ended by Lord Roberts—had been drawn up by the German Emperor, and, if this were so, would the Minister of War, Haldane, publish the document? The Minister answered that no such document could be found in the War Office archives, nor in the possession of any department connected therewith. " Consequently," Haldane continued, " I am not in a position to fulfil the wish of those who want the document published." To this answer Hansard added: (" loud laughter from all parts of the House.") Though this laughter doubtless expressed the private feelings of their government on the whimsies of the German Kaiser I am bound to admit that, officially, the English remained correct and friendly. I was informed confidentially, through the English Ambassador in Berlin, that the government would do all in its power to ease my position, which the article had rendered so delicate, and would in any case put a stop to complications. I caused the following to be published on the front page of the *Norddeutsche Allgemeine Zeitung*:

A considerable section of the home and foreign press has directed severe criticism against the person of His Majesty the Emperor, in connection with a recent article, published in the English *Daily Telegraph*, on the false supposition that the Emperor had permitted its publication without foreknowledge of those responsible for the Foreign Policy of the Empire. This belief is altogether unfounded. A private citizen of England had submitted to His Majesty an article in which were summed up a series of conversations our Emperor had had, at different times, with various other persons in England. The intention behind the request was to make these observations of His Majesty known to as wide a circle of English readers as possible, thus furthering the cause of good Anglo-German understanding. His Majesty forwarded the article to the Chancellor, who submitted it to our Foreign Office with the request that it should be carefully read through. Since no objection was raised in the report returned by the Foreign Office permission to publish was given, and it appeared in the *Daily Telegraph*. When the Imperial Chancellor learned of its publication and contents he informed His Majesty that he, personally, had never seen the draft of the article, and that, had he seen it, he would have advised against its publication, but that he considered himself solely responsible for what had occurred, and absolved the officials and departments under him. At the same time the Imperial Chancellor tendered his resignation to His Majesty, which the Emperor refused to accept, but consented to Prince Bülow's proposal that the latter, by making public the above statement of the facts, should be enabled finally to dispose of any criticism directed against the person of our Emperor.

Loebell, and above all Hammann, were very much against publishing the above, and considered that I took more blame than was due to me. Hammann remarked: " Does Your Excellency really think it necessary to commit *hara-kiri* like this, simply in order to shield the real culprits?" Bethmann-Hollweg, then Vice-Chancellor, and Secretary of State for the Interior, said much the same to me. He advised me, I am convinced with the best intentions, to sacrifice the Foreign Office officials, instead of shielding them and taking all the blame on myself. But I have never considered it very estimable to behave like the Russian peasant who, with wolves on his track, first throws to them his sheep, then his child, and finally his wife, to save himself. I wanted most of all to keep the Crown well out of the firing line. But it had only too soon become apparent that this would be beyond my power, and would, I may add to-day, have been just as impossible to any other Minister, in the circumstances.

The tempest which this article raised in Germany was not caused by the mere error committed in its tactless publication. Such political observations and remarks as the Emperor had made in the *Daily Telegraph* were only the decisive drops in a cup already filled to the brim with discontent at the ever-recurring aberrations, the gossiping imprudence, of His Majesty. This publication, as by some sudden slap in the face, had roused the whole nation to the memory of all the political faults, through a reign that had lasted twenty years, which William II had permitted himself to commit. All the warnings, all the dismal prophecies, of the man he had dismissed from office, Prince Bismarck, returned into the public mind. A dark foreboding ran through many Germans that such clumsy, incautious, over-hasty—such stupid, even puerile speech and action on the part of the supreme Head of the State, could lead to only one thing—catastrophe. The Emperor himself, if only for a passing instant, felt the earth tremble beneath his feet. He had intended,

at the end of October, to pay a short visit to Kiel and Hamburg, but
he abandoned the idea, on receiving a letter from Ballin persuading
him against the latter city where hostile demonstrations might be
expected.

This *avis au lecteur* gave the Emperor an unpleasant shock.
On 31st October, two days after the article's appearance, on the day
that followed my announcement in the *Norddeutsche Allgemeine
Zeitung*, he paid me a call which lasted two hours. He was, as he
always was at moments of crisis, very pale, very pitiable. I assured
him that I was ready, now as ever, not only to do my plain duty and
shield him as well as I could, but to draw off the fire on to myself,
to insist on the mistakes of my officials. But I did not conceal from
him the fact that there was bound to be yet another full dress debate
in the Reichstag on the so often criticized personal rule of His
Majesty. I reminded him how, exactly two years before, on 14th
November 1906, I had declared in the Reichstag that a Minister
might well be embarrassed, in the very interests of Monarchy, by
any excessive personal intervention of the sovereign, any overween-
ing conception of monarchic privilege. Such a Minister, I had
said, might not feel equal to shouldering his weight of responsibility
before the Crown, the nation, and history. And this time also I
should be forced to speak in the same strain, and that in the Imperial
interest. His Majesty answered very calmly: " Go ahead; say what
you like." But, almost with entreaty, he added, " But, however
you do it, get us out of this; bring us through! " This trustful,
childlike attitude touched me more than I can say, all the more since
he had not said a word of reproach on the blunder of the Foreign
Office, a department which as a rule he rather disliked.

Here I must confess another fault, but this time intellectual, not
moral. I ought to have insisted, unconditionally, on the Emperor's
staying in Berlin during the crisis which, by this time, was upon us.
If he had, I could have guided him further. He would have been
forced to see for himself the state of public opinion in the capital,
the feeling in parliament, the high tension and excitement, even in
intellectual circles, and so might have judged very differently, and
much more justly than he did, my conduct and whole line of action.
But he saw it all from the safe haven of Donaueschingen, surrounded
by men many of whom were frivolous and ignorant. His Majesty
had been extremely anxious to meet the Archduke Francis Ferdinand
once again, and had urged that, in view of the Bosnian crisis, such a
meeting was quite essential. He was also longing for Donaueschingen where fox-hunting, cabaret entertainments, and every kind of
amusement were in prospect. I yielded to his wish because I told

myself that at a time of such agitation in every political sphere and
in parliament, the burdens I had to shoulder would be easier if I
were not forced to make a daily journey from Berlin to the Neues
Palais at Potsdam, where the Court, unless it were travelling, always
remained till after Christmas.   And before the Emperor left Berlin
I warned him, both verbally and in writing, not to make any kind of
agreement or promise on the subject of the Dardanelles, neither in
Vienna nor at Konopischt, nor to the Austrians staying at Donaueschingen, one of whom was Count Ottokar Czernin, later Minister
of Foreign Affairs.   On this point at least I insisted that we must
keep our hands entirely free.   As far as the Dardanelles were concerned there must be no active opposition to Russia's wishes.

Before I speak of the Reichstag debate on the article in the
Daily Telegraph I should like to give a brief account of what happened
to the officials responsible.   As a sequel to our somewhat stormy
interview, immediately after its appearance, Klehmet sent me a long
memorandum, which on the whole merely repeated his excuse that
His Majesty had seemed " most peremptorily " to demand that
that effort should be published.   He had had no other aim, in his
first submission to the Chancellor, than to leave me free, should I
so desire, to edit " certain passages " myself.   Klehmet himself
had been convinced that the Emperor most particularly wished to
profit to the full by this interesting offer from an Englishman.   He
had concluded from an article—unknown to me—which had
appeared in *Fleischer's Review*, that the essential points in the English
article had already become known to the public, and had, consequently, all the less reason to oppose the " peremptory " wishes
of the Emperor.   He had further believed it to be a question of
appeasing English sentiment, *à tout prix*, in view of the projected
naval agreements attempted by Haldane and Lloyd George but
rejected by His Majesty and Tirpitz.   It might therefore be a case
for applying the old Bismarckian principle of achieving one's main
object first, *i.e.*, in this case of working for the immediate improvement of our whole relationship with England to the exclusion of all
other considerations, including both the Russian and the French.
By the fact that it was guaranteed by Wortley it had seemed almost
certain that the article would produce a good effect among the
English.   He had had no decisive argument with which to oppose
His Majesty's view: had supposed that no one wanted his opinion
on the advisability of publication: had been unable to delete certain
passages since the whole made a " closely knit argument."   The
plan of campaign which the Emperor was said to have elaborated
had seemed to him indispensable, because it formed the " culminat-

ing point in the demonstration." Besides, had not two such highly
placed officials as the Secretary of State, von Schön, and Stemrich,
the Under-Secretary, signed, without any modification, the précis
he had drawn up to submit to them? He had also said to himself
that there could be no question of the authenticity of Imperial declarations; that such declarations, even if the Emperor refused his
permission to have them published, would be sure to get published
elsewhere, and that, therefore, it was more dignified for His Majesty
to admit their authority at once without having to be obliged to do so
later. In conclusion Klehmet reminded me that the Wolff Agency
had issued the *Daily Telegraph* article without any reference to him,
or any authorization from the Chancellor, on the sole authority of
Geheimrat Hammann.

These last observations were justified. It is certain that the
Emperor's oft-repeated assertions, made with such precision and
emphasis, and in so sensational a form in the hearing of so many
different Englishmen, must in the end have leaked out and reached
the public. It is also true that Wolff's Agency had reproduced the
contents of the article without having asked my permission, or even
Klehmet's advice. Holstein, who was always delighted to say anything bad against the people with whom he happened to be on bad
terms, tried to the day of his death, to persuade me that Hammann,
of malice aforethought, had " forgotten " to get my authorization
in order to create trouble for me. I prefer to think that that was just
a blunder on the part of the occasionally blundering Hammann.

But lamer, far, than Klehmet's excuses was the pitiable attempt
to defend himself I received from the Minister, von Müller, whose
responsibility was certainly far greater than that of any Councillor
of Legation. Müller began by saying that he had had no time to
examine the manuscript with the care which my instructions enjoined. When I asked him next day, very pointedly whether, really,
he had examined the thing at all, with anything like care and
sufficiency, he had been too ashamed to confess that, in fact, he had
omitted to do so. He " lay low " until my retirement, when he sent
my wife a lachrymose letter to say how very deeply he regretted it.
For years he had shared my joys and sorrows, even the political,
etc. The struggles I had had to endure had aroused Müller's
deepest sympathy. He added a consoling acknowledgment of the
numerous " acts of kindness " he had received, for so many years,
in my house, in which he had known unfailing friendship. Such
kindness would never be absent from his memory. It had earned
us his " unchanging gratitude; when once you have made this
painful break with the habits and connections that were dear to you,

I am happy in the thought that sunnier days await you, either on the North Sea, in the villa which you have so charmingly enlarged, or else in the Eternal City."

But most lamentable of all was the attitude of the Secretary of State, von Schön. He simply took to his bed. His Belgian wife wrote to me, in her very indifferent German, that her husband had had an " *arrêt de coeur.*" Imagining he suffered from a dangerous heart attack I sent von Schön my doctor and friend Geheimrat Renvers. In half-an-hour Renvers returned, with a smile, to tell me that I need not worry. The illness of the Secretary of State was nothing graver than " nerves," brought on by his terror of the difficulties his carelessness had caused. He was simply scared at the thought of having to defend the Foreign Office and its methods before the Reichstag. He was even more afraid of the coming friction between myself and the Emperor. I sent Schön away on long leave and summoned Kiderlen-Wächter, our Minister to Bucharest, to Berlin, where I put him in temporary charge of the Foreign Office. Least culpable of all was Stemrich, the Under-Secretary, who had only been in office a short time and could not have been expected to appreciate the full gravity of the article. This excellent fellow was soon to be taken ill, and he died prematurely. Klehmet, whom I really rather pitied, I ensconced, not long before my retirement, in Athens, as German delegate to the International Financial Commission. There he lived many happy years:

> " *im Schatten des Ölbaums*
> *wo flüsternd leis zu der Ulme sich neigt die Platane.*" [1]

Long after the *Daily Telegraph* affair Felix von Müller shot himself. But I am very far from believing that self-reproach and remorse at his own bad service were what put the pistol into his hand. He was no Brutus to fall on his own sword. His mother was a member of the Stumm family which has produced several distinguished men, among others Baron Ferdinand von Stumm-Halberg, nicknamed " King Stumm," the well-known industrialist and deputy, one of the ablest and most high-principled men in the economic life of Germany. But among the Stumms there were several inflicted by hereditary insanity. I am inclined to think those people right who told me that Felix von Müller took his life in a fit of madness.

---

[1]   " . . . in the shade of the olive
Where, whispering softly, the plane-tree bends to the elm."

CHAPTER XXIV

Discussion of the situation in the Commission for Foreign Affairs of the Bundesrat; confidential discussion between the leading Ministers— The feeling in the Prussian Ministry—Particularly sharp criticism in the Conservative press—Debate in the Reichstag on Imperial conversations in England—Another indiscreet interview: I manage to prevent its publication.

BEFORE the re-assembly of the Reichstag there took place, according to old custom, a meeting of the Commission for Foreign Affairs of the Bundesrat, in the course of which I presented detailed information regarding our Foreign Policy, the Bosnian problem, the Casablanca affair, and our whole relationship with England. The Commission were unanimous in expressing to me the gratitude of the Federal Governments and their absolute confidence in myself. All evinced the lively and sincere desire that I might continue for many years to direct the home and Foreign Policy of the Empire. Before they left the hall, after the meeting, the members began a frank, informal discussion of the situation created by the Emperor's conversations in England. On all sides I was warned, with moderation, but none the less seriously and forcibly, that things could not continue as they were, that the Emperor must learn, at last, to control his attitude and his words, or the Monarchist idea in Germany, and with it the Empire itself, would sustain very serious hurt. From several quarters it was suggested that the German princes would do well to appear, *in corpore* in Berlin, and personally express their anxiety to the Emperor. Rather sharply I opposed this suggestion, which, I said, I could not even discuss. Such a " raising of shields " on the part of the Federal Princes would recall the bad old days of the Empire. Abroad it would be interpreted as a demonstration of particularism on the part of the Princes against the Imperial Crown. Since this crown was the symbol of German unity, things would go from bad to worse. I announced that I would make myself fully responsible for inducing the Emperor to conduct himself in a quieter, more seemly fashion in future. That same evening I gave a dinner-party, to which I invited all the members of the Bundesrat present at the Commission for Foreign Affairs and the members of the Prussian State Ministry. These worthy gentlemen were so moved by what had happened in England that they importuned,

351

not only me, but my wife, who always kept well apart from politics. Herr Bethmann-Hollweg, the Secretary of State for the Interior, was among the most emotional of them all. He exclaimed to her, with solemnity and pathos: " You must keep on repeating this to your husband, the prince, whom I respect so deeply: ' You are not Court Chancellor but National Chancellor! ' "

Later, this same Bethmann had not the courage to justify, or even defend to the Emperor, my attitude in the November debate.

Even greater excitement was shown by the Prussian State Ministry. The Ministers, at a meeting to which I summoned them, all declared that, as Royal Prussian Ministers, it was their duty to warn His Majesty most emphatically against further errors of the kind, in the interests—nay it might even be for the salvation—of the Prussian Crown. The necessity for greater self-control, more seriousness of purpose, must be urged. The Kaiser must be implored to remember his great ancestors and follow the example they had bequeathed him. The Minister for War, von Einem, announced that, even among officers, there was growing discontent in the army with the actions and attitude of His Majesty, with his abuse of personal prerogative, his temperamental outbursts and caprice. Their effect was demoralising, even dangerous. Undoubtedly the famous and honourable traditions of our army were still alive and potent in its ranks: if it ever came to actual war the officers would behave as magnificently as they had done in 1870, in 1866, in 1813, and throughout the whole Seven Years' War. But the prestige of the Crown, the monarch's position with his officers, was less firmly established than it had been, and that was His Majesty's fault. Prussian kings had been more gifted or less gifted in the military sense, but no past king of Prussia had been content with merely " playing at soldiers," with working out sham manœuvres, with such puerile externals as new uniforms, " silly trifles " like the changing of parade formations; or had so confused appearance and reality in this, the most important of all spheres. The Secretary of State, von Tirpitz, spoke in the same sense. He declared that the Navy, " His Majesty's pet arm," thought just as the Army did. Sailors were certainly very grateful for the Emperor's interest in the Fleet, for all that he had done, and still was doing, for it. But almost all naval officers were convinced that the most important thing their Kaiser could do, for the lasting benefit of both services, would be to maintain a greater reserve, to show a more serious, discreet and practical spirit in politics.

Herr von Bethmann-Hollweg concluded the meeting with the remark that the first duty of any Premier was to say quite frankly to His Majesty: "So far but no further!" The Chancellor's duty was to make it clear to the Reichstag that, in future, the Emperor would abstain from speech or action both dangerous to the authority of the Crown and the peace of the country. But I must not omit to add that, a few months later, when I asked to see the report of the speeches at this memorable meeting, the Under-Secretary of State at the Prussian Ministry replied, not without a certain embarrassment that, at the earnest request of several members, the Ministry had suppressed the report, "in the interests of the dignity of the Crown." On 6th November, the *Konservative Korrespondenz*, the organ of the Conservative party, printed a semi-official announcement in which the following occurred: " We see with some anxiety that certain declarations of His Majesty, despite the fact that, assuredly, he spoke with the noblest motive, have tended to compromise our Foreign Policy, partly because of the false interpretations put upon them. Urged as we are by our desire to safeguard Imperial authority from criticism and debate which do not beseem it, and firmly convinced that we have a duty to shield the German nation from every embarrassment and injury, we feel obliged to express (though most respectfully) the wish that in future the Emperor will maintain greater reserve in his conversations."

Commenting on this manifesto from the Conservative leaders the *Kreuzzeitung* declared: " Such a courageous attitude on the part of our Conservative chiefs is a thing for which we must be profoundly grateful. May their courage be of benefit to our Fatherland! Whether or not it achieves the result at which it aims it has shown, at least, that the whole Conservative party may rest assured of the insight and disinterested action of its leaders, just as these, in their turn, may trust the party as their guide."

Indignation against the Emperor spread far and wide. It was sharpened by several tactless accounts in the press of the entertainment offered to His Majesty by Prince Max Fürstenberg at Donaueschingen. In these there was no mention of anything but the splendid fox-hunting, the brilliant and amusing performances of a cabaret show, brought over from Frankfurt to the Fürstenberg's castle for the occasion, etc. Via August Eulenburg, the Chief Marshal of the Court and Minister of the Household, I called the attention of those in control at Donaueschingen to the bad effect these frivolities were having on the nation, whereupon the Emperor, with his usual impulsive change of front, offered what he called " a sop," to public opinion and, on the day on which it was my duty to reply in the Reichstag to an interpellation on his English interview (8th November 1908), he took occasion to honour Count

Zeppelin, whom before he had always pooh-poohed and taken little notice of, with a most melodramatic bestowal of the Black Eagle. After the investiture he thrice embraced the Count, and delivered a speech in which (*anno* 1908!) he called him the greatest German of the twentieth century. It seemed a little premature.

On the same day the debate began in the Reichstag. National-Liberals, Independents, Socialists, Conservatives, and the Party of the Reich, had all many questions to ask. The Chief of the National-Liberals, Ernst Bassermann, opened the debate in a measured and dignified speech. He said that the Imperial Chancellor had pursued, throughout his whole term of office—and notably in the dangerous Bosnian crisis—a policy which was generally approved; a policy of realism and firmness. He then protested against the incautious and dangerous statement of the Emperor that the majority of the German nation were unfriendly or even hostile to England. The gravest thing of all, said Bassermann, was not that such a remark should have been published but the fact that it should ever have been made. " Even if such words had escaped publicity the fact remains that, in England, they would have been carried from mouth to mouth. And how many other sayings of the kind may not be lying recorded, at this moment, in the secret archives of foreign countries! " Bassermann, at the end of his speech, protested against the Emperor's remark that our fleet was destined to carry out a policy of German Imperialism in the Pacific. The Reichstag ought to declare explicitly that the German Naval Law was defensive in character, that the mission of the German fleet was to guard our coasts, our rivers, and our ports. But, above all, that the great majority of sensible and peace-loving Germans was far from feeling any hostility against either England or Japan.

The Socialist leader, Herr Singer, spoke very moderately. He may have felt that the more the Sovereign " put his foot in it " the better it would be for Socialists. But it is also possible that he spoke from motives less selfishly partizan. On the morning of 10th November my friend Renvers certainly told me how, on the previous evening, he had met Herr Singer at the house of some friends, and that Singer had quite spontaneously assured him that the Social-Democrats would create no further difficulties for me, and had no intention of any violent attack. The Socialists, so he had said, did not want war, and they considered that in spite of our profound political differences, my Chancellorship was the best guarantee of peace amid the difficulties of the Foreign situation.

Herr von Heydebrand, the Conservative spokesman, spoke far

more severely than Herr Singer. In his opinion the anxiety which
had spread throughout all Germany was most grave. This excitement could not truly be understood if related merely to present
happenings. It must be openly said that we were dealing with a
state of unrest that had been gathering force for many years. This
feeling had even spread to circles most attached to the Kaiser and
the Reich. A mere Foreign Office blunder was not the gravest
aspect of this case. Its real importance lay much deeper. Conservatives had always seen my point when I had touched on this very
serious question of how far a Chancellor could be answerable for
the spontaneous declaration of the Emperor. "But," continued
Herr von Heydebrand, "it is possible that now, on looking back,
the Chancellor has himself begun to feel that he did not always show
sufficient energy; that, perhaps, it would have been wise to speak still
more strongly; that, in future, directness will be necessary if such
unfortunate incidents are to be avoided. It would be most unjust if,
at this moment, we forgot all that Prince Bülow has achieved for
the Empire and the German people, if we let this single incident
efface the significance of so much toil, so much loyalty, talent, and
patriotism." Herr von Heydebrand concluded in the wish that the
Chancellor's reply would be sincere and definite, and give reason to
hope for the future.

The speech of Prince Hatzfeldt, Grand Duke of Trachenberg,
the leader of the Empire group, was as flat as the lemonade in
Schiller's play. He contented himself with saying that, in his
opinion, what mattered most was the affirmation of monarchist
loyalty in Germany and that, in present circumstances, he felt he
had nothing to add. That meant that the noble duke had not yet
given up all hope of one day filling the corner seat on the ministerial
bench of the Reichstag, and that, feeble though his prospects might
appear of ever becoming Imperial Chancellor, he did not intend to
spoil them with his sovereign. Wiemer too, the leader of the Independents, would blow neither hot nor cold.

I spoke after Hermann Hatzfeldt. I think I may say that, in
parliament, I have always had a flair for what Italians call the *am-
biente*—the feeling around one in the place where one speaks, the
"atmosphere in the auditorium." I was aware that I must be frank,
and very serious, and indeed I felt so. Above all it was my duty to
calm the resentment provoked abroad by the indiscretions of the
Emperor, and to remove the mistrust he had aroused in England,
Russia, France, and Japan. I declared that nothing the Emperor
had related about Franco-Russian intervention at the time of the
Boer War was new. All that had been known for some time, and

could not be called a " revelation," though His Majesty had indeed laid on the colours rather too thickly. I also corrected the story of a plan of campaign. There had been no question of a properly worked out and detailed plan, but simply of " maxims," of " purely academic conceptions." Here I was interrupted by the laughter of the Social-Democrats, whom I called to order, reminding them that this was a serious debate, that the matters we were discussing were very grave, and of far-reaching political significance. I begged the house to hear me in silence, and it did. I next said that the Chief of the General Staff, General von Moltke, and his predecessor, General Count Schlieffen, had both reported that, though the Staff had drawn up a memorandum for the Emperor on the subject of the Boer War, it had been only the kind of memorandum which it drew up on every war, great or small. Both had assured me, however, that the General Staff had neither examined nor transmitted to England any plan of campaign or other similar work of His Majesty on the subject of the war in South Africa, or any document which bore any resemblance to such a plan. This was an exact statement of the facts. Actually all that William II had told his English friends about the share he claimed in the crushing of the unfortunate Boers had been mere bragging humbug from end to end. Further I said that many expressions of opinion in the *Daily Telegraph* article had been most unhappily chosen. " This applies particularly," I declared, amid loud applause from all parts of the House, " to the passage where the Emperor alleges that the majority of the German people is hostile to England. Between Germany and England there have been misunderstandings—serious and regrettable misunderstandings—but I know I have the whole House with me in saying that the entire German nation desires peaceful and cordial relations with England, relations based on mutual esteem, and I recognize that the speakers of all parties have expressed themselves in that sense to-day. The passage which treats of our interests in the Pacific is couched in the most exaggerated terms. This passage has been interpreted in a sense unfriendly to Japan. Such interpretation is quite unjustified, since we have had no other aim in the Far East than to obtain and hold for German commerce its fair share in Far Eastern trade, in a region with a great economic future. We have never had the least idea of risking naval adventures in the Pacific. Aggressive designs in the Far East can be deduced from German Naval construction as little as aggressive designs in Europe. His Majesty moreover fully agrees with those responsible for conducting German Foreign Policy in honouring the tremendous progress which the Japanese people has made by its political energy and military valour. German policy is in no sense directed towards depriving the Japanese people of the full enjoyment and development of what it has won."

Having thus toned down, and rectified as best I could, the most harmful of the Emperor's remarks—I use the word in the sense of their effect on foreign countries, even more than of that on the Reichstag—I went on, once I felt that the passion of my hearers was abating, to a direct defence of His Majesty. " You do grievous injustice to the Emperor," I cried to the Reichstag, " if you doubt the sincerity of his motives, his idealism, his deep love of his country." And I uttered the words which, once the storm had passed, were to be used against me by every toady and sycophant, every intriguer and time-server who played on the Emperor's conceit. I spoke them in the full conviction, a conviction I retain today, that to say them was a sheer necessity, if confidence were ever to be restored in either the Reichstag or the nation; if William II and his people were ever to understand each other again.

" Gentlemen," I said, " it is certain that the appearance of this interview in England has not produced there the effect His Majesty desired; that here in Germany it has caused the profoundest emotion, the gravest heart-searchings and regrets. His knowledge of this—these last few days have convinced me of it—will cause His Majesty, even in future *private* conversations, to maintain that reserve indispensable to the interests of any consistent Foreign Policy, and to those of the authority of the Crown. (Here a burst of applause, particularly from the benches of the Right.) " But if this were not so," I added, to the prolonged acclamation of both National-Liberals and Conservatives, " neither I myself, nor any successor of mine could accept the responsibility of office." I then admitted that, immediately after the *Daily Telegraph* article had appeared, I had asked to be allowed to resign, since I could not doubt its disastrous effects for an instant. I had taken this step without regret, though, later, at the express desire of His Majesty, I had made what was perhaps the gravest, most unwilling decision of all my political life, the decision to remain in office. This I had done solely because I felt it my public duty to continue in the Emperor's service, to remain at my country's disposal through this unusually vexed and difficult crisis. (Here again loud applause.) I did not know how long I should keep my post. I would only add one word, which had to be added: "At an hour, when much in the world was again in a state of vexed uncertainty, an hour at which it behoved us to guard our position abroad, to show no sign of aggression and yet to maintain our interests calmly and firmly—an hour at which the general situation caused deep anxiety, and demanded the most serious attention—we had no right to let ourselves become demoralized, to allow an unlucky episode to become a catastrophe. I felt I must refrain from all criticism of those extravagances of which we had just been made the victims; but certainly no one could neglect the warning we all had received in the last few days." (I emphasized the words " no one " and " all.")   " Yet none of this was any justification for showing the world a divided, disconcerted front, a front which could not fail to give our adversaries the impression that at home and abroad the Empire had received a crippling blow."   I ended with the words: " It is for qualified representatives of the nation to show a prudence which befits the seriousness of the hour.   I do not speak for myself, I speak for the country.   At this juncture your support is not a favour; it is a duty which this august assembly cannot escape."

When, amid a roar of cheering, I sat down, I felt that the battle had been won.

The next speaker was von Hertling of the Centre Party.   He was calm and moderate.   He agreed with Bassermann that the substance of the English article was more important than the blunder of the Imperial Chancellery in having allowed it to be published.   In spite of all the tension then existing between the Centrists and myself, Herr von Hertling added: That the Imperial Chancellor had " most loyally " made himself responsible for the blunder of his subordinates, as well as for the indiscretions of the irresponsible Emperor.   The significance and inner meaning of the incident in the realms of Ministerial responsibility must be that in future, for those answerable there must exist a " thus far, but no further."   He assumed that I had offered my resignation less on account of my failure to prevent the publication of the article than because of what it contained.   He also supposed that when I yielded to His Majesty, and consented to remain in office I had obtained definite guarantees for the future.   The German people had a right to demand that an Imperial Chancellor should never again be put in the position of having to prevent such incidents.   At the end of the debate the anti-Semite, Liebermann von Sonnenberg, delivered a crude and insolent speech, handling the Emperor far more roughly than Singer or even than Hertling and Wiemer.

As I walked home through the Tiergarten I met Ernst Bassermann.   He shook my hand with the words: " Your speech to-day was a masterpiece of oratory and politics."   Then he added thoughtfully, " But how will things go now between you and the Emperor? " When I said I could only hope that His Majesty would set political necessity and the welfare of the Empire above petty personal feeling Bassermann answered: " Yes, if he were at all like his father and grandfather. But he's so vain." And Bassermann was right. For a time in the first days after the debate and throughout the winter that followed it, the more generous side of William II's nature prevailed. In the end wounded pride and morbid vanity got the better of him—though I must add, in justice, that this was mainly due to the influence of self-seeking *arrivistes*. So destiny followed its course. Exactly ten years after I had spoken thus in the Emperor's defence—in the November, that is to say, of 1918— under a grey, dismal sky, in pouring rain, William II was crossing the Dutch frontier as a fugitive.

Next day (11th November 1908) the debate in the Reichstag continued. Miquel, who possessed a basic knowledge of the German parliamentary system, once said to me that the art of public speaking had been so little cultivated and appreciated in Germany, that our political temperament was so dull, our political gift so mediocre, that every Reichstag debate ended flatly on the second day. In this second day's debate the deputy von Normann read the following, in the name of the Conservative party: " We consider that yesterday's speech from the Imperial Chancellor expressed the position as a whole, and need therefore only add our hope that Prince Bülow will give us such a sequel as the welfare of the country demands."

Herr von Normann was a man who did honour to his party and to Parliament. He had formerly been in the Red (Zieten's) Hussars, when, as orderly-officer to Prince Friedrich Karl, on the eve of the battle of Königgrätz, he had taken a daring ride through the enemy outposts, to inform the Crown Prince of the spot where Prince Friedrich, on the following day, hoped to join forces with his cousin. After him came the Württemberg Democrat, Konrad Haussmann. For many years he and his brother, Friedrich, had exercised a certain influence over the policy of the South German People's Party, in conjunction with Herr von Payer, a man of no exceptional ability, but honest, and well-intentioned, who later, in the last transition period before the Revolution, became Vice-Chancellor.

Konrad and Friedrich Haussmann were twins. August Stein, the *Frankfurter Zeitung* correspondent, who ought to have known, since he himself was a Democrat, used to say that, of the brothers Haussmann, Karl was the one who knew even less about politics. His speech on 11th November certainly achieved no heights above the level of the average pleading solicitor in a little Swabian town. Then, after a solid and fairly restrained speech by the Socialist

Heine, there followed an unfortunate little incident the unwilling hero of which was my friend Kiderlen.

Because I knew that Kiderlen was a strong-nerved and courageous man who was always ready with a speech, I had asked him if he would care to say a word on behalf of the Foreign Office which had been so sharply, and for the most part so unjustly, criticized. Kiderlen consented at once with delight, and at the end of the debate on 11th November, he rose to speak. What he said was really not bad. He spoke far more fluently than Tschirschky, than the Hereditary Prince of Hohenlohe-Langenburg, than Stübel, Jagow, and others who, before or since, have defended the Foreign Office. But he took the wrong tone. On his declaring himself empowered to announce to the deputies that the government intended to begin their reform of the Foreign Office, which the Reichstag as a body had demanded, by submitting proposals to increase the Foreign Office staff, there was a general outburst of hilarity. Since then we have seen, again and again, that no German republican government ever considers any drastic reform of the Foreign Office, but that each, on the contrary, has doubled and trebled its staff to find jobs for republican party-members, and that without protest from the Reichstag. But poor Kiderlen aroused even more and greater merriment by his praises of the conscientious spirit and industry of Foreign Office officials and, worse still, of our wonderful system of organization, a system which was the envy of other lands, whose Foreign Ministers strove without success to copy it. At last there was such a burst of laughter that Kiderlen was forced to break off his speech. But this mirth had another cause besides the actual arguments of the speaker. Though the Reichstag, before the November revolution, never indulged in such wild, unbridled scenes as occurred from time to time in the French and Italian Chambers, it did not mind an occasional joke. This jollity was of much the same kind as that which reigned at student gatherings, at banquets in the regimental messes, at the many kinds of association dinner, in the old, happy, pre-war Germany. Kiderlen's débâcle was also due to his pronounced Swabian accent, and, *horrible dictu*, to the extraordinary yellow waistcoat he wore.

While the House remained in this rather undignified mood I was asked by several members to speak after Kiderlen, so as to refute any attack against the Emperor, but more definitely than on the previous day. On the evening before, I had already dictated a few final words in this sense to Hammann, and was therefore prepared for all eventualities. Both Hammann and Loebell had strongly advised me to end the debate on such a note. But my deputy to the Reichstag, Herr von Bethmann, had been just as definite in opposing them. I have since often been told that Bethmann-Hollweg intentionally gave me bad advice. That, I have never believed, and I still refuse to believe it, though I have since lost many illusions on Bethmann-Hollweg. And I am still of opinion that I was right in adding nothing to what I had said the day before. Certainly this well-considered silence of mine was used by those who crept away into mouse-holes during the storm, to persuade the Emperor that I was a tepid and ineffective defender. But I need not add that, had I spoken a second time, these intriguers would have suggested to His Majesty that I was spoiling the effect of my first speech, that I had been misled by my vanity, my notorious inclination to be forever standing up in the Reichstag in order to let it admire my eloquence, and so, without any good reason, had made him again the central figure in the debate. I therefore repeat: I should have weakened the effect of my first speech by consenting to make a second. The nation would have seen in such a speech no more than a concession to the Emperor whom it wanted to alter his methods of ruling. I should have forfeited the great confidence it had placed in me. Finally any fresh speech on my part would have meant fresh answers from the deputies, and the debate would have gone on for ever. I was right in not speaking a second time, especially in what was, then, the obvious state of feeling in parliament.

My speech of 10th November was acclaimed by the whole Right Wing press. The Socialist papers reproached the Reichstag with not having demanded guarantees that this would be the end of personal rule; it had let itself be bluffed by Prince von Bülow. The chief Vienna newspaper, the *Neue Freie Presse*, commented on the debate as follows: "Prince von Bülow, who never gave a more sympathetic impression than at this moment, in one of the most difficult situations with which any Minister could be faced, spoke not as a courtier but as a statesman, responsible for the conduct of a policy."

The Paris *Figaro* declared: "*Le discours du Prince de Bülow semblera un peu étrange dans sa forme brutale, à peine voilée par quelques précautions de langage. Mais il faut reconnaître qu'il correspondait à une situation non moins étrange et à peu près sans précédent. Le ministre n'avait qu'un moyen d'en sortir: La franchise entière. Et il en a heureusement usé.*" The whole English press treated my speech as a sign of the friendly attitude of the German government towards England, and expressed the hope that the German people shared that attitude. Such bold criticism of Imperial mistakes, not only in the

German press but in the Reichstag was, it declared, a happy omen for constitutionalism and parliamentary freedom in Germany.

For the moment not a word came from the Emperor. From his suite I learned that he was by turns excited and depressed. His gloom had been increased by his discovery that the public honours paid to Count Zeppelin, had failed, through their very exaggeration, in the effect for which His Majesty had hoped. Most Germans considered it an excellent thing that their Kaiser should duly honour that tireless, never discouraged, never despairing pioneer of aviation. But these same shrewd, ordinary intelligent people shook their heads as they read, in the address to Zeppelin, issued at once through Wolff's by Imperial orders: " It cannot be sufficiently emphasized that what we have witnessed to-day has been one of the greatest moments in human culture. I thank my God, with every other German, that He has thought our people worthy of making it ours."

When this further piece of Imperial eccentricity (11th November 1908) became known to Berlin it had a bad effect on the Reichstag. The country, too, only saw in it a further proof of the Kaiser's mental instability.

Meanwhile the whole foreign press continued to criticize the personality, behaviour, and methods of government of the Emperor, more sharply than it had ever done before. The English papers still maintained that Imperial protestations of friendship for England appeared merely a somewhat undignified endeavour to curry favour. In any case the opinions he had expressed could only be welcomed by his adversaries. France and Russia would lose all confidence in German discretion, as a result of these, all too candid, revelations of their plans for intervention in the Boer War. Japan would once more become mistrustful. The alleged " plan of campaign " was simply an incredible story, an insult to England. Even in unimportant English papers the Emperor was mocked as the " real winner of the Boer War." At the same time it was reported that Lord Roberts had been deeply offended, and had only with difficulty been dissuaded from returning His Majesty the Black Eagle, with which he had been invested seven years previously, to the deep disgust of German public opinion, then all in favour of the Boers.

The great French newspapers were ironic over what they called the " fantastic romanticism " of the Emperor's " personal " policy. In Russia the greatest, most influential Russian newspaper, the *Novoie Vremia*, declared that no Russian could ever have believed such words the Emperor's, unless he had seen them officially in print. William II had dealt " tactlessly and treacherously " with

France and Russia. The Italian press was equally severe in its judgments of the Emperor's policy and rule: William II appeared to be doing his best to embroil Germany with the whole world. The Japanese papers declared that the Kaiser's remarks on the Far East were profitless and would do much harm. What the Japanese could not understand was why it should seem good to the Kaiser to arm against Japanese development and the awakening of China.

But precisely, and above all, in England did these fresh out-pourings of William II produce the effect of a hailstorm in early summer. Their result would have been even more disastrous had I been unable, just in time, to prevent the publication of an inter-view given by the Emperor to an American journalist, Hale, in entire contradiction of the opinions formerly expressed at High-cliffe. In it that same William II, who before had expressed such violent, undying friendship for the English, said just the opposite to the Americans. He warned them against English trickery, against English hostility to America, advising them to seek German protection from the wiles of perfidious Albion. The well-intentioned proprietor of the American *Century Magazine*, who had obtained possession of this interview was, at last, persuaded to relinquish it and forego the joys of publication. At about the same time Herr Bünz, the German Consul-General in New York, reported that the " famous interview," before it reached the *Daily Telegraph*, had been in the hands of the proprietor of the *Daily Mail*, Mr. Harmsworth, who later, as Lord Northcliffe, achieved such sad distinction in the World-War. The *Daily Mail* " with regret " had given up the idea of publishing it when Mr. Harmsworth had been told by the English Foreign Office that its publication was not desired.

CHAPTER XXV

*Serious effects of the Imperial observations abroad—The friendly
speeches of English statesmen delivered a short time previously—My
interview with Sidney Whitman—Audience with William II—
Official statement in the " Norddeutsche Allgemeine Zeitung "—
Financial reform in the Reichstag—The Kaiser suggests abdication—
The Crown Prince comes out of his shell—The banquet at the Rathaus
—For the first time William II reads his speech—Letters and ad-
dresses on the events of November—His Majesty recovers his spirits.*

THE disservice which, like the bear in the fable, William II
had done my policy and our whole relationship with England
was rendered still more regrettable by the fact that, throughout this whole summer of 1908, a series of incidents had shown
clearly that, in England, influential people were doing their best to
reassure their public opinion on the subject of the German naval
programme. Thus, in July, Mr. McKenna, in reply to an alarmist
speech by Lord Charles Beresford, declared in the House of Commons, in the name of the Admiralty, that the great superiority of
England in the older classes of battleship, and the possession,
against Germany's nine, of twelve English Dreadnoughts and
Invincibles, gave England, for 1911, full security. Undoubtedly,
said Mr. McKenna, such unconditional security was a matter of
life and death for Great Britain, but to go beyond that would simply
be waste. On 27th July Sir Edward Grey, the Secretary of State
for Foreign Affairs, said emphatically in the House of Commons
that he did not aim at isolating Germany. On 15th August, at a
miners' meeting at Swansea, the President of the Board of Trade,
Churchill, who till then had been very bellicose, sharply criticized
a recent speech by Lord Cromer in the House of Lords, concerning
the alleged German peril: " For both countries and for the world,
a war between England and Germany would be an appalling
catastrophe. Despite the growling and snapping in the press and
in the London clubs neither nation has any reason at all to fight the
other. In Germany there are scarcely ten thousand people who
really seriously contemplate a crime so deeply accursed; and in
England I do not believe there are so many." At the end of September 1908 Mr. Harcourt, a member of the Government, and First
Commissioner of Works, protested at Lancaster against the " half

cowardly half chauvinist " noise in the English yellow press. He declared: " Within the last ten years there has been no time, and I speak from first-hand knowledge, and with the consciousness of full responsibility for what I say, at which our relations with Germany have been on a firmer or more friendly basis than to-day. Although in both countries there is a tiny clique of publicists who, because of their selfish lack of true patriotism, stir up hostile feelings, these are simply the footpads of politics and foes of humanity. Keep your heads cool, your ships ready, your tongues courteous, and you need not be alarmed at these yelping curs who befoul the kennel in which they live."

I had taken advantage of this friendliness to speak frankly but tactfully on the German side, in an interview on Anglo-German relations which I gave to the *Standard*, through the pacificist and pro-German journalist, Sidney Whitman, who had been educated at the Vitztum college in Dresden, and had often been used as his mouthpiece by Prince Bismarck. The tone of the interview made a good impression in England.

When at last in November 1908, William II returned to Potsdam, I applied for an audience, which he granted me in the Neues Palais. This took place on 17th November. Since our long conversation on 31st October he had only twice, as far as I was concerned, shown signs of life. He had telegraphed, through the Minister von Jenisch that, in all the discussion aroused over the *Daily Telegraph* affair, far too little emphasis had been laid on the fact that the desire for publication had come, not from our side, but from the English, and that in England the prevailing opinion had been that to publish would be to do service to the cause of Anglo-German understanding. On the evening before the debate in the Reichstag the Emperor had wired to me in English that I must never forget the silver lining behind even the blackest cloud!

At our interview (17th November 1908) I met His Majesty on the terrace in front of the Neues Palais. Beside her Imperial husband stood the Empress. She came forward quickly and whispered: " Be really kind and gentle with the Emperor. He is quite broken up." Then the Emperor invited me to follow him to his study. Arrived there, we sat down. The Kaiser indeed looked quite dejected. He was very pale and evidently expected a severe lecture from me.

It would have been a breach of taste to have lectured him at such a time, so I contented myself with remarking that already we had discussed many times all the problems and subjects now the cause of so much acrimonious complaint. He answered me simply and frankly: " Yes," he said, " you told me it was all going to happen." Then he hesitated, and asked, with obvious anxiety: " But what now? What's going to happen? Shall we win through?"

I told him that I had no doubt of it, provided that His Majesty made up his mind, once and for all, to be more discreet and cautious in future. This especially applied to Foreign Policy. The " Hun " speech and the " trident " speech were far more serious matters than the Swinemünde telegram or the speech on pessimism, though even these were, naturally, not to be recommended. But the joke about " admiral of the Atlantic " and the personal letter to Lord Tweedmouth had done far more damage than occasional indiscretions in Germany.

The Emperor nodded agreement. He declared that most certainly he intended to put a guard on his tongue in future, and avoid offending people: " But what is it that makes them all so annoyed? "

I replied that the indignation, which certainly existed, was not all due to political mistakes. I alluded to his excessively outspoken, excessively violent attitude towards the modern trend in art and literature. This is one of the points on which Germans are especially susceptible, on which they resent dictation from above. Here, for the first time, the Kaiser protested, saying that it was not only his right but his duty to denounce the influence of Hauptmann and Liebermann, since such people were poisoning the soul of the German nation. I answered that, none the less, Max Liebermann had certainly painted some very beautiful pictures; that Gerhart Hauptmann was both a thinker and a poet, who had given the stage profound and striking plays of real significance. It is always dangerous, I added, to attack genius and talent, and certainly the Kaiser would get the worst of it if he could only oppose Knackfuss to Liebermann, and Major Lauff to Gerhart Hauptmann. Liebermann's *Net Menders*, I continued, and his *Old Man's Refuge*, would always find admirers; while Hauptmann's *Hannele*, *The Sunken Bell*, *The Weavers*, and *Florian Geyer*, would for long continue to move their audiences. All this I said without sharp insistence, and on a note of easy conversation, referring all the time to our many previous talks on the subject. But I could feel at once that, with the Emperor, this topic was dangerous ground, and so turned back the talk to politics which, for me, were of far greater importance.

I gave him a long exposé of the difficulties with which we were bound to be faced in the coming winter. Of questions of internal policy the most pressing was the reform of Imperial finances; its solution was an immediate necessity. The German people did not take kindly to taxation. Should we content ourselves with fresh indirect taxation, or impose a direct tax? Both politically and socially it seemed dangerous to base such an important fiscal reform on nothing but indirect taxation. But such direct taxation as I envisaged would with difficulty be got through the Reichstag, since it could not fail to arouse strong opposition in the Conservatives: that might give the Centre Party their chance of provoking a political crisis by taking advantage of any split in the government *bloc*.

The Emperor stressed the fact that he wished the *bloc* to be maintained. I agreed, and said my efforts were all directed towards re-establishing some *modus vivendi* with the Centre Party, while at the same time, and without ever alienating the Independents, I maintained the present friendly relationship between Conservative and National-Liberal. As to the Centre we had already paved the way to such an arrangement by our careful regard for the rights of the Catholic Church and for Catholic feeling. I also hoped that my personal friendship for Cardinal Kopp, for whom I had the deepest respect, and the benevolent feeling of the Pope and the Curia towards myself, would lighten our task of gradually reconciling the Centre Party. In such an event I would take the liberty of suggesting that the Prussian Legation to the Holy See should be transformed into a German Embassy. I had even a candidate in view for the Ambassadorship—the Reichstag deputy, Herr von Hertling. The Emperor did not seem to have any objections.

I proceeded to discuss Foreign Policy. This, more than anything else, I said, demanded our most serious attention. By that time the Bosnian crisis had reached its acute stage. Nevertheless I was still quite confident that we could bring it to a peaceful conclusion, without sacrifice of the rights and security of the Hapsburg Monarchy, or damage to our relationship with Russia. I did not try to conceal from His Majesty that the effect of his conversations at Highcliffe had been that of a spring frost in the night, nipping in the bud that understanding which the last few months had seemed so fairly to promise, between the two great peoples on either shore of the North Sea. But none of this was irreparable, I said. The English Ambassador had told me in confidence that King Edward was still firm in his intention of showing, *urbi et orbi*, his desire for Anglo-German " peace and goodwill." He therefore intended a most ceremonious visit to Berlin, and would be accompanied by Queen Alexandra.

" Splendid! " cried the Emperor, obviously very much relieved. But he still seemed uncomfortably to expect that I should impose on him something disagreeable as my condition for remaining in office.

For a moment we both were silent. Then the Emperor, who clearly had deeply pondered the question, asked: " Must I issue a proclamation to the country? Do you want a Cabinet Order concerning yourself? I am ready for anything you like." He spoke quite amiably.

I replied that I should not think of asking my Sovereign to issue any sort of capitulation, still less an undignified *Pater peccavi*. What I proposed was a statement in the *Norddeutsche Allgemeine Zeitung*, that His Majesty had given me the opportunity to describe to him the emotion produced in the German people by the interview in the *Daily Telegraph*, and to explain to him my attitude in the subsequent Reichstag debate. It might further be added that the Emperor considered it his duty to maintain his constitutional responsibilities towards the Empire, and the continuity of German policy, and that he continued to honour me with his confidence. Already, on the previous day, I had drafted an announcement in that sense. It ran as follows: " In the course of an audience granted to the Imperial Chancellor His Majesty, our King and Emperor, heard a report, which lasted several hours, presented to him by Prince von Bülow. The Chancellor described the emotion produced in the minds of our people by an interview in the English *Daily Telegraph*. Prince von Bülow then explained the attitude he had taken in a subsequent Reichstag debate on interpellations relative to this interview. His Majesty gave serious consideration to these statements and explanations of his Chancellor, and he announces his pleasure as the following: Uninfluenced by the exaggerations of public criticism, which seem to him unjustified, His Majesty the Emperor regards it as his chief Imperial task to assure the continuity of Imperial policy, while, at the same time, maintaining his constitutional responsibilities."

He gave me his immediate and eager consent to this. Indeed he seemed surprised at having come through the affair so easily. When I read over the draft to him a second time I added, in the first sentence, after the word " emotion " the additional phrase " and its causes." I also proposed a conclusion to the announcement, and this, as he assured me, the Emperor particularly approved. This is how I worded it: " His Royal and Imperial Majesty has accordingly approved all declarations by the Imperial Chancellor in the Reichstag, at the same time assuring Prince von Bülow of the continuance of his confidence."

He insisted on adding his formal " Agreed, William I. R.," to the draft, though I told him I considered this unnecessary. " But I agree with every word in it," he said, " and there ought to be a permanent record of my assent in the archives."

The Imperial study adjoined the room in which the Emperor Frederick had lain dying. Its door played a pleasant little tune every time it opened or shut. As we entered he had grasped my hand convulsively. " Help me! Save me! " he had exclaimed. Now, as I was just about to leave him, he embraced me, and gave me a hearty kiss on both cheeks, a thing I have only known him do twice —then, and in 1901, when he gave me the customary salute, on investing me with the Order of the Black Eagle. As I bowed myself out he repeated twice: " Thank you! Thank you with all my heart."

Back in the Chancellor's palace I said to my wife who, through my often stormy career, has never failed me in loyalty and affection: " I've managed, once more, to get the Crown and the Emperor out of a scrape. But I shouldn't care to say how long we shall be staying in this palace." Forty-eight hours later the Reichstag began its debate on the proposed reform of Imperial finances. I opened it with a speech which lasted for over two hours.[1] As always, I spoke extempore. For months I had studied the question at issue, turning it over and over in my mind. I have sometimes heard it said that financial reform caused my downfall, since my life's preoccupations had been such that I had never had time to master the subject. Even good friends have sometimes told me that my personal indifference in questions of money and finance had an unfortunate influence on my method of handling the Finance Reform of the Reich. This is incorrect. In my preparatory work, and in the business of getting the Customs tariff through parliament, I certainly did not examine every detail. I have already said that, for a statesman, charged with the general direction of a policy, it is unwise to lose oneself in details. " Le détail est une vermine qui ronge les grandes choses." I repeat, it is not necessary for a leader to know every tree in the forest. His duty is far more difficult—he must avoid not seeing the wood for trees. And that error is typically a German one—the defect of just those qualities which give us our failures and our successes. I could have carried through financial reform as successfully as the previous tariff and commercial treaties if the Conservatives, in 1908 and '9, had shown the same intelligence as eight years before; and if the Emperor had given me his steadfast support.

But, already in the spring of 1908, months before the appearance

[1] Prince von Bülow, *Speeches*. Complete Edition, iii, 141 *et seq*. Compressed Edition, v, 89 *et seq*.

of the *Daily Telegraph* article, my Imperial master had said with annoyance to his Minister of War, von Einem: "Bülow is getting too big for me." General von Einem had told me this in the strictest confidence, with the good intention of putting me on my guard. The Emperor first turned from me, then against me, when, as the result of the Reichstag debate, his morbid self-conceit had been exacerbated; when intriguers, jealous rivals, and toadies had rubbed into the wound their poison of suspicion and calumny. In the winter of 1908 he still wore a benevolent mask.

At this session (19th November 1908) I had just stood up in the Reichstag to announce my intention of formulating and defending the proposed financial reforms, when one of the Chancellery staff came to my side and whispered: "His Majesty informs Your Highness, by telephone message, given by the Chamberlain Schultz, that he intends to abdicate." I had only the time to whisper in reply: "Telephone back urgently that nothing must be done precipitately; that, in any case His Majesty must wait till after the banquet in the Rathaus, the day after to-morrow." In the same instant came the voice of the President: "The Imperial Chancellor has the floor."

I began by explaining in broad outline the fundamental facts of our international position. Parvenus, as a rule, were not beloved. The German Empire, the youngest of the European family, had received more respect, more fear, than benevolence, so far. Germany, once a happy hunting-ground for the dabblers in foreign intervention, had grown into a formidable competitor. Bismarck himself had not been able to extinguish the "*revanche*" idea in France, to prevent the wave of anti-German feeling that swept through Russia at the end of the Russo-Turkish War. Nor was it really unnatural that, when, as a result of our growing population and our productive energy, we had achieved economic expansion, a section at least of the English people had ceased to be so friendly as formerly, and were showing a certain anxiety. Such enmity, in the last resort, was due to elementary causes, but, in my opinion, was in no way impossible to remove. Time would heal or mitigate many reasons for it. "What we need is presence of mind, courage, consistency, and peace at home and abroad." I roused deep emotion in the House by evoking that profound image of Albert Dürer, the greatest of our German painters, which shows a knight in full armour, riding calm and fearless through a valley, in company with death and the devil. With that picture I compared another, which I had recently seen in a French paper—a caricature showing a German cuirassier, with gleaming sword and polished helmet, but in a tattered uniform, and stretching out his hand like a beggar to strangers, who pass on their ways with haughty gestures of refusal. That was how many foreigners judged of our financial position and, with it, of our ability to defend ourselves, of our real preparedness for battle. That was a danger which we, and only we, could remove. This time we had the will and saw the necessity of ordering our own financial house. No one in the world doubted that the German nation was strong enough to shoulder the burden made necessary by a fundamental reform of Imperial finance. Everyone knew that, year in year out, three milliards of marks were spent in Germany on beer, spirits, and wine. Germans smoked the cheapest cigars in the world. In Germany the tax on tobacco amounted to a little more than 1.50 m. a head. In Austria it was almost five marks, in Great Britain well over six; in France nearly eight. In Germany the tax on beer per head of the population amounted to scarcely 1.50 m., while in Great Britain this same tax was over six and a half marks. As to spirits, our average tax was little over two and a half marks per head, as compared with six and a half in France, and eight and a half in Great Britain. All this at a time when German wealth was increasing by leaps and bounds. I estimated, at nearly four milliards of marks a year, the increase of our national income. The value of private deposits in the banks rose yearly by 400 million marks. Every year about three milliard marks were invested in Stock Exchange securities alone. To these must be added the new deposits in the savings banks, amounting to 500 million marks and, in the joint stock banks, to about 225 millions. Such a land was not poor; such a land could bear much heavier burdens in the interests of its security and prestige. There was nothing in all that to point to bankruptcy! Nothing that even hinted at decline! But moral bankruptcy might threaten us unless we could work a transformation, and ceased to base our national economy on debts. I referred to my friend, the Independent deputy, and *Prorektor* of the Freiburg University, Professor von Schulze-Gävernitz, who had recently stated that the deficit in German finance arose, not from inability, but from reluctance to endure taxation. I also referred to Professor Adolf Wagner, my old patron and friend, who had spoken of German " stinginess " and " niggardliness " in the matter of evading taxes. I urged the Reichstag, and with it the whole German people, to greater economy. We had grown rich almost in a night; we were like those heirs who imagine themselves richer than they are, spend wildly, and suddenly find themselves in debt. We had been poor too long not to give way to the temptation of living, like our rich neighbours, in luxury: " I tell you frankly that there is too much love of material ease and pleasure in Germany. Such over-estimation of material things is a source of deep anxiety to anyone who has at heart the real treasure of our people, its treasure of intellectual culture. We must all live more simply."

Here I was interrupted by the Socialists, and retorted: " I except no one. Simplicity of life is nobler, more dignified, and worthier of a German." I recalled the fact that, at all times, wealth has been a means to national power. With every decade this would be more and more the condition of a people's greatness, since with every decade economic and industrial factors increased in importance, in international groupings and relationships. I praised the admirable thrift of the French, the effects of which I had observed during my long stay in France, that " *force d'épargne*," in every French man and woman, which offered us so useful an example. I invited the experts to substantiate and complete what I had said by their personal observations and experience. Amid Socialist applause I declared that my warnings against extravagance had been principally addressed to the upper and middle classes. I spoke here from personal observation, since I remembered how simply things had been managed in our Club House at Bonn in the old days, when I was still in the King's Hussars, as a lieutenant. This reminiscence provoked laughter on certain of the benches, so I repeated that this was a very serious charge; that it was very sad, and unworthy of the German nation, of its culture, its glorious spiritual tradition, if we had sunk to the point at which people are only respected according to income, if such standards, or lack of standards, of social morality prevailed among us. I concluded in the firm belief that the Reichstag would see for itself how urgent and important was this task; that it would achieve it with all the dignity of a great and pacific people, whose eyes were turned upon the future.

My speech was followed by one from the new Secretary of State for the Imperial Treasury, Sydow. I ought here to add that I had made a mistake in choosing him. When I first saw the absolute necessity for a fundamental reform of our finances, and for what, in those days, was considered a heavy increase in taxation, I had perceived at once that such a task would be beyond the powers of Stengel, hitherto the Secretary of the Imperial Treasury. He was a good and conscientious official, but his long years as Bavarian plenipotentiary to the Bundesrat had so fixed him into the rut of the old system that, as an instrument of Financial Reform, he would have been useless. He was, moreover, in close touch with the Centre Party, which desired to bring me down on the question of Financial Reform, and by means of it.

As Stengel's successor I at first considered Walter Rathenau, who often came to my house, and had given me repeated demonstrations of his deep and ardent respect. On the evening of 17th November he had sent me a charming bouquet with his card, on which he had written the words: " To the saviour of the Fatherland, from his ever loyal, Walter Rathenau." To-day I still feel he would have done better if he had become Secretary to the Treasury; far better than later on, as Foreign Minister. The Emperor liked him. I think I have already mentioned the fact that the Kaiser was very far from entertaining any religious bigotry or race prejudice. Especially was he free from anti-Semitism. But he thought that the appointment of a Jew to what was, at the present juncture, the very important office of Secretary of the Treasury, would arouse ill-feeling in the Right, already restive about the new taxes. For that reason he rejected the very able banker, Carl Fürstenberg, and even his favourite, Albert Ballin. Besides I am not sure whether either of these latter—both first-rate men, and men for whom I had a profound respect—would have consented to serve if I had appealed to them. I had asked another distinguished banker, Herr Waldemar Müller, of the Dresdner Bank. He refused because, for the moment, he could not leave his bank which, shortly before, had lost two of its chief directors. I was therefore obliged to choose a civil servant, and my choice had fallen on Sydow, then Under-Secretary. Sydow was an honourable, diligent, and conscientious man, who possessed many of the excellent, traditional qualities of the Prussian Civil Servant, but also many characteristic failings of the bureaucrat. He was stiff, hidebound, and would lose himself in masses of detail, and so confuse the outlines of a subject. He was clumsy, and excessively " thorough "—had never pondered that pregnant remark of a French poet, a remark which, I admit, it is hard for worthy Germans to understand:

" *Glissez, heureux mortels,*
n'appuyez pas."

The maiden speech which he delivered on 19th November had obviously been prepared with much burning of midnight oil. It was very long, and bristled with facts; was uninteresting, and so failed in its effect. While the words pattered from his lips in a steady and relentless shower, I left the House. As I strolled away from the Reichstag in the direction of the Grosser Stern, to stretch my legs, and get a little air, a man approached me, whom I recognized as one of the royal footmen, though he wore ordinary clothes and not

livery. He handed me a letter. I saw at once that the envelope had
been addressed by the Empress. The letter inside it contained only
the following words: " I should like to speak to you. The messenger will tell you the rest. V." We walked side by side. A few
minutes later my companion stopped a closed cab, which drove us
to the Potsdam Station, whence we took the Wannsee train to Potsdam. We travelled second class, so as not to be recognized. From
the station at Potsdam another closed cab to the Neues Palais. Her
Majesty the Empress received me on the ground floor. Her eyes
were red with tears, but her bearing was entirely regal. She asked
me at once: " Must the Emperor abdicate? Do you wish him to
abdicate? "

I told her emphatically, and without a second's hesitation, that
such a thing had never occurred to me, nor could I see the slightest
necessity for it. The Empress sat down, and asked me also to be
seated. She told me that the Emperor had had " a nervous breakdown," " a collapse." This had happened to him already several
times, after moments of emotional crisis, as the result, for instance,
of his Brandenburg speech, and after the Swinemünde telegram.
But this time, she said, it was more serious. The Emperor had taken
to his bed with cold shiverings and hysteria. I explained the whole
position to the Empress. It was not necessary to give her the reasons
why public feeling had been so stirred. Despite her superb loyalty
and unbounded devotion to the Emperor, her fine instinct and
exceptional good sense precluded any possible illusion in her, as to
the dangerous side of her august husband's nature. I was fully
convinced, I told her, that this storm would soon have blown itself
out. Since my speech in the Reichstag it had already begun to
abate. She could be assured that I would never consent to any curtailment of the traditional, constitutional rights of the Prussian
Crown. It was certainly necessary for the Emperor to cultivate
more calm; to be more discreet and moderate in his attitude, his
speech, his writings, and all his actions. I should consider it useful
for him to appear at the banquet in the Berlin Rathaus, on 21st
November, in two days time. The Empress said that she did not
know if His Majesty would have recovered sufficiently in two days
to be able to appear in public. I reassured her by pointing out that
her husband had a most resilient nature. Let Her Majesty soothe
him a little, and there could be no doubt that he would be well
enough to undertake this task at the Rathaus. And I knew that
he would discharge it excellently. I had a fine speech ready prepared for him.

When Her Majesty dismissed me she was calmer, and seemed

much easier in her mind. I returned to Berlin as I had come. My absence had been unnoticed by the House, which merely supposed that I had gone for a longish walk in the Tiergarten, a thing I very frequently did alone, unaccompanied even by the stout, plain-clothes officers who protected me.

On 20th November I received a visit from the Crown Prince. Neither he nor the Emperor knew anything of my yesterday's interview with the Empress. He had come to be informed of the situation. He was, as usual, modest and polite, in contrast to his Imperial father; discreet, and somewhat hesitant in manner, a listener rather than a talker. But I saw at once that he would not have been unwilling to govern, at least for a time. While, in cautious but lucid terms, he unburdened himself on the widespread feeling of irritation, of bitterness even, against his father, I was reminded of the famous scene in Shakespeare, where the Prince of Wales, the future Henry V, sitting beside the bed of the sleeping king, sees the crown lying on his pillow, grasps it, and sets it on his own head:

" Lo, here it sits,
Which God may guard."

The Crown Prince asked me whether I considered that the Emperor, attacked so wildly—mainly, indeed, by Maximilian Harden, but by others too—could go on reigning, just as though nothing had happened. Was not a break, possibly a longish break, advisable? Or even necessary? . . . I answered that I felt certain that, by tomorrow or, in any case, by the end of the following week, the Emperor would be perfectly ready to resume the duties of his high office, and perform them all, without exception. Should His Majesty, the Emperor and King, permit himself to adopt a more moderate attitude he would continue to reign, not with diminished, but with greatly increased, authority. The Prussian Crown was forged from the most resistant metal. It was a symbol of the glorious history of five centuries. From Fehrbellin to Mars la Tour the blood of the men of the Mark, and of Prussians, had been poured out in streams to defend it. Around that Imperial Crown which William I, with Bismarck's aid, had brought back from the Kyffhäuser, there was still a magic, a halo without compare. It would need " some enormous blunder " to destroy that magic and that halo; to shake that loyalty.

As he left me the Crown Prince looked rather disappointed. His memory plays him false when he states, in his *Memoirs* that, after the November days, he received, as deputy for his father, a deeper and most disquietening insight into the workings of the governmental machine. I do not recall at that time, having handed him a single detailed report, and certainly no report of real consequence. In any case the Emperor was completely restored to health before I had occasion to ask the Crown Prince to consider any important decision.

On November 21st, at the Berlin Rathaus, there was celebrated the hundredth anniversary of the Prussian Municipalities' Ordinance. The Emperor attended as punctual as he always was. He was still very pale, but greeted all those present with cordiality. To the address delivered by the burgomaster he did not, as he had usually done before, reply with an improvised speech, but took from my hands the text of the answer I had prepared for him, which he read in a loud voice, but quite naturally. It contained the following :

" . . . The evidence given by my ancestor, in this grant of municipal self-government, of the confidence he placed in his people, and the appeal which he then addressed to the forces, both moral and intellectual, of the citizen body as a whole, have borne rich fruits. True gold is purified by fire. And the gold of German loyalty and capacity which distinguishes the citizens of our towns was refined, both in the War of Liberation and in a century of hard, unselfish toil for the commonwealth. Though, in the words of our Prussian national hymn, ' the bright sun cannot always shine,' and there must be occasional days of gloom and depression, no settled cloud shall ever cast its shadow between myself and my people. May God prosper my city of Berlin." All the Councillors, even those of the Left, were loud in their applause of this speech. When he had finished the Emperor beckoned me to his side and handed me back my manuscript, at the same time shaking me by the hand. He intended to show that he felt himself a constitutional monarch.

The excitement which these November events had aroused in the German people was revealed in the veritable deluge of letters and addresses I received, and from which I will only pick out a few specimens.

The upright, and very patriotic King Wilhelm of Württemberg, wired: " Cannot refrain from expressing my deep satisfaction that Your Highness is to continue your experienced guidance of Imperial policy."

His distinguished Prime Minister, Weizsäcker, also wrote of his " profound relief " at my remaining in charge of affairs. The government of Baden spoke of its " sincere pleasure " at the thought of my continuance in office : " May your Highness long be spared for your sure and balanced guidance of German policy, to the prosperity of the Empire and the furtherance of peace between the nations." In the Saxon Lower House, Count Hohenthal, the Minister of State, speaking in a debate on Imperial policy declared : " At a meeting of the Foreign Affairs Commission of the Bundesrat, Prince Bülow, in a very frank speech lasting four hours, gave exhaustive information of all that had taken place during recent years in the domain of Foreign policy. What he said was strictly confidential. But I may say that in the ensuing discussion, in which every member of the Commission took part, it was shown beyond any doubt that the conduct of our Foreign policy could be in no better hands than those of our present Imperial Chancellor. And if, though with a heavy heart, he has consented, after these last critical days, to continue to shoulder the burden of office, he has done so out of the purest patriotism, from sheer duty and loyalty to the Emperor."

The Bavarian Envoy was commissioned by the aged Prince-Regent to convey to me his earnest desire that I should remain in office. Two veterans of journalism, men who had been active in Bismarck's day, Paul Lindau and Ludwig Pietsch, congratulated me with the same warmth, as did Eugen Zimmermann, afterwards the Emperor's collaborator in His Majesty's *Erscheinungen und Gestalten*.

Dr. Oertel, the editor in chief of the Agrarian *Deutsche Tageszeitung*, an able Conservative parliamentarian, also wired to congratulate me on my decision to remain: " not only in Your Excellency's interests but in those of the Kaiser and the Reich." He " prayed I might be granted strength and vigour to retain for many years my difficult office, so that these last, anxious days might not in the end prove fruitless." Another wire in the same sense came from Otto Roese, the editor of the Conservative *Schlesische Zeitung*.

Some of the letters were humorous. An " English admirer " sent me the following verses, inscribed in "art" lettering on parchment, with big initials:

For the Kaiser.[1]

Something to remember :

> If your lips you'd keep from slips
> Five things observe with care:
> Of whom you speak, to whom you speak
> And how, and when, and where.

Albert Ballin wired that he was " happy and profoundly grateful" to think that I should remain in my high office for the Fatherland.

[1] English in text.

General von Kracht, a veteran of the war in '70, and a free citizen of
Zerbst, sent me a post-card with a picture of the old Prussian colours,
which his forefathers had carried into battle. He added that, in the
circles in which he moved, he heard only expressions of satisfaction
at the thought of my still being Chancellor. A worthy old clergy-
man in Lower Franconia thanked me for the " manliness of my
action " both in the Reichstag and at the Neues Palais. I had placed
my personal interests below those of the Fatherland, and had done
immeasurable service to the nation and Monarchy. He added:
" My faith as a Christian which shows me the Lord of Lords, the
King of all Kings, as the true guider of our destinies, impels me to
express as follows my thanks and good wishes to Your Highness :—
May God prosper your every future effort for the well-being of our
German Fatherland, may He grant you, and His Majesty the
Emperor, strength and wisdom for every praiseworthy act."

A professor in the old and oft-beleaguered town of Flensburg
wrote: " Out of this day of gloom was born a great day, perhaps
your greatest. I and my wife and children are among those many
thousand Germans who this night, in admiration and gratitude, turn
their eyes towards the Statesman and the man. In spirit at least
I shake your hand." Another professor wrote to me from the
Rhineland : " May the firm assurance never fail you that, both now
and in after time, all you have done, and will do, for Germany,
cannot cease to be acclaimed by all true men. May God protect
you." He signed himself: " German who stands apart from café
politics and parties, who refuses to flatter, but is filled with a deep
respect for anything genuine and sincere."

As gradually the storm abated which had swept the whole
German nation, His Majesty's physical health began to improve.
The day after the banquet at the Rathaus, he sent me a telephone
message to trouble him with no other documents save those that
concerned his Achilleon villa at Corfu. He never wanted to hear
the word " politics " again. But a few days later August Eulenburg
wrote to tell me how much brisker the Kaiser was, and how much he
enjoyed playing with his terriers. In this, at least, I could sympathize
with His Majesty's feelings. I am fond of all animals, as fond of
dogs as I am of horses, and, of dogs, next to my poodle, I love my
dachshund. Since the beginning of my married happiness I have
always been surrounded with dogs. In St. Petersburg there was little
" Erda " whom we had to bury in the Mokhovaia, where she slept
while the Russia of the Tsars was transformed into the Russia of
the Soviets. " Waldi I " accompanied us to Bucharest, and then to
Rome, where he found his last resting place in the gardens of the

Palazzo Caffarelli, the home, for so many years, of Prussian and
German ambassadors, but which we were to lose in the World-War.
In the garden of the Imperial Chancellery we buried the intelligent
" Froh," at the side of Prince Radziwill's greyhounds and Prince
Bismarck's huge " Tyras." " Erdmann " rests in peace in the
garden of the Villa Malta, near the palm tree planted by Goethe,
—" Erdmann," who in Norderney and Berlin, so often bit our
visitors' legs, or at least tore holes in their trousers. And now to
keep me company I have " Waldi II," who, for ten long years, has
still remained the true and faithful friend of a Chancellor retired
from office. For all my dogs I keep a tiny, but abiding, corner in
my heart.

CHAPTER XXVI

Change in the Emperor's feeling towards me—Influences and intrigues at court—The duties of a statesman—Further development of the Bosnian Crisis—Isvolski goes from capital to capital—His visit to Berlin—Lunch with the Emperor—My instructions to the German Ambassador in Vienna—The attitude of the Great Powers—A visit from the Russian Ambassador, Count Osten-Sacken—Russia's unconditional agreement (24th March 1909)—The warlike feeling in Vienna—Aehrenthal.

BY degrees the Emperor recovered in mind and body from the effects of the trouble in November. I once read the pleasant little story of an Alpine climber, who found himself hopelessly stuck on the point of a peak, somewhere in the neighbourhood of Chamonix. He promised his guide a hundred thousand francs if only he could bring him down in safety. When they were past the worst glaciers and ridges he reduced his offer to fifty thousand. Down in the valley he felt ten thousand more than enough: he began to feel very angry with the guide for having exaggerated the danger, and accused him of not knowing the right paths. No sooner had the crisis provoked by the Emperor's Highcliffe indiscretions passed its acute stage than attempts began to be made to undermine my position by the use of its moral effect on his Majesty.

Of these, the first result was that it grew increasingly difficult to pass financial reform in such conditions as would have been either economically, or above all, financially, fruitful. I had always felt most strongly, that I could not, and would not, accept any modification of that reform which might lead to bad economic, or politically harmful, results. I have never thought much of ministers who " will always consider an alternative." A minister, especially a Chancellor, must on any difficult question both form a conviction and abide by it. The man at the helm of state should never veer from the course on which he has seriously embarked: he has no right to sail down every wind of opinion in questions which, he feels, entail the future of his country. So that, with this conception of the proper scope and duties of my office, combined with my knowledge of the instability and fickleness of William II, I was obliged, in 1908, to give some serious thought to resignation. All the more anxious was I, therefore, to have everything as shipshape as possible when I handed over to my successor. I wanted in home politics to be sure of Liberal, as well as of Conservative support, since it seemed to me risky to have a government based only on lords temporal and spiritual. It also seemed wise to keep open the *aditus ad pacem* to the Centre Party, and, with it, the Catholic part of the nation, by a reasonable, just, and accommodating attitude towards the Catholic Church, the Hierarchy, and the Vatican. Abroad, in the Bosnian Question, some solution would have to be found which, without damaging our relations with Russia, would assure the continuance of Austria. I was no less anxious for a good understanding with England on the naval question, and especially on the " slowing down " of construction.

I turn first to the Bosnian question which recently (end of October 1908) had been the subject of a long audience with His Majesty. "Woe unto them that are wise in their own eyes and prudent in their own sight," says Isaiah in warning, while St. Paul lays down among other golden rules, the following precept for the guidance of the young Christian community in Rome: " Be not wise in your own conceits." Whether the first readers of the Epistle to the Romans took this lesson to heart we do not know, but on the other hand the kings of Judah did not follow the counsels of the greatest of Old Testament prophets, and so they repented of their folly. Isvolski considered himself very clever, and did, in fact, possess a certain dose of that Slav cunning which mainly consists in the ability to lie spontaneously and fluently, and to present extravagant demands as though they were nothing,—methods to which many honest Germans have succumbed, in the course of history. Sometimes we have been taken in by Russians, sometimes by Czechs, and Serbs; most frequently of all by Poles.

But Isvolski, in spite of all his feints, made blunder on blunder after his meeting with Aehrenthal at Buchlau. As I have already pointed out, it was an error not to have obtained a definite statement from Aehrenthal, at the famous meeting of September 15th 1908, as to when and how he intended to carry out the annexation of Bosnia and Herzegovina. A still greater stupidity of Isvolski's was his not having returned at once to St. Petersburg, there to defend his policy like a man, before the Tsar and the Duma, after Aehrenthal had sprung on him the surprise of suddenly proclaiming the annexation, on October 5th 1908.

But, instead of this, our new Ulysses took a series of almost comic journeys—zigzagging here and there from one European capital to the next. From Vienna he rushed first to London, then back to Paris, with the object of getting, if he could, the means of satisfying Russian greed in the Dardanelles. But he had no success, either on the Thames or on the Seine. He was informed in London that the English Liberal Cabinet must give weight to the left wing of the Liberal Party, and could not, therefore risk any offence to the Young Turks by countenancing Russian ambitions in the Dardanelles. The Young Turks had, indeed, as the heroes of Liberal independence, become as dear to the British radical heart as formerly the Sultan, " that bloodstained tyrant,"[1] had been odious to it. In Paris the same result! And in both the Western capitals he only got on everybody's nerves, with his incessant complaints against Aehrenthal, and inopportune insistence on the Dardanelles. " Isvolski is a great boar "[1] was London's verdict; and, in Paris :—" *Isvolski nous embête.*"

Yet Isvolski could not bring himself to refuse invitations to " selected parties,"[1] offered by the English country houses. Still less could his uxorious heart deny the petitions of his wife to do her Christmas shopping in Paris. Mimi Isvolski was a charming woman, an excellent wife and a good mother, and, at the same time, pretty and smartly dressed. Later, when Isvolski had been made Ambassador in Paris, the gallant French nicknamed her " *le sourire de Paris.*" But, in the autumn of 1908, she did no great service to her husband in delaying his return to St. Petersburg.

On October 24th 1908 Isvolski arrived in Berlin, and came to see me. He seemed a broken man:

> " *In den Ozean schifft mit tausend Masten der Jüngling.*
> *Still, auf gerettetem Boot, treibt in den Hafen der Greis.*"[2]

But the more distressed he became, the more I endeavoured to treat him with calm and quiet consideration, not out of any natural feelings of good nature and Christian long suffering, but because this seems to me expedient. He reminded me how, in a far less difficult position, before his transfer to Tokio, he had asked my advice, which he had found not merely kindly but wise. To-day, he assured me, he was really in a tight corner: " *Alors je me trouvais devant une tâche difficile. Aujourd'hui je suis dans un affreux pétrin,*" I answered that I was really anxious to help him, not only because we were old friends but, above all, because I wished to safeguard the traditional understanding between Russia and Germany. This relationship was essential to both countries; but, naturally, I could

---

[1] English [*sic*] in text.
[2] "Youth puts out with a forest of masts to the Ocean Quiet, in the boat from the wreck, the old man rows to the shore."

not leave our Austrian ally in the lurch. I added smiling: " And neither do you wish to desert the French."

I could not blame this Russian Minister for answering that the refusal to renew Bismarck's Re-Insurance Treaty had come from our side, not from theirs, that it was the work of Caprivi, Marschall, and Holstein. But I cut short his appeal to the past by reminding him of the fact that, in the Bosnian Question, the Hapsburg Monarchy had on its side not only the actual wording of a treaty, but some other diplomatic trump cards, notably the letter in which Isvolski himself had invited Aehrenthal to make the occupation an annexation.

Isvolski could say very little; his mistakes were too evident to defend. He could only keep on repeating: " *Le sale Juif m'a troupé, il m'a menti, il m'a mis dedans, l'affreux Juif.*" In his excitement, with his red and distorted face, he looked like a furious ape. I closed up my ears with my two forefingers, and said to him, quietly and gravely: " *Tant que vous direz du mal de mon ami Aehrenthal, je me bouche les oreilles. Mais je vous promets que, si Aehrenthal se servait jamais de termes aussi inconvenants sur mon ami Isvolski, je me boucherais égale- ment les oreilles.*" Little by little he calmed down. Clearly he could find no new explanation of the diplomatic errors he had committed. He repeated that he had " unluckily " trusted to the sense of honour and upright character of Aehrenthal, but had been most cruelly disap- pointed. That, from a Russian Minister, sounded almost comic, when one remembers that the most famous Russian diplomat of the last fifty years, Ignatiev, was extremely proud of the soubriquet "Father of Lies," which had been bestowed on him by the Turks, and that Gortshakov, Saburov, and many other Russian statesmen have not been distinguished as truth-lovers. I slipped in a question to find out how successful he had been in obtaining in London and Paris positive results on the Dardanelles. He replied with a show of uneasiness that, in London, they had told him that the attitude of the English Liberal electorate made it impossible for an English government, at the moment, to back up any demands which would be a source of annoyance to the Young Turks, and likely to increase their difficulties. As for Paris, the French had affirmed that, without England, they could do nothing in the Dardanelles, and that the French government had always to take account of its small rentier class, heavily committed to Turkish securities. Without falling into the manner of the Pharisee, who thanks his God he is not as this publican, I did not conceal from the Russian Minister my own point of view as to the Dardanelles: I took my stand, in this question on the Bismarck Re-Insurance treaty. In the matter of the Straits Germany had no primary interest. Our attitude here must depend both on the alignment of the powers and the general situation, and on the way in which we were treated by Russia. We should not oppose Russian policy in the Straits. But Isvolski himself could hardly expect us to favour it in the present situation in Europe, since France, his ally, was opposed to any limitation of the full Turkish sovereignty, either in the Straits or Sanjak. "*Je ne vous dis pas : Lâchez la France et nous lâcherons l'Autriche, mais je vous dis: soyons, vous dans l'Entente, nous dans la Triple-Alliance, un élément de paix et de conciliation.*" Isvolski put out his hand to me with the words: "*Votre langage est non seulement celui d'un homme d'Etat, mais aussi celui d'un ami de la Russie. J'ai pleine confiance en vous, et mon souverain a pour vous les mêmes sentiments que moi.*" Next day, when he paid me a second visit, he was in far better spirits than before. I took advantage of this fact to discuss the whole position from A to Z with him, and entered on a series of special points. As to the suggestion of a conference, I said I had no objections in principle, but that before we could proceed to such a step it would be necessary for the Powers to decide together what questions such a conference would discuss.

It is impossible to begin a concert until the instruments are in tune. I told him he was wrong in imputing also to Germany all the actions of the Dual Monarchy. I did not hold him personally responsible for all that was done, hoped for, and fostered in Paris. Austria-Hungary was as great and independent a Sovereign Power as France. Her policy in the Balkans was her own affair. No good purpose could be served by retrospective criticism of this Austro-Hungarian initiative. "There is no use crying about spilt milk."[1] If we had definitely stated that we supported Austria-Hungary in her present crisis such an attitude had been forced upon us, not merely for reasons of loyalty but of statesmanship. But there was no need for us to intervene further on behalf of the Turks, since England had them under her special protection. "*Les Anglais,*" I said, "*sont devenus plus Turcs que les Turcs.*" Isvolski nodded his approbation. And since, I continued, we had no direct political interests in Turkey, we were free for any policy with regard to it, though, naturally, we should always have to safeguard our essential economic interests. It seemed to me, however, in the interests of peace, and of all the Powers, that Turkey should receive guarantees for the integrity of her territory in Europe. Isvolski pounced on this remark, which I had thrown out casually in a tone of mere conversation. He said he had lived too long in the East not to know how

[1] English in text.

selfish, unreliable, and utterly democratic and radical were the Balkan peoples. All Bulgarians and Serbs, Greeks and Rumanians, were equally good for nothing, and equally fickle. If the Dardanelles Question were to be solved in a fashion acceptable to Russia, then the *status quo* in the Dardanelles and the continuance of Turkey were, on the whole, the best that Russia could hope. When I informed Isvolski that Turkey had already begun to negotiate with Austria-Hungary and Bulgaria (by French advice, as far as Bulgaria was concerned), he shrugged his shoulders and answered with a melancholy smile. Finally I assured him, with perfect truth, that I had been very glad that Aehrenthal had informed me so late on the subject of his plan of annexation, since this relieved me of all responsibility and left me with my hands free. We parted on the very best of terms. Since he kept repeating that, in St. Petersburg he looked forward to real hell; that he did not think he would remain Foreign Minister much longer, and that his assistant Tcharikov was only waiting to step into his shoes, I consoled him: "*Vous serez encore ministre ou ambassadeur, quand je planterai mes choux dans le jardin de la villa Malta.*" He threw up his hands in a gesture of protest and answered: "*A Dieu ne plaise. Restez à votre poste, nous avons tous besoin de vous.*"

The Emperor asked Isvolski to lunch. I had begged His Majesty not to be drawn into any comprehensive political talk with the Russian Foreign Minister and to speak only in general terms of the Bosnian crisis. I emphasized the fact that he must insist on our desire for peace and general friendship with Russia, and must, above all, treat the Russian with quiet friendliness. He unfortunately neglected my advice. At bottom he was entirely out of sympathy with all Foreign Ministers as such. They were his natural enemies, since he would have preferred to handle Foreign Policy directly with other Sovereigns. " I am at my best," he would always say, " when I talk straight out to my colleagues." But all the same, I gratefully admit that the Emperor, as long as I was in favour, was quite willing to ask my advice; though that did not imply that he would follow it. At this lunch in the Royal Palace (25th October 1908) he made an elaborate show of not having heard the political observations, references, and still less the questions of Isvolski, and, again and again, brought back the talk to commonplaces. To vary this delightful entertainment he made stale puns and told comic chestnuts, to the great joy of all the German guests, who had been warned in advance that His Majesty would use this method of " chipping " Isvolski. I was not present at this luncheon party.

Isvolski said as he took leave of me: "*Vous avez été charmant pour moi. Quant à l'Empereur, il s'est beaucoup égayé à mon sujet. J'ai eu l'honneur de lui servir de tête de Turc.*"

Ever since the Bosnian crisis began I had repeatedly assured His Majesty that the issue was one of neither letting the Austrians lose their nerve, nor, on the other hand of allowing any step to be taken which would lead to a general war. To avoid the first of these dangers I sent (2nd December 1908) an instruction to Herr von Tschirschky, the Imperial Ambassador in Vienna, in which I characterized as attempts at intimidation the rumours spread abroad from the English, but especially from the Russian side, as to the possibility, even the probability, of a war in the following spring. To judge from the general tenor of our information on Russia no serious statesman really considered war, notwithstanding a fiery speech by Isvolski, whose self-esteem had been so wounded. As I learned from Paris, from certain well-informed financial circles there, Russia, by spring at latest, would have been forced to borrow heavily in the European money market. The redemption of the Treasury bonds held in France, was due in May, and could hardly be delayed much longer. The deficit on the extra budget—about one hundred and fifty million roubles—would have to be covered. An agreement had already been made with France for a loan of a milliard marks to be used for the purpose. It was thus in the best interests of both countries to see that the present political tension eased. But precisely because Russia did not really intend warlike action, Isvolski rattled his sabre the more industriously for the purpose of scaring the Dual Monarchy. *Rebus sic stantibus*, firmness was Austria's best policy. On the other hand the Dual Monarchy might well show itself conciliatory to Turkey in all matters of finance. I suggested that she would also be well advised to get Bulgaria, Greece and Rumania on her side by a skilful and accommodating policy. Austria should neither drive too hard a bargain with Turkey, nor neglect and ruffle the Balkan States. The Rumanians under the Crown of St. Stephen ought to be more gently treated, and Austria should be very amenable in the matter of commercial treaty negotiations with Rumania. Greece could be thrown back on Albania. Naturally the Vienna Cabinet ought to give Italy a free hand in Tripoli, since there, though she might be inconvenient to England on account of Egypt, and to France on account of Tunis, her presence was in no way prejudicial to Austrian or German interests. Bulgaria, like Rumania, must be treated, formally at least, in a friendly manner by Austria. I concluded this instruction to von Tschirschky, who was to read it to the Minister Aehrenthal, with the assurance of my con-

ALEXANDER PETROVITCH ISVOLSKI

Imperial Russian Minister of Foreign Affairs

viction that the crisis could be successfully resolved by a judicious blend of firmness and compromise.

The end of December 1908 brought our first reliable information that Isvolski was in retreat. He addressed a circular to the Powers, sharply criticising Austria's action, and giving precise reasons for his proposal to convoke a European conference. But, at the same time, he announced himself ready to consider Austrian wishes to the extent that the Conference should agree to accept the *fait accompli*—the annexation—without debate. Discussion could take place beforehand between the individual Cabinets.

In a speech delivered in the Duma on 25th December 1908, he took refuge in similar phrases, but these were really heavy artillery giving the signal to retire. Throughout the whole Bosnian crisis King Edward had busied himself assiduously with pouring oil on the flames. His passion for political intrigue and gift for poisoning the well-springs of political relationships came out in a very clear light. He would have liked most of all to unseat Aehrenthal, and replace him by the Austrian Ambassador in London, Count Albert Mensdorff, who as a distant connection of the English Royal Family, enjoyed, as I have already said, the full favour of the English Court. More discreet and cautious was the attitude of Sir Edward Grey, the English Foreign Secretary. Sir Edward was, no doubt, very anxious not to see things forced to a head. Sir Charles Hardinge too, the then Under-Secretary to the Foreign Office, the hero of the conversation on the billiard table at Homburg, with the Emperor, worked hard for peace, although Nicolson, the English Ambassador in St. Petersburg, was inflaming the Russians not only against Austria, but, even more, against ourselves. Let me anticipate a little and say here that Nicolson's appointment as Permanent Under-Secretary to the Foreign Office (he succeeded Hardinge, soon after my retirement) was almost as ominous a sign as the appointment, two years later, in 1913, of Delcassé as Ambassador to St. Petersburg. During the whole crisis the attitude of Rumania, or, to be more precise, of King Carol, was above reproach. The King, in its very first stages, let me know that I could depend on his maintaining a correct attitude because he was convinced that, though I should remain quite loyal to Austria, I would not let the peace of the world be endangered. Italian policy found itself in a difficult situation. In the debate on Italian Foreign Policy held in the Chamber of Deputies at the beginning of December 1908, both Barzilai, the Irredentist, a refugee from Trieste, and the Radical, Fortis, an ex-Foreign Minister, made furious attacks on Austria. But, aided by the imperturbable calm of Giolitti, the Premier, the skill of the then

Minister of Foreign Affairs, Tittoni, at that time President of the Senate, later Ambassador in London and Paris, steered successfully between Scylla and Charybdis, between Italy's obligations to Austria and the anti-Austrian feeling, so widespread through all classes of Italians. A general feeling of relief was apparent in Italy, and, with it, a higher appreciation of the value of the Triple Alliance, at my having had the good fortune to settle the Bosnian crisis without any grave results or damage to the Hapsburg Monarchy. Sydney Sonnino, then the leader of the Constitutional opposition, and later Minister for Foreign Affairs, said in a letter to his constituents: "During recent years the Triple Alliance has been able to contribute effectively towards maintaining the peace of the world. It is therefore in every way desirable that diplomacy should succeed, as soon as possible, in dissipating even the faintest doubt, misapprehension, or suspicion, which may have arisen among the allies. Relationships of trust and cordiality must, without delay, be re-established between the Italian government and the neighbouring Empire (Austria). Such an atmosphere will, in itself, do much to facilitate the solution of every problem, even the most delicate and involved." Guicciardini, a former Foreign Minister (later he again held that post) delivered a speech to his constituents at San Miniato, in which he declared that he considered the Triple Alliance not only a sure guarantee of peace, but also a great factor of development. But, in spite of all such favourable symptoms, no quiet and perceptive observer of international relationships and the world situation could doubt that, if Austria invaded Serbia and so precipitated a crisis, the Italians would not be kept in the Triple Alliance without heavy concessions to Italy.

On 14th March 1909 the Russian Ambassador, Count Osten-Sacken, asked for an interview with me. In the conversation we had that same day he appealed for our support in order to extricate the Russian Foreign Minister from a very painful situation—painful both politically and personally. He confided that the Austrian Foreign Minister had threatened, in order to prove his sincerity, on which Russia had been casting some aspersions, to publish a series of secret documents in which Isvolski had not only given his full acquiescence to the annexation of Bosnia and Herzegovina, but had literally encouraged Aehrenthal to take the step, if not to precipitate it. I answered the Ambassador, *fortiter in re, suavissime in modo*, that I would gladly act as mediator for Isvolski, and do my best to extricate him from the difficulty in which he had managed to involve himself. This would help keep the peace and particularly would be of use in preserving traditional Russo-German friendship. It would be too ridiculous to oppose, for purely formal reasons, an annexation which, in actual fact, in no way altered the *status quo* in the Balkans, and might very well lay the foundations of a future cordial understanding between the Powers directly concerned. It would be an outrage to common-sense to fling a Europe, avid for peace, into a war of which only one thing was certain—that it would necessitate gigantic sacrifice and leave only misery and ruin. But, naturally, the preliminary condition for any intervention on our part was that Russia, as well as she could, should restrain the Serbs. If Isvolski could give us no binding assurance of this we scarcely, though to our very great regret, saw any other possible course than that of leaving Austria-Hungary free to pursue whatever policy she thought best. But, if Russia were genuinely willing to check the Serbs, then I too was very ready to discuss, in a friendly fashion, with Isvolski how best to bring energetic pressure on Belgrade without seeming in open contradiction to the policy hitherto pursued by Russia. With a little skill and good feeling on both sides a *combinazione*—to use the Italian *terminus technicus*—ought not to be difficult to find. And if Russia undertook to use her influence with the Serbs the rewards of the compromise would go to the St. Petersburg Cabinet. If, by official declarations, the Powers agreed to the Bosnian annexation, there was no need for any European conference. The cause of dispute, which had been immeasurably exaggerated, could best be appeased in this fashion. I requested only, and for obvious reasons, that Isvolski should tell the English Ambassador nothing of my suggestion until he himself had considered it and made up his mind. It was a good omen for the peaceful solution of the crisis that Isvolski did, in fact, refrain from saying anything on the subject to Nicolson.

Ten days after my talk with Count Osten-Sacken the unconditional consent of Russia to the annexation of Bosnia and Herzegovina reached both Vienna and Berlin. Only then was Nicolson informed of it. He vented his ill-temper and disappointment by spreading the lie that Germany had brought Russia to heel by threats, by a thrust with the " mailed fist." No one had asked us to intervene, etc.

I cannot decide whether Isvolski did not help to spread this legend. He abstained in any case from taking definite steps to contradict it. Consequently I got our ambassador to enquire of Herr von Tcharikov if, now, it would not be proper to explain, by simultaneous publication of identical and relevant documents dealing with the actual facts, how well-intentioned, friendly, courteous and successful had been the mediation we had undertaken at Russia's

request, and so put a definite end to the malicious insinuations
spread abroad. It became apparent in further conversations between
Isvolski, Herr von Tcharikov, and our ambassador, that the
Russians were extremely anxious to have certain alterations made
in the documents in question. I therefore refrained from publication, since my chief anxiety in the matter was that the Bosnian crisis
should leave no shadow of resentment between the Russians and
ourselves.

So ended the first act of the Bosnian imbroglio. The danger had
been avoided that Russia would egg on the Serbs to further resistance to Austria. Above all there had been no breach with Russia,
a possibility which had seemed to me very grave, and which I had
taken the greatest pains to avert. I never saw Isvolski again after
our memorable conversation on 26th October 1908. Then, as he
was leaving, he had said to me: " Between Russia and Aehrenthal
the breach is complete, as much on personal grounds as for reasons
of policy. Aehrenthal has behaved without loyalty and without
gratitude. As attaché, as Secretary, as chargé d'affaires, as ambassador in St. Petersburg, he was for ever assuring us that he was the
true friend of Russia and the inflexible advocate of good relationships between his Monarchy and the Russian Empire. When he left
St. Petersburg to become Foreign Minister we gave him the Cross of
St. Andrew. As thanks, all he could do was to betray and insult us.
He has behaved so treacherously that war would have broken out
if it had not been for your friendly and able intervention. War
would have meant the greatest possible misfortune to the world and
all the three Empires."

To these words of Isvolski I add *ex post* that neither the Russian
court nor Russian diplomacy ever forgave Aehrenthal his action
during the Bosnian crisis. Not long after this crisis had been
resolved a Russian Grand Duke passed through Vienna. He
informed the Russian Ambassador that he would be very glad to
pay his humble respects to His Imperial and Royal Apostolic
Majesty, and also delighted to meet Austrian and Hungarian
dignitaries and statesmen, but that any meeting with Aehrenthal
was out of the question as far as he was concerned. Aehrenthal
would have liked to induce his Imperial master to renounce the
pleasure of any visit from the Grand Duke who so pointedly refused
to meet him. But the old Emperor had no wish to let a diplomatic
quarrel breed discord between the two courts and dynasties. He
received the Grand Duke with his usual kindness and distinction.

On the relations between Austria and Russia Isvolski had assured
me at our last meeting that he still fully endorsed all that I had

previously said to him on the grave dangers to the survival of the Monarchic principle and order, latent in any conflict between the three Imperial Powers. Monarchist and conservative Russia had nothing to gain from war, as such, with the Hapsburg Dual Monarchy. Till now, in spite of many conflicting interests and occasional bitterness of feeling, there had been no war between Austria and Russia. Its avoidance should be just as possible in the twentieth as in the eighteenth and nineteenth centuries. But the first condition for such avoidance was that Austria should not attempt to drive Russia entirely out of the Balkan peninsular. Prince Bismarck, long ago, had advised that a *modus vivendi* be sought between the two powers on the basis that, in Bulgaria, Russia should be given a free hand, and in Serbia, Austria. But in the meantime, first by the Battenberg episode, then by the election of Prince Ferdinand of Coburg as head of Bulgaria, Austrian influence in Sofia had become stronger than Russian. There was a similar position in Bucharest where the inclination was towards Berlin and Vienna rather than St. Petersburg. Thus the old Bismarckian formula no longer applied. In any case Austria, having achieved such a brilliant success in the Bosnian affair, ought not to press Serbia further. *Ne bis in idem!* Serbia had yielded all along the line; she was humiliated, she had been punished enough. To kick her when she was down would be cruelty. Austria Hungary, therefore, would really be acting in her own interests if she made a few economic concessions to Serbia. Would a tiny port for Serbia on the Adriatic coast really constitute such a grave danger for the great Austro-Hungarian Monarchy? Isvolski said to me—I give his own words:—" *Si j'avais des arrière-pensées, je me réjouirais des maladresses des Autrichiens et des Hongrois vis à vis des Serbes qu'on pousse ainsi dans nos bras. Mais dans l'intérêt de la paix Européenne et des grandes dynasties je voudrais que l'Autriche soit un peu plus habile.*" Isvolski ended this last conversation by assuring me that German-Russian relations remained as before. He was very grateful for my conciliatory attitude. As before I enjoyed the confidence and goodwill of the Tsar. " *Vous avez la pleine confiance de l'Empereur Nicolas qui sait ce que vous devez à l'alliance avec l'Autriche, mais qui sait aussi que vous êtes l'ami de la Russie et un homme d'état sage et habile. Nous espérons tous que vous resterez encore longtemps à la tête des affaires.*" Pointing to an album of photographs of my Roman villa, which was lying on the table, Isvolski added: " *N'allez pas de sitôt jouir de votre belle villa. Restez à Berlin!*"

The following are the last words I ever said to Isvolski: " *Je vous le répète et le Prince Bismarck l'a dit avant moi: Dieu seul sait comment finirait militairement une guerre entre les trois empires. Mais ce que l'homme réfléchi et prudent peut prévoir est ceci: Ce seront en tout cas, et quelque soit l'issue militaire du conflict, les trois dynasties qui payeront les pots cassés."*

Isvolski lived long enough to see for himself how true my prophecy was. He was destined to live through the defeat and fall of Tsarism and watch the old proud and mighty Russia crash into a sea of blood and tears. He died, as a dismissed ambassador, sick and embittered, in a very modest flat, in a little town in Southern France where he lived on a small allowance from the French Government—a miserable reward for all his feverish activities throughout the war and immediately before it, a reward which seemed still more wretched when compared with the millions which, for decades, had flowed from Russia into the pockets of grasping French journalists and politicians.

Having evaded the danger of war in the North we had, in 1909, to restrain Vienna. There, too, there was a danger of war. I was well aware that certain Austrian generals were as eager to fight in 1908 and 1909 as they had been in the second half of the 'eighties. Conrad von Hoetzendorff, the Chief of the Austro-Hungarian General Staff, reproached me for years with having let slip the right moment for war. This same reproach had been made, twenty years previously, by Austrian generals to Prince Bismarck. Von Hoetzendorff had his eye chiefly on Italy, though he also longed to strike at Russia, via Serbia, of course, which must be " chastised." His arguments were the same as those used in Berlin two decades before, by Count Alfred Waldersee in his struggle against Prince Bismarck. Through the winter of 1908-9 he preached the " inevitability " of a reckoning with Serbia, Italy and Russia. The longer the delay the worse the position would become. With every day that passed the enemies' strength was increasing, whereas the Central Powers had achieved the furthest point of military expansion. Therefore: Strike now before it becomes too late.

I opposed him. I had no intention of letting Germany be intrigued into a war of incalculable dimensions, of whose results only one was certain—that we had little to gain which could not be won, without war, in the course of our natural development. We should risk enormously by war, we should hazard incalculable values. I had a serious talk along these lines with the Austro-Hungarian ambassador Szögyényi, as soon as I knew that Russia had given way. I also got my brother, Karl Ulrich, who for seven years had been German military plenipotentiary in Austria, to write to Vienna in this sense. He had good Viennese connections,

especially in the entourage of the Archduke Francis Ferdinand. To
the ambassador, an old and experienced diplomat, who fully agreed
with me in his heart, and privately reported my remarks to friends
in the suite of Francis Joseph, I spoke as follows: Ten to one any
Austrian march on Serbia would mean immediate war with Russia.
A war with Russia would almost inevitably be a world-war. I could
only consent to be involved in so monstrous a game when we had
played our last trump card in the policy of the Central Powers.

I appealed to Article VII of the Triple Alliance agreement,
which laid down that in any case of Austro-Hungarian expansion,
Italy had the right to increase her territory. Austria could not evade
that obligation by maintaining that the crushing of Serbia, such a
Serbian invasion as the Austrian generals seemed to contemplate,
was not aggrandisement in the sense provided against in the agreement. Such a contention would be mere sophistry, the sort of
cunning that would prove useless in our great questions as affecting
the destinies of nations. Naturally the conquest of Serbia, and even
the invasion of Serbia, would shift the balance of power in the Balkan
peninsular. Did Austria intend to assure Italy an equivalent? The
former bishopric of Trient, for instance? Or Görz, Gradiska, Pola,
Trieste? And the same applied to Rumania. Was Austria willing
to compensate Rumania with the Bukovina? To assure the genuine
co-operation of Rumania with Austria it would at least be necessary
to accord the Hungarian Rumanians better treatment and a stronger
representation in the Hungarian parliament.

In my successful endeavours to restrain Austria-Hungary from
rash action I was supported both by the heir to the throne, Francis
Ferdinand, and by Aehrenthal. The latter, as a result, was attacked
by those Vienna newspapers inspired by the Austrian General Staff
with a virulence which poisoned the last days of that Minister,
already stricken down by a fatal illness. The comic papers, especially, surpassed themselves in the meanest ridicule and slander of the
dying statesman. But he did not give way.

Aehrenthal, from the very first, had completely understood my
attitude to the Bosnian crisis. When the Bavarian Centrist deputy,
Speck, who never saw an inch beyond his nose, reproached me
loudly and angrily in the Reichstag with half-heartedly supporting
our ally Aehrenthal wrote to the ambassador, von Szögyényi:

Prince Bülow is perfectly right in describing as too trans-
parent a manœuvre these nonsensical attacks on the Imperial
policy in the Reichstag for half-heartedly supporting Austria. Any
deviation from the course which Prince Bülow had laid down for

himself would, as he saw very clearly, have been most inopportune, for two reasons:—first the abandonment on the part of the German government, of its policy of discretion and reserve, would have been regarded as an attempt at tutelage, and so have created bad blood; while, on the other hand, such a change in the German attitude would certainly not have furthered our direct negotiations with Turkey. The acceptance in principle of our proposals in the matter of Bosnia by the Grand Vizier and the vote of confidence in that statesman passed by the Turkish parliament, are striking proofs that the methods used by Prince Bülow in regard to the support to be assured us, were in every way the right ones.

CHAPTER XXVII

My visits to Rome and Vienna—Audience with Pius X—The Heir to the Hapsburg throne—The Bosnian Question in the Reichstag (23rd March 1909)—Germany's " Nibelungen Troth "—Franco-German agreement on Morocco-Casablanca—The Crown Prince criticizes this agreement—The character of the Crown Prince—The question of William II's abdication—A letter, concerning Herr von Kiderlen, from the Crown Prince—My answer—England's attitude in the Bosnian Crisis—More letters from Count Metternich on the Naval Question—King Edward and Queen Alexandra visit Berlin—Geheimrat Renvers and the death-bed of the Empress Frederick.

LIKE the Austrian Minister of Foreign Affairs, the heir to the Austrian Throne, the Archduke Francis Ferdinand, fully approved of the line I had taken in the Bosnian Question, and particularly of my efforts to preserve European peace. I had taken advantage of the Easter recess of the Reichstag (1908) to pay two short visits to Rome and Vienna. At Rome I had had long audiences with King Victor Emanuel, with the Premier, Giolitti, and the Foreign Minister, Tittoni, whose visits to me in Homburg and Baden-Baden I returned. As the official Agenzia Stefani pointed out, these visits revealed our complete agreement in point of view and ideas. An audience with Pius X, who received me and my wife with moving kindness—my wife was one of this grey-haired pontiff's own flock, but, even to a non-Catholic like myself he seemed a true successor of the Apostle—gave His Holiness a chance to assure me of his abiding confidence and goodwill. He was in no way influenced, he said, by the opposition shown me by the Centrists. German Catholics were, the Pope declared, among the truest and best sons of the Church; but their parliamentary representatives were plainly sometimes rather wrong-headed (*ostinati*). Naturally it was not I who made the first mention of my differences with the Centre Party; the remark came spontaneously from His Holiness, accompanied by a smile of understanding.

In Vienna the Emperor Francis Joseph received me with his usual kindness. In March 1908 I had a long talk with the Archduke Francis Ferdinand, who had always been most graciously disposed towards me. The Archduke had had the kindness to invite me to afternoon tea. I remained for about two hours alone with him and his wife, the Duchess of Hohenberg. How clearly I can still see that meeting! The Archduke, an upright, manly figure, very handsome, with passionate—perhaps too passionate—eyes, quick energetic movements of the hands, a face of great sincerity and openness; the duchess, not precisely a beauty, but very charming, very gracious, very well dressed, and with all the breeding of the "*fesche*"[1] Austrian Countess of good family. I remember that the Archduke constantly returned to the subject of the Bosnian crisis. He did not conceal his resentment against the Magyars, and his preference for the Slavs; but he complained about the Russian (*i.e.*, Pan-Slav) agitation in Galicia, Bohemia, and particularly Bosnia and Herzegovina. The Duchess of Hohenberg fully agreed with what he said. She was particularly indignant at the obstacles which the schismatic clergy put in the way of the missionary activities of "the good Franciscans." In her opinion the Franciscans had perhaps more to contend against in the religious indifference of Hungarian statesmen and Austrian functionaries, blinded by the traditions of Joseph II, than under the domination of the Moslems. It was in the main their warm interest in the Catholic cause which, six years later, drew this unlucky pair to Sarajevo, where, to quote Heine's *Lamentations*: "Thanatos, evil death, on his pale charger," awaited them. It seems all the more senseless that the Serbs should have murdered this Archduke when one remembers that he undoubtedly preferred the Slavs to the Magyars, the Italians, or even at bottom, the German Austrians. This Slavophil tendency in the Archduke was one of the reasons which induced him to give such staunch support to my efforts towards the maintenance of European peace. In this, in spite of certain minor differences, he was of the same mind as the old Emperor, who was so delighted with my policy that he wanted to give me some public token of his approval. Since I already possessed all the Austrian Orders—the Order of St. Stephen with brilliants, and the Emperor's photograph, beautifully framed and autographed by himself, as well as his statue in bronze—the old gentleman honoured me, after the successful resolution of the Bosnian crisis, with an over lifesize portrait of himself in the uniform of his Prussian regiment, and wearing the sash of the Order of the Black Eagle. This portrait was the work of the Hungarian painter, Leopold Horovitz, and is of genuine artistic merit.

Some foolish attacks had been made on me in the Reichstag by the Bavarian Centrist deputy Speck, because of my alleged failure

---

[1] Austrian slang approximating to "thoroughbred."

to support our Austrian ally. Speck was a highly placed customs official. If defence had been necessary I should have been amply reassured by the tribute paid to me by one of the ablest of Austrian statesmen, Baron von Chlumecky, who was by turns Minister of Agriculture and of Commerce, and for many years leader of the German Liberals in the Vienna Chamber, at first Vice-President, then President of the Austrian Parliament. When the crisis was over he wired me: "Deep and heartfelt gratitude from an old Austrian for all that Your Excellency has done for your ally and for your brilliant speeches in the Reichstag."

In my Reichstag speech [1] of 29th March 1909 I had declared that ever since the beginning of the Bosnian difficulties we had stood loyally by our Austrian ally. In this speech I used the expression " Nibelungen troth," which later was worked to death in and out of season, but which made its effect at the moment at which it was coined. I had shown, above all, that Serbia was not worth a war, still less, therefore, a world conflagration; it would be intolerable if European peace were jeopardized because of Serbia, especially since the annexation of these two provinces was no cynical act of spoliation, but merely the logical conclusion of thirty years of civilizing influence, and had been done with the blessing of the Powers. In this connection I made it clear that I had been obliged to inform the Russian Minister that, in the matter of a conference, we could not break with Austria; but I added emphatically: " For the rest M. Isvolski and I were agreed that Russian policy is in no way aimed against Germany; that, on the contrary, our old friendly relations must be maintained. Once again the Russian Minister assured me that no agreements, public or secret, exist between Russia and England that could be turned against German interests."

Throughout the crisis the attitude of the French Government had not been unfriendly to Germany. This was evident even in those French newspapers which as a rule were most anti-German. The Paris press, in this matter of the Austro-Serbian conflict, was calmer than the English. The *Temps* announced in a few dry phrases that a great war would not be in the interests of France, who would stand to lose more by it than England, and would besides have to bear a heavier military and financial burden. The help of the French army would be invaluable to England in any war; but should France become engaged in a European conflict, English military aid would be far less useful to her. I had been fortunate enough to get the above very sensible article into the columns of a leading French

[1] Prince Bülow's *Speeches*, complete edition, iii, p. 179; Réclame edition, v, p. 117.

newspaper through the assistance of a lady with whom I had long
been acquainted. The French ambassador to Constantinople,
M. Constant, remarked to his German colleague, Baron von
Marschall: "*Si les Russes croient que nous allons faire la guerre pour
leurs beaux yeux ils se fourrent le doigt dans l'oeil.*" This discreet
and reserved French attitude, at a moment when a great war had
come within the range of possibilities, was also attributable to the
negotiations which I had opened with France after the unpleasant
Casablanca incident, and which, finally, on 9th February 1909
resulted in the improved agreement concluded with the French on
the subject of Maghreb el Aksa. We allowed them in this pre-
cedence in all matters of politics, without yielding them complete
dominion over the country, whose integrity and sovereignty were
once more guaranteed by the French Government. Against this
France promised us complete equality in Morocco in matters of
trade, to which we attached supreme importance.

On 2nd October 1908, during these negotiations with France
over Morocco, I received a letter from the Crown Prince, in which
he referred to an alarmist article in the Pan-German and ultra-
chauvinist *Rheinisch-Westfälische Zeitung*, demanding the despatch
of a German cruiser to Casablanca, and reproaching me with having
given our "once chivalrous and fearless nation" the idea that
peace and tranquillity were more desirable than war and honour.
The Crown Prince expressed himself as follows:

> First of all I must ask Your Excellency to forgive me for
> writing to you in pencil, but in the hunting-box where I am at
> present there is a sad lack of writing material. You have always
> been so kind and frank with me, and we have discussed together
> so many political issues, that I feel I may write to you quite freely.
> I am firmly convinced that this Casablanca incident was pre-
> meditated. The French are really trying to find out how far they
> can tax our patience, our love of peace. I write this in all serious-
> ness, after due reflection, and in the knowledge that later I must
> abide by the consequences. If the French manage to pull this
> off, without giving us entire satisfaction and a formal apology,
> our prestige will be impaired for many years. Our honour is
> deeply involved, and it is high time that this insolent clique in
> Paris should be made once more to feel what a Pomeranian
> grenadier can do. Believe me, Your Excellency, a great part of
> the nation thinks as I do, and the whole army is longing to " get
> at 'em." If this business had happened to an English consul four
> English cruisers would have been sent off at once to Casablanca

with their decks cleared for action. Such is my firm conviction. I hope you will not be angry, and that you will understand me. I earnestly entreat you to demand the fullest satisfaction, and, unless you get it, threaten them with energetic measures. It appears that our German merchants are already asking desperately if their Fatherland will leave them in the lurch. It is open to Your Excellency to point out that all this is no business of mine, but after all, sooner or later, it is I who will have to take the consequences; and if once one gets the reputation of being " entirely a peace lover," it is difficult to win back one's position.

With many loyal greetings,
Yours,
WILLIAM.

On 11th October 1908 I answered this letter as follows:

I was very pleased to receive Your Royal and Imperial Highness' letter from Gross-Mützelburg. I ask to be allowed to express my most dutiful thanks, and to reply in the same frank spirit to the confidence which Your Imperial and Royal Highness has placed in me. In the particular case under discussion matters are not quite so simple as the Press has made them appear. From the standpoint of international law it is somewhat doubtful if our consulate in Casablanca was justified in helping French deserters to get away. In any case it should have been careful to avoid giving such assistance to any non-German deserter. In the strictest confidence—since luckily the French are still ignorant of it— I may add that, in error as I hope, a false declaration was issued by the German Consulate, in which Austrian subjects, among others, were declared to be German nationals. Of course the French also are not free from blame in this matter, and that is why we have laid some claim. But our consulate certainly did not act in an entirely unimpeachable way, and those Germans on whose behalf it acted do not really deserve much sympathy since they are deserters and not simply German subjects. Again in the strictest confidence (since it is better that the French should not learn it) I may add that, in Prince Bismarck's time, the methods used in dealing with deserters, by the application of general instructions for consuls contained in the Consulate Laws of 1871-73, were far more drastic than to-day. By the terms of these instructions our consulates must on no account receive deserters, and, in particular, not repatriate them into Germany, since Prince Bismarck held that such people did not deserve to be considered German subjects. His Imperial and Royal Majesty has also announced his will and pleasure to the same effect in a marginal note.

So far for this particular case. But I would also beg to be allowed to express the following general considerations: I entirely agree with Your Imperial and Royal Highness that it is inadvisable too frequently to express one's love of peace, since this gives others too great a feeling of self-assurance. I too am convinced that, if a case involves one's country's honour it is necessary to strike, *coûte que coûte*, and whatever the chances may seem to be. But, unless our honour is engaged, we should always ask ourselves what is to be expected from a war. No war in Europe can bring us much. There would be nothing for us to gain in the conquest of any fresh Slav or French territory. If we annex small countries to the Empire we shall only strengthen those centrifugal elements which, alas, are never wanting in Germany. Naturally such considerations could not prevent our declaring war if it were forced on us, or if our national honour demanded it. But prudence is essential in such questions.

In 1866 and 1870 there was a great prize to be won. To-day that is no longer the case. Above all we ought never to forget that nowadays no war can be declared unless a whole people is convinced that such a war is necessary and just. A war, lightly provoked, even if it were fought successfully, would have a bad effect on the country; while if it ended in defeat, it might entail the fall of the dynasty. History shows us that every great war is followed by a period of Liberalism, since a people demands compensation for the sacrifices and effort war has entailed. But any war which ends in a defeat obliges the dynasty that declared it to concessions which before would have seemed unheard of. It is enough to remind you of those which His Majesty, the Emperor Francis Joseph, was obliged to make after 1859 and 1866, and the consequences which to-day the war with Japan is producing in Russia. It is for these reasons that Prince Bismarck, who took on himself the responsibility for two great wars, declared all wars to be dangerous unless dictated by reasons of state or some vital interest of the country. He particularly warned us against taking any passing incident too seriously, no matter what passions it may rouse. In affairs of this kind the opinion of the army cannot be decisive. It is excellent, no doubt, that the army should not feel its sword has rusted in the scabbard: it is necessary even that soldiers should be bellicose. But the task of a leader of policy is to get a clear view of consequences. *Quidquid agis, prudenter agas et respice finem!* In 1875 many officers were already feeling that France must be crushed a second time, since, weak as she was, her chauvinism had already raised its head. Since then we have managed to live at peace with France for thirty-three years, years in which our prosperity and our population have increased by leaps and bounds. Both in 1887 and 1888 Prince Bismarck was bitterly reproached with not having declared what was called a " prophylactic " war, against Russia. At that time everyone said such a war was inevitable. Yet for twenty years we have lived at peace with Russia. I repeat that if ever we are obliged we will fight like Frederick the Great against a world in arms, if need be. But war to-day would be a serious matter, far more serious than it was in 1870, since, meanwhile, the French army has much improved. Moreover, to-day it is improbable that we could ever fight France single-handed. We should have to fight England as well. And if we attacked France, Russia would come in on her side. Consequently, and in view of the very difficult situation in Europe to-day, I feel that the main thing is to keep our powder dry—make every endeavour to have our army in as high a state of efficiency as possible, and see that we do not lose our heads.

The Crown Prince had neither his father's exceptionally quick intelligence nor power as a speaker. He also lacked that personal charm which gained William II so many friends, especially at first, before they had got to know him better and perceive the weakness and faults that lay beneath. But from his sensible mother the Crown Prince had inherited a cold prudence which unluckily his father entirely lacked, and in addition to this his nerves were stronger than the Emperor's. Like all his brothers, like his uncle Prince Henry, like the Emperor Frederick and the Emperor William I, like Prince Frederick Charles, and Prince Albert—the Crown Prince was absolutely fearless. Had he ever succeeded he would have astonished the world less than his father, would have drawn less attention, done less to alienate other sovereigns, ministers and peoples. It would have been easier to rule with him than with William II. Since the disasters which overtook our country, I have often been asked why I did not use the November crisis to set the Crown Prince in his father's place. I answered, and answer still, that I had sworn an oath of fealty to William II, and that in no case could I have violated that oath, taken to my Emperor and King. I should never even have thought of trying to bring about an abdication by persuasion, urgent suggestion, surprise or artifice. Had any third party attempted to force such an issue I should have opposed him by every means, even by violence. But in any case I do not think that in 1908 it would have been possible to get William II to abdicate, especially since the Empress would have fought against any such suggestion with all the means which a woman has at her command—especially a woman so full of character as she. I may add to-day, even after all that has happened since, that in 1908 the vast majority of Germans did not want their Emperor to abdicate. The nation would never have understood such a gesture. Germany wanted the Monarchy, which stood for so much honour, glory, and prosperity, and which without any question was, and still remains for our people, the only really satisfying and profitable form of government. I do not say this out of prejudice. Nor do I speak *ex parte*, as a believer in divine right, especially as conceived by the Stuarts and Bourbons, and by the last Guelph king: my opinion is based on my study of history, and my experience. The power of the Imperial idea was so strong in Germany that the nation, once the November crisis was past, hastened to forget and forgive all the mistakes of its incarnate representative. The case of Prince Felix Schwarzenberg has been cited, who, in 1848, persuaded the Emperor Ferdinand of Austria to abdicate, and his brother, the Archduke Francis Charles, to renounce his title to the throne, which he proceeded to fill with the eighteen-year-old Archduke Francis Joseph. In answer to this I say that William II was not a half-wit, like Ferdinand I and the good Archduke Francis Charles, but, on the contrary, despite his many faults and weaknesses, an unusually gifted man.

And in 1908 we were in no such case as was the Austrian Monarchy in 1848, when Austria was in the midst of civil war, at war with rebellious provinces, at war with a neighbouring state. The German Federal princes and people only wanted, in the autumn of 1908, more self-control and prudence, a calmer, more reflective attitude, from their sovereign. Nor did the November crisis fail to have its salutary effect on the man who was chiefly afflicted by it. If, in that fatal summer of 1914, the whole world, but, alas, particularly Germany, had not through a lack of vision, prudence and adroitness, almost unknown before in human history, become involved in the worst catastrophe of centuries, William II might have continued to reign in honour for many years. But he was not personally equal to such a test of endurance as the world-war. Himself incapable of steering his ship through the storm, he was equally unable to set men of real capacity at her helm, so that the good ship Germany foundered.

My personal relations with the Crown Prince were always excellent. Among other very good points in his character was an

absence of touchiness and conceit. He liked to be seen on a difficult horse; he was a bold rider, and good at every kind of physical
exercise, would wear his service cap at a jaunty angle like a dashing
lieutenant of the Hussars of the Guard or the Life Guards, was very
gallant with pretty girls and beautiful ladies. But besides his
outward simplicity of manner he was free of intellectual pride or
vanity. He detested all pose and ceremony; perhaps too much,
since people like to see their princes invested with a certain aureole
and surrounded by a certain *grandezza*. These qualities the
German people expects, even of its Ministers and Chancellors.
My old friend, Prince Arenberg, often said to me: "You aren't
majestic enough. You should pose more. You're too natural!
German deputies, as well as German higher civil servants, differ
from those of England, Italy or France. Our people's representatives, from Lieber to Eugen Richter and Bebel, have been
philistines. They affect that cold dignity which, in Schiller, the
Maiden from Afar finds useful in repelling undue familiarities."
Up to a point I admit that Arenberg's criticism was just, but I have
never wanted to change, and never been able to, since one's natural
disposition will always end by breaking through. " *Chassez le
naturel, il revient au galop*," said old Destouches, who also loved
the phrase I quote so often, that art is hard and criticism easy. But
just because, in so many matters, I was on the best of terms with
the Crown Prince, since what the French call " *les atomes crochus* "
united us, I could be more frank with him than with his father when
there was any real difference between us. I remember how, in the
winter of 1908-9, he wrote me a somewhat excited letter, enclosing
a newspaper article which, in a spiteful and trivial manner, attacked
the Minister Kiderlen, whom I had just summoned to replace the
incapable Secretary of State, von Schön. Kiderlen was accused of
an immoral relationship with his housekeeper, the widow Kypke.
The Crown Prince felt it to be his duty to call my attention to the
position " which simply cannot be allowed to continue." I ought,
he said, to intervene at once: " I have already taken the liberty of
calling Your Excellency's attention to these facts, which have been
confirmed to me by several serious and well-informed people. It
seems to me very dangerous to reply with an official denial, which
would risk being easily disproved." I answered as pugnaciously
as possible that I hoped, if in the distant future the Crown Prince
ever ascended the throne of his ancestors, that he would have
learned not to sacrifice able and proved officials to every mean
and trivial piece of scandalmongering: that I certainly refused
to sacrifice Kiderlen because some malicious competitor, or per-

haps merely a journalist out of work, had been throwing mud
at him.

To his credit be it said that the Crown Prince took my letter in
good part. Later I learned that the author of all these intrigues was
the ambitious Baron von Wangenheim—at that time he was Minister
in Athens, and later Ambassador to Constantinople—who would
himself have liked to be Secretary of State, and in any case tried to
put Kiderlen out of the running, as far as Constantinople was concerned. Wangenheim had a very pretty wife, the daughter of
Baron Spitzemberg, who was for many years Württemberg Minister
to Berlin, and the Crown Prince was one of this lady's most ardent
admirers—though, of course, in quite an honourable sense. Having
quashed this intrigue I told Kiderlen all that had happened. He
answered with a smile, in the broadest of Swabian accents: " Excellency, if I were to produce the *corpus delicti* for your inspection I
think you would find it rather hard to believe in any illicit relationship between me and a fat old woman like that. She is a most
worthy old Swabian who has long since passed the age of consent.
My sister, the Baroness Gemmingen, got her for me as housekeeper."

I have had few such capable colleagues as Kiderlen. With his
immense and never-flagging industry, his quick understanding and
rapid judgment, Alfred von Kiderlen-Wächter could seize my
thoughts almost before they were spoken. But I admit that he was
like those horses who refuse every rider but the right one. Under
Bethmann-Hollweg, who knew nothing of Foreign Affairs, and was
afraid of him, Kiderlen gave too free a rein to his rough and sometimes brutal temperament, and was apt to be coarsely violent in
expression.

It had not escaped my notice that, in the Bosnian crisis, the
Russian, even the French, attitude towards us had been more
friendly than the English. By this I do not mean the English
government, nor yet the great majority of the people. Sir Edward
Grey, the Foreign Secretary, had made special efforts to prevent any
grand conflagration because of Serbia. But Nicolson, the English
Ambassador in St. Petersburg, had excited the Russians against
Austria, and even more against Germany, and had spared no effort,
intrigue, or calumny to make our intentions appear suspect. And
King Edward had watched all this with a smile: he had even done
his best to encourage it. To-day, after all we have since had to
suffer, I still do not think that, in 1908, Edward VII was deliberately aiming at a war. But he feared nothing so much as the drawing
together and friendship of Germany and Russia. Nothing pleased

him more than " incidents " and misunderstandings between the
two great Powers of the North. I never believed that England
would attack us; I did not even believe it in the days of the " naval
scare," when the fear of German attack had grown so strong in
England; not even when our impressionable, and very excitable
Kaiser saw the German fleet already wiped out by the English, and
Tirpitz was counting the years and months ahead of us, before we
could reckon ourselves safe. On the other hand I never doubted
that, if we went to war with Russia, and in consequence also with
France, and that if, above all, we invaded Belgium quicker than the
French did, the English would be on the other side. So that now,
in this winter of 1908-9, feeling that I might soon have ceased to
be Chancellor, I knew it to be one of my first duties to make sure,
within the limits of the possible, that our future peace with England
had been secured. The best guarantee for such a peace appeared to
be an understanding with England, on the basis of a slowing down
in naval construction, as against England's assurance of neutrality,
if ever we were attacked by the French. Metternich had written
on 2nd November 1908:

> England, militarily, and politically, is preparing herself to
> face the situation which, in the unshakable opinion of English-
> men, is created for their country by the growth of the German
> fleet, within the limits we have assigned to it. The best thing we
> can do is to consider this a permanent state of mind, and one that
> we can do nothing to alter. The Englishman is " matter of
> fact." [1] He considers that our programme constitutes a menace
> to his country, and is resolved, in order to avert it, to still further
> immense financial sacrifice and effort.

On 25th January 1909 our London Ambassador reported:

> It seems to me more and more certain that we shall never
> succeed in getting England to promise political neutrality, even
> by concessions on the naval question, so long as the Morocco
> question remains unsolved. The " *revanche* " idea is losing its
> hold, and will die all the more quickly if, by a peaceable settlement
> of Moroccan differences, there ceases to be the prospect of
> English help. If the apple of discord in Morocco can be re-
> moved the immediate consequence will be an Anglo-German
> *détente*, and consequent slowing down of the rate of our naval
> construction. It is my firm conviction that the English Govern-
> ment will never abandon France as long as the French feel our

[1] English in text.

pressure in Morocco. The sooner we give up our preconceived ideas on the perfidy of English policy the better for our own interests. If once the English Government can be brought to admit our honourable intention of caring no further about Morocco politically, once we have obtained all possible guarantees from the French for the protection of our economic interests, I am inclined to think that England, in any negotiations to such an end, will adopt much the same sort of attitude as she took up between Austria and Turkey, *i.e.* ' We give our consent to all that seems acceptable to France." (Even though such negotiations were confined to the French and ourselves, they would be sure to keep the English fully informed.) The existence of hostility between France and Germany in Morocco is useful to England only for so long as she sees in us a possible military opponent. Otherwise it has no object. If we get an understanding on the naval question then our military opposition to England fades into the background. It now remains to be seen how best to obtain such an understanding. Among other things it is most necessary that our intentions be kept strictly secret till the moment when we seriously think of making a definite suggestion. No preliminary " feelers," therefore, in the press. Further, we must be careful not to look as though we were making a virtue of necessity, that is to say, there must be a " *bon mouvement* " from our side inspired by a genuine wish to come to a settlement with England. Such a step would produce a deep impression here. It seems to me of very great importance, in strengthening our position with England, that the Financial Reform which you are urging should receive the sanction of the Reichstag. Then we could show to all the world that our capacity for taxation is not exhausted, that we have no need to base our financial existence on credit. But if we do not manage to put our financial house in order, and then proceed to ask England to negotiate on the naval question, the English will at once conclude that we are at the end of our tether financially, and therefore, in any case, compelled to slow down the building of our fleet, whether or not we achieve an understanding with them. German financial reform is being followed here with close attention. I need scarcely add that, should this happen, it would not create the best of atmospheres in which to achieve a naval settlement. The next English budget, so I hear, is to be based solely on taxation of the rich, so that there is already great uneasiness in the possessing classes. Incomes above a certain level are to be heavily taxed. This year, unless I am mistaken, the death duties have already reached the enormous yield of £22,000,000. I gather that all this tends to drive English capital abroad. The legacy duties you are demanding are very modest compared to those in England. And, against death duties in themselves, the English scarcely raise any objection. What disquietens them is their exorbitant rise, which threatens to ruin English landowners, and along with them the power of the great families who have given England some of her best statesmen. There can be no more indirect taxation here without recourse to Protection, whereas we in Germany have an almost virgin field for this in such articles as beer, tobacco and wine. Your programme of allowing the broad shoulders of the majority to bear part of the burden of indirect taxation, instead of loading everything directly on to the shoulders of the " chosen few," [1] though you make these also contribute with a moderate and considered death duty, is far sounder, economically than the English, and less likely to be resented as class taxation. But if, as usually happens in Germany, everyone wants to pass on the new taxation to the next man, the result can only be—nil. In regard to the *modus vivendi* of naval settlement I would suggest a preliminary conversation with Asquith rather than with Grey, and that we speak quite academically and intimately, without precise and special instructions. The possibility of our ever reducing our fleet should remain a close secret for the present. It will be quite enough if we use, as our bargaining instrument, a possible slowing down of the *tempo* of naval construction. But here, of course, we must cease to proceed on the assumption that whatever we may not build in the first three years we shall be able to build in the next three. That would not be a method of bargaining, but at best a suggestion to the English that with every year the danger is increasing. Any slowing down of *tempo*, likely to be of use to us here would mean, I suppose, our consent not to build more than two battleships a year.

On 9th February 1909 the King and Queen of England arrived in Berlin, where they were received by the Emperor and Empress, the Crown Prince and Princess, and all the Princes and Princesses of the Royal House. As the train steamed slowly into the Lehrter Bahnhof, Metternich, who in obedience to etiquette, had come to Berlin to be present at their Majesties' visit, and was standing between myself and Tirpitz, said to the Secretary of State for the Navy: " Unless you make it possible for Prince Bülow to bring off the naval agreement he wants with England, and is doing his utmost

---

[1] English in text.

to get, this will probably be the last time that an English king comes here to visit a German emperor."

As soon as he had greeted our Sovereigns, King Edward came straight up to me and said how pleased he was to see me again. At a banquet held that same evening in the White Saloon of the Royal Castle, the Emperor delivered a toast, which he and I had composed together as follows: " Your Majesties may rest assured that, with myself, my capital and seat of residence, together with the whole German Empire, sees in Your Majesties' presence here a sign of that feeling of friendship which has induced Your Majesties to visit us. The German nation greets the ruler of the mighty British Empire with all the respect that is due to him, and considers this visit a new guarantee for the maintenance of pacific and friendly relations between our two countries and peoples. I know how much our wishes for the maintenance and strengthening of peace are in agreement, and I can offer Your Majesty no fairer welcome than by expressing my confident conviction that Your Majesty's visit will contribute to the realization of such wishes. In expressing the hope that the wide realm over which Your Majesty rules will continue to thrive and prosper, I raise my glass to the health of Your Majesty and Her Majesty."

The King, whom I had caused to be informed beforehand of the Emperor's speech, replied, also in German:

Although I have the most pleasant memories of my frequent visits to Kiel, Wilhelmshaven and Cronberg, it gives me new and special pleasure that the Queen should have been able to accompany me on this present visit, and that we should have been welcomed here in this ancient castle, the seat of Your Majesty's ancestors, in the centre of Your Majesty's capital, and city of residence, Berlin. Your Majesty's words as to the aim and purpose of our visit, and the results which we hope it will achieve, have so ably expressed my own feelings that I can only repeat that our sojourn here is intended not merely to remind the world of that close tie of kinship which links our houses, but to strengthen afresh the friendly relation between our countries for the maintenance of the peace of the world, to which my whole effort is directed. With the wish that the prosperous development of Your Majesty's Empire may continue, I raise my glass to your health, to the health of Her Majesty the Empress, to your whole house.

During this banquet the Emperor drank my health with an elaborate show of cordiality. A happy coincidence had enabled me to sign the already mentioned Franco-German agreement on Morocco on the very day of the English Sovereigns' arrival. In the conversation which King Edward accorded me after dinner he expressed his entire satisfaction with the agreement I had arrived at with France. "You have," he declared with a smile, "won a diplomatic success on which I personally congratulate you. No doubt you will come equally well out of the Bosnian affair." Still smiling, he added, fingering one of the knots of my tunic: "But keep a sharp look out on *him*, and see that he doesn't get too uppish about it." As he said these words King Edward looked across at his nephew the Emperor, who was standing some little distance away from us. Till then our conversation had been in English, but, in giving me this gentle hint, His Majesty had used the Berlin expression: "*Dass er nicht zu sehr prampiert.*"

On 10th February King Edward visited the Rathaus. The Emperor, not particularly pleased at his uncle's visiting "The Red House," did not put in an appearance at the ceremony. But the King had willingly gone at my suggestion. He seemed much less constrained, among the aldermen and councillors of Berlin, than he had been at the ceremonial banquet in the castle: he was gay and amiable, almost familiar, as he talked with the worthy City Fathers. His German cousins at Coburg, Darmstadt, or Strelitz could not have chatted in their castles in a pleasanter circle after dinner. To the toast of the Bürgermeister, Kirschner, the King only gave a brief reply, but he spoke in a deep, clear voice, and most expressively: "I thank you for having given me this chance of letting you know how sincerely grateful I am for the magnificent reception of yesterday, and for letting me see your beautiful City Hall. I am very glad to be back in Berlin. My chief desire is that the relations between our two countries may always be the friendliest possible."

This speech was received with general cheers. When the musical programme was beginning the King asked me to come and sit beside him. Several times he turned to me, and said: "Very nice, very nice indeed."[1] And again: "They seem to be very good people and quite reasonable."[1] Obviously his Imperial nephew had been making some disparaging remarks about the municipal council of Berlin, which the Emperor could never bring himself to like because it had several times opposed his wishes for the further embellishment of his capital, and he suspected it of inclinations to make a *fronde* against him. Opposite King Edward there stood a certain number of well-known Berliners who had been invited to this reception. I named them all to His Majesty, and among them

---

[1] English in text.

Privy Councillor Renvers. No sooner had he heard the great
doctor's name than the King asked me to beckon him over to us,
telling me how eager he was to meet the distinguished physician, so
devoted in his care for his dear eldest sister, the Empress Frederick,
throughout her last painful illness. Renvers approached the King,
who shook him very warmly by the hand, thanked him, and said:
" You, with your art, your skill, your devotion, your kindness, did
all that was humanly possible to assuage the terrible sufferings of
the poor Empress."

When, next morning, the Berlin papers, not having received any
official indication on the subject, spontaneously reported the King
of England's visit to the Rathaus, one or two of them included in
their accounts these gracious words of King Edward to Professor
Renvers. One such report had been submitted to the Emperor,
not by me, in the usual morning batch of press-cuttings. He
scribbled a highly indignant marginal note: " Nonsense! My
mother never knew Renvers." I showed this in confidence to
Renvers. He seemed much perplexed. " This is terrible," he
said, " it is almost pathological." He continued that, in 1899, he had
been entrusted, by the Emperor's consent, with the care of the
Empress Frederick, who was suffering from carcinoma, and added—
I give his exact words—" In 1901, the year in which the Empress
died, the Emperor gave me a long audience before embarking on
his North Sea trip. He made me give a solemn promise to report
to him at once if his mother's state became sufficiently grave, so that
he might see her again while she still lived. I gave him this promise,
and I kept it, and His Majesty the Emperor stood beside me, the
physician in charge, for many hours at the dying Empress's bedside,
through the whole of her last agony." After his mother's death,
the Emperor had had another very long conversation with Renvers
on the nature of cancer—and now, this marginal note. I asked
Renvers how, as a doctor, he would explain the case, and he answered:
" If the Emperor were an ordinary patient I should diagnose
Pseudologia phantastica." When I asked him to explain this technical
term, he said with a laugh: " A tendency to live in phantasy. Or,
to put it quite bluntly, to lie." We discussed what was best to be
done. Renvers, an experienced neurologist, explained to me that
such tendencies to phantasy are common enough with all neurasthenic patients, but do not prevent their living to a ripe old age,
displaying great activity, and real talent in certain fields, since such
infirmities are entirely compatible with unusual, even brilliant gifts,
though certainly they are not desirable in a ruler. But what was the
remedy? Renvers told me that he had often spoken about it with

the old physician in ordinary to the Emperor, Surgeon-General von Leuthold, and that he only knew of one remedy for nervous diseases of the kind:—bodily and mental quiet; composure; self-discipline. " If," said Renvers, " you could persuade the Emperor to read a serious book alone for two hours every day—the sort of book on which one has to concentrate—you would have done a very great deal."

At the first suitable opportunity I suggested such mental hygiene to the Emperor, though scrupulously avoiding the tone of a pedagogue. I even mentioned certain books to him—Schopenhauer's *Parerga* and *Paralipomena*, Wilhelm von Humboldt's *Letters to a Friend*, Thucydides, and certain of Plato's dialogues, Wilhelm Meister's *Lehrjahre*, etc. But I do not think my Imperial master listened.

CHAPTER XXVIII

Lunch at the British Embassy—Conversation with Edward VII—Lord Crewe—The English visit to the Reichstag—Problem of an agreement with England as to the tempo of naval expansion—Report from Walter Rathenau on his English impressions—Letter of William II —Conference on the naval question, of all departments concerned.

AT the wish of King Edward only my wife and I had been invited to the luncheon given at the British Embassy on 12th February. The King commanded me to take the Queen's arm and himself conducted my wife to table. He was in a very good humour. He talked to my wife at length of his dead sister, the Empress Frederick, whose close friend she had been, and added: " Your husband has not a particularly easy time of it with my nephew, the Kaiser." He thought the Kaiser very gifted but often " very imprudent." Through the *Daily Telegraph* affair, or rather through all he had said at Highcliffe, the Emperor had placed his principal minister in an extremely difficult, a really painful situation. After lunch the King drew me aside and said: " Shall you remain? I wish you'd remain for the benefit of your country and for peace in Europe. How do you get on with the Emperor? It does not seem to be very easy for his ministers to get on with him." [1] It would have been both unwise and in bad taste if I had replied with banal remarks about his nephew whom the King knew as well as I did. I preferred to tell him that the Kaiser was certainly sometimes careless in his utterances, that he was prone to exaggeration, was too excitable and altogether still very young in spite of his fifty years. " But," I continued, " there is one thing that I can assure Your Majesty quite frankly and certainly—the Emperor is peacefully disposed for the simple reason that he takes his duties as a Christian and a monarch very seriously. He is by no means an intriguer by nature. There is nothing he desires more sincerely than good relations with England, and his natural temperament and the whole of his upbringing incline him towards them." The King said he thought I was right and that the Kaiser's intentions were almost always of the best. But he needed careful, experienced, advisers. He must not imagine that in these days a sovereign at the head of a

---

[1] English in original.

great empire could govern entirely by himself. " That will never do in modern times." [1]

Then the King said that he would send me bronze busts of Queen Alexandra and himself as a souvenir both of this visit and of his many years acquaintance with me and my still older acquaintance-ship with the Queen. During our conversation it struck me that the King looked ill. His breathing was heavy, he seemed over-fatigued, exhausted. When our talk came to an end he sat down in a big arm-chair, while I went across to another part of the room to talk to the gentlemen of his suite. But even from there I could observe how His Majesty's pallor increased; at last he seemed to be asleep. An English doctor who had been with us at lunch asked all those present to leave the room. After a good quarter of an hour the guests were recalled. The King made no reference to his attack. He made a sign to Daisy, Princess Pless, who had arrived at the Embassy after lunch. Princess Daisy was one of the prettiest women I have ever met, tall with a lovely figure, exquisite complexion, magnificent hair, splendid teeth, a typical English beauty. She had been a Miss Corn-wallis-West of the Earls of De La Warr and was the wife of one of the Kaiser's closest friends, Prince Hans Heinrich of Pless, the eldest son of the Duke of Pless, and Fräulein von Kleist. Prince Hans Heinrich, in contrast to his distinguished father, was superficial and common-place. In his castle at Pless, furnished with Oriental luxury, William II wasted a great deal of his time during the war, instead of visiting the troops in the trenches or at least sweeping out the bases with an iron broom, or inspecting the wounded in field-hospitals. The Silesian headquarters of William II were very different from those of his great ancestor during the Seven Years' War.

One hundred and fifty years after the Battle of Leuthen, six years before 1914, the beautiful châtelaine of Pless, full of anxiety for the health of the ruler of her own country, curtsied gracefully in the English Embassy in the Wilhelmstrasse in front of Edward VII. The head of the British Empire inspected her with all the satisfaction of an old connoisseur of female beauty. It was the last time I ever saw King Edward and that picture remains in my mind. The King was neither as wicked nor as wise as he was thought to be, particularly in Germany, but he possessed two very valuable quali-ties—a knowledge of men and how to handle them with prudence and tact. These would have made him equally successful as the director of a big industrial trust; as it was they made of him a successful constitutional monarch of a World Empire under parliamentary government.

[1] English in original.

Among the King's suite was the head of the Privy Council, the Earl of Crewe, son-in-law of Lord Rosebery, who had been Foreign Secretary in 1886 and 1892, and Prime Minister from 1894 to 1895. Lord Crewe was a good type of those aristocratic English statesmen who, for centuries, have maintained and enlarged the British Empire with their policy of " common-sense," unshakeable calm, and traditional understanding of what makes for a healthy, practical policy. Lord Crewe talked to me in just as peaceful and matter-of-fact a strain as his sovereign, but he too stressed the fact that a naval agreement between us would be eminently desirable. He admitted that English anxiety over the German Navy, still so much weaker than the British, was much exaggerated. But I must not forget that the British Empire, the Motherland herself, would stand or fall by British security—absolute security—at sea. Britain must be the impregnable mistress of the ocean. England had no wish to diminish, still less destroy, German industry, German commerce, the German navy, nor indeed the German Empire in any way. Was not Germany England's best customer and *vice versa*? But the Germans had special talents for organization, and the young German navy was quite an excellent one: it was precisely because it was so excellent that the English did not wish to repeat at sea the experience of the Austrians and French on land in 1866 and 1870.

When, a few weeks later, the Reichstag discussed the estimates for the Imperial Chancellery I took the opportunity of mentioning the English royal visit, which had gone very well, as in every way a happy event. The speeches made by the King in Berlin, re-enforced by his speech at the opening of parliament in London, and the subsequent debate in the House of Commons, had again shown clearly to both peoples how much reason they had for mutual respect; for being content with peaceful competition. I continued: " The network of their connections has become so tightly enmeshed that it will not be easy to destroy, however much malice may try to do so. Apart from all ethical considerations there were scarcely two other countries so dependent on each other as England and Germany. Germany, as I showed, statistics in hand, was the best client of the United Kingdom, while, on the other hand, no other nation took so large a proportion of German exports as England. The figures I gave were my proof of values whose power to unite the two peoples had been practically tested for many years. Most certainly, just as with us, there were in England, though her people are politically so advanced, fanatics who could not realize our common interest. But these, I sincerely hoped, would never succeed in gaining decisive influence on English political thought. The impressions I had gained in England in a number of political conversations there, strengthened me in this hope which, in any case, I was not expressing for the first time in the Reichstag.

The question nearest my heart during the whole of my last period in office was the conclusion of an Anglo-German naval understanding. In the spring of 1909 Albert Ballin, who had just heard from Sir Ernest Cassel, the intimate friend of King Edward, told me that the former had written again to him that our naval programme was " the Alpha and Omega of all English mistrust, as of all English machinations."

Not long afterwards Ballin sent me a long and brilliantly written report from Walter Rathenau, describing his impressions of England. Rathenau stressed the point that England was obsessed by two anxieties—the economic and the colonial. What was the situation economically? Modern industry, highly grouped and organized—machine-making, for instance, and chemical and electrical production—was based on two factors: technique and organization—that is to say on the efficiency of the technical and commercial employé. In the older branches of industry, which supplied detailed commodities, England still maintained her position. But in great sections of modern industry, whose more highly organized methods of production enabled them to supply manufactured goods to the finishing trades, she was behind Germany. As for the Colonies the centrifugal forces were becoming stronger every day, and to check these, England had only her Navy on which to rely, so that, with every ship that Germany built, a stone was loosened in the masonry of the Colonial edifice. Against these two great anxieties England had only two means of self-preservation. One was a protective tariff, feasible in principle but probably not to be recommended. The other was naval expansion, but this was perhaps not so easily carried out as appeared at the first glance. England was no longer so lavish in expenditure as formerly.

Rathenau concluded as follows:

It is to be noted that both these anxieties—the industrial and the colonial—force England to study Germany. Germany is a competitor and a rival. This feeling has been apparent in all my conversations with cultured Englishmen. Sometimes it takes the form of a compliment, sometimes it is said ironically, sometimes it becomes a direct reproach. " You'll soon be passing us." " You have passed us," etc. A third important point should be added, of which we, in Germany, are not always conscious—the impression we Germans make on foreigners. Outsiders who cast their eyes over Europe see a seething mass, a people of restless activity, and enormous spiritual and mental vitality, hemmed in by older, more stagnant nations. Eight hundred thousand fresh Germans a year! Every five years an additional population nearly equal to that of Scandinavia or Switzerland! And one asks how long declining France can withstand the atmospheric pressure of such a neighbour. So that every English discontent is beginning to be crystallized and summed up in this one concept—Germany. What, in the educated classes, has become a reasoned conviction, comes out, in the rank and file, in provincials, and in young people, in the form of prejudice, hate, fantastic misconception, to an extent far surpassing our own best journalistic efforts. It would be superficial and futile to hope that small acts of friendliness, visits of deputations, or press manœuvres, could dam up a dissatisfaction that flows from so deep a source. Only the ensemble of our policy is capable of at last giving England the impression that, on Germany's side, there is no irritation, no fear, no pressing need to expand and take an offensive attitude. Such a policy, though it will not convince the masses, may, at least bring governments to a consciousness of their responsibilities.

I gave all the more weight to these opinions since Rathenau, very ambitious and therefore careful not to clash with the opinions of his sovereign, was obviously, in this memorandum, striving not to come into conflict with desires and aspirations known to exist in the most exalted quarter. He closed, in words which might have been dictated by Tirpitz, affirming that, with every year that passed, the relationship between the two fleets would be more in our favour, and that this would bring about " a gradual consolidation." Before this came the clever sentence: " If it is exact that, since wars of conquest ceased, war in Europe has been declared chiefly because, in their embarrassment at having mismanaged a situation, governments did not know what else to do, it appears that, once again, nothing must be left undone which can in any way contribute to peaceful politics."

I took this report as the basis for a longer immediate report to His Majesty. The Kaiser agreed with my favourable verdict of Rathenau's impressions. But unluckily William II refused to see that it was time, high time, to come to some sensible naval agreement with England. The more our shipbuilding worried England the more did the Kaiser seek a scapegoat for this uncomfortable and undesirable state of affairs. He found one, quite wrong-headedly, in our Ambassador in London, Paul Metternich, whom he had formerly approved, but whom, now, he began to reproach with not opposing English fears and misconceptions with the necessary energy. A reflection of this attitude is to be found in the following letter, which I received from His Majesty at the beginning of April.

To-day, before Tirpitz came to you, I went through this whole filthy English naval and Dreadnought business again with him, in the presence of von Müller and Plessen, and empowered him to discuss these matters with you, too, in the same sense. We all concluded, on the basis of the sequence of dates, that Metternich actually does deserve part of the blame for the present involved situation. I had made a tremendous personal concession—that in 1912 no amendment should be issued—and I had impressed it upon him that he must make some eventual use of it. Instead of which, for no reason, he has simply thrown this card away, with nothing from the English in exchange for it but lies, calumnies, and insults galore. The whole thing has been mismanaged, he has forced himself and us into a corner. (1) The English, although they form the constitutional state *par excellence* made the most blatant political blunder at Cronberg in ignoring both constitutional usage and all properly qualified personalities—that is to say yourself, Schön, Tirpitz, and others, and in taking me, the Supreme War Lord and monarch, directly to task in a menacing and commanding tone with: " You must stop building." [1] That ought never to have happened, since it was not, as is now maintained in Parliament, " an offer of negotiations," but a one-sided demand on England's part, which we could only answer as we did. In the autumn, when England approached Metternich with all sorts of officious questions and suggestions, the ambassador ought to have rubbed that into the English government, in the plainest, most brutal and energetic fashion possible, and have seen to it that we received an apology for this indescribable behaviour towards ourselves. Only then could we have accepted any official proposition from London and allowed negotiations to proceed. (2) Since unfortunately the ambassador omitted to act as I have indicated, the English still adopt the tone and attitude of Cronberg, and Metternich, and through him, Ourselves, are being constantly assailed with new masked demands, to do as they would have us do. All this means that, although we committed ourselves to nothing, there has been no question of two equal powers discussing a suggestion, but always the same somewhat haughty demand of a stronger party

[1] English in the original.

to a weaker, who is not considered as an equal. Hence our refusal, since our personal honour was nearly always at stake. (3) The English suggestions, though expressly they committed to nothing, having always assumed the character of demands to be fulfilled as soon as possible, never once showed any intention of negotiations on an equal footing, and equally binding to either party: so that, neither at Crönberg, where we are told "You must stop building," nor later, in the course of the winter and autumn negotiations, did the English show the slightest sign of any intention to stop arming at the same time as ourselves. On the contrary they always gave us to understand that it was in their interest that we should disarm, so that they, of course, could maintain their advantage with as little trouble and expense as possible! That is a point of view we cannot accept either from the military or national standard of honour. (4) Every English intrigue and machination is bent on forcing us to accept the Two Power Standard. This we neither will nor can consent to, unless we are prepared to capitulate before the world and forfeit our national honour—and we will not. Let England, as much as she will, assert her supremacy at sea. Let her build ships accordingly, and base her programme on any kind of ratio she chooses—that is her business. But I utterly and finally refuse to recognize the Two Power Standard, above all as applied solely against us, and still more to consolidate it for ever by any kind of written agreement. "They may have a certain start of us—granted! But the Two Power Standard—never!" . . . such are the words that Tirpitz used before witnesses. (5) From the whole of the above it is clear that England, hitherto, has made no single honest suggestion for binding negotiations between equals, but has tried, in an informal and underhand fashion, to corner us and prevent us from building. We could not consent to play this game. But now, after having spoken with Tirpitz and studied the technical suggestions he lays before me, both I and he are perfectly ready to negotiate with England if she asks us frankly to treat with her. We would discuss on the basis of three to four ships of the line, withdrawing the suggestion made last autumn, by which we renounced an amendment for 1912. That can be settled elsewhere according to Tirpitz's plan.

I would therefore suggest that Your Excellency should let Tirpitz work you out a formula which ignores figures and types for the time being, and lays down, on a broad basis, our proposals, should the English government give us a fresh opportunity, of an official and formal nature, to offer our opinion on the subject.

But of course they must promise us sincerely to cease building so extravagantly on their side.

To resume then: Courteous negotiations between equals instead of peremptory desires imposed by one party only. That is the sense of von Tirpitz's report to myself, with which I agree.

WILLIAM I. R.

I may add, in explanation, to the above Imperial letter, which I have reproduced textually, that the Müller named at the beginning of it was Chief of the Naval Cabinet, and Plessen, whom I have already described in full, for many years Adjutant-General de service and Commander at Imperial Grand Headquarters.

On the 3rd June 1909 I summoned a conference at the Chancellor's Palace on the subject of an understanding with England. In addition to myself there were present Tirpitz, Metternich, the Secretaries of State for the Interior and for Foreign Affairs, Bethmann-Hollweg, and Schön, the Chief of the Military Cabinet, Vice-Admiral von Müller, and General von Moltke, the Chief of General Staff. Here is the official protocol of these proceedings:

The Imperial Chancellor opened the discussion, after pointing out briefly the great importance of the subject, with the reading of a letter written by His Majesty the Kaiser on 3rd April 1909. In this letter His Majesty expresses his agreement with the opinions submitted to him by Admiral von Tirpitz on an eventual understanding with England, and instructs the Imperial Chancellor to request Admiral von Tirpitz to draw up a formula which may serve as basis for negotiations. The letter censures the diplomatic method of the Ambassador in London, Count Metternich, who obtained from English statesmen no equivalent for our eventual relinquishment of a naval amendment and demanded no redress for the unconstitutional procedure of Sir Charles Hardinge at Cronberg. The Imperial Chancellor next read a communication from Count Metternich in which this gentleman upholds his attitude. The Imperial Chancellor stressed the fact that among those present there must be no thought of personal susceptibilities. All were united in the single endeavour to serve Emperor and Fatherland to the best of their ability. But he wished to leave no doubt on one point: the first duty of a representative of His Majesty abroad is to report the truth and describe conditions as they are. An Ambassador who acts in this manner must always be supported by the Imperial Chancellor, whether or not his reports make pleasant reading, since it is useless to grumble at a barometer because it indicates bad weather. The first question to be debated was whether Admiral

von Tirpitz's suggestion to establish a relation of three to four with
England could be regarded as a basis for understanding, leaving out
the relinquishment of an amendment.   In the opinion of Count
Metternich any such suggestion made to England would lead very
quickly to war.   The Imperial Chancellor himself points out that,
judging by all accounts he has received, public opinion in England
is very seriously inflamed against us.   This ill-feeling is grounded
on the supposition that our naval construction approximates too
dangerously to the English.   Under the impression of this anxiety
England, throughout the whole world, has recently shown herself
inimical to us, and has been trying to bring other Powers into conflict with us.   This state of affairs has been proved by several quite
recent documents.   People who must be taken seriously in England
are predicting a war with Germany.   What remains to be ascertained are our chances in case of such a war.   Admiral von Tirpitz
had expressed his view that for the next few years we could not
regard any conflict with England with equanimity.   The question
therefore was paramount whether an understanding with England
were possible.   It is manifest that diplomatic measures no longer
suffice to calm the English.   An agreement might perhaps be
achieved on the basis of a simultaneous slowing-down of the tempo
of naval construction.   The best course would be to reach such an
agreement in conjunction with an understanding on other questions,
those for instance touching colonial or commercial policy, and those
of an universally political nature.   An agreement might take the
form of a convention of neutrality.   The Chancellor is of opinion
that our relations with England are the only dark cloud on the
horizon of our foreign policy which, in other respects, is more serene
than it has been for many years past.   Not for twenty years had we
been so respected and feared in the world as to-day.   But the question of our relationship with England obscures the whole of our
future.   Count Metternich, on the invitation of the Imperial Chancellor, next gave his impressions on the state of public feeling in
England.   Twenty years ago this was still favourable to Germany
and the Triple Alliance.   But it had become impaired through
the Krüger telegram and the German attitude to the Boer War.
English feeling against us had not, however, become thoroughly
and seriously inimical till the moment when our naval programme
and public agitation on its behalf had given the English the constantly increasing impression that our fleet would mean a serious
menace to England, for whom absolute security and supremacy at
sea were matters of vital importance.   It was not so much German
rivalry in international markets, though this too was certainly

disagreeable to the English, but actually the German naval policy which had caused this deep-seated mistrust.

Admiral von Tirpitz suggested that misunderstandings might arise from His Majesty's letter. He personally had always striven to convince His Majesty of the unwisdom of refusing *a priori* any discussion on the question of naval armaments. On the 3rd April 1903 he had made, at the Chancellor's instigation, an immediate report, and had suggested to the Chancellor, at that time, that by the autumn of 1908 it might be possible to admit as a basis of negotiation the proportion of three to four. This proposition would no doubt have had some chance of being accepted by England, since the English, at that moment, only wanted to build four new ships. But at present things were otherwise. It would have been preferable to have given no promise to refrain from an amendment in 1912 and to have used this as a lever for negotiations. In the Admiral's opinion Count Metternich over-estimated the danger of war with England. The Admiral's personal observations lead him to conclude that English bad temper is the result of German economic and political competition, and that the present agitation is essentially due to the intrigues of Sir John Fisher who represents the Admiralty and works against the Germans with every under-hand method. The more we strengthen our fleet the less ready England will be to quarrel with us. The Admiral thinks that the " navy scare " has died down in England. He could only repeat his regret that Count Metternich should have given the assurance that for 1912 no amendment was proposed, without getting anything in exchange, and that he, as a Secretary of State, should not have been consulted at the time instructions were issued to Count Metternich. The Admiral considers it inopportune, even dangerous, after the attitude adopted this spring by the English government, to take the initiative in any agreement with England. England should take the first step. We should listen to their proposals and then make our offer.

In any case our new constructions for 1912 will fall from four units to two, and this represents a slowing-down, and should have been pointed out to the English as such. In the Admiral's opinion we should not count on a new attempt at agreement. We could in no case enter into an understanding with England without obtaining sufficient military counter-concessions. On the whole he is for waiting quietly in present circumstances. Count Metternich repeated that he had received from His Majesty definite instructions to assure the English that the Emperor has no intention of going beyond the established naval programme. He had never heard, until a few days ago, of any projected amendment for 1912. Admiral von

Tirpitz declared that the whole world, and with it the English, must be aware that 1911 will be a critical year in which an amendment might be expected. In his report of his conversation with Sir Charles Hardinge, dated 30th June 1908, the Ambassador had already clearly stated that the English fear within a few years a new amendment in addition to the German Navy Law.

The Imperial Chancellor pointed out that, hitherto, the conversations and notes which he has exchanged with the Secretary of State for the Marine Office, have never given him the impression that a desire in that quarter existed for a naval understanding with England. It astonished him to hear at present that the Secretary of State for the Marine Office had, last autumn, considered such an understanding possible and even desirable; he, the Chancellor, had had no idea that this was so. On the other hand he cannot understand why that which, at the time, the Secretary of State considered both possible and useful, should now be repudiated by him. English disquiet was not due to the machinations of Sir John Fisher. It unfortunately sprang from a profoundly rooted conviction in the English that our increase of naval power threatened the foundations of the British Empire. On this point we should be under no illusion. One may pursue all sorts of policies but never that of the ostrich. In spite of the efficiency of our navy, recognized and admired by us all, we are not, by Admiral von Tirpitz's own showing, at present in a position to come out of a fight with England as victors. To bridge the period of danger between to-day and the achievement of our fleet, understanding with England is desirable. Such understanding, of course, can only be based on mutual agreements. He felt no need to stress the point that he, the Imperial Chancellor, would never recommend a step, nor accept a solution, unless it were in full accord with the dignity of the nation. The manner in which, for twelve years past, he has carried on the foreign affairs of the country should vouch for this. Admiral von Tirpitz declared that he is well aware of the present danger, that he has already pointed it out, and that it induced him to discountenance the agitation raised by the Navy League at the instigation of General Keim. He, also, desires to see a pause. In connection with this, and the remarks of the Imperial Chancellor, he indicates the written report sent to His Highness on the 20th of January 1909 in which he announced himself in entire accord with the view of the Imperial Chancellor that it would not be possible to refuse England should she suggest a fresh reduction of naval construction in both countries, by mutual agreement. Such a refusal would, indeed, be detrimental to the moral prestige of Germany. He had added in this report that, from the end of September 1908, he had endeavoured to set this point of view before the Emperor. The proposal made in it—to continue in the proportion of three to four—would, within ten years, have given the English almost their desired Two Power Standard, *i.e.*, the ratio 2 : 3·6. The Cabinet Minister, von Bethmann-Hollweg, considered any initiative on our part for an agreement, only advisable if we are able to make a definitely formulated proposition. But the present discussion had not got as far as that. Perhaps a certain relaxation of the present tension with England might be achieved in the matter of the Colonies and commercial policy. For the last, however, the primary condition—England's adoption of protective tariffs—was lacking. Count Metternich was of opinion that an understanding on these colonial and commercial questions, though desirable, would be insufficient to allay English anxieties. This could only be achieved by a naval agreement. Would it not be possible to make a concession to England by slowing down our rate of construction? Admiral von Tirpitz answered this by pointing out that, in 1912, there will be a reduction of from four to two ships. The Chancellor suggested that Count Metternich be empowered to say informally to the English that we are ready to discuss naval questions. The Ambassador should make no concrete proposals but should let it be understood that our concessions might take the form of a gradual slowing-down in construction and of our giving up additional amendments. The Minister, von Bethmann-Hollweg, here queried whether any reduction of speed in building would be possible without a modification of the Navy Law. General von Moltke was of opinion that we have no chance of coming victorious out of a conflict with England, and that consequently, he too is in favour of an honourable agreement, perhaps on a basis of reduction of the time taken in building. We must certainly not conceal from ourselves the fact that a failure to reach such agreement might mean war.

The Imperial Chancellor again pointed out the dangers of the position. At this moment the only dark cloud on our horizon lies across the English Channel, but it is a storm cloud. Admiral von Tirpitz stressed the annually increasing value of our navy, including the reserve formations. An eventual delay of five years in building, placing the final achievement of our programme in 1925, such as Count Metternich seemed to have in mind, would mean to us the loss of fifteen Capital Ships. With such a delay our whole naval programme becomes worthless.

Herr von Bethmann-Hollweg: The growing strength of our navy is precisely what the English have perceived, and what causes them so much anxiety. What could our Admiralty offer if a friendly feeler on England's part should lead to a fresh discussion?

Admiral von Tirpitz: Our eventual offer can only depend on the English proposal and cannot be formulated in advance.

Herr von Bethmann-Hollweg: Is not a reduction in speed possible, in the sense of our building three new ships next year instead of four, on condition that the English, on their side, limit themselves to four—I mean Capital Ships, of course?

Admiral von Tirpitz then explained that such a slowing-down need not necessarily mean a modification of the Navy Law, and that a reduction of four to three might be made to tally with the Budget. The Chancellor suggested that such a measure would therefore be possible without debates in the Reichstag and without too much publicity. Admiral von Müller emphasized the fact that it must be clearly understood that any entente with England on the matter of slowing-down naval construction will only be possible if England offers a mutual concession on the same lines, *i.e.*, a reduction in her own naval programme. This suggestion is unanimously approved. The Chancellor then repeated that England must promise us entire reciprocity not only in the matter of armaments but in political assurance as well. Admiral von Tirpitz stated that in his opinion the danger zone in our relationship with England would have been crossed within five or six years, that is to say, by about 1915, after the widening of the Kaiser Wilhelm Canal and the completion of our arrangements in Heligoland. Even within two years we should be in a less dangerous position.

The Imperial Chancellor: That is very nice. But the question still remains. How are we to get out of our present difficulties? Admiral von Tirpitz considers that these can be evaded by means of an understanding about new ships in the proportion 3:4.

The Imperial Chancellor asked the Secretary of State for the Navy to work out a formula for agreement according to the commands of His Majesty. At the same time, however, His Highness called attention to the fact that no diplomacy in the world can bring the English Government to accept a formula which would appear to menace England's existence.

Admiral von Tirpitz replied that, for the moment, he considers a formula of no value, above all because of the misunderstandings it might occasion when put into practice in the course of negotiations, conducted by a third party, with the English. A formula of this kind could only be regarded as preparatory to the possibility of any real English *démarche* towards an understanding with us on the question of armaments. Only after gauging the measure of the

English approach would it be possible to judge how an eventual formula should be drawn up. The Secretary of State, Admiral von Tirpitz, finally repeated, in this connection, the argument already brought forward (page 5 of Protocol), that, judging by the attitude of the English Government this spring, the initiative cannot come from our side. In conclusion the Imperial Chancellor begged that this debate and the subject matter discussed be kept rigorously secret.

CHAPTER XXIX

H.M. on this Conference—A change in the Imperial attitude towards me —Difficulties arising therefrom in the performance of my duties— New Chiefs of Department—The difficulties at the Foreign Office— Privy Councillor Hammann—Audience and conversation with the Kaiser—Their Majesties dine with us—H.M. again in the best of tempers.

THIS conference of 3rd June 1909 remains an indelible memory. Count Metternich had been calm, almost phlegmatic, but clear and altogether matter-of-fact. He had known quite well that he risked being soon out of favour, after having been in his sovereign's good graces for some time, for opposing the ever-increasing audacity of the Kaiser's naval policy. But he preferred his conviction to his career. Tirpitz, deeply moved in reality, had outwardly seemed equally cold, sometimes crabbed, but full of burning ambition and glowing patriotism, confident as to his own work and the future of the German people, great, even in his errors, but one-sided. The two Secretaries of State for Home and Foreign Affairs, Bethmann-Hollweg and Schön, had been equally afraid of offending either His Majesty or the Chancellor, since no one could be certain whether I might not remain in office after all: "*par nobile fratrum*," to use the words as ironically as Horace! Moltke had been well-intentioned, lucid and reasonable, but, unfortunately, he was not a man of action. The Chief of the Naval Cabinet, von Müller, at that time a satellite of von Tirpitz, was to become his treacherous enemy when the sun of Imperial favour ceased to shine on the man who had created our fleet.

I thought it my duty to give His Majesty a personal report of this conference, my reasons for summoning it, and my attitude during the discussion. The immediate audience I requested was not granted till a week later, on 11th June. On this audience I transferred to my archives the following note: " H.M. replied as follows to my observations on the dangers created for us by English anxieties as to our naval programme. H.M. cannot believe in any such dangers; the English will never attack us alone; at the moment they will not find any allies. In any case we have nothing to fear if they do attack us for, even now, we could do them great damage at sea. The alleged English agitation about our naval programme

was simply bluff, for reasons of English domestic policy. Such is
the opinion of Admiral von Tirpitz, and H.M. is in entire agreement."

But this note is merely the outline of my long and exhaustive
verbal report to His Majesty on 11th June 1909. Basing my
remarks on history and statistics, I stressed the immense resources
of England, her enormous power of action, and the efficiency she
had displayed in all her wars, from those against Louis XIV and
Napoleon down to the Boer War. I told His Majesty that I still
did not believe that the English would attack us unexpectedly,
without warning, as he had sometimes feared they might, but that
undoubtedly, if the race for naval armaments continued at its
present speed, it was to be feared that England would range herself
on the side of our enemies the moment we had the slightest difficulty with any other foreign power, especially Russia. This
paralysed our policy in the present and was a grave danger for the
future, since it was certain that a war on two fronts, against England
and France on the one hand and Russia on the other, would present
very serious dangers. The Kaiser pooh-poohed my fears. He referred me to our General Staff. I answered that even staff-officers
were not infallible, that they underestimated the French *forces
noires*. According to the General Staff, France would not find any
good soldiers in Africa; she might even be obliged to leave more
of her own troops there on garrison duty than she could recruit
natives for her army. I considered this opinion incorrect in view of
impressions I had gained on a journey in Tunis and Algiers. I
had the highest opinion of the Prussian General Staff, the clever
brain of the army, but it had been the traditional mistake of Prussian
military circles to underestimate the military strength of western
powers, particularly the English.

Here I must add, in brief parenthesis, that future events, to my
great sorrow, were to prove me right in all I said. By the Christmas
of 1914 there were five hundred thousand English in France; by
1917 nearly two million. In the Great War England put over six
million men into the field, and more than another three million
from her colonies, her Dominions, and India. In all she mobilized
ten million men.

Again and again I had presented reports to the Emperor on the
advantages of an understanding with England, which we could have
obtained by slowing down our naval programme. I always spoke
as unemotionally as possible, strove to be lucid, serious, and em-
phatic. But very often His Majesty would listen impatiently, and

sometimes with real irritation. More than once I reminded him of our very first interviews on naval policy, in the June of 1897, at Kiel, on my recall from Rome. Faced with the problem of constructing our navy without coming into conflict with England we must not, as I had reminded him in the words of the Roman poet, "*propter vitam vivendi perdere causas.*" Now, twelve years later, I told the Emperor that I felt obliged to repeat this warning emphatically, more emphatically than ever before. We had constructed our fleet for our own defence, I said, but we must not let this protective weapon become a cause of complete estrangement from the English.

My last seven months in office can only be really understood in conjunction with the peculiar emotional, unbalanced, and incoherent temperament of William II. On the surface his behaviour towards me remained the same; in many ways he was even more considerate, contradicted me rarely and unwillingly, and only showed irritation when I began to broach the naval question. But at the same time, he seemed over-anxious about my health, although I had never felt better in my life.

On 6th February 1909, my wife's birthday, he visited us with the Kaiserin, to congratulate her, bringing a handsome bouquet of red carnations, his favourite flower. But on all sides I heard that, behind my back, the Emperor not only spoke of me with disfavour but had begun to tell all sorts of stories concerning the November crisis and my attitude while it lasted. All this made my work extremely difficult. It was harder in any case than it had been when I could count on the solid support of the three Chiefs of Cabinet, Lucanus, Hülsen, and von Senden. Of these the last had often complicated my foreign policy by his tactlessness and anti-English prejudice, but, notwithstanding, had felt it necessary, in the interests of the Empire and the dynasty, that I should remain at the head of affairs, and so had always opposed intrigues against me. His successor, Admiral von Müller, was more suave and pliable but less dependable, and entirely sycophantic towards the Kaiser. But, at bottom, the admiral was a muddle-headed pietist and pacifist, tendencies which, no doubt, did infinite credit to his good-heartedness, but which scarcely qualified him to represent that brilliant spirit of active resolution which distinguished our navy. Count Hülsen-Haeseler had succeeded Adjutant-General von Hahnke. Von Hahnke, much older than myself, I had felt as a benevolent and thoroughly reliable guide. Hülsen had been my personal friend for many years. During the November crisis he died suddenly of an apopleptic stroke, at the castle of Donaueschingen, only a few hours after having implored the Emperor not to part with me. His successor, General von Lyncker, was a good and honourable soldier, but without initiative. He regarded himself always and only as a good, loyal, and dutiful Adjutant-General, awaiting orders. Lastly the highly intelligent and skilful Lucanus had been replaced by Herr von Valentini.

A witty Russian friend, Ernest Meyendorff, once said to me: *" Une longue expérience m'a prouvé qu'on ne réussit jamais à tuer, son successeur."* Lucanus knew how changeable His Majesty was. When he noticed that the Emperor had taken a special liking to Herr von Berg, His Majesty's corps fellow at the University, who still remained a close favourite, and had become Councillor in the Civil Cabinet, he thought he would do his best to supersede him. As his successor Lucanus had chosen the Regierungspräsident at Frankfurt on the Oder, Herr von Valentini who seemed to him too insignificant ever to be made Chief of the Civil Cabinet. And von Berg did in fact become chief shortly before the Revolution, so Lucanus had no success with his scheme. As for Valentini, for ten years he had all too many opportunities of showing himself a nonentity, and a very feeble one at that.

Here is the last letter I ever received from Lucanus, shortly before his death:

> Your Excellency has given me great pleasure in expressing so warm an interest in my health. I am now able to leave my bed, and hope that I shall soon be about again. How many and how great are the problems awaiting your solution. May God's protection and blessing assist you. In unchanging regard, and constant affection I remain,
>
> Your Excellency's devoted and loyal friend,
> LUCANUS.

More painful still than the loss of my three Chiefs of Cabinet was the death of Field-Marshal General von Loë, my beloved Colonel in 1870, and for many years a friend whom I had loved as a father. Deeply moved, I sent the following telegram to his widow, who did not follow her husband till fourteen years later, when she was nearly ninety:—" The news of your husband's death has touched me deeply. The Field-Marshal's name will live eternally in the history of Prussia and of Germany. He was a knight, *sans peur et sans reproche*, loyal to his God, his sovereign, and his Fatherland. He was a living proof of the indissoluble attachment of the Rhineland to the Monarchy. Personally I shall always cherish the most grateful and affectionate memories of the man who, ever since 1870, had been to me a true friend and a father. My wife sincerely joins me in condolence."

May that chivalrous soldier and faithful son of the Catholic Church, the loyal servant of four Prussian kings and of three Emperors, that ardent Prussian and German patriot, Field-Marshal General von Loë be taken as their model by the sons of the fairest of Prussian provinces, till such time as, on the German Rhine, delivered from its shame and from its bondage, there shall arise that monument which, to-day, we can only raise to Walter Loë in our hearts!

At the Foreign Office my difficulties had increased. Herr von Schön, like Tschirschky his predecessor, was primarily interested in never offending the Emperor rather than in doing his duty, the only difference being that Tschirschky had been what the French call " *un rond de cuir*," that is to say an official automat who at least feels bound to spend his days on the high stool at his office desk, whereas " *le baron de Schön* " was equally flighty and inadequate. Finally, during my last winter in office, my Chief of Press, Otto Hammann, as the result of unfortunate private complications, lost his head. Soon after I was made Secretary of State, Hammann's wife had died suddenly, on a walking tour through the Black Forest. Holstein, who would say anything about people he did not like, and who had quarrelled with Hammann, his erstwhile *fidus Achates*, by whose side he had struggled against the deposed Bismarck, was always trying to persuade me that Frau Hammann had not died a natural death. I never believed it, and contradicted all such hints with energy; but the truth of the matter, as I see it, was that the poor woman's grief and worry, at seeing her husband's love for somebody else, had contributed to hasten her end. Hammann, now a widower who, though he did not look like a Lovelace apparently possessed a passionate soul, urged his mistress to divorce her husband. The latter, one of Germany's foremost architects, refused a divorce. Finally some kind of pecuniary arrangement was arrived at, by which the lady remained in separation, and was to receive maintenance on condition that no intimate relations occurred between herself and her lover until she should be free to marry him. As may be imagined the deserted husband was not in the best of tempers. His jealousy, very naturally, continued. He engaged an excellent detective to discover the secret meeting-place of the lovers, then rented a room, above the one where their amorous encounters took place, and proceeded to bore a hole in the floor through which to view the proceedings, though they certainly cannot have given him much pleasure. All this might have furnished Boccaccio with the material for a very pleasant tale. But unluckily the Public Prosecutor intervened to charge a Privy Councillor with perjury. Hammann had sworn an oath that he and his Dulcinea were platonic. I was urged on all sides to relieve my Press Chief of his post. Schön, the virtuous Secretary of State, refused to sit at the same table as Hammann as a member of the Reichstag Budget commission.

The position was difficult, but I could not leave Hammann in the lurch. He had stood by me pluckily on the day of my fainting-fit, and had served me loyally. I make it my rule never to forget a service rendered. Together we found a way out. Hammann himself requested to be temporarily excused duty. He was acquitted, but, through weeks of anxiety, during which he already saw himself in prison, he had not the mental alertness and peace of mind necessary for his work as head of a department, in circumstances difficult in themselves and a stormy political crisis.

Having rewarded Hammann for his loyalty to me in April 1906 I also helped him on to his feet again. He remained under Bethmann-Hollweg with whom he even obtained more political influence than in my time, since from me, in foreign affairs, he had only received the necessary hints to enable him to give a lead to the Press, and was accorded no nearer insight into the inner workings of my policy. But Hammann had neither the tact, diplomatic experience, nor knowledge of foreign countries necessary, to broach complicated questions of diplomacy, let alone the major issues of foreign policy, and I fear that, in the summer of 1914 he contributed to that series of clumsy mistakes which led to the ultimatum to Serbia. Bethmann's unfortunate speech on 4th August 1914 reminded me in its construction and contents, of Hammann's drafts for official press articles which had not yet been censored by myself. During the war, Hammann, advanced to the rank of Excellency, was unfortunate in his direction of our press-propaganda abroad. The various books which, later, he published on contemporary politics are written under the influence of whatever political constellation prevailed for the moment in Germany. When his first book, *The New Trend* [1] (*i.e.* the Caprivi trend) was published, the Kaiser still felt himself completely master of the situation. *Rebus sic stantibus*, Hammann treated Bismarck's dismissal in the tone of an officious loyalist of 1891: "His Majesty, according to Constitution, dismisses or appoints the Imperial Chancellor—so what has all the fuss been about?" Bötticher himself could not have said it more prettily!

[1] *Der Neue Kurs.*

In a later book, dealing with events that led up to the war, His Majesty again is handled very tenderly indeed. But *For the Kaiser's Sake*,[1] which appeared after the November revolution, deals severely with the fallen monarch. None of these three books is of any permanent value, but there is considerably more merit in one which appeared later, *The Misunderstood Bismarck*,[2] whose title Hammann borrowed from me. In my Reichstag speech of 14th November 1906 I had said: " Dogmatising about Prince Bismarck has, if I may be allowed the truth for once, become not only a mania but a calamity. We are suffering from the misunderstood Prince Bismarck. That is a sure sign of our national tendency to turn everything into a system."

The youngest child of Hammann's muse, *Pictures from the Last Days of the Empire*,[3] also makes very light reading, but is entertainingly written. The letters and instructions from me reproduced in these *Pictures*, though published without my consent, are quite authentic in origin.

All these changes in the Kaiser's entourage and at the Foreign Office, of so much importance to a Chancellor, increased my difficulties and multiplied the points of friction. But a source of really personal grief, which touched me to the very core, was the death of my old friend and physician, Renvers, who died in the prime of life, in the spring of 1909. Renvers, throughout the whole of my Chancellorship, which took so high a toll of health and strength, had advised and aided me with the highest degree of medical skill, and with a kindness that never once flagged. I am naturally healthy and had taken little care of my health; Renvers, with masterly psychological insight, made me observe myself and live hygienically. He used to insist that at fifty a man who cannot be his own physician is a fool. He was for moderate eating and still more moderate drinking, for three-quarters, or at the very least, for half an hour's gymnastic exercise a day: he recommended riding and walking. But he was also a physician of the soul, and in many personal and political difficulties he had understood, and really helped, me with his advice. Renvers, who cared for me scrupulously, who had restored so many others to health and life, died young as the result of his own neglect of the internal complaint from which he suffered. He, whose diagnosis passed for infallible, who had sometimes told me jokingly that medical science had made very little progress since Hippocrates but that surgery alone had really advanced, allowed himself to be operated too late. When, under his charge, I had com-

---

[1] *Um den Kaiser.*   [2] *Vom missverstandenen Bismarck.*
[3] *Bilder aus der letzten Kaiserzeit.*

PROFESSOR DR. VON RENVERS

Physician to the Empress Frederick and Prince von Bülow

pletely recovered from the effects of my fainting-fit in the Reichstag,
my wife gave a little dinner to which, besides his charming wife and
Renvers, a number of other friends were invited. I proposed a
toast in which I quoted Schopenhauer's saying that the lawyer sees
mankind in all its baseness, the theologian in all its stupidity, and
the doctor in all its weakness. I declared that in spite of my admiration of Schopenhauer as an acute thinker and a great master of
prose, I considered his dictum on the lawyer and theologian unjust.
But above all I was sure that the doctor might sometimes see man
in all his gratitude, and that such was my deepest feeling towards
Renvers. I shall never forget him.

In view of the Centre's opposition, on principle, and the strong
Conservative dislike both of the electoral reform I intended in
Prussia, and of my proposed Death Duties Bill, the *bloc* was only
to be upheld if the Crown supported me firmly. At the outset the
Centre had not been against such a measure. When, in 1905, I
undertook the so-called "minor fiscal reform," I had made a
speech, at the first discussion of the Budget, on 6th December,
candidly expressing my misgivings on the subject of death duties.
Herr Spahn, the leader of the Centre, had paid me some very
graceful compliments on the clarity with which I had treated this
difficult theme. In his opinion I had even managed to make its
dullness come alive. But he could not understand my objection to
death duties.

I told him that, a few days previously, I had received a petition
from the Rhenish-Westphalian knights of the Maltese order pro-
testing against this tax on the grounds that it was levelled against
the family. I had also heard that the hierarchy were against it and
suspected it. Spahn replied with a certain humour. "Well, of
course you won't get very far if you consider the Knights of Malta's
families, or even the bishops!" Later this point of view was
revised, and things began to look different. The death duties I
now proposed, for practical reasons and after mature thought,
appeared to the Centre a good opportunity for coming into line
with the Conservatives and so bringing about my downfall.

To put through financial reforms of a kind which should be
really adapted to the true interests of Crown and Empire, *i.e.* the
Death Duties Bill, and to ensure against all future eventualities by
securing a naval agreement with England, were my two chief
tasks before my retirement from office.

But to achieve these ends it was necessary to clear up my personal
relationship with the Emperor. I determined to take the bull by
the horns. On 11th March 1909 after I had given His Majesty a

report on Foreign Affairs, I requested him to hear me a few moments longer on a personal matter. I had, I said, the impression that, though after the events of November he had seemed convinced that my attitude had been just, and above all absolutely loyal, he no longer placed the same confidence in me. Whether, or by whom, I had been libelled was a question I did not care to discuss. But I could not continue to shoulder the heavy burden of office unless I felt convinced that I had the entire confidence of my sovereign. I might have erred in this or that individual matter, since nobody is infallible, but I had never desired anything but to prevent serious discord between the Throne and the people. All my efforts had been directed towards preserving for the Emperor the confidence of the Federal princes, towards calming their growing agitation and that of precisely those Germans best disposed towards His Majesty and the Empire. I wished the Kaiser to retain his people's confidence and love. Such had been the course I had tried to steer through past storms, and I felt that now, more than ever before, the Throne, enjoyed the affection and reliance both of the princes and of the nation as a whole. But if the Emperor had ceased in any way to trust me I begged him to be gracious enough to allow me to resign. This he could do without misgivings. I should neither start a *fronde* against him nor cause him any other unpleasantness. I should retire with the heartfelt wish to see him enjoy a long and happy reign.

The Emperor thanked me for my candour. It was a relief to him to be able, on his part too, to speak frankly. He certainly had had the impression that I had not shown sufficient energy in contradicting, as entirely without foundation, all the attacks levelled against his person.

In the course of the conversation which followed this, I observed, respectfully but plainly, that the opinions he had expressed to various people, in the course of his stay in England, the opinions which Colonel Stuart Wortley had summed up in the *Daily Telegraph* article, had been of a nature to create agitation in Germany, and to cause us grave difficulties abroad. His Majesty answered that, at the time, he had either wired or written to me from England all that had subsequently appeared in the *Daily Telegraph*. I was obliged to deny this most decisively, and the Emperor admitted that he had either announced to me beforehand what he thought he was going to say, or had told me what he had said when he had said it. But even this was not exact, and so I was obliged to inform him. He then began to speak of the injustice with which the world in general so often treated him. I pointed out a number of recent incidents (the Swinemünde telegram, the Lippe affair, several speeches, etc.) which had not only distressed public opinion but that of the Federal governments. This I had suggested more than once to him, and had begged him to be more prudent and reserved. I showed him how, little by little, irritation had increased in Germany through the course of the November days, till at last the storm, happily a passing storm, had burst, with many exaggerations and injustices. His Majesty could not recall these events in detail, particularly not the Swinemünde telegram whose existence he began by denying altogether. He declared that, in any case, the facts had been grossly exaggerated. Again I begged him to accept my resignation if he felt that he had any grounds for dissatisfaction or blame. But the Emperor answered that that was out of the question, that for many years, I had rendered the most distinguished services, that, especially throughout the last winter, I had directed foreign policy " in a masterly fashion," that he knew that my intentions had always been of the best and most sincere, and that he would refuse to allow his judgments of me to be influenced. In conclusion I thanked His Majesty sincerely for this renewal of his gracious confidence, and the Kaiser assured me that I enjoyed his entire trust.

The above is an exact resumé of this audience, and I placed it in my archives that same day. The Emperor had talked most graciously, and I had remained entirely calm. I have even somewhat toned down, in dictation, the expressions of hearty recognition His Majesty was good enough to bestow on me. I remember his constantly repeating that I was " a past master of foreign policy," that he did not know what foreign affairs would do without me, etc. We had talked walking up and down the White Drawing-Room of the Berlin Palace. At the end of our official conversation, the Kaiser still continued for some time, pointing out, most amiably, the embellishments he had recently been adding to this apartment, which had witnessed so many important events in Prussian history. " That too is thanks to yourself," he added, " since it is you who by keeping the peace have enabled me to encourage art."

But I intentionally refrained from putting into the archives, in my official account of this audience of 11th March 1909, a passage which I ask to be allowed to reproduce in these pages, because it is so very characteristic of that mixture of naïve egotism and romantic sentimentality peculiar to William II. In the course of our conversation he said: " Froben would not have spoken as you did at the Reichstag debate on 10th November." I asked him gravely if His Majesty really meant to imply that I should hesitate to die for my sovereign. The Kaiser protested most cordially that such an idea had never crossed his mind: " What I wanted to say was simply this. If Froben, the royal equerry, who mounted the piebald horse of the Great Elector at Fehrbellin, to attract bullets away from his master, had had to face the Reichstag as Chancellor, he would certainly have declared that it was he who had advised his Emperor to speak in England as he did." To which I answered: " I beg to be quite candid. When the bombshell of the *Daily Telegraph* article burst, I suggested two courses to my subordinates: firstly, to tell the truth about the whole business, and nothing but the truth —(here the Kaiser shrugged his shoulders)—Yes, Your Majesty! At a time of such grave crisis we had no right to deceive the country; and, secondly, I gave instructions to do everything possible to divert attacks from the Crown." The Kaiser: " Well—you see! " I: " I have explained to Your Majesty repeatedly that the *Daily Telegraph* article contained four particularly serious points. There was the statement that Your Majesty is probably the only German who really feels friendly towards England. This was not only contrary to reality but contrary to all I had been saying for years in the Reichstag, in my conversations with English statesmen, and in interviews. Your Majesty next declared that you were constructing your navy against Japan. How could I possibly have advised you to say any such thing—I, who ever since I took office, have given repeated warnings against irritating Japan unnecessarily? You further assured the English that you had prevented England's being humbled into the dust by Russia and France. I have always requested Your Majesty not to talk about *B* to *A*, and then about *A* to *B*, since *A* and *B* may always meet and confide in each other with the result that they both lose all confidence in Your Majesty. Finally at Highcliffe you announced yourself the real conqueror of the Boers, since the plan of campaign by which Lord Roberts defeated them had been worked out by you. It seems to me utterly impossible that anybody either in Germany or England could suppose me capable of having advised Your Majesty to say any such thing." The Kaiser: " Which simply means you consider me a donkey, capable of blunders you yourself could never have committed." I: " I am far from suggesting that. *Non omnia possumus omnes*, or, if you would rather not have it in Latin, Schiller remarks that the gifts of this life are most unevenly distributed. Your Majesty surpasses me in many respects; not only, of course, in naval and military knowledge but, above all, in natural science. I have often listened in admiration when Your Majesty explained the barometer, or wireless telegraphy, or the Röntgen rays. I am

shamefully ignorant in all branches of natural science, have no notion
of chemistry or physics, and am quite incapable of explaining the
simplest of natural phenomena. But, in compensation, I possess
some historical knowledge, and perhaps certain qualities useful in
politics, but especially in diplomacy."

The Kaiser heartily admitted it. He was again in the very best
of tempers. He said: "Haven't I always told you that we complete
one another famously? We should stick together, and we will."
He shook my hand warmly several times, and rode straight off
to lunch with the Minister of Justice, Dr. Beseler, where he had
arranged to arrive at one o'clock.

Meanwhile it was half-past-one, for my audience had lasted a
long time. When he reached the Ministry, where everybody was
anxiously awaiting his arrival, His Majesty went straight up to the
Head of the Chancellery, my faithful collaborator Loebell, and
gave him his hand, with the words: " I've just been having it out
with the Imperial Chancellor, and everything has been put to rights
between us. If anyone says anything to me against Prince Bülow
after this, I shall punch his nose for him! " He illustrated this with
a gesture.

Next day my old war comrade and faithful friend, Bodo Knesebeck told me how, on the previous evening, he had dined, as the
only stranger present, with Their Majesties and the royal children,
and that the Emperor, turning towards him, and towards his sons,
had said with an expression of real relief: " There's a great weight
off my mind. You can all congratulate me. The Chancellor and
I have made it up, and everything is explained." Knesebeck went
on to say that the Kaiserin had seemed equally glad, and had
expressed the liveliest satisfaction.

On 12th March, Count August Eulenburg, bringing a magnificent bouquet, called on my wife from the Emperor to ask whether
Their Majesties could dine with us, *en petit comité*, that evening.
My wife asked Eulenburg to express her thanks and her pleasure.
As a matter of fact, she really felt rather embarrassed, since she did
not know whether, at such short notice, a dinner fit for royalty could
be managed. She summoned our chef, of many years' standing,
M. Cholin, and asked him what was to be done. He replied with
dignity: " *Je n'en suis nullement étonné, cela ressemble bien à Sa
Majesté; elle n'en fait jamais d'autres. Mais je m'en tirerai à mon
honneur.*"

Not only was the dinner excellent but everything went off most
harmoniously. The Emperor greeted my wife with the words:

" How happy I am to be here again! What a terrible winter this has been. But now it's all going to be perfect." He stayed from eight till half-past twelve o'clock. Next day Count August Eulenburg came back again, by Imperial orders, to my wife, to tell her how happy it made the Emperor to feel that we were completely reconciled.

Rarely, during my long official and personal connection with him, had I seen William II in a better and gayer frame of mind than he was during the next few weeks. The first little cloud to sully this clear horizon was news, from a reliable source, of His Majesty having sent the following telegram to his brother, Prince Henry, on the evening of 11th March, the day when we had had our long interview: " Have just forgiven Bülow after he begged my pardon in a paroxysm of tears."

I mentioned this quite inexact but very strange statement to August Eulenburg who did not seem to attach any great importance to it. In his opinion the Kaiser, after the many unpleasant and derogatory things he had lately told him of me, had not known how to explain our reconciliation to his brother, and so, to get out of the difficulty, had invented the " paroxysm of tears."

" The most exact lover of truth in the world must always experience great embarrassment if he has to give an account of an absurdity. He must strive to clothe it in an idea, and hence in some sort of significance, while in reality it is a cipher, a nullity which wants to be mistaken for something." The foregoing is a remark in Goethe's *Italian Journey*, where he begins to describe the Villa Pallagonia at Palermo, whose grotesque eccentricities cause the normal human being to shake his head.

CHAPTER XXX

The feeling in the country—Schmoller and Harnack—The position of Finance Reform—The Conservatives make trouble—Their leaders visit me (29th April 1909)—An interview with Herr von Heyde-brand alone—The Reichstag franchise and Prussia.

THE growing difficulties I had now to encounter with the political parties, in view of the approaching decision on the Death Duties, did not make me swerve from the path I had always pursued, ever since I began my term of office.

My course was determined by the conviction that it is the duty of an Imperial Chancellor to lead, and not be led by deputies who, in Germany, are all too often narrowly selfish, and usually very short-sighted. I was also convinced—and the elections of 1907 had confirmed me—that the people, as a whole, are more sensible than their politicians. " *Le pays est sage, les partis ne le sont guère*," said Thiers, in 1872 or '3, at the time when he was President of the Republic, to Harry Arnim, who was then our Ambassador in Paris. Bismarck endorsed this wise remark.

Even in the last days of my Chancellorship I had the country on my side. An excellent caricature in *Simplicissimus* reflected the opinion of wide sections of the German people. It showed a stout Germania, anxiously clinging about her Chancellor's neck, with the words: ' Don't leave me Bernard! The wicked men are knocking at the door already.' Through the window two bur-glars are seen peeping into the room; a Social-Democrat, with a peasant's stockinet cap on his head, and a parson in a shovel hat.

I could sense this opinion in many pamphlets which reached me from all over Germany. But it will be enough if I quote a single letter from the Bavarian Minister of the Interior, Count Feilitzsch, dated 31st March 1909, in which he says:

Since the Franco-Prussian War founded German unity and prosperity, no such important event has occurred as the peaceful solution of the Balkan problem. This we owe to the energy and consistent policy of Your Highness. Germany has shown her-self strong enough to dictate peace to Europe and save us from war. You have silenced the grumblers. These last broad-minded speeches of Your Highness in the Reichstag won you admiration not only in parliament but in every German and

439

foreign newspaper, and also with every real patriot. May this be some small compensation for the spiteful attacks and suspicions, the heavy burden of labour and trouble, which lately you have had to endure. Your truest satisfaction will be your consciousness of having done a great service to Germany. Will you permit a man who went through the war of 1870 and who, as Minister and Federal representative under four Chancellors, has had the good fortune to witness the growing power and expansion of our Fatherland, to congratulate you warmly on this magnificent success? It will now be necessary to settle yet another grave question, a question as important as it is difficult. Important because in the future Germany's position will depend on it, difficult because, even on the very gravest subjects, divided opinion is a disease which our country finds it difficult to cure. I mean Financial Reform. Your Highness, in the Reichstag speech I have just read, has pointed the way both clearly and convincingly. We are all agreed that reform is absolutely necessary. We are nearly all of us of opinion that a consumer's tax as well as a tax on property is necessary. Nobody except yourself has made one feasible suggestion in any other direction, and yet no agreement can be reached. We in South Germany only approached the Death Duties reluctantly, and yet they seem an absolute necessity, since there appears no other way of raising the necessary hundred million. I hope and believe that this whole Conservative resistance, or most of it at least, may be overcome. Your Highness's speech, yesterday, may help to do so. Here we are doing our best to carry the proposed reforms. Forgive me for taking up so much of your valuable time, but my mind was too full of all this not to write to you. In deepest devotion,

Your Highness's most obedient servant,
Dr. Count von Feilitzsch.
(ex-Minister.)

Count Feilitzsch, a statesman of many years standing and rich in experience, had not been wrong in his estimate of the favourable effects of my speech on the general feeling in the country. In the last period of my term in office I always made a point of speaking over the heads of my immediate hearers and addressing the nation as a whole. I would hold up before the eyes of our people those great and fundamental truths on the recognition of which our future depended. In my speech [1] of 30th November 1907 I had epito-

---

[1] Prince Bülow's *Speeches*, complete edition, iii, 93 *et seq.*; Réclame edition, v, 43 *et seq.*

mized as follows the aims of my internal policy, which formed, at the same time, the core and essence of the *bloc* policy:

"Against the scorn so often directed at our formula of an union of Liberal and Conservative I should like to relate an incident which I count among the deepest, most lasting experiences of my life. As I stood in the room in which Prince Bismarck died—that bare, austere little room in the Sachsenwald—I happened to glance at a picture on the wall opposite the bed. It was a woodcut—a portrait of Ludwig Uhland. That singer of our old traditional rights—the man who, in St. Paul's Church in Frankfurt, had declared that no crown should ever shine over Germany unless the head that bore it had been anointed with a thick drop of democratic oil, looked down on the bed where a great man of action had lain dying—the man who gave our century-old dream to the German people. In these two, who faced each other there, had lived again the whole of German history, which only the united effort of the conservative Prussian will to action, and Prussian discipline, with the wide and tolerant Liberal German spirit, can lead onwards into a happy future."

On 26th March 1908 [1] I had answered Bebel's affirmation that it would be no misfortune to the world if the Prussian State were to vanish for all time: "The Empire cannot do without Prussia, nor Prussia without the Empire. Such is the beneficent, the glorious culmination of both German and Prussian history, in the last two hundred and fifty years. It is the fruit of the labours and genius of the Great Elector, of the Great King, and the men of 1813. Above all it is the result of Bismarck's policy. In this unity lies the future of the nation, this unity forms our highest good; the unity—and this I emphasize not only to those at home but to those abroad—which neither foreign attack nor domestic crisis will ever again have power to shake."

I had the same object in view in a speech to the Chamber of Deputies (19th January 1909) in the Budget [2] debate on the position and significance of the Crown. I had never, I said, since I first took on myself responsibility for the conduct of the policy of the State, tried to shirk the obvious duty of shielding the wearer of the Crown. "But it is also my duty," I continued, "to watch that no dissension arises between the wearer of the Crown and the desires and sentiments of the people, since division would be fateful to both sides. A responsible Minister must see to it that the Crown does

[1] Prince Bülow's *Speeches*, complete edition, iii, 132 *et seq.*; Réclame edition, v, 65.
[2] *Ibid.*, complete edition, iii, 174 *et seq.*; Réclame edition, v, 189 *et seq.*

not misunderstand the country, nor the country the wearer of the crown. He must see that the constitution is upheld, not only according to its letter, but that its spirit is honoured and respected. Above all else a Prussian Prime Minister must make sure that the Crown's historic glory, the legacy of a splendid past, the foundation of our power and our well-being, the basis of our unity and future, be not tarnished, discredited, and worn threadbare." I then reminded them that Prussia had grown great through her rulers. I emphasized the noble aims, the idealism, the many services of our present Emperor and Sovereign—his efforts to keep the army in constant readiness, to create a fleet, to foster science and industry, commerce, art, and technical progress. I closed with the words: " In the past our strength was based on the mutual trust which existed between Sovereign and people: on the deep seriousness with which both regarded this relationship, on the fact that the Prince felt himself the First Servant of his country, that the country knew that its interests —and these alone—were the guide and aim of the Prince. Such is the rock on which our past glories have been built; from that we take our strength, the strength which is to go to make our future."

When, a few days later, I met my excellent friend, Gustav Schmoller, he described my speech as " the testimony of a true Monarchist," and said that it had moved him profoundly.

> *" Der eine fragt: was kommt danach?*
> *Der andre : was ist recht?*
> *Und dadurch unterscheidet sich*
> *Der Freie von dem Knecht."* [1]

Soon after the November crisis I had asked Gustav Schmoller and Adolf von Harnack to dine with me. Schmoller, with all the freedom of sincerity, had expressed his agreement with my speech and attitude in the November crisis. I had done my duty to country as well as to Kaiser—both as Prussian Minister and German Imperial Chancellor. He reminded me of the fact that, apart from Bismarck, other Prussian Ministers had seen the necessity for standing up to their kings. Both Count Brandenburg and Freiherr von Manteuffel had, more than once, opposed Frederick William IV. The great Freiherr von Stein and Wilhelm von Humboldt had stood out against Frederick William III; Count Robert Zedlitz and the Minister of Public Worship, von Gossler, as well as the War

---

[1] One asks : what follows after ?
The other : what is right ?
And, by their words, you know them
For varlet or for knight.

Minister, Bronsart von Schellendorff, had opposed William II. Harnack sat uneasily, saying nothing, though as a theologian, it might have been supposed that he would have been able to call to mind many passages, both from the Old and New Testaments, in which truth and frankness are made the duties of a Christian. A few days later I heard from a member of the suite that Harnack had been assuring the Kaiser, through his intimate friend Theodore Schiemann, whose Baltic origin he shared, that he would never have accepted my invitation had he received it after I had delivered my November speech. But, since the invitation had come first, it had been very difficult to refuse. Even this silly excuse was not the truth. I had invited Harnack *after* my speech had been delivered, and his trepidations only began when he had listened to our little talk. The rats left the sinking ship.

In the meantime the preliminary sittings of the Finance Committee of the Reichstag were lumbering on their way as ponderously as that postchay which, in the old days, had lumbered along through the sandy Marches between Oranienburg and Berlin—the postchay which had brought me back to school, at the good old Pädigogium at Halle, from my parents' house in Neu-Strelitz, after the holidays. Sydow had not the gift of adjustment, he could not overcome difficulties or conceive and put into effect what Italians call a *combinazione*. Bismarck would always ask about anyone suggested for a leading position, " Is he any good at taking corners? " Sydow was not. Bismarck would also say that, in certain contingencies, it was a Minister's business to make " *flèche de tout bois*." When once, at the time of the conflict, he expressed this maxim to the then Crown Prince the latter was shocked to the very depths of his highly conscientious, idealistic, and entirely ethical soul by it. It applied, however, to the business of the Finance Commission. But Sydow was neither good at taking corners nor was he an " *homme à expédients*." This explains the fact that, without being unpleasantly " a stickler " he was very, very anxious to remain " a big pot," to use the Berlin expression. And he succeeded. After his fall, as State Secretary to the Treasury, on the occasion of the Death Duties Bill, Sydow was proposed by Bethmann-Hollweg, to whom he was spiritually akin, for advancement to the post of Minister of Commerce, in which function he replaced Clemens Delbrück, who was made Secretary of State for the Interior. William II was always well-disposed towards Sydow, especially after Bethmann had repeated his remark to His Majesty: " I should never even think of resigning. I should wait until H is Majesty demanded my resignation." And Sydow did, in fact, outlast all his colleagues, as a Minister. He was, unless I am mistaken, the last Prussian Minister to receive the Black Eagle from his Sovereign, shortly before the flight into Holland, in the autumn of 1918.

Our difficulties in the matter of Finance Reform, which had now begun to dominate home politics, came, above all, from the Conservatives. Bismarck said once that politicians would not shrink, in the interests of their party, from actions which, in private life, they would never even have dreamed of considering. This was proved in the Conservative attitude towards me in the winter of 1908-9. Conservatives had been the first to sound the tocsin, in their party organ, *Konservative Korrespondenz*, on the publication of the Kaiser's indiscretions at Highcliffe. In the Reichstag debate of 10th and 11th November, Conservatives had protested sharply— far more sharply even than the Socialists Heine and Singer or than the members of any other party—against such Imperial back-slidings. But when a few days later the Conservatives, who never lacked Court information, had learned that it was not quite certain whether His Majesty would afterwards not take offence at my attitude during the debate, this same *Konservative Korrespondenz* reproached me with not having been sufficiently zealous in defending my sovereign in the Reichstag. To be sure both the chief Conservative paper, the *Kreuzzeitung*, and the Agrarian *Deutsche Tageszeitung* stood out against this perfidious suggestion, but it was already clear that Herr von Heydebrand had begun to shift his ground.

Ernst von Heydebrand und der Lhasa, of Klein-Tschunkawe, in Upper Silesia, at that time fifty-eight years of age, was a man of distinguished intelligence, many-sided interests, and wide know-ledge. He was very well-read and, better still, had thought out his reading. He had a solid grounding in all branches of political economy, in political and administrative jurisprudence, in econo-mics and banking. He was interested in history, in philosophy even. He was one of the readiest debaters I have ever had to en-counter. His speeches were often sarcastic, but never banal and, still less, coarsely aggressive, always worded with fastidious care, and the work of a highly-educated man. He was a personality. With all his accomplishments he should have had a great executive future.

He had worked for several years in the administrative service at Oppeln, under Count Robert Zedlitz, who was very much struck with his capacities. From 1887-95 he had been Landrat of Militsch-Trachenberg and, in this capacity, had fought a never-ending battle with the two biggest landowners in the district, Count Andreas von

Maltzan-Militsch, and Prince Hermann von Hatzfeld-Trachen-berg. He was a squabbler. In 1895 he had said good-bye to the Service, to devote himself entirely to politics. I have often been annoyed with him, but never found him personally unsympathetic. But the " party angle " was the thing he always considered of most importance, perhaps without knowing it himself. His *raison d'etat* was party interest, and just as he had convinced himself that Prussia, and with Prussia the whole of Germany, could only hope to see salvation as the result of a decisive Conservative policy, so was he equally certain that he himself was the best, if not the only possible, Conservative leader. Not that he would ever have consented to become a Minister. He would have refused such a request with disdain, or at any rate, with annoyance. What he wanted was a place behind the scenes, from which to direct our home policy. Herr von Heydebrand was a very short man. Old Georg von Koller, for years President of the Chamber of Deputies, the stout archetype of all Pomeranian junkers, was always saying what a pity it was that Heydebrand should have been so small. It made him be for ever striving to show himself " little but fiery." Friedrich von Moltke, when he became Minister of the Interior, said that if ever he wanted something out of Heydebrand, he always took care to arrange the interview so that he could sit, and Heydebrand could stand and look down on him. Otherwise the gigantic Moltke would find himself handicapped from the start, and Heydebrand in a very bad temper. In the last days before my retirement Heydebrand insisted on two points: he was anxious that the Conservatives should not forfeit their complete control of the Chamber of Deputies, and he utterly refused, in the Reichstag, to hear a word on either Death Duties or the tax on unsettled property. This was to avoid offending the " Agrarian League," which formed his chief political support.

At the end of April 1909 an interview took place between myself and the President of the Upper House, Freiherr Otto von Man-teuffel, together with Herr von Heydebrand and Herr von Nor-mann. The minutes of this meeting were drawn up as follows for my archives:

The Imperial Chancellor expressed himself somewhat as follows: He had heard that on Friday, 30th inst., a meeting had been called of the General Committee (committee of fifty) of the Conservative Party, to discuss the Conservative position on the subject of Finance Reform. He had no idea what kind of resolu-tions had been proposed, or what attitude the meeting would adopt. But from articles in the Conservative press the Chancellor had some reason to fear that Conservatives intended to make a stand against any increase in the Legacy Duties. He therefore considered it his duty to enlighten the gentlemen present on the state of the political situation. It was certain that if the Conservative party persisted in opposing Death Duties, that would make it impossible for both personal and objective reasons, for the Chancellor to realize any project for the reform of Imperial finance. It was generally agreed that, of the five hundred million marks to be raised, one hundred should be raised on landed property. But on the method of applying such a tax much had been written and debated. He, the Imperial Chancellor, had little liking for Death Duties as such. It had needed a considerable effort to make him admit to himself that they were necessary: but, to that he had been forced by *dira necessitas*. If we had had a war or a fresh rising in South West Africa, he would equally have been forced to act as he did. In the opinion of the Federal governments, and especially of the larger Federal States, there was no other practical or feasible tax on property which would be likely to yield the sums required. The proposed Conservative tax on increased valuation of property was certainly worth consideration. For some time now this suggestion had been mooted, but many good and practical reasons, based on facts which he proposed to submit to them, all pointed against its ever being realized. He, the Imperial Chancellor, was convinced that such considerations were preponderant; above all that such a tax would not nearly approach the sums required in the Reichstag; that it would be far more likely to give a maximum yield of twenty-five millions. It was already plain that a tax on the increased value of share-certificates would simply be impossible to collect. Such taxation, therefore, could not be considered a satisfying alternative to the Death Duties. A further rise in the quota was out of the question. Another less direct form of quota was the Federal Tax, intolerable in its incidence on the smaller and medium states. So that the Chancellor, if the Death Duties failed, would be forced to regard Finance Reform as abortive. He could not pass any reform with the help only of the Conservatives, the Economic League, the Poles, and the Centre. It would be a blow to his whole policy if now he were to allow the Poles to save the situation for him. The National-Liberals must be with him, but they would never consent to join such a majority. He did not wish even this reform to be carried in opposition to the Conservative Party. Should Conservatives continue to oppose him he might be unable to see his way towards the further control of Imperial Affairs. For that the Conservative Party would be responsible. Since, if he resigned, it would be his duty to advise the Emperor on future policy, as well as on the choice of personalities entrusted with its further conduct, he would ask the gentlemen present three questions: Firstly. What programme did they propose, in the event of this reform not being carried, for the ordering of Imperial Finances? Secondly: With which of the parties did they propose to carry through their programme? Thirdly: Which men would they suggest should be put at the head of affairs in order to achieve their object? To-day's conversation must not be regarded as implying that the Chancellor felt himself converted to any parliamentary method, or intended submission to any parliamentary faction—even Conservative. But he had felt it his duty to explain matters fully to these gentlemen since, till now, throughout the whole of his Chancellorship, he had carried out a Conservative-Agrarian policy, with the help of the Conservative party. All the gossip about an "anti-Conservative" government was either stupid or slanderous. Every intelligent man knew perfectly well that, both in method and policy he, the Chancellor, had always applied Conservative principles. In spirit the present government was both Agrarian and Conservative, and had been carried on, as any of the gentlemen present would find himself obliged to carry it on, in the event of his becoming a Minister, if he desired to make political progress. Herr von Heydebrand himself, in the Chancellor's place, would not have been able to govern solely by the principles of the Conservative party-programme. He, Prince Bülow, considered it his duty to re-establish normal relationships between the Conservative Party and the Crown. He desired to make no reforms against the Conservatives, but also none in conjunction with the Poles and the Centre. If this reform were defeated, Conservatives must take the responsibility, and would then have to prove how feasible their own programme really was. There was much talk, at present, of dissolution. He could not, with an easy conscience, recommend such a step to His Majesty, since it would mean the decimation of the Conservatives and a great re-enforcement of Socialism, whose previous advance had been stemmed by his, the Chancellor's policy, which had weakened, discredited, and at the last election halved the Socialist numerical strength. Dissolution, at the present time, would contradict his whole previous policy. He could only give the Emperor such advice as tallied with his political convictions. He therefore begged an answer to his questions.

The three gentlemen answered unanimously. To (1): They hoped that in place of the Death Duties, to which they took the strongest objection, it would be possible to suggest a suitable tax on values, which might preferably be incident on the Bourse. To (2): They did not consider reform a feasible matter without the co-operation of the Centre. To (3): They could express no opinion.

More significant still was the conversation I had, a few days later with Herr von Heydebrand. In this he announced himself obdurate both on the Death Duties and on any suggestion of a change in the Prussian franchise. His attitude to both must be determined by the wishes and convictions of his party members, who would hear nothing either of Death, or Inheritance duties, or of any change in the Prussian electoral system. I told him his attitude reminded me of a *mot* of the Paris *préfet de police*, Caussidière who, in 1848, had wandered the boulevards in the midst of an unruly mob. Asked by a friend how he could associate himself with such a following he had answered: " *Je suis leur chef ; il faut que je les suive.*" And I continued: " You believe that you know the feeling in home politics better than I do. I wont argue about that. My long residence abroad may have prevented me from knowing my way as you do through all the ins-and-outs of party *cliques*. But, believe me, I see further than you can. You want to sever the bond which unites National-Liberals and Conservatives, and you forget the fact that Bismarck always set the highest possible value on the co-operation of precisely these two parties. You think you are going to do better by rushing into the arms of the Centre Party. I have nothing at all against the Centre in itself—on the contrary I remember the Centre as one thinks of a once-loved mistress, from whom one has only parted with regret, and who always keeps a corner in one's heart. I might even remind you of the day when, during the debate on the abrogation of paragraph 2 of the Jesuit Law, you confronted me with so much force and conviction: " Thus far, Mr. Chancellor; but no further! Your easy-going complaisance and tolerance of the Catholic part of the nation have reached the uttermost limit of what is supportable." That was how you spoke in the March of 1904. And to-day I should still not think of denying that I have always been extremely careful to respect Catholic feeling and Catholic principles—if only because, in Germany, the Catholics are in a minority. But such consideration as I have shown —my sympathetic respect for the greatness of the Catholic Church —can in no way influence my attitude to the party-politics of the

Centre. I know the Centre better than you, Herr von Heydebrand!
This alliance you contemplate with the Centre will not be of very
long duration. *Au fond* there are more points of contact between the
Centre and certain Liberal factions than between the Centre and the
Conservatives. The distance between Erzberger and Haussmann
or Payer is shorter than that which leads from Klein-Tschunkawe
to the influential members of the Centre Party. I can tell you in
advance where your break with the National-Liberals will lead you:
to just that Coalition which was one of Bismarck's worst night-
mares, between Windthorst, Richter, and Grillenberger."

Herr von Heydebrand answered: " This is a case of conviction
against conviction: one standpoint opposed to another. I think
I am a better judge of the situation." I reminded him that, even
he, had sometimes been mistaken in his prophecies. He had, for
instance, (13th December 1906) declared that the dissolution could
only lead to a heavy government defeat, a rout of the Conservative
Party. But just the opposite had happened. Heydebrand answered,
rather huffily, that he did not consider himself infallible, but that, at
least he could be certain of this—that the next elections would show
a very good, even a " brilliant " Conservative majority, if the party
made just that move to which I objected *i.e.*, if it left the National
Liberals and went into alliance with the Centre. I made one last
appeal to the Head of the Conservative Party. I said to him: " Of
course, from the political standpoint, nothing could have been
stupider than my having let you, Normann and Manteuffel, know
in advance that I do not intend a dissolution or to fight the Conservatives at the polls. I am not such a fool that I can't see that; nor
am I, as a rule, considered stupid or a faulty tactician. But I have
no wish to *finesse* with the Conservative Party. Above all, I can't
betray my conviction of what conduces to the well-being of the
State, and of what is likely to damage it. A dissolution, at the
moment, would be in the interests neither of the Prussian State nor
German Empire: nor of the Crown. As a Prussian, a loyalist, a
German Chancellor, I cannot dissolve the Reichstag. But, as a man
who stands or falls by his conviction, I refuse to remain in office if
at present you destroy the *bloc*, instead of waiting till it come to its
natural end; if you render impossible any intelligent financial
reform, if you frivolously risk all our gains at the last elections."

Herr von Heydebrand left me with the remark that he did not
mind my occasional bluntness of expression, partly because he
could well appreciate the natural embitterment of a statesman, overburdened with work, and harassed with many different anxieties,
and partly, too, because he had never doubted my fundamental

loyalty and Prussianism. But he also must abide by his convictions.

Heydebrand, in contrast to Wilhelm von Kardorff-Wabnitz, to Count Limburg-Stirum, Count Kanitz-Podangen, Count Udo Stolberg, Count Mirbach-Sorquitten, had not learned in the Bismarck school. His opinions had their roots in the habits of thought of Julius Stahl, of Karl von Bodelschwingh, of Count Leopold Lippe, of Ludwig von Gerlach. Had he been born twenty years earlier, in the days of the Conflict, he would have been an enthusiastic supporter of the Bismarck-Schönhausen Ministry which, as a good Prussian, he would have supported, even to Sadowa. But, in the 'seventies he would have gone into opposition, and would have signed the *Kreuzzeitung* declaration. For all his exceptional gifts, and all his conviction Heydebrand, in the end, through sheer blind obstinacy, *parti pris*, and narrowness of vision, helped to dig the grave of the old Prussia. In this matter of the Death Duties it was more his enslavement to the Agrarian League than any deeply personal conviction which made him adopt so intransigeant a standpoint. The League opposed the Death and Legacy duties because of its wish to stir up opinion. In the course of years I had satisfied every legitimate and reasonable aspiration of the German farmer. But, to keep any hold over an organization so based on agitation as the League, some object of attack and point of conflict had continually to be held up before the eyes of its members. The battle-cry: " No Death Duties! No tax on inheritance! " seemed the best slogan to use in an eventual election. But Heydebrand's opposition to any reform of the Prussian electoral system came from the very depths of his soul, was founded on his dearest wishes, passions, and convictions. He wanted, *à tout prix* to assert his dominant position in the Diet. It was only possible if the Conservatives could command an absolute majority, and this, in its turn, depended on the system never being modified.

I had had no thought of applying Reichstag franchise to Prussia. This I had already said quite plainly on 26th March 1908—and not in the Diet, which would have echoed my opinion almost unanimously, but in the Reichstag, whose majority, in theory at least, would have liked to see its franchise applied.[1] I affirmed emphatically, with full conviction and sincerity, that the Federal governments had no intention of changing the present system of election to the Reichstag. But I proceeded to stress the excellent reasons for a certain restriction of this in Prussia although, in the Empire as a whole, the broadest franchise was justified. And I did not attempt

[1] Prince Bülow's *Speeches*, complete edition, iii, 122 *et seq.*; Réclame edition, v, 54 *et seq.*

to hide the fact that the principle, even of direct, secret, and universal suffrage was not a dogma—no fetish, no idol to be worshipped. I am no idolator, no high-priest of any cult of fetishes, nor do I believe in political dogma of any kind.   There is no absolutely just system of franchise, valid for all lands and in all circumstances.   I reminded the deputy Friedrich Naumann, who had been especially zealous in his demands for the application to Prussia of Reichstag franchise, that secret, equal, and universal suffrage existed neither in England, Italy or Belgium.   To the great amusement of the House I asked Naumann whether he really believed that the Mecklenburg he so abhorred, because of its patriarchical constitution, was really worse governed than Haiti.   Haiti had its complete electoral system, universal, equal, and direct.   I reminded the Independents of the fact that every radical change in the Prussian franchise led on, most urgently, to the question whether three-class franchise in the districts had really so much as a leg on which to stand.   I further recalled the fact that no other country in the world had so honest, thorough, and capable a municipal system as our own; that an overwhelmingly Liberal majority had not cared to tamper with our municipal constitution.   I said: " Just try and imagine a Berlin municipal council elected on equal, universal suffrage, and then see if you still want our, admittedly imperfect, three-class franchise replaced by a system which, in more than one area, could result in the domination of only one party, and that the most intolerant of them all."   To-day I think I may add the following question to these remarks of 26th March 1908: " Is there to-day in Germany one Democrat who feels satisfied with the results obtained by the introduction of the Reichstag franchise into municipal affairs—particularly those of Berlin—in the sphere of municipal government? Is there one Democrat who rejoices at the parliamentary tone which, since the introduction of equal, universal suffrage, dominates on every Berlin municipal council? As I dictate these lines a newspaper lies before me on the table containing the report of an incident at a recent sitting of the Berlin City Parliament.

" In the course of a debate on the disturbance at the Circus Busch the Socialist deputy, Ullrich, suddenly hurled himself on his Right Wing colleague, Herr Luedtke, pummelled him to earth with his fists, kicked him in the back, and shouted: ' I'd like to tear you to bits, you lousy scalliwag.' "   The aggrieved Luedtke took action before the magistrate's section of Berlin (Central).   The examining magistrate treated the incident very leniently.   He admitted that this Socialist boor had shown " a certain lack of self-restraint," but suggested that such incidents are apt to bring discredit,

both at home and abroad, on German parliamentary methods. No
doubt he had in mind the saying of the Chancellor, Joseph Wirth, that
the enemy is always to the Right. His final suggestion was a mere
six weeks' imprisonment. The tribunal, however, imposed a higher
fine or, on non-payment of this, a longer sentence. My humble
suggestion is that Comrade Ullrich should have been ordered to
spend a few more months at the Board School, there to learn that
though, as a died-in-the-wool " Red " one has every right to threaten
the lives of one's colleagues, it is more effective to do so in good
German.

I had intended in this matter of Prussian franchise to introduce
such desirable and necessary reforms as would put an end to the sole
domination and preponderance of the Conservative Party, without
however taking away their chance to form a majority, if they chose,
by the help of either the Liberals or the Centre Party. In those
days such a result might have been reached along several quite
feasible and moderate paths. It was, above all, the Liberal party
which, during my last years in office, officially desired some moderate
well-considered measure of franchise reform. But Professor Robert
Friedberg—a decade later he was Vice-President of the Prussian
State Ministry under Hertling—the leader of the National-
Liberals, explained to me: " We National-Liberals can only
lose by any alteration in the franchise. If we vote for any such
measure we shall be sawing away the branch on which we sit. So
please, at least, lay down some straw for us to fall on, so that we
don't have to break our necks." One of the most intelligent and
influential Independents, Reinhart Schmidt-Elberfeld, elected in
1895 as the first, from '98 to 1900, as the second, Vice-President of
the Reichstag, said to me once that the introduction of Reichstag
franchise into Prussia would be sure to bring in its train its further
municipal extension, and so threaten the position and influence of
bourgeois democracy, in the very place where its strength was most
firmly rooted. " May heaven grant," said Schmidt-Elberfeld, " that
the government stands firm on this question, and never lets it get as
far as that! Don't be misled by the fact that we read declarations
demanding the extension of Reichstag franchise. You mustn't take
it too seriously. You, above all, need not fear our opposition in this
matter, any more than you did in the matter of the Customs' Duty."
Schmidt-Elberfeld also cited Eugen Richter, who was also, so he
said, a silent opponent of any extension. Friedrich Naumann, alone
of the Independants, zealously and sincerely championed the introduction of universal suffrage, and of the secret direct ballot into
Prussia. When I asked my old friend Albert Ballin to explain why

ALBERT BALLIN

President of the Hapág
(Chairman of the Hamburg-America Line)

so idealistic and highly educated a man as Naumann should be stupid enough to fling that apple of discord, the suffrage question, among the parties of the *bloc*, Ballin answered in his broadest Hamburg accent: " But, Highness, hadn't you ever noticed that good old Naumann is enormously stupid politically?" He pronounced the word " enorm " (enormous) in the Hamburg fashion: " eno-o-o-rm." Twice during the world-war, Ballin was destined to complain of the " enoormous " political obtuseness of Dr. Naumann—once when the latter published his very superficial book on Central Europe, and again when, in conjunction with Hans Delbrück, Riezler-Rüdorffer, and other ninnies of that ilk, he urged the rescussitation of Poland. It was Naumann who sabotaged the *bloc* with his foolish Left-Wing tactics, while Herr von Heydebrand, from the Right, untroubled by all I had said, or the serious warning I had given him, officially informed the National-Liberals, through von Normann, that the Conservative party would never consent to any taxation of property and that, especially, they would oppose, tooth and nail, any suggestion for legacy or death duties. Naturally, that meant the beginning of the end for the *bloc*, as Conservatives themselves had to admit.

While thus the situation in home politics was drifting towards a dangerous crisis the Kaiser had once again, for the time being, become trustful and friendly towards myself. This, above all, was the result of favourable developments in our Foreign Policy. The solution of the Bosnian crisis had favoured both our interests and prestige. Soon after 14th March—so important for its final resolution—I received, during a sitting of the Reichstag, a telephone invitation to dine at the Neues Palais, that same evening. I answered with the request to be excused, since I should be bound to be detained at the Reichstag, but the Kaiser sent another telephone message, saying that dinner should be kept back for me. He would send two cars to fetch my wife and myself; if one broke down *en route*, we could always get into the other. We did not reach Potsdam till 9 a.m. When my wife apologized to the Kaiserin she answered: " It was a pleasure to wait for you and your husband. The Emperor is so delighted to see him and thank him." Soon after this came the Kaiser, radiant with satisfaction, to tell me that he had just received a wire from the Tsar who had, on his own initiative, proposed a meeting in the Baltic. " I should never have dared to hope it," said His Majesty, " it is far more than I ever expected. You handled this Bosnian affair magnificently."

The Kaiser's good-humour was still further increased by the fact that the recent Navy Estimates had slid, without trouble, through the Reichstag.   All the bourgeois parties had voted for them;   the Socialists had abstained, but had raised no serious opposition.

This very fact, that the attitude and vote of the Reichstag had now rendered it possible for us to make some advance to England, on the question of slowing down construction, without thereby exposing ourselves to the risk of seeming to make a virtue of necessity; such a moment as that on which, in his letter of 26th January 1909 Metternich had laid special weight, decided me to open an exhaustive and serious correspondence with Tirpitz.   I wished, just because I was uncertain how long I should direct our Foreign Policy, to stress yet again the desirability of a friendly understanding with England or, in any case, to set some future check on the forced *tempo* of our naval programme.   In essence, my suggestions amounted to this:—that the Naval Cabinet at least should notify us of how long it would take to reach the naval strength necessary for national defence.   I recalled my earlier speeches to this effect.   I also reminded Tirpitz of all I had done, both negatively and actively, in the cause of naval construction: actively by arousing the nation to a sense of the necessity for a fleet, strong enough to defend the country, and by laying the necessary estimates before the Reichstag; negatively by making it possible, in the midst of acutely difficult circumstances, for that fleet to be constructed without war.   But Tirpitz answered me evasively.   He was unwilling to commit himself in any way, and wished to keep all avenues open, spurred on by the noblest ambition, the deepest patriotism, a brilliant knowledge of his work in a highly specialized branch; but unable to estimate the dangers which, in the event of any European conflagration, threatened us from an England already galled and rendered mistrustful by our programme.

CHAPTER XXXI

My farewell visit to Holstein—Meeting with Tittoni, in Venice—William II arrives in Venice—-He suggests a Chancellorship to Monts—The further adventures of Count Monts—The Emperor sails for Corfu—von Wangenheim's report—The meeting of William II with the Italian Sovereigns at Brindisi—The Emperor in Vienna—The state of Finance Reform—William II, at Wiesbaden, receives my report on the subject—The musical festival at Frankfurt-am-Main; the cordial reception of the Emperor—The Federal Princes in Berlin to celebrate the Emperor's birthday—The intrigues against me increase.—The " League of Loyalists "—Rudolf Martin and Prince Fürstenberg—Meeting of William II and Nicholas II—My " Ten Commandments " for the Emperor.

ON the advice of Renvers, who was both my doctor and best friend, I had made up my mind to spend the Easter recess in Venice. Venice is the best of all cities in which to rest, collect one's thoughts, and soothe the overtaxed nerves. Since I had heard that Holstein was unwell I went to see him before leaving. It was long since he had paid me a visit, though only because of his poor state of health. I myself, though we had known each other for thirty years and more, had never been to see him at his quarters. He who, under Hohenlohe, under Caprivi, under Bismarck, had been one of the most powerful men in the State and who, in my time still pulled many wires, this man whose extensive personal connections, wide experience, quickness of perception and, last not least,[1] decision, cunning, and ruthlessness, had set him in a position of high authority, lived far off, in two little rooms, on the third storey of a house in the rather shabby Grossbeerenstrasse—rooms which many a lower-grade official might have despised. In the hall I ran into Frau von Lebbin, Holstein's intimate friend of many years standing. She had brought two buttered rolls along with her, wrapped up in paper, for her lunch, to be eaten with a glass of beer and a bit of cheese. In the next room Holstein lay in bed. On the wall there hung only three pictures:—a portrait of Paul Hatzfeldt, the Ambassador, the German diplomat with whom Holstein was most in sympathy, another of Count Launey, for many years Italian Am-

---

[1] English in text.

bassador in Berlin, whom he took as his model of a balanced and far-seeing statesman and, finally, a photograph of my brother Alfred and my wife, feeding pigeons in the Piazza San Marco, in Venice. Such photographs, as everyone knows, are done for a few lire at short notice. Holstein's eyes glittered with fever, his cheeks looked very flushed. Frau von Lebbin had already told me how, in order to get the strength to speak to me, he had had to stimulate his heart with strong injections of camphor.

His first question was whether I intended to remain in office. That, I said, would not depend on me alone. Holstein, with obvious effort, adjured me in his most insistent manner, not to resign, in any circumstances, while the foreign situation remained as it was. It mattered nothing whether or not the Kaiser still had faith in me— nothing that the Reichstag might refuse to endorse my project for Finance Reform. I replied that a situation might arise in which it would be impossible to remain. I wished, after twelve years in office, either to stand or fall an honest man. I could not set my name to legislation, or even approve any suggestion for new laws which I felt would do lasting damage to the country. Above all I would take no part in developments which I knew to be mistaken and harmful. Old Holstein answered in a voice of stuttering excitement: " You must stay! You must, I tell you! Who, except yourself, could ever steer the country to-day, with such an unstable and reckless Kaiser; with a nation as politically foolish as ours is, and a Reichstag childishly ignorant of Foreign Policy? At least stay another five years! You handled this Bosnian crisis so brilliantly! And yet, at the same time, you knew how to get us a better understanding with Russia than we'd ever had since Bismarck's days. Even Harden, who hasn't set eyes on you, who for the last twelve years, ever since you took office, has always attacked you mercilessly, has just been saying in the *Zukunft*: that, in the ' Balkan stakes,' as he calls them, you were the only real winner. King Edward has met with his first check as a ruler, Isvolski has come out with the reputation of a spiteful fool, Clemenceau only managed to scrape through, and Aehrenthal has paid a big price for having got what he wanted. You were the only one, Harden says, who achieved every object you had in view, and you have proved yourself again an indispensable master of diplomacy. You must stay, I tell you! Even Harden says it—your enemy, Maximilian Harden! At least they must give you time to reach a naval agreement with England. Then you can go to the devil for all I care. But for the moment we can't afford to lose you."

I had no desire to exhaust this dying man with contradictions.

I therefore only repeated what I had said to him: that I could not consent to bend my neck under the Caudian yoke of Kaiser and opposition, whether one or the other laid it on me. That was the last time I ever saw Holstein, whom I had got to know well thirty years before, at the time of the Berlin Congress. In the hall, as I said good-bye to Frau von Lebbin, I could still hear the hoarse, stuttering voice: " You must stay . . . stay." My last encounter with this strange, and to me uncongenial, personality, whose great political gift I had never been able to deny. Soon after this he died. To everyone's amazement Joseph von Radowitz came to his funeral— the man whom, for thirty years, he had hated and persecuted. Some saw in this a fulfilment of the precept from the Mount, which enjoins us to love our enemies; others said that von Radowitz wished to make certain that Holstein was really gone—at last!

I reached Venice on 12th April. Soon after my arrival Tommaso Tittoni, at that time the Foreign Minister, called on me. He was " *romano di Roma*," a true son of the Eternal City, level-headed, cautious, and subtle. He had finished his education at Oxford, spoke English, and had been, for some time, Italian Ambassador in London. He preferred conciliatory policies and knew, both as Minister and Ambassador, how to maintain good relations with the Vatican. We had always liked each other and agreed. This time also we both felt certain that, provided the men at the helm would pursue a calm and reasoned policy, neither German relations with Italy nor the peace of Europe need be in danger.

Not long after this the Emperor arrived in Venice on the " Hohenzollern," accompanied by the Empress. When I left him, eight or ten days previously, His Majesty had seemed in excellent spirits and full of confidence in myself. Yet now I found him less expansive, touchy, and visibly ill-humoured and mistrustful. Later I learned that, during our short separation, my enemies at Court, in particular Prince Max Fürstenberg, Eugen Röder, the Master of Ceremonies, and other such members of the Suite, had once more succeeded in making him change his opinion of me. On the other hand His Imperial Majesty was as chivalrous and cordial as ever in his manner to my wife. Our Ambassador to Italy, Count Monts, had reached Venice at the same time as I did. During my previous year's visit to Rome I had already been reluctantly convinced that Monts had not made himself beloved there. In all Italian official circles, both governmental and parliamentary, he had literally managed to get himself detested; and in society it was even worse. Then, to put the finishing touch, he had quarrelled with the German colony. He himself longed to get clear of Rome, his next objective being Vienna. But against the realization of this hope was a frank dislike of Monts, already mentioned, in both Austrian and Hungarian governments, and the, if possible, even stronger antipathy of the old Emperor Francis Joseph, not to mention that of the Heir Apparent, Francis Ferdinand. Nobody in all Austria-Hungary, it seemed, would so much as hear the " detestable " name of Monts. He was commanded to dine on board the " Hohenzollern " on the same night as my wife and myself. We had taken our leave and were making our way back to our hotel when I saw the Emperor bear down rapidly on Monts, who bowed low, far too low, before him. Next day I heard, from a very reliable friend in the suite, that the Emperor had said to Monts, in a voice which could be heard by everyone: " Bülow has betrayed me. You must replace him. He, like yourself, was Ambassador in Rome at the time when he was created Chancellor." Monts had replied without altering his posture of submission, in a voice of almost cringing devotion: " Your Majesty has given me leave to speak. I've never thought much of Bülow myself." Thus Monts, to the very end, took " Cousin Anselmo " as his model, that " Anselmo " in whom Chamisso has created the repulsive pattern of all time-servers and *arrivistes*.

In Chamisso, however, it is " Yglano " who ends by striking " Cousin Anselmo " in the face, and having him shown the door. In the case of Monts these functions were discharged by fate itself. A radiant Monts left Venice on 15th April 1909, glowing with the heartening assurance that he would soon become Imperial Chancellor. Back in Rome he hurried off to call on his mother-in-law, and tell her that it would not be very long before he could leave the Palazzo Caffarelli. Nor would he sneak out by the back stairs, but ascend thence to ever greater heights—to the very summit! He made preliminary arrangements for his promised move to Berlin, and laid the intellectual foundations for the future discharge of his high office by exchanging ideas with several trusted friends in the world of finance. But in actual fact—I may as well say it at once— William II had thought at first of considering Monts as my successor when, two months later, I resigned. His hopes were shattered by Valentini who, though as a rule he was all too ready to fall in with any Imperial suggestion, this time declared firmly that His Majesty could not possibly consider for the Chancellorship a person so utterly deficient in both *savoir faire* and talent as Count Monts; a man who was everywhere disliked; alike in Vienna and in Budapest, in Oldenburg, in Munich, and now in Rome, and who was, moreover, so lacking in all capacity as a speaker that he had to

KAISER WILLIAM II AT A FANCY DRESS DANCE AS GREAT ELECTOR

sweat blood and tears to get out a few lame words on the Emperor's birthday, for the benefit of the German colony there. So the Emperor did not insist on his suggestion, and caused Valentini to write to Monts that he regretted not to be able to make him Chancellor, since he needed somebody rather better acquainted with the German domestic situation. But His Majesty promised himself the pleasure of often listening to the distinguished suggestions of Count Monts, whom he invited to pass the following winter in Berlin. Monts, now retired but full of hope, appeared at the first Court ball in 1910, where the Emperor honoured him with a long and much commented conversation. At the second ball the Emperor passed him by with a few words. At the third he paid no attention at all to him. Monts ended his days in the neighbourhood of Munich where, even as an ex-diplomat, he found means of making himself so very *mal vu* that the good and worthy Prince-Regent, Luitpold, had to threaten to strike his name off the list of invitations to Court.

Let me return to Venice whence, on 15th April 1909, William II sailed in the " Hohenzollern " for Corfu. Since he had bought his beautiful "Achilleon" the Emperor could scarcely await the moment for setting out to that Phaeacian shore, there to recover from the fatigues of a Berlin winter. In this spring of 1909 his impatience for the blessed strand where once the royal virgin Nausicaa took pity on the sea-worn Ulysses, was more than usually acute. The November crisis, as His Majesty repeatedly assured me, had affected him even physically. As early as in February 1909, on the margin of an account from Paris, of the forthcoming Mediterranean trip arranged for Frederick Augustus, King of Saxony, he had scribbled the melancholy note: " Lucky man! If only *I* could get away at once and sail the blue Mediterranean." On the humours and occupations of the Emperor, throughout those four halcyon weeks which His Majesty passed in Corfu, Baron von Wangenheim, then Minister to the Greek Court and later Ambassador to Constantinople, wrote as follows, to Flotow, my Chief-of-Staff:

I should like to add a few hasty notes to my Corfu reports, which leave in half-an-hour. I write to you because you are in closest touch with the Chancellor. Naturally all I say is strictly confidential. My reports were drawn up at the wish (three times expressed) of the Emperor, who absolutely insisted that the Chancellor should be apprised of his successes at Corfu. H.M. for the last few days had been so enchantingly gracious to myself that obviously he had had some end in view. He wanted me to give him full marks in my reports. I am not sure whether His

Majesty has a retrospective sense of his duties as a constitutional monarch, or whether he only wished to display his "Achilleon" and the political successes which, in Corfu, he claims to have obtained. Whichever way it may be, his order was so positive and formal that I could not do otherwise than obey it. As I took my leave, His Majesty said to me again, that he would ask to be shown my reports. This was a hint as to the note I should be expected to strike. You can imagine how much I relished such an order. This is the first time I have ever sent in a report which contained descriptions of floral decorations, folk dances, etc. But His Majesty insisted that all these trifles should be mentioned. It was harder still to relate the conversations conducted by His Majesty. I have made it sound in my description as though H.M., in his high wisdom, had always promptly given correct answers. But such was by no means always the case. On the contrary Jenisch and myself were obliged to be continually retouching, to give the Greeks an exact conception of the Imperial words. At once, on the first meeting with King George, the latter so moved the Emperor's heart that he had already given him the promise to recommend to all the other Cabinets the rapid solution of the Cretan question in a sense favourable to Greece. Then, after having talked it over with Jenisch and myself, H.M. made an adroit *volte-face*. During three whole weeks I had to work to persuade His Majesty that we can do nothing for Greece so long as the Cretan question remains unsolved, and there is still the possibility of difficulties between Greece and Turkey. At first His Majesty seemed in complete agreement with this, but now, in these last few days, he has taken the bit between his teeth again, offering an admiral to the King and Theotoki, and returning to the naval question. Theotoki, who is far too intelligent not to see that any Greek finessing with Germany would at once provoke resistance from England and, along with it, fresh difficulties over Crete, replied evasively and put off discussion with the Emperor. I could not say any of this in my account. I was obliged, on the contrary, to put in a few white lies, and do a little falsification of history by making the Emperor appear as the " great and wise man." But when H.M. reads my *compte rendu* I think he will be pleased to see how logically he appears to have spoken especially if, when occasion arises, the Chancellor compliments him on his cleverness. Corfu was interesting but not always very agreeable. This time the Greeks have been better treated. In the end Jenisch was nervous about Brindisi, and the Emperor's intention of giving Tittoni a sore head. What happened?

Von Wangenheim was not far wrong in feeling that H.M.'s policy in Corfu had been inopportune. William II longed, in 1909, to champion Greek aspirations in Crete as warmly as, twelve years previously, he had supported Turkish rights in the Isle of Minos. He loved extremes, so that he had to be kept continually in check, unceasingly watched and guided.

In Brindisi where, on 12th May, there was a meeting of the German and Italian sovereigns, Jenisch, who accompanied the Kaiser as our Foreign Office representative, managed to shield the Italian Foreign Minister, Tittoni, from the lecture with which the Kaiser threatened him. But he still could not prevent His Majesty from exclaiming loudly to his Suite, as the Italian King hailed the " Hohenzollern ": " Look out! Let's watch how the little fellow climbs aboard." An Italian officer attached to the Kaiser's guard of honour was forced to overhear this piece of rudeness. He turned to a comrade at his side and said, very clearly and emphatically: " *Ich verstehe Deutsch.*" The incident ended there: at the ensuing banquet, on board the Italian warship " Vittorio Emmanuele," the most correct of toasts were exchanged. But relations between the two Sovereigns were, and remained, uncertain and frigid.

On 13th May, *via* Polo, the Emperor reached Vienna, where he gave a fresh, and to me even exceptional proof of his astonishing, ingenuous, *desinvoltura*. He, who at the beginning of the Bosnian crisis, had suddenly, without warning, overnight, wished to reverse our whole Foreign Policy, and send Austria-Hungary straight into the arms of the *Entente*, now made a speech in the Hofburg, which fairly bubbled over with enthusiasm for the " august person of the venerable Emperor Francis Joseph " and the " golden Viennese heart "; a speech in which he declared that if the peace of Europe had been kept, it was because he, William II, had stood shoulder to shoulder with Austria-Hungary, and confronted the world in shining armour. Tschirschky, our Ambassador in Vienna, supposed with reason that this trumpet-blast would get on my nerves and, with the full consent of the Austrians, softened the above passage for Wolff's Agency, as follows: " All are aware how far, in these last months, our Alliance has contributed to preserve peace in Europe."

The homage of the City of Vienna—one of whose streets, in reference to my " Nibelungen " phrase, had been re-christened " Nibelungenstrasse "—was received with satisfaction by His Majesty. He commanded Tschirschky to send off a detailed report to the Chancellor " so that he may know that here, at least, there are still people who appreciate me."

While the Emperor William passed, in the most literal sense of Bismarck's phrase, " merry days " on the Phaeacian shores of Corfu, my attention and efforts were concentrated on the most important question of the day—the reform of Imperial finances. The country was being more and more won over to this reform, and that by the method which I had suggested for it, *i.e.* by Death Duties. I concentrated, not without success, on strengthening this feeling among the people, by means of interviews with the most influential leaders of our economic life in all its branches, men of every shade of opinion. At that time I would receive from ten to twelve people a day for private discussion. Wider circles I sought to win by letters and telegrams, all of which were published in the press. To a telegram from the deputy Bassermann who, in the name of the National-Liberals promised me whole-hearted support and confidence, I answered: " Stronger than any dismay at the height of the difficulties to be scaled is my firm belief in the future of the German people. In this belief I shall continue to work, with confidence, at the task of reform already begun. I congratulate myself on the knowledge that you have promised me your support." Similar assurances on all sides reached me from every quarter of the Reich.

On 20th April I had received, in the Congress Hall of the Chancellor's Palace, deputations from Bavaria, Saxony, Baden, Württemberg, and Thuringia. Among those present were many notable personalities in the financial and industrial worlds; the trusted spokesmen of wide sections of the German people. In a long speech to these assembled gentlemen I emphasized the fact that I saw in them, not the representatives of their parties, but men, for whom their country's well-being was most precious, and who would therefore not consider Finance Reform a party question. I warned them against the doctrinaire formula " No monopolies." That was a phrase, I said, which had lost its meaning in this age of cartels and trusts. I begged the Agrarians to remember how I had furthered their interests, and with what unflagging, scrupulous attention. I exhorted the Conservatives not to turn deaf ears to the voice of the middle classes. These serious and influential men accepted all my warnings with approbation, punctuating my words with their applause, at the end of almost every sentence. Especially in the matter of the Land Tax did my suggestions meet with full approval. It is melancholy to-day to recall a passage in one of my speeches at that time. I was answering the reproach of " Socialism," recently levelled at my policy by the Conservatives, because I had suggested placing such a " weapon " as the Death Duties in the hands of a Reichstag, elected by universal suffrage. In this connection I spoke as follows: " As long as Social-Democrats do not control the Federal Council and the Reichstag there will be no danger of any confiscatory methods in the application of these duties. But should a Socialist government ever take this matter in hand, heirs will very soon find out whether or not my proposals are really Socialist. So let us have done with this accusation of Socialism! We need fear that as little as did Prince Bismarck." These words were based on the results of the 1907 election. I may add to-day that, if narrowness of vision and stupidity in the ranks of all the bourgeois parties had not scattered the harvest of that election, things might have taken a very different course from that which we were all compelled to witness in the years that followed my retirement. My personal attitude towards the Death Duties had already been summed up in the words: " If, in the most various countries of the world—in the Hansa cities, in Alsace-Lorraine, in the German-speaking cantons of Switzerland, in Austria-Hungary, France, and England, this tax has been applied for decades, without in any way weakening the family, in Germany, too, it will come to be regarded as a normal, just, and bearable tax. Later generations will scarcely be able to understand our present excitement at the thought of it."-

So positive and unmistakable an assertion naturally left no doubt that I, personally, would stand or fall by the Death Duties. After this meeting, on 20th April in the Congress Hall at the Palace, I had long, personal talks with several of the gentlemen. I received, again and again, the firm and sincere assurance that an overwhelming majority of our people agreed with the line I had adopted.

But, in the Reichstag, it was all the other way. In the latter half of April 1909 I had asked Herr von Heydebrand and Mehnert, the leader of the Saxon Conservatives and President of the Saxon Second Chamber, to dine with me. The Saxon Conservatives were among my most faithful adherents and they stood undismayed on my side, even in the matter of the Death Duties. They knew why. At the 1907 election the bourgeois parties in Saxony had won back not less than thirteen seats from the Socialists. As Mehnert came upstairs to me with Heydebrand he urged on him the dangers of my retirement, both to the further successful pursuance of our Foreign Policy and, above all, to the home situation. The Conservative Party, he said, would be taking a very grave risk if it made itself responsible for that. Heydebrand answered: " What you say is perfectly right as far as it goes. But you forget that, even if we allow the Chancellor to pass his Death Duties, we shan't be saving him.

The Emperor has finally decided to part with Bülow. We are about
to dine with a corpse. There is, therefore, no need to throw either
the Death Duties or Prussian Franchise Reform into his grave with
him." Such was Mehnert's story, as he told it, after my retirement,
to my old friend, the President of the Saxon Upper House, Count
Friedrich Vitzthum. Heydebrand had very exact information on
His Majesty's attitude towards me. He had been at school with
Count Anton Monts and, although they were at opposite poles
politically (Monts was inclined to be Left-Wing), they had always
remained good friends. When, in Venice, the Emperor enflamed
him with the idea that he might possibly succeed me, Monts had
written straight off to Heydebrand saying that he might count it a
certainty that His Majesty would dispense with my services. He
had not, however, betrayed the fact that he deluded himself with
the hope of succeeding me, since he knew how unenthusiastic
Heydebrand would be at the idea. He had only left him in no
doubt that my position with the Kaiser was badly shaken.

Many, all too many, straws in the wind, so clearly showed that
my present difficulties could be traced back to the one exalted
source, that I decided to clear things up once and for all. I requested a private audience, which was granted, on 18th May at
Wiesbaden. I found the Emperor in high spirits. He greeted me
with the assurance that, this time, his Vienna reception had " really
and truly " surpassed all he had ever encountered on such occasions,
in the way of enthusiastic devotion. He was also very proud of his
political successes in Corfu. He had won the Greeks for ever to our
side, and they formed a major acquisition to our political credit
account. On the strength of my former residence, of nearly two
years' duration in Greece, I suggested that the modern Greeks, by
reason of their political disorders, their military weakness, and the
little reliance to be placed in them, recalled rather the Graeculi of
the Roman Empire than the heroes of Marathon and Thermopylæ,
and that therefore we should be ill-advised to make them a serious
factor in our policy. His Majesty's good humour vanished at once,
nor did his temper improve when I began to broach the subject of
Finance Reform which, in itself, both wearied and annoyed him.
But I made him understand, quite plainly, that I should have to
present a detailed report. Several times he showed clear signs of
impatience, and twice or three times scarcely managed to stifle a
yawn. I did not pay the slightest attention to this, and talked to
him for a good hour on the attitudes of the various parties, the
situation in the Reichstag, and its repercussions on myself. My
exposé may perhaps have been too detailed, but I made things as

clear and unambiguous as I could. I went on to say that the whole political situation was rendered far harder by the Conservatives, whose vision was limited and unstatesmanly. Here His Majesty brusquely interrupted, to tell me that he could not consent to a dissolution. I answered that I had not suggested one; that I should not consider it an advantage, either to the country or the Crown. But it was quite another question whether I either should or would accept a line of policy begun with the severance of the *bloc* and ending with the rejection of the Death Duties. As I said this I studied the Emperor's face. I knew my Imperial master far too well not to see the inner conflict that arose in him. On the one hand he longed to be rid of me; on the other he wished to be the one to determine the moment and occasion of my retirement.

Four days after this we met again at the Frankfurt-am-Main musical festival. I have rarely seen so cordial a reception of the Emperor as this, at the contest of choral societies, in the ancient city of the Electors—the city in which Emperors were crowned—the beautiful city on the Main in which I had spent my childhood. The jubilation was indescribable. As Wagner's magnificent " Imperial March " rang out, the Empress squeezed my hand. " It's all turning out just as you prophesied it would in the Neues Palais," she said to me, with tears in her eyes. She had spoken almost in a whisper, glancing uneasily at the Emperor, who was standing a little way off, proclaiming in a sonorous voice to the Suite, how certain he was that the German people would follow him through thick and thin. His Majesty grew more and more self-satisfied. Of this he had given striking proof, not long after the last birthday celebrations, in a very characteristic marginal note. I had made the confidential suggestion that the Federal Princes as a body might come to Berlin for the fiftieth birthday of their Emperor—27th January 1909. They came and their presence in no small measure contributed to the splendour and success of the occasion. Prince Ludwig of Bavaria, who deputized for his father, the Regent Luitpold, whose great age had prevented his being present, read a very excellent speech, expressing in the most moving terms the idea of Imperial unity.

After the banquet a reception was held in the picture gallery, where almost every German Federal Sovereign expressed to me the deepest patriotism. Most, at the same time, evinced the hope of seeing me, for many years their Chancellor, for the good of the Empire. Especially cordial in expression were Prince Ludwig of Bavaria, King Wilhelm of Württemberg, and the Grand-Duke of Baden. The King, as patriotic as he was intelligent, devoted to the Emperor from the circumstance that he had served as an Hussar of the Guard, but equally devoted to the Empire, said to me: " We all hope and pray you will remain, and the people hope and wish it too. In my State there are even a number of Centre Party electors who, as I gather from certain Württemberg Catholics, would like to keep you, if only on account of our Foreign Policy." The Emperor came and went among the Sovereigns with a very evident strut of satisfaction. My friend Knesebeck whispered, pointing towards this grandson of the modest and retiring William I: " Isn't he just like a peacock spreading its tail?" And this true and sensible friend added, with a melancholy smile: " Unfortunately he reminds me of the young Lord Edenhall in Uhland's poem. *Absit omen*!"

A few days later the Prussian Ministers at the various German courts slipped into their reports discreet allusions to the suggestion which had done most to bring about this reunion of Federal Sovereigns in the Imperial castle at Berlin. But the Emperor scribbled in the margin that it had been useless to bring pressure on the Princes, since they all knew perfectly well what their " damned duty " (to their Imperial Lord and Master) was.

In the meantime Herr von Heydebrand's policy, which he followed against the advice of many Conservatives (Schwerin-Löwitz, Kanitz-Podangen, Kaphengst, Hohenlohe-Oehringen, Pauli, etc.) of a stubborn *rapprochement* with the Poles and Centre against the Liberals, had made progress. It grew to seem more and more unlikely that the reform of Imperial finances would be carried in the manner I had prescribed, *i.e.* with the Death Duties I suggested. Count Udo Stolberg, President of the Reichstag, since the election swing-over in 1907, and who, for thirty-eight years, had been a deputy—one of the most adroit and experienced champions of the Conservative Party and principles—had already written to Herr von Loebell on 22nd May 1909: " My one hope of things not going to pieces is centred in the Chancellor himself. I am in the same position as Ballestrem, who could see his friends' mistakes without being able to alter them. I trust you not to show this letter to anyone; or, if you do, not before my death, since then it will make no difference to me." At the same time, and more than ever before, there were intrigues against me round the Kaiser. A certain *clique* had come together to this end who called themselves the " League of Loyalists." Prince Max Fürstenberg played a leading part in this *côterie*. He, as I have already mentioned, à propos of poor Philip Eulenburg's disgrace, had now become the Emperor's favourite. The death of his cousin, Karl Egon, had left him heir to the big property of Donaueschingen. But his sympathies were entirely Austrian. His upbringing had been Austrian; his mother had been a Khevenhüller, his wife was a Schönborn-Buchheim—all Austrians, *pur sang*! He had often made himself a nuisance to me by his pro-Austrian attempts to set the Kaiser not only against Italy but Russia, while on the other hand, wherever he could, he would champion Poland. The Chamberlain, Reischach, married to a Ratibor, whose mother had been a Fürstenberg, felt very proud of being able to boast about his " cousin " Prince Fürstenberg, and did whatever he could to assist the intrigues of the Emperor's favourite. It mattered very little to His Majesty that Max Fürstenberg should be in financial difficulties. Second only to Fürstenberg in the " League of Loyalists " were the Master of Ceremonies, Eugen Röder, and his sister, Countess Paula Alvensleben. Röder had already intrigued against the Bismarcks, both father and son, and now began to scheme against myself, although, for several years, he had been most stupidly obsequious. Whenever I went to a court ball he would be waiting for my wife and myself at the charming Eosander's entrance to the castle, his feathered hat in hand to have, as he put it, " the privilege," of escorting my wife to the White Saloon. When once I warned him not to catch a cold in his head he laid his hand on his heart, and answered in the accents of a hero: " I would rather get congestion of the lungs than, for an instant, forget my duty to Princess Bülow." Through Eckardstein, who had come to such grief in England, the League of Loyalists got into touch with Rudolf Martin. Martin had been a Saxon official whose climbing propensities had made him unpopular with his superiors. The Saxon government managed to " praise him out " of Saxony, and hang him up in the Imperial Home Office. There he came into conflict with Count Posadowsky, who soon sized up his general unreliability and uselessness, and put him on the shelf, in a very subordinate department. Martin, in revenge, published a brochure against him and, having heard that there were differences of opinion between us, he had the impertinence to send me a copy of it, in the hope of currying favour with me by stabbing his chief in the back. Naturally I took disciplinary proceedings against him, which led to his being turned out of the service.

Eugen Zimmermann, then the Head of the Scherl Publishing House, who later collaborated with the Emperor in his book *Gestalten und Erscheinungen* and who, during my last months as Chancellor, became my zealous and incisive defender in the press, both wrote and said to me that such men as Rudolf Martin and Eckardstein were backed by the Silesian magnates, who resented what they considered my " Socialist " policy. I never gave much weight to these suggestions, and certainly did not allow them to influence my personal friendship with such influential Silesians as Prince Guido Henckel-Donnersmarck, and others.

It is certain that this same Count Oppersdorff who, ten years later, betrayed his country and went over to the Poles, was one of the most zealous members of the Loyalists' League. He had made friends with the Alsatian, Wetterlé who, as everyone knows, flew across the frontier from Colmar, at night, as soon as war was declared. He remained in France throughout the war and carried on propaganda against us. To this day he still lives in Paris, in the aura of a French patriot and deadly enemy of the " Boches." Through the influence of Calmette, its editor, this Abbé Wetterlé caused articles to be published in the *Figaro* at the request of von Oppersdorff, which were destined to be read by the Emperor. These were not unskilfully contrived to produce an effect on the childish fantasy of His Majesty. I remember one which, as a " horrible warning " to the Kaiser, described the fate of a Merovingian King, whose wicked Chancellor, Gonthram-Bose, first enmeshed him in a net of guile and fooled him, then lamed his strength by means of a finely-spun conspiracy, and finally had his head shaved, and sent him into exile in a cloister. This sad story is to be found at greater length in Augustin Thierry's *Récits des temps mérovingiens*. Thierry describes the wicked Gonthram as follows: " *Gonthram-Bose présentait dans son caractère une singularité remarquable. Germain d'origine, il surpassait en habilté pratique, en talent de ressources, en instinct de rouerie, si ce mot peut être employé ici, les hommes plus déliés parmi la race gallo-romaine. Ce n'était pas la mauvaise foi tudesque, ce mensonge brutale accompagné d'un gros rire ; c'etait quelque chose de plus raffiné et de plus pervers en même temps, un esprit d'intrigue universel et en quelque sorte nomade, car il allait s'exerçant d'un bout à l'autre de la Gaule. Personne ne savait mieux que cet Austrasien pousser les autres dans un pas dangereux et s'en tirer à propos. On disait de lui que jamais il n'avait fait de serment à un ami, sans le trahir aussitôt, et c'est de là probablement que lui venait son surnom germanique. Bose, en Allemand moderne " boese," signifie malin, méchant.*"

So the parallel lay there, ready to hand, between the cunning Gonthram-Bose and Prince Bülow, the German Kaiser's wicked (böse) Chancellor. Several of the League of Loyalists were afterwards punished, or at any rate exposed, by fate. Not to mention Calmette who, shortly before the beginning of the war, was shot by

Mme. Caillaux, Eckardstein, soon after war broke out, was put under lock and key by the military authorities, on suspicion of having betrayed his country. Rudolf Martin, on the outbreak of the November revolution rushed over from the Loyalists' League to the Socialists. Count Hans Oppersdorff was universally despised in Silesia, where he got the nickname " Oppersdorffski."

I have already said how delighted William II was at having received a spontaneous invitation from his "colleague Nicky," to a friendly meeting in Russian waters. Since the Reichstag situation was a difficult one the Emperor, on his own initiative, excused my being present at this interview, in a letter which he caused to be written to me, on 2nd June 1909, by the Head of the Civil Cabinet:

> I have the honour of informing Your Highness that His Majesty would have been most happy to feel he had Your Highness beside him at his forthcoming interview with the Emperor of Russia. But, His Majesty, having learned that the Reichstag is to resume its sittings on the 15th inst., believes Your Highness's presence indispensable, by reason of the exceptional importance of the present debates on fiscal reform. In these circumstances His Majesty, the Emperor, abstains most regretfully from suggesting that Your Highness should accompany him to Danzig, and begs Your Highness to allow yourself to be represented on that occasion by the Secretary of State for Foreign Affairs.
> I must beg Your Highness to believe that I remain,
> always, Your most devoted,
> (Signed) VON VALENTINI.

This letter was in typescript. Valentini had added the words " most regretfully " in ink.

To Herr von Schön, who accompanied His Majesty in my stead, I gave the following short instruction, under the heading " Ten Commandments." This decalogue, a copy of which I sent to the Emperor, was drawn up as follows:

(1) Be pleasant to the Russians, especially Isvolski. We shall have to talk politics to Isvolski, since that is what his sovereign brings him for. Of course be prudent with him. Let him do the talking.

(2) Say nothing to the Russians which might be repeated in Vienna, either directly or indirectly through London and Paris, and might arouse mistrust in the Viennese government.

(3) Do not broach the subject of the Dardanelles. If the Russians mention it first answer them pleasantly, that that is an European

Question, but that certainly there will be no obstacle from our side to prevent Russia from fulfilling her aspirations, in so far as the further development of Russo-German good relations permits us to show ourselves amenable to her.

(4) No mention of the Cretan Question. Should the Russians begin to discuss it say that, since Crete is not under our protectorate, we have no interests in the matter.

(5) Any Russian complaints on the subject of Austria to be answered with sighs or smiles, according to their seriousness and intensity; shoulders may be shrugged, but no positive agreement expressed.

(6) Re-emphasize the traditional German feeling of friendship for Russia as the basis of the Monarchic principle in the world and, at the same time, the guarantee of peace. An alliance of the three Emperors remains our ideal: but let the Russians make some advances. We cannot, at the moment, consider a separate under-standing with Russia, only one in conjunction with Austria.

(7) If the Russians declare that the situation in Turkey is uncer-tain and may, at any moment, breed surprises, do not contradict them, but be calm in the discussion of recent Turkish events. We are not irrevocably committed in Turkey.

(8) Not a word against England. It would go straight home and would only serve to confirm the Russians in their present pro-English attitude.

(9) We have no interest in opposing Russia in Persia or any-where else in the Near East. The Persian situation does not interest us in any way. *Nescio quid nobis magis farcimentum sit.*

(10) I would not recommend dwelling too insistently on the events of last winter. Should the Russians pursue the subject tell them that we have been loyal to Austria and at the same time, open and friendly with Russia. No returning to Björkö!

The meeting took place on 17th June off the rocky Finnish islands before Frederikshaven. It was the last which, before my retirement, took place between the Emperor and the Tsar, and it passed off very well.

His Majesty obeyed my ten commandments. At my express wish he did not improvise a speech, but read a toast I had composed for him at my leisure, with a clear head, and sent after him. At previous interviews the Tsar had been repeatedly irritated by the Emperor's evident satisfaction in displaying his talents as an orator, whereas he, who was no Demosthenes, had to hold a big sheet of paper and laboriously read from it his toast. But this time both

Monarchs read their speeches to the great satisfaction of the Tsar.

In the course of the political conversations, begun after dinner, the Tsar gave the Emperor " his most sacred word " that he would endorse no demand from France or England which implied hostile intentions towards Germany. He affirmed, that for the Emperor William he had always felt a deep and trusting sympathy; that the Emperor's friendship was most precious to him, his Empire, and his Crown; that, through thick and thin, he would always remain the Emperor's friend, as he begged him, sincerely, to believe. Isvolski, too, had a talk with Baron von Schön in the course of which he mentioned Aehrenthal, whom he still considered " indiscreet " and " unreliable," and whom he accused of blackmail, because he had threatened to publish strictly confidential Russian documents. Aehrenthal had for ever forfeited the favour of the Russian Court, which had felt itself entitled to expect very different treatment at the hands of this Ambassador to St. Petersburg on whom, for so many years, the Russian government had showered favours. For the moment this attitude of Aehrenthal had forced down to zero relationships between Austria-Hungary and Russia; they were now on a footing of formal correctness, and that was all. Nevertheless Russian policy still remained peaceful, though to be sure, the St. Petersburg Cabinet hoped and believed that, if necessary, the German government would prevent Austria from taking any further aggressive step in the Balkan peninsula, since Russia, a Slav and Orthodox Power, could not, without forswearing her tradition, look on with folded arms at any such further attempt.

Herr von Schön, inspired by my instructions, replied that Austria had renounced all thoughts of advance on Salonica; that in the matter of the recent annexation it had simply been a question of concluding a matter agreed upon, long since, in principle; that extraneous circumstances had pushed Austria to complete her liquidation of a contract, by making the matter *de facto*; and that, finally, we had not been in concert with Austria-Hungary, either in the matter of the Sanjak or in that of the annexation. The Russian Foreign Minister asked von Schön to give me his formal assurance that the Anglo-Russian Agreement was exclusively concerned with certain matters already well known, and connected with Central Asia; that he had never had the intention of developing this *entente*, and that there had been no question of it, even at Reval. He declared that he had no wish to interfere with German economic interests in Persia, defended by us as he admitted, with great moderation. Nor had he the slightest inclination to interpret the good relationship with England in a sense hostile to ourselves. The *Triple Entente* was merely a journalist's myth. Neither he nor the Emperor Nicholas would be willing to commit themselves permanently to any irrevocable grouping of Powers. The Prime Minister, Stolypin, assured both the Emperor and von Schön of his real pleasure at this interview of the Sovereigns which had, indeed, passed off very agreeably. He added that, for Russia, it was essential, for reasons both of domestic and foreign policy, that the two neighbouring Powers of the North should remain on a footing of peace and amity. As he sailed out of Russian waters the Emperor received the following telegram from the Tsar:—

> Glad to hear you arrived safely. Alix and I were most happy to have received you. We thank you heartily for the great pleasure you gave us by your visit and for your kindness to all our children, who kiss their uncle.
>
> Your loving and devoted friend,
NICKY.[1]

At the same time the Russian Ambassador in Berlin handed me a confidential letter from Isvolski expressing to me the deep satisfaction felt by his Imperial master with regard to the results of the interview. This letter, written in French, contained the following: "*Pour la première fois nous avons vu l'Empereur Guillaume lisant en langue française un toast préparé d'avance, et presque calqué sur celui de notre Auguste Maître dont on nous avait demandé le texte.*"

---

[1] English in text.

CHAPTER XXXII

*The taxation problems in the Reichstag (16th June 1909)—My last
speech in the Reichstag—The Question of the Eastern Marches—
My Expropriation Scheme—William II's attitude towards it—My
earlier speeches on the question (1907-1908)—Declarations on the
adoption of an expropriation policy—Contradictory attitude of William II towards me—Intrigues against me—Erzberger, Röder,
Martin—Who will be Chancellor?—A letter from Count Wedel.*

ON 16th June, the day before the interview off Finland, the
second reading of my taxation scheme began in the Reichstag. I spoke [1] at the very beginning of this session, in
order to make my whole position clear to the great bourgeois
parties. I told the Centre that I had never had the slightest wish
to reject its collaboration and support in the matter of Finance
Reform. The Centre, at my express suggestion, had from the
start, like all the other bourgeois parties, been apprised of the
Federal Government's intentions. I had made it my rule never to
hinder the constructive effort of any party—from the Social-
Democrats, even, I would welcome any concrete suggestion. I
reproached the Centre with the suspicions excited against me by
some of its party-members. These had done nothing to weaken
my political standpoint; I was used to slander. I had begun, little
by little, to grasp the true inwardness of Bismarck's words when he
said to a distinguished man who showed small eagerness to accept
a Minister's portfolio: " I can quite understand your not wanting
to fall in within range of the mud-slingers." Nor had I let myself
be daunted by the fact that certain members of the Centre Party had
broken off their social connection with me. " The fact that I have
lived so long abroad may perhaps contribute to my surprise that
people should avoid each other socially because they happen to
disagree in politics and hold opposite views on economics or policy.
I can only hope that, in this respect, our manners as a nation may
improve, that even Germany, in time, will have reached a point long
since achieved in other countries. In England, for instance, people
are not so narrow-minded as to carry their political differences into
society with them. Even here, I hope, we may one day become

[1] Prince Bülow's *Speeches*. Complete edition, iii, 214. Compressed edition,
ii, 194.

sufficiently civilized to perceive that, though a man may not agree with us in political, economic, and social questions, that does not necessarily prove him a fool or a knave. That would be a very marked step in the direction prescribed by Goethe when he suggested that we should cut the nets of the Philistine: but, up to now, we have never managed to take it." The rest of my speech made it clear that I was resolved to direct affairs in such a manner that the Liberals should not find themselves excluded from a collaboration which seemed to me infinitely desirable in the interests of our quiet and healthy development. To boycott the Liberal spirit in our legislation and public life would, I said, be an historic injustice, as well as a political error.

"That which was possible and even advantageous in old Prussia is not always so in the Federal German Empire. South Germany and Central Germany must both be given a high—a far higher—opinion of the value of Conservative Prussia. And Conservative Prussia herself must not forget that those Liberal forces which weld the various racial factors of Germany are an absolute necessity to the Empire." After which I settled accounts with the Conservatives. I reminded the Right how, almost as soon as I was made Minister, I had eased the tension which, in those days, existed between Conservatives and the Crown; how, by years of industry and patience, I had straightened out the tangle of the Canal Question how, since the very first day of my Chancellorship—or, literally, since the very first hour of it—I had made myself the champion of Agriculture. Amid hearty applause and a burst of laughter from the Left, I attacked the Conservatives as follows: "You will have to wait a very long time before you get another Chancellor to defend Conservative interests—I mean real Conservative interests—as consistently and successfully as I have done: a Chancellor who will promote, as I have promoted, the real interests of Agriculture. Yes, I have defended your interests, but without forgetting those of the State. Not even the Conservative Party can prove itself superior to the country: not even Conservatives shall make me neglect my duty and forget the well-being of all Germany."

Conservatives were wrong, I continued, if they supposed that mere adherence to party principles could justify a political blunder. The victory of the moment often meant the defeat of the future. But I did not shrink, in spite of the noisy protests of the Left, from affirming that, under the guidance of their Sovereigns, the junkers— yes, the much-maligned junkers—had built up the power of the Prussian State and with it that of the German Empire. I was well aware how much those elements which composed the backbone of the Conservatives had contributed to Prussia throughout the centuries. But if their party closed its eyes to every just demand, if it had not the sense to abandon untenable positions, it would itself be digging its own grave.

I then addressed that warning to Conservatives which later developments have only too tragically confirmed: "Your 'inacceptable' may perhaps succeed in impeding these Death Duties, for the moment. But you will only be laying down the road which leads on to new and crushing taxation in future—taxation directed against you, and laid on you without your consent, and which will take far less count of your desires than the duties I propose to you to-day. The Conservative attitude towards this great national question will make a deep impression on our whole people. It may be that you are calling into being a reaction against the Conservative Party, that you are breeding a deep and sure antagonism, and with it, such a crop of radical tendencies as neither you nor I may be willing to answer for to history. This morning I read in a newspaper that my suggestion of a Conservative-Liberal alliance had been nothing but a piece of party tactics, made to procure that momentary re-grouping which would favour my own policy in the Reichstag. That is untrue. My desire for such an understanding is born of the simple wish, not only to see the Liberals collaborate, and to admit political necessities, but to lead the Conservative party into the paths of a sane and healthy progress. I wished to avert such future struggles and antagonisms as may shake the very foundations of Germany. My concept was the concept of a statesman. The future will show that I was right, and it will matter little that the man in whom this concept first became articulate should have retired from the political scene a few years earlier or later."

Once again I stated clearly and unmistakably my reasons for adhering firmly to the Death Duties. I refused to let my name be associated with taxes that would damage trade or commerce, which would burden industry, and prejudice our whole economic position.

" I consider it as my duty in equity and as a social and political necessity to see to it that any new tax laid on the community as a whole be borne proportionately by a considerable section of the possessing classes. It is not possible to derive five hundred millions of fresh taxation solely from the taxes on consumption, or from other indirect levies which bear on the middle-class and on the people, in greater proportion than on the rich. I insist on Death Duties, not from obstinacy and desire to be always in the right, but because they are socially just. I hope that in the Reichstag the solidarity and social sense of the nation will triumph over narrow party interests." I concluded: " Should I be convinced that I, personally, am an obstacle to this; that any other man would achieve this object more easily—should the course of this debate be such that I cannot and will not accept its conclusions, it will be possible then, to convince the Sovereign of the expediency of my resignation—and I shall wish my successor luck as sincerely and heartily as, till now, I have endeavoured to serve my country."

That was the last time I ever spoke in the Reichstag. The first half of my speech was often interrupted by Social Democrats and Centre, but they ended by listening in silence. Neither did these two hostile parties hiss my conclusion ; while both Liberals and the majority of Conservatives broke into loud applause. Among other evening papers the Democratic *Berliner Tageblatt* declared that it would not be in the least surprising if, even this time, Prince Bülow, though he played with the idea of resigning, in the end proved master of the situation. The Conservative *Kreuzzeitung* reassured : " The eminent merits of this Chancellor in the domains of Economic and Foreign Policy will secure him for all time the thanks of the nation, including the Conservative Party. We hope and trust that, even now, his statesmanlike adroitness and acumen will enable him to discover ways and means of achieving a thorough reform of imperial finances by a method satisfactory to all."

The leading clerical organ *Germania*, stigmatized my speech as a new affront to the Centre. The *Post* which expressed the Independent Conservatives, wrote :—" Everyone could see that the time had come to settle accounts, when Prince Bülow, in a powerful speech, put down his cards on the table. He spoke very clearly and trenchantly,—like a leader. Each faction was given plainly to understand, and without any beating about the bush, what its proper position really was, and shown exactly where it had gone wrong. Its errors were pointed out to each, before the Prince defined his own standpoint."

Through these months preceding my resignation I could contemplate with a certain satisfaction the position of our Eastern Marches question. More than once, since I had taken over the control of Prussian Affairs, I had declared that I considered this the most important question of Prussian internal policy. The essential thing was to promote the work of colonization in a resolute and consequent fashion. But, the further colonization proceeded, the more the Poles redoubled every effort to prevent the passing of Polish territory into German hands. Above all they sought to prevent Germans from acquiring large holdings at the expense of

LAST SPEECH OF BÜLOW IN THE REICHSTAG, 16TH JUNE 1909,

On his attitude towards the parties

Poles.   Yet just such acquisition as this was necessary to secure the land needed for colonization against any Polish encroachment. I had, for some considerable time, been discussing this question *à fond* with the two Oberpräsidenten of Posen and West Prussia how best to overcome Polish resistance.   Herr von Waldow and Herr von Jagow both belonged to the best class of old Prussian Civil Servant, and that is saying a great deal.   When Bill Bismarck was Oberpräsident of East Prussia, Herr von Waldow had been his right-hand man as Regierungspräsident. He had told me that Herr von Waldow was of the stuff of which Prince Bismarck liked his officials to be made.   People who did not like him had nicknamed him " the frozen towel," because of his somewhat rigid manner; but he was a man.   And Jagow was no less reliable.   Three members of his old and excellent Brandenburg family were, at that time, in the service of the State :— W. P. Jagow, Oberpräsident of West Prussia, P. P. Jagow, the Berlin Chief of Police and A. A. Jagow, who later became a Secretary of State in the Foreign Office.   The two first did honour to their family and the March of Brandenburg, but A. A. Jagow possessed a shrinking soul in a feeble body.

Convinced of the necessity for fostering German colonization in the Eastern Marches, I had decided to lay the draft of a law for expropriation before the Landtag.   This was, I admit, the law which I sponsored with most regret throughout the whole of my long career.   On all sides it aroused hostility ; first from the Centre and Liberals, by tradition opposed to any vigorous action in the Eastern Marches, and, in this matter, oblivious of the *salus publica*, by reason of their own party-interests, their doctrinaire conceptions and prejudices.   But other politicians opposed it—men of intellect, devoted to the State, and in other ways favourable to the government.   Their objections to my project had great weight with me. But what other means had I of acquiring, in spite of the resistance of their owners, holdings which the Poles bought up and kept with the sole object of obstructing and generally embarrassing the State ?   To-day, as I look back on all this, I must even admit that I consider my scruples of those days with regard to expropriation, somewhat exaggerated.   In that same *Berliner Tageblatt* which violently opposed my Expropriation Law I read as follows, in the December of 1922 : " Seven hundred thousand Germans have been driven out of Posen and West Prussia alone, by the Poles, since they obtained possession of these provinces : an appalling figure, indicative of the human tragedy now being played out behind the frontiers of the new Poland."

"You see, we savages are better men than you are," as Seume makes his "Canadian" exclaim.

In conjunction with Arnim-Krieven the Minister of Agriculture, and Rheinbaben, the Finance Minister, I delivered a verbal report on expropriation to the Emperor, setting forth, with all due seriousness and candour, those first scruples, which it had needed an effort to surmount when I saw myself faced with *dira necessitas*. His Majesty had no such hesitations. "Go ahead. Don't spare them," he said to me. "Go for them. Go for the whole. I've been wanting such a law for a long time." As, after our audience, we descended the broad curves of marble staircase, which lead from storey to storey of the palace, the zealous and loyal Rheinbaben asked me, with an almost vexed surprise: "What on earth induced Your Excellency to keep pouring your absinthe of hesitation into the bubbling champagne of the Emperor's enthusiasm for our expropriation project?" I answered that I had considered it my duty, in this as in every other bold suggestion, to lay the pros and cons before His Majesty. "Let us be thankful," I added, "if the Kaiser remains so resolute. It is always easy enough to fire his enthusiasm for any new and unusual idea, but far harder to rely on his seeing it worked out to the bitter end, and not going back on his word, as soon as he becomes aware of the dangers and difficulties entailed." And indeed it was not so very long before William II, under the influence of his favourite, Prince Max Fürstenberg, had begun to vaccillate in the expropriation question, criticize my scheme, and wish to cancel it. After I had retired, these proposals were the pet theme of His Majesty, whenever he felt it necessary to demonstrate my political lack of vision and moral impriority. However: *Quod licet Jovi, non licet bovi.* The rights and liberties of Jupiter are considered unseemly in the ox.

Loebell, the Head of the Imperial Chancellery, both understood and gave full weight to my hesitations in the matter of expropriation—though, at the same time, the Reporting Councillor of the Chancellery, Wahnschaffe—nicknamed "handsome Wahnschaffe"—surpassed in zeal the most fervent anti-Poles. More than once I was obliged to remind him that I did not admit expropriation except in the case of such property as had very recently passed from German into Polish hands, or of estates whose Polish landlords were absentees, and lived abroad in Paris or Monte Carlo. If Wahnschaffe had had his way he would have laid hands on all Polish property whatsoever, without distinction. This same zealous Wahnschaffe, however, as the faithful henchman of Bethmann-Hollweg, caused my book *German Policy* to be banned during the

war, within the radius of the Eastern High-Command because
the chapter on our policy in the Eastern Marches, though
written with extreme moderation, might hurt the feelings of
" our chivalrous Polish friends." And it was Privy Councillor
Wahnschaffe who, as Head of the Chancellery, under the orders
of Prince Max of Baden, refused, in November 1918, to leave his
telephone box, and rang up Spa, again and again, to find out how
long it would take the Kaiser to make up his mind, at last, to
abdicate.

By reason of the peculiar difficulties attached to this expropriation scheme I decided to defend it myself, both in the Upper
House and Chamber of Deputies. I had already (26th November
1907)[1] discovered that, since my Chancellorship, about twice as
many German peasant families had been established in the German
Eastern March as in all the previous years since 1886, the year
in which Prince Bismarck began to colonize. On that day I had
declared, in my speech, that we had every reason to hope that,
thanks to our policy in Posen, we had succeeded in checking that
movement of population which had been, since 1867, unfavourable
to Germanization. But I went on to prove statistically that, in the
last analysis, only the proportion of small holdings could decide
whether our Eastern Provinces were going to be German or Polish.
As things were moving at present German holdings, within twenty
years, would be reduced to *fidei commis* and domaines, and would be
infinitely smaller than the Polish. I said quite plainly amid a chorus
of protest from the Poles: " We cannot, by free purchase, satisfy
our need for more land, so that therefore, in the superior interests
of the State, the Commission for Colonization must be authorized to
proceed to expropriatory measures." The Prussian State would
neglect its first duty—the duty of self-preservation—if it abandoned
its most efficacious means of protecting itself—its policy, that is to
say, of colonization—at the very moment when it seemed to promise
lasting results. I thanked, on behalf of the Royal government, those
parties which, till then, had backed my policy, for the unanimity
with which, in spite of some serious hesitations, they had declared
themselves ready to give me a free hand, in any further colonizing
effort. This was the only method, I said, by which Prussia could
remain what she was in reality—a national State. The minutes of
this session, of 16th January 1908, contains the following note
à propos of my speech[2] in the Chamber of Deputies on the second

---

[1] Prince Bülow's *Speeches*. Complete edition, iii, 45 *et seq*. Réclame edition, iv,
257 *et seq*.

[2] *Ibid.* Complete edition, iii, 90 *et seq*. Réclame edition, iv, 286 *et seq*.

reading of my Expropriation Scheme: "Decisive applause from the Right and National-Liberal benches; commotion from Polish and Centre Party benches. Renewed applause from the Right, and National-Liberals; hissing from the Poles and Centre. Stormy applause from the Right and National-Liberals." Even in the Reichstag I have never known a stormier debate.

In the Upper House the scheme encountered even greater difficulties. Here it was opposed, though very moderately, with dignity and restraint, but still decisively, by my revered friend, Cardinal Kopp. The ex-Minister of Agriculture, Lucius, and my old friend, Count Mirbach-Sorquitten, not to mention such distinguished people as Leo Buch, opposed it sharply. But, in hourlong debates, extending over the whole of three days, I still held fast to my principle: without permission to expropriate there could be no efficient colonization policy, and so no chance of holding our Eastern Marches. I had to speak five or six times in the Landtag, and in the Upper House several times in the same sitting. To certain juridical objections I replied: "Its strong sense of justice is a noted characteristic of our people—it is, perhaps, the finest of German qualities. But it has its reverse side in our tendency—often a dangerous one politically—to lose our way and slip back into formalism. I allude to our inveterate habit of judging even great political questions solely from the standpoint of private equity. One cannot reason thus on those great problems which involve the very existence of a country. The first, the supreme duty, of a State is to persist. Other countries have taught themselves this lesson; unless we too can learn it we shall slip under the Juggernaut wheels." I parried the suggestion that our policy in the Eastern Marches was displeasing to Austria, and would discredit us there. "It is an excellent thing to keep one's weather eye on Foreign Policy, to note every sign of fair or stormy and, above all, to keep a sharp look out for thunder claps. But to tremble every time the foreigner frowns— that is not what beseems a great people. Our duty is to pursue a calm, just, and reasoned policy, of the kind that will win us confidence and respect, and thus to collaborate with the world in the great work of civilization. But, neither to individuals nor to nations, is it possible to disarm all jealousy, to draw the sting from every hate. What we need is a calm, proud, resolute national consciousness, ready to hold fast what it has won."

Finally I succeeded in getting Adicke's compromise accepted by both Chambers of the Landtag. By this the area of possible expropriation ceased to be limited to the nine districts of Posen and West Prussia, and the government was given the right to proceed, in the whole territory of these provinces, to expropriations, up to a parity of 70,000 hectars. Herr von Oldenburg, in contrast to several of his Agrarian and Conservative friends, was an incisive champion of the Expropriation Scheme. With his racy originality he was one of the best types of junker. He had spoken from the soul when he ended a speech with the words:

> *" Der Adler Preussens wendet sich zum Lichte*
> *Schwer ist sein Flug, er trägt die Weltgeschichte."* [1]

On the adoption of the Scheme I received a letter of thanks from the director's committee of the Eastern Marches League. The League congratulated me on my " devotion," my " determination to see the Scheme right through." By making this project law I had done an immense and historic service to the whole Teutonic race, and had lifted a great weight off the minds of the vast majority of Germans in the Eastern March, who felt as if delivered from a nightmare. General Count Wartensleben, a veteran of eighty, the glorious Chief of the Head Quarters of our First Army during the war of 1870, wrote to me:

> With all my heart I congratulate Your Highness on your difficult but decisive victory in the matter of the Eastern Marches. For some time I had put down my name to speak on the 26th but, alas for my eighty-one years, I was taken ill at the wrong moment, and my doctor expressly forbade the journey to Berlin. It was very painful to me to have been prevented from doing my duty on that occasion. But the essential thing is yesterday's result, which seems even better than we had hoped. Believe me Your Excellency's most sincerely devoted:
>
> COUNT WARTENSLEBEN.
> (Cavalry General.)

Prince Lichnowsky told me in confidence that, shortly after the acceptance of the scheme, his younger sister, married to the Pole, Lanskoronski, had written to tell him the opinions of her relatives, friends, and neighbours in Galicia. They all agreed that, if the law were passed at once, and applied for the next ten years without unnecessary severity, but with ordinary vigour and persistence, Germanism would have gained the Eastern Provinces. Such was the position in East Prussia when Heydebrand, with his henchman Westarp, helped by the Poles, procured my downfall, and so laid

---

[1] The Prussian Eagle strives into the light
The history of the world weighs down his flight.

the seeds of those events which led on to the restoration of Poland, and the loss of our Eastern Marches.

The nearer we seemed to a solution of the Death Duties' problem, the higher waxed the excitement in the country, whose best elements, without any question, would have liked to see me remain in office. But my enemies, above all those at court, redoubled their efforts to unseat me. His Majesty's attitude became more and more contradictory. I gave orders to submit to the Emperor every article in the serious press which either dealt with me, personally, or discussed the situation as a whole—and above all those which took me to task. In the margins of the ones which sang my praises the Emperor would always scribble a note: " Bravo! Bravissimo! That's what they all ought to say." Against the others: " Lies! Slander! Miserable scribbling journalists, etc." I remember one, in a Viennese newspaper, which affirmed that the Emperor was too high-minded and patriotic to bear me any grudge for my attitude in the November crisis. In the margin, in the Emperor's handwriting: " Excellently put." Another suggested that His Majesty would not really be very sorry to part with me, since he still resented the line I had taken in November 1908. In the margin : " Rascal! Miserable slanderer! " But, unluckily I had other information which did not seem to tally with marginal protests. Count August Eulenburg confided that the Emperor had granted a long private audience to that same Eckardstein whom he had wanted to turn out of the Service, at the time of his divorce-court scandal and all the other wretched incidents connected with his public reputation. I also learned that one of my most spiteful enemies, Count Hans Oppersdorff, had been commanded, with his wife, to dine *en petit comité* at the Palace, and that the Emperor had had a long talk with him. To explain this invitation to the Kaiserin, who wanted very much to see me remain, Her Majesty was informed that Countess Oppersdorff had had twelve children in fourteen years, and that among them there had been two pair of twins. The Empress Augusta Victoria, who was what Holy Writ calls " the joyful mother of children," was very eager to meet a lady who had also done so much to increase our population. Countess Doda Oppersdorff (*neé* Princess Radziwill) was, however, a good and charming woman, very different from her spiteful husband.

Most malicious of all was the Master of Ceremonies, Eugen Röder. He had had several secret meetings with my worst enemy in the Centre Party, Erzberger, to whom he explained that, at bottom, His Majesty disliked me, and would be only too grateful to the Centre if it managed to bring about my downfall. This inspired the deputy for Biberach—at that time he was only thirty-four—to make a very violent speech, in which, alluding to Uhland's famous poem, he compared me to the wicked squire, who killed his master because he longed to be a knight. This might have passed as a joke, though a very poor one, of the same kind as the *Figaro* article's comparison of me with Gonthram-Bose, the wicked Chancellor, but for Rudolf Martin, who attacked me in a very clumsy pamphlet, in which he " unmasked my baseness " in the style of the penny novelette. I had, it seemed, deliberately induced the Emperor to give declarations in England, which I had then intentionally made public through the article in the *Daily Telegraph*. My scheme had been so to compromise my Sovereign that the *bloc* I had specially formed to such an end, would force him to abdicate,—my final object being the proclamation of a German republic, with myself as president.

I cannot remember the exact title of this slander, nor precisely how the case was made out. Such libels have never left very much impression on me—this thing of Martin's as little as an even sillier pamphlet, published thirteen years later by Professor Halle, of Tübingen. Against such shafts I have Goethe's consolation, who says that, since the whale itself has parasites, the puny human has no right to resent the sting of a gnat. At the same time it was not a good symptom that His Majesty should have described Martin's scribbling as " a very good book " which threw fresh light on the November crisis.

Yet how could all this tally with the obstinate friendliness of the Kaiser, and especially with his marginal notes? I do not think there was conscious guile in His Majesty. He was no Louis XI nor, in spite of the foolish pamphlet against him, published by the free-thinking Professor Quidde, soon after he came to the throne, could he really be considered a Caligula. He was like nothing less than a Roman Emperor in delirium. He was only, as an English lady of my acquaintance, who had known him as a boy, once said of him: " Not false but fickle." [1] He was a weathercock whose direction at any given moment very largely depended on the people with whom he happened to associate. Ballin would say of him: " Whenever I have to go and see the Emperor I always try and find out whom he's just been with, because then I know exactly what he's thinking."

I must add that the Loyalists' League, which united my enemies in the Suite, contained differences—profound differences—of opinion. Some of these people were merely the instruments of the

---

[1] English in text.

others, more highly placed, who despised the tools with which they worked. When, several years after my retirement, the Emperor paid a visit to Switzerland, he took Röder with him, as a reward for having been so faithful. Röder's father had been German Minister to Switzerland, and a very good Minister he was. But, at the time of this Imperial visit, my brother Alfred was German Minister in Berne. One day, when His Majesty and the Suite were inspecting a Swiss farmyard where, in rustic innocence, a manure pit was displayed, my brother, noticing that Röder had strayed too close to this ill-savoured, perilous ditch, expressed the fear that he might fall into it. "Oh let him be," said Prince Max Fürstenberg, who was standing at my brother's side, "the best place for a swine is in the pig-wash." On my birthday I had received an unusually cordial telegram from the Kaiser. I have already told how, after my retirement, I returned His Majesty all the telegrams and letters I had received from him while in office, preserving only a very few copies. But I distinctly remember how in this, my last birthday telegram as a Chancellor, His Majesty expressed the hope that I should remain at his side for many years. There followed the most energetic assurance that he would never let himself be influenced by attacks of which I was the object—neither by yapping journalists nor votes in the Reichstag. Loebell begged my permission to publish this proof of Imperial favour and confidence, but I refused since, in November 1908, I had adjured His Majesty—as much for the Crown's sake as the country's—not to figure too frequently in politics. I felt that it would be undignified to seem to use him as a shield.

For as long as I remained a Chancellor, my birthday meant a heap of congratulations. *Donec eris felix multos numerabis amicos*! 3rd May 1909, brought an unusual number of good wishes. Adjutant-General von Plessen wrote: "As your classic witness of the never-ending cares and labours heaped increasingly on your shoulders, I tremble at the thought that a day may come on which you will shake off such a burden. May God grant that yet another year of your life be devoted to the Emperor and the Fatherland. If not I do not see what is to happen. May the Princess, who for so long has shared and relieved your heavy task, still contribute her selfless aid to the good cause. Please tell her this from me, with all good wishes."

Bethmann-Hollweg, whom I had just congratulated on the acceptance of his Stock Exchange and Assembly Law, wired in reply, with birthday greetings: "Collaboration in our domestic policy re-shaped by you, and so releasing to fresh activity many

WILLIAM II

Portrait by P. A. Lazló

forces that were once warped and embittered—forces which will build a new bridge over the Main—I reckon as my chief and greatest recompense."

Naturally the obtrusive Professor Schiemann was also anxious to wish me joy, though recently I had had to rap him over the knuckles on account of yet another tactless article. For my sixtieth birthday he sent me the most submissive good wishes and added:

I know that I always try to write very carefully, and am still not quite sure where I went wrong. It would be intolerable to think that I had hindered instead of helping you. This feeling it is which inspires me to sign myself, in unchanging respect for Your Highness,

Your very devoted,
THEODOR SCHIEMANN.

Hammann, the head of my press-bureau, insisted on sending me written in addition to his verbal congratulations. In the midst of all the worry entailed by the perjury proceedings against him he found time to write me the following:

Your Highness may be certain that I remain one of those who, from the bottom of their hearts, well wish both the man and the statesman. You have triumphed over this difficult year in the full and blessed possession of all your faculties and gifts—of body, mind, and inner strength. May this coming year see Your Highness still yourself, both humanly and politically, and as full of labours and success. In grateful devotion,

Your most obedient,
HAMMANN.

August Stein, for years the *Frankfurter Zeitung* correspondent, who, though we had not always agreed politically, had still always remained my friend, had celebrated, shortly before my birthday, his twenty-fifth year of work on the staff of the great Frankfurt newspaper. To the good wishes I had sent him on that occasion, in which I had jokingly referred to his " silver wedding with the *Frankfurt lady*," hoping that I should also see the golden one, August Stein replied:

Will Your Highness accept my very best thanks for all the kind things you say to me on my married life with the *lady of Frankfurt*. You must excuse me, however, if I say " No—the thing is impossible." Another twenty-five years of this, and another Imperial Chancellor who likes me, and to whom I am

personally so devoted in spite of all political ups and downs—
Vota diis exaudita malignis! No German journalist goes unpunished if he honours, and is favoured by, German statesmen.
I do not long for any successor. The Socialist *Leipziger Volkszeitung* recently called me—" next to Mohrchen, the most faithful
of all the Chancellor's house-trained dogs." That made me
laugh; but I am worried by the thought that another Chancellor
might prefer another breed of domestic pet, for the kind Social-
Democrats to compare me with. The next I should certainly
oppose. And, since I hate to be in opposition, I hope that
perhaps Your Highness may be induced to remain a few years
longer in office and, in the meanwhile, will accept the sincerest
homage of your ever devoted,

A. STEIN.

Gustav Schmoller who, with Ulrich von Wilamowitz, had been,
since Mommsen's death, our greatest scholar, wrote to my wife:

I cannot send off this letter without congratulating you very
sincerely on the Chancellor's latest speech. He has surpassed himself. All Europe admires him as a peace-maker, and very rightly.
I hope his great gifts as a statesman will secure him a fresh success
in domestic policy and Finance Reform. The more difficult our
position becomes, internationally, the more mere party intrigue
hinders and impedes all great reform, the more indispensable is
Prince Bülow. His knowledge of how to handle men and parties
is of as high an order as is his eloquence, to both of which he adds
such saving humour, such a really compelling force of historical
argument.

Naturally, ever since the November crisis, the question of my
successor had been discussed, and it preoccupied many ambitious
people, since His Majesty's unfavourable criticisms had begun to
be passed from mouth to mouth. At about that time I received a
letter from Count Wedel, the Statthalter of Alsace-Lorraine, which
I here reproduce, in testimony of his frank sincerity and patriotism.
He was an exceptional man.

MY DEAR BÜLOW,
Our long friendship gives me the assurance that you will
understand me if I write quite frankly on a matter which may
strike you at first as a little odd. I had thought of asking your
brother, Karl Ulrich, to act as my intermediary. But, on mature
reflection, I consider it better and simpler to write to you directly,
in confidence. I am even obliged to do so, since you know that

I am not simply your friend, but, in many ways your ever grateful debtor. But let me get to the point. I have noticed that, for some time, certain newspapers have suggested me as your possible successor. That, in itself, is not important, since the papers are always full of silly stories. But the same thing has been said to me privately, and some equally silly suggestions have been made, to all of which I either listened indifferently, or else, quite plainly contradicted them. But what really troubles me is this: I have heard it said that, a few months ago, you suggested me as the eventual Chancellor. I had been rather hoping that, during our long *tête-à-tête* in January, you would have dropped a hint, if this were so since, naturally, I could not be so tactless as to broach the subject myself. Had you begun to talk of it I could at once have given you a plain answer, and should not have been obliged to write this letter. But perhaps you never intended to suggest that I might eventually succeed you. In that case, of course, I have no real reason for writing to you at all about the matter, and yet I feel the need for a clear understanding with you. Without boasting I think I may say that I have always had a sense of duty and patriotism. I am therefore always ready to make a sacrifice in the interests of my Emperor and country. Yet I also feel it the first duty of any sincere and fully developed adult to examine and know himself, as far as possible. To accept a post for which I could never really feel myself fitted would, in my opinion, be a frivolous and unpatriotic act, since no one has the right to take chances where the highest interests are involved. What use is other people's confidence unless one can be confident in oneself? What use is it to will, unless one can be certain of performing? You see how I feel. *Sapienti sat!* If therefore I were suggested for the Chancellorship my only sincere reply would be an unshakeable " no," even if I were to lose my present post by it. For long I have had no ambitions, and though I still feel the urge and necessity to work, I should retire without any great regret, in the knowledge that, by refusing to be Chancellor, I was really serving my country. And I have other reasons which make me hope and believe that this offer will never come my way. If you have been tempted to suggest me I must earnestly beg you not to put my name on your list a second time, and so spare me the painful necessity of having to give a definite refusal. Luckily, for the moment, all this is the sheerest hypothesis, and I wish with all my heart, that you may long remain at the head of affairs, however crushing your present burdens may seem to you. I know that there are intrigues against you, and that efforts are

being made to prejudice a certain personage. I have also enough
psychological insight to realize how annoyed the personage in
question must be feeling. But all that will settle itself in time
when your further successes show how indispensable you are,
and serious reflection on all the facts has removed the reproaches
levelled against you, of having been a tepid defender of the
interests it is your business to guard. Apart from which, to take
things just as they seem, the method, which you followed, produced results, since never, until these last few months, has there
been such calm, and such consistency, in spite of serious difficulties
at home and abroad. As a faithful servant of our Sovereign and
country I am glad of this, as much for the sake of the one as of the
other. In the hearty wish that this great task of Finance Reform
may reach its successful accomplishment, that it may be your
distinction to have given that necessary strengthening to the
Empire which will render it indifferent, and if need be, imper-
vious to storms.

I remain your old and very devoted friend,
Carl Wedel.

CHAPTER XXXIII

William II still outwardly supports me — Franco-German relation-
ships — Letters from Count Metternich — The die is cast in the
Reichstag—The division of 24th June 1909—I give in my resigna-
tion—Audience with the Emperor in Kiel—Bethmann-Hollweg de-
cided on for the Chancellorship—Herr von Valentini—Luncheon on
board the " Alice "—I bid farewell to the Emperor—My last sugges-
tions to him—Valentini begs me not to retire before the autumn.

THE nearer came the Reichstag division, which should decide
the fate of the Death Duties, the more zealous grew the
efforts of my enemies to spread abroad the Kaiser's criticisms.
Nor could I doubt that these were authentic, although, almost up
to the moment when the Duties were definitely rejected, His
Majesty's official declarations were all very cordially on my side.
As late as on 22nd June 1909, at a banquet of the North German
Yachting Association, held in Cuxhaven, on board the Hamburg-
American steamer " Deutschland " which, ten years earlier, I had
christened at the Vulcan wharf in Stettin, the Emperor expressed
the hope that the national spirit would prevail in the teeth of narrow
party interests and carry this measure of reform, so necessary to
Germany's well-being at home and abroad. In this same speech,
in vibrant terms he announced to the assembled sportsmen that his
interview with the Tsar of all the Russias, among the rocky islands
off Finland, had led to their complete agreement for an energetic
defence of peace. " As monarchs we both feel responsible for the
weal and woe of our peoples. All the nations need peace. We two
therefore will ever strive, with God's help, to promote and preserve
it. And, of course, peace is good for yachting."

So that William II was in sincere agreement with my policy of
keeping the peace. At my wish he even endeavoured to promote it
by sinking his old antipathy for " the Japs," and inviting two
Japanese princes, who were visiting Germany that spring, to an
audience at the Neues Palais, in Potsdam. He received them very
graciously indeed, allowed them to watch a Potsdam review, and
even bestowed on them the Black Eagle. It was a little drop of oil
on the troubled waters of Japanese susceptibility, so wounded by
His Majesty at Highcliffe and, as such, it was thankfully received.

Together with my thanks for his docile behaviour on this

occasion, I was able to announce to the Emperor that the very painful Casablanca incident had now been satisfactorily resolved, even in form. On 29th May, as I have said, the two governments had signed a protocol in Berlin, expressing their mutual regrets for the attitude of their officials in Casablanca, in so far as these had incurred the censure of the Court of Arbitration at the Hague. This satis- factory ending of the affair showed that even so vexed a question as this, involving up to a point, national honour, and whose rights and wrong were very hard indeed to disentangle, was capable of solution by arbitrament. I can scarcely remember any other period at which Franco-German relations were so peaceable as in this same spring of 1909. At the invitation of the Central Committee for Improved Franco-German relationships, the French senator, Baron d'Estour- nelles de Constant, had spoken in the Emperor's Hall of the Prussian Upper House, on the theme: " Franco-German *rapprochement* as the basis for world-peace." D'Estournelles was an old friend. I had met him during a delightful journey which, in the spring of 1884, I had taken through Tunis and Algiers as First Secretary of our Embassy in Paris. He had very pleasantly done me the honours of Tunis, where he held the post of Legation Secretary to the French resident Minister. Later we met again several times—our last meet- ing had been at Kiel, at the interview in 1904 between King Edward and the Emperor. D'Estournelles had accompanied King Edward, who had thought very highly of him since the days when he was Secretary of the French Embassy in London. The baron was a convinced pacifist; he wanted peace between Germany and England —peace throughout the whole world; above all peace, and the gradual reconciliation of France to Germany, by means of a slow and tactful *rapprochement*. His lecture in the Emperor's Hall was a masterpiece of tact and common-sense and, next day, he talked equally well, on the same lines, to a few friends I had invited to dinner to meet him. At our parting he made me a present—a copy of Stendhal's *Chasseur Vert*, in a charming Parisian binding. He knew how much I admire that great writer who gave, not only France but the world, two such masterpieces as *Le Rouge et le Noir* and *La Chartreuse de Parme*. To this day *Le Chasseur Vert* stands on my bookshelf, but it remains the only relic of our friendship. In 1914, as soon as we had declared war on France, d'Estournelles de Constant, like all French pacifists, did just what might have been expected by anyone knowing France and the strength of her patriotism—he became the fieriest of patriots who joined, with fervour in his country's cry: " *Aux armes, citoyens!*"

At about the time when my friend d'Estournelles delivered his excellent lecture in Berlin, I had received a personal telegram from the Tsar, to tell me in the warmest terms that, as a sign of his particular trust and esteem he conferred on me the Order of St. Andrew with brilliants. The Russian Ambassador, when he came to me a few days later, to bring me this handsome decoration, set in the finest diamonds, told me in confidence that the Tsar had had, besides his esteem, another special object in conferring it on me. The Tsar had, of course, no right whatever, nor any intention to interfere in the conduct of German home affairs; but he had wished to give me a definite indication of how very much he desired me to remain the German Chancellor, both in the interests of Russo-German relations and the peace of Europe as a whole. Hence this exceptional distinction. It was in much the same fashion that, at that time, the Rumanian Minister brought me the Order of Charles, on behalf of King Carol—the first occasion on which that prudent monarch, whose esteem I had long enjoyed, had conferred it on any but a sovereign.

Already, during the previous winter, my friend Schorlemer had written to me, from Rome, that Pius X, on receiving William II's congratulations on the occasion of his episcopal jubilee, had spoken to him with obvious gratification of my audience in the spring of 1908, when His Holiness had received me with my wife. His letter continued: " Cardinal Rampolla made a very good impression on me. He told me how happy he was at Your Highness's success in settling the crisis in November. Other diplomats whom I met at the Austrian and Spanish Embassies, also expressed their very real pleasure at Your Highness's remaining Chancellor."

That spring Cardinal Kopp wrote me the following: " My one wish is that Your Highness has really managed to recruit your strength and gain tranquillity in Venice." He added that the Vatican still retained its good impression of my last year's visit to Rome; that His Holiness in particular felt reassured as to the position of the Catholic Church in Prussia. The letter ended:

> I feel happy and easy in my mind at the thought that Your Highness is at the helm, and beg you to remain assured of my respect, and very faithful attachment.
>
> G. Cardinal Kopp.

During the days which led to the final Reichstag decision there was an important exchange of letters between myself and our London Ambassador. In my letter of 23rd June 1909 I told Metternich that I had received the impression that England still wished an *entente* with Germany, which would bring her a certain measure of relief from the anxieties entailed in her maintenance of inviolable naval supremacy, and from the financial burdens imposed on her by the too-rapid increase of her fleet. I had already many times assured the ambassador that many Germans wished the same. Their desires were as vivid as ever. It seemed to me prudent to announce in the proper quarter, in England, that we should not be hostile to an equable naval agreement. I wrote:

I am convinced that, with goodwill on both sides, and provided the English will avoid all that could seem to suggest threats or coercion, a general understanding on the subject of naval construction is practical politics. I therefore beg that, as soon as German Finance Reform is decided, you will take steps not to summon, *à tout prix*, a conference of directing personalities on naval armament, but to make it generally felt that an *entente* on the Naval Question is not impossible, provided it is combined with a general orientation of English policy in a sense more favourable to Germany. Please keep strictly to my last instructions, in any talks with Sir Edward Grey or Sir Charles Hardinge. Speak as though you had not desired the interview, so that they do not receive the impression that we have ended by changing our minds. If Grey and Hardinge open the subject with you, you can speak in the sense I have just defined, even before the vote on Finance Reform, but avoid allowing these two statesmen to feel that your interest in the matter arises from our being at the last gasp financially. The final steps will largely depend on such answers and proposals as you may receive and, on this I await your report with interest.

A week later Paul Metternich answered:

Within a few days you should receive a detailed report or a private letter on the position here in regard to the naval question, and I shall write to you at the same time on the subject of the valuable indications contained in your last letters to me. To-day I can only express my real regret at the news I have just seen in the paper, of your resolve to give in your resignation, after carrying through Finance Reform. I hope that, in spite of all, the situation may turn out to be such that you can decide to reconsider your decision, even although, according to the latest accounts, it is irrevocable. I fear that you have been impelled to make it by some special circumstance of the last few days, and not only by the disagreeable party-squabbles in the Reichstag. But, of course, this is mere surmise. If I felt that this would be of use politically I could always have a talk with Lord Knollys, and tell him how very regrettable your final resignation would be— especially since you are in no way opposed to a naval agreement. But I will do nothing in this matter unless I hear from you.

Lord Knollys was a friend—perhaps the most intimate friend— of King Edward. But I wrote at once to the ambassador asking him to take no such steps, since I did not wish my retirement or decision to remain, to depend in any way on foreign suggestions.

The dice fell on 24th June 1909. In the name of the Conservatives Herr von Richthofen opened the debate on the second reading of my Death Duties, which, little by little, had put into the shade all other suggestions for Finance Reform. Heydebrand preferred to remain behind the scenes at the crucial moment, but he pulled the strings. Baron Karl Richthofen-Damsdorf was a Conservative of the good old school, the owner of a nobleman's estate, a member of a Students' Corps, squadron-leader of the reserve of the Cuirassiers of the Guard. He had been in turn, assessor, Regierungsrat, and Oberregierungsrat. He managed his estate in Silesia, and was generally highly esteemed as a member of the Agricultural Chamber and District Council. In the 1907 election he had ousted the Socialist deputy for the Schweidnitz-Striegau district in Silesia. I do not think that, at bottom, Herr von Richthofen was in real agreement with Heydebrand, but, in conformity with our German tradition in politics, he slavishly obeyed his party leader. His speech was weak and ineffective. To the jeers of the Left he declared that the Conservatives had never had the intention of unseating a Minister; all they had wanted was to do their duty to the Fatherland. There was every reason to hope that, once the Death Duties had been rejected, the bourgeois parties would come together to pass Finance Reform by other methods. For the moment, however, the great Conservative majority would vote against the measure, as suggested. The Secretary to the Treasury, Sydow, answered in a short speech—the one good speech he ever made in that capacity. The Death Duties were the fairest blossom in the bouquet of government proposals, and could therefore not be torn petal by petal. Foreigners were simply unable to understand the German resistance to such a tax. Germany, too, would have to get accustomed to Death Duties. Prince Hatzfeldt, in the name of the Empire Party, read a weak declaration according to which, though his friends had no liking for the Death Duties, they would nevertheless, with a few exceptions, vote in favour of them as a last attempt to have done with Finance Reform. This declaration was so expressed as to compromise as little as possible His Grace's chance, slender as it was, of succeeding me.

After him came Freiherr von Hertling. He, as the most Conservative Centre deputy, had been put forward by his party with the object of soothing and gaining the Right. For him too the day was no red letter one. Herr von Hertling began by announcing that many felt this sitting to be decisive for the fate of Finance Reform. As to that he could say nothing: the future was dark and mysterious. Here the Left benches shouted: " It is," and this provoked a shout of laughter all over the house. Hertling went on to hint mysteriously that this was not simply an isolated fiscal question, but a matter of principle, of a great clash of power between Right and Left. This was, of course, intended to send shivers down the Conservative spine. In fact, as is now well known, this Conservative move towards the Centre led in the end to a very different political regrouping—an alliance of the Centre with Socialists and Democrats, to the exclusion of the Conservative party; a situation which later made it possible for Herr Wirth, the strongest of the Centre Party deputies, to give as his *mot d'ordre*, from the Reichstag tribune: " The enemy is to the Right." Hertling went on to say that he considered it natural enough that, on such an issue, the Centre should go with Prussian Conservatives. There was a fresh burst of laughter when somebody shouted: " It's just the opposite. The Conservatives are going with you." Dr. David, one of the most sympathetic figures of the Socialist party, had little difficulty in disposing of Hertling's feeble argument.

Then came the division. The first rejections were the preamble and heading of the draft bill. The Vice-President, Paasche, ruled that this left nothing of the draft, and that therefore it would not be possible to allow the third reading. The paragraphs on the Death Duties were put to the vote. National-Liberals, Independents, and Socialists voted, *en bloc*, in favour: the Centre and the Poles, *en bloc*, against. The majority of Conservatives voted against. I give the following names of Conservative deputies who voted in favour of Death Duties, and by their vote showed themselves honourable patriots, whose country's welfare meant more to them than their party:—von Kaphengst, Prince Hohenlohe-Oehringen, Pauli (Potsdam), Arnold (Reuss, elder branch), and two Saxons: Wagner (Freiberg) and Giese (Oschatz-Grimmen). Of National-Liberals the deputies Cornelius Heyl zu Herrnsheim and Count Waldemar Oriola abstained from voting because they wished to keep all doors open and offend nobody. Of the Economic Alliance and the Reform Party the Anti-Semites, Liebermann, von Sonnenberg, Bindwald, Köhler, and the two brothers Vogt, voted against me. The Death Duties were rejected by 195 to 187 votes.

I had left the Reichstag in the middle of Hertling's speech. I felt perfectly calm. The man who is at one with himself is the possessor of a peace which cannot be shaken.

> " Denn Recht hat jeder eigene Charakter
> Der übereinstimmt mit sich selbst,
> Es gibt kein Unrecht als den Widerspruch." [1]

as " Countess Terzky " says to " Wallenstein." But contradiction not only breeds injustice, it is the source of all inner conflict, all uncertainty—the source, in short, of moral weakness which, in politics, constitutes the sin against the Holy Ghost.

I went home through the Tiergarten, and felt pleased to note how well it was kept up. I rejoiced in the sight of ancient trees, some of them veritable giants, of the well kept flower-beds, the charming lake which encircles the Rousseau Island, the spruce and knightly-looking officers galloping up and down the Rider's Mile. It was pleasant to me to notice the well-being, the air of health and vigour of passers-by. Germany was, in truth, what Heine had always boasted she was, a country, sound and healthy to the core. A solid country, with her beeches, oaks, and limes. When I reached home I found my wife in the little garden room on the ground floor; that room in which Prince Anton Radziwill who, to Goethe's joy composed the music for his *Faust*, had listened to his daughter Elise, the first love of our good old Kaiser, play on her harpsichord and sing. My wife awaited events as calmly as I did. She, too, had long been used to set peace of spirit beyond outward storms and tribulation. It was a lovely day in June. Sunbeams, caught amid green branches, patterned, with the mighty shadows of old trees, the trim lawns of the Palace garden.

As we sat together, chatting of indifferent matters, a sealed portfolio was brought into me containing a report from the Head of the Chancellery, of the final rejection of the Death Duties. I sent for one of my secretaries and dictated a telegram to the Kaiser, in which I announced the result of the division to His Majesty and, reminding him of the audience he had granted me on 18th May at Wiesbaden, requested another, at which to tender my resignation. Next day I received the somewhat frigid answer that the Emperor

---

[1] That man whose mind is still at unity
Whose spirit is an undivided whole—
Is right. 'Tis contradiction breeds injustice.
SCHILLER.

would receive me at Kiel, on 26th June, on the " Hohenzollern."
By the 25th many letters and telegrams had reached me, all expressing regret, and irritation at the Reichstag vote; all blaming the
Centre, as unpatriotic in its attitude, and censuring the Conservatives
even more. The slogan of a " black-blue Coalition " became current
at about that time, as well as the assurance that the nation would
never submit to such a yoke.

> " *Kaisers alten Landen*
> *Sind zwei Geschlechter nur entstanden,*
> *Sie stützen würdig seinen Thron ;*
> *Die Heiligen sind es, und die Ritter ;*
> *Sie stehen jedem Ungewitter*
> *Und nehmen Kirch und Staat zum Lohn.*" [1]

Thus, in the second part of *Faust*, the Chancellor addresses
his Emperor. But such times are past, and to anyone who could see
into the future it was clear enough that Herr von Heydebrand's
policy could in the end profit one party only—the Socialist. Even
in the first days after the vote I received many letters from Conservatives, expressing their disgust at having been betrayed by their
party. Such Conservatives as Count Kanitz and Count Schwerin-
Löwitz, to name only two of the best, had been rather taken by surprise than convinced, by Herr von Heydebrand. At the second
vote, which was the decisive one, many Conservatives had voted
against me because they had been deluded into the belief that there
would still be another division. Heydebrand's right hand in his
struggle to reject my scheme was Count Cuno Westarp. Westarp
was the son of the *mésalliance* of a Prince von Anhalt-Bernburg-
Schaumburg-Hoym, who had married a bourgeoise, Fräulein
Westarp. He was a facile speaker, though not a convincing one, since
he had no new ideas to express. He could sometimes be biting, but
never witty; was always lucid and superficial, wrote a vivacious,
common-place style, and was one of those embittered politicians who
suffer from disappointed hopes which, at times, seem to fill them
with dull resentment. He had been compared with an unjustly super-

---

[1] . . . . Two only races
Have in the Empire kept their places
And prop the throne with worthy weight.
The saints and knights are they: together
They breast each spell of thunder weather,
And take for pay the Church and State.
                              GOETHE's *Faust*, Part II, sc. 2.
                                  (Bayard Taylor translation.)

annuated police-inspector and had, in actual fact, as a young man, been district commissaire, and later, police prefect of Schöneberg. He had begun as assistant to a Landrat, and himself become Landrat of Bomst, a little town in the government district of Posen, on the sluggish Obra, one of the most depressing and ill-famed provincial holes in our Eastern Provinces. Westarp had never managed to become Regierungspräsident and this he considered a grave injustice. He may have had some reason for thinking so, since he was hard-working, punctual, and accurate. I had never met him before his election to the Reichstag, but had heard his merits praised in the service. Several times I had suggested his promotion in the Council of Ministers, but my colleagues had always opposed it. The pale and rather peevish-looking Westarp was considered too pushing by his colleagues, and this had rendered him unpopular. He had entered the Reichstag at a by-election. On the death of the Conservative deputy, von Gersdorff, all the German parties in the Meseritz-Bomst district voted for him, and he obtained a two thousand majority over his Polish opponent. It was therefore all the less excusable that he should have supported such a tactic as Heydebrand's, who, with Polish help, caused the downfall of the most decided and resolute champion of a vigorous policy in our Eastern Marches.

On 26th June I left for Kiel. Before leaving Berlin I received a visit from Bethmann-Hollweg, the Secretary of State for the Interior. I have read *Hamlet* and seen it on the stage, and in life I have also met many hesitant people, but never one so undecided as Bethmann-Hollweg. Did he want to succeed me? Or not? Even now I cannot be certain. Almost in the same breath he begged me not to think of suggesting him, and warned me against considering Schorlemer, on account of his " Catholic blinkers," or Rheinbaben, whom he considered ambitious, and who " could scarcely manage to sit still, he wanted so badly to be Chancellor." Bethmann was all hesitant uncertainty, though under it all, there was something pushful, vain, and full of susceptibilities. He asked my permission to go to the station with me, and I gave him a lift in my car. His last words to me were: " On the whole perhaps it would be better not to. . . . Unless. . . . Let me put it this way."

On the platform I met the Cabinet Councillor, Valentini. He had seen the Kaiser, to whom he had gone to ask for orders, immediately after the Reichstag vote. How many Ministers out of favour had not Lucanus, his predecessor, ferried across the Styx, in the course of his twenty years' activities? Valentini was obviously proud of having a Chancellor to conduct on his first official trip to Hades, and wanted to be as nice to me as possible. When we were alone in my compartment he assured me how much he regretted my departure, especially on account of Foreign Policy, which had really begun to make him feel uneasy. He proceeded to mention the *Daily Telegraph* affair—saying that he did not consider it the real reason of His Majesty's displeasure: the Emperor knew perfectly well that I had shown " the most admirable dexterity " and " a wonderful mixture of calm and energy " in getting him through that crisis; that I had indeed played the part of " a faithful servant." But my domestic policy, ever since the 1907 elections, had been causing him more and more uneasiness—grave uneasiness. He feared that I might try to stray from the paths of a " vigorous monarchist " (that is to say personal) régime, and attempt to introduce parliamentary methods, along English, Italian, or Belgian lines.

I reproduce this talk with Valentini from some notes which I placed in my private archives on 27th June 1909. I answered him: " I have never had the least desire to introduce English parliamentary methods, since I am quite aware that their primary condition is lacking here. Neither do I favour the kind of régime prevailing in Italy, Belgium, Rumania, etc., since I know how this would prejudice the army, and the whole of Prussian organization—even, perhaps, the unity of our Empire. But I certainly consider that it would be good to make more use of parliamentarians, to introduce, little by little, with all due prudence and circumspection, greater parliamentary freedom into Germany. Why should Spahn, for instance, not be made Prussian Minister of Justice, Schwerin-Löwitz, Minister of Agriculture, Fischbeck, Minister of Commerce? Had not the National-Liberal, Miquel, been made Minister of Finances? And a very good Minister he was. Why, in our Empire, should we not have Bassermann as Secretary of State for Justice? Heinrich Carolath or Hertling as Under-Secretary of State for the Foreign Office? Or Gamp, as Minister for Public Works? Or Kanitz, or Udo Stolberg as Secretary of State to the Treasury? Heckscher, Dove, Dohrn, Mommsen, and other Liberals would all make excellent Secretaries, or Under-Secretaries of State. Once three or four deputies have obtained ministerial rank, there will, I said, be a higher proportion of capable people putting up for election to the Reichstag, our parliamentary average will be higher, and that will be a good thing in every way. I could not even see much objection to making any really capable Socialist— Huë, for instance, or Legien, head, or reporting Councillor at the Home Office. For this the present moment would be well chosen, after the crushing Socialist loss at the last elections." Valentini

(beside himself): " But His Majesty couldn't think of such a thing!"
Myself: " I don't suggest its being done in a hurry. Step by step,
you know! Let me remind you that I managed to bring His
Majesty safely through the November crisis, without the least curtailment or circumscription of the rights of the Crown. But I
should certainly not consider it loyal to use that crisis to build up a
Liberal government." Valentini: " His Majesty wants the opposite of such plans. He wants to accentuate still more what you have
just described as ' personal ' government." Myself: " That's
really serious. Where does he want to get? To a state of affairs
like that in Russia? " Valentini: " Well not precisely the same as
in Russia; but more or less that sort of thing, you know—taking
into account all the differences between the two countries. Above all
we must bridle the Reichstag. For some time past His Majesty
has been feeling that your tendency is to cajole the Reichstag too
much. He feels you speak there too often and too successfully."
Myself: " All the same, the speeches of which you complain have
managed, in the last twelve years, to get almost everything His
Majesty wanted there, and all that was in the interests of the State.
What more do you need? " Valentini: " I quite admit it. But
those results have been due to Your Highness's own talent and
facility as a speaker; and to your personality. They were not
obtained in any obedience to principle—or to the Emperor. With
Your Highness as Chancellor the deputies have grown too insolent,
and His Majesty has felt for some time that Your Highness was
rather too much *en évidence*." Myself: " *Vous vous plaignez que
la mariée soit trop belle*." Valentini (who had obviously not understood the gist of this): " I can assure Your Highness that, like all
patriots, I feel the deepest respect for your exceptional merits, in so
many different branches . . . that I honour you, and that your resignation has really alarmed and worried me." Here we shook
hands; he with emotion and I very politely. As the train steamed
into Kiel station Valentini told me that he had been unable to
broach the question of my successor, since His Majesty wished to
discuss it with me personally. He added, with a smile, in a low
voice: " I've made him give up all idea of Monts . . . and it wasn't
very difficult either. Our Imperial master sometimes gets the
strangest ideas." Before us lay the Kieler Föhrde—the queen of
all the harbours in the Baltic. The port was full of battleships, as it
always was when the Emperor was there for the Kiel Regatta. One
mighty cruiser stood anchored beside the next. I looked thoughtfully out at this great fleet, and said: " Just twelve years ago to-day
—on 26th June 1897, I was entrusted, on board the " Hohen-

zollern," with the conduct of Foreign Affairs." Valentini was too close an observer not to see what I was thinking yet would not say. " Your Highness," he replied with a certain solemnity, " may well say to yourself with pride—on 26th June 1909—that this whole magnificent fleet which, in twelve years, has grown up without conflict with England, is your work, since it was you who made it possible to build it, you who kept the peace, encouraged our economic development, and yet safeguarded our place as a nation." Once more we shook hands. In the meantime Admiral von Müller, the Head of the Naval Cabinet, had approached us, whose duty it was to conduct me on board the " Hohenzollern." He seemed preoccupied. He was worried, he told me as soon as Valentini had departed, at the thought of our future Foreign Policy. He knew, as the result of his years as Prince Henry's adjutant that, at bottom, neither the English nor Russian Courts placed any deep confidence in our Emperor, whom they both considered independable. Nor was he popular with either since, in both, his tactlessness and arrogance had ended by getting on everybody's nerves—on the ladies' as well as on the gentlemen's. "Your Highness will be missed," he kept repeating. I soothed him who, by the way, was soon enough to become an enthusiastic supporter of Bethmann's policy. " If," I said, " our policy is reasoned and prudent, and at the same time fearless, we shall win through, by the grace of God."

The Kaiser was awaiting me on deck, visibly impatient, nervous, and agitated, with a hint of embarrassment in his manner. I was struck by his violent gestures. There ensued the following dialogue, textually copied from my notes of 27th June 1909.

His Majesty: " As for your successor, my dear Bülow, you needn't worry yourself about the report which no doubt you have ready prepared for me. I've decided to appoint Bethmann-Hollweg. I'm sure you'll agree with me. He is true as steel; thorough, through and through, a tremendous worker, and yet full of ' go.' He'll soon put the Reichstag down a peg or two. Besides I shot my first roebuck at his place in Hohenfinow." Myself: " If Your Majesty has already made his choice I can only say with Hamlet: ' The rest is silence.' "[1] H.M.: " How aptly you always manage to fish up quotations. Wonderful! But you needn't look so sorrowful, you know. Tell me why you object to Bethmann. As a matter of fact I'm rather in a hurry; in an hour I have to lunch with the Prince of Monaco . . . but still, I always like to hear what you have to say." Myself: " As far as domestic policy is concerned Bethmann-Hollweg is perhaps the best man. He'll be able to keep the

[1] English in text.

Left in order, and he'll manage to conciliate the Centre. As far as I know the Conservatives have nothing against him either. The only thing is that he understands nothing of Foreign Policy." H.M. (with a laugh): "You leave Foreign Policy to me. You've managed to teach me something, you know. That will be all right." Myself: ":I hope it will. But, all the same, Your Majesty will need a good assistant as Secretary of State for Foreign Affairs. Schön is incapable." H.M.: "Well I think he did very well in the Bosnian Question." Myself: "Yes, under my direction." H.M. (rather irritated, for the first time): "My dear Bülow, what went so well under your orders will, no doubt, go equally well under mine." Myself: "As auxiliaries in the Foreign Office I would suggest either Mühlberg or Kiderlen to Your Majesty." H.M.: "I don't intend to have either of them." Myself: "Then Bernstorff. And, if necessary, he would make an excellent Chancellor." H.M.: "I'll make a note, I like Bernstorff." Myself: "Brockdorff-Rantzau is also talented." H.M.: "I don't care for him. He's the nephew of Therese Brockdorff, my wife's Mistress of the Robes, and I don't like personal relationships between the Foreign Office and my people at court." Myself: "Now as to policy—I have two very serious recommendations to make to Your Majesty. H.M. (impatient; glancing at his wrist-watch, and on the defensive): "My dear Bernhard . . . I really haven't the time." Myself: "I'm sorry for that. But I will do my best to read you only extracts, 'in winged haste,' as poor Dietrich Hülsen used to put it. Do all you can to reach a 'naval agreement'[1] with England." H.M. (very annoyed): "Why must you end by harking back to that? Haven't I told you again and again, verbally, and in letters and marginal notes, that I don't intend to let naval construction be interfered with! All such proposals are an affront to me and to my navy." Myself: "I have never advised Your Majesty to do anything that could affect our national honour. But an affair of such seriousness and difficulty cannot be entirely decided by the students' duelling code. (His Majesty frowned). Besides how could our honour be affected if we succeed, *avec un beau geste*, spontaneously, in reaching such an understanding with England as will diminish English anxieties at the present *tempo* of our naval programme and so, to a great extent, weaken the ever-latent danger of war?" H.M. (in a tone of great decision): "I don't believe in any danger of war!" As he said these words His Majesty glanced at the fleet, which lay surrounding the "Hohenzollern." With a wave of his hand towards the mighty battleships he cried, raising his voice, and

[1] English in text.

proudly throwing back his head: " Whoever looks out, as I do now, on the fruit of years of painful effort has a certain right to feel proud of himself." I could not help remembering Schiller's " Polycrates " who, from the roof of his palace, looks down on Samos and his fleet. I answered: " I don't suggest that England will make any sudden attack on us, as Nelson attacked the little Danish fleet, off Copenhagen. What I fear is this: That if we force— I stress the word ' force '—our naval construction, we shall succeed in so irritating and disquietening the English that they will turn against us, if any great international complication gives them a chance to do so." H.M.: " But, my dear Bülow, I want us to part in peace and *sans rancune*. Why therefore insist on dwelling on this subject ? " Myself: " Because this is a favourable moment to come to an agreement with England. My resignation—another Chancellor—all that will permit of ' a new departure.' [1] In any case no one supposes at the moment that, if we slow down our naval construction it means that we are at the end of our tether financially. Our coffers are full again." H.M.: " I cannot, and will not allow John Bull to give me orders on how many ships I am to build." Myself: " It is not a question of ' orders ' or compulsion, but of a benevolent and amicable arrangement." H.M. (very impatiently): " You're simply playing with words. Please stop. We want to part good friends—don't we ? " Myself: " *Dixi et salvavi animam meam*." H.M.: " Another quotation ! Well, and what's the great pedagogue's second lecture ? " Myself: " Don't repeat the Bosnian business." H.M. (mistrustful): " That was a triumph for you." Myself: " Situations in Foreign Policy seldom repeat themselves. Last winter we had a set of circumstances which probably will never be so favourable to us again. *Ne bis in idem*." H.M. (once more quite friendly and pleasant): " You quote on to the last, but always appositely. At least you have no rivals there. So you think I ought to be careful in the Balkans ? " Myself: " Yes. There more than anywhere. The danger is there ! I hope Your Majesty will be mindful of what Bismarck said on the subject —of all that he wrote, all his warnings; his telegram to good old General Deines, my friend and comrade at arms and Your Majesty's distinguished general aide-de-camp. I think it was in 1905, after the Coblenz manœuvres, that I read Your Majesty the copy I had taken of that telegram, and which I begged Your Majesty to preserve." H.M. (again with a glance at his wrist-watch): " All right! All right. I shan't forget. You needn't worry. Now I really must be off. I can't keep Monaco waiting. But let me take

[1] English in text.

you with me in the boat." Myself: "Your Majesty is far too gracious. I have only one thing more to say to you. Precisely because, to my deep regret, you refuse any naval agreement with England, you must be doubly prudent with the Russians. I say again that I do not think it likely that England will suddenly attack us. But I do think that the English will be so irritated by the rate of our naval construction that they are likely to take the other side if ever we come to war with Russia. Finally I would say this. Have you really made up your mind to Bethmann? Karl Wedel would be much better." H.M. (as we got into the launch): " I consider him obstinate and you've known that for a long time." Myself: " Or Schorlemer? His vision is wider than Bethmann's. Or Rheinbaben? He's pluckier." H.M.: " No. I've said Bethmann. Just wait till you see that great long fellow stand up in the Federal Council, or in the Reichstag and glare at all the ' honourable members.' Why he'll scare them to death. They'll run off and hide in their mouse holes. And quite time they did. But come on."

In a few minutes we were on board the " Alice "—the Prince of Monaco's steam-yacht. The Prince who was entirely French in his sympathies, had a number of French guests aboard. Others had come over from the yacht of Menier, the rich chocolate manufacturer, which had also come to anchor in Kiel harbour. All knew that I was in Kiel in order to hand in my resignation, and they watched us curiously, and somewhat maliciously, to see how the Emperor treated his ex-Chancellor. Of course I was perfectly calm, and did my share of the conversation. The Emperor was in high spirits, and laughed loudly at some of my stories. When we rose from table one of the French guests—unless I am mistaken he was called Jules Roche, or a name very like it—came up to me and said: " *Ma foi, ce déjeuner a été délicieux, nous avons cru assister à une scène de théâtre, à un drame de Scribe ou de notre grand Hugo. J'ai vu plus d'un ministre s'en aller, mais pas un dans une aussi belle attitude. Vous avez été parfait, mon prince, le sourire sur les lèvres et le front haut. Je vous en fais mon compliment.*"

I was conscious of a peculiar sensation; as Imperial Chancellor and President of the Council I had eaten the condemned man's last meal in the midst of foreigners. Apart from His Majesty, myself, and the Emperor's aide-de-camp there had only been Frenchmen present.

I took leave of the Emperor on board the " Alice " to return to the " Hohenzollern " where I met Valentini again, and General von Plessen. Von Plessen said to me: " You know how I wished you to remain in office. But now I tell you, you are perfectly right to retire. Your relations with the Emperor had become impossible. What I really admire is the way you have kept your dignity to the end."

Valentini asked to be allowed to come to the station with me. *En route* for it he asked whether I knew that His Majesty had chosen Bethmann-Hollweg. I answered "yes," and Valentini said with decision: "Anyway, Bethmann is by far the best; there can be no doubt of it." Bethmann and Valentini were close friends. I believe, though I may be wrong, that they had been students together. Now that his mind was easy on that score Valentini asked whether I would not consent to remain in office until the autumn— adding that, if I did so, I should of course have to sponsor Finance Reform, in the shape it had received from Conservatives and Centre before the Reichstag and the country. It was naïve to ask me such a question and showed the lack of statesmanly qualities which had always been Valentini's characteristic. I answered that it would not be possible—that, in my opinion, the rejection of the Death Duties and severing of the *bloc*, engineered by the Conservatives, were fatal mistakes. Since such was my conviction I must abide by it; a Minister may resign, but must not forswear himself. My refusal to fall in with his suggestion seemed to disappoint and depress Valentini. I told him, in the plainest of terms, that I had not wished to give as my reason for retirement any disagreement with the Emperor or His Majesty's declining favour. I preferred to allege the rejection of the Death Duties. Valentini answered that, certainly, it was better to retire on such an issue than because of any friction with the Sovereign, but that, all the same, he did not consider it a good reason—it savoured of parliamentary methods. Once more he begged me to remain, at least until the Reichstag re-assembled. I might use the millions offered by the new Reichstag majority. Surely that was the proper solution. It would be the solution desired by my successor, Bethmann-Hollweg, who wished to wait for the autumn before he shouldered his heavy burden of office. Since Valentini would not stop insisting and had become almost indiscreet, I said to him finally: "But surely, Excellency, you can't ask me to castrate myself?"

Just as the Berlin train was leaving the platform Valentini announced that the Emperor would shortly again receive me at the Castle in Berlin for my ceremonial farewell audience. "That will be," he added, "a grave yet beautiful hour in Your Highness's life!"

Back in Berlin I at once noted down all my impressions of this varied and interesting day. I have used those notes to compile the present narrative.

CHAPTER XXXIV

Official intimations of a change of Chancellor—The Press—Third
reading of the Finance Reform Bill—The Conservative attitude—
My interview with Herr von Eckardt—Proclamation of my retirement
in the "Reichsanzeiger" (14th July 1909)—An autograph letter from
His Majesty—My farewell audience—Their Majesties dine with us
for the last time—A talk between the Kaiser and my wife—Our
farewell visit to the Empress—We leave Berlin (17th July 1909).

AFTER I left Kiel, Valentini caused Wolff's bureau to publish
a statement that the Chancellor had begged His Majesty
to accept his immediate resignation. Prince Bülow's request
had, however, not been granted for the moment. His Majesty
could not further consider it until such time as fresh efforts at
reforming the finances of the Reich should have led to some positive
result, acceptable by the Federal Governments. I at once inserted
a paragraph, under the heading " More definite information," on
the front page of the *Norddeutsche Allgemeine Zeitung*, intimating
that His Majesty had indeed asked Prince Bülow not to resign till
Financial Reform had been achieved, and that the Chancellor had
felt unable to refuse this Imperial request. " Nevertheless, in view
of the political situation revealed by the vote on the death duties,
Prince Bülow is irrevocably determined to resign, as soon as
financial reform has been accomplished."

My first visitor in Berlin was Bethmann-Hollweg. He seemed
dejected. Again and again he asked me if I could not retain my
post until the autumn. He begged that, at least, I would take
responsibility before the country for the project of financial reform,
in the sense given it by the Conservatives and Centre Party. I
declined, but he returned to the assault in a lachrymose and rather
confused letter, and finally sent me all the documents relative to the
project, in an envelope, on the cover of which was scribbled in
pencil: " With the respectful and urgent request that Your Highness furnish the necessary signatures, and so set your great name to a
great work."

I returned the envelope and its contents without any accompanying letter, since I felt that quite enough had been said on the subject.
I received an impression of gloom in Berlin circles. An article in
the *Frankfurter Zeitung* pointed out that, behind the deputies who

had rejected the new death duties, there had been scarcely four million voters, against seven million, in round figures, behind those who had voted in their favour. Of course the democratic *Frankfurter Zeitung* obtained from these figures the conclusion that it was a matter of urgent necessity to draw up a new division of electoral areas. The movement for such a re-shuffling did indeed begin at about this time, whereas I, during my long term of office, had had no difficulty whatever in rejecting all such proposals from the outset. The *Germania*, the leading organ of the Clerical Centre, had spread the lie that there had always existed bad feeling between myself and the members of the Federal Diet, particularly the Bavarian Minister, Lerchenfeld. Count Hugo Lerchenfeld, an old friend of many years standing and a man of unblemished reputation, made a spontaneous declaration in the Reichstag which relegated this to the world of fable. He stated that for twelve years Prince Bülow had been on the best and most confidential terms with all members of the Federal Diet: that he, Lerchenfeld, in particular, most definitely refuted the myth of any personal disagreement with myself.

More serious was the storm which broke on 3rd July. It was caused by Sydow, who till then had been a Secretary of State. At the second reading of the bill on the spirits duty, he tried to justify the attitude of the Federal governments, who were now renouncing the death duties, which they had begun by demanding so insistently, and yet accepted fiscal reform in the terms proposed by the Conservatives and Centre. The noise in the Reichstag was such that Sydow could scarcely make himself heard. When at last, very nervous indeed, he began, less to speak than stammer out: " The Federal governments stand firm on their conviction that this standpoint "—Singer, the chief of the Social-Democrats, interrupted in stentorian tones, " You're not standing on anything, you toppled over long ago!" The shout of laughter that followed lasted for several minutes. Poor Sydow clung to the railing of the tribune incapable of further speech. It was years since there had been such a noise in the Reichstag.

In Saxony the Conservatives were in an especially bad position. They announced that they had never had any intention of causing Prince Bülow whose merits were incontestable, to resign. But none of that did them any good. In 1907, as I have said in an earlier chapter, the bourgeois parties had won thirteen seats in Saxony. In 1912 they lost nearly all these seats to the Socialists. To-day Saxony oscillates between a Socialist and a Communist government, and has even, at times, become the playground of that German Rinaldo Rinaldini, Herr Max Hölz. Heydebrand may perhaps have felt that he had made a great mistake, since he used the third reading of the Finance Reform Bill (10th July) to rehabilitate himself as far as possible. Dialectically his speech was most adroit. But the elections of 1912 were soon to show that there are cases in which all chop logic is as naught. He threw to me " the eminent and distinguished Chancellor " many bouquets of the floweriest praise. " Conservatives could never forget—(voice from the Left: " That they overthrew him.")—" No," said Heydebrand, " we shall never forget how much this statesman has done for us. This House has often been swept away by his eloquence; we have all of us been witness often enough of that lucid and penetrating intellect devoted to the service of the Empire not only at home but abroad." And Conservatives could never forget how much this Chancellor had done in the economic interests of his country; with what devastating eloquence he had fronted the Social Democrats. Most of all the whole Conservative party were unanimous in their gratitude for the " firm and manly way " in which Prince Bülow had often stood up to the King and Emperor. In an obvious and hesitating embarassment, very different from his usual manner Heydebrand strove, if not to justify, then to excuse the Conservative alliance with the Poles. This partnership was " rather haphazard." It would not in the least prevent Conservatives from being what they had always been hitherto—the champions of German culture in the Eastern Provinces. If need be they would fight " to the last man " in defence of this culture. Twenty-four hours after this very feeble string of excuses the *Dziennik Berlinski*, the official organ of the Polish Party, wrote on its behalf and in its name: " We emphatically declare that the Polish members of the Reichstag aimed solely at the overthrow of Prince Bülow in the division which decided the fate of the Death Duties Bill."

Indeed, as I have already pointed out, this Bill, on 24th June, had been rejected by 195 to 187 votes; that is to say, by a majority of only 8. It would have passed without the Polish vote. The deputy Raab, the speaker for the Economic Association, followed the example of Heydebrand. He reproached me, at this same sitting, with my illusions on the subject of the Liberals, but added: " We, too regret the loss of this Chancellor. Who knows when we shall get another like him! We are not responsible for his fall; it was brought about by the Left."

On 13th July the Reichstag rose. On the following day I renewed my application to retire. On the same day I gave Felix von Eckardt, the Chief Editor of the *Hamburger Korrespondent*, my views on the political outlook. With this interview I pursued a double policy. I wished first of all to refute the widespread, and not entirely groundless, opinion that my real reasons for resigning were to be found in the Kaiser's attitude towards me. The better to shield the Kaiser and the Crown, I therefore said that my only reason for having resigned was the attitude adopted by the Conservatives. " Nobody regrets more than I do," I told Herr von Eckardt, " the rejection of the Death Duties Bill. It was a just and moderate project for taxation, and its rejection will have serious consequences. I am not surprised that the Centre did not want it. The Centre refused to see the undeniable advantages of such a tax. They have forgotten how, for many years past, the most widely read and varied Catholic newspapers have officially prophesied its necessity, how from both the sociological and fiscal standpoints such a measure is in accordance with Catholic policy. But the Centre with its usual elasticity felt that, by opposing this measure, it could win the Conservatives to its side and so cause my retirement. I feel no grudge against the Centre any more than I do against the Poles who, although not opposed to the death duties, as such, voted against them to get rid of me. *A la guerre comme à la guerre.* I had expected nothing different from that quarter. But I confess that the Conservative attitude is rather less easy to understand, nor will it be easy to make the country understand it. The indelible impression will remain that the Conservatives have helped the Centre back to the decisive position in Parliament which it desired. If now the Conservatives declare that they regarded the exclusion of the Centre, on principle, as a political error, they can only intend a *bloc* policy. And I never made the political mistake of excluding the Centre on principle. If on the other hand the Conservatives consider a *bloc* policy an error, I cannot understand why they pursued it for two and-a-half years, and sanctioned it by providing the first president. I can recognize neither political logic nor consistency." I further indicated that the question of increasing the death duties, whose principle the Conservatives had admitted, in no way involved an attack on those other basic principles on which the Conservative Party was built up. " The whole matter has been artificially exaggerated by the leaders of the Conservative Party. And if now, after the event, a debating point is scored by the introduction of the principle of the method of election to the Reichstag, at a moment when mass consumption is already considerably overburdened, that only brings grist to the mills of Socialist agitation. The country will come to recognize more and more that, if the Conservative attitude had been different, our financial reforms could have been satisfactorily achieved, without any change in the *bloc*, without any change of government, without relinquishing all the hopes of the 1907 election, and the prosperity these hopes implied."

I stressed the anxiety caused by the Conservative attitude throughout the country. " The country is well aware of all the dangers which such an attitude may provoke, both for the party itself and for the Fatherland. We may see bitter conflict within the parties, re-groupings of an unnatural sort, detrimental to the country's well-being. Prince Bismarck said more than once that it is impossible to judge whether any political action was wise or unwise at the moment. Its effects as a rule were not perceived for many years. That certainly applies to this present action of the Conservative Party against me. We shall see at the next elections how good or bad it was for the country." I reminded Herr von Eckardt that I had not only defeated Socialism in my speeches, that my triumphs had been more than oratorical; that I had caused its heavy defeat at an election, a defeat entailing many practical consequences. And I added: " To have reduced the strength of the Socialists from eighty to forty seats is a proof that this party can be fought and conquered without any necessity for police regulations or special laws. We shall see how successful the next elections are in this respect. Socialism is, for the moment, in low water. It is possible that the ebb may continue. And we shall also see whether the progress of Germanization in our Eastern Provinces, on which the Oberpräsident of Posen and West Prussia has given such a favourable report, will continue to maintain itself and develop. We shall see if the Guelphs can still be kept out, who were swept away in 1907! If all this happens nobody will be more pleased than I. I shall see in it a proof that my policy was on the right lines, that its good effects continue, in spite of Conservative mistakes. If not, the result may be regarded as the evil consequence of the Conservative attitude, which will then be seen as frivolous trifling with the interests of the Empire and the Fatherland. We shall meet at Philippi."

As to-day I ponder these words in retrospect I still consider them justified, even though a balanced historical judgment cannot deny that the Kaiser must take his share of the blame. The allusion to Philippi was, of course, not a hope but a warning. Cassandra herself did not desire that Troy should fall. She feared it, as Schiller's ballad so beautifully puts it, " with mournful clarity." My interview with Herr von Eckardt closed with the following words, which I addressed directly to him: " I retire in the wish that the German people will triumph over all obstacles and perils, that it will remain prosperous, conserve its strength, go forward on its path of progress, and hold its place in the world." I cannot even to-day withdraw the reproach that Heydebrand and Westarp trifled with the interests of the Fatherland in the winter of 1908-9. I can only add that the action of these Conservative leaders was not merely frivolous but stupid.

On 14th July the *Reichsanzeiger* published my resignation, with the news that the Emperor had awarded me, on retirement, the diamonds of the Order of the Black Eagle, at the same time promoting Bethmann-Hollweg from Secretary of State to Imperial Chancellor. The Minister of Commerce, Delbrück, became Secretary of State for the Interior. Sydow, the Secretary to the Treasury, Prussian Minister of Commerce, and Wermuth, the Under-Secretary of State for the Interior, Secretary to the Treasury.

Valentini, as Cabinet Councillor, transmitted the following autograph letter from his Majesty:

My dear Prince—I learn, to my pained regret, from your renewed application to retire, that you are finally resolved to lay aside your heavy burdens as Imperial Chancellor, President of the Prussian Council, and Secretary for Foreign Affairs. Difficult as it is to renounce your valued collaboration in the direction of Imperial affairs, and of those of the Prussian State, and to sever those bonds of mutual confidence which for so many years have bound me to you, I consider it right to give full weight to your motives in wishing to resign your Chancellorship, and, in view of the important reasons which have led you to confirm your decision, not to refuse your urgent request any longer. I have therefore granted your petition, and inform you that you are free to retire.

It is, however, my heartfelt wish to express on this occasion my warmest thanks to you for all the self-sacrifice and devotion with which you have served myself, my ancestors, and the Fatherland, in the most various posts and offices, throughout your long, honourable and fruitful career. May God grant you yet, after so richly active a life, many years of quiet, untroubled happiness. As an outward sign of my grateful recognition and affection I have awarded you the Imperial Order of the Black Eagle with brilliants, and herewith transmit to you the insignia of that Order.

I remain your always well-disposed and grateful King and Emperor.

WILLIAM I.R.

Herr von Valentini, who brought me the above, remarked of his own accord before I had read it that the terms of this *lettre de congé* in no way corresponded to my merits. He had, he told me, presented another draft to the Emperor, which had been far more appreciative in tone. But this His Majesty had refused, demanding a less cordial letter. Valentini added that he attributed this humour of His Majesty mainly to the insinuations of Professor Schiemann, who, since the day when it had seemed certain that I would retire, had changed from an enthusiastic toady into a treacherous enemy.

On the following day I had my farewell audience with the Kaiser. He received me in the little garden attached to the so-called " Green Hat," a minor annexe of the Palace. It is said that this name originated in the colour of the old copper roof, oxidized with age, which crowns this small, tower-shaped building. The little garden at its foot can be seen from the Elector's Bridge. Opposite the " Green Hat " stands the oldest hotel in Berlin, " The King of Portugal," which dates back to the seventeenth century. To begin with, until the first half of the eighteenth century, it was a modest inn, with a bar parlour. Then it was granted the honour of lodging under its roof the Portuguese Chancellor to the Court of Prussia and, charmed at receiving such distinction, it re-christened itself " The King of Portugal." I do not know if this homage to Lusitania was recognized by the Portuguese Chancellor of those days, the famous José de Carvallo Emello, Count of Oeyras and Marquis of Pombal, the friend of enlightenment and enemy of the Jesuits. But it is to the favour of the Elector Frederick III, who afterwards became first King of Prussia, that the little " King of Portugal " owed its origins. For its construction the Elector Frederick granted a loan of 2,000 thalers to an honest Berlin widow, Frau Hammerstein the wife of his deceased *valet de chambre*. A fairly large sum for those days. So that the oldest hotel in Berlin owes its being to a kindly act performed by a great prince. This brought it good luck. Gotthold Ephraim Lessing lodged under its roof. It is the setting of his " Minna von Barnhelm." Here too was written one of Hauff's most delightful stories, *The Singer*. Hoffmann would drink on alternate nights at Lutter and Wegener's, and " The King of Portugal." King Frederick William IV would often turn in here and call for his favourite meal of Sauerkraut and sausages, a typical Berlin dish, washed down by a glass of " cool blond." Legend says that one day, as he left the inn, he was attacked by a most disloyal bull and only escaped its horns by a hasty and undignified retreat. Above the main entrance of the Inn there stands the

inscription " Free House " : to the left of it " Halls for banquets "
and " Superfine, and Plain City Cooking." This quietly charming
setting, an idyll of the Berlin of 1830, lay around me as I faced
William II, a dismissed and retired Imperial Chancellor. The sight
of the " Green Hat " and the " King of Portugal " would have
soothed me had I not already been in full possession of myself. The
Emperor, on the other hand, seemed nervous, abrupt, and gruff.
His day, he said, would be a very busy one; he had several
other audiences to get through. In particular he would have to
explain to the Federal representatives the meaning of this change
of Chancellorship, which they seemed unable to understand. In
any case it was unheard of that his summer plans should have been
suddenly upset by this crisis. He would be obliged to postpone his
North Sea trip, and this was most inconvenient—most annoying.
Only half-an-hour before, he had written to his friend, the Archduke
Francis Ferdinand, and told him how lucky he was to be born a free
man. I was dismissed with the words: " The Kaiserin wants to
dine with you again. See that your famous cook does himself
justice." When the Kaiser dismissed me, on my way out of the
palace, in the antechamber, I ran into the representatives of Bavaria,
Württemberg, Saxony, and Baden.

Next day one of these gentlemen told me that the Kaiser had
made them a very " mixed up kind of speech," informing them that
he had had to part with me because I had completely lost my
memory. At times I did not even know what I had said the day
before. I had become " quite confused," almost " senile." He
was perfectly willing to admit that, in the past, I had rendered the
Empire certain services; and he largely attributed this impairment
of my faculties to overwork. But he had considered it his " duty as
a Christian," not to oppose my return to private life. According
to the Emperor I had made some quite unheard of suggestions for
appointments to various posts. For instance I had suggested, as
ambassador, a certain Herr von Rath, a former private secretary to
Herbert Bismarck, and a notorious gambler and drunkard.

The statement as to my memory was absurd. As for Herr von
Rath, it is true that he had been attached to Herbert Bismarck, as
his Secretary of Legation, for special duties. Like his chief, von
Rath was fond of an occasional glass. Once, in Bucharest or Belgrade,
I cannot be quite certain in which city, he had lost a large sum at
bridge or *ecarté*, but he was well off, and paid up at once. I had
never considered him for an embassy, and certainly never suggested
him for one, and, for exactly twenty-two years, I had not set eyes on
him. He had, however, in a series of well-written articles, in the

Berlin and Hamburg newspapers, supported our policy during the
Bosnian crisis, and, in recognition of this, the Foreign Office had
proposed, since he was already Councillor of Legation, to confer on
him the title of Resident Minister.   Naturally I had signed the
report concerning him, which contained besides, a number of other
small distinctions conferred in the lower ranks of the Service on
officials who had proved their merit.   When I think that, by such
trifles as this, His Majesty sought to justify his attitude towards me,
I can only, once again, repeat with Goethe:—" The most exact
lover of truth in the world must always experience great embarrassment if he has to give an account of an absurdity.   He must strive
to clothe it in an idea, and hence in some sort of significance, while,
in reality, it is a cipher, a nullity which wants to be mistaken for
something."

I left this farewell audience with a feeling of bitterness.   The
attitude and behaviour of the Emperor had been those of a badly
brought up little boy.   I remembered the Latin tag with which
Prince Bismarck, seventeen years before, had expressed his opinion
of the speech in which the Kaiser had called him—the man of genius,
of overwhelming strength,—"a pigmy," and threatened to crush him:
" *Sunt pueri pueri, pueri puerilia tractant.*"   Bismarck had written
this on the margin of the newspaper article in which these insults
had been reported.   I thought, too, of the wise old Queen Victoria,
who had called her eldest grandson " an overgrown schoolboy."

To divert my mind from such unpleasing impressions I went
home on foot from the " Green Hat."   I stopped and looked up at
the equestrian statue of the Great Elector.   With him had begun
that heroic progress from Brandenburg to the Prussian kingdom.
I passed beneath the statues of the generals of 1815, Blücher,
Gneisenau, Bülow-Dennewitz, Yorck, and von Scharnhorst—perhaps the noblest of them all.   I looked up at the corner window
in which our dear old Kaiser had shown himself in the last years
of his happy reign.   I saw the magnificent statue of the great
Frederick, and that simple palace in which, for so many years, had
lived that other Frederick, our dear Emperor, the knightly conqueror
of Wörth.   So on, through the Brandenburg Gate, through which,
three times in seven years, victorious Prussian armies had returned;
the gate on which stood the Quadriga, stolen from us by the French,
and which we had brought back from Paris in 1814.   Then down
the Wilhelmstrasse where, almost opposite the house in which
Bismarck created our Empire, the heroes of the Seven Years' War
testify to their own immortal fame.   These memories of so great
a past restored all my peace, all my serenity.

Although neither I nor my wife were in the mood for banquets, I did not want to leave office without having seen my collaborators once more. On 6th July I had arranged a dinner-party of forty-eight covers, to which were invited the Prussian State Ministers and the members of the Federal Diet. On the 10th, the members of the Foreign Office, attended a dinner for which fifty-two invitations had been sent out. I made a special point, at this dinner, of inviting those lower-grade officials who, for so many years, had supported me with such unswerving loyalty and industry. In reply to a speech by the Secretary of State, von Schön, I recalled the old and closely-knit relationship which bound me to the Foreign Office Staff. I had entered it thirty-six years ago, more than a generation there-fore, as a young attaché, at the time when my father was at its head, as Secretary of State for Foreign Affairs. Two decades later I had myself become Secretary of State. I had grown up in the Foreign Office, and owed gratitude to each one of its officials; I thanked them all, and begged them not to think too badly of me. " I bid you all farewell in the firm hope that the Foreign Office will never turn its eyes from that great figure, the figure of the greatest of all Germans, the first Imperial Chancellor who set, by his example and admonishment, his seal on the German Foreign Office; that our Foreign Office may be ever in the forefront where German interests are concerned, and the honour and well-being of our people, Kaiser, and Empire."

These hopes, alas! were unfulfilled. Under Schön, who after my retirement, no longer felt himself controlled, the Foreign Office became slack. Kiderlen brought a temporary improvement in discipline. With Jagow as Secretary of State, the Foreign Office, notwithstanding the sense of duty of the able Under-Secretary, Zimmermann, was the breeding-ground of that disastrous policy, begun with the ultimatum to Serbia, and which brought about Germany's ruin.

On 15th July, Their Majesties dined with us for the last time. They themselves had expressed the wish to be received once more as my guests. This command created a difficult position for my wife, since silver, liveries, etc., had already, in part, been packed, to be sent to Norderney, Flottbeck, or Rome, where, in 1904, as my loving and far seeing companion, she had busied herself with the purchase of a Tusculum—the Villa Malta. The Kaiser arrived with a splendid bouquet, and presented it to my wife with the words: " This morning during my morning walk, I bought roses, at Rothe's in the Tiergarten street in order to lay them at your feet." At the same time he presented her with a handsome gold bracelet, attached to which was his portrait in enamel, surrounded by brilliants. The Kaiser looked very pleased with himself, the Kaiserin seemed depressed. As soon as he had given my wife the bracelet His Majesty began the following conversation with her, which she entered that same night in her diary. I reproduce it word for word, without having even altered her own small slips of style:—His Majesty: " Well this is a farewell dinner. What about it?" Myself: " I feel very sad at having to part from Your Majesty, and I thank you warmly for all the kindness you and Her Majesty the Empress have shown me during my twelve years stay in Berlin." H.M.: " Well I feel even worse than you do. I've fought against it tooth and nail, but Bernhard was determined to go." Myself: " That was because he was convinced that he could not be of use to Your Majesty any longer. The Reichstag has rejected the Death Duties. The *Bloc* is broken up. Bernhard could not stay under such circumstances." H.M.: " Yes the Reichstag is pretty wild. Such a thing has never happened to me before in my whole reign." Myself: " Herr von Heydebrand was so obstinate in the way he led the Conservatives." H.M.: " Heydebrand's crazy. But seriously, listen to me. You mustn't go and think that the *Bloc* or the Death Duties are what really made Bernhard retire. The real reason must be sought in the events of last November. You see, those fellows let me know privately that they didn't really mind the Death Duties. They overthrew him because they didn't think he'd shown enough zeal in defending me, his Imperial master." Myself: " But Your Majesty, surely the Conservatives were ruder than anyone else in November, it was they who drew up that address."—(Here my wife is alluding to an official declaration of the Conservative Party, very severe and critical of the imprudent declarations of the Emperor on Foreign Policy: it had been published on 6th November, four days before the debate in the Reichstag, in both the *Konservative Korrespondenz* and the *Kreuzzeitung*.)—H.M.: " That's quite a different kettle of fish. I'm going to talk to those fellows and send them away with a flea in their ear." Myself: " Your Majesty I know nothing about politics, but I can assure you of one thing at least; that Bernhard is devoted, body and soul, to Your Majesty. For twelve years he has had no other thought than the thought of serving you faithfully. He suffered very much in November and, day and night, he could think of nothing, except how best to save Your Majesty, and restore your good relationship with the nation. And he succeeded. Your Majesty is as respected as ever." H.M.: " Yes, now that they see they did me an injustice." Myself: " But what does Your Majesty suggest that Bernhard

should have done in the November crisis?" H.M.: "He ought
to have declared in the Reichstag: 'I wont have any more of this
insolent speech about the Emperor. How dare you speak like this?
Quick march! Get out!' Bernhard should have declared that he
stood shoulder to shoulder with me. He knew perfectly well what
that article in the *Daily Telegraph* contained. I had written from
Highcliffe to tell him." Myself: "But Bernhard got no such letter."
H.M.: "Well, if I didn't write I said it to him. I can show you
the very tree in your garden under which I talked to him about it."
Myself: "All this winter people have been poisoning Your
Majesty's mind against Bernhard. The Conservatives didn't want
to pay the Death Duties. When they saw that that was making them
unpopular they made it look as though it was really the November
debate that made them overthrow Bernhard. And of course the
Centre wanted to be revenged for the dissolution. But surely it is
impossible for Your Majesty to let yourself be taken in by these
intrigues and misrepresentations and slanders. You have known
Bernhard for so many years. Surely you won't let party hatred and
intrigue make you suspect the loyalty of such a true patriot and
faithful servant of Your Majesty. It would be a terrible pity if
wretched intriguers were allowed to gain such a victory." H.M.:
"Well if you really want to know the ins-and-outs of it I advise you
to read Martin's book. I don't understand much about these
political manœuvrings myself, and I'm sure you understand even
less. Suppose we go in to dinner."

I sat facing the Emperor. To my left, some distance away, sat
Professor Schiemann, whose name the Kaiser had caused to be
placed at the head of the list of guests he wished invited. During
dinner Schiemann turned straight to the Emperor with the words:
"Believe me Your Majesty. The English are a lot of cowards."
The last of these words he spoke with a strong Baltic accent ("*faije*,"
instead of "*feige*"). The Kaiser began to look embarrassed. I
said to Schiemann, "The English can be reproached with many
things, they may be called self-centred, egoists, sometimes even
hypocrites and brutes, but I've never heard that cowardice is one
of their weaknesses. In all their wars, on sea or land, from Mal-
plaquet to Trafalgar and Waterloo, or even the Boer War, from
Marlborough, Nelson, and Wellington, down to Sir Henry Have-
lock and Lord Roberts, they have always fought bravely and
stubbornly." Schiemann looked annoyed and said nothing. But
soon after this he started again: "Your Majesty, I have very good
and reliable news. The British Empire is cracking from end to
end. In South Africa they're brewing up for a great insurrection

of the Boers. Canada wants to join on to America. Australia is going to declare her independence. India is seething with unrest. The whole British Empire is going to pieces." The Emperor looked the other way. I said, rather sharply, to Schiemann: " I'm sorry for more than one reason at having to part from His Majesty. But I'm sorrier still not to be near him when I hear the kind of nonsense you've just been talking." He turned as red as a turkey cock. After dinner the Empress came over to me and said: " I was so glad to hear you rap that terrible Schiemann over the knuckles. People like that do nothing but poison the Emperor's mind. He, with his goodness and generosity, pays far too much attention to Schiemann, who is so obtrusive. Cissy—(this was the nickname given in the Imperial family to the Princess Victoria Louise, who later became Duchess of Brunswick)—always says: ' Professor Schiemann runs after father like a young man after his fiancée.' I told Cissy that a little girl had no business to know how young men run after their fiancées." And, after a short pause the Empress added: " Be on your guard against Schiemann. He looked very spiteful after you'd put him in his place."

That evening Her Majesty had a fairly long talk with my wife. With all her usual goodness and simplicity she begged her not to forget how much the Emperor had suffered during the November days; how he had " cried like a child," he had been so hurt by the ingratitude and injustice he had received from all quarters. To get the right idea of his present conduct we must always remember what he had been through then. Valentini said to my wife that during her talk with the Emperor she had lost her usual gentle, and kind expression, and that her face had looked very severe. She told him that though she was quite willing to leave the Chancellor's Palace, she simply could not listen without a protest to unjust and exaggerated criticism of her husband, even from the lips of His Majesty. Valentini shrugged his shoulders and answered: " Good Lord, you must never get too upset by anything His Majesty says. In any case I shouldn't mind betting that, within two years, you'll be back in the Chancellor's Palace."

The Emperor stayed with us till eleven. As usual I escorted him to his car. All the time we were going downstairs he talked in a most excited manner of a certain Spanish *Infante*, who had married one of his cousins, the charming Princess Beatrice of Coburg, and who had had to forfeit his military honours, and his Order of the Golden Fleece, for having married a heretic. " Nice sort of allies Heydebrand has gone out to collect," the Emperor added with a laugh. I answered that the Centre Party, in which there were many

honourable and very patriotic men, must not be held responsible
for the fanaticism of Spanish *exaltados*, a century behind their times,
and who still imagined themselves in the age of the Inquisition, and
auto da fés. He squeezed my hand and got into his car, in which he
had so often pulled up in front of my windows with a cheerful,
" honk-honk; honk."

On 16th July my wife and I were received in farewell audience
by the Kaiserin. That kind and generous woman seemed really
moved, and told me with genuine warmth, and certainly with entire
sincerity, how much she deplored and regretted my retirement.
" If I had had my way," she said with a melancholy smile, " you
would have remained for another twenty years." I answered that
His Majesty the Emperor would not have found an eighty year old
Chancellor much use to him. Her Majesty had heard, presumably
from some hostile quarter, that I intended to put up for the Reichstag. In a voice which really touched me she begged: " But you
won't make speeches against the Emperor in the Reichstag, will
you? " I replied, as I kissed her hand, that neither in the Reichstag
nor elsewhere, would I create any difficulties for His Majesty, that
I was, and would always remain, a Monarchist. She also said, still
with her air of charming candour and honesty, that she had " nearly
always " felt in agreement with me, but that since she understood
nothing about politics, I should probably not consider her praise
worth much. In only two matters had she been unable to share my
opinion: she had sometimes thought me too friendly to England.
She herself was convinced that England was not to be trusted. I
answered that, taken as a whole, English policy was no slier than
any other: *tutto il mondo è paese*, but that, if England really were so
treacherous, there was all the more reason for treating her with
caution. Her Majesty's second reproach was that I had proposed
the Death Duties Bill, which would ruin the nobility, the support of
altar and throne, and at the same time destroy family life. Here of
course Her Majesty was only repeating something she had been
told by foolish courtiers.

Next day I said good-bye to Berlin. I had given instructions
not to communicate to the Press either the hour or the day of my
departure, since I wanted to avoid all demonstrations. Nevertheless
the rumour had leaked out that I should be leaving Berlin on 17th
July for Norderney. As I drove away with my wife from the Chancellor's Palace, thousands of people were lined up along the Wilhelmstrasse, in front of the Brandenburg Gate, the Bismarck Monument, and the Lehrter Bahnhof. The crowd shouted acclamations.
The station was full of people. There were my colleagues, the

Prussian Ministers, the Bundesrat, the diplomatic corps, personal friends, above all many officers, and also many faces unknown to me. Outwardly I was calm enough. But, within myself I felt very agitated and, let me admit it, full of dark forebodings. The train steamed out. The crowd took off their hats and burst forth into the national hymn. As we rumbled out of the station its last notes sounded in my ears:

> " *Von der Maas bis an die Memel,*
> *Von der Etsch bis an den Belt,*
> *Deutschland, Deutschland über alles,*
> *Über alles in der Welt.*" [1]

[1] From the Meuse to the Niemen.
From the Adige to the Belt.
Germany, Germany over all—
Over all else in the world.

INDEX

LONDON: CHARLES WHITTINGHAM AND GRIGGS (PRINTERS), LTD.
CHISWICK PRESS, BRUNSWICK PARK ROAD, N. 11